KT-546-912

★ ABOUT THIS BOOK

Franklin Gothic (designed by American Morris Fuller Benton, 1872–1948) is once again the main type family used throughout this year's edition. The headers and boxed features use Novarese – a serif font that hints at chiseled Greek lettering – by the Italian type designer Aldo Novarese (1920–95).

Novarese also designed the Microgramma typeface used in our text block (above). It is a solid, masculine typeface that was designed in the 1950s and is evocative of television screens, architecture and aircraft windows of that era. It captures the post-war enthusiasm for new technology and a brighter future – the optimistic ideal of the technological revolution of those times.

This idea of looking to the future from the past also permeates the design of this year's pages. Our designers, Keren and Lisa at Itonic, took inspiration from the "steampunk" genre and created a lush, visually rich environment inspired by Victoriana and 1950s' fantasy and sci-fi. It's a bold look that synthesizes the old and new – perfect for visualizing the 2010 edition.

The prospect of a new decade also inspired us to look back over the past 10 years of record breaking – a period longer than many of our younger readers have been alive. Look out for special "decade" features such as video clips, interviews and free downloads scattered throughout the book.

FIRST...

BLOCKBUSTER

Steven Spielberg's (USA) movie *Jaws* (USA, 1975) – the story of a small seaside community terrorized by a great white shark – is considered the first summer blockbuster. It became the **first film to earn over $100 million** (then £58.1 million) at the box office and won three Oscars – Best Film Editing, Best Music (Original Score) and Best Sound (it was also nominated for Best Picture). Fans queued around the block to see the movie, giving rise to the term "blockbuster".

ASSASSINATION ATTEMPT

The earliest recorded assassination attempt was against Amenemhat I, a Pharaoh of the Middle Kingdom of Egypt, Around 2000 BC.

★ NEW RECORD
UPDATED RECORD

ALPHABET

The earliest known example of an alphabet – that is, a writing system in which a small number of symbols is used to represent single sounds rather than concepts – dates back to around 1900 BC and was found by John Darnell (USA) in the early 1990s carved into limestone in Wadi el Hol near Luxor, Egypt.

BANK NOTE

Paper money has existed in China since the 9th century, but the first bank to issue a banknote (or *banco-sedlar*) was the Bank of Palmstruch in Stockholm, Sweden, in July 1661. The oldest surviving note is one of the denomination of five dalers, which is dated 6 December 1662.

CLONED ANIMAL

A Finn Dorset sheep called Dolly was the first animal to be successfully cloned from an adult cell, as revealed in February 1997 by Dr Ian Wilmut (UK, pictured right) at the Roslin Institute in Scotland, UK. Born on 5 July 1996, Dolly survived to maturity and gave birth to lambs of her own via natural means. She was euthanized on 14 February 2003, aged six and a half, after developing a progressive lung disease.

MANNED FLIGHT

Frenchman Jean-François Pilâtre de Rozier is widely regarded as the first person ever to have flown. On 15 October 1783, he rose 26 m (84 ft) into the air in a tethered hot-air balloon built by Joseph and Jacques Montgolfier (France).

BEAUTY CONTEST

The earliest international beauty contest was staged by PT Barnum (with the public as the judges) in the USA in June 1855.

IN-FLIGHT MOVIE

The first film to be shown on a flight was First National's *The Lost World* (USA, 1925), a dinosaur adventure based on Sir Arthur Conan Doyle's (UK) book of the same name. It was shown during an Imperial Airways flight in a converted Handley-Page bomber, which flew from London, UK, to Paris, France, in April 1925.

The Lost World is also considered the **first full-length feature film to use stop-motion animation**; the first use of the technique was in the 1908 short *Humpty Dumpty Circus* (USA).

HUMAN CANNONBALL

Rosa Richter, a 14-year-old acrobat performing under the stage name "Zazel", became the first human cannonball when she was shot a distance of about 6.1 m (30 ft) at Westminster Aquarium, London, UK, on 2 April 1877.

GUINNESS WORLD RECORDS

FERRIS WHEEL

The original ferris wheel was designed by George Washington Gale Ferris Jr (USA, 1859–96), a bridge and tunnel engineer, and was erected for the World's Columbian Exposition of 1893 in Chicago, Illinois, USA. The "Ferris Wheel", as it became known, reached a maximum height of 80 m (264 ft), with a diameter of 76 m (250 ft) and a circumference of 240 m (790 ft). Each of the 36 fully enclosed gondolas carried up to 40 passengers.

AIR CONDITIONER

US inventor Willis Haviland Carrier designed and built the first air-conditioning system in 1902. It was devised for a printer in New York, USA, who had found that temperature fluctuations were causing his paper to warp.

FEATURE FILM

The world's first full-length feature film, running for more than an hour, was *The Story of the Kelly Gang*, made in Melbourne, Australia, in 1906. This biopic of the notorious bushranger Ned Kelly (Australia, 1855–80) opened at the Melbourne Town Hall on 26 December 1906. It was produced by local theatrical company J & N Tait on a budget of £450 (then $2,185).

★ PERSON TO BE KILLED BY A POWERED AEROPLANE CRASH

Lieutenant Thomas Etholen Selfridge (USA) was an army observer on a plane piloted by Orville Wright (USA) on 17 September 1908 when, four minutes into the performance test of the aircraft *Wright Flyer*, the propeller snapped a rudder control wire, which led to the plane nose-diving into a field. Selfridge died from internal injuries and a fractured skull within three hours of the accident.

ASCENT OF MOUNT EVEREST

The summit of Mount Everest was first reached at 11:30 a.m. on 29 May 1953 by Edmund Percival Hillary (New Zealand) and Sherpa Tenzing Norgay (Nepal).

Reinhold Messner (Italy) and Peter Habeler (Austria) made the **first ascent of Everest without oxygen** on 8 May 1978.

EMAIL

In 1971, Ray Tomlinson (USA), an engineer at the computer company Bolt, Beranek and Newman, sent the first ever email. It was an experiment to see if he could get two computers to exchange a message. It was Ray who decided to use the @ symbol to separate the recipient's name from their location. The message was: "QWERTYUIOP".

★ PERSON KILLED IN A CAR ACCIDENT

The first person to be killed by a car was Bridget Driscoll (UK, circled above), when she walked into the path of a vehicle moving at 6.4 km/h (4 mph) in the grounds of Crystal Palace, London, UK, on 17 August 1896.

SIGNIFICANT FIRSTS

One of the main criteria for a Guinness World Records achievement is that the record must be breakable. The only exception to this rule is when the achievement is considered a "significant first" within that category. For example, the first ascent of Mount Everest is significant within the climbing community; the first person to play the banjo at the top of Everest is not a significant first within either the music or climbing communities.

NOBEL PRIZE

The first Nobel prizes were awarded on 10 December 1901 for contributions to Physics (Wilhelm C Röntgen, Germany), Chemistry (Jacobus H van't Hoff, the Netherlands), Physiology or Medicine (Emil A von Behring, Germany), Literature (Sully Prudhomme, France) and Peace (Jean H Dunant, Switzerland and Frédéric Passy, France).

MILLION-SELLING RECORD

The first record to sell over 1 million copies was "Vesti la giubba" from Leoncavallo's *I Pagliacci*, sung by Enrico Caruso (Italy, 1873–1921). It was recorded in November 1902. The **first million-selling CD** was Dire Straits' (UK) *Brothers in Arms* in 1985.

DOG IN ORBIT

Laika, a stray Siberian husky-mongrel mix, became the first dog – and the first living Earthling other than microbes – to orbit the Earth on 3 November 1957 on board Russia's *Sputnik 2*. Laika (which means "Barker" in Russian) reached an altitude of 3,219 km (2,000 miles), earning her the nickname of "Muttnik" from the US media. The spacecraft was not designed to return to Earth, and Laika died from overheating and stress just a few hours into the mission – a fact not released by the Russians until October 2002.

British Library Cataloguing-in-Publication Data:
A catalogue record for this book is available from the British Library

ISBN: 978-1-904994-49-7

For a complete list of credits and acknowledgements, turn to p.276

If you wish to make a record claim, find out how on p.14. Always contact us before making a record attempt.

Check the official website www.guinnessworldrecords.com regularly for record-breaking news, plus video footage of record attempts. You can also sign up for the official GWR mobile phone services.

Sustainability
The trees that are harvested to print *Guinness World Records* are carefully selected from managed forests to avoid the devastation of the landscape. For every tree harvested, at least one other is planted.

The paper contained within this book is manufactured by UPM Kymi, Finland. The production site has been awarded the EU Flower licence, is Chain-of-Custody certified, and operates environmental systems certified to both ISO 14001 and EMAS in order to ensure sustainable production.

The European Eco-label distinguishes products that meet high standards of both performance and environmental quality. Every product awarded the European Eco-label must pass rigorous environmental fitness trials, with results verified by an independent body.

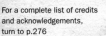

Made of paper awarded the European Union Eco-label reg.nr FI/11/1

Pictured opposite: The **smallest species of chameleon** is the tiny leaf chameleon (*Brookesia minima*, top), with an average length of 18 mm (0.7 in). The **largest known land gastropod** is the African giant snail (*Achatina achatina*, bottom); the largest recorded specimen measured 39.3 cm (15.5 in) in length, and weighed exactly 900 g (2 lb).

© 2009 Guinness World Records Ltd

THE JIM PATTISON GROUP

EDITOR-IN-CHIEF
Craig Glenday

MANAGING EDITORS
Matt Boulton, Ben Way

EDITORIAL TEAM
Harry Boteler, Rob Cave, Rob Dimery, Carla Masson, Gary Werner, Matt White

INDEX
Chris Bernstein

DESIGN & CONCEPT CREATION
Keren Turner and Lisa Garner at Itonic Design Ltd, Brighton, UK

COVER DESIGN
Yeung Poon Design

DIRECTOR OF PRODUCTION
Patricia Magill

PRODUCTION MANAGER
Jane Boatfield

PRODUCTION EXECUTIVES
Erica Holmes-Attivor, Raj Kumar

PRODUCTION CONSULTANTS
Roger Hawkins, Esteve Font Canadell, Salvador Pujol, Julian Townsend

PRINTING & BINDING
Printer Industria Gráfica, Barcelona, Spain

COVER PRODUCTION
Spectratek Technologies, Inc., USA

COLOUR ORIGINATION
Resmiye Kahraman at Colour Systems, London, UK

PICTURE EDITOR
Michael Whitty

DEPUTY PICTURE EDITOR
Laura Nieberg

PICTURE RESEARCH TEAM
Anna Wilkins, Fran Morales

ORIGINAL PHOTOGRAPHY
Richard Bradbury, Rob Fraser, Paul Michael Hughes, Ranald Mackechnie, John Wright

EDITORIAL CONSULTANTS
Earth, Science & Technology:
David Hawksett

Life on Earth: Dr Karl Shuker

Human Body: Dr Eleanor Clarke;
Robert Young (gerontology)

Adventure/Exploration:
Ocean Rowing Society,
World Speed Sailing Records Council

Weapons & Warfare:
Stephen Wrigley

Arts & Entertainment:
Dick Fiddy (TV)

Music: Dave McAleer

Sports & Games: Christian Marais;
David Fischer (US sports)

RECORDS MANAGEMENT
VP of Records
Marco Frigatti (Italy)

Adjudications Manager
Andrea Bánfi (Hungary)

Records Management Team
Gareth Deaves (UK)
Laura Farmer (UK)
Danny Girton (USA)
Ralph Hannah (UK)
Kaoru Ishikawa (Japan)
Tzeni Karampoiki (Greece)
Olaf Kuchenbecker (Germany)
Carlos Martínez (Spain)
Mariamarta Ruano-Graham (Guatemala)
Talal Omar (Yemen)
Chris Sheedy (Australia)
Lucia Sinigagliesi (Italy)
Kristian Teufel (Germany)
Aleksander Vipirailenko (Lithuania)
Wu Xiaohong (China)

SALES AND MARKETING
Senior VP Sales, Marketing & Licensing:
Samantha Fay

UK Marketing Director:
Paul Kenny

US Marketing Director:
Laura Plunkett

English Language Sales Director:
Nadine Causey

Licensing Director:
Frank Chambers

National Accounts Manager:
John Pilley

PR Manager:
Amarilis Espinoza

International Licensing Manager:
Beatriz Fernandez

US Licensing Manager:
Jennifer Gilmour

Business Development Managers:
Stuart Claxton (USA)
Erika Ogawa (Japan)

International Marketing Executive:
Justine Bourdariat

PR Executive:
Karolina Thelin

Marketing & PR Assistants:
Damian Field (UK)
Jamie Panas (US)

GUINNESS WORLD RECORDS

Managing Director:
Alistair Richards

VP Finance: Alison Ozanne

Management Accountant:
Jason Curran

Finance Manager: Neelish Dawett

Asst Finance Manager:
Jack Brockbank

Director of IT: Katie Forde

Developer: Jai Singh

Webmaster: Aadil Ahmed

IT Analyst: Fazal Khadbai

Director of HR: Kelly Garrett

Legal and Business Affairs:
Raymond Marshall,
Tom Harris, James Howell

Contracts Administrator: Lisa Gibbs

Director of Television: Rob Molloy

Digital Content Manager:
Denise Anlander

Television Assistant: David Chabbi

Talent Researcher: David Taylor

Office Administrators:
Lorna Springall (UK)
Danielle Pointdujour (US)

GUINNESS WORLD RECORDS 2010

GUINNESS WORLD RECORDS

ACTUAL SIZE

ACTUAL SIZE

GUINNESS WORLD RECORDS 2010
CONTENTS

smallest snake p.52

Pierced people! See pages 63–4

BIGGEST burger in the world – p.143

EXTENDED FEATURES ONLINE

Unlock special extended features on our new-look website whenever you see these symbols:

TOP 100 Records of the Decade

TOP 100 RECORDS OF THE DECADE
Find out more about the 100 most significant records of the past 10 years. Go online to vote for your top record in each of the 10 categories.

View this clip

VIEW THIS CLIP
Watch exclusive video footage of specially selected records.

DOWNLOAD IMAGES
Download pictures as a desktop or mobile wallpaper.

To unlock these exclusive features, visit www.guinnessworldrecords.com/2010 and enter this key code:

6762571984

Could this be the world's smallest mammal? Mmm, not sure... Find out on p.59

"I still buy and read the Guinness Record book every year, because it's become like an old friend that I like to catch up with..." – reader review on amazon.com

GUINNESS WORLD RECORDS

Pennies from heaven? Not quite! See p.156

Dog-eared, p.140

Check me out on p. 259

ENGINEERING & TECHNOLOGY

Don't miss out on the FIRSTS and LASTS spreads at the very front and back of the book!!

TOP 100 Records of the Decade

TOP 10 RECORD HOLDERS OF THE DECADE

	RECORD HOLDER	NO. OF RECORDS*	AS SEEN ON...
1	Ashrita Furman (USA, above)	164	p.145
2	Alastair Galpin (New Zealand)	38	p.137
3	Suresh Arulanantham Joachim (Canada)	36	p.111
4	Paddy Doyle (UK)	25	p.240
5	Rob Dyrdek (USA)	20	p.260
6	Jim DeChamp (USA)	14	p.261
7	Stephen Hyland (UK)	13	p.15
8	Anthony Kelly (Australia)	12	p.17
9	Terry Grant (UK)	10	p.260
9	Zdenek Bradac (Czech Republic)	10	p.78

It's been a fantastic decade for record breaking and what better way to honour our most prolific claimants than by including 10 of them in our Top 100 Records of the Decade? All 10 record breakers feature at various points in this book, some more than once. Frequent record smasher Ashrita Furman (above) claimed to his 100th current Guinness World Records feat on 14 April 2009 when he was one of 111 participants earning the title for the ★ **poem/literary passage recited in the most languages.** Can you beat Ashrita? Turn to p.14 to learn how to be a record breaker.

*Figures include only records set between 1 January 2000 and time of press.

INTRODUCTION

TALL TEENS, TALLER TURKS AND EVEN TALLER TOWERS – IT'S BEEN A BIG YEAR FOR RECORD BREAKING AND, AS EVER, WE WERE THERE WITH OUR TAPE MEASURES AT THE READY

Some record holders are like buses (indeed, some record holders *are* buses, such as the 32.2-m-long (104-ft) Super CityTrain buses of the Democratic Republic of Congo, the **longest bus**, but that's not important right now).

Take, for example, the category of tallest man: you wait years for a new one, then five claimants come along at once. This was the situation that faced us this year after we announced that we were disqualifying a Ukrainian claim of 257 cm (8 ft 5.5 in), due to a lack of sufficient evidence.

Almost all of the claims we then received looked certain to beat the height of the default tallest man Bao Xi Shun (China) – 236.1 cm (7 ft 8.9 in). However, we decided that we could no longer rely on the testimony of witnesses or even medical professionals when it came to measuring the tallest or shortest people

RED NOSE DAY

Anyone who criticizes record breaking as a frivolous waste of time need only see the amount of money raised for charities by people indulging in record-breaking feats – literally thousands, if not millions, of pounds are raised on behalf of campaigns such as Comic Relief's *Do Something Funny for Money* for Red Nose Day. Above, GWR's Lucia Sinigagliesi adjudicates at the **most T-shirts worn at once**.

GORDON'S F-WORD

GWR adjudicator Ralph Hannah risked the wrath of Gordon Ramsay (UK) as he judged record attempts by the celebrity chef and his guests on the TV shows *The F-Word* and *Cookalong Live*. Gordon failed spectacularly in all of the challenges, but his talented guests set records for a variety of culinary skills – find out which on p.144.

– someone from Guinness World Records had to be present at every measurement. Only then could we be sure.

So, after a year of globetrotting with my tape measure, I can reliably claim to have measured the world's tallest living man – and I can vouch for it personally, because I did the measuring! This case study shows what we're most proud of at Guinness World Records – no one else invests such a high degree of care or professionalism to

(Continued on p.10)

SMASHING NEWS

Guinness World Records returned to UK TV screens in 2009 with *Guinness World Records Smashed*, an exciting new format created by Outline Productions and shown exclusively on Sky1. Hosts Steve Jones and Konnie Huq enlisted the help of GWR's Marco Frigatti to arrange hundreds of records – and even set a few new world records of their own. Celebrities, unsuspecting members of the public, wannabe record breakers and even the studio audience were all given chances to get their names in the record books. Well done to all those who succeeded!

GUINNESS WORLD RECORDS SMASHED

Jan 1: Cosmonaut Sergei Avdeyev (Russia), born on the first day of 1956, has completed 11,968 orbits of the Earth during his career – the **most orbits around the world**. Many happy returns!

Jan 2: More than 200 million people were left without electricity when a power station failed in Uttar Pradesh, India, on this day in 2001 – the **largest power cut** ever.

2,802: the number of new and updated records added to the GWR master database in the past 12 months.

★ **NEW RECORD**
★ **UPDATED RECORD**

BLUE PETER

Congratulations and thanks to everyone who succeeded in breaking records on *Blue Peter* (1958–current), the **longest running children's magazine show**. Pictured is guest chef Aldo Zilli (Italy) after setting the record for the **most pancakes tossed in 1 minute** (117) on the show on 24 February 2009.

X-REF
Check out the records from our new TV consultant on **What's on TV?** (p.198), **Comedies & Soaps** (p.200) and **Game Shows & Reality TV** (p.202)

HE PINGPING & SVETLANA TOUR THE WORLD

To help us celebrate the launch of the 2009 book, we enlisted the support of a rather unique pair: Svetlana Pankratova (Russia), owner of the **longest female legs** (132 cm; 51.9 in), and He Pingping (China), at 74.61 cm (29.3 in), the world's **shortest mobile man**. The unlikely twosome proved such a hit in London that they were both invited to photoshoots and TV shows around the world and are now famous faces everywhere. Well done to Svetlana and Pingping on their success.

9

Jan 3: In 2007, Michael Perham (UK, b. 16 March 1992) became the **youngest person to sail the Atlantic solo**. He sailed from 18 November 2006 to 3 January 2007, aged 14 years 247 days.

Jan 4: In 1991 on this day, Fu Mingxia (China, b. 16 August 1978) became the **youngest diving world champion**, winning the world title for platform diving at Perth, Australia, aged 12 years 141 days.

EXTENDED FEATURES

With our TV shows, websites, podcasts and magazine spin-offs, we're more than just a book of records. And this year, our online presence is bigger than ever.

At every available opportunity this year, we sent our film crew along to capture record-breaking in action – including the measuring of the van Kleefs, the world's **tallest married couple** (below). Whenever you see the film symbol, log on to www.guinnessworldrecords.com/2010 and enter the code printed on p.6.

MALT BALLS & FAST TONGUES

A big thank you is due to all those radio DJs who hosted a Guinness World Record attempt this year. David Moore of Dublin's 98FM morning crew blew us away with his record 7.36 m (24 ft 2 in) **furthest Malteser blow with straw**; and BBC Newcastle DJ Jon Harle (inset), set the ★**fastest time to recite the first verse of a song** with **fastest talker** Sean Shannon (Canada), who recited alternate words of "Rock Around the Clock" on GWR Day 2008 in 7.06 seconds!

ratifying records across such a wide spectrum of subjects. We've been doing it for over 50 years now, and have built up an unrivalled global reputation.

Yet, like those buses, half a dozen or so new "record-ratification" companies have also come along this year, some of them even claiming association with Guinness World Records. I'd like to make it clear that GWR does not ratify records for anyone else. We have a dedicated team of inhouse Records Managers who process thousands of claims each year (find out more about what they do on p.14), and they investigate any claim that fulfills our criteria. We also have a fantastic team of Consultants from around the world who scour the globe for superlatives (see p.4 for a full list). We literally go to the ends of the earth to bring you this book, so please beware of pale imitations!

Well, what's new in this year's edition? As we're approaching a new decade, it seemed the perfect time to look back over the noughties and pick out what we consider the most inspiring, awesome, significant, and world-changing records and record breakers from the past 10 years. I remember as a child the excitement of the 1970s turning into the 80s (there were even TV ads to celebrate the new era!), and I know our younger readers will have the same excitement at facing their first new decade.

So packed is this year's book that we've overspilled some of the content on to our website. Use your unique code on p.6 to access this year's "extended features" such as downloadable wallpapers,

TALL TALES

The ★**tallest man-made structure** (p.178) topped out this year, and records for the ★**tallest cake** and ★**tallest cookie tower** both fell; find out more on pp.144–5. As tall as these towering constructions have been, I have never felt as short as I did when I flew round the planet to meet the new ★**tallest man** (below right), the ★**tallest married couple** (left) and the ★**tallest girl** (below left) and ★**boy** (p.73), the last two both under the age of 18. On a sadder note, while we were working on this book we learned of the passing of Sandy Allen (USA), the **tallest woman**. Sandy was always a good friend of Guinness World Records and will be much missed.

Jan 5: On 5 January 2008, Los Angeles-born singer/songwriter Josh Groban became the **first artist to have five tracks on the US Top 30 Adult Contemporary chart at once**.

Jan 6: The **youngest director of a feature-length film** is Kishan Shrikanth (India, b. 6 January 1996), who directed the movie *C/o Footpath* (India, 2006) when he was 9 years old.

5,023,333: the number of viewers – of at least 237 TV shows – who watched footage from Guinness World Records Day 2008!

PAUL O'GRADY

One of the perks of working at Guinness World Records – or one of the more daunting tasks, depending on your point of view – is that you could be called at any moment by the king of teatime TV himself to be on *The New Paul O'Grady Show*. Almost everyone at GWR has adjudicated on Paul's show, and whatever happens, we're guaranteed a good time! Pictured is Paul with his guests and a few of the GWR team.

SUN-KISSED!

It's always a pleasure to work with the UK's number one newspaper, *The Sun*, as we're always guaranteed a fun time. This year, for Guinness World Records Day, *The Sun* enlisted the help of model Ruth Reynolds to attempt the **most kisses given in a minute**. Despite the chance of some time off work, and a kiss from the beautiful Ruth, only 42 members of the paper's staff volunteered so it didn't take long for her to give them all the kiss off.

streaming videos and exclusive record-holder interviews. Look out for the following icons throughout the book – they denote where there is extra material available on our website.

To keep the content of the book as fresh and as relevant as possible, we've focussed a lot on the major news topics of the year – environmental concerns (**Planet in Danger**, p.148; **Eco-transport**, p.166), the global economy (**Economy**, p.150), piracy (**Boats**, p.170) and **Terrorism and Warfare** (p.154). We've also logged all the major achievements in the adventuring world – see the **Travellers' Tales** chapter (pp.90–101) for

more – and the latest scientific discoveries and achievements (see **Space,** pp.20–29 and **Technology and Engineering** on pp.164–191).

All your favourite sections are back as usual – including **Sports** (pp.220–275), **Animal Planet** (pp.46–60), **The Body** (pp.60–73) and **Human Achievements** (pp.74–89). We welcome onboard a new entertainment consultant by the name of Dick Fiddy, the British Film Institute's TV historian who helped us stay on top of our **TV records** (pp.198–203). And the **Sports Reference** (pp.266–275) and **Gazetteer** sections (pp.102–137) round off the book.

Finally, I'm pleased to say that GWR made it back on to British TV screens this year after a

few years' hiatus with an original production on Sky1. Thanks to everyone involved on the show, and especially Outline Productions, who produced the 12-part series. You'll find records from the show peppered throughout the book.

Thanks, indeed, to everyone who has helped make this year's edition so special. It's a global production that relies on a cast of thousands and the unrivalled quality of our record breakers to make it all happen. Perhaps that's why we're still the only universally-respected records validation and ratification company in the world...

Craig Glenday
Craig Glenday
Editor-in-Chief
GWR

CHILDREN IN NEED

Guinness World Records is a proud partner of Children in Need, and over the last year we helped with the fundraising by getting Britain record-breaking! We took part in the world's **largest pillow fight** (3,706 people) at Minehead Butlins, the **most people belly dancing** (535) in Malvern for BBC Hereford and Worcester, and measured the **tallest sugar cube tower** (146.5 cm; 57.6 in) in the West Quay centre in Southampton. Congratulations to everyone involved!

Jan 7: When he took over as manager of England's national side on this day in 2008, Fabio Capello (Italy) also became the **highest paid football manager**, with a reported salary of £6 million ($11.8 million).

Jan 8: The **largest plasma screen** measures 381 cm (150 in) diagonally, and was unveiled by Panasonic on this day at the 2008 International Consumer Electronics Show in Las Vegas, USA.

The Unbreakables

MOST GUINNESS WORLD RECORDS ARE BREAKABLE, AS THOUSANDS OF PEOPLE PROVE EVERY YEAR. SOME FEATS STAND THE TEST OF TIME, THOUGH, AND ARE UNLIKELY TO BE BEATEN ANY TIME SOON. WE PRESENT SOME OF HISTORY'S MOST ENDURING RECORDS...

Unbroken for 1,550 years – the longest held record in our archives

Longest pole sit St Simeon the Stylite (c. AD 386–459) spent 39 years on a pillar on the Hill of Wonders, near Aleppo, Syria.

Unbroken for 658 years

Largest pandemic From 1347 to 1351, the pneumonic form of plague, aka the Black Death, killed around 75 million people.

Unbroken for 635 years

Worst dance mania In July 1374, an outbreak of tarantism (dancing mania) in Aachen, Germany, saw thousands quite literally dancing uncontrollably in the streets.

Unbroken for 399 years

Most prolific female murderer From c. 1585 to 1610, Countess Elizabeth Báthory (Hungary) allegedly killed over 600 virgins. She was later locked up in her castle, where she died in 1614.

Unbroken for 195 years

Youngest doctorate On 13 April 1814, Carl Witte of Austria was made a Doctor of Philosophy (PhD) of the University of Giessen, Germany, aged just 12.

Unbroken for 120 years

Lightest person Lucia Xarate (or Zarate, aka "The Mexican Lilliputian", Mexico, 1863–89), an emaciated ateleiotic dwarf, weighed just 2.13 kg (4.7 lb) at the age of 17.

Unbroken for 126 years

Loudest noise Have you heard that the eruption of the island-volcano Krakatoa, in the Sunda Strait, Indonesia, on 27 August 1883, was audible 5,000 km (3,100 miles) away?

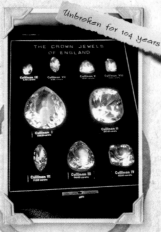

Unbroken for 104 years

Largest diamond No larger diamond has ever been found than the 3,106-carat Cullinan unearthed on 26 January 1905 at the Premier Diamond Mine in South Africa.

Unbroken for 34 years

Largest audience to attend a circus Ladies and gentlemen, a round of applause, please, for the largest circus crowd. A total of 52,385 people attended the Ringling Bros. and Barnum & Bailey Circus at the Superdome in New Orleans, Louisiana, USA, on 14 September 1975.

4.5 billion years ago: most astronomers now believe that at around this time a planet the size of Mars collided with our own world, resulting in the largest ever impact on Earth.

Largest production car When it comes to size, one car leaves its rivals in the dust. First built in 1927, the Bugatti "Royale" type 41 is more than 6.7 m (22 ft) in length. Its bonnet is over 2.13 m (7 ft) long.

Highest box office Taking inflation into account, epic weepie *Gone with the Wind* (USA, 1939) is the top-grossing movie ever, having taken $5,362,000,000 (£2,916,000,000) at the box office.

Largest plane by wing-span The H4 Hercules flying boat, aka the *Spruce Goose*, has a wing-span of 97.51 m (319 ft 11 in) and a length of 66.65 m (218 ft 8 in). It flew just once, on 2 November 1947.

Best-selling single by a group Recorded on 12 April 1954, "Rock Around the Clock" by Bill Haley and his Comets (USA) has sold an unaudited 25 million copies. That's what we call a record!

Jan 9: Ben Gold (USA) became the **first video-game world champion** when he won the North American Video Game Olympics in Ottumwa, Iowa, USA, on 8–9 January 1983.

TALLEST MAN EVER

He's perhaps the single most famous record holder in the history of GWR. Robert Pershing Wadlow (USA) was the **tallest man** ever recorded, standing 272 cm (8 ft 11.1 in) tall, with a weight of 199 kg (439 lb) at his peak. Wadlow's hands (unsurprisingly, the **largest hands** ever measured) were 32.3 cm (12.75 in) from the wrist to the tip of his middle finger and he wore a size-25 ring (pictured). This remarkable man was also the owner of the world's **largest feet**: he wore US size-37AA shoes (UK size 36, or approximately a European size 75), the equivalent to 47 cm (18.5 in) in length. Indirectly, it was his outsize feet that brought about Wadlow's untimely demise. He died after he developed a blister on his left foot while he was making a round of public appearances. The blister became infected, Wadlow's health deteriorated dramatically and he died in his sleep on 15 July 1940, aged just 22.

ACTUAL SIZE

Highest batting average Australian cricketing legend Sir Donald Bradman holds the highest Test batting average: 99.94 from 52 Tests – or 6,996 runs in 80 innings – from 1928 to 1948. It's unlikely that anyone will catch him…

HOW TO BE A RECORD BREAKER

LONGEST HOT DOG

On 27 September 2008, Empacadora Ponderosa (Mexico) created a 114.32-m-long (375-ft) hot dog in Monterrey, Mexico. GWR's Danny Girton was on hand to measure the outsize snack and to declare it officially as a new world record.

GWR'S ADJUDICATORS SPEND THE WHOLE YEAR TIRELESSLY ROAMING THE GLOBE TO BRING YOU THE HOTTEST RECORDS ON THE PLANET. MEET THE TEAM!

1. GET IN TOUCH

If you fancy setting, or breaking, a world record, the first step is to log on to our website: **www.guinnessworldrecords.com**. Then, click on "Break a Record" and simply follow the instructions. Please tell us as much as possible about your claim.

2. FOLLOW THE RULES

Do you want to break an existing world record? If so, we'll send you the guidelines that the current world record holder followed. If you have a brand-new record that you're just itching to try – and if we like the sound of it – we'll send you a set of new guidelines for you to follow. Once you've got them, you can begin!

3. POST US THE EVIDENCE

After you've completed your record attempt successfully, we'll need you to post us the evidence. So please remember to film your attempt, take lots of photographs and have two independent witnesses on hand to certify your achievement. Depending on the nature of your record attempt, we might also need some extra evidence – if we do, though, we'll tell you when we send you our guidelines.

4. WAIT

This might be the hardest part! You now have to wait while our expert Records Management Team assesses your claim and decides whether or not to award you a Guinness World Records certificate. Unless, of course, you've already arranged for an adjudicator to be a judge at your record attempt (see *opposite page*). Good luck!

★ **NEW RECORD**
UPDATED RECORD

RMT AT YOUR SERVICE

Our dedicated Records Management Team (RMT) assesses, adjudicates and approves all GWR record attempts. Much of the work takes place at our London, UK, headquarters, but RMT members – 10 of whom are seen here – find themselves adjudicating records in all four corners of the globe. From left to right: Kaoru, Tzeni, Andrea, Ralph, Marco, Talal, Mariamarta, Gaz, Laura and Lucia.

Jan 10: Ann and Claire Recht (both USA) were measured on 10 January 2007 and each found to be 2.01 m (6 ft 7 in) tall, making them the **tallest twin sisters**.

LONGEST SKIS

GWR's Denise Anlander visited Örebro, Sweden, on 13 September 2008 to measure a pair of 534-m-long (1,751-ft 11-in) skis. They were worn by 1,043 skiers in an event organized by Danske Bank.

INVITE A GWR JUDGE!

Arrange for a GWR adjudicator to attend your record attempt and you'll enjoy a whole different Guinness World Records experience:

• Instant confirmation that you're an official Guinness World Records holder (if you're successful) – and you'll receive an iconic GWR certificate on the spot.

• International media coverage for your record attempt. You could find yourself becoming one of the headlines of the day!

• A full write-up about your record on our website. See: **www. guinnessworldrecords.com/ register/login.aspx**.

• Expert support: your record attempt will be assigned to a member of our Adjudications Team, who will guide you through the unique experience of planning and – hopefully – breaking a world record.

• One of our adjudicators will also be available to carry out interviews and press conferences on your big day – a fantastic way to maximize publicity.

Please note that GWR charges a fee for adjudicators to attend record attempts. To find out more about this premium service, visit **www. guinnessworldrecords.com/ member/services_adjudications.aspx**.

You can now liaise with us in nine languages – English, French, Italian, German, Spanish, Portuguese, Arabic, Mandarin and Japanese – via our website. Simply click on the flag of your choice in the top-right corner to find out what's happening in your chosen country.

Finally, don't forget about the *Guinness World Records Gamer's Edition*. If you're aiming for a record-breaking high score, why not have a GWR adjudicator there to make it official?

MARCO FRIGATTI (ITALY)

Marco leads RMT, the people who collectively decide what constitutes a record. "It's a massive job," he admits, "with more than 1,000 applications pouring through every week." As well as his native Italian, Marco speaks English, German, French, Dutch and is learning Mandarin. And what does he most like about his work? "Meeting record holders. They are very passionate about the most disparate things. Record holders are special people I look up to."

ANDREA BÁNFI (HUNGARY)

Andrea's role as Adjudications Manager sees her play a key role in setting up record attempts as well as attending them: "I coordinate the company's adjudication service. If a record is witnessed by one of our adjudicators, you can be certain that I am involved in it." For Andrea, adjudications can inspire moments of real magic too: "Every event has the potential to become the most extraordinary moment in your life." She is fluent in German, English, Romanian and her native Hungarian.

TALAL OMAR (UK, B. YEMEN)

Based in London, Talal specializes in adjudications in the Middle East – appropriately, as he is fluent in both English and Arabic. "The Middle East is one of the fastest-growing areas for record-breaking in the world," he reveals. "The people are passionate about working together to be the best at what they do – such as the team from Al Jana bakers in Qatar, who successfully made the ★ **longest pitta bread in the world**" (128.5 m; 421.5 ft). What does Talal like best about GWR? "You will never have the same day twice!"

CARLOS MARTINEZ (SPAIN)

It was sport that kick-started Carlos's fascination with GWR. His earliest memory of the book was starting a collection of GWR stickers; the sports records always attracted him most. "One of my favourite memories is seeing so many sporting greats assembled for the **largest gathering of sport titles and awards** in Spain," he says. "All my heroes were there." This boundlessly enthusiastic adjudicator speaks Spanish, English, Italian and Portuguese and is based in our New York, USA, offices.

LUCIA SINIGAGLIESI (ITALY)

"During my school and university years I used to take every opportunity I had to travel to different countries," says Lucia. That restless appetite for globetrotting drove this Adjudications Executive from her home in the Marche, Italy, to London, UK, via much of the rest of the world – and made her a perfect candidate for the GWR team. Lucia speaks three languages – Italian, English and French – and is based in our London, UK, offices.

DANNY GIRTON (USA)

"I love to see history in the making and to personally meet the people who make it happen," says Danny, who handles record attempts from the northernmost stretches of Canada through to the southernmost tip of South America. Danny, who joined GWR some 18 months ago, is based in our New York offices, and speaks English and Spanish.

Jan 11:
The **youngest person to trek to the South Pole** without dogs or motor vehicles is Sarah Ann McNair-Landry (Canada, b. 9 May 1986), who was 18 when she reached the Pole on this day in 2005.

Jan 12:
The **oldest person to begin primary school** was aged 84. Kimani Ng'ang'a Maruge (Kenya) enrolled into Standard One at Kapkenduiyo Primary School, Eldoret, Kenya, on 12 January 2004.

RECORD-BREAKING TELEVISION

USA

British TV star Fearne Cotton (below) popped across the Atlantic to introduce the spectacular countdown show *Guinness World Records Live – Top 100* on NBC. Featuring the 100 greatest records ever seen on TV, the two-hour special culminated in a nerve-wracking, blood-boiling – and live! – attempt at the **longest motorcycle ride through a tunnel of fire** – an incredible 60.96-m (200-ft) stunt by US rider Clint Ewing (left).

GERMANY

Guinness World Records – Die größten Weltrekorde attracts the cream of the international record-breaking community, as well as a host of celebrity guest stars. Pictured are Markus Ferber and Clarissa Beyelschmidt (both Germany) setting the record for the ★ **longest time holding a person vertical overhead** (59.34 seconds), and Marco and Andrea adjudicating an attempt at the **most eggs crushed with the wrist**.

BE ON TV

If you've got a record-worthy skill or body part or plant or pet, then capture it on video and upload it to the GWR community – www.guinnessworldrecords.com/community.
If we like what we see, our talent scouts will get in touch to ensure you get official recognition as a Guinness World Records holder. Get posting!

UNITED KINGDOM

Sky1 is now officially the home of record-breaking in the UK, thanks to the Outline Production *Guinness World Records Smashed*. This exciting new format, hosted by Steve Jones and Konnie Huq (left), is a high-energy studio show that invites *you*, the public, to prove your record-breaking prowess. Submit your video applications online and you might find yourself on national TV trying to beat Shaeen Sadough's (UK, right) record for the ★ **most T-shirts worn in 1 minute** (83) or Zara Phythian's (UK) ★ **most objects kicked off the head in 1 minute** (43).

Jan 13: The **oldest couple to run a marathon** were Japan's Shigetsugu Anan (83 years 11 days) and his wife Miyoko (78 years 71 days), who ran the Ibusuki Nanohana Marathon on this day in 2008.

Jan 14: Yogesh Sharma (India) shook hands with 31,118 different people in eight hours – the **most handshakes by an individual** in this time period – on 14 January 1996.

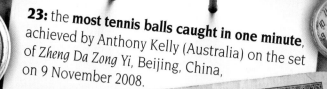

23: the **most tennis balls caught in one minute**, achieved by Anthony Kelly (Australia) on the set of *Zheng Da Zong Yi*, Beijing, China, on 9 November 2008.

CHINA

Proving that record-breaking is a global obsession is *Zheng Da Zong Yi – Guinness World Records Special* on CCTV in China. Pictured is the ever-ready Marco Frigatti awarding a certificate to Chen Yun (China, above) for the ★**most Diabolo juggling catches on the back in 1 minute** (67) and scrutinizing Wang Weibao (China, right) as he successfully completes the ★**longest duration standing on four fingers** (19.23 seconds).

SPAIN

Guinness World Records: El Show de los Records, goes from strength to strength, with hosts Carmen Alcayde and Luis Muñoz introducing ever more awesome skills and thrills each year. Pictured (from the bottom up) are *cortadore de jamón* (ham cutter) Nico Jiménez Rodríguez (Spain) creating the ★**longest slice of meat** (13.32 m; 43 ft 8 in); Daniel Browning Smith (USA), the **most flexible man**; and Chloe Bruce (UK) performing the ★**most martial arts kicks in one minute using one leg** (192).

ITALY

Senior adjudicator Marco Frigatti returns to his native Italy to film *Lo show dei Record*, a no-expense-spared showcase of talent from a global line-up of record breakers. Claimants from as far afield as China and New Zealand, Finland and Lithuania descend upon Milan for this most glamorous of TV events. Leading the proceedings is host Barbara D'Urso, who introduces records such as ★**most car rolls in 5 minutes (solo)** – seven by Austria's Franz Muellner (above) – and the ★**most bowls broken by one finger in one minute** – 102 by the Chinese martial arts expert Fan Weipeng (right).

Jan 15: Thomas Syta of Van Nuys, California, USA, managed to keep a single Lifesaver sweet in his mouth for a record 7 hr 10 min – with the hole intact – on this day back in 1983.

★ **NEW RECORD** ★ **UPDATED RECORD**

17

GUINNESS WORLD RECORDS 2010
GWR DAY

🇨🇦 Canada
LARGEST GAME OF LEAPFROG

On 14 November 2008, the Toronto Zoo welcomed over 800 participants who leapfrogged for five minutes. Despite just falling short of setting a new record for Guinness World Records Day, the event was a great success and helped to raise awareness for amphibian conservation.

🏴 England
★ LARGEST GATHERING OF PEOPLE WEARING UNDERPANTS

Raising awareness for the Fair Trade Organization "Pants to Poverty" campaign, 116 people gathered at St Pancras train station, London, wearing just their underwear on Guinness World Records Day, 13 November 2008.

🇺🇸 USA
★ LONGEST DREADLOCKS (FEMALE)

When measured in Davenport, Florida, USA, on 13 November 2008, Asha Mandela (USA) was found to have dreadlocks 2.59 m (8 ft 6 in) long.

🇮🇪 Ireland
★ LARGEST IMAGE MADE OF LED LIGHTS

Tesco Ireland, in conjunction with Disney and Make a Wish Foundation, made an image of Donald Duck using 26,981 LED lights in Dublin on 13 November 2008.

🇺🇸 USA
LARGEST DOG WEDDING

This record attempt took place in Illinois on 8 November 2008, but freezing temperatures meant that only 87 dog couples attended. The record of 178 dog weddings therefore still stands.

🇩🇪 Germany
MOST STEINS CARRIED 40 M BY A WOMAN

Anita Schwarz (Germany) carried 19 steins over 40 m (131 ft 3 in) in Mesenich on 9 November 2008 to mark Guinness World Records Day.

🇧🇷 Brazil
★ LARGEST BREAD

A loaf of bread weighing 1.571 tonnes (1.731 tons) was made by Joaquim Goncalves (Brazil) in Curitiba/Parana on 13 November 2008.

Jan 16: The **largest ice cream cake**, weighing 8,750 kg (19,290 lb), was made by Beijing Allied Faxi Food Co., Ltd for Beijing Children's Art Theater Co., Ltd in Beijing, China, on this day in 2006.

Jan 17: The **fastest row across the Atlantic** in any direction, land to land, is 33 days 7 hr 30 min. A 14-man UK/Irish team rowed from Spain on 15 December 2007, arriving in Barbados on 17 January 2008.

View this clip

103: the **most people dressed as superheroes,** who gathered at Bournemouth University, Poole, UK, in celebration of GWR Day.

FEATS OF ACHIEVEMENT

• The **farthest golf ball blow** is 5.835 m (19 ft 1 in), achieved by Alastair Galpin (New Zealand) in Auckland on 2 November 2008.

• The **most kisses given in a minute** is 94, achieved by Valentin Pasquier (France) in Nantes, France, on 12 November 2008.

• The **longest distance that a person has been pulled by a horse during a full body burn** is 472.8 m (1,551 ft 2 in) by Halapi Roland (Hungary) in Kisoroszi, Hungary, on 12 November 2008.

★ **NEW RECORD**
★ **UPDATED RECORD**

✠ *England*
★ LARGEST CUP OF TEA

A cup of tea measuring 1.22 m (4 ft) in diameter, 1.22 m (4 ft) in height and with a volume of 400 litres (88 gal) was made by Lancashire Tea at an Asda supermarket in Preston, UK, on 13 November 2008.

☪ *Turkey*
CONCRETE BLOCK BREAKING

As part of Turkey's celebrations for GWR Day, strongman Ali Bahçetepe (Turkey, above left) set a new record for the **most concrete blocks broken in a single stack** in Datça, Turkey, on 14 November 2008. At the same event, Norway's Narve Laeret (Norway, above right) broke the record for the ★ **most concrete blocks broken in 1 minute** with 700 blocks smashed. (Laeret's record has since been broken by Bahçetepe, with 888 on 9 January 2009.)

🇫🇷 *France*
★ LONGEST SCOUBIDOU/ BOONDOGGLE

A scoubidou (aka boondoggle or gimp) is a lanyard braided and knotted from brightly coloured strands of plastic. The longest was made by Manuela Dos Santos (France) and was measured at 510 m (1,673 ft 2 in) in Brancourt on 11 November 2008.

View this clip

Check out **guinnessworldrecords.com** to download videos and photos from various GWR Day events.

🇨🇳 *China*
★ HIGHEST WATERFALL DIVE

The highest waterfall dive was 12.19 m (39 ft 11 in) and was achieved by Di Huanran (China) at the Diaoshuilou Waterfall of Jingbo Lake, Mudanjiang City, on 5 October 2008.

United Arab Emirates
★ MOST CHILDREN READING WITH AN ADULT

The record for the most children reading with an adult is 3,032, which was achieved by The Kindergarten Starters School at Global Village in Dubai, United Arab Emirates, on 12 November 2008.

Jan 18: The **fastest crossing of the Antarctic continent** (also first **solo and unaided**) was achieved by Børge Ousland (Norway), who completed the 2,690-km (1,675-mile) trek on this day in 1997.

SPACE

CONTENTS

★ MOST DURABLE MARS ROVER

This image was taken by NASA's *Opportunity* rover which, along with its twin (*Spirit*), touched down in January 2004. They are both still operational as of March 2009, despite being designed to last just three months.

The photograph – which has been false-coloured to highlight the differences in the planet's surface materials – shows the rim of the Victoria impact crater. At the top of the crater lies loose, scattered rocks; at the base is hard bedrock. In between is a band of bright pink rock. Geologists believe that this pink rock represents what used to be the surface of the planet until the impact which created the 730-m-wide (2,395-ft) crater buried it beneath its ejecta blanket tens of millions of years ago.

★ NEW RECORD   UPDATED RECORD

5 cm/sec (1.9 in/sec): the maximum velocity of the twin Mars Exploration Rovers *Spirit* and *Opportunity*, holders of the **land-speed record on Mars**.

DEEP SPACE

★ LARGEST SPACE MIRROR

The primary mirror built for ESA's Herschel Space Observatory measures 3.5 m (11 ft 6 in) across. It was constructed from a single piece of silicon carbide ceramic, making it much lighter than glass. The mirror will allow the observatory to study objects in the Solar System as well as deep space in the infrared spectrum. Successfully launched on 14 May 2009, Herschel is expected to last for three years with its instruments cooled by liquid helium down to just 2 K (−271.15°C; −456.07°F).

★ SHORTEST DISTANCE BETWEEN TWO BLACK HOLES

In March 2009, astronomers reported that the quasar (short for "quasi-stellar object") SDSS J153636.22+044127.0, a galaxy emitting vast quantities of electromagnetic energy, appears to contain two black holes (a binary black hole) at its centre. The black holes weigh the equivalent of around 50 million and 20 million Suns respectively, yet are separated by only one third of a light year.

★ DENSEST GALAXIES

Ultra Compact Dwarf (UCD) galaxies are a class of galaxy discovered in 1999 by a team of astrophysicists led by Dr Michael Drinkwater (Australia). Dozens of UCD galaxies, which are possibly leftover building blocks that once formed much larger galaxies, are now known to astronomers. These small galaxies contain around a hundred million stars in a space just 200 light years across, but

★ MOST COMMON TYPE OF GALAXY

Of the few hundred billion galaxies in the Universe, spiral galaxies – like our own galaxy, the Milky Way – make up roughly 77% of them. They are characterized by spiral arms wound around a brighter core, with about half of all spirals also containing a bar across their centres. Spiral galaxies can contain several hundred million stars, along with dust and gas.

astronomers suggest that billions of years ago these galaxies had a density of perhaps one million stars per cubic light year – one million times higher than the density of the Milky Way.

★ GALAXY WITH THE HIGHEST LEVEL OF STAR FORMATION

Astronomers studying the light from the galaxy J1148+5251 have estimated that stars are being formed there at a rate of around 1,000 solar masses per year – roughly a thousand times greater than the rate of star formation in our own galaxy. J1148+5251 is a distant active galaxy known as a quasar. At 12.8 billion light years away, astronomers are watching its star-forming activity as it was 12.8 billion years ago.

DEEP SPACE?

There are various definitions of "deep space". Some use it to describe anything beyond the gravitational influence of Earth; however, many astronomers, and Guinness World Records, use the term for the Universe outside the Solar System.

★ OLDEST BROWN DWARF

Brown dwarfs are "failed stars", rather like gas supergiants that never became large enough to produce the internal pressures necessary for nuclear fusion. One brown dwarf in the sparse halo surrounding our galaxy (the Milky Way) is 2MASS 1626+3925. Measurements of the weak infrared light it emits suggest that this failed star is around 10 billion years old: more than twice as old as our Solar System.

LARGEST LAND-BASED TELESCOPE

The twin Keck Telescopes on the summit of Hawaii's dormant Mauna Kea volcano are the world's largest optical and infrared telescopes. Each of these telescopes, designed to observe deep-space objects, is eight storeys tall and weighs 272 tonnes (300 tons). Both Kecks have a 10-m-wide (32-ft) mirror, made up of 36 hexagonal segments that act together to create a single reflective surface.

★ NEW RECORD
UPDATED RECORD

Jan 19: The **fastest speed at which a spacecraft has departed from Earth** is 58,338 km/h (36,250 mph). It was achieved by NASA's New Horizons spacecraft, which launched on this day in 2006.

Jan 20: Francis Joyon (France) sailed solo and non-stop around the world in 57 days 13 hr 34 min 6 sec from 23 November 2007 to 20 January 2008 – the **fastest circumnavigation sailing solo**.

299,792,458 m/sec (983,571,056 ft/sec): the speed of light in a vacuum, the **fastest speed possible in the Universe**. A light year is the distance light can travel in a year.

protons and electrons in the atoms in a star's core are fused together into neutrons. Since neutrons comprise much of an atom's mass, neutron stars are small and dense, usually the size of a large city, but containing as much mass as the Sun. Pulsar PSRJ0108-1431, in the constellation of Cetus, is just 280 light years away from the Earth.

★ HIGHEST-ENERGY GAMMA-RAYS

Launched on 11 June 2008, NASA's Fermi Gamma-ray Space Telescope can detect gamma-rays from violent events in the Universe at energies from 8,000 electron volts to greater than 300 billion electron volts, the highest-energy wavelengths yet studied. A map of the whole sky at gamma-ray energies of more than 150 million times greater than visible light (above) was released in March 2009, representing three months of Fermi data.

★ BRIGHTEST ACTIVE GALAXIES

Active galaxies are galaxies that have a highly luminous (bright) centre and emit energy over the electromagnetic spectrum. They are also believed to house supermassive black holes at their cores. These black holes are in the process of sucking in matter surrounding them and ejecting jets of ionized gas at close to the speed of light.

When the jet of one of these galaxies is pointing towards the Earth, the galaxy appears more luminous to observations than other galaxies. Such galaxies are known as "blazars". Pictured above is a NASA conceptual image of blazar PKS 2155-304.

DID YOU KNOW?

Although "blazars" appear bright to us on Earth, the magnitude or level of their brightness is highly variable.

of the Sun. With the exception of the supermassive class of black holes at the heart of galaxies, this is more than double the size of any known black hole.

NEAREST PULSAR

Pulsars are a type of neutron star that emit beams of radiation as they rotate. They are formed in supernovae explosions where

★ MOST DISTANT OBJECT IN THE UNIVERSE

On 23 April 2009, NASA's *Swift* satellite detected a 10-second-long gamma-ray burst and its subsequent X-ray afterglow eminating from star GRB 090423. Later analysis revealed GRB 090423 to be roughly 13.035 billion light years away, which means the explosion occurred close to the when the Universe is estimated to have formed (see below). This also makes GRB 090423 the ★ **oldest object in the Universe** yet detected.

★ FASTEST APPROACHING GALAXY

Despite the overall expansion of the Universe, there are only a small number of galaxies that are approaching our own. M86, a lenticular (lens-shaped) galaxy around 52 million light years away in the Virgo Cluster, is moving towards the Milky Way at 419 km/s (260 miles/s).

★ HEAVIEST BLACK HOLE

In February 2008, astronomers announced their discovery of a black hole in the dwarf galaxy IC 10 that has a mass estimated to be as much as 33 times that

MOST ACCURATE MEASURE OF THE AGE OF THE UNIVERSE

TOP **100** Records of the Decade

The *Wilkinson Microwave Anisotropy Probe* (*WMAP*, illustrated below) was designed to measure the Cosmic Microwave Background of the Universe – the radiation echo of the Big Bang. The first results from *WMAP*, released on 11 February 2003 and pictured right, reveal minute temperature differences in the early Universe. This has allowed scientists to estimate the age of the Universe at 13.7 billion years old, with a degree of error of just 1%.

Jan 21: Tommy Clowers of Ramona, California, USA, achieved the **highest jump on a motorcycle** with a leap of 7.62 m (25 ft) at Van Nuys Airport, California, on this day in 2001.

EXTRASOLAR PLANETS

★ NEW RECORD ★ UPDATED RECORD

★ CLOSEST EXTRASOLAR PLANET TO ITS PARENT STAR

Extrasolar planets, or exoplanets, are any planets that do not orbit our Sun. In 2007, astronomers using the Hubble Space Telescope took part in the Sagittarius Window Eclipsing Extrasolar Planet Search (SWEEPS), a project to monitor 180,000 stars for a week in the direction of the centre of the Milky Way. Hubble watched for the dimming of light from the stars caused as planets crossed in front of them. Of the 16 planets discovered in this project, one of them, SWEEPS-10, orbits its star at a distance of only 1.2 million km (745,000 miles). It hurtles around its orbit in only 10 hours. For comparison Mercury takes 88 days to orbit the Sun.

★ LIGHTEST EXTRASOLAR PLANET

Gliese 581e, whose discovery was announced in April 2009, is the fourth planet discovered to date orbiting the star Gliese 581. Estimates of its properties reveal that it could have the same mass as just 1.9 Earths; however, this rocky planet orbits too close to its star to have conditions suitable for life.

Generally, extrasolar planets are named after the star they orbit in the order that they are discovered ("a" is not used as it refers to the star itself). So, the first planet detected orbiting Gliese 581 is Gliese 581b, and so forth. There are many ways of naming stars, but the system of adding a letter at the end to denote objects in the orbit is standard.

★ MOST ELONGATED EXTRASOLAR PLANET ORBIT

HD 80606b, the first extrasolar planet on which real-time weather changes have been observed (see column, left), lies 190 light years away in the constellation Ursa Major. It has a highly elliptical (oval-shaped) orbit, similar to that of a short period comet. During each orbit, the planet ranges in distance from its star from just 4.5 million km (2.8 million miles) at its closest point to 125 million km (78 million miles) at its most distant point. HD 80606b's year – that is, the time it takes the planet to orbit its star – lasts a mere 111 days.

FACT

Extrasolar planet-finding techniques should soon be able to detect extrasolar planets smaller than the size of the Earth.

★ HOTTEST EXTRASOLAR PLANET

HD 149026b is a gas giant orbiting a yellow sub-giant star 257 light years away. Orbiting close to its parent star, it achieves a temperature of around 2,040°C (3,704°F), well above the melting point of iron. The planet is probably metal-rich and very dark and likely to have dark clouds of metal oxides that absorb the star's radiation efficiently, contributing to its immensely high temperature.

OLDEST EXTRASOLAR PLANET

The oldest planet yet discovered is an extrasolar planet in the globular cluster M4, some 5,600 light years from Earth. With an age estimated to be at least 10 billion years, this distant planet is more than twice as old as our Solar System. Its discovery was announced in July 2003.

★ FIRST REAL-TIME WEATHER CHANGES SEEN ON AN EXOPLANET

Space telescope observations of the gas giant HD 80606b have revealed weather changes within its atmosphere as it passed close to its star. Over an eight-hour period, the planet's cloud tops went from temperatures of 520°C (968°F) to around 1,220°C (2,228°F) – hotter than molten lava.

moon
Earth
COROT-Exo-7b

★ SMALLEST EXTRASOLAR PLANET

In February 2009, scientists working with the Convection, Rotation and Planetary Transits (COROT) satellite announced the discovery of a planet orbiting a star 456 light years away in the constellation Monoceros. Known as COROT-Exo-7b, this world has a diameter estimated at just 1.7 times that of Earth's.

Jan 22: Happy birthday George Blair (aka Banana George, USA, b. 22 January 1915)! George is the world's **oldest active snowboarder**, snowboarding between 45 and 60 days a year.

Jan 23: The **deepest manned ocean descent** was achieved by Jacques Piccard (Switzerland) and Donald Walsh (USA). They descended to 10,911 m (35,797 ft) in the Mariana Trench on this day in 1960.

★ FIRST CONFIRMED DISCOVERY OF AN EXTRASOLAR PLANET

In 1992, astronomers announced they had discovered two planets orbiting pulsar PSR B1257+12. The pulsar is a supernova remnant 980 light years from Earth that weighs around 1.4 times the mass of the Sun but is only around 30 km (18 miles) across. It spins once on its axis in just 6.22 milliseconds (9,646 rpm). The pulsar was previously a giant star that went supernova around 800 million years ago.

★ LARGEST STAR WITH A PLANET

In January 2003, astronomers announced their discovery of a planet orbiting the orange giant star HD 47536. This star is expanding at the end of its life and currently measures around 33 million km (20 million miles) across. HD 47536b, one of two planets spotted in the system, is 300 million km (186 million miles) from its star but will eventually be consumed in a few tens of millions of years as the star continues to expand into a red giant.

★ FIRST MAP OF AN EXTRASOLAR PLANET

In 2007, NASA's Spitzer infrared space telescope was pointed at the star HD 189733 and its accompanying planet, HD 189733b, and observed the system for 33 hours. The resulting observations were converted into a temperature map showing a range from 700 to 940°C (1,292 to 1,724°F). The planet was discovered by the transit method, in which the planet passes between the Earth and the planet's star, reducing the light visible from the star by 3%.

★ COLDEST EXTRASOLAR PLANET

OGLE-2005-BLG-390Lb, named in part from the Optical Gravitational Lensing Experiment (OGLE) observatory that played a role in its discovery in 2006, orbits a cool red dwarf star 21,000 light years from Earth. The low energy of its star coupled with the size of its orbit, farther out from its star than Mars is from our Sun, means its surface temperature is just -220°C (-364°F). Its mass is estimated at around five times that of Earth's and it probably has an icy surface, rocky core and thin atmosphere.

★ WINDIEST EXOPLANETS

HD179949b, HD209458b and 51 Pegasi b are all gas giants orbiting different stars within 150 light years of Earth. Each orbits its star within around 8 million km (4.5 million miles) – far closer than Mercury orbits the Sun. Results released in January 2007 show that the temperature difference between day and night on these planets is tiny. To explain this, some scientists suggest that supersonic winds of up to 14,500 km/h (9,000 mph) are constantly transferring heat from the planets' day sides to their night sides.

FIRST DETECTION OF AN EXOPLANET ATMOSPHERE

In November 2001, astronomers used the Hubble Space Telescope to detect light passing through the atmosphere at the edge of the planet HD 209458b as it passed in front of its star. Spectral analysis of this light revealed the presence of sodium in the atmosphere of this scorched gas giant, which orbits its star in just 3.5 days. Subsequent observations of this planet have suggested the presence of water vapour in its atmosphere.

★ FIRST PLANET HUNTER SPACE MISSION

Designed specifically to find planets around other stars by the French Space Agency CNES, the Convection Rotation and Planetary Transits spacecraft (COROT) was launched on 27 December 2006 into a polar orbit 827 km (513 miles) above the Earth. The probe, which uses transits to identify extrasolar planets, reported its first planet discovery, COROT-Exo-1b, in May 2007.

★ FIRST VISIBLE LIGHT IMAGE OF EXTRASOLAR PLANETS

In November 2008, two discoveries announced at the same time revealed the first images taken in visible light of planets orbiting other stars. Scientists using the Hubble Space Telescope captured the dust disk surrounding the star Formalhaut, 25 light years from Earth (main picture), and found a world about the size of Jupiter (inset) orbiting within it. Another team using the Keck and Gemini telescopes directly imaged three planets around the star HR 8799, 129 light years from Earth.

Fomalhaut b Planet
2006
2004

Jan 24: The **largest hora dance** involved 13,828 participants, who danced in the town of Slatina, Romania, on 24 January 2006.

EXPLORING THE SOLAR SYSTEM

★ FIRST DETECTION OF PLANETARY LIFE BY A SPACE PROBE

When the *Galileo* spacecraft, bound for Jupiter, made a fly-by of Earth in December 1990, mission scientists used *Galileo*'s sensors to study Earth for signs of life as if it were being probed for the first time. The spacecraft detected the infrared signature of chlorophyll, molecular oxygen and methane in the atmosphere, and radio signals of an unnatural origin – all of which are key indicators of life.

★ NEW RECORD
UPDATED RECORD

★ FIRST THUNDER HEARD ON ANOTHER PLANET

The USSR's *Venera 11* lander touched down on Venus on 25 December 1978. Among its instruments was an acoustic detector capable of registering sound in the Venusian sky and on its surface. During its parachute descent, the detector heard the sound of the wind and it picked up the noises of the lander's other equipment operating just after touchdown. Roughly 32 minutes after landing, another sound of unknown origin with a level of 82 decibels was detected. A Venusian thunder clap is the most likely explanation.

★ FIRST MISSION TO STUDY A DWARF PLANET

NASA's *Dawn* spacecraft was launched on 27 September 2007. Its goal is to reach the asteroid Vesta in the asteroid belt between Mars and Jupiter, study it from orbit and then break orbit to rendezvous with Ceres, the largest object in the asteroid belt. Ceres, like Pluto, was reclassified as a dwarf planet in 2006. Despite launching later than NASA had hoped, *Dawn* will reach Ceres in February 2015, five months before the *New Horizons* spacecraft reaches Pluto.

★ MOST DISTANT PLANET STUDIED FROM ORBIT

The exploration of the Solar System by unmanned spacecraft began with simple fly-by missions in which a probe would hurtle past a planet, gathering

FACT

Cassini has been in orbit of Saturn since 1 July 2004, taking many images, such as this composite image of Titan, Saturn's largest moon.

MOST REMOTE PLANETARY LANDING

The European Space Agency (ESA) probe *Huygens* landed successfully on Saturn's largest moon, Titan, on 14 January 2005. It sent back science data and images of the surface during both its parachute descent and from the ground. *Huygens* was carried to Titan, which is on average 1.433 billion km (890 million miles) from the Sun, by the NASA/ESA spacecraft *Cassini*.

data. Fly-bys are eventually followed by orbiter missions: as their name suggests, a spacecraft collects planetary data while in orbit. In July 2004, upon the arrival of NASA's *Cassini* orbiter, Saturn (on average 1.43 billion km; 888 million miles from the Sun) became the most distant planet to be studied from orbit.

FARTHEST DISTANCE FROM EARTH REACHED BY HUMANS

The crew of the ill-fated *Apollo 13* (pictured here on Earth with their families) reached a distance of 400,171 km (248,655 miles) above the Earth's surface, at 1:21 am BST on 15 April 1970. An explosion in an oxygen tank on the service module forced the crew to abandon their Moon landing and shift to a free return trajectory enabling them to use the Moon's gravity to slingshot their vessel back to Earth. The manoeuvre took them to within 254 km (158 miles) of the lunar surface on the far side of the Moon and to a distance that is the absolute record for the highest altitude achieved by a human. For more record highs and lows, turn to pp.92–93.

Jan 25: Luuk Broos (Netherlands) and his team created the **tallest champagne fountain**, consisting of 43,680 glasses forming 63 storeys, in Wijnegem, Belgium, on this day in 2008.

MOST REMOTE MAN-MADE OBJECT

NASA's *Voyager 1* spacecraft (pictured, bottom), launched on 5 September 1977 (right), encountered Jupiter in March 1979 and then Saturn in November 1980. Those fly-bys flung the probe out of the plane of the Solar System. As of 1 February 2009, *Voyager 1* was 16.247 billion km (10.095 billion miles) from the Sun. Still operational, the craft has enough power to operate until around 2025.

FASTEST DEPARTURE SPEED FROM EARTH

The fastest speed at which a spacecraft has ever departed from Earth is 58,338 km/h (36,250 mph). It was achieved by NASA's *New Horizons* spacecraft, which launched from Cape Canaveral on 19 January 2006, beginning a nine-year flight to Pluto and its moons Charon, Nix and Hydra.

LARGEST SPACE STATION

The *International Space Station* (ISS) has been under construction since its first component, the *Zarya* module, was launched in November 1998. On 31 May 2008, NASA astronauts attached the *Kibo* module, made by the Japan Aerospace Exploration Agency (JAXA), bringing the total mass of the ISS so far to 298,000 kg (657,000 lb).

LONGEST COMET TAIL (MEASURED)

The longest comet tail ever measured was 570 million km (350 million miles) long and belonged to the comet Hyakutake. This is more than three times the distance from the Earth to the Sun. The tail was discovered by Geraint Jones of Imperial College, London, UK, on 13 September 1999, using data gathered by the ESA/NASA spacecraft *Ulysses* – on a chance encounter with the comet on 1 May 1996. Although other comets undoubtedly have longer tails, this is the longest ever measured.

SPACE TOURISTS

Businessman Dennis Tito (USA) became the **first space tourist**, flying to the International Space Station on a trip that lasted from 28 April to 6 May 2001.

Anousheh Ansari (Iran) became the **first female space tourist** on 18 September 2006 with a 10-day visit to the International Space Station.

The ★ **most prolific space tourist** is Charles Simonyi (USA), who has successfully completed two trips into space. Simonyi departed on his first expedition on 7 April 2007 and his second on 26 March 2009.

★ CLOSEST FLY-BY OF MERCURY

On 14 January 2008, the *MESSENGER* spacecraft performed a gravity-assist fly-by of Mercury, closing to just 200 km (124 miles) above its surface at closest approach. Because Mercury is deep within the Sun's gravity well, achieving orbit is difficult. *MESSENGER* has performed two fly-bys of Mercury so far, with a third due in September 2009. These will adjust the spacecraft's trajectory so it can enter the orbit of Mercury in March 2011.

MOST COMETS DISCOVERED BY A SPACECRAFT

The ESA/NASA spacecraft *SOHO* (Solar and Heliospheric Observatory) was launched in December 1995 to study the Sun from close to the L1 point – a position between the Sun and Earth where the gravities of the two bodies cancel each other out. The probe has produced near real-time solar data for space weather prediction, and its discoveries of comets have been incidental. On 25 June 2008, the spacecraft accidentally discovered its 1,500th comet.

THE NEW MISSION

NASA scientists hope that *Voyager 1* will remain operational long enough to reach, and prove the existence of, the heliopause – the theoretical boundary of our Sun's influence and the point at which its solar wind is overpowered by that of other stars.

Jan 26: The **largest diamond** was found on this date in 1905 at the Premier Diamond Mine near Pretoria, South Africa. Named The Cullinan, it was graded at 3,106 carats.

Jan 27: Clint Ewing (USA) drove 60.96 m (200 ft) to complete the **longest motorcycle ride through a tunnel of fire** at Universal City, Los Angeles, USA, on this day in 2008.

27 WWW.GUINNESSWORLDRECORDS.COM

MARS

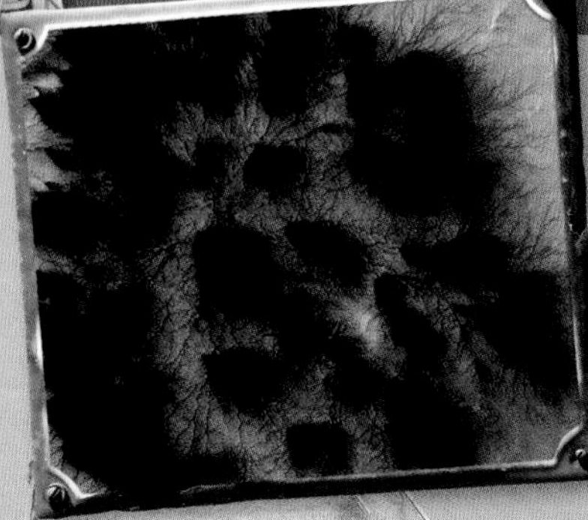

WELCOME TO MARS

The fourth planet from the Sun, Mars is a rocky world like Earth but around half the size. Its thin atmosphere of carbon dioxide blankets a dusty surface stained red by iron oxide. In the night sky, Mars' red colour is distinctly visible to the naked eye. When space probes began visiting the red planet in the 1960s, they gradually unveiled a world of titanic geology, prehistoric rivers and conditions that could support primitive life.

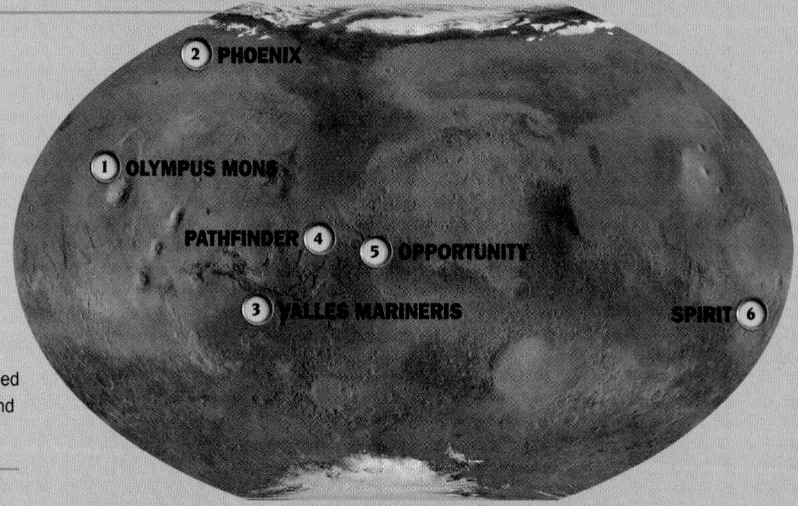

② PHOENIX

① OLYMPUS MONS

PATHFINDER ④

⑤ OPPORTUNITY

③ VALLES MARINERIS

SPIRIT ⑥

★ LARGEST AREA OF SURFACE ICE

Almost all of the ice on Mars' surface is located at the poles. The southern ice cap is the largest of the two and is around 420 km (260 miles) across, and contains enough water to cover the entire planet in a layer 11 m (36 ft) deep.

Martian ice consists of water ice and a seasonal coating of carbon dioxide "dry" ice, which accumulates during each polar winter. The dry ice can erode the terrain as it sublimates (converts directly from ice to vapour) every spring. The troughs in the image above, captured by the *Mars Reconnaissance Orbiter*, are believed to have been eroded by dust-rich gas flowing beneath the seasonal ice to openings where the gas can escape.

LONGEST TIME SURVIVED ON MARS BY A ROVER

The twin Mars Exploration Rovers, *Spirit* ⑥ and *Opportunity* ⑤ (the **largest planetary rovers**), touched down successfully on the surface of Mars on 4 and 25 January 2004, respectively. Since then, they have each travelled across the Martian surface, taking scientific images and measurements. By April 2009, the *Opportunity* rover had travelled 15,805 m (51,853 ft) over the surface – far farther than it had been originally designed for. As of May 2009, both rovers are still operational.

★ LARGEST IMPACT CRATER

One of Mars' most striking features is the stark difference between its low-lying plains of the northern hemisphere and the ancient cratered highlands of its southern hemisphere. Analysis of data from NASA's orbiting probes suggests the whole northern hemisphere could be a vast impact basin 8,500 km (5,300 miles) across – significantly lower than the southern hemisphere. This impact would have happened more than 3.9 billion years ago and would have required an object larger than the dwarf planet Pluto to create.

★ MOST RECENT EVIDENCE OF WATER ON MARS

An image taken by *Mars Reconnaissance Orbiter* of a dry gulley in the Promethei Highlands suggests liquid water flowed on Mars as recently as 1.25 million years ago. The gully looks like it formed as ice melted, flowed downhill and deposited sediment before evaporating in the thin Martian atmosphere.

★ FIRST AVALANCHE WITNESSED ON ANOTHER PLANET

The HiRiSE camera on NASA's *Mars Reconnaissance Orbiter* took images of a 700-m-tall (2,296-ft 7-in), steep slope near the north pole on 19 February 2007. Upon analysis, it was found that the orbiter had accidentally captured clouds of debris fanning from the base of the slope, where ice and dust had broken loose and fallen just seconds before.

★ FIRST MARS ROVER

NASA's Mars *Pathfinder* ④ mission landed in Ares Vallis on 4 July 1997. The lander deployed a small mobile laboratory, or rover, called *Sojourner*, capable of travelling a few hundred metres from the lander. *Sojourner* weighed just over 10.6 kg (23 lb 5 oz) and was able to conduct basic experiments such as measuring the chemical compositions of Martian rocks. *Pathfinder* (pictured below) and the *Sojourner* rover operated until contact was lost on 27 September 1997.

Jan 28: At 21 years 155 days, Jamal Lewis (USA, b. 26 August 1979) of the Baltimore Ravens became the **youngest player to ever appear in the Super Bowl** at Super Bowl XXXV on 28 January 2001.

90–100 km (55–62 miles): the altitude of Martian clouds discovered by ESA's *Mars Express Orbiter*, the **highest clouds in the solar system**.

★ FIRST EXTRATERRESTRIAL DUST DEVILS OBSERVED

First seen from orbit by the *Viking* spacecraft in the 1970s, the "dust devils" (whirlwinds of dust) on Mars can tower above the landscape. They are produced by the Sun warming the dust and ground, causing the loose dust to rise into clouds with the warm air. A dust devil passed over the *Spirit* rover in 2005, blowing off the dust on its solar panels and improving its power levels.

★ NEW RECORD
UPDATED RECORD

HIGHEST MOUNTAIN IN THE SOLAR SYSTEM

The peak of the Martian volcano Olympus Mons ① is 25 km (15 miles) above its base – nearly three times the height of Mount Everest. Olympus Mons is designated a shield volcano because of its shape. Despite its great height, it has a very gentle slope – Olympus Mons is over 20 times wider than it is high.

★ FIRST SUCCESSFUL POLAR LANDER

NASA's *Phoenix* spacecraft ② landed in the Vastitas Borealis, the great world-wrapping lowland plain in the northern polar region, on 25 May 2008. It entered the atmosphere after a nearly nine-month journey at 21,000 km/h (13,000 mph), using a heat shield, then parachute and retro rockets to slow to just 8 km/h (4.9 mph) for touchdown. Contact was eventually lost with *Phoenix* on 2 November 2008.

★ FIRST MARTIAN AURORA

In June 2006, ESA announced that its *Mars Express Orbiter* had detected localized aurorae on Mars. On Earth, the northern and southern lights are caused by charged particles from the Sun interacting with the planet's magnetic field, making parts of the upper atmosphere glow like a neon tube. Mars has no magnetic field; instead, its aurorae are caused by the solar particles interacting with regions of locally magnetized rock – remnants from when Mars had a magnetic field of its own.

LARGEST CANYON IN THE SOLAR SYSTEM

The Valles Marineris ③ on Mars is the largest canyon in the Solar System. It has an overall length of around 4,500 km (2,800 miles). At its widest, it is 600 km (370 miles) across and up to 7 km (4.3 miles) deep. It is named after the *Mariner 9* spacecraft that first discovered it in 1971.

★ FIRST IMAGE OF A LANDING ON ANOTHER PLANET

While NASA's *Phoenix* polar lander ② was making its descent toward the surface, the orbiting *Mars Reconnaissance Orbiter* used its high-resolution camera to take an oblique snapshot of the event from 310 km (192 miles) above the planet (below). The image shows the lander suspended beneath its parachute, which had opened 46 seconds earlier, with *Phoenix* just 52 seconds away from touchdown.

★ MOST SPACECRAFT ORBITING THE SAME PLANET

When NASA's *Mars Reconnaissance Orbiter* entered Martian orbit in March 2006, there were three other functioning spacecraft orbiting the red planet: *Mars Global Surveyor*, *Mars Odyssey* and *Mars Express*. In addition, there were two rovers also operating on the planet's surface, making the total number of active spacecraft exploring the same planet six.

MOST DURABLE ORBITER

NASA's *Mars Global Surveyor* was launched in 1996 and entered Martian orbit on 11 September 1997. It was due to spend just two years mapping and monitoring the planet but, because of the success of the mission and the quality of its science, it was granted multiple extensions.

Contact was lost with the spacecraft on 2 November 2006 – by which time it had sent more than 250,000 images of the red planet back to Earth after more than nine years in orbit.

Jan 29: The record for the **most consecutive rolls by an aeroplane** is 408, achieved by Zoltán Veres (Hungary) during the Al Ain Aerobatic Show in Al Ain, UAE, on this day in 2007.

Jan 30: The **greatest annual net loss by a company** is $98.7 billion (£60 billion), reported by AOL Time Warner on 30 January 2003.

17,000 m³/sec (600,000 ft³/ sec): the rate of flow at the Boyoma Falls, Democratic Republic of the Congo – the **largest waterfall**.

HIGHEST WATERFALL

The Salto Angel ("Angel Falls") in Venezuela, on a branch of the Carrao River in the Canaima National Park, is the highest waterfall (as opposed to vaporized "bridal veil") in the world. It has a total drop of 979 m (3,212 ft), with the longest single drop being 807 m (2,648 ft). The Angel Falls were named after the pilot Jimmie Angel (USA, 1899–1956), who recorded them in his log book on 16 November 1933. Known by the natives as Parakupa-vena or Kerepakupai merú, the Falls had been reported by Venezuelan explorer Ernesto Sanchez la Cruz as early as 1910.

CONTENTS

COMPACT CONTINENT

Europe is the second smallest of the world's seven continents (Oceania is smaller, Asia is the largest), with a land area of approximately 10.1 million km² (3.9 million miles²), which accounts for about 6.8% of Earth's land area.

★ LOWEST COUNTRY

The Netherlands has a total area of 41,526 km² (16,033 miles²), around 27% of which actually lies below sea level. The country is famous for its extensive systems of dykes, which are either man-made or natural earth walls that hold back the sea and rivers, and protect land for arable and other uses. Humans have been building dykes in the Netherlands for more than 2,000 years.

★ NEW RECORD
UPDATED RECORD

★ OLDEST LAND ANIMAL

The fossil of a 1-cm-long (0.39-in) centipede found near Stonehaven, Scotland, UK, by bus driver and amateur palaeontologist Mike Newman (UK) is thought to be 428 million years old and the earliest evidence of a creature living on land rather than in the sea. Formally named *Pneumodesmus newmani* in 2004, the anthropod had spiracles – primitive air-breathing structures on the outside of its body – making it the oldest air-breathing creature yet to be discovered.

Newman made his find on the foreshore of Cowie Harbour in 2004 and placed the specimen in the charge of the National Museums of Scotland in Edinburgh, UK.

LARGEST HOT SPRING

The largest boiling river issues from the hot, alkaline Deildartunguhver spring at Reykholtsdalur, north of Reykjavik, Iceland, at a rate of 245 litres (65 gallons) of boiling water per second. The water, which is piped up to 64 km (40 miles) away to provide heating, is warmed by underground volcanic activity.

HIGHEST COLD WATER GEYSER

The highest cold water geyser is the Geysir Andernach, which typically blows water to heights of 30–60 m (98–196 ft) in Germany's Mayen-Koblenz district.

Unlike naturally occurring hot water geysers, cold water geysers are formed by cold ground water dissolving large amounts of carbon dioxide (released through cracks from the Earth's upper mantle) and effectively "charging" the water (similar to a soda bottle); this charged underground water then erupts from a drilled well.

The Andernach well is 350 m (1,148 ft) deep and the highest eruption of the geyser was 61.5 m (201 ft 9 in), recorded on 19 September 2002. The average volume of water ejected per eruption is 7,800 litres (2,060 US gallons; 1,715 UK gallons) and the average interval between eruptions is 90–110 minutes; one eruption lasted 7–8 minutes.

HIGHEST RAISED BEACH

The High Coast in Västernorrland, Sweden, has a shingle beach some 260 m (853 ft) above sea level. Its high elevation is a result of land rising after the last Ice Age, when the vast weight of the ice sheets was lifted. The region is still rising, at a rate of around 1 cm (0.39 in) per year, and will continue rising for around another 10,000 years or so.

★ LARGEST BRACKISH SEA

Brackish water has a salinity (salt level) between that of fresh water and sea water. The Baltic Sea, in northern Europe, with a surface area of around 377,000 km² (145,560 miles²), is the largest area of brackish water in the world. Its salinity ranges from around 0.6% to 1.5%. For comparison, sea water contains around 3.5% salt. The low salinity of the Baltic is due to the mixing of sea water with the freshwater run-off from its surrounding countries.

LARGEST CONIFEROUS FOREST

The vast coniferous forests of northern Russia, which lie between Lat. 55°N and the Arctic Circle, cover a total area in the region of 4 million km² (1.5 million miles²).

LARGEST GLACIAL GROTTO

In terms of area, the largest artificial cave made inside a glacier measures 5,500 m² (59,200 ft²). It is located inside the Fee Glacier in Switzerland and was constructed by the glaciologist Benedikt Schnyder (Switzerland). The grotto includes a 54-m-long (177-ft) tunnel that forms an art gallery 8 m (26 ft) below the surface of the glacier.

Jan 31: Mehmet Ozyurek's (Turkey) nose was 8.8 cm (3.46 in) long from the bridge to the tip when measured on 31 January 2001, making it the **longest nose** in the world.

Feb 1: Thomas Edison's "Black Maria", a frame building covered in black roofing-paper, was completed in West Orange, New Jersey, USA, on this day in 1893 – making it the **first film studio**.

45,000 m³/sec (1.6 million ft³/sec): the flow of water from the Vatnajokul glacier, Iceland, in 1996, following a volcanic eruption – the **fastest melting glacier**.

DEEPEST CAVE

In September 2007, cavers of the Ukrainian Speleological Association reached a new record depth of 2,191 m (7,188 ft) inside the Krubera Cave in the Arabika Massif, Georgia. Over 2.5 km (1.5 miles) of new cave passages were explored in this 29-day underground expedition.

The effort of reaching the lowermost chambers of this cave is likened by speleologists to "climbing an inverted Mount Everest".

DEEPEST SHAFT

Vrtoglavica (meaning "vertigo") is an unbroken vertical shaft that plunges to a depth of 643 m (2,110 ft) in the Kanin mountain range in Slovenia, making it the world's deepest naturally occurring shaft. It could comfortably accommodate two Eiffel Towers.

LARGEST ISLAND CREATED BY VOLCANIC ERUPTIONS

The entirety of Iceland was formed from volcanic eruptions from the mid-Atlantic Ridge, upon which it sits. With an area of 64,051 km² (39,800 miles²), Iceland is essentially ocean floor exposed above the surface of the ocean.

★ LARGEST MANTLE PLUME

Mantle plumes are regions of warmer rock in the Earth's mantle that slowly rise because of their decreased density. The head of the plume can melt upon reaching the surface and they are believed to provide a means for the Earth to lose internal heat. Today, the largest such plume sits beneath Iceland and is responsible for its formation. The Iceland Plume has been studied extensively – particularly using seismic data. It is characterized by an approximately cylindrical structure, about 160–240 km (100–150 miles) across, and extending to a depth of about 400 km (248 miles) or more. Within this region, the rock is some 150–250°C (302–482°F) hotter than the surrounding mantle.

X-REF
You've read about Europe's incredible natural extremes, now find out about the amazing people who live there in the Gazetteer, starting on p.102.

MOST TORNADOES BY AREA

Incredibly, the world's tornado hotspot is the UK, which is hit by a record of one tornado per 7,397 km² (2,856 miles²). The equivalent figure for the USA is one tornado per 8,663 km² (3,345 miles²).

★ MOST NORTHERLY BOTANICAL GARDEN

The Tromsø Botanic Garden (69°40'N 18°56'E) in Norway lies within the Arctic Circle but benefits from the warming effects of the Gulf Stream. Operated by the Museum of Tromsø University (the world's **most northerly university**), it houses arctic and alpine plants from across the northern hemisphere.

LONGEST FJORD

A geological feature evident chiefly along the coastline of Nordic countries, fjords are long, thin inlets that have been carved out by glacial movement and erosion. The longest fjord is Greenland's Nordvest Fjord, which extends 313 km (195 miles) inland from the sea.

LONGEST PERIOD OF VOLCANIC ERUPTIONS

Mount Etna is a stratovolcano on the Italian island of Sicily. With a summit height of around 3,329 m (10,922 ft), it is the largest active volcano in Europe. Etna is also one of the world's most active volcanoes, and has erupted around 200 times since its first recorded eruption in 1500 BCE.

LAVA FLOW

The longest lava flow in historic times reached a distance of 65–70 km (40–43 miles) during the eruption of Laki in southeast Iceland in 1783. The lava was a mixture of pahoehoe (twisted cord-like solidifications) and aa (blocky lava) – both terms taken from Hawaiian.

Feb 2: The **fastest transatlantic crossing made completely under solar power** is 29 days by the catamaran sun21 (Switzerland), sailing from Gran Canaria to Martinique and arriving on this day in 2007.

PLANET EARTH
NORTH AMERICA

1872: the year Yellowstone Park, Wyoming, USA – the **oldest national park** – was opened to the public.

★ MOST CLIMATICALLY SIGNIFICANT ISTHMUS

Around three million years ago, volcanic activity and sediment deposition closed the gap between North and South America, creating a strip of land called the Isthmus of Panama. This narrow land barrier prevented circulation between the Atlantic and Pacific Oceans and forced the formation of the Gulf Stream, which increased the temperature of European winters by around 10°C (18°F).

LARGEST GRASSLANDS

The grasslands of the Great Plains of North America stretch for 3 million km² (1,158,300 miles²) from southern Canada through the USA to northern Mexico. The Great Plains are the **largest temperate grasslands**, meaning they experience warm, dry summers and are found inland.

By contrast, the **largest tropical grasslands** – that is, grasslands that grow nearer the coast, have higher rainfall and often include woodland – are the savanna grasslands of northern Australia, which measure 1.2 million km² (463,320 miles²).

MOST COLD-TOLERANT TREES

The larches (genus *Larix*) are an incredibly hardy group of trees. In particular, the tamarack larch (*L. laricina*), native to northern North America and predominantly Canada, can survive winter temperatures down to at least –65°C (–85°F) and commonly occurs at the Arctic tree line, the most northerly point at which trees grow.

OLDEST LIVING TREE

A bristlecone pine (*Pinus longaeva*) christened "Methuselah" was found by Dr Edmund Schulman (USA) in the White Mountains, California, USA, and dated in 1957 as being 4,600 years old, although some scientists claim to have found even older specimens. The location is kept secret to protect the tree from vandalism. The annual growth rings of trees such as bristlecone pines provide an insight into our changing climate.

WORST CYCLONE DISASTER BY DAMAGE TOLL

Hurricane Katrina, the category 5 hurricane that devastated the coast of Louisiana, USA, on 29 August 2005, caused damage in the region of $45 billion (£25 billion), according to the insurance company Swiss Re.

★ FASTEST MAJOR GLACIER

The Columbia Glacier, located between Anchorage and Valdez in Alaska, USA, was measured by glaciologists from the University of Colorado to be flowing at an average rate of 24 m (80 ft) per day in 2005.

LARGEST WATERFALL EVER

Around 18,000 years ago, near the end of the last Ice Age, a huge lake was formed in North America, near the present-day city of Missoula, Montana, USA. The lake was formed when a huge advancing glacier dammed a river, resulting in a trapped body of water some 2,000 km³ (500 miles³) in volume. When the water broke through the ice dam created by the glacier, the lake, "glacial Lake Missoula", emptied in a catastrophic flood. As the water drained away, some flowed over what is now known as Dry Falls, resulting in a waterfall measuring 5.6 km (3.5 miles) long by 115 m (380 ft) high. By comparison, the Niagara Falls measures 1.6 km (1 mile) wide by 50 m (165 ft) high.

★ LARGEST HYDROTHERMAL EXPLOSION CRATER

Hydrothermal explosions are caused when underground water is subjected to very high temperatures and pressures by interactions with molten rock. When this superheated water reaches close to the surface of the Earth, the resulting drop in pressure can cause an explosive expansion of the water into steam. The Mary Bay explosion crater complex in Yellowstone National Park, Wyoming, USA, measures 1,929 x 944 m (6,330 x 3,100 ft) and was formed around 14,000 years ago by a series of hydrothermal explosions.

LARGEST ISLAND

Although controlled by Denmark, Greenland forms part of the North American continent and is the world's largest island. It has an area of 2,175,600 km² (840,000 miles²).

★ HIGHEST CONCENTRATION OF PLAYAS

Playas are dry lakebeds with hard, smooth surfaces that generally form in arid and semi-arid conditions. They vary in composition from mud flats to salt flats and many contain shallow lakes during the winter. Eastern New Mexico and the southern high plains of Texas, USA, contain almost 22,000 of these features. A playa in the White Sands National Park, New Mexico, USA, is pictured above.

★ NEW RECORD
★ UPDATED RECORD

TOP 100 Records of the Year

★ OLDEST ROCK

A track of bedrock found on the eastern shore of Canada's Hudson Bay contains the oldest known rocks on Earth, formed 4.28 billion years ago. Some scientists have speculated that the rocks could be remnants of Earth's primordial crust, which formed on the planet's surface as it cooled soon after forming.

★ FASTEST GLACIAL REBOUND

The weight of ice pressing down on the land in south east Alaska during the Little Ice Age, roughly between 1300 and 1650, caused it to be squashed downwards. When the ice retreated the land that was covered started to rebound – that is, spring back upwards. Global Positioning System measurements reveal that the area is rising at a rate of 32 mm (1.25 in) every year.

TALLEST LIVING TREE

A coast redwood (*Sequoia sempervirens*) was discovered by Chris Atkins and Michael Taylor (both USA) in the Redwood National Park, California, USA, on 25 August 2006 and named Hyperion, after the Greek god. The tree currently measures 115.5 m (379 ft 1 in).

★ SMALLEST ORCHID

The orchid family is the second largest family of flowering plants after Compositae (daisies), with around 25,000 species. The world's smallest orchid species is the jungermannia-like platystele (*Platystele jungermannioides*), found in the lower cloud forest of Mexico, Guatemala, Costa Rica and Panama at an elevation of 200–1,000 m (656–3,280 ft). Growing around 6.3 mm (0.25 in) high and 20 mm (0.78 in) wide, it blooms in the spring with just two or three tiny flowers that are a mere 2.5 mm (0.09 in) wide.

ACTUAL SIZE

★ LONGEST "SAILING STONE" TRAILS

The Racetrack Playa in Death Valley on the Nevada-California border is famous for its bizarre "sailing stones". The flat surface of this dry lakebed is home to rocks that seem to have moved across the ground without human intervention, leaving trails in the dried surface. No-one has seen these rocks move but monitoring results published in 1996 revealed that a rock, nicknamed "Diane", had left an 880-m-long (0.5-mile) trail. Strong winds – up to 145 km/h (90 mph) – coupled with occasional wet conditions are the likely causes of this phenomenon.

NORTH AMERICA

There is some debate over which countries constitute North America but Guinness World Records defines it as Canada, the USA, the Caribbean countries, Greenland and the Central American countries of Belize, Costa Rica, El Salvador, Guatemala, Honduras, Nicaragua, Mexico and Panama.

Feb 3: The **first images from the surface of the Moon** were taken by the Soviet robotic lander Luna 9, which landed on the lunar surface on this day in 1966.

Feb 4: On this day in 1990, the *Voyager 1* spacecraft took a picture of our home planet from a distance of almost 6.5 billion km (4 billion miles) – making it the **most distant image of Earth**.

Feb 5: Ridden by Captain Alberto Larraguibel Morales (Chile), the horse Huaso ex-Faithful achieved a record 2.47-m-high (8-ft 1.25-in) jump on 5 February 1949, the **highest jump by a horse**.

SOUTH AMERICA

★ SOUTHERMOST PERMANENTLY INHABITED PLACE

Discounting Antarctic research stations, the farthest south that people permanently live on Earth is the small hamlet of Puerto Toro (55°04'59S) on the island of Navarino on the southern tip of Chile. In the last census taken in the area (2002), its population was recorded as just 36 people.

HIGHEST ACTIVE VOLCANO

The Ojos del Salado on the border between Chile and Argentina is the world's highest active volcano at 6,887 m (22,595 ft) high. It experienced some minor activity in 1993.

DRIEST PLACE

For the period between 1964 and 2001, the average annual rainfall for a meteorological station in Quillagua in the Atacama Desert, Chile, was just 0.5 mm (0.019 in). This discovery was made during the making of the TV series *Going to Extremes* by UK company Keo Films in 2001.

FACT
Pictured is the Strait of Magellan as it flows through the Torres del Paine National Park, Chile. For more icy records, see Polar Regions on pp.44–45.

★ MOST PRODUCTIVE COPPER MINE

The two open pit mines of Escondida and Escondida-Norte in the Atacama Desert, northern Chile, produced 1.483 million tonnes (1.634 million tons) of copper in 2007. In September 2008, the US Geological Survey reported that there may be as much as 750 million tonnes (826 million tons) of undiscovered copper in the Andes Mountains.

HIGHEST LAKE

The highest commercially navigable lake is Lake Titicaca, which lies at a height of 3,810 m (12,500 ft) above sea level on the Andean border between Peru and Bolivia. Its surface area covers approximately 8,300 km² (3,200 miles²) and has an average depth of around 140–180 m (460–590 ft). The freshwater lake also sustains an archipelago of more than 40 floating "islands" made entirely from totora reeds, which are home to the indigenous Uros tribe. These islands – the **largest man-made reed islands** – fluctuate in size, as the bottom layers of reeds rot away and their surfaces are constantly replenished.

★ SOUTHERNMOST STRAIT

The Strait of Magellan is a natural passage of water separating mainland South America from Tierra del Fuego. Measuring around 530 km (329 miles) long and between 4 and 24 km (2.4 and 14.9 miles) wide, it has historically been the most important shipping route that connects the Atlantic and Pacific Oceans. Despite the importance of the man-made Panama Canal, the Strait of Magellan is still used extensively today by ships rounding South America.

LARGEST AQUATIC INSECT

The largest aquatic insect is the giant water bug (*Lethocerus maximus*), a carnivorous species that inhabits Venezuela and Brazil. It has been measured up to 11.5 cm (4.5 in) long, but, as it is relatively long and narrow, it is not as heavy as some of this continent's burly terrestrial beetles and stick insects.

WIDEST RIVER

While not in flood, the main stretches (i.e. not its tidal reaches, where an estuary/delta can be much wider) of the Amazon River in South America can reach widths of up to 11 km (7 miles) at its widest points.

LARGEST HERB

The puya (*Puya raimondii*), pictured far left, is a rare species of giant bromeliad growing at a height of around 3,960 m (12,992 ft) in the Bolivian mountains. Although it is a herbaceous plant, it has a panicle – stalk or trunk – up to 4 m (13 ft) high, bearing thousands of flowers and millions of seeds. The puya takes around 150 years to bloom, making it the **slowest plant to flower**; once it has blossomed, the plant dies.

Feb 6: Danny Wainwright (UK) popped the **highest skateboard ollie** at 113 cm (44.5 in) on this day in 2000 to win the Reese Forbes Ollie Challenge in Longbeach, California, USA.

Feb 7: Concorde took 2 hr 52 min 59 sec to travel the 6,035 km (3,750 miles) between New York and London on 7 February 1996, the **fastest transatlantic flight by a commercial aeroplane**.

3,631 m (11,913 ft): altitude of La Paz, the administrative centre of Bolivia and the world's **highest capital city**.

★ **NEW RECORD**
UPDATED RECORD

LARGEST PRE-COLOMBIAN LINES

The so-called "Nazca lines" are a group of gigantic figures engraved on the ground of the Nazca desert in Peru, representing plants, animals, insects and a variety of geometric shapes. Most can only be appreciated from the air. The designs occupy a 500-km^2 (193-mile^2) piece of land and average 180 m (600 ft) in length.

GREATEST SPECIES ENDEMISM

The area of the world considered to have the highest species endemism is the Tropical Andes stretching across Venezuela, Colombia, Ecuador, Peru, Bolivia and a small section of northern Argentina. So far, scientists have identified 20,000 vascular plants, 677 birds, 68 mammals, 218 reptiles and 604 amphibians that are endemic to the area, covering 1,257,957 km^2 (485,700 miles^2).

NARROWEST COUNTRY

In terms of comparing its length to its width, the narrowest country is Chile. Measuring an average of 4,345 km (2,700 miles) long by 175 km (108 miles) wide, the country forms a ribbon shape that extends down the entire straight western coastline of South America.

LARGEST RIVER BASIN

A basin is an area of land where water – usually from rain or melting snow or ice – drains into a significant body of water, typically a river. The largest river basin in the world is the Amazon basin, which covers around 7,045,000 km^2 (2,720,000 miles^2) – almost the size of Australia. It has many tributaries, including the Madeira, which at 3,380 km (2,100 miles) is the world's **longest tributary**.

LONGEST MOUNTAIN RANGE

The Andes is the world's longest range of mountains. At 7,600 km (4,700 miles) in length, it spans seven countries and includes some of the highest mountains on Earth. Over 50 of the Andes peaks reach over 6,000 m (20,000 ft) high. The range is around 300 km (200 miles) in width along most of its extent.

LARGEST SWAMP

Located principally in Brazil but with small areas within Bolivia and Paraguay, the Pantanal (which is Spanish for "marshland") covers a surface area of 150,000 km^2 (57,915 miles^2) – greater than the total surface area of England. During the rainy season, 80% of the Pantanal is flooded.

LONGEST COLUMN OF ANTS

Army ants in the genus Eciton, from Central and South America, and driver ants in the genus Dorylus, from Africa, have a reputation for travelling in highly organized columns. These can be up to 100 m (328 ft) long and over 1 m (3 ft 4 in) wide and may contain as many as 600,000 individuals, which frequently take several hours to pass one spot.

★ HIGHEST RATE OF DEFORESTATION

According to the 2009 State of World's Forests report by the Food and Agriculture Organization (FAO) of the United Nations, Brazil experiences the greatest rate of deforestation. For the years 2000 to 2005, Brazil underwent a loss of 3,103,000 hectares (7,667,680 acres; 31,000 km^2, or 12,000 miles^2) – an area the size of Belgium – per year.

The report reveals that the planet lost 745,000 hectares (18.04 million acres) of forest between 2000 and 2005, equivalent to 200 km^2 (77 miles^2) – more than 37,000 football fields or the area of Washington, DC, USA – every day.

★ LARGEST NEW WORLD CIVILIZATION

Because of their "recent" discovery by western civilizations, the Americas and Australasia are collectively known as the New World. The most successful and largest empire in these regions before discovery by the West was the Incas, who started as a tribe founded in the city of Cuzco around the year 1200. At their height, around 1460, the Incas ruled over 10 million people throughout an area of western South America similar in size to the Roman Empire. Pictured are the remains of the Inca city of Machu Picchu in Peru.

Feb 8: On this day in 2005, astronomers from the Harvard-Smithsonian Center for Astrophysics (USA) announced a star travelling at over 2.4 million km/h (1.5 million mph) – the **fastest recorded star**.

AFRICA

★ LARGEST TROPICAL LAKE

With a surface area of around 68,634 km² (26,500 miles²), Lake Victoria is the biggest lake in the world that lies within the tropics. Containing some 2,750 km³ (660 miles³) of water, it is ranked as the seventh largest freshwater lake in the world. It is the main source of the River Nile.

★ LONGEST INHABITED CONTINENT

Africa is regarded as the cradle of civilization and is the continent on which human ancestors as well as the great apes first evolved millions of years ago. Modern humans, *Homo sapiens*, first appeared there around 200,000 years ago.

LARGEST DESERT

The Sahara in north Africa is the largest hot desert in the world. At its greatest length, it is 5,150 km (3,200 miles) from east to west; from north to south, it is between 1,280 km and 2,250 km (800–1,400 miles). The area covered by the desert is about 9.1 million km² (3.5 million miles²). The Sahara also boasts the **highest sand dunes**: in Isaouane-n-Tifernine in east central Algeria, the dunes can reach a height of 465 m (1,526 ft).

HIGHEST RECORDED TEMPERATURE

The highest shade temperature ever recorded is 58°C (136°F) at Al'Aziziyah in the Sahara Desert, Libya, on 13 September 1922.

★ HIGHEST CONCENTRATION OF HEATHERS

The fynbos (Afrikaans for "fine bush") plant ecosystem, exclusive to South Africa's Cape floristic region, contains more than 600 species of heather (*Erica*, see photograph above). Only 26 species of heather occur in the rest of the world.

★ HIGHEST CONCENTRATION OF ENDANGERED PLANT SPECIES

The world's highest concentration of endangered plant species occurs in South Africa's Cape Flats. A total of 15 species per square kilometre in the region are threatened by extinction.

★ SMALLEST PLANT KINGDOM

The South African is the smallest of the six floral kingdoms (Boreal, Neotropical, Paleotropical, South African, Australian and Antarctic). It also has the **★ highest concentration of plant species**, with over 9,000 species, 6,200 of which occur nowhere else, in an area of 46,000 km² (17,750 miles²). This equates to 1,300 species per 10,000 km² (3,861 miles²); in comparison, the rainforests of South America contain only 400 plant species per 10,000 km².

★ OLDEST DESERT

The Namib Desert, covering some 80,807 km² (31,200 miles²) of Namibia and Angola, has been arid or semi-arid for at least 80 million years. A coastal desert, it receives less than 10 mm (0.4 in) of rain each year. Its hyper-arid state is caused by descending dry air, cooled by the frigid waters of the southern Atlantic's Benguela current. Such conditions lead to thick coastal fogs that provide just enough moisture to support the survival of a number of highly adapted life forms, such as *Welwitschia*, which Darwin named "the vegetable Ornithorhynchus" – the platypus of the plant kingdom.

PLATYPUS PLANT

The leaves with the longest lifespan belong to the welwitschia (*Welwitschia mirabilis*) of the Namib. This strange plant lives for an estimated 400–1,500 years and produces two leaves per century, which it never sheds, hence its Afrikaans name *tweeblarkanniedood* ("two-leaf-cannot-die").

Feb 9: On this day in 1995, Fred Hale (USA) became the world's **oldest driver** when he had his licence renewed... at the grand age of 104 years old!

3,798,994 hectares (9,387,520 acres): the area of the Kgalagadi Transfrontier Park in Botswana and South Africa, the world's **largest cross-border park**.

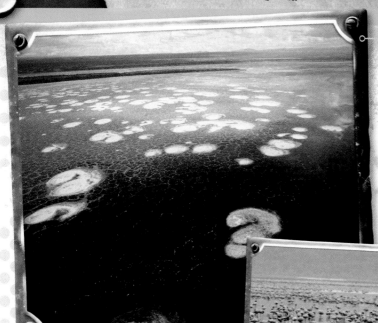

★ LAKES WITH THE HIGHEST LEVELS OF ALKALINITY

The Magadi–Natron basin in the Rift Valley of Kenya–Tanzania contains saline (salt) bodies of water with temperatures as high as 50°C (120°F) and alkalinity as high as pH 10–12, strong enough to blister or burn human skin. The corrosiveness of these lakes – particularly Natron, Magadi and Nakuru – is caused by high concentrations of sodium carbonate (soda), sulphur, chlorine and phosphorus produced by the active volcanoes in the Rift System (see right). Lake Natron's characteristic deep-red colouration (pictured) is the result of pigments produced by algae thriving in the hypersaline environment. The pigments also account for the pink colouration of the lesser flamingoes (*Phoenicopterus minor*, inset) who feed off the algae.

LONGEST RIFT SYSTEM

The East African Rift System is approximately 6,400 km (4,000 miles) long with an average width of 50–65 km (30–40 miles). The escarpments around the edge of the valley have an average height of 600–900 m (2,000–3,000 ft). Also known as the Great Rift Valley, it begins in Jordan and extends to Mozambique in east Africa. This extensive rift system has been gradually forming for around 30 million years, as the Arabian peninsula has separated from Africa. As a result, the area is dotted with volcanoes, including Oldoinyo Lengai (see **coldest erupting lava**, left), hot springs and highly alkaline lakes.

CONTINENT MOST AFFECTED BY DESERTIFICATION

Desertification – the transformation of arable land to desert – has a number of natural causes, such as climate variation and soil erosion. Human activities – including over-intensive farming, deforestation and even the migration of refugees during wartime – can also give rise to conditions that make desertification possible. The situation is at its worst in Africa, where two-thirds of the continent has been reduced to desert or dry land.

MOST THUNDEROUS COUNTRY

In the Tororo district of Uganda, an average of 251 days of thunder per annum was recorded for the 10-year period 1967–76, making it the most thunderous place on Earth.

FACT

More than 4 million flamingoes flock to the Magadi-Natron basin each season. The birds have adapted to endure pH levels of up to 10.5 or 11.

COLDEST ERUPTING LAVA

Common basaltic lavas erupt at temperatures of 1,100–1,200°C (2,010–2,190°F), but the natrocarbonatite lava of the volcano Oldoinyo Lengai in Tanzania erupts at just 500–600°C (930–1,110°F). Oldoinyo Lengai is the only active carbonatite volcano on Earth. The bizarre carbonatite lavas look rather like molten chocolate upon eruption. It is extremely runny and has the lowest viscosity of any lava. As it cools it turns white in colour.

THIN CRUST

The Great Rift Valley of northeast Africa has the **thinnest continental crust** at just 15 km (9 miles) thick. On average, continental crust on Earth is around 35–40 km (21–24 miles) thick.

Feb 10: The **largest snowball fight** took place on this day in 2006 between 3,745 participants at Michigan Technological University in Houghton, Michigan, USA.

Feb 11: The **first traffic lights** were trialled on this day in 1928 in Wolverhampton, UK. Within a month, the first permanently operated lights were turned on in Leeds, West Yorkshire, UK.

PLANET EARTH
ASIA

COLDEST HOT DESERT

In the Gobi desert, winter temperatures can drop below -20°C (-4°F). The Gobi extends over southern Mongolia and certain parts of northern and north-western China and is the world's fifth largest desert. The Himalayan mountain range prevents rain-laden clouds from reaching the Gobi, which for this reason is referred to as a "rain shadow" desert. Pictured is a bactrian camel, which grows a shaggy winter coat during the colder months.

LARGEST CONTINENT

Continental masses cover 41.25% of the Earth's surface, or 210,400,000 km² (81,200,000 miles²). The largest of these continental masses is Asia, which covers an area of 45,036,492 km² (17,388,686 miles²).

LARGEST HYDROELECTRIC PROJECT

TOP 100 Records of the Decade

The Three Gorges Dam in China is the largest hydroelectric power station in the world, and is set to generate power for China's expanding economy as well as control flooding in the Yangtze River. The huge dam wall, measuring 2,309 m (7,575 ft) long by 185 m (607 ft) high was completed in May 2006.

COUNTRY WITH THE MOST VARIED TOPOGRAPHY

China is the world's least flat country, with an altitude range of 9,002 m (29,534 ft) from the Turpan Depression at 154 m (505 ft) below sea level to the peak of Mount Everest at 8,848 m (29,028 ft) above sea level.

★ LARGEST VERTICAL EXTENT

Both the highest and lowest points on the Earth's exposed surface are in Asia. Mount Everest, with its peak at 8,848 m (29,028 ft) above sea level, and the Dead Sea, with its surface at 422 m (1,384 ft) below sea level, give Asia a vertical extent (that is, the distance between its highest and lowest points) of 9,270 m (30,413 ft).

★ MOST CONICAL VOLCANO

Mount Mayon (2,462 m/8,077 ft; 13°15'24"N 123°41'6"E) is the most active volcano in the Philippines. It is almost perfectly conical – with a base 130 km (80 miles) in circumference – and is known to volcanologists as the "Perfect Cone". Situated in Albay on the island of Luzon, the majestic Mayon is a stratovolcano (one composed of layers of erupted material) with a characteristic small crater peak and steep sides. It last erupted between July and October 2006.

★ HIGHEST GLACIER

The head of the Khumbu Glacier, located between the peaks of Mount Everest and the Lhotse-Nuptse Ridge in the Himalayas, is situated at an altitude of around 7,600 m (24,934 ft) above sea level and runs for 17 km (10 miles) to the west and south, terminating at around 4,900 m (16,076 ft) above sea level.

Feb 12: On this day in 2002, palaeontologists led by Prof. Peter Doyle (UK) announced they had found 160-million-year-old fossilized vomit from an ichthyosaur, a large marine reptile – the **oldest vomit**.

Feb 13: The **tallest woman ever** was Zeng Jinlian (China, b. 26 June 1964). When she died, on this day in 1982, she measured 2.48 m (8 ft 1.75 in).

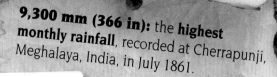

9,300 mm (366 in): the highest monthly rainfall, recorded at Cherrapunji, Meghalaya, India, in July 1861.

LARGEST LANDLOCKED COUNTRY

Kazakhstan, which has an area of 2,724,900 km² (1,052,100 miles²), is bordered by Russia, China, Kyrgystan, Uzbekistan, Turkmenistan and the landlocked Caspian Sea (see below). It has no border access to the open ocean.

LARGEST LAKE

The largest inland sea or lake in the world is the Caspian Sea (in Azerbaijan, Russia, Kazakhstan, Turkmenistan and Iran). It is 1,225 km (760 miles) long and has an area of 371,800 km² (143,550 miles²). Of this total area, some 143,200 km² (55,280 miles²), or 38.5%, is in Iran. Its maximum depth is 1,025 m (3,360 ft) and the surface is 28.5 m (93.6 ft) below sea level.

Lake Baikal in the southern part of eastern Siberia, Russia, is the **deepest lake**. It is 620 km (385 miles) long and between 32 km and 74 km (20 miles and 46 miles) wide. In 1974, the lake's Olkhon Crevice was measured by the Hydrographic Service of the Soviet Pacific Navy and found to be 1,637 m (5,371 ft) deep, of which 1,181 m (3,875 ft) is below sea level.

LONGEST EARTHQUAKE

The Sumatra-Andaman Islands earthquake in the Indian Ocean on 26 December 2004 was the longest-lasting quake ever recorded. Its duration, monitored by seismometers all over the world and announced in the journal *Science* in May 2005, lasted between 500 and 600 seconds. The earthquake had a magnitude of between 9.1 and 9.3 on the Richter scale.

★ LARGEST FROZEN PEAT BOG

The western Siberian sub-Arctic region is a vast area of frozen peat bog covering around 1 million km² (386,102 miles²), roughly the area of France and Germany combined. In 2005, scientists discovered that this region is thawing for the first time since its formation 11,000 years ago.

HIGHEST TREE

The highest altitude at which trees have been discovered is 4,600 m (15,000 ft). A silver fir (*Abies squamata*) was located at this height in south-western China, and specimens of the closely related *A. spectabilis* have been found at an altitude of 4,267 m (14,000 ft) in the Himalayas. Himalayan birch trees (*Betula utilis*, right) have also been discovered at these altitudes.

LAND FARTHEST FROM SEA

The land location most remote from open sea is at Lat. 46°16.8'N, Long. 86°40.2'E in the Dzungarian Basin, which is in the Xinjiang Uygur autonomous region in the far north-west of China. It is at a great-circle distance of 2,648 km (1,645 miles) from the nearest open sea – Baydaratskaya Guba to the north (Arctic Ocean), Feni Point to the south (Indian Ocean) and Bohai Wan to the east (Yellow Sea).

★ LARGEST NATURAL GAS FIELD

The South Pars/North Field gas field covers an underground area of 9,700 km² (3,745 miles²) straddling the jurisdictions of Iran and Qatar. As well as oil deposits equivalent to 360 billion barrels, its total reserves of natural gas are around 51 trillion m³ (1.8 quadrillion ft³), or enough to fill the fuel tanks of more than 230 million Boeing 747s.

LARGEST AREA OF DRY STEPPE

Steppe land is treeless, savannah grassland with hot, dry summers and cold, snowless winters. The largest area of dry steppe land on Earth is the Kazakh Steppe of central Asia, which measures 804,500 km² (310,600 miles²). Before some areas were cultivated for crop farming in the 1950s, the Kazakh Steppe ran from the Ural River in the west to the Altai foothills in the east.

★ LARGEST TERRESTRIAL BIOME

Biologists divide the world into its major regions of distinctive zones or "biomes", such as desert, tundra, grassland and mangrove. The largest is the taiga, the great boreal coniferous forest that encircles the world's land south of the northern tundra. It occurs mostly in northern Siberia, where it covers around 5.9 million km² (2.3 million miles²) – around one-third of the world's forested area.

★ LARGEST CONTINENTAL COLLISION ZONE

Around 40–50 million years ago, the Indian subcontinent collided with the Eurasian continent. The collision, which is still ongoing along a zone around 2,400 km (1,491 miles) long, created the Himalayan mountains.

TAKE THE HIGH ROAD

The **highest road** in the world is in Khardungla pass at an altitude of 5,682 m (18,640 ft). It is one of the three passes of the Leh–Manali road in Kashmir, completed in 1976.

★ HIGHEST RIVER

Of the world's major rivers, the highest is the Yarlung Zangbo, which begins in Tibet and runs for around 2,000 km (1,242 miles) in China, with an average elevation of around 4,000 m (13,123 ft), before entering India, where it is known as the Brahmaputra River. It enters the ocean at the Bay of Bengal, where it forms the world's **largest delta**.

Feb 14: Valentine's Day! The **longest hug** was achieved by Paul Gerrard and Sandra Brooke (both UK), who hugged for 24 hr 1 min at Paddington Station, London, UK, on 13–14 February 2008.

OCEANIA

★ RAREST MAMMALS

The five species of the order Monotremata are an incredibly rare group of primitive mammals that lay eggs instead of producing live young. The group consists of four species of echidna (a type of spiny anteater) and the only species of platypus (above). The entire Monotreme group is found exclusively in Australia and New Guinea.

FACT
Male platypuses have venomous spurs on their hind legs, making them one of the few venomous mammal species.

★ MOST SOUTHERLY WETLANDS

Home to many rare species, such as the cushion plant Donatia, Waitunu Lagoon and its associated wetlands on the southern tip of South Island, New Zealand, are the southernmost recognized wetlands. Comprising lagoons, ponds, lakes, streams, peatlands and coastal beaches, the wetlands cover an area of 3,556 ha (8,787 acres).

LARGEST EXPOSED SANDSTONE MONOLITH

Uluru, aka Ayers Rock, is a sandstone monolith that rises to a height of 348 m (1,142 ft) above the surrounding desert plain in Northern Territory, Australia. It is 2.5 km (1.5 miles) long and 1.6 km (1 mile) wide and is considered sacred by the local Aboriginal people. Only one-third of the rock can be seen – two-thirds of it extends down beneath the surface of the desert. It has a total volume of 0.54 km^3 (0.12 miles^3) – over 215 times that of the Great Pyramid of Giza in Egypt.

★ FLATTEST LANDMASS

Australia is the only major landmass in the world to lack a significant mountain range. The highest point on the Australian mainland is the summit of Mount Kosciuszko (pictured above) in New South Wales at an elevation of 2,229 m (7,313 ft) above sea level. Australia's average elevation is just over 200 m (656 ft) above sea level.

★ **NEW RECORD**
★ **UPDATED RECORD**

★ CONTINENT WITH THE FEWEST LAND BORDERS

Of the major regions of the Earth, Oceania contains the fewest international land borders. According to the United Nations definition of the continent of Oceania, the only land border in the region is that between Papua New Guinea and Indonesia.

HOTTEST PLACES

On an annual-mean basis, with readings taken over a six-year period from 1960 to 1966, the temperature at Dallol, Ethiopia, was 34°C (94°F); in Death Valley, California, USA, maximum temperatures of over 49°C (120°F) were recorded on 43 consecutive days between 6 July and 17 August 1917. But at Marble Bar, Western Australia, 160 consecutive days with maximum temperatures of 37.8°C (100°F) or higher were recorded between 31 October 1923 and 7 April 1924 (maximum 49.2°C; 120.5°F). And at Wyndham, Western Australia, the temperature reached 32.2°C (90°F) or more on 333 days in 1946.

HIGHEST WATERSPOUT

The highest waterspout of which there is a reliable record was one observed on 16 May 1898 off Eden, New South Wales, Australia. A reading from the shore gave its height as 1,528 m (5,013 ft). Waterspouts occur when tornadoes appear at sea, sucking a column (vortex) of water into the clouds. Although associated mostly with minor tornadoes, waterspouts pose a significant risk to shipping.

LONGEST REEF

The Great Barrier Reef off Queensland, north-eastern Australia, is 2,027 km (1,260 miles) in length. It is not actually a single reef but consists of thousands of separate reefs. It is also the **largest marine animal structure**, consisting of countless billions of dead and living stony corals (order Madreporaria or Scleractinia). Over 350 species of coral are currently found there and its accretion is estimated to have taken 600 million years.

HIGHEST DENSITY OF CRABS

Around 120 million red crabs (*Gecarcoidea natalis*) live on the 135-km² (52-mile²) Christmas Island, a density of approximately one crab per square metre for the whole island. Each year, millions of the crabs swarm out of their forest burrows to the coast to mate and spawn. Many of the crabs, which are unique to the island, die on the way, but some survive and return to the forest.

Feb 15: On this day in 2003, the **largest anti-war rally** took place in Rome, Italy, where a crowd of 3 million gathered to protest against the USA's threat to invade Iraq.

163,000 ha (402,781 acres): the area of Fraser Island, **the largest sand island**, off the coast of Queensland, Australia.

★ LARGEST SUBMARINE PLATEAU

The Ontong Java Plateau, a large flat area on the floor of the Pacific Ocean, is a vast volcanic formation north of the Solomon Islands. It covers an area of around 2 million km^2 (772,204 miles^2), roughly the same size as Mexico, and is believed to have formed around 125 million years ago.

MOST FORESTED COUNTRY

The country with the highest percentage of forested land is the Cook Islands in the South Pacific Ocean, with 95.7% of the country covered as of 2000.

TALLEST GEYSER

Waimangu geyser in New Zealand regularly erupted to a height in excess of 460 m (1,500 ft) every 30–36 hours in 1903. However, in 1904 the geyser fell inactive and has remained so ever since.

LARGEST CLOUD

Soliton clouds are rare, solitary cloud forms that maintain their shape while moving at a constant velocity. The best-known soliton cloud is Morning Glory, which forms in the Gulf of Carpentaria, Australia. This backward-rolling cloud formation can be 1,000 km (620 miles) long, 1 km (3,280 ft) high and travels at up to 60 km/h (37 mph).

REMOTEST SPOT FROM LAND

An area in the South Pacific, 47°30'S, 120°W, is 2,575 km (1,600 miles) from the nearest points of land, namely Pitcairn Island, Ducie Island and Peter I Island. Centred on this spot is a massive circle of water with an area of 20,826,800 km^2 (8,041,200 miles^2), which is larger than Russia.

OCEANIA

There is much debate as to what countries fall within the continent of Oceania. According to the UN, the continent includes Australia, New Zealand, Papua New Guinea and the island groups of Melanesia, Micronesia and Polynesia.

★ MOST EASTERLY COUNTRY

The Republic of Kiribati is an island nation of around 100,000 people living on a collection of atolls in the Pacific Ocean. In 1995, its government moved the International Dateline so that all of its islands were in the same time zone. As a result of this, the International Dateline now bulges eastward around Kiribati.

★ LARGEST CONCENTRATION OF MARSUPIAL SPECIES

Marsupials are a group of mammals whose young are not fully developed at birth. Female marsupials, including the kangaroo, wallaby and koala, carry their newly born young in a pouch. Scientists estimate that there are around 330 species of marsupials, more than two thirds of which are found exclusively in Australia and its surrounding islands.

★ LARGEST HUMAN ART FIGURE

A giant outline of a naked Aborigine man, 4.2 km (2.6 miles) in length and so vast that it can only be seen from the air, appeared at Finniss Springs, near Marree, South Australia, in July 1998. The lines of the figure are 35 m (115 ft) wide and measure 28 km (17 miles) around. No-one has yet owned up to the "Marree Man" and theories about its creation still abound.

LONGEST WILDERNESS HORSE TRAIL

The Australian Bicentennial National Trail is the longest marked horse-trekking trail in the world at 5,330 km (3,312 miles). The trail, which is also used by hikers and mountain bikers, winds through wilderness areas from Cooktown in North Queensland to Healesville in Victoria, following historic coach and stock routes, pack-horse trails and country roads.

★ LARGEST SUBMERGED MICROCONTINENT

New Zealand represents just the highest part of the microcontinent of Zealandia. Although it has an area of some 3,500,000 km^2 (1,351,357 miles^2) – about half the size of Australia – around 93% of Zealandia is under water and forms a shallow coastal shelf around New Zealand. A microcontinent is a fragment of land broken off from the main continental landmass.

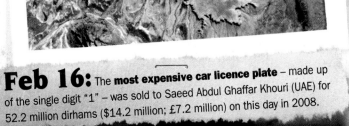

Feb 16: The **most expensive car licence plate** – made up of the single digit "1" – was sold to Saeed Abdul Ghaffar Khouri (UAE) for 52.2 million dirhams ($14.2 million; £7.2 million) on this day in 2008.

Feb 17: A group of 72 volunteers built the **largest self-supporting domed igloo** on this day in 2008. The igloo had an internal diameter of 7.85 m (25 ft 9 in) and a height of 4.17 m (13 ft 8 in).

POLAR REGIONS

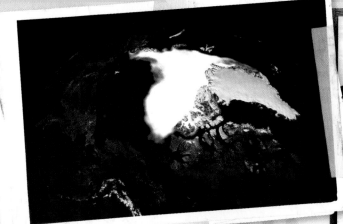

★ SMALLEST RECORDED ARCTIC ICE-CAP

The Arctic ice-cap (above) is mainly composed of sea ice floating on the Arctic Ocean. Because of the changing temperatures of the Earth's seasons, this cap shrinks in the summer and grows in the winter. In the summer of 2007, the ice-cap shrank to a record low in extent, covering 4.11 million km^2 (1.59 million miles^2). The average summer area for the Arctic ice-cap between 1979 and 2000 was 6.7 million km^2 (2.6 million miles^2).

★ NEW RECORD
★ UPDATED RECORD

★ CONTINENT WITH THE FEWEST COUNTRIES

The continent of Antarctica has no native population, and no countries are recognized below the latitude of 60°S. Although various countries have claimed parts of Antarctic territory, the Antarctic Treaty, signed by 45 nations in 1959, pledges to keep the continent open for peaceful scientific investigation and precludes military activity.

THICKEST ICE

On 4 January 1975, a team of seismologists measured the depth of ice in Wilkes Land in eastern Antarctica and found it to be 4,776 m (15,669 ft; 4.76 km; 2.96 miles) deep, equivalent to 10 Empire State Buildings!

★ FIRST AIRCRAFT FLIGHT OVER THE NORTH POLE

On 12 May 1926, an expedition led by Roald Amundsen (Norway) flew over the North Pole in the Airship *Norge*, piloted by its designer, Umberto Nobile (Italy). Among the 16 crew members who undertook the trip was the US explorer Lincoln Ellsworth, who also helped to finance the flight.

★ FIRST EXPEDITION TO THE ANTARCTIC POLE OF INACCESSIBILITY ON FOOT

The Antarctic Pole of Inaccessibility is the exact centre of the Antarctic land mass. It was first reached on foot (assisted with kite skis) by Henry Cookson, Rupert Longsdon, Rory Sweet (All UK) and Paul Landry

(Canada), who dragged their supplies behind them on 120-kg (264-lb) sleds, on 19 January 2007. The team – N2i – covered 1,700 km (1,056 miles). The Pole of Inaccessibility is more remote and more difficult to reach than the geographic South Pole, and was reached for the first time in 1948 by a Soviet team.

LARGEST...

GLACIER

First discovered by an Australian aircraft crew between 1956 and 1957, the Lambert Glacier has an area of 1 million km^2 (386,100 miles^2). Draining about a fifth of the East Antarctic ice sheet, it is up to 64 km (40 miles) wide and, with its seaward extension (the Amery Ice Shelf), it measures at least 700 km (440 miles) in length, which also makes it the world's **longest glacier**.

★ LARGEST ANTARCTIC BASE

McMurdo Station is the USA's permanent research station on the southern tip of Ross Island. It was first established in 1956 and has since grown to be Antarctica's largest permanently inhabited facility. In winter its population is less than 200 but this grows to around 1,000 during the summer. Its inhabitants are scientists and support personnel. The station contains three airfields, a harbour and more than 100 buildings, as well as a nine-hole golf course.

SINGLE BODY OF FRESH WATER

The Antarctic ice-cap holds approximately 30 million km^3 (7.25 million miles^3) of fresh water, around 70% of the world's total supply of fresh water.

★ OLDEST CONTINUOUSLY OCCUPIED ANTARCTIC STATION

Mawson Station, operated by the Australian Antarctic Division, is located in Mac Robertson Land, East Antarctica. It was first established as a permanent base on 13 February 1954 and currently houses around 20 people in the winter and 60 during the summer.

TOP 100 Records of the Decade

Feb 18: The USA's Powerball prize stood at $365 million (£209.6 million) when it was drawn on this day in 2006, the **largest national lottery jackpot** prize.

167 m (550 ft): the height of the tallest iceberg, measured off western Greenland by the US icebreaker East Wind in 1958.

★ LARGEST RUPTURED EPISHELF LAKE

Epishelf lakes are created when an ice shelf blocks the entrance to a salt-water lake or fjord. Fresh water entering the lake is locked in and forms a layer of fresh water above the heavier sea water. The epishelf lake in the 32-km-long (19.8-mile) Disraeli Fjord in Canada had a layer of fresh water 43 m (141 ft) deep, held in by the Ward Hunt ice shelf. Between 2000 and 2002, fracturing of the shelf caused 3 billion m³ (105 billion ft³) of fresh water to drain into the ocean.

★ SUBGLACIAL RIVER

In April 2006, scientists from University College London and Bristol University (both UK) released the results of satellite studies of lakes under the Antarctic ice. The data showed the lowering of the ice surface over one subglacial lake by 3 m (10 ft) and simultaneous bulges over two other lakes 290 km (180 miles) away. The scientists think these observations could be explained by the presence of a subglacial river. A flow of 1.8 km³ (0.43 miles³) of water over 16 months could account for the phenomenon.

ICEBERG

As of April 2005, iceberg B15-A in the Ross Sea off Antarctica measured around 120 km by 20 km (75 miles by 12 miles), with an area of approximately 2,500 km² (960 miles²).

ANTARCTIC STATIONS

While Antarctica has no permanent population, it has been continuously occupied since 1943 by scientists living on various bases. The seasonal population varies but can reach up to 4,000.

HIGHEST CONTINENT

Excluding its ice shelves, Antarctica has an average elevation of 2,194 m (7,198 ft) above the OSU91A Geoid – a means of measurement similar to, yet more accurate than, measuring from sea level. The highest point on the continent is Vinson Massif, at 4,897 m (16,066 ft) above sea level.

AREA OF SEA ICE

During the winter, between 17 and 20 million km² (6.5 and 7.7 million miles²) of the Southern Ocean is covered by sea ice. This area decreases in size to between 3 and 4 million km² (1.1 and 1.5 million miles²) during the summer. The Arctic Ocean, by comparison, is covered by between 14 and 16 million km² (5 and 6 million miles²) of ice in the winter, decreasing to 7–9 million km² (2.7–3.5 million miles²) in the summer.

SUBGLACIAL LAKE

Lake Vostok in Antarctica was discovered in 1994 by analyzing radar imagery of the icy continent. Located beneath Russia's Vostok Station, it is buried under 4 km (2.5 miles) of the East Antarctic Ice Sheet and is one of the oldest and most pristine lakes on Earth, having been completely isolated from the rest of the world for at least 500,000 years and perhaps much longer. Covering an area of some 14,000 km² (5,400 miles²), it is the 18th largest lake in the world and has a depth of at least 100 m (330 ft).

★ SUBGLACIAL MOUNTAIN RANGE

The Gamburtsev Mountains in eastern Antarctica extend for some 1,200 km (745 miles) across the continent. They reach up to 2,700 m (8,858 ft) high and are permanently buried under more than 600 m (1,968 ft) of ice. First discovered by a Soviet team using seismic surveys in 1958, the mountains are believed to be around 500 million years old.

★ MOST SOUTHERLY CASH MACHINES

The most southerly, and isolated, cash machines are located in McMurdo Station, Antarctica, at a latitude of 77°51'S. The two ATMs, provided by the bank Wells Fargo, do not charge a fee for dispensing money.

Feb 19: The **longest time to spin a basketball on one finger (maintaining spin)** is 4 hr 15 min by Joseph Odhiambo (USA) on 19 February 2006 in Houston, Texas, USA.

Feb 20: Rally driver Juha Kankkunen (Finland) hit speeds of 321.65 km/h (199.86 mph), the **fastest speed for a car on ice,** on the frozen Gulf of Bothnia in Kuivaniemi, Finland, on this day in 2007.

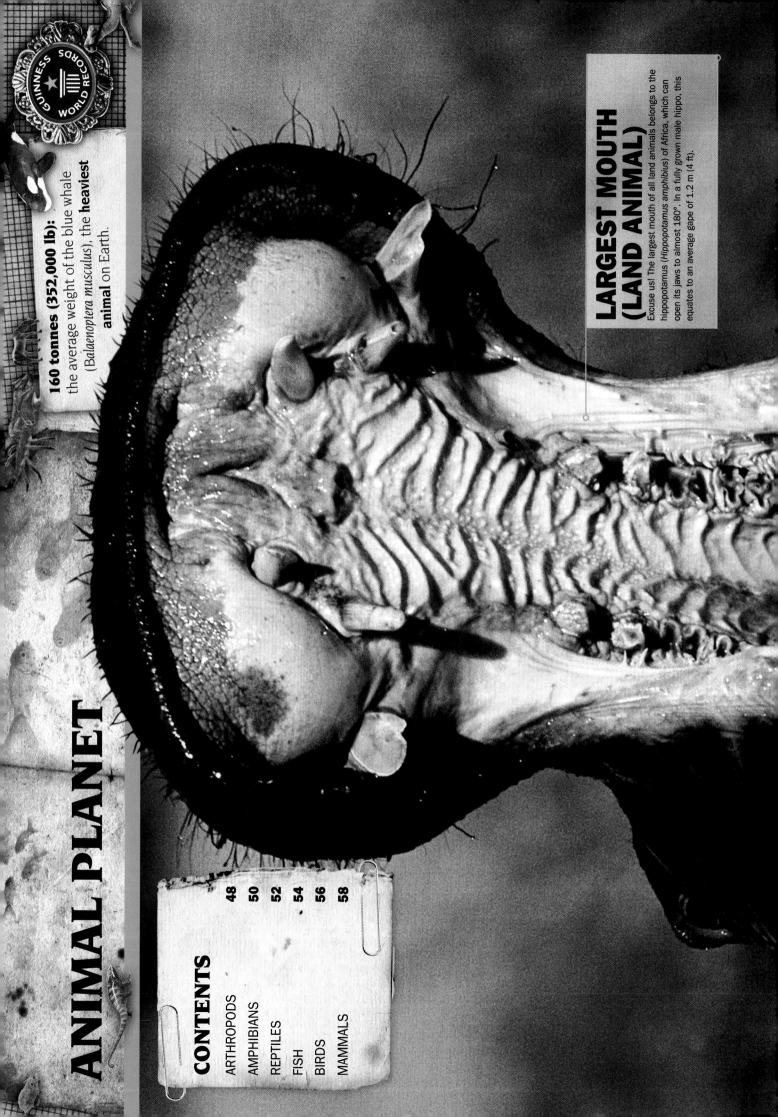

ANIMAL PLANET

160 tonnes (352,000 lb): the average weight of the blue whale (*Balaenoptera musculus*), the **heaviest animal** on Earth.

LARGEST MOUTH (LAND ANIMAL)

Excuse us! The largest mouth of all land animals belongs to the hippopotamus (*Hippopotamus amphibius*) of Africa, which can open its jaws to almost 180°. In a fully grown male hippo, this equates to an average gape of 1.2 m (4 ft).

CONTENTS

ANIMAL PLANET
ARTHROPODS

1,933: the number of people killed in Mexico in 1946 by scorpion stings. Around 1,000 people are currently killed by scorpions every year.

★ GREATEST COLOUR VISION

Stomatopod crustaceans, which include the mantis shrimps, possess the greatest extent of colour vision. Whereas, by comparison, the eyes of most mammals contain two types of colour photoreceptor, humans and other primates have three (and most birds and reptiles have four), stomatopod eyes contain no less than eight different types of colour photoreceptor. These afford the marine coral reef-dwelling crustaceans an unparalleled range of colour vision, enabling them to distinguish numerous shades within the electromagnetic spectrum's ultraviolet waveband – which is entirely invisible to humans.

NEWEST ANIMAL PHYLUM

In November 2006, studies of an obscure genus of small, worm-like creatures revealed not one but two species. *Xenoturbella* had first become known to science when dredged up from the Baltic Sea and named in 1949. The two species – *X. bocki* and *X. westbladi* – are so different from all other species of animal that they required the creation of an entirely new phylum – the highest category of animal classification – all for themselves; this is a rare occurrence, as only a few new phyla have been discovered in the past 50 years.

LIGHTEST INSECT

The male bloodsucking banded louse (*Enderleinellus zonatus*) and the parasitic wasp *Caraphractus cinctus* each weigh as little as 0.005 mg (5,670,000 to an ounce). Eggs of the latter each weigh 0.0002 mg (141,750,000 to an ounce).

★ FIRST USE OF BEE-VENOM THERAPY

The earliest use of apitherapy (or bee-venom therapy, BVT, the pharmacological use of honeybee products to treat illnesses) was by the ancient Chinese, Greeks and Romans. Greek physician Galen (AD 129–200) is said to have used honey and bee venom to treat baldness. Bees are still used today as a type of "insect acupuncture" and BVT is particularly popular in the alternative treatment of auto-immune diseases such as MS and arthritis.

★ LARGEST BUTTERFLY FARM

Opened in March 1986 and occupying 0.8 hectares (2 acres), the world's largest butterfly farm is on the Malaysian island of Penang. It contains over 4,000 living specimens belonging to more than 50 different species.

SMALLEST BUTTERFLY

The tiny grass blue (*Zizula hylax*) has a forewing length of 6 mm (0.25 in). Its upperside is steely blue-grey in colour, with a light grey and scattered dark speckling underside.

LARGEST SPIDER

A male goliath bird-eating spider (*Theraphosa blondi*) collected by members of the Pablo San Martin Expedition at Rio Cavro, Venezuela, in April 1965 had a leg-span of 28 cm (11 in) – wide enough to cover a dinner plate.

The **smallest spider** known is *Patu marplesi* of Western Samoa. A male specimen found in moss at Madolelei on the island of Upolu in January 1965 measured 0.43 mm (0.017 in) overall – about the size of the full-stop at the end of this sentence. While considered rare, it may just be that *Patu marplesi* is just very difficult to detect and collect.

★ LARGEST FAMILY OF SPIDERS

The largest zoological family of spiders is Salticidae, which contains the jumping spiders. Over 4,400 species are currently known to science, and most live in the tropics. Uncharacteristically for spiders, jumping spiders hardly ever spin webs, catching their prey not by entrapment but by actively leaping at them.

LONGEST INSECT

On 16 October 2008, the UK's Natural History Museum announced a new holder for the record of the longest stick insect: *Phobaeticus chani* – aka Chan's megastick – from the rainforests of Borneo. The longest of the three known specimens (pictured with the museum's Orthoptera curator George Beccaloni) measured 56.6 cm (22.3 in) with its legs stretched; its body alone measured 35.5 cm (14 in) – also a record for the insect class.

STRONGEST SPIDER

The Californian trap-door spider *Bothriocyrtum californicum* has been proved to be able to resist a force 38 times its own weight when defending its trap-door: a silken structure covering the entrance to its underground burrow. This equates to a man trying to hold a door closed while it is being pulled on the other side by a small jet plane.

MOST DANGEROUS BEE

The Africanized honey bee (*Apis mellifera scutellata*) will generally only attack when provoked but it is persistent in pursuit. Its venom is no more potent than that of other bees, but it attacks in swarms and death can result from the sheer number of stings inflicted.

HEAVIEST INSECTS

The goliath beetles (family Scarabaeidae) of equatorial Africa – *Goliathus regius, G. meleagris, G. goliathus (G. giganteus)* and *G. druryi* – are the heaviest insects. In measurements of one series of males (females are smaller), the lengths from the tips of the small frontal horns to the end of the abdomen were up to 11 cm (4.33 in), with weights of 70–100 g (2.5–3.5 oz).

LARGEST MARINE CRUSTACEAN

A specimen of *taka-ashi-gani* or giant spider crab (*Macrocheira kaempferi*) discovered in Japan in 1836 had a clawspan of 3.69 m (12 ft 1.5 in) and weighed 18.6 kg (41 lb). It is thought to have a life expectancy of up to 100 years.

LARGEST LAND CRUSTACEAN

The robber, or coconut, crab (*Birgus latro*), which lives on tropical islands and atolls in the Indo-Pacific, weighs up to 4.1 kg (9 lb) and has a leg-span of up to 1 m (39 in), making it the largest land arthropod.

★ SMALLEST BEE

The world's smallest species of bee is *Perdita minima* (pictured left), a minute species of solitary bee just under 2 mm long and weighing only 0.333 mg. It is native to southwestern USA, where it constructs a tiny nest in sandy desert soils and feeds upon the nectar and pollen of spurge flowers.

The **largest bee** is the female king bee (*Chalicodoma pluto*), which can attain a total length of 3.9 cm (1.5 in). This species – found only in the Moluccas Islands of Indonesia – was first discovered in 1859 by naturalist Alfred Russel Wallace (Great Britain), after which no specimen was recorded until February 1981, when two enormous females were seen by entomologist Dr Adam Messer (USA).

LARGEST BUTTERFLY

Queen Alexandra's birdwing (*Ornithoptera alexandrae*), native to Papua New Guinea, has a wing-span in excess of 28 cm (11 in). The female specimens are so big (the size of a domestic pigeon) that tribesmen bring it down from the high tree canopies where it usually flies by shooting it with a bow and arrow. The first specimen obtained by scientists was brought down using a shotgun! Inset is the birdwing's mature larva (caterpillar).

ACTUAL SIZE

ACTUAL SIZE

LONGEST INSECT EGG

In terms of length, the largest egg laid by an insect belongs to the 15-cm-long (6-in) Malaysian stick insect *Heteropteryx dilatata* – the Malaysian jungle nymph or giant thorny phasmid – and measures 1.3 cm (0.5 in). This makes it larger in size than a peanut!

ACTUAL SIZE

Feb 21: The **oldest person ever** was Jeanne Louise Calment (France), who lived for 122 years 164 days. She was born on this day in 1875 and died on 4 August 1997.

Feb 22: The **fastest solo unsupported ascent-descent of Mount Kilimanjaro** was completed in a time of 9 hr 21 min 47 sec by Simon Mtuy (Tanzania) on 22 February 2006.

Feb 23: A record 462,572 people took part in the largest **toast at multiple venues** when they gathered in pubs, restaurants, bars and concert halls across the USA on this day in 2001.

AMPHIBIANS

52: the age of a giant Japanese salamander (*Andrias japonicus*) in Amsterdam, Netherlands – the oldest **documented age for an amphibian.**

★ **NEW RECORD**
★ **UPDATED RECORD**

ACTUAL SIZE

FARTHEST TRIPLE JUMP BY A FROG

The greatest distance ever covered by a frog in a triple jump is 10.3 m (33 ft 9 in) – about half the length of a basketball court! The jump was accomplished by a South African sharp-nosed frog (*Ptychadena oxyrhynchus*) named Santjie at a frog derby held at Lurula Natal Spa, Petersburg, South Africa, on 21 May 1977.

FACT
The California newt's typical diet includes **snails, slugs, sowbugs, bloodworms, earthworms and mosquito larvae.**

★ MOST POISONOUS NEWT

The world's most poisonous species of newt is the California newt (*Taricha torosa*), whose skin, muscles and blood contain tetrodotoxin, a highly toxic and powerful nerve poison. Although the newt itself is immune to the effects of the poison, one tiny drop of this substance will kill several thousand mice.

SMALLEST FROG

The world's smallest frog, and the **smallest known amphibian**, is *Eleutherodactylus limbatus* of Cuba, which is 8.5–12 mm (0.33–0.47 in) long from snout to vent when fully grown.

★ HEAVIEST FROG EVER

The heaviest species of frog ever known to have existed was *Beelzebubo ampinga*, which lived in Madagascar during the late Cretaceous Period (65–100 million years ago). Formally described by science in 2008 and currently known from some 75 bones and other fossil fragments, females of this mega-species may have grown to over 40 cm (15.7 in) long and weighed 4 kg (8.8 lb). Its mouth was so expansive that it was probably capable of preying upon small juvenile dinosaurs that co-existed there at the time.

★ MOST CONSECUTIVE JUMPS BY A FROG

An adult spring peeper (*Hyla crucifer*) newly captured on a grassy lawn in eastern USA performed 120 consecutive jumps, as documented in 1952 by biologist Stanley A Rand (USA). Not surprisingly, the distance covered by each jump gradually decreased, but it remains a prodigious feat of endurance nonetheless.

FARTHEST GLIDING AMPHIBIAN

Certain species of flying frog are able to glide up to 15 m (50 ft) using the extensive webbing on their feet to cause drag and sustain their flight.

★ MOST FERTILE AMPHIBIAN

The world's most fecund species of amphibian is the inappropriately named marine toad (*Bufo marinus*), which is not marine. A female can lay up to 35,000 eggs a year.

ACTUAL SIZE

LARGEST FROG

A specimen of the African goliath frog (*Conraua goliath*), captured in April 1889 on the Sanaga River, Cameroon, by Andy Koffman of Seattle, Washington, USA, had a snout-to-vent length of 36.83 cm (14.5 in) and an overall length of 87.63 cm (34.5 in) with its legs extended. On 30 October 1889, it weighed 3.66 kg (8 lb 1 oz). The average length for this species is 30 cm (11.8 in), about the size of a rabbit.

WHAT ARE AMPHIBIANS?

Their name comes from the Greek for "both lives", since amphibians are born as water breathers, then mature to air-breathing adults. Cold-blooded, they usually have four limbs and lay their eggs in water, and include the frog, toad, newt, (water-dwelling) salamander and (limbless) caecilian families.

MOST COLD-RESISTANT AMPHIBIAN

The wood frog (*Rana sylvatica*) is the only amphibian able to survive after it has been frozen. These frogs live north of the Arctic Circle and survive for weeks in a frozen state. Glucose in their blood acts as a kind of antifreeze that concentrates on the frogs' vital organs, protecting them from damage while the rest of the body freezes solid.

SMALLEST TOAD

The smallest toad is the sub-species *Bufo taitanus beiranus* of Africa, the largest specimen of which measured 24 mm (0.94 in) long

LARGEST TOAD

The largest known toad is the cane or marine toad (*Bufo marinus*) of tropical South America and Queensland, Australia (introduced). An average specimen weighs 450 g (1 lb), but the largest ever recorded was a male named Prinsen owned by Håkan Forsberg (Sweden). In March 1991, it weighed 2.65 kg (5 lb 13 oz) and measured 38 cm (1 ft 3 in) from snout to vent and 53.9 cm (1 ft 9 in) when fully extended.

RAREST AMPHIBIAN

The golden toad (*Bufo periglenes*) is notable in its genus for being both sexually dichromatic and visually striking. Male colouration is characteristically bright orange while female pigmentation ranges from greenish-yellow to black. It is found in a small area (less than 10 km²; 4 miles²) contained in the Monteverde Cloud Forest Preserve in Costa Rica's Cordillera de Tilaran. Its numbers have mysteriously plummeted, with the last recorded sighting of one specimen between 1988 and 1989.

★ AMPHIBIAN WITH THE MOST RESTRICTED DISTRIBUTION

The Peaks of Otter salamander (*Plethodon hubrichti*) is entirely confined to a 19-km-long (12-mile) expanse of temperate forest in the Blue Mountains of Virgina, USA. This is the most restricted distribution for any species.

★ LARGEST NEWT

The Spanish ribbed newt (*Pleurodeles waltl*), found in central and southern Iberia and Morocco, ranges in length from 15 cm to 30 cm (6–12 in). The females are longer and thicker than the males and have smaller tails relative to body length. The Mexican lungless salamander (*Bolitoglossa mexicana*) is the world's **smallest newt** or salamander. It attains a maximum length of about 2.54 cm (1 in), including the tail.

LARGEST CAECILIAN

Caecilians are limbless and rarely seen, although they are often mistaken for earthworms. The largest is Thompson's caecilian (*Caecilia thompsoni*) of Colombia, which measures approximately 1.5 m (5 ft) long and 3 cm (1.8 in) wide. The **smallest caecilian**, *Idiocranium russeli* of west Africa, attains a length of just 98–104 mm (3.9–4.1 in).

★ FIRST LUNGLESS FROG

The first species of lungless frog was confirmed in 2008. Previously known only from two specimens, *Barbourula kalimantanensis*, an aquatic species from Borneo, obtains all of its oxygen by direct absorption through its skin and hence has no need for lungs. This was verified by studies following the recent discovery of two new populations of this species in Kalimantan, Borneo.

★ LONGEST GESTATION

The longest gestation period for an amphibian, and the **longest gestation for any terrestrial vertebrate**, is 37–38 months by the alpine salamander (*Salamandra atra*), native to the Swiss Alps. This is at least a year longer than that of the Asian elephant, for which the maximum gestation period on record is 25 months, the **longest for any mammal**.

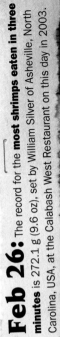

Feb 26: The record for the **most shrimps eaten in three minutes** is 272.1 g (9.6 oz), set by William Silver of Asheville. North Carolina, USA, at the Calabash West Restaurant on this day in 2003.

Feb 25: Christopher Eddy (USA) scored a field goal from a distance of 27.49 m (90 ft 2.25 in) on 25 February 1989 – the **longest basketball goal ever thrown**.

Feb 24: The record for the **largest tea party** is 32,681 participants, set by Dainik Bhaskar (India) for the City of Indore at Nehru Stadium in Indore, India, on this day in 2008.

ACTUAL SIZE

★ SMALLEST SNAKE

A species of threadsnake, *Leptotyphlops carlae*, recently discovered on the Caribbean island of Barbados, measures just 10 cm (4 in) long and is as thin as a strand of spaghetti. This tiny non-venomous snake is thought to be close to or even at the physiological minimum size possible for any snake.

HEAVIEST SNAKE

The green anaconda (*Eunectes murinus*) of tropical South America and Trinidad has an average length of 5.5–6.1 m (18–20 ft). A female shot in Brazil *c.* 1960 was 8.45 m (27 ft 9 in) long with a girth of 111 cm (44 in) and was estimated to have weighed 227 kg (500 lb).

★ LARGEST TURTLE CONGREGATION

The largest congregation of turtles (or, indeed, of any chelonian – turtles, tortoises and terrapins) ever recorded took place on a 10-km (6-mile) stretch of beach at Gahirmatha in Orissa, India, in 1991, when 610,000 specimens of olive ridley turtles (*Lepidochelys olivacea*) were counted nesting there. Each February, the turtles emerge from the sea at night to lay their eggs (over 50 million of them) on the beach, returning to the sea by dawn.

★ LARGEST SNAKE OF ALL TIME

The largest snake ever known to have lived is *Titanoboa cerrejonensis*, a prehistoric species of boa known from the fossils of 28 specimens found in the coal mines of Cerrejón in La Guajira, Colombia. Their discovery had been made by an international scientific expedition led by Florida University vertebrate palaeontologist Dr Jonathan Bloch and was formally announced in early 2009. The fossils revealed that *Titanoboa*, which lived 58–60 million years ago during the Palaeocene Epoch, reached a maximum length of 12–15 m (39 ft 4 in–49 ft 2 in), measured approximately 1 m (3 ft 3 in) across at the thickest portion of its body and weighed around 1,135 kg (2,502 lb, or 178 st 10 lb). These measurements dwarf those of both the reticulated python, the world's **longest living snake**, and the anaconda, the world's **heaviest living snake**.

FASTEST LIZARD

The highest burst of speed recorded for any reptile on land is 34.9 km/h (21.7 mph), achieved by *Ctenosaura*, a spiny-tailed iguana from Central America.

MOST VENOMOUS LAND SNAKE

The small-scaled snake (*Oxyuranus microlepidotus*), which measures 1.7 m (5 ft 7 in) and is found mainly in the Diamantina River and Cooper Creek drainage basins in Queensland and western New South Wales, Australia, is the world's most venomous land snake. In a single strike, it can inject 60 mg (0.00211 oz) of venom, sufficient to kill a small marsupial in seconds, but also more than enough to wipe out several human adults. The average venom yield is 44 mg (0.00155 oz) but one specimen yielded 110 mg (0.00385 oz), enough to kill 250,000 mice or 125 men. Fortunately *O. microlepidotus* only lives in the deserts of central eastern Australia and no human death has been reported from its bite.

MOST ENDANGERED REPTILE

The Abingdon Island giant tortoise (*Geochelone elephantopus abingdoni*) is represented by a single living specimen, an aged male called "Lonesome George", making it the world's **rarest reptile**.

TOP 100 Records of the Decade

BIG SNAKE...

Biologists and staff of the biological research station El Frio in Los Llanos, Venezuela, hold a live green anaconda measuring 5.3 m (17 ft 4 in), which is about average for an adult of the species.

Feb 27: The **longest time heading a football without stopping** is 8 hr 32 min 3 sec by Tomas Lundman (Sweden) at the Gångsatrahallen, Lidingo, Sweden, on this day in 2004.

Feb 28: The final episode of *M*A*S*H* aired in the USA on this day in 1983. An estimated 125 million people tuned in, taking a 77% share of all viewing, the **largest rating share for a TV audience**.

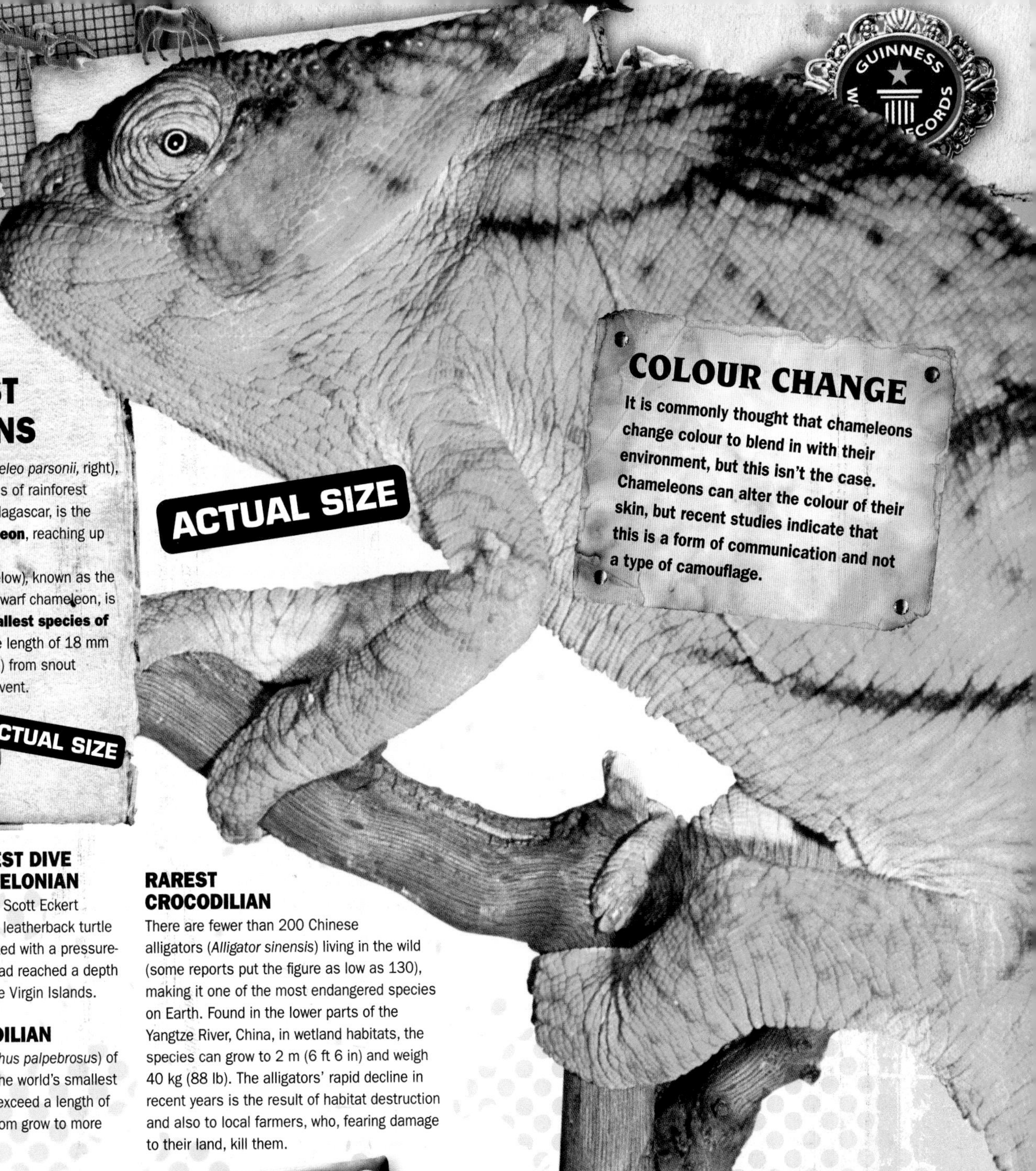

★ LARGEST & SMALLEST CHAMELEONS

Parson's chameleon (*Chamaeleo parsonii*, right), which is native to small areas of rainforest in eastern and northern Madagascar, is the **largest species of chameleon**, reaching up to 68 cm (27 in) in length.

The *Brookesia minima* (below), known as the tiny leaf chameleon, or the dwarf chameleon, is acknowledged to be the **smallest species of chameleon**, with an average length of 18 mm (0.7 in) from snout to vent.

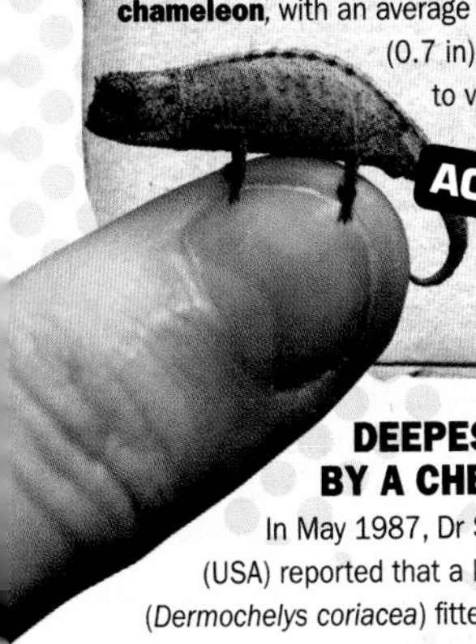

ACTUAL SIZE

ACTUAL SIZE

COLOUR CHANGE

It is commonly thought that chameleons change colour to blend in with their environment, but this isn't the case. Chameleons can alter the colour of their skin, but recent studies indicate that this is a form of communication and not a type of camouflage.

DEEPEST DIVE BY A CHELONIAN

In May 1987, Dr Scott Eckert (USA) reported that a leatherback turtle (*Dermochelys coriacea*) fitted with a pressure-sensitive recording device had reached a depth of 1,200 m (3,937 ft) off the Virgin Islands.

SMALLEST CROCODILIAN

The dwarf caiman (*Paleosuchus palpebrosus*) of northern South America is the world's smallest crocodilian. Females rarely exceed a length of 1.2 m (4 ft) and males seldom grow to more than 1.5 m (4 ft 11 in).

RAREST CROCODILIAN

There are fewer than 200 Chinese alligators (*Alligator sinensis*) living in the wild (some reports put the figure as low as 130), making it one of the most endangered species on Earth. Found in the lower parts of the Yangtze River, China, in wetland habitats, the species can grow to 2 m (6 ft 6 in) and weigh 40 kg (88 lb). The alligators' rapid decline in recent years is the result of habitat destruction and also to local farmers, who, fearing damage to their land, kill them.

★ **NEW RECORD**
UPDATED RECORD

★ NEWEST IGUANA

In 2009, it was announced that a new species of iguana, rose-pink (*rosada*) in colour and up to 1.75 m (5 ft 8 in) long, had been discovered living on a single volcanic mountain called Volcan Wolf on the island of Isabela in the Galapagos chain. Genetic tests confirmed that it is a very distinctive species, dating back over 5 million years. Interestingly, the pink iguana, which has been named *Conolophus rosada*, had first been seen on Isabela in 1986 by park rangers, but had been dismissed as nothing more than a freak variety of the familiar yellow land iguana (*Conolophus subcristatus*).

Feb 29: The **first posthumous Oscar** was awarded to Sidney Howard for his screenplay of *Gone With The Wind* (USA, 1939) on this day in 1940.

53

WWW.GUINNESSWORLDRECORDS.COM

ACTUAL SIZE

SMALLEST FISH

In 2006, the discovery in Indonesia of a fish of the genus *Paedocypris* (below) measuring 7.9 mm (0.31 in) long was announced. However, according to research published by Prof. Theodore Pietsch of the University of Washington, USA, in August 2005, the smallest fish – and the **smallest vertebrate** – is a mature male *Photocorynus spiniceps*, collected from the Philippine Sea. The tiny male measured 6.2 mm (0.24 in) long.

SMALLEST SEAHORSE

An adult pygmy sea horse (*Hippocampus denise*) is typically just 16 mm (0.63 in) long – smaller than an average human fingernail. It is the smallest seahorse on record and a rival to the world's smallest fishes, and was discovered in 2003 in the delicate corals of the Flores Sea, off the coast of Indonesia. It lives among the deeper corals and is a master of camouflage.

LARGEST FISH

The **largest cartilaginous fish**, and also the **largest living fish** of all, is the whale shark (*Rhincodon typus*). The largest recorded example measured 12.65 m (41 ft 6 in) long, 7 m (23 ft) around the thickest part of the body and weighed an estimated 15–21 tonnes (16.5–23.1 tons). It was caught near Karachi, Pakistan, in 1949. Cartilaginous fish (Chondrichthyes) have skeletons made from cartilage and include sharks, rays and skates.

The **heaviest bony fish** in the ocean is the sunfish (*Mola mola*), which has been recorded weighing 2 tonnes (2.2 tons) and measuring 3 m (10 ft) from fin tip to fin tip. Bony fish (Osteichthyes) are characterized by a mostly calcified skeleton and include sturgeons and most of the common fishes.

★ SHORTEST LIFE SPAN

The shortest-lived fishes are various species of toothcarp, including several South American species of the genus *Nothobranchius* that only live for about eight months in the wild. These small fishes thrive in temporary pools of water, such as drainage ditches and even water-filled animal footprints. As soon as these pools dry up, however, the fishes die, but the eggs that they have laid survive in the mud at the bottom of the dried-up pool. When rain fills them up again, the eggs hatch. The new-born fish rapidly grow to their full size, then spawn quickly before their homes dry out once more.

FISH WITH THE MOST EYES

The six-eyed spookfish (*Bathylychnops exilis*), which inhabits depths of 91–910 m (300–3,000 ft) in the north-eastern Pacific, was only discovered in 1958. A slender 45-cm-long (17-in) pike-like species, it has a pair of large principal eyes and a second, smaller pair (known as secondary globes) positioned within the lower half of its principal eyes, each possessing its own lens and retina. Lastly, located behind the secondary globes is a third pair of eyes, which lack retinas, but divert light into the fish's large principal eyes.

★ FASTEST-EATING FISH

Frogfishes (family Antennariidae) can open their mouth and engulf prey in under 6 milliseconds – the fastest recorded time for eating documented for any fish. It was confirmed following frame-by-frame analysis of high-speed cinematography (800–1,000 frames per second), part of research conducted by Theodore Pietsch and David Grobecker (both USA).

FACT

The pygmy seahorse's camouflage is so effective that the species wasn't actually discovered until its soft coral host was being examined in a laboratory. Can you spot it in the photograph above?

DEEPEST-LIVING

The fish that lives at the greatest recorded depth is the *Abyssobrotula galatheae* species of cusk eel (family Ophidiidae). The 20-cm-long (8-in) fish has been collected from the Puerto Rico Trench at a depth of 8,370 m (27,460 ft).

STRONGEST BITE

The strongest fish bite ever has been estimated at 5,300 N – the equivalent to a downward force of about 540 kg (1,200 lb). It belonged to the prehistoric *Dunkleosteus terrelli*, an armoured fish that lived 360–416 million years ago and grew to lengths of up to 11 m (36 ft). Scientists Philip SL Anderson (USA) of the University of Chicago and Mark W Westneat (USA) of the Field Museum of Natural History created a computer-generated model of *D. terrelli*'s skull based on fossilized jaw bones from the fish, and published their measurements on 28 November 2006.

LARGEST SNEEZING FISH

The only species of fish that can sneeze is the hagfish, or slime eel (*Myxine glutinosa*), a primitive species of jawless fish that lacks true fins or scales. The largest known species is *Eptatretus goliath*, with a specimen recorded at 127 cm (4 ft 2 in). The hagfish bores inside other fish and eats their internal organs until they are completely hollow. It then slips out of the host by secreting vast amounts of slime to lubricate its body so that it can ease out of its prey's empty carcass. It prevents itself from suffocating in its own slime by sneezing it out of its primitive respiratory slits.

Mar 1: On this day in 1987, ice skater Marie-Jose Houle (Canada) leapt 13 barrels spanning a distance of 6.84 m (22 ft 5 in), the **most barrels jumped over by a woman on ice skates**, at Lasalle, Quebec, Canada.

Mar 2: At 1:47 pm on this day in 1958, a party of 12 led by Sir Vivian Ernest Fuchs (UK) completed the **first surface crossing of the Antarctic continent**.

★ LARGEST FISH EVER

The biggest fish ever known to have lived is a specimen of the marine fossil species *Leedsichthys problematicus* that was discovered in claypits near Peterborough, UK, in 2008. Dating back 155 million years, this particular specimen (artist's impression above) was 22 m (72 ft 2 in) long, almost twice the length of the whale shark (*Rhincodon typus*), the **largest living fish** (see opposite). The *Leedsichthys problematicus* was first made known to science back in the 19th century. It belongs to an extinct group of bony fishes known as the pachycormids but is believed to have been a plankton feeder, comparable to the basking shark and also the baleen whale.

FISH WITH THE GREATEST SENSE OF SMELL

Sharks have a better sense of smell, with more highly developed scent-detecting organs, than any other fish. Well known for their ability to detect blood from great distances, they can sense one part of mammalian blood in just 100 million parts of water.

★ LARGEST PLACODERM

Placoderms constitute a class of prehistoric armoured fish known today only from fossils, and lived from the mid-late Silurian Period to the close of the Devonian Period, 360–416 million years ago. They were characterized by thick articulated plates of armour that covered their head and body. By far the largest species – often looked upon as the world's first vertebrate super-predator – was *Dunkleosteus terrelli*, which measured 8–11 m (26–36 ft) long and had a near-worldwide distribution.

MOST ABUNDANT FISH

The 64-mm-long (2.5-in) deep-sea bristlemouth (*Cyclothone microdon*) numbers in the billions and has an almost worldwide distribution. It would take about 900 adults to weigh 453 g (1 lb).

MOST VENOMOUS FISH

The stonefish (family Synanceiidae), and in particular *Synanceia horrida*, of the tropical waters of the Indo-Pacific have the largest venom glands of any fish. Direct contact with the spines of its fins – which contain a strong neurotoxic poison – can prove fatal.

LARGEST FRESHWATER FISH

The Mekong giant catfish (*Pangasius gigas*) of the Mekong River basin, and *P. sanitwongse* of the Chao Phraya River basin, both in south-east Asia, are reputed to attain a length of 3 m (9 ft 10 in) and weigh 300 kg (660 lb). However, *Arapaima giga* of South America is reported to reach 4.5 m (14 ft 9 in) long, but weighs only 200 kg (440 lb).

★ SMALLEST LAMPREY

The Miller Lake lamprey (*Lampetra minima*) is less than 10 cm (3.9 in) long when mature. Originally known only from Miller Lake in Oregon, USA, this species was believed extinct after 1958. Fortunately, small populations have been found in Oregon's Upper Williamson River and other rivers close by since the early 1990s.

★ NEW RECORD
UPDATED RECORD

★ FIRST LIVE FISH BIRTH

An extremely well-preserved 25-cm-long (9.8-in) placoderm (prehistoric armoured fish) fossil, uncovered in the Gogo area of Western Australia, clearly shows the presence of an embryo attached to its mother via an umbilical cord. Pictured is Dr John Long, Head of Sciences at Museum Victoria, Australia, inspecting a model of the 380-million-year-old placoderm. An artist's impression of the live birth is shown above. The remarkable fossil represents a new species and was named *Materpiscis attenboroughi* after British TV wildlife presenter Sir David Attenborough.

Mar 3: The **most goals scored by a National Hockey League team in a single match** is 16, by the Montreal Canadiens in their 16–3 victory over the Quebec Bulldogs on 3 March 1920.

ACTUAL SIZE

SMALLEST BIRD

Male bee hummingbirds (*Mellisuga helenae*), which inhabit Cuba and the Isle of Youth, measure just 57 mm (2.24 in) in total length, half of which is taken up by the the bill and tail, and weigh just 1.6 g (0.056 oz). This is believed to be the lowest weight limit for any warm-blooded animal.

ANIMALS IN DANGER

The annual Red-List, published by the International Union for the Conservation of Nature (IUCN), is the world's most authoritative report* on extinction risk to wildlife. It is used by many organizations to inform their conservation efforts.

★ **NEW RECORD**
   UPDATED RECORD

★ LONGEST TIME TO LEARN TO FLY

The longest known interval between hatching from an egg and gaining the ability to fly is exhibited by the wandering albatross (*Diomedea exulans*), whose chicks take 278–280 days on average to make their first flight after hatching. Because it takes so long for the young albatross to take wing, adults breed only once every two years.

★ LONGEST MIGRATION BY A BIRD NON-STOP

A satellite-tagged female bar-tailed godwit (*Limosa lapponica baueri*) known as "E7" was recorded flying directly across the Pacific Ocean from Alaska to New Zealand in a nine-day, non-stop migration flight that covered 11,500 km (7,145 miles) in mid-September 2007. The recording of this migration was made during a study of godwit migration (from their summer breeding grounds in Alaska) by the US Geological Survey, PRBO Conservation Science (USA) and researchers from New Zealand's Massey University.

★ LARGEST EGG COLLECTION

The world's largest scientific collection of bird eggs is that of the Natural History Museum in London, UK, which contains over 1 million different specimens.

★ MOST INDIGENOUS BREEDING SPECIES (COUNTRY)

Colombia in South America is home to over 1,700 indigenous breeding species of birds. In comparison, Canada and the USA combined, yielding a total area vastly in excess of Colombia's, contains fewer than 600 indigenous breeding species.

★ FEWEST INDIGENOUS BREEDING SPECIES (REGION)

The most sparsely populated geographical region for birds is the Antarctic, comprising Antarctica and those islands south of the Antarctic Convergence, which supports just three indigenous breeding species of bird. In comparison, the Neotropical region, comprising tropical Mexico, the Caribbean, Central America and South America, is home to more than 3,400 indigenous breeding species of bird, far more than any other geographical region in the world.

★ RAREST BIRD OF PREY

According to BirdLife International 2006 and the 2007 IUCN Red List of endangered species, the Californian condor (*Gymnogyps californianus*) is classified as Critically Endangered. A conservation programme following the species' removal from the wild into captivity in 1987 has seen this condor recently reintroduced into the wild.

FASTEST BIRDS

● The **fastest bird in level flight** is the grey-headed albatross (*Thalassarche chrysostoma*); a satellite-tagged specimen sustained a speed of 127 km/h (78.9 mph) for over 8 hours while returning to its nest at Bird Island, South Georgia, in the middle of an Antarctic storm.

● The **fastest bird in a dive** is the peregrine falcon (*Falco peregrinus*), which has a terminal velocity of approximately 300 km/h (186 mph) when in a diving stoop, making it the fastest animal on earth.

● The **fastest bird on land** is the (flightless) ostrich (*Struthio camelus*), which can reach speeds of up to 72 km/h (45 mph) when at full stride – up to 7 m (23 ft) per step.

● The **fastest-running flying bird** is the North American roadrunner (*Geococcyx californianus*), which has been clocked at 42 km/h (26 mph).

● The **fastest swimming bird** is the gentoo penguin (*Pygoscelis papua*), which has a maximum burst speed of 27 km/h (17 mph).

★ FIRST BIRD LEG-RINGED

The earliest known example of a bird being leg-ringed is a grey heron (*Ardea cinerea*) that was ringed during the early 18th century in Turkey (then the Ottoman Empire). The bird was subsequently identified by its ring in 1710 when observed in Germany. In more modern times, the record for the **most birds ringed by a single person** goes to Òskar J Sigurösson (Iceland), the principle bird-ringer for the Icelandic Institute of Natural History. Since 1953, Sigurösson, lighthouse keeper at Stórhöföi on Heimay in the Westmann Islands, had ringed 65,243 birds as of 26 February 1997.

Mar 4: The **longest Oscars acceptance speech** lasted 5 min 30 sec and was made by Greer Garson (UK) after winning Best Actress for *Mrs Miniver* (USA, 1942) on this day in 1943.

3.63 m (11 ft 11 in): the wing-span of the male wandering albatross (*Diomedea exulans*), the **largest wing-span of any living bird species**.

BIG BIRDS

● The large-limbed, extinct elephant bird, or vouron patra (*Aepyornis maximus*), that lived around a 1,000 years ago in Madagascar had an estimated weight of 450 kg (1,000 lb) – three times that of a similarly shaped ostrich – and was the **largest modern-day bird**.

● The **largest living bird** is the North African ostrich (*Struthio camelus camelus*). Male examples of this flightless (ratite) sub-species have been recorded up to 2.75 m (9 ft) tall and weighing 156.5 kg (345 lb).

● The **heaviest flying bird** was a male kori bustard (*Ardeotis kori*) that weighed 18.2 kg (40 lb) when documented in 1936.

● The **largest species of penguin** was *Anthropornis nordenskjöldi*, which lived about 24 million years ago. It stood 1.5–1.8 m (5–5 ft 10 in) tall and may have weighed as much as 90–135 kg (198–298 lb).

HIGHEST FLYING BIRD

A Rüppell's vulture (*Gyps rueppellii*) flying at an altitude of 11,300 m (37,000 ft) collided with a commercial aircraft over Abidjan, Ivory Coast, on 29 November 1973. The impact damaged one of the aircraft's engines but the plane landed safely. Sufficient feather remains of the bird were recovered to allow the American Museum of Natural History to make a positive identification of this high-flier, which is rarely seen above 6,000 m (20,000 ft).

MOST ABUNDANT

The red-billed quelea (*Quelea quelea*), a seed-eating weaver of Sub-Saharan Africa, has an estimated adult breeding population of 1.5 billion. At least 200 million of these birds, sometimes dubbed "feathered locusts", are slaughtered annually without having any impact on this number.

★ STRANGEST DIET

An internal examination conducted on a dead ostrich (*Struthio camelus*) that had been living at London Zoo, UK, revealed that during its life it had swallowed (among other things) an alarm clock, a Belgian franc, two farthings, a roll of film, three gloves, a handkerchief and a pencil!

★ FARTHEST HEAD TURN

Several species of owl can rotate their heads by as much as 280° and then swiftly rotate them back again in the opposite direction, creating the appearance of more than 360° rotation. Despite many popular claims, however, no species can rotate its head through a full 360°.

LARGEST NEST

A mating pair of bald eagles (*Haliaeetus leucocephalus*) built a nest that measured 2.9 m (9 ft 6 in) wide and 6 m (20 ft) deep near St Petersburg, Florida, USA. It was examined in 1963 and was estimated to weigh more than 2 tonnes (2.2 tons).

LARGEST EAGLE

Named after the famous German botanist Georg Steller, the world's largest species of eagle is Steller's sea eagle (*Haliaeetus pelagicus*), which weighs between 5 kg and 9 kg (11–20 lb) and has a wing-span of between 2.2 m and 2.45 m (7 ft 2 in–8 ft 3 in). Although it breeds mainly in Russia, where it is a protected species, the eagle has also been spotted in Korea, Alaska in the USA and in Japan, where it is considered a national symbol. The International Union for the Conservation of Nature classifies the bird as vulnerable with an estimated population of 5,000 specimens.

Mar 5: Ken Edwards (UK) ate 36 cockroaches – the **most cockroaches eaten in one minute** – on the set of *The Big Breakfast* (C4, UK), London, UK, on 5 March 2001.

Mar 6: The **most expensive human skull** – that of Swedish philosopher Emanuel Swedenborg (1688–1772) – was bought for £5,500 ($10,664) on this day in 1978.

★ LARGEST SQUIRREL

The Indian, or Malabar, giant squirrel (*Ratufa indica*), found exclusively in deciduous and evergreen forests in India, can grow to 1 m (3 ft 3 in) in total length – about the size of a large domestic cat – two-thirds of which consist of its long, bushy tail. Rarely coming down from its home in the upper canopy of the forest, it moves from tree to tree by way of huge leaps of up to 6 m (20 ft).

★ FIRST HUMAN-SHEEP CHIMERA

In March 2007, Prof. Esmail Zanjani from the University of Nevada, USA, announced that his team had created the world's first human–sheep chimera – a sheep that contains sheep cells (85%) and human cells (15%). (Chimera in Greek mythology had a lion's head, a goat's body and a serpent's tail.) Its creation brings ever closer the prospect of animal organs being transplanted into humans. Zanjani and his team have spent seven years and $7 million (£5 million) perfecting the technique required to produce this chimera, which involves injecting adult human cells into the foetus of a sheep.

★ LARGEST INVASIVE SPECIES

Colombian drugs baron Pablo Escobar stocked his huge estate with hundreds of exotic animals, including a lake of four African hippopotamuses. After he was killed in 1993, his estate passed into government hands and all the animals disappeared – except for the hippos. They currently number 19, and roam the area at night in search of food.

★ LARGEST MAMMOTH SKELETON

Known colloquially as the West Runton elephant, the world's biggest – and most complete – mammoth skeleton was discovered in Cromer, Norfolk, UK, in 1990. *Mammuthus trogontherii* stands 4 m (13 ft 1 in) at the shoulder and is approximately 600,000 years old.

★ LONGEST MAMMAL MIGRATION

The humpback whale (*Megaptera novaeangliae*) migrates up to 8,200 km (5,095 miles) each way when journeying back and forth between its warm breeding waters near the equator and the colder, food-rich waters of the Arctic and Antarctic regions.

FACT
The incredible photograph above shows a humpback whale swimming backstroke. This species is particularly acrobatic, indulging in playful diving and tail-splashing. It is also famed for its beautiful singing.

LARGEST PREHISTORIC RODENT

The world's largest-ever rodent is a newly named 2-million-year-old fossil species named *Josephoartigasia monesi*. Although currently known only from a single skull measuring 53 cm (21 in) long, the complete animal probably weighed a massive 1 tonne (1.1 tons). Related to today's much smaller pacarana (*Dinomys branickii*), it lived in coastal Uruguay, in what was then lush forested swampland, and probably fed on soft vegetation as its jaws, though huge, lacked chewing power.

OLDEST PIG EVER

The oldest pig is "Hoofer", who was 18 years 8 months 23 days old when he died on 2 March 2008. He lived with his owners Shawn Burton Wygrys and Allen Wygrys (both USA) in Sugar Land, Texas, USA, until his death.

ON THE RUN

On account of their dangerous nature, there is now concern that the Escobar hippos will attempt to colonize other lakes and rivers and thus spread farther through the Colombian countryside. One was recently shot by a farmer several kilometres away from their lake.

★ **NEW RECORD**
UPDATED RECORD

Mar 7: Roy Makaay (Netherlands) scored the opening goal for Bayern Munich against Real Madrid in just 10 seconds in Munich, Germany, on 7 March 2007 – the **fastest Champions League goal**.

Mar 8: The **largest decorated Easter egg**, made by Freeport in Alochete, Portugal, was 14.79 m (48 ft 6 in) long and 8.40 m (27 ft 6 in) in diameter when measured on 8 March 2008.

★FIRST RHINO BORN
FROM ARTIFICIAL INSEMINATION

A calf born in Budapest Zoo, Hungary, on 23 January 2007 was the first successful birth of a rhinoceros via artificial insemination. Lulu – the mother – had already given birth to a dead calf conceived using the same process in 2005. Vets used artificial insemination as there was no chance for natural breeding owing to the brother–sister relationship of the zoo's rhinos.

★RAREST ELEPHANT

The rarest elephant on record is Motty, a male calf born at Chester Zoo, Cheshire, UK, on 11 July 1978. He is considered the "rarest" because he is the only known example of a hybrid between the African elephant (*Loxodonta africana*) and the Asian elephant (*Elephas maximus*). His father was Jumbolino, a bull African elephant, and his mother was Sheba, a cow Asian elephant, and he lived for 10 days before dying from necrotic enterocolitis and an *E. coli* septicaemia.

Motty possessed a fascinating combination of features from both species of elephants and his skin was preserved as a mounted taxiderm specimen, which is housed at the Natural History Museum, London, UK. Until Motty's birth, it was not believed possible that interspecific elephant hybrids could occur, and none has been recorded since.

★OLDEST BAT EVER

The world's oldest bat was an Indian fruit bat (*Pteropus giganteus*) that died at London Zoo, UK, on 11 January 1979, aged 31 years 5 months. In the wild, a little brown mouse-eared bat (*Myotis lucifugus*) found dead in a cave on Mount Aeolus in Vermont, USA, on 30 April 1960, is known to have been at least 24 years old because it had been banded back on 22 June 1937, when it was already fully mature.

★OLDEST PONY EVER

The oldest pony ever was Sugar Puff (1951–2007), an Exmoor Shetland owned by S Botting (UK) of Chichester, West Sussex, UK.

★LARGEST ORANGUTAN SANCTUARY

The world's largest sanctuary for orangutans (*Pongo pygmaeus*) is the Sepilok Orangutan Rehabilitation Centre in the Malaysian state of Sabah in northern Borneo. Since it opened in 1964, it has rehabilitated over 100 rescued orphaned orangutans back into the wild.

The centre is also actively involved in public education on conservation, as well as research and assistance in relation to other endangered species. The sanctuary currently employs more than 37 staff, including a wildlife officer, a vet and wildlife rangers.

★NEWEST TAPIR

For more than a century, only four species of tapir have been known to science (see box, right), but a fifth species was identified in 2008. Known as the black dwarf lowland tapir (*Tapirus pygmaeus*), it was found in Brazil's lowland Amazonia by Dutch zoologist Dr Marc van Roosmalen. It can be distinguished from the common tapir by its smaller size, unique dentition (teeth arrangement) and lack of white marks on its ear tips.

WHAT ARE MAMMALS?

Mammals are a class of vertebrate animals. The name is derived from the animal's mammary glands, with which it feeds its young. Animals in this order also have sweat glands, hair, three middle-ear bones for hearing and a neocortex region in the brain.

★LARGEST TAPIR

The largest of the five species of tapir, the Malayan tapir usually grows to 1.8–2.4 m (6–8 ft) long, 90–107 cm (3–3 ft 6 in) high and typically weighs 250–320 kg (550–700 lb), although it can weigh up to 500 kg (1,100 lb).

LARGEST RODENT

The capybara, or carpincho (*Hydrochoerus hydrochaeris*, above left) of Argentina, Brazil and Uruguay, has a head and body length of 1–1.3 m (3 ft 3 in–4 ft 3 in) and can weigh up to 79 kg (175 lb). One exceptional cage-fat specimen attained 113 kg (249 lb). Several species vie for the title of **smallest rodent**. In particular, the northern pygmy mouse (*Baiomys taylori*, left) of Mexico, Arizona and Texas, USA, and the Baluchistan pygmy jerboa (*Salpingotus michaelis*) of Pakistan. Both have a head–body length of as little as 3.6 cm (1.4 in) and a tail length of 7.2 cm (2.8 in).

ACTUAL SIZE

Mar 9: The **youngest individual athletics world record holder** is Wang Yan (China, b. 9 April 1971), who completed the women's 5,000 m walk in 21 min 33.8 sec, aged 14 years 334 days in China on 9 March 1986.

1952: the last time that India's Shridhar Chillal (**longest nails on a single hand**) – cut the nails of his left hand.

TOP **100** Records of the Decade

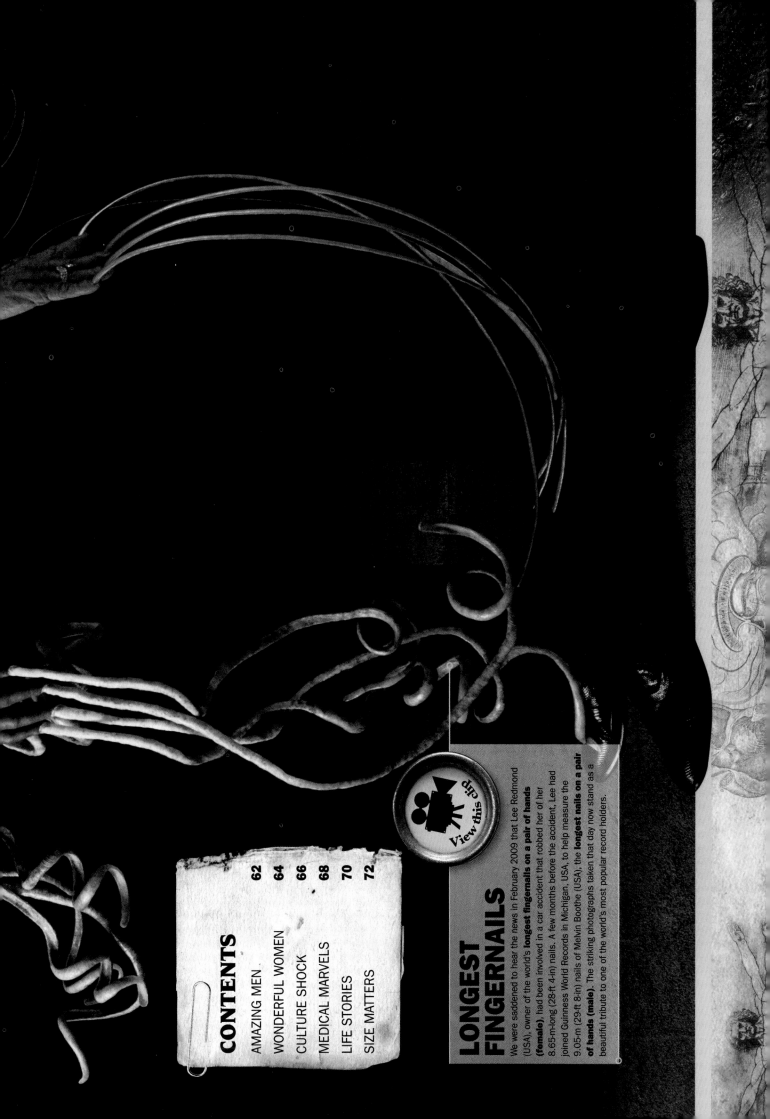

CONTENTS

LONGEST FINGERNAILS

We were saddened to hear the news in February 2009 that Lee Redmond (USA), owner of the world's **longest fingernails on a pair of hands (female)**, had been involved in a car accident that robbed her of her 8.65-m-long (28-ft 4-in) nails. A few months before the accident, Lee had joined Guinness World Records in Michigan, USA, to help measure the 9.05-m (29-ft 8-in) nails of Melvin Boothe (USA), the **longest nails on a pair of hands (male)**. The striking photographs taken that day now stand as a beautiful tribute to one of the world's most popular record holders.

View this clip

AMAZING MEN

LONGEST EAR HAIR

Antony Victor (India) has hair sprouting from the centre of his outer ears (the middle of the pinna) that measures 18.1 cm (7.1 in) at its longest point.

Victor is a retired headmaster from Madurai in the Indian state of Tamil Nadu. He regained his record in 2008, having previously held it in 2002, when his ear hair was measured at 11.5 cm (4.5 in), signifying a growth of 6.6 cm (2.5 in) over six years.

LONGEST BEARD

After being soaked in water and combed several times, the beard of Sarwan Singh (Canada) measured a record 2.33 m (7 ft 8 in) from the end of his chin to the tip of the longest hair. The beard was measured on 11 November 2008; to unveil his whiskers in full, Singh stood on a box and allowed the hairs to flow down freely.

LARGEST FEET

Robert Wadlow (USA, 1918–1940), the **tallest-ever man**, wore US size 37AA shoes (UK size 36 or approximately a European size 75). Wadlow also holds the record for the **largest-ever hands** – his measured 32.3 cm (12.75 in) from the wrist to the tip of his middle finger. *See p.13 for more on Robert Wadlow.*

The **tallest living man**, Sultan Kösen (Turkey, see pp.72–73), also has the **largest hands** (27.5 cm/10.8 in from wrist to finger tip) and **feet** (36.5 cm/14.4 cm, heel to toe) of a living person.

★ MOST WEIGHT LOST IN A LIFETIME (MALE)

The "yoyo" dieting habits of Michael Hebranko (USA) has resulted in an estimated total weight loss over his lifetime of 2,268 kg (5,000 lb; 357 st; 2.2 tonnes). His first major documented weight loss – of 321 kg (50 st 6 lb; 709 lb) – was a record at the time (1990). He regained this weight, and more, by 1999, to reach a peak of 500 kg (78 st 7 lb; 1,100 lb). However, his current diet has seen him lose a further 291 kg (642 lb; 45 st 12 lb). The accumulated weight that Hebranko has lost in his lifetime equates to that of 35 average males!

TOP 100 Records of the Decade

LONGEST MOUSTACHE

Ram Singh Chauhan (India), a Rajasthan state tourism official, started growing hair on his upper lip in 1982. When measured in November 2008, his moustache was 3.50 m (11 ft 6 in) long.

CAN YOU BEAT THIS?

If you think your moustache is longer than Ram Singh Chauhan's, these are the guidelines you'll need to follow if you want to claim the record:

1. Measurements must be made by a suitably qualified individual, such as a medical professional.
2. The total length of the moustache should be measured from tip to tip.
3. Take a photograph of your moustache alongside an accurately calibrated measuring tape.
4. Provide a signed letter confirming the measurement, countersigned by two independent witnesses.

For full instructions on how to make a claim, go to p.14.

Mar 10: The **shortest radio advertisement** lasted 0.954 seconds and was made by BBDO Oslo Reklamebyrå AS. It was first broadcast in Norway on this day in 2006.

Mar 11: The **youngest person to have a pacemaker fitted** is Stephanie Gardiner (UK), who was four hours old when she was fitted with a pacemaker the size of a stamp on 11 March 1995.

8.4 cm (3.4 in): the amount by which J J Bittner (USA) can open his mouth – giving him the world record for the **widest human gape**.

SHORTEST LIVING MAN (MOBILE)

The shortest known mobile living adult is He Pingping (China, b. 1988), who was measured by a team of doctors in Hohhot, Inner Mongolia, China, and found to be 74.61 cm (2 ft 5.37 in) tall on 22 March 2008.

★ WIDEST TONGUE

Australian Jay Sloot's tongue measured 7.9 cm (3.1 in) at its widest point when examined on the set of *Guinness World Records* in Sydney, Australia, on 23 August 2005.

In February 2009, the UK's Stephen Taylor set the record for the ★ **longest tongue**, measuring 9.8 cm (3.85 in) from lip to tip.

LARGEST WAIST

Walter Hudson (USA, 1944–91) measured 302 cm (119 in) around the waist at his peak weight of 545 kg (1,197 lb; 85 st 7 lb).

★ MOST 18-GAUGE SURGICAL NEEDLE BODY PIERCINGS

Robert Jesus Rubio (USA) had 900 18-gauge, 1.2-cm-long (0.5-in) surgical needles inserted into his body in Texas, USA, on 29 May 2008. Rubio beat the previous record of 745 needles, held by Benjamin Drucker (USA), which had stood for five years.

MOST TATTOOED MAN

Fire-eating, unicycling, chainsaw-juggling Lucky Diamond Rich (Australia) has spent over 1,000 hours having his body modified by tattoo artists. Rich has 100% coverage of black ink, including his eyelids and his gums, and is now being tattooed with white designs on top of the black and coloured designs on top of the white!

LONGEST HAIR

● **Nipple**: A hair growing from the nipple of Douglas Williams (USA) was found to be 12.9 cm (5.07 in) long when measured in New York City, USA, on 26 May 2007.
● **Leg**: The longest leg hair is 16.51 cm (6.5 in) in length and belongs to Wesley Pemberton (USA), as measured on the set of *Lo show dei record* in Madrid, Spain, on 9 February 2008.
● **Arm**: Robert Starrett (USA) has an arm hair that had grown to a length of 13.5 cm (5.31 in) when measured in Mequon, Wisconsin, USA, on 7 December 2006.
● **Chest**: A chest hair belonging to Richard Condo (USA) measured 22.8 cm (9 in) when verified in New Jersey, USA, on 29 April 2007.
● **Eyebrow**: The longest eyebrow hair belongs to Toshie Kawakami (Japan) and was confirmed to be 15.1 cm (5.94 in) at the Guinness World Records Museum in Tokyo, Japan, on 22 January 2008.
● **Eyelash**: Stuart Muller's (USA) left upper eyelash was 6.99 cm (2.75 in) when measured on 7 December 2007.

LONGEST NOSE

Mehmet Ozyurek's (Turkey) nose measured a record 8.8 cm (3.46 in) long from the bridge to the top of the philtrum when officially assessed in his home town of Artvin on 31 January 2001.

The **longest nose ever** belonged to circus performer Thomas Wedders (UK, c. 1770s) and was reportedly 19 cm (7.5 in) long.

★ **NEW RECORD**
★ **UPDATED RECORD**

MOST PIERCED MAN

The world's most pierced man is 78-year-old John Lynch (UK), who was found to have 241 piercings, including 151 in his head and neck, when examined in London, UK, on 17 October 2008. A former Barclays Bank manager, Lynch gave up his "regular" lifestyle in the late 1990s after reading a book on piercings.

FACT

John Lynch (UK, b. 9 November 1930) worked in a bank for 30 years before retiring and getting his first piercing in his nose. Lynch hated the conformity of the work place and developed an interest in extreme body modification as a way of "standing out from the crowd". Although the piercings came after he left the bank, Lynch got his first tattoo when he was in his 40s.

Mar 12: Rapper 50 Cent (USA) had three singles in the US Top 5 on this day in 2005, the **most simultaneous Top 5 hits by a solo artist**. The tracks were "Candy Shop", "How We Do" and "Disco Inferno".

TOP **100** Records of the Decade

WWW.GUINNESSWORLDRECORDS.COM

THE BODY
WONDERFUL WOMEN

★ NEW RECORD
UPDATED RECORD

GETTING THE POINT

Elaine Davidson, a former nurse from Brazil, claims that she never removes her rings and studs, which she estimates weigh a total of 3 kg (6 lb 9 oz), and she insists that she sleeps soundly with all of her piercings in place.

Elaine also sleeps on a bed of nails, walks on fire, lies on broken glass and holds a black belt in Judo, which she earned in Japan. She is well known in Edinburgh, UK, where she runs a shop specializing in aromatherapy, piercings, tattoos and hair braiding.

LONGEST LEGS

Svetlana Pankratova (Russia) has the world's longest legs, verified as measuring 132 cm (51.9 in, or 4 ft 6 in) in Marbella, Spain, on 3 February 2008. An estate agent currently living in Torremolinos, Spain, Svetlana used to play basketball for the USA's Virginia Commonwealth University from 1992 to 1995.

SHORTEST LIVING WOMAN

Madge Bester (South Africa, b. 26 April 1963) is only 65 cm (25.5 in) tall. However, she suffers from *osteogenesis imperfecta* (characterized by brittle bones and other deformities of the skeleton) and is confined to a wheelchair. Her mother, Winnie, is not much taller, measuring 70 cm (27.5 in), and is also confined to a wheelchair.

SHORTEST WOMAN EVER

Pauline Musters (Netherlands, b. 26 February 1876) measured 30 cm (12 in) at birth. At nine years of age, she was just 55 cm (21.5 in) tall and weighed only 1.5 kg (3 lb 5 oz). She died on 1 March 1895 in New York City, USA, at the age of 19, and a post-mortem examination showed her to be exactly 61 cm (24 in) tall – there was some elongation after death.

SMALLEST WAIST

Cathie Jung (USA), who stands 1.72 m (5 ft 8 in) tall, has "trained" her waist to a circumference of 38.1 cm (15 in) when corseted. Cathie began tightening her corsets to replicate the narrow hour-glass shape popular in Victorian England.

SMALLEST WAIST EVER

The smallest waist of a person with normal stature was 33 cm (13 in) and belonged to Ethel Granger (UK, 1905–82). A measurement of 33 cm (13 in) was also claimed for the French actress Emile Marie Bouchand (1881–1939).

HEAVIEST WOMAN EVER

Rosalie Bradford (USA, 1943–2006) is claimed to have registered a peak weight of 544 kg (1,200 lb, or 85 st 10 lb) in January 1987. In August 1987, she developed congestive heart failure and was rushed to hospital. She was consequently put on a carefully controlled diet and by February 1994 her weight was down to 128 kg (283 lb, or 20 st 3 lb).

★ LONGEST DREADLOCKS

The longest dreadlocks belong to Asha Mandela (USA). When measured in Davenport, Florida, USA, on 13 November 2008, the dreadlocks were 2.59 m (8 ft 6 in) long.

MOST PIERCED WOMAN

Since her first piercing in January 1997, Elaine Davidson (UK) has had so many additional procedures over and inside her body that she has lost count of them all. When Guinness World Records was last able to examine and count her piercings, in October 2004, she was found to have 2,520 in total.

Mar 13: On this day in 2007, the **shortest concert** took place. A performance by The Who (UK) in Tampa, Florida, ended after 13 seconds when lead vocalist Roger Daltrey (UK) realized that he was too ill to sing that night.

TOP 100 Records of the Decade

104.75 dB: the **loudest burp by a female** was achieved by Jodie Parks (USA) on 16 February 2008. By way of comparison, a pneumatic drill is around 100 dB.

★ OLDEST COMPETITIVE FEMALE BODY BUILDER

At 73 years 4 months of age, Ernestine Shepherd (USA, b. 16 June 1936) is the world's oldest competitive body builder. She started training when she was 56 as she wanted to see if she could get her body into shape and delay the ageing process.

LARGEST TUMMY TUCK

Surgeons at the Hospital de Cruces in Barakaldo, Spain, removed an "apron" of fat weighing 60 kg (132 lb) from an obese woman in March 2006. Small cranes were used to help remove the flesh, which hung down to the patient's knees. The excised skin weighed the same as an average 17-year-old girl, and had an energy content of 462,000 calories.

OLDEST PERSON TO GROW A NEW TOOTH

Mária Magdolna Pozderka (Hungary, b. 19 July 1938) had an upper right canine tooth erupt at the age of 68 in March 2007.

★ MOST TATTOOED SENIOR CITIZEN

Isobel Varley of Stevenage in Hertfordshire, UK, has an estimated 76% of her body tattooed – everything except her hands, face, neck and the soles of her feet. After 10 years, she has had over 200 designs inked on to her body, including an owl on her leg and tigers on her stomach. The only tattoo she regrets is an "unrealistic frog" on her stomach. Apparently, the most painful area to have done was her toes!

LIGHTEST PERSON EVER

Lucia Xarate (or Zarate, Mexico, 1863–89), an emaciated ateleiotic dwarf (a person of short stature with normal human proportions) standing just 67 cm (26.8 in) tall, weighed 2.13 kg (4.7 lb) at the age of 17. She managed to increase her weight to 5.9 kg (13 lb) by her 20th birthday.

TALLEST WOMAN EVER

Zeng Jinlian (China, b. 26 June 1964) of Yujiang village in the Bright Moon Commune, Hunan Province, China, measured 2.48 m (8 ft 1.75 in) when she died on 13 February 1982. This figure represented her height with assumed normal spinal curvature because she suffered from severe scoliosis (curvature of the spine) and could not stand up straight.

TALLEST TWINS (FEMALE)

Ann and Claire Recht (both USA, b. 9 February 1988) were measured both horizontally (lying down) and vertically (standing) on three occasions over the course of the day on 10 January 2007 and each was found to have an average overall height of 2.01 m (6 ft 7 in).

HEAVIEST MODEL

US model Teighlor (aka Debra Perkins) reached a peak weight of 326.14 kg (719 lb, or 51 st) in the early 1990s and forged a successful modelling career, appearing in films, on greeting cards and in advertisements.

FACT
Ernestine began her fitness regime by walking every day, which then progressed to running, and she now regularly competes in 5-km and 10-km races.

LONGEST FEMALE BEARD

After the death of her mother in 1990, Vivian Wheeler (USA) stopped trimming her facial hair and grew a full beard. The longest strand of hair was found to be 27.9 cm (11 in) in 2000. Vivian prefers to tie the beard up, to allow her to continue with her day-to-day routines, and often adorns it with ribbons and bows.

The "bearded lady", Janice Deveree (USA, b. 1842), had the **longest ever female beard** – it measured 36 cm (14 in) in 1884.

FARTHEST EYEBALL POP

Kim Goodman (USA) can pop her eyeballs 12 mm (0.47 in) beyond her eye sockets – a "talent" she discovered once while yawning! Her eyes were measured most recently in Istanbul, Turkey, on 2 November 2007.

LONGEST TOENAILS

Since 1982, Louise Hollis (USA) has been growing her toenails to great lengths. When measured at their longest, in 1991, the combined length of all 10 toenails was 220.9 cm (87 in).

LONGEST HAIR

The world's longest documented hair belongs to Xie Qiuping (China) at 5.627 m (18 ft 5.54 in) when measured on 8 May 2004. She has been growing her hair since 1973 from the age of 13.

Mar 14: The **longest-lasting rainbow** was visible for six hours continuously, from 9.00 a.m. to 3.00 p.m., over Wetherby, UK, on 14 March 1994.

Mar 15: David Schummy (Australia) threw a boomerang 427.2 m (1,401 ft 6 in) on this day in 2005 in Queensland, Australia – the **farthest distance any object has been thrown by hand.**

CULTURE SHOCK

★ MOST ENDANGERED TRIBE

Just six members remain of the Akuntsu tribe of Rondônia state, western Brazil (five of the six are pictured right). They live in a single community, sharing just two malocas (communal houses) made of straw, and cultivate a small garden of corn and manioc. They are also keen hunters of wild pig, tapirs and agouti. The cause of the tribe's demise was a massacre by cattle ranchers, who bulldozed the forest and caused near genocide among the indigenous population in the 1980s.

★ NEW RECORD
UPDATED RECORD

★ LANGUAGE WITH THE MOST SOUNDS

!Xóõ (aka Ta'a), which is spoken by about 4,000 Khomani people in southern Africa, contains 74 consonants, 31 vowels and four tones (pitches).

DID YOU KNOW?

The Akuntsu was discovered in 1995, when they numbered just seven. One of the group later died when a tree fell on their home during a storm.

★ FIRST EVIDENCE OF HOMINID CANNIBALISM

In the foothills of the Sierra de Atapuerca in northern Spain is a series of prehistoric caves in which a human ancestor – *Homosapiens antecessor* – lived up to 800,000 years ago. Among the hominid remains are bones and skulls displaying a series of gouges and scars that suggest a tool had been used for skinning, scraping flesh and extracting marrow from bones. The same pattern of markings is mirrored in animal bones found nearby.

★ LARGEST VOODOO FESTIVAL

On Voodoo Day, celebrated at the peak of the annual 10-day voodoo festival in Ouida, Benin – the West African home of this ancient religion – upwards of 10,000 worshippers gather for sacrifices, blessings and prayers. An estimated 60% of Benin's population practise voodoo (more accurately referred to as Vodun), which worships and honours a supreme god as well as ancestors and ancient spirits (loa), each of which is associated – and invoked – with a particular song and dance.

★ MOST FAMILY MEMBERS TO WALK ON ALL FOURS

Five (out of 19) adult siblings of the Ulas family of Turkey – four sisters and a brother – walk on their feet and the palms of their hands. This quadrupedal gait (known as "bear walk") is unique to the Ulases and is different to the "knuckle walk" witnessed in the great apes. The five siblings also suffer from congenital brain impairment and have trouble balancing on two legs. The condition is known as Uner Tan Syndrome, after the Turkish professor at Çukurova University, Turkey, who first studied the family in 2005.

★ MOST ISOLATED TRIBE

Survival International, a charity dedicated to maintaining tribal societies, points to the inhabitants of the 72-km^2 (28-mile^2) North Sentinel island in the Andaman chain, located in the Bay of Bengal, as the most likely candidates for the most isolated tribe. The Sentinelese – who want no contact with the rest of the world – have inhabited their island for over 60,000 years. Video evidence taken in the aftermath of the 2004 tsunami that destroyed much of the Andaman archipelago confirmed that the tribe continues to cling to life.

LARGEST LIP PLATES

The Surma people of Ethiopia wear lip plates to signify wealth. The process of inserting these plates (made by women from local clay) begins approximately a year before marriage; the final size indicates the number of cattle required by the girl's family from her future husband. Plates typically reach up to 15 cm (6 in) in diameter, which would require a payment of 50 cattle.

LABRETS

Lip piercings, plugs and plates are known collectively as labrets (LAY-brits). A small piercing is made in either the upper or lower lip, and a wooden plug inserted. Once the wound heals, increasingly larger plugs are substituted until the lip is stretched wide enough to accommodate a plate.

Mar 16: Wim Hof (Netherlands) swam 57.5 m (188 ft 6 in) under ice in a lake near Kolari, Finland, on 16 March 2000, the **farthest distance swum under ice without breathing equipment.**

1.3 million: estimate for the number of people who celebrated Thaipusam at the Batu caves near Kuala Lumpur, Malaysia, in 2007.

HIGHEST PERCENTAGE OF WOMEN WITH BOUND FEET

The practice of foot binding, which began in 10th-century China and persisted until it was banned in 1911, prevented women's feet from growing more than 10 cm (3.9 in). A study in 1997 of 193 women (93 were over 80 years old, 100 were aged 70–79) in Beijing, by the University of California, San Francisco, USA, found 38% of the women in the over-80 group and 18% in the younger group had feet that had become deformed by foot binding.

★ LONGEST RELIGIOUS CEREMONY

Every 60 years or so, the Dogon peoples of Mali celebrate the Sigui, a mask festival to mark the handing over of the cult's secrets from one generation to the next. The ceremony takes many years to complete – the last Sigui ran from 1967 to 1973, with the next due in 2032 – as the initiates (male only) must learn a secret language and carve a Great Mask, several metres in length. Each initiate wears his own mask and performs in a series of dances from village to village.

★ MOST RECENT TRIBAL "FIRST CONTACT"

There are around 100 known but uncontacted tribes in the world, and the most recent to make contact was a sub-group of the Ayoreo-Totobiegosode peoples of the Chaco, a forest stretching from Paraguay to Bolivia and Argentina. In March 2004, a group of 17 Indians – five men, seven women and five children – were ousted from the Paraguay forest after cattle ranchers forcibly colonized their territory and occupied their waterholes.

SHORTEST TRIBE

The Mbutsi pygmies from Zaire have an average height of 1.37 m (4 ft 6 in) for men and 1.35 m (4 ft 5 in) for women, with some groups averaging only 1.32 m (4 ft 4 in) for men and 1.24 m (4 ft 1 in) for women.

TALLEST TRIBE

The tallest major tribe in the world is the Tutsi (also known as the Watussi) of Rwanda and Burundi, Central Africa, whose young adult males average 1.83 m (6 ft).

LONGEST NECK

The maximum known extension of a human neck is 40 cm (15.75 in) and was created by the successive fitting of copper coils, as practised by the women of the Padaung or Kareni tribe of Burma as a sign of beauty. Their necks eventually become so long and weak that they cannot support their heads without the coils.

FEWEST TOES

The two-toed syndrome exhibited by some members of the Wadomo tribe of the Zambezi Valley, Zimbabwe, and the Kalanga tribe of the eastern Kalahari Desert, Botswana, is hereditary via a single mutated gene.

★ LARGEST THAIPUSAM FESTIVAL

The Thaipusam Hindu festival, widely celebrated by the Tamils, honours Subrahmanya – aka Murugan – the son of Siva and Parvati. Devotees practise mortification of the flesh by impaling their cheeks with skewers. The largest of the festivals starts at the Sri Mahamariamman Temple in Kuala Lumpur, Malaysia, which attracts up to 1 million devotees.

Mar 17: The **largest sandwich** weighed 2,467.5 kg (5,440 lb) and was made by Wild Woody's Chill and Grill, Roseville, Michigan, USA, on this day in 2005.

Mar 18: The **first spacewalk** was carried out by Lt-Col. (later Maj. Gen.) Alexei Arkhipovich Leonov (USSR), from Voskhod 2, on this day in 1965.

GUINNESS WORLD RECORDS

MEDICAL MARVELS

★ FIRST QUINTUPLE KIDNEY TRANSPLANT

The first five-way "domino" organ transplant took place at John Hopkins Hospital in Baltimore, USA, in November 2006 led by chief transplant surgeon Robert Montgomery (USA, pictured in front of a chart showing the passage of the five kidneys from patient to patient). It took 12 surgeons, six operating rooms, five donors and five recipients to achieve the ground-breaking surgery. *See Kidney Swap box (right) for more details.*

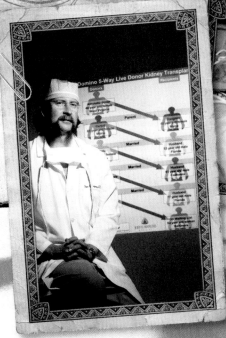

NEW RECORD
UPDATED RECORD

★ FIRST PLASTIC SURGERY

A World War I gunnery warrent officer named Walter Yeo (UK) was the first person to have plastic surgery. Skin grafts were transferred from his shoulder to his face in order to replace both upper and lower eyelids, which he had lost while manning the guns aboard HMS *Warspite* in 1916 during the Battle of Jutland. The groundbreaking surgery was performed by Sir Harold Gillies (New Zealand), regarded today as the father of plastic surgery.

★ HEAVIEST KIDNEY STONE

Wazir Muhammand Jagirani (Pakistan) had this kidney stone (below), weighing 620 g (21.87 oz), removed from his right kidney at the Nephro-Urology Chandka Medical College Hospital in Sindh, Pakistan, on 24 June 2008.

KIDNEY SWAP

In this procedure, four of the patients had a relative willing to offer a kidney (the fifth was on the waiting list for a dead donor), but in each case the donor kidney was incompatible with the patient. However, with the help of one new donor, enough compatible matches were found to complete a five-way swap.

MOST EXPENSIVE KIDNEY STONE

On 18 January 2006, it was announced that *Star Trek* actor William Shatner (USA) had sold a kidney stone that he had passed through his body the previous year for $25,000 (£12,700) to online casino GoldenPalace.com. Shatner donated the money to the Habitat for Humanity housing charity.

ACTUAL SIZE

★ FIRST BIONIC HAND

In 2008, the i-limb hand, created by Touch Bionics (UK), became the first commercially available bionic hand. Each finger is powered by its own motor; it has a credit-card grip for narrow objects and a power hold for larger objects. It is now used by over 400 patients worldwide.

ACTUAL SIZE

Mar 19: Representatives of Swatch Japan cooked the **heaviest Spanish omelette**, which weighed 11.036 tonnes (12.169 tons), at Minato Mirai, Yokohama, Japan, on this day in 1994.

Mar 20: Robert G Davis (USA) completed the **longest snowmobile journey**, which totalled 19,574.45 km (12,163 miles), on his Yamaha RS Venture snowmobile on this day in 2008.

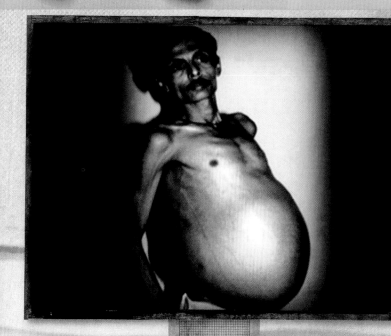

OLDEST UNDISCOVERED TWIN

Sanju Bhagat from Nagpur, India, lived for 36 years with a grossly distended stomach that defied any explanation. In June 1999, his condition became a medical emergency, as his enlarged abdomen began to crush his diaphragm and leave him breathless. Upon operating, Dr Ajay Mehta of Tata Memorial Hospital in Mumbai, India, encountered the foetus of Bhagat's unborn twin, which had continued to grow parasitically inside his abdomen. The twin weighed 4 kg (9 lb), of which 1 kg (2 lb) was hair.

★ MOST BLOOD DONATED

A dedicated blood donor, Anthony Davis (UK) has donated a total of 601 units of blood and blood components as of 3 July 2008.

★ LONGEST SALIVA STONE

Saliva stones are mineral deposits that develop in the saliva ducts. They usually measure a few millimetres long, but the longest on record measures 37 mm (1.45 in). It was removed from a 43-year-old male patient by Dr Kyprianos Kakouris (Cyprus) at the Evangelistria Medical Centre in Cyprus on 20 November 2006.

X-REF
From twins to octuplets, from the very youngest to the very oldest, turn the page to find out some more amazing Life Stories...

★ LONGEST CONFINEMENT IN A WHEELCHAIR

As of 21 November 2008, William Borrelli (USA, b. 4 March 1925) had been confined to a wheelchair for 76 years 173 days. He was hit by a bus at the age of seven while running an errand but has gone on to live a full life, including fathering four children.

FIRST SUCCESSFUL PARTIAL FACE TRANSPLANT

Isabelle Dinoire (France) underwent a face transplant at Amiens University Hospital, France, on 27 November 2005. Ms Dinoire was left severely disfigured after being bitten by her dog. Surgeons worked through the night to remove skin, fat and blood vessels from the donor and then placed them over Ms Dinoire's skull and muscle before re-connecting the blood vessels.

TOP **100** Records of the Decade

BLOOD BANK
The American Red Cross is the world's **largest provider of blood,** plasma, and tissue products with more than 4.5 million donors supplying 3,000 hospitals.

★ HIGHEST PERCENTAGE OF BODY BURNS SURVIVED

Two people have survived burns to 90% of their bodies. David Chapman (UK) was burned after a petrol canister exploded and drenched him with burning fuel on 2 July 1996. Surgeons spent 36 hours following the accident removing his dead skin. Tony Yarijanian (USA) underwent 25 surgeries, including multiple skin grafts, after suffering similar injuries in an explosion at his wife's beauty spa in California, USA, on 15 February 2004.

★ MOST TUMOURS REMOVED

Dr Charitesh Gupta (India) removed a total of nine brain tumours from his 78-year-old patient H S Agarwal (India) in a single operation performed at the Himalayan Institute of Medical Sciences in Dehradun, India, on 9 December 2006.

★ HEAVIEST HUMAN HAIRBALL

A "trichobezoar" – the correct medical term for a hairball – occurs as a result of "trichophagia" – the eating of one's own hair (from the Greek *tricha-* hair, and *phagin-* to eat, also known as Rapunzel syndrome after the Brothers Grimm fairy tale). The largest ever removed from a human was a trichobezoar weighing 4.5 kg (10 lb) found in the stomach of an 18-year-old woman treated at Rush University Medical Center in Chicago, Illinois, USA, in November 2007. The excised trichobezoar measured 37.5 x 17.5 x 17.5 cm (15 x 7 x 7 in).

★ LARGEST TONSILS REMOVED

Justin Dodge (USA) had tonsils that measured 3.2 cm (1.3 in) long, 2.6 cm (1 in) wide and 2.1 cm (0.8 in) thick when they were surgically removed at St Francis Hospital, Milwaukee, Wisconsin, USA, on 18 December 2008.

ACTUAL SIZE

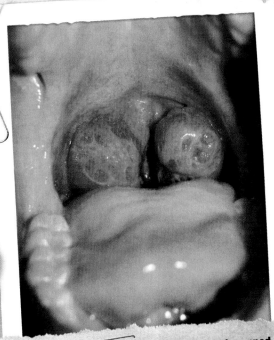

Mar 21: The **largest slot machine payout** is $39,713,982.25 (£25,361,761), won on the Megabucks slot machine at the Excalibur Hotel-Casino, Las Vegas, Nevada, USA, on this day in 2003.

Mar 22: Valeriy Poliyakov (Russia) took the **longest manned flight** when he flew to the *Mir* space station on 8 January 1994 and returned on this day in 1995, a trip lasting 437 days 17 hr 58 min 16 sec.

★ MOST CHILDREN SURVIVING FROM A SINGLE BIRTH

Nadya Suleman (USA, below) claimed headlines across the world on 26 January 2009 when she gave birth to six boys and two girls at the Kaiser Permanente Medical Center, Bellflower, California, USA. The babies were conceived with the aid of *in vitro* fertilization (IVF) treatment and were nine weeks premature when they were delivered by Caesarean section.

The **most children born at a single medically recorded birth** is nine, to Geraldine Brodrick (Australia) at the Royal Hospital for Women, Sydney, Australia, on 13 June 1971. None of the children lived for more than six days.

★ FIRST MARRIED MAN TO GIVE BIRTH

A controversial figure, Thomas Beatie (USA) was born female but legally became a man in his home state of Oregon, USA. He underwent sex reassignment surgery in 2002 but did not have his female reproductive organs removed. As a man, Beatie was legally able to marry Nancy, his female partner, in 2003. Nancy had previously had a hysterectomy, so when the couple wanted to start a family, it was Thomas who, with the help of an anonymous sperm donor, conceived and carried the child. The couple's daughter, Susan, was born on 29 June 2008.

The ★ **first publicized case of a man giving birth** was that of Matt Rice (USA). Rice was also born female and became pregnant through artificial insemination, giving birth to a boy named Blake in 1999.

★ FIRST MOTHER-CHILD SUPERCENTENARIANS

Supercentenarians are people who have attained an age greater than 110. Mary P Romero Zielke Cota (USA, b. 1870) died in 1982, aged 112 years 17 days; her daughter, Rosabell Zielke Champion Fenstermaker (USA, b. 1893), was equally long-lived and died in 2005, aged 111 years 344 days.

★ OLDEST FATHER EVER

The oldest man to father a child was reportedly Les Colley (Australia). Colley was 92 years 10 months old when his ninth child, a son named Oswald, was born. The boy's mother was Colley's third wife, and the couple first met in 1991 through a dating agency when Colley was 90. "I never thought she would get pregnant so easy, but she bloody well did," he told newspaper reporters when the birth was announced.

★ OLDEST MOTHER TO CONCEIVE NATURALLY

On 20 August 1997, Dawn Brooke (UK) became the oldest natural mother when she gave birth to a son by Caesarean section at the age of 59 years. She conceived accidentally, having managed to ovulate past her last period.

HEAVIEST BIRTH

Anna Bates (Canada, 1846–88), who measured 2.27 m (7 ft 5.5 in) tall, gave birth to a boy weighing 10.8 kg (23 lb 12 oz) at her home in Seville, Ohio, USA, on 19 January 1879, but the baby died 11 hours later. The **heaviest baby to survive** is a boy born to Carmelina Fedele (Italy) at Aversa, Italy, who weighed 10.2 kg (22 lb 8 oz) at birth in September 1955.

FACT

On 13 November 2008, Beatie again shocked the world with news of his second pregnancy just months after giving birth to his first child.

MOST PREMATURE BABY TO SURVIVE

The normal human gestation period is usually around 280 days (roughly 40 weeks). However, James Elgin Gill was born to Brenda and James Gill (all Canada) 128 days premature and weighing just 624 g (1 lb 6 oz) on 20 May 1987 in Ottawa, Ontario, Canada. Much of James's body was still developing when he was born, including his skin, hands, ears and feet. His eyes were still fused shut and he required an operation shortly after his birth to seal off a small artery leading from his heart to his lungs.

TOP 100 Records of the Decade

OLDEST WOMAN TO GIVE BIRTH TO HER OWN GRANDCHILDREN

At the age of 56 years, Jacilyn Dalenberg (USA) acted as surrogate mother for her daughter, Kim Coseno (USA), carrying and delivering her own grandchildren – three girls named Elizabeth Jacilyn, Carmina Ann and Gabriella Claire. Born nine weeks early by Caesarean section at Hillcrest Hospital in Cleveland, Ohio, USA, on 11 October 2008, the triplets weighed between 0.9 kg and 1.29 kg (2 lb–2 lb 14 oz).

Mar 23: Sen to Chihiro no Kamikakushi, aka Spirited Away (Japan, 2001), is the **first anime to win an Oscar**; it took the prize for Best Animated Feature on this day in 2003.

7.2 million: the number of people killed by ischaemic heart disease, based on estimates from the United Nations Health Report 2004, making it the world's **deadliest disease**.

★ NEW RECORD
UPDATED RECORD

★ OLDEST LIVING FATHER

In August 2007, Nanu Ram Jogi (India) celebrated the birth of what he believes is his 21st child, a daughter named Girija, at the grand old age of 90. This achievement makes him the oldest known dad in the world. He fathered his first child in 1943 and hopes to continue having babies until he reaches 100 years old. His current wife (the fourth) was previously married to one of his sons, who died in 1997.

★ TOP 10 OLDEST LIVING PEOPLE
As of 19 June 2009

	NAME/NATIONALITY	SEX	BORN	AGE
1	Gertrude Baines (USA, above)	f	6 April 1894	115 y 74 d
2	Kama Chinen (Japan)	f	10 May 1895	114 y 40 d
3	Mary Josephine Ray (USA)	f	17 May 1895	114 y 33 d
4	Olivia Patricia Thomas (USA)	f	29 June 1895	113 y 355 d
5	Neva Morris (USA)	f	3 August 1895	113 y 320 d
6	Chiyo Shiraishi (Japan)	f	6 August 1895	113 y 317 d
7	Maggie Renfro (USA)	f	14 November 1895	113 y 217 d
8	Eugenie Blanchard (France)	f	16 February 1896	113 y 123 d
9	Lucia Lauria Vigna (Italy)	f	4 March 1896	113 y 107 d
10	Daisey Bailey (USA)	f	30 March 1896	113 y 81 d

★ OLDEST MAN

Henry Allingham was born in London, UK, on 6 June 1896, and took the world title of oldest living man on 19 June 2009 (upon the death of Tomoji Tanabe of Japan) aged 113 years 13 days. A veteran of World War I, Allingham served in the Royal Navy and was a founding member of the Royal Air Force.

★ OLDEST PEOPLE TO SHARE A BIRTHDAY

Camille Loiseau (France) and Toyo Endo (Japan) were both born on 13 February 1892 and were the oldest ever people to share a birthday. Toyo was the first to pass away, aged 112 on 3 January 2005; Camille was aged 114 when she died on 12 August 2006.

★ OLDEST MOTHER OF TRIPLETS

In September 2008, an unnamed woman of Asian descent gave birth to triplets at the Cochin maternity hospital in Paris, France, at the age of 59 years. The triplets, two boys and a girl, weighed 2.3 kg (5 lb 1 oz), 2.1 kg (4 lb 9 oz) and 2.4 kg (5 lb 3 oz).

★ OLDEST LIVING SINGLE TWIN

Leona Adams Gleed (USA, b. 28 March 1900) became the oldest living half of a twin on 27 January 2009. Her twin, Leo, died aged 89 in 1990 but the 108-year-old Leona continues to thrive in Norfolk, Nebraska, USA.

MOST PROLIFIC MOTHER EVER

The greatest officially recorded number of children born to one mother is 69, to the wife of Feodor Vassilyev (b. 1707– c. 1782), a peasant from Shuya, Russia. Amazingly, Vassilyev's wife also holds the records for the **most sets of quadruplets born**, with four sets, and the **most sets of twins**, with 16 pairs. While this miraculous mother also gave birth to seven sets of triplets, the record for the **most triplets** is 15 sets, by Maddalena Granata (Italy, 1839–86).

OLDEST WOMAN TO GIVE BIRTH

The oldest mother whose age has been verified is Maria del Carmen Bousada Lara (Spain, b. 5 January 1940), who gave birth by Caesarean to twin boys, Christian and Pau, aged 66 years 358 days, in Barcelona, Spain, on 29 December 2006. The births followed a controversial course of IVF treatment.

Mar 24: The **largest inflatable castle** is 12 m (39 ft) tall and 19 m² (62 ft²) at the base and was first opened to visitors to the Roundhouse in Camden, London, on this day in 1997.

GUINNESS WORLD RECORDS

TOP 100 Records of the Decade

TOP 100 Records of the Decade

71

SIZE MATTERS

DO YOU MEASURE UP?

- Claimants for a **Tallest** record must be prepared to be measured three times in one day (morning, noon and evening; standing position).
- The measurements must be made in the presence of a Guinness World Records adjudicator.
- Only claims that exceed the current record (and if supported by written, medical confirmation) will be measured.

272 CM: TALLEST MAN (EVER)

Weighing 3.85 kg (8.5 lb) at birth, Robert Wadlow (USA, see p.13) started growing abnormally at the age of two, following a double hernia operation. His height chart reveals his incredible growth until his death aged 22:

AGE	HEIGHT
5	163 cm (5 ft 4 in)
8	183 cm (6 ft)
10	199 cm (6 ft 5 in)
12	210 cm (6 ft 10.5 in)
14	226 cm (7 ft 5 in)
16	240 cm (7 ft 10.24 in)
18	253 cm (8 ft 3.5 in)
20	261 cm (8 ft 6.75 in)
22.4	272 cm (8 ft 11.1 in)*

*Still growing while terminally ill

Wadlow died at 1:30 a.m. on 15 July 1940 as a result of a septic blister on his right ankle caused by a brace, which had been poorly fitted only a week earlier.

View this clip

★ 208 CM: TALLEST GIRL

The tallest female under the age of 18 years is Malee Duangdee (Thailand, b. 22 December 1991), whose height of 208 cm (6 ft 10 in) is attributable to an inoperable tumour on her pituitary gland. She is pictured here towering above GWR Editor-in-Chief Craig Glenday (170 cm; 5 ft 7 in), who measured the teenager at the Chulalongkorn Hospital in Bangkok, Thailand, on 16 January 2009. Drug therapy can slow or even halt Malee's growth but it is expensive and currently beyond the means of her family.

248 CM: TALLEST WOMAN (EVER)

Zeng Jinlian (China, 1964–82) measured 248 cm (8 ft 1.75 in) when she died. This figure represented her height with assumed normal spinal curvature because she suffered from severe scoliosis (curvature of the spine) and could not stand up straight.

Zeng began to grow abnormally from the age of four months and stood 2.17 m (7 ft 1.5 in) when she was 13.

118–234 CM: MOST VARIABLE STATURE

Adam Rainer (Austria, 1899–1950) measured just 118 cm (3 ft 10.5 in) at the age of 21 but suddenly started growing at a rapid rate. By 1931, he had nearly doubled to 218 cm (7 ft 1.75 in). He became so weak that he was bedridden for the rest of his life. At the time of his death, he measured 234 cm (7 ft 8 in) and was the only person in history to have been both a dwarf and a giant.

228.6 CM: TALLEST NBA PLAYER

With the recent retirement of Gheorghe Muresan (Romania), Yao Ming (China) of the Houston Rockets (USA) has become the tallest player in the National Basketball Association (NBA), standing at 228.6 cm (7 ft 6 in) tall. He made his pro debut in 1997.

223.5 CM: TALLEST MALE TWINS

Identical twins Michael and James Lanier (USA, b. 27 November 1969) of Troy, Michigan, both stand 223.5 cm (7 ft 3 in). Both boys played collegiate basketball – Michael for the University of Denver, Colorado, and James for the University of California in Los Angeles.

213 CM: TALLEST WBA HEAVYWEIGHT CHAMPION

The tallest person to become the World Boxing Association's Heavyweight Champion is Nicolay Valuev (Russia), who measures 213 cm (7 ft) tall and weighs 150 kg (330 lb). Nicknamed the "Beast of the East" by commentators, Valuev was a former basketball player who, at the age of 16, had already reached 201 cm (6 ft 7 in) tall as a result of a pituitary gland disease.

404.7 CM: TALLEST MARRIED COUPLE

Wilco (Netherlands) and Keisha van Kleef-Bolton (UK) have a combined average height of 404.7 cm (13 ft 3.3 in), making them the world's tallest married couple. They met after Keisha contacted the UK's Tall Persons Club in search of a dance partner. Shortly afterwards, the tall twosome were married by the Reverend Brian Shipsides (also pictured) in All Saints Church, Forest Gate, London, UK.

73 cm (2 ft 5 in): the difference in height between 248-cm-tall (8-ft 2-in) Don Koehler (USA) and his fraternal (non-identical) twin sister – the **greatest height differential between twins**.

236.2 CM: TALLEST WOMAN

Yao Defens (China) reportedly stands at a height of 236.2 cm (7 ft 8.9 in), which would make her the tallest woman on the planet. GWR has yet to confirm her actual height – repeated attempts to measure her have been abandoned due to ill health. Most recently, in April 2009, Ms Yao was injured in a fall that left her temporarily unable to stand.

204 CM: TALLEST NHL PLAYER

Standing 204 cm (6 ft 9 in) tall, Zdeno Chara (Slovakia) of the Boston Bruins (USA) is the tallest player in NHL history.

201 CM: TALLEST FEMALE TWINS

Ann and Claire Recht (USA, b. 9 February 1988) were measured, both horizontally and vertically, three times during 10 January 2007 in Oregon, USA. Each of the twins was found to have an average overall height of 201 cm (6 ft 7 in).

194 CM: TALLEST LEADING ACTOR

Two actors currently hold this title, standing at 1.94 m (6 ft 5 in) – Christopher Lee (UK), who has played most of the major horror characters in films since 1958; and Vince Vaughn (USA), whose first leading role was in *Return to Paradise* (USA, 1998). The **tallest actor (ever)** was Matthew McGrory (USA, 1973–2005), who stood at 229 cm (7 ft 6 in) when he starred in Tim Burton's *Big Fish* (USA, 2003).

182 CM: TALLEST LEADING ACTRESS

Margaux Hemingway, Sigourney Weaver, Geena Davis (all USA) and Brigitte Nielsen (Denmark, see p.207) all stand at 182 cm (6 ft) tall.

211 CM: TALLEST AFL PLAYER

The tallest player to play in the Australian Football League is Aaron Sandilands (Australia) at 211 cm (6 ft 11 in) tall, playing for Freemantle in 2003–05. He shares the record with Tasmanian Peter Street of St Joseph's.

208 CM: TALLEST TENNIS PLAYER AT WIMBLEDON

Ivo Karlovic (Croatia) measured 208 cm (6 ft 10 in) when he played in the 2003 Wimbledon Tennis Championships.

View this clip

★225.1 CM: TALLEST BOY

At just 13 years old, Brenden Adams (USA, b. 20 September 1995) is already 225.1 cm (7 ft 4.6 in) tall – taller than Robert Wadlow (the **tallest man ever**) was at his age. Brenden suffers from an extremely rare chromosomal disorder (he is currently the only known case), but his growth rate has slowed to 0.5 cm (0.25 in) per year.

GROWING PAINS

Sultan has a condition known as "pituitary gigantism", which is the result of an over-production of growth hormone. Growth hormone is released from the pituitary gland in the brain; if the gland is damaged by, say, a tumour, it can release too much (or too little) hormone. The effects of over-production include large hands, a thickening of the bones and painful joints.

246.5 CM: TALLEST MAN

Sultan Kösen (Turkey) officially reigns supreme as the world's tallest living man – and tallest living human – reaching an average height of 246.5 cm (8 ft 1 in) when measured by GWR in Ankara, Turkey, in February 2009. Kösen was born on 10 December 1982 in Kiziltepe Köyü, in the Mardin Province of east Turkey. As a teenager, his height excused him from military service but drew the attention of scouts from the basketball team Galatasaray; he was signed up to play but proved too ungainly and never made it on to court.

TOP 100 Records of the Decade

HUMAN ACHIEVEMENTS

CONTENTS

★ HEAVIEST VEHICLE PULLED OVER 100 FT

Lutheran pastor Reverend Kevin Fast (Canada) started competing in heavy events in 1996 and claimed his first Guinness World Records crown in 1998. Currently, Reverend Fast holds the record for the heaviest vehicle pulled over a level 100-ft (30.48-m) course, which he set when he successfully pulled a truck weighing 57,243 kg (126,200 lb) over that distance on the *Live with Regis & Kelly* television show in New York City, USA, on 15 September 2008.

7,710 kg (16,997 lb): the weight of a truck that Kevin Fast pulled using just one arm on 25 February 2008.

STRENGTH

★ FASTEST TIME TO PULL AN ARTICULATED BUS OVER 50 M

Pascal Laloux (Belgium) pulled an articulated bus a distance of 50 m (164 ft) in 43.09 seconds in Namur, Belgium, on 13 April 2008.

HEAVIEST TRUCK PULLED BY ARM

Using an arm-wrestling move, the Rev. Kevin Fast (Canada) managed to pull a 7,710-kg (16,997-lb) truck in Cobourg, Ontario, Canada, on 25 February 2008. See pp.74–75 for another incredible feat of strength by Rev. Fast.

★ HEAVIEST VEHICLE PULLED BY THE EYELIDS

Using ropes attached to hooks that were inserted into his lower eyelids, Dong Changsheng (China) pulled a car weighing 1,500 kg (3,307 lb) a distance of 10 m (33 ft) in Changchun, China, on 26 September 2006.

HEAVIEST VEHICLE PULLED BY HAIR

The heaviest vehicle to have been pulled by the hair alone over a distance of 30 m (98 ft) is a double-decker bus weighing 7,874 kg (17,359 lb) by Letchemanah Ramasamy (Malaysia) at Bruntingthorpe Proving Ground, Leicestershire, UK, on 1 May 1999.

★ LONGEST TIME TO HOLD A PERSON ABOVE THE HEAD

Markus Ferber held Clarissa Beyelschmidt (both Germany) above his head for 59.34 seconds in Cologne, Germany, on 13 September 2008.

HEAVIEST WEIGHT LIFTED BY TONGUE

Thomas Blackthorne (UK) lifted a 12.5-kg (27-lb 8.9-oz) weight that had been hooked through his tongue on the set of *El Show Olímpico* in Mexico City, Mexico, on 1 August 2008.

★ HEAVIEST WEIGHT LIFTED BY NIPPLES

For five seconds, Sage Werbock (USA), who performs as "The Great Nippulini", lifted a total weight of 21.9 kg (48 lb 4.2 oz) suspended from his pierced nipples at Tritone Bar in Philadelphia, Pennsylvania, USA, on 20 May 2003.

HEAVIEST WEIGHT SUPPORTED ON THE SHOULDERS

Franz Muellner (Austria) supported an average of 560 kg (1,234 lb) on his shoulders for 30 seconds, while a helicopter landed on a frame which he was partly supporting. The record was achieved on the set of *El Show Olímpico* in Mexico City, Mexico, on 31 July 2008.

★ HEAVIEST WEIGHT SUSTAINED BY THE BODY

Eduardo Armallo Lasaga (Spain) sustained 71 concrete blocks and four people – 1,459 kg, or 3,216.5 lb – on his body in Madrid, Spain, on 30 January 2009.

★ LONGEST HOLD OF THE "HUMAN SCALE"

Jessica and Hartmut Held (Germany) maintained the punishing acrobalance position of "human scale" for 38.5 seconds on the set of *Guinness World Records: Die Größten Weltrekorde* in Germany, on 18 December 2008.

HEAVIEST COMBINED WEIGHT BALANCED ON THE HEAD

For one hour, UK strongman and record holder John Evans balanced a total of 5,180.09 kg (11,420 lb) on his head at Lowestoft Seafront, Suffolk, UK, on 23 July 2000.

★ MOST LIFTS OF A 100-KG WEIGHT WITH TEETH IN ONE MINUTE

Using just his teeth, Georges Christen (Luxembourg) managed to lift a 100-kg (220-lb) weight 24 times in one minute on the set of *L'Été De Tous Les Records* in Benodet, France, on 22 August 2005.

GREATEST WEIGHT OF BRICKS LIFTED

Fred Burton (UK) held 20 bricks weighing a total of 102.73 kg (226 lb 7 oz) at chest height for two seconds on 5 June 1998 at Cheadle, Staffordshire, UK.

★ TIGHTEST FRYING-PAN ROLLS

Scott Murphy (USA) took a 30-cm (12-in) aluminium frying pan and, with his bare hands, rolled it into a tube with a circumference of 17.46 cm (6.87 in) in 30 seconds. The feat took place at the NXB Team Training Center in Myrtle Beach, South Carolina, USA, on 30 July 2007.

The ★ **tightest circumference of two 30-cm (12-in) aluminium frying pans** rolled together with bare hands in 30 seconds is 30.5 cm (12 in), set by Jon Pritikin (USA) at Rectory Road Park in Sittingbourne, Kent, UK, on 11 July 2007.

Mar 25: Peggy Ashcroft (UK) won an Academy Award for *A Passage to India* (UK/USA, 1984) on this day in 1985, aged 77 years 93 days – the **oldest winner of a Best Supporting Actress Oscar.**

580: the number of times Mark Anglesea (UK) lifted the rear of a car clear of the ground in one hour on 3 October 1998.

★ MOST CONCRETE BLOCKS BROKEN IN A SINGLE STACK WITH THE HEAD

The record for the most concrete blocks broken in a single stack using just the head is seven, achieved by Narve Laeret (Norway) in Horten, Vestfold, Norway, on 3 July 2008. Laeret beat his own record of five set the year before.

★ GIANT HULA HOOP – MOST ROTATIONS IN A MINUTE

In Jamaica, New York, USA, on 30 April 2008, Ashrita Furman (USA) rotated a custom-built hula hoop with a diameter of 3.5 m (11 ft 6 in) a total of 64 times in one minute.

★ HEAVIEST WEIGHT PULLED WITH THE EYE SOCKETS

Chayne Hultgren (Australia) pulled a rickshaw loaded with people, weighing a total of 411.65 kg (907 lb), using ropes attached to fish hooks that were hooked on to the lacrimal bones underneath his eyes, in Milan, Italy, on 25 April 2009.

LONGEST TIME RESTRAINING A CAR

While appearing on the *El Show Olímpico* television show in Mexico City, Mexico, on 28 July 2008, Franz Muellner (Austria) managed to restrain a Ferrari 360 Modena that was at full throttle for a total of 13.84 seconds.

MOST BENCH PRESSES OF A PERSON

Fernando Saugar (Spain) bench-pressed a person sitting on a specially designed bench with a combined weight of 106.28 kg (234 lb 5 oz) 111 times in one minute. Saugar achieved the record on the set of *Guinness World Records – El Show de los Records* in Madrid, Spain, on 25 May 2006.

★ MOST DOMESTIC APPLIANCES THROWN IN ONE MINUTE

Taking the art of domestic-appliance-throwing one stage farther, Oliver Gratzer (Austria) tossed 24 different household appliances in one minute on the set of *Guinness World Records – Die Größten Weltrekorde* in Cologne, Germany, on 13 September 2008.

FARTHEST WASHING-MACHINE THROW BY AN INDIVIDUAL

Bill Lyndon (Australia) managed to toss a washing machine weighing 45.3 kg (99 lb) a distance of 3.36 m (11 ft 0.24 in) in Sydney, Australia, on 26 June 2005.

★ FASTEST TIME TO COMPLETE THE GWR FITNESS CHALLENGE

Robin Simpson (UK) finished a 2-mile swim, a 110-mile cycle ride, a 12-mile run, a 12-mile walk, a 20-mile row, 20 miles of Nordic track (elliptical) training, 136,077 kg (300,000 lb) of lifts (no leg lifts), 1,250 push-ups, 3,250 abdominal crunches, 1,250 leg lifts and 1,250 star jumps in 18 hr 25 min 40 sec in Leeds, UK, on 28 November 2008.

★ MOST VEHICLES TO RUN OVER THE STOMACH

Tom Owen (USA) had eight vehicles run over his stomach in Phoenix, Arizona, USA, on 17 October 2008. The total weight of the eight vehicles was 32,658 kg (72,000 lb).

LONGEST TIME SPENT RESTRAINING TWO CESSNA AIRCRAFT

Chad Netherland (USA) used just his own unaided strength to prevent the take-off of two Cessna aeroplanes pulling in opposite directions for 1 min 0.6 sec.

The record was set at Richard I Bong Airport in Superior, Wisconsin, USA, on 7 July 2007.

N12839

View this clip

Mar 26: The **shortest papal reign** was that of Pope Stephen II, who was elected on 24 March 752, following the death of Pope Zacharias... and died two days later.

Mar 27: The **longest TV commercial** was for Lipton Ice Tea Green, which lasted for 24 minutes when it was broadcast by the Yorin television channel in the Netherlands on this day in 2005.

ODD TALENTS

TOP
100
Records of the Decade

★ LOUDEST BURP (MALE)

Paul Hunn (UK) produced a burp measuring 107.1 dBA on the set of *The New Paul O'Grady Show* in London, UK, on 24 September 2008.

★ FASTEST TIME TO ARRANGE A DECK OF PLAYING CARDS

Zdenek Bradac (Czech Republic) arranged a deck (52 cards) of shuffled playing cards into the order Ace through 10, Jack, Queen, King of Diamonds, Clubs, Hearts and Spades in 36.16 seconds at Sheffield Castle College, South Yorkshire, UK, on 15 May 2008.

★ FASTEST TIME TO ESCAPE FROM A SUITCASE

Contortionist Leslie Tipton (USA) "folded" herself into a standard suitcase, which was then zipped shut. She managed to escape from the case in 7.04 seconds. The feat was achieved on 31 May 2008 in Los Angeles, California, USA, during Book Expo America.

MOST TORCHES EXTINGUISHED WITH THE MOUTH

Hubertus Wawra (Germany), aka "Master of Hellfire", extinguished 68 fire torches with his mouth in one minute on the set of *Guinness World Records: Die Größten Weltrekorde* in Cologne, Germany, on 13 September 2008.

★ GREATEST DISTANCE TRAVELLED WITH A POOL CUE BALANCED ON THE CHIN

Ashrita Furman (USA) travelled 1,668 m (1 mile) with a pool cue balanced on his chin at the Joe Austin Playground in Jamaica, New York, USA, on 6 July 2008. The 500-g (17.6-oz) cue was balanced with just the leather tip touching the chin.

★ LONGEST FULL-BODY ICE CONTACT

Wim Hof (Netherlands) spent 1 hr 42 min 22 sec in direct, full-body contact with ice on the set of *Guinness World Records* in Madrid, Spain, on 23 January 2009. Hof has been involved in extreme outdoor activities for over 20 years. He uses the "inner fire" yoga technique to keep his body temperature at a normal 37°C (98.6°F) even in extreme cold.

★ FASTEST 100 M HURDLES WEARING SWIM FINS (FEMALE)

Maren Zänker (Germany) completed the 100 m hurdles wearing swim fins in 22.35 seconds on the set of *Guinness World Records – Die Größten Weltrekorde* in Cologne, Germany, on 13 September 2008. By contrast, the fastest "normal" 100 m hurdles (female) was run in 12.21 sec by Yordanka Donkova (Bulgaria) in 1988.

Mar 28: On this day in 1977, the **only posthumous Best Actor Oscar** was awarded to Peter Finch (UK) for his work on *Network* (USA, 1976). He died on 14 January 1977 of a heart attack.

HAVE A GO!

Have you got an odd talent or party trick that could be recognized by Guinness World Records? If so, tell us about it at guinnessworldrecords.com. If we like the idea, we'll write the official guidelines that you – and others – must follow when making the attempt. If you're successful, you could see your name here next year!

21: the **most tennis balls held in one hand**, achieved by Rohit Timilsina (Nepal) for 14.32 seconds in Kathmandu, Nepal, on 14 June 2008.

★ FASTEST TIME TO BURST THREE HOT WATER BOTTLES

Using only his lung power, Brian Jackson (USA) inflated three hot water bottles until they burst in 1 min 8 sec, on the set of *Lo Show Dei Record*, in Milan, Italy, on 19 April 2009.

★ MOST SMARTIES/ M&Ms EATEN IN ONE MINUTE

John Muller (USA) ate 27 M&Ms in one minute using chopsticks in New York City, USA, on 14 November 2008. The record was part of GWR Day 2008 and taped live on the set of *CW11 Morning News*.

★ MOST JUGGLING CATCHES WHILE SUSPENDED

Ashrita Furman (USA) achieved 601 catches juggling three balls while suspended upside down by gravity boots in Jamaica, New York, USA, on 6 May 2008.

★ MOST SPOONS BALANCED ON THE FACE

Joe Allison (UK) balanced 16 spoons on his face simultaneously. This classic cutlery record was achieved in Totnes, Devon, UK, on 1 April 2008.

★ MOST WATERMELONS SMASHED WITH A FIST

Our UK television show, *Guinness World Records Smashed*, really lived up to its name on 2 April 2009 when Ricky O'Brien (UK) literally smashed his way through 45 watermelons in one minute before a live audience at Pinewood Studios, London, UK.

MOST SCORPIONS HELD IN THE MOUTH

Maged Elmalke (Saudi Arabia) held 22 scorpions in his mouth in Riyadh, Saudi Arabia, on 1 September 2008. Guidelines state that all the scorpions must be in the mouth for at least 10 seconds.

MOST SWORDS SWALLOWED SIMULTANEOUSLY

Chayne "Spacecowboy" Hultgren (Australia) swallowed 17 swords in one go at Calder Park Raceway, Melbourne, Australia, on 28 March 2008. The next day he broke the record for the ★ **heaviest weight dangled from a swallowed sword** when he swallowed a non-retractable 40.5-cm-long (15.9-in) sword and then held two gas canisters weighing 22.4 kg (49 lb 6 oz) attached to the sword handle for five seconds at the Crusty Demons Night of World Records at the same venue.

★ FASTEST TIME TO SKI 100 M BACKWARDS

Winter sports fanatic Andy Bennett (UK) skied 100 m (328 ft) backwards downhill, navigating through a course that included four slalom gates, in 9.48 sec at the SNO!zone indoor snow slope in Milton Keynes, UK, on 27 April 2009. The challenge was recorded for *Guinness World Records Smashed*.

★ MOST MAGGOTS MOVED WITH THE MOUTH IN ONE HOUR

Charlie Bell (UK) shifted 17 kg (37 lbs 7 oz) of maggots between two containers placed 1 m (3 ft 3 in) apart in one hour, on the set of *Guinness World Records Smashed* at Pinewood Studios, London, UK, on 7 April 2009. The hot studio lights prompted the maggots to pupate and turn into flies, making Charlie's challenge even harder!

★ MOST CANDLES BLOWN OUT IN ONE BREATH

V. Sankaranarayanan (India) blew out 151 candles at the Press Club in Ramnathapuram, India, on 18 January 2008.

MOST CHAINSAW JUGGLING CATCHES

Aaron Gregg (Canada) achieved 88 chainsaw juggling catches on the set of *El Show Olímpico* in Mexico City, Mexico, on 28 July 2008.

★ NEW RECORD
★ UPDATED RECORD

MOST RATTLESNAKES HELD IN THE MOUTH

Jackie Bibby (USA) held 11 diamondback rattlesnakes in his mouth by their tails without any assistance for 10 seconds on the set of *Guinness World Records: Die Größten Weltrekorde* in Germany, on 20 December 2008. Bibby was born in Texas, USA, in 1950 and has been handling snakes since 1968. He is currently the president of The Heart of Texas Snake Handlers.

Mar 29: Henry Fonda (USA) was the **oldest Best Actor Oscar winner** on this day in 1982 for his performance as Norman Thayer Jr in *On Golden Pond* (USA, 1981), aged 76 years 317 days.

Mar 30: The **greatest amount paid by a single cheque** was £2,474,655,000 ($3,971,821,275). Issued on this date in 1995, the cheque was a payment by Glaxo plc to Wellcome Trust Nominees Ltd.

SUPER STUNTS

★ FASTEST TIME TO THROW 10 KNIVES AROUND A HUMAN TARGET

The Reverend Dr David R Adamovich, aka "The Great Throwdini" (USA), threw 10 35-cm-long (14-in) throwing knives around his partner, "Target Girl" Tina Nagy (USA), in 4.29 seconds on the set of *El Show Olímpico* in Mexico City, Mexico, on 29 July 2008.

★ HEAVIEST VEHICLE PULLED USING A SWALLOWED SWORD

Ryan Stock (Canada) swallowed a 43.18-cm-long (17-in) sword on the TV show *Guinea Pig* filmed in Las Vegas, Nevada, USA, on 28 October 2008. He then tied the sword using ropes to a 2002 Audi A4 that weighed 1,696.44 kg (3,740 lb) and dragged the car 6.38 m (20 ft 11 in) in 20.53 seconds.

HIGHEST SHALLOW DIVE

Darren Taylor (USA) beat his own world record by diving from 10.83 m (35 ft 6.6 in) into just 30 cm (11.8 in) of water in Tokyo, Japan, on 7 December 2008.

TOP 100 Records of the Decade

MOST PINE BOARDS BROKEN WITH THE HEAD IN 30 SECONDS

The most pine boards broken across the forehead in 30 seconds is 32 by Kevin Shelley (USA) on the set of *El Show Olímpico* in Mexico City, Mexico, on 30 July 2008.

★ HIGHEST REVERSE BUNGEE JUMP

The greatest height to which a human has been catapulted by reverse bungee is 54.25 m (178 ft), achieved by Ben Shephard (UK) in London, UK, on 3 October 2008.

★ SHORTEST GAP BETWEEN AEROPLANE AND MOTORCYCLE DURING A RAMP JUMP

The closest that a motorcycle has ever come to an aircraft during a ramp jump is 2.42 m (7 ft 11 in), when Hungary's Veres Zoltán (piloting an Extra 300) and Gulyás Kiss Zoltán (riding a Yamaha YZ250F cross motorbike) crossed in mid-air during a stunt in Etyek, Hungary, on 7 September 2008.

★ FASTEST TIME TO RUN THROUGH 10 LOCKED AND BURNING DOORS

In a punishing test of fitness, fearlessness and foolhardiness, Sandra Kier (Germany) ran through 10 locked, burning doors in just 23 seconds on the set of *Guinness World Records: Die Größten Weltrekorde* in Germany on 18 December 2008.

★ NEW RECORD
★ UPDATED RECORD

GOING UP...

A reverse bungee involves anchoring yourself to the ground, strapping yourself securely to a bungee cord and stretching the cord upwards (usually using a crane) to its limit. Only then do you release the rope, which catapults you high into the air (see insets).

Mar 31: On this day in 1997, Switzerland's Martina Hingis (b. 30 September 1980) became the **youngest woman to be ranked world tennis number one** at the age of 16 years 182 days.

★ LONGEST TIGHTROPE CROSSING BY BICYCLE

FACT
The tightrope was set up between two cranes at a height of 41.15 m (135 ft) – that's 13 storeys high!

Nik Wallenda (USA), a seventh-generation member of the Flying Wallendas circus acrobat family, cycled 71.63 m (235 ft) along a tightrope in Newark, New Jersey, USA, on 15 October 2008.

HIGHEST JUMP WITHOUT A PARACHUTE ON FILM

Movie stuntman A J Bakunas (USA, 1950–78) jumped from a height of 70.71 m (232 ft) without a parachute while doubling for Burt Reynolds in *Hooper* (USA, 1978). He fell on to an air mattress.

HIGHEST FREEFALL ON FILM

Working as a stuntman in the film *Highpoint* (Canada, 1979), Dar Robinson (USA) jumped 335 m (1,100 ft) from the summit of the CN Tower in Toronto, Canada. His parachute opened just 91 m (300 ft) from the ground after six seconds of freefalling.

HIGHEST SKI BASE-JUMP ON FILM

For a sequence in *The Spy Who Loved Me* (UK, 1977), James Bond – aka stuntman Rick Sylvester (USA) – skied down a slope and jumped off the edge of a 609.6-m (2,000-ft) cliff, Asgard Peak on Baffin Island in Canada, before opening his Union Jack canopy.

LOWEST DEATH-DIVE ESCAPE

Robert Gallup (Australia) was leg-manacled, handcuffed, chained, tied into a secured mail bag and then locked in a metal cage before being thrown out of a C-123 transport plane at 5,486 m (18,000 ft) above the Mojave Desert, California, USA. With less than a minute before impact and travelling at 240 km/h (150 mph), Gallup escaped from the sack and cage to reach his parachute secured on the outside of the cage and was able to deploy it with enough altitude to land safely.

★ MOST CARS LOADED INTO AN AIRCRAFT IN ONE HOUR

The delivery company TNT and the TV show/magazine *TopGear* (both Italy) had just one hour to load a Boeing 747 with smart cars at Liege Airport in Belgium on 23 October 2008. The team of seven staff actually filled the hold with 30 cars in a time of just 35 min 45 sec.

GOING DOWN...

Tyler achieved his record-breaking descent (pictured here using multiple exposures) by staying to the far left of the waterfall and landing in a safety zone (or "cushy foam pile" as he called it), where the water pushes away from the waterfall's base. "It was a lot softer landing than I expected," he reported.

LONGEST WATERFALL DESCENT BY CANOE

The longest descent over a waterfall in canoe is 32.6 m (107 ft) by Tyler Bradt (USA) at the Alexandra Falls on the Hay River in Canada's Northwest Territories on 7 September 2007. To succeed in this attempt, Bradt had to remain in his Dagger Nomad kayak at all times.

Apr 1: The **largest operational mousetrap** was built by Bio Tec-Klute GmbH (Germany) and measured 4.25 m (13 ft 11 in) long and 2.10 m (6 ft 10 in) wide when unveiled on 1 April 2007.

Apr 2: Emilio Scotto (Argentina) completed the **longest ever journey by motorcycle** on this day in 1995. He'd started his trip on 17 January 1985 and covered over 735,000 km (456,700 miles).

18

MASS PARTICIPATION 1

MOST PEOPLE DRESSED AS SUPERMAN

On 15 June 2008, Steven Kirk (USA) organized an event that was attended by a record 122 people dressed as the "Man of Steel". The Superman celebration was held in Metropolis, Illinois, USA, the self-proclaimed "Hometown of Superman".

★ DRESSED AS SUNFLOWERS

The most people dressed as sunflowers was 116, a record set at The Nursery on the Green in London, UK, on 13 August 2008.

★ PATTING THEIR HEADS AND RUBBING THEIR STOMACHS

In total, 159 participants convened at the Windmill Public House in Clapham Common, London, UK, on 27 October 2007 to pat their heads while rubbing their stomachs at the same time.

★ SITTING ON ONE CHAIR

The most people sitting on one chair is 1,058 in an event organized by the Tampines West Constituency Sports Club at Springfield Secondary School, Singapore, on 16 August 2008. To achieve this record, one person sits on a chair, someone else sits on their lap, another on *their* lap and so on...

★ WITH TEAM COLOURS PAINTED ON THE FACE

A record 29,688 people gathered at the Stade de France in Paris, France, on 7 June 2008 to have their faces painted in the Stade Français Paris Rugby Club colours of blue and pink. The record attempt was organized in collaboration with Fanbrush face-paints, the Stade Français Paris and the Stade de France.

★ MOST PEOPLE DRESSED AS SMURFS

On 18 July 2008 at the Muckno Mania Festival in Castleblayney, Co. Monaghan, Ireland, 1,253 people dressed as Smurfs and paraded through the town's streets.

★ MOST PEOPLE ON SPACE HOPPERS

On 4 July 2008, at an event organized by the Shepway School Sport Partnership at the Cheriton Road Sports Ground in Folkestone, Kent, UK, a total of 1,008 people gathered to bounce on their space hoppers.

Also known as a hoppity-hop, hop ball and kangaroo ball, the inflatable rubber toy – invented in Italy in the late 1960s – serves no real purpose: they do not allow you to travel higher or faster than you can do on foot!

MOST PEOPLE...

★ IN A CUSTARD PIE FIGHT

The most participants in a single custard pie fight is 120. The feisty pie-flingers did battle during the filming of the music video for the track *Troublemaker* by the band Weezer in Los Angeles, California, USA, on 21 August 2008.

★ PLAYING DOMINOES

At the 6th annual World Domino Tournament – hosted by the International Domino Federation and the National Domino Federation (both USA) – at Walt Disney World in Orlando, Florida, USA, on 10 July 2008, a total of 332 people played dominoes simultaneously.

FACT

In 1979, Superman was the first Superhero to get his own video game. for more gaming records see p. 218–19.

Apr 3: The **first portable telephone handset**, or mobile phone – invented by Martin Cooper (USA) of Motorola – was used for the first time on this day in 1973.

1,752: the number of people at the Wave for Wales event in Margam County Park, UK, dancing the "Locomotion" on 24 June 2007.

★ MOST PEOPLE DANCING WITH HULA HOOPS

On 12 April 2008, to celebrate the DVD release of *Alvin and the Chipmunks* (USA, 2007), Twentieth Century Fox organized an event at Chessington World of Adventures, Surrey, UK, during which 342 people danced with hula hoops!

★ SOLVING CROSSWORDS SIMULTANEOUSLY

On 28 September 2008, 443 people were solving crosswords simultaneously for Gewista Werbeges.m.b.H at a Vienna Recordia event held in Vienna, Austria.

★ DANCING THE WALTZ

The largest waltz consisted of 242 couples who danced for an event organized by Non Profit Verein Rueff unter der Patronanz des Verband der Tanzlehrer Österreichs (VTÖ) (Austria) at Austria Center Vienna, Austria, on 26 April 2008.

★ JUMPING ON SPRING-LOADED STILTS

The Shao Lin Tagou Martial Arts School of Dengfeng City, Henan province, China, organized 103 people to simultaneously jump on spring-loaded stilts on 17 September 2008.

★ PLAYING MAHJONG SIMULTANEOUSLY

A simultaneous game of mahjong was played by 492 participants at the Hong Kong International Trade & Exhibition Centre Rotunda Hall 2 in Hong Kong, China, on 20 July 2008.

★ PLAYING WOOD BLOCK/ CHINESE BLOCK

The record for the most people playing wood (Chinese) block at the same time was achieved by 240 participants at the event Ngong Ping Buddha's Birthday Celebration in Hong Kong, China, on 11 May 2008.

★ RECEIVING A FOOT MASSAGE

And relax... A total of 1,000 lucky people received a 40-minute reflexology foot massage at an event organized by the Taiwan Tourism Bureau at Taipei Arena, Taipei, Taiwan, on 1 July 2008.

★ TOSSING DIABOLOS

A record 223 students and staff at Manor Field Primary School in Burgess Hill, UK, tossed diabolos on 13 July 2008. A diabolo is a spool- or yoyo-like juggling prop that is kept airborne and spinning using a piece of string tied to two sticks; a stick is held in each hand.

★ IN A GOLF LESSON

John Roethling (Germany) really got into the swing of teaching when he gave a golf lesson to a record 562 people at Baustert, Rhineland-Palatinate, Germany, on 8 June 2008.

LARGEST GATHERING OF WALLYS

If you've been wondering "Where's Wally?" recently, then you should have had your eyes peeled at the record attempt organized by the ACUITY insurance company at their corporate headquarters in Sheboygan, Wisconsin, USA, on 10 December 2008 – a total of 577 people turned up dressed as the elusive children's book character aka Waldo/Walter/Efi/ Charlie/Holger, depending on which country you're in)!

★ NEW RECORD
UPDATED RECORD

Apr 4: The **largest crowd for a basketball match** is 80,000 for the European Cup Winners Cup final in Athens, Greece, between AEK Athens (89) and Slavia Prague (82) on this day in 1968.

Apr 5: The world's **oldest adopted person** is Jo Anne Benedict Walker (USA), who was aged 65 years 224 days when she was adopted by Frances Ensor Benedict (USA) on 5 April 2002.

MASS PARTICIPATION 2

LARGEST BALLET CLASS – BARRES

On 24 August 2008, 989 dancers from Cape Town City Ballet and 65 ballet schools and studios took part in a single ballet class organized by Andrew Warth (South Africa) at Canal Walk Shopping Centre, Cape Town, South Africa.

★ AQUA AEROBICS DISPLAY

On 5 April 2008, 273 people took part in the largest ever aqua aerobic display at LifeCenter Plus health and fitness facility in Hudson, Ohio, USA. The event was organized to raise money for, and awareness of, a diabetes charity.

★ CHEERLEADING CHEER

On 23 April 2008, just a few months prior to the Beijing Olympics, a team of 1,200 people dressed in red and took part in a 5-minute-long "I'm Lovin' it When China Wins" cheer at Beijing Olympic Sports Centre – a pom-pom's throw from the Bird's Nest Olympic Stadium in Beijing, China.

★ AIR GUITAR ENSEMBLE

An air guitar ensemble involving 318 participants collectively rocked out to "I Believe in a Thing Called Love" by Justin Hawkins (UK) on the set of *Guinness World Records Smashed* in London, UK, on 3 October 2008.

★ BOLLYWOOD DANCE

Organized by Sapnay School of Dance (UK) during *Big Dance 2008*, 278 dancers performed a Bollywood dance routine in Trafalgar Square, London, UK, on 6 July 2008.

★ SKI LESSON

A record 594 skiers were instructed by Hansjürg Gredig (Switzerland) of the Swiss-Snowsport School at Sarn-Heinzenberg (Graubünden), Switzerland, on 23 February 2008.

★ DANCE-MAT ROUTINE

A simultaneous dance-mat routine involving 100 participants established a new Guinness World Record at the NOKIA Theater LA Live in Los Angeles, California, USA, for the FOX television show *So You Think You Can Dance* (USA) on 19 May 2008.

★ SCAVENGER HUNT

A group of 183 participants took part in an urban scavenger hunt at the Hanashobu shopping centre in Osue-Chou Hikone-Shi, Japan, on 22 June 2008.

DANCING BY NUMBERS...

1,217 *Head, Shoulders, Knees and Toes* singalong, Taiwan, 1 Jul 2008

221 ★ Yowla dance, UAE, 22 Feb 2008

186 ★ Longsword dance, UK, 26 Sep 2003

146 Maypole dance, UK, 21 May 2008

★ NEW RECORD
★ UPDATED RECORD

LARGEST...

★ SPEED DATING EVENT (MULTI-VENUE)

At an event organized by Fast Impressions to celebrate the 10th anniversary of the dating organization RSVP, a total of 1,240 single people from across Australia went speed-dating on 14 February 2008 to help raise funds for Drought Relief.

LARGEST PARADE OF INLINE SKATERS

On 15 June 2008, a total of 1,188 inline skaters rolled their way into the record books when they came together on the streets of Paris, France. The participants – organized and led by Rollers & Coquillages (France) – skated *en masse* for 20.4 km (12.68 miles) in a circuitous route starting and finishing at the Place de la Bastille.

MOST PEOPLE

STATIC CYCLING

During their annual Esporta Health & Fitness conference in Gloucester, UK, 412 company employees came together to take part in a 45 minute spinning (static cycling) workout on 19 February 2009.

Apr 6: The **longest recorded boxing fight** – between Andy Bowen and Jack Burke (both USA) – began on this day in April 1893 in New Orleans, USA. It lasted 110 rounds and took 7 hr 19 min!

3,264: the number of people who took part in the **largest Haka** in Ngaaruawaahia, Waikato, New Zealand, on 16 February 2008.

LARGEST SANTA GATHERING

In 2007, Christmas came early for the people of Derry City, Northern Ireland, UK, when 13,000 people dressed as Santa gathered in the Guildhall Square on 9 December.

★ LARGEST BHANGRA DANCE

On 31 August 2008, a total of 763 dancers from the Nachdi Jawani Association and Punjabi Virsa Arts and Culture Academy (both Canada) participated in a Bhangra dance at the Powerade Centre in Brampton, Ontario, Canada.

CAN YOU BEAT THIS?

Every year, thousands – if not millions – of people take part in mass-participation record events, often raising millions of pounds for charity. If you want to organize an event of your own, here are the basic guidelines:
1. You need to demonstrate to us an accurate method of counting participants.
2. Each person involved should write their name in a log book.
3. Stewards – one for every 50 people – must be made available to ensure that everyone present is actually taking part in the event.
For a full list of rules, visit www. guinnessworld records.com

GATHERING OF ZOMBIES

In total, 1,227 people dressed up as zombies in Nottingham, UK, as part of the city's GameCity festival on 31 October 2008.

GAME OF DODGEBALL

Two teams of 50 people (100 total) played against each other during the filming of the pop video "Troublemaker" by Weezer in Los Angeles, California, USA, on 21 August 2008.

FACT

On 13 April 2008, Ian Sharman (UK) ran the London Marathon in **3 hr 12 min 27 sec** – while dressed as Santa Claus.

★ GATHERING OF NINJA TURTLES

On 10 April 2008, at an event staged at Rutgers University in New Jersey, USA, 786 people attended wearing full Ninja Turtle costume.

★ GATHERING OF PREGNANT WOMEN

The "Your Baby" show in Johannesburg, South Africa, was the location for a gathering of 1,164 pregnant women on 17 May 2007.

★ WINE-TASTING EVENT (MULTI-VENUE)

A wine-tasting event organized by the JD Wetherspoon pub group saw 17,540 people tasting wine in 409 UK pubs on 21 May 2008.

LARGEST CPR TRAINING CLASS

A cardiopulmonary resuscitation (CPR) training session involving 3,692 participants was organized by Norwegian Air Ambulance at Valhall indoor stadium in Oslo, Norway, on 26 May 2008.

Apr 7: The **shortest title of any Oscar-winning film** is Z (Algeria/France, 1969), directed by Costa-Garvas (Greece), which won two Academy Awards on this day in 1970.

Apr 8: On this day in 1998, David Holleran (Australia) completed the **longest triathlon** – a 42-km (26-mile) swim, 2,000-km (1,242-mile) cycle and 500-km (310-mile) run in 17 days 22 hr 50 min.

IN AN HOUR

MOST PANCAKES MADE BY AN INDIVIDUAL

Bob Blumer (Canada), host and co-creator of the adventure television series *Glutton for Punishment*, made a record-breaking 559 pancakes in one hour at Rope Square in Calgary, Alberta, Canada, on 10 July 2008.

★ GREATEST WEIGHT DEADLIFTED (INDIVIDUAL)

The greatest weight deadlifted in one hour is 31,500 kg (69,445 lb) by Eamonn Keane (Ireland) at Powerhouse Gym in Dublin, Ireland, on 29 September 2007. He also bench-pressed 138,480 kg (305,300 lb) in an hour at World Gym, Marina del Rey, California, USA, on 22 July 2003 – the ★ **greatest weight bench-pressed by an individual in one hour**.

★ GREATEST DISTANCE MOONWALKED

Krunoslav Budiselic (Croatia) moonwalked for one hour at the Athletic Stadium Mladost in Zagreb, Croatia, on 10 September 2006, and managed to cover 5.255 km (3.265 miles).

★ FARTHEST DISTANCE STATIC CYCLING

Holden Comeau (USA), from the New York Sports Clubs/Cadence Cycling Team, covered 65.48 km (40.69 miles) in one hour during "Saints & Spinners – The 24-Hour Spin Party and Benefit" in New York City, USA, on 18 January 2008.

★ GREATEST DISTANCE CYCLING BACKWARDS

Markus Riese (Germany) cycled 29 km (18 miles) backwards in one hour at the VC Darmstadt 1899 e.V. cycling club, Darmstadt, Germany, on 24 May 2003.

MOST KNEE BENDS ON A SWISS BALL

On 13 November 2008, Stephen Buttler (UK) achieved 1,502 knee bends at Hope House, Shropshire, UK.

MOST...

★ BALLOONS INFLATED BY THE NOSE

Andrew Dahl (USA) inflated 308 balloons using just his nose in one hour on the *Live with Regis & Kelly* TV show in New York City, USA, on 16 September 2008.

★ HEADS SHAVED

Anne Armstrong (UK) managed to shave a record 44 heads in one hour at Maginns of Castlewellan in Castlewellan, Co. Down, UK, on 25 April 2008.

★ CHIN-UPS

Stephen Hyland (UK) achieved 908 successful chin-ups in one hour in Stoneleigh, Surrey, UK, on 2 January 2009.

MOST STEP-UPS WITH A 40-LB PACK

The most step-ups completed in one hour with an 18-kg (40-lb) pack is 1,805 by Arran McLellan (Canada) on a 38.1-cm (15-in) bench at Club Phoenix Gym in Victoria, B.C., Canada, on 21 February 2009.

FACT

The record for the largest pancake toss is 405, achieved by Bram Zwiers in Almere, the Netherlands, on 24 October 2008.

★ BUNGEE JUMPS

Veronica Dean (South Africa) performed 19 bungee jumps in one hour at Bloukrans River Bridge, South Africa, on 9 May 2003. The bungee cord used was approximately 36 m (118 ft) long.

★ BASKETBALL LAY-UPS (TEAM)

UBALL (Utrecht BasketBALL) under-18 boys team recorded 2,640 basketball lay-ups in one hour at Sporthal Galgenwaard, Utrecht, the Netherlands, on 24 May 2008.

★ BASKETBALL THREE-POINTERS

Vladislav Raiskiy (Russia) made 835 three-pointers in one hour at Tauras-Fitness Ltd, St Petersburg, Russia, on 23 November 2008.

★ BASKETBALL FREE THROWS

Appearing on the set of *Unbelievable* at the Fuji TV studios, Tokyo, Japan, Fred Newman (USA) made 1,663 free throws in one hour on 17 September 2008.

★ PIZZAS MADE

Donald Mark Rush (USA) made 142 pizzas in one hour at Domino's Pizza, Gulfport, Mississippi, USA, on 2 August 2008.

Apr 9: The **oldest voice recording** is that of a woman singing "Au Claire de la Lune" ("By the Light of the Moon"). It was made on 9 April 1860 by Edouard-Leon Scott de Martinville (France).

38.632 km (24 miles): distance covered by Mauro Guenci (Italy) on inline skates in one hour at Senigallia, Italy, on 11 June 2005.

MOST LEGS WAXED IN ONE HOUR

Beautician Susanne Baird (UK) successfully waxed 40 pairs of legs at the Grange Cricket Club in Stockbridge, Edinburgh, UK, on 14 April 2008. She actually managed 42 pairs, but two were rejected as the hair had not been completely removed.

UNDERWATER HAIRCUTS

The most haircuts given under water in one hour is 27, achieved by David Rae (UK) at the London School of Diving, London, UK, on 12 November 2007.

RUGBY TACKLES

Students from Scots College (all Australia) at Sydney, New South Wales, Australia, made 4,130 rugby tackles in one hour on 15 March 2007.

MOST INVERTS ON A SIT-DOWN HYDROFOIL

Greg Gill (Australia, left) managed 589 inverts in one hour on the Maroochy River, Maroochydore, Queensland, Australia, on 26 June 2008. Gill also performed backside rolls and gainers in the attempt.

★ **NEW RECORD**
UPDATED RECORD

FACES PAINTED

Gary Cole (USA) painted a total of 217 different faces, using a minimum of three colours per face, at Almondvale Shopping Centre in Livingston, West Lothian, UK, on 1 September 2007.

★ WEIGHT LIFTED BY INCLINE DUMBBELL FLYES

An incredible 27,890 kg (61,486.9 lb) was lifted by Eamonn Keane (Ireland) in one hour at Lough Lannagh Fitness Centre, County Mayo, Ireland, on 22 May 2008. Eamonn also set the record for the ★ **most weight lifted by a barbell upright row in one hour** on 10 June 2008, with 18,485 kg (40,752.5 lb).

RUBIK'S CUBES SOLVED

David Calvo (Spain) solved 185 Rubik's cubes in one hour while appearing on the Spanish television show *Donde Estas Corazon* on 14 November 2008.

★ PUSH-UPS (USING BACKS OF HANDS, CARRYING A 40-LB PACK)

Strongman and multiple record holder Paddy Doyle (UK) managed 663 push-ups on the backs of his hands carrying a 18-kg (40-lb) pack at Stamina's Boxing Martial Arts Club in Birmingham, UK, on 13 May 2008.

WEIGHT LIFTED BY STANDING BARBELL PRESS

The greatest weight lifted by standing barbell press in one hour is 45,000 kg (99,208 lb) achieved by Robin Simpson (UK) in Manchester, UK, on 25 October 2008.

WAVE RIDERS

A sitdown hydrofoil is towed behind a speed boat. When moving across the water, the hydrofoil lifts the rider and board above the surface of the water. Balance is crucial to staying upright, because slight body movements have a great effect on the position of the hydrofoil.

MOST HUGS GIVEN BY AN INDIVIDUAL IN ONE HOUR

At an event held at Boardman Stadium in Boardman, Ohio, USA, Jeffrey Ondash (USA) hugged 1,205 people to help raise money for the American Cancer Society on 16 May 2008.

Apr 10: Andrzej Makowski (Canada) earned his driver's license on this day in 1974. He passed his test at Namyslow, Poland, aged 14 years 235 days, making him the **youngest licensed driver**.

Apr 11: The **largest Rock, Paper, Scissors tournament** featured 793 players in an event organized by Renee Tomas at Brigham Young University, in Prove City, Utah, USA, on 11 April 2008.

IN A DAY

★ MOST TIME SPENT DRIVING A BUMPER CAR

On 30 September 2007, Sebastian Bösch (Austria) spent 24 hours driving a bumper car during the event Vienna Recordia in Vienna, Austria, making it the longest bumper car marathon on record.

GREATEST DISTANCE...

★ PUSHING A CAR (INDIVIDUAL)

Record-breaking powerhouse Ashrita Furman (USA) pushed a car 27.45 km (17.06 miles) in 24 hours at the Old Bridge Township Raceway Park in Englishtown, New Jersey, USA, on 6 March 2008.

TRAVELLED ON A SKATEBOARD

James Peters (USA) travelled 296.12 km (184 miles) on a skateboard in 24 hours on 11 May 2007. The amazing skating feat was achieved on the Greenlake bike trail in Seattle, Washington, USA.

COVERED BY WHEELCHAIR

Mario Trindade (Portugal) covered 182.4 km (113.34 miles) in a wheelchair in 24 hours at the Vila Real Stadium in Vila Real, Portugal, on 3–4 December 2007.

TRAVELLED ON A HUMAN-POWERED VEHICLE

In 24 hours, Greg Kolodziejzyk (Canada) covered 1,041.24 km (647 miles) riding *Critical Power*, his specially designed HPV (human-powered vehicle), at Redwood Acres Raceway in Eureka, Alberta, Canada, on 18 July 2006.

PADDLING A BATH TUB

The greatest distance covered by paddling a hand-propelled bath tub on still water in 24 hours is 145.6 km (90.5 miles) by 13 members of Aldington Prison Officers Social Club, near Ashford, Kent, UK, on 28–29 May 1983.

★ RUN THREE-LEGGED

The record for the longest distance run three-legged – that is, two people tied together at the ankle – in 24 hours is 100.13 km (62.22 miles), which was achieved by Steven and Suzanne Eltis (both Australia) at Eatons Hill State School in Eatons Hill, Brisbane, Queensland, Australia, on 24–25 October 2008. The husband and wife team attempted the record to raise awareness and funds for Epilepsy Queensland.

GREATEST DISTANCE TRAVELLED RIDING A UNICYCLE

Sam Wakeling (UK) covered 453.6 km (281.85 miles) riding a unicycle in a 24-hour period at Aberystwyth, Wales, UK, from 29 to 30 September 2007.

MOST TREES PLANTED BY A TEAM

The record for the most trees planted in 24 hours by a team of 300 people is 348,492, achieved by CONAFOR (Comision Nacional Forestal) and citizens from the state of Durango at Predio San Manuel, Estado Durango, Mexico, on 29–30 August 2008. On hand to present the official GWR certificate was adjudicator Ralph Hannah (pictured, on the left).

Apr 12: The **most expensive car** is a 1931 Bugatti Type 41 "Royale" Sports Coupé by Kellner, which sold for $15 million (£9,135,200) on this day in 1990.

9,088: total revolutions on a wheel of death in 24 hours, as experienced by Joey Kelly and Freddy Nock (both UK) on 24 November 2006.

★ MOST COSMETIC MAKEOVERS BY A TEAM

A record 856 cosmetic makeovers were carried out in 24 hours by a team of make-up artists in an event organized by Alpha Marketing Company in Hong Kong, China, on 3 May 2008.

★ GREATEST DISTANCE COVERED IN A PEDAL-POWERED BOAT

Greg Kolodziejzyk (Canada) used pedal power to propel his boat *Critical Power 2* a distance of 245.16 km (152.33 miles) in 24 hours on Whitefish Lake, Montana, USA, from 8 to 9 September 2008. Greg's next record goal is to pedal his way across the Pacific!

MOST...

HAIR DONATED TO CHARITY

The most hair collected for charity in a day is 48.72 kg (107 lb) – the weight of an average 14-year-old boy – when 881 people donated their ponytails at the Mississippi Institute for Aesthetics, Nail and Cosmetology in Clinton, Mississippi, USA, on 21 May 2007. The event was organized in support of the Pantene Beautiful Lengths campaign, which aims to provide free wigs to women who have lost hair following cancer treatment.

HOLES OF MINIATURE GOLF PLAYED (INDIVIDUAL)

David Pfefferle (USA) played 4,729 holes of miniature golf in 24 hours at Westerville Golf Center, Westerville, Ohio, USA, on 28–29 May 2008. During the 24 hours, David – who owns the golf course – walked an estimated 88 km (55 miles) and raised over $6,000 (£3,357) for charity.

RADIO INTERVIEWS (PAIR)

On 31 October 2008, Patrick Stump and Pete Wentz (both USA) from the Chicago-based band Fall Out Boy spoke with 72 different American radio stations. The topic of discussion was the band's new album, *Folie à Deux*, released on 15 December 2008.

★ TATTOOS BY A SINGLE ARTIST

John McManus (USA) of the Joker's Tattoo Studio in West Monroe, Louisiana, USA, tattooed 775 two-coloured stars in a 24-hour period starting on 31 October 2008. He beat the record of 726 set the previous week by Derek Kastning (USA) at Rat-A-Tac-Tat Tattoos in Tyler, Texas, USA.

★ VISITED WEBSITE WITHIN FIRST 24 HOURS OF LAUNCH

The most unique (individual) visitors to a website within its first 24 hours is 483,424, registered by MySkip.com on 30 April 2008. The site is a virtual skip into which unwanted goods can be dumped or picked up for repurposing.

★ WEIGHT SQUAT-LIFTED BY AN INDIVIDUAL

On 6 November 2008, Kevin Machate (USA) squat-lifted 45,999.71 kg (101,412 lb) in 24 hours at Gold's Gym in Garland, Texas, USA.

★ CONSECUTIVE HAIRCUTS

The most consecutive haircuts in 24 hours by an individual is 340 and was achieved by Ivan Zoot (USA) at Men's Grooming Center in Austin, Texas, USA, on 22–23 August 2008. During the course of the day, Ivan also broke Guinness World Records marks for the **fastest single haircut** (doing so eight times, finally achieving a record time of 55 seconds) and the ★ **most haircuts in one hour** (34).

★ NEW RECORD
UPDATED RECORD

FARTHEST DISTANCE TRAVELLED ON A HAND-CRANKED CYCLE

Keane West (USA) travelled 518.85 km (322.40 miles) on a hand-cranked cycle in 24 hours during the Bike Sebring 12/24 Hours event in Sebring, Florida, USA, from 16 to 17 February 2008.

Apr 13: Paula Radcliffe (UK) ran the **fastest ever marathon by a woman** in London, UK, on 13 April 2003, in a time of 2 hr 15 min 25 sec.

Apr 14: On this day in 1991, 20 paintings, worth $500 million (£280 million), were stolen from the Van Gogh Museum in Amsterdam, the Netherlands, in the **greatest ever art robbery**.

★ DEEPEST UNDERWATER CYCLING

Who says you shouldn't cycle in the wet? The greatest depth at which submarine cycling has been carried out is 66.5 m (214 ft 10 in) and was achieved by Vittorio Innocente (Italy) in Santa Margherita Ligure, Liguria, Italy, on 21 July 2008. He also holds the record for the **farthest distance cycled under water**, having pedalled 2 km (1.24 miles) on a bicycle at the bottom of the Naviglio canal in Milan, Italy, on 4 May 2003, in a time of 36 min 38.15 sec. Vittorio is pictured here performing an underwater wheelie at the London Aquarium, UK – alongside some of the residents.

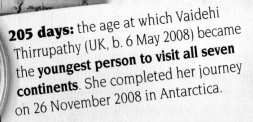

GUINNESS WORLD RECORDS

CONTENTS

★ **NEW RECORD**
☆ **UPDATED RECORD**

WWW.GUINNESSWORLDRECORDS.COM

UPS & DOWNS

4,983 m (16,050 ft): the altitude of the *Neste Enterprise* at the source of the Yangtze River, China, on 11 June 1990, the **highest altitude reached by a hovercraft.**

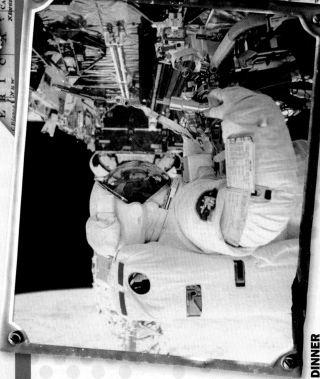

HIGHEST...

ALTITUDE (MALE): 400,171 KM

The *Apollo 13* crew of Jack Swigert, Jim Lovell and Fred Haise (all USA) travelled beyond the Earth at an altitude of 400,171 km (248,655 miles), farther than any other humans. Turn to p.26 for the amazing details on this fantastic feat of flight.

AIRCRAFT: 37,650 M

The official FAI (Fédération Aéronautique Internationale) altitude record for an aircraft is 37,650 m (123,523 ft) by Alexandr Fedotov (USSR) flying a highly modified MIG-25 "Foxbat" (designated E266M) from Podmoskovnoe Aerodrome, Russia, on 31 August 1977.

GLIDER FLIGHT: 15,460 M

Serial record breaker Steve Fossett (USA) set the absolute altitude glider flight record at 15,460 m (50,721 ft) over El Calafate, Argentina, on 29 August 2006.

HELICOPTER FLIGHT: 12,442 M

Flying an Aérospatiale SA315B "Lama" helicopter over Istres, France, Jean Boulet (France) achieved an altitude of 12,442 m (40,820 ft) on 21 June 1972.

CONCERT: 12,192 M

Norwegian band Magnet (aka Even Johansen) celebrated the launch of his album *The Simple Life!* by performing at an altitude of 12,192 m (40,000 ft) onboard a flight from Oslo, Norway, to Reykjavik, Iceland, on 27 March 2007.

CYCLE RIDE: 7,008 M

Siegfried Verheijke, Luc Belet (both Belgium) and Martin Adserballe (Denmark) rode their mountain bikes to an altitude of 7,008 m (22,992 ft) on the slopes of the Muztagata peak in the Xinjiang province of China on 11 August 2000.

HIGHEST HOT-AIR BALLOON: 21,027 M

Dr Vijaypat Singhania (India) achieved the altitude record of 21,027 m (68,986 ft) in a Cameron Z-1600 hot-air balloon over Mumbai, India, on 26 November 2005.

PARACHUTE ESCAPE: 17,100 M

On 9 April 1958, the RAF's J de Salis and P Lowe parachuted out of an English Electric Canberra bomber flying at 17,100 m (56,102 ft) over Monyash, Derby, UK.

HIGHEST HEAD-FIRST HIGH DIVE: 35 M

Professional divers regularly flock to La Quebrada, a cliff top in Acapulco, Mexico, 35 m (115 ft) high to exhibit their skills. Divers must dive out 8.22 m (27 ft) from the cliff to ensure they clear the jutting base rocks and time their dive into the 3.65-m deep (12-ft) water to coincide with an incoming wave.

HIGHEST ALTITUDE (FEMALE): 611.16 KM

Kathryn Thornton (USA) attained an altitude of 611.16 km (379.75 miles) after an orbital engine burn on 10 December 1993 during the space shuttle *Endeavour* mission STS 61. Thornton was the only female crew member on STS 61, the first shuttle mission to service the Hubble Space Telescope.

DINNER PARTY: 6,805 M

Butler Joshua Heming (UK) served a formal meal to Henry Shelford, Thomas Shelford, Nakul M Pathak, Robert Aitken, Robert Sully (all UK) and Caio Buzzolini (Australia) at a height of 6,805 m (22,326 ft) on Lhakpa Ri, Tibet, on 3 May 2004.

BASE JUMP: 6,640 M

Glenn Singleman and Heather Swan (both Australia) took part in a wingsuit BASE jump from a ledge at an altitude of 6,604 m (21,666 ft) on Mount Meru, Garwhal Himalaya, India, on 23 May 2006.

BUNGEE JUMP: 6,632 M

Curtis Rivers (UK) performed a bungee jump from a hot air balloon at 4,632 m (15,200 ft) over Puertollano, Spain, on 5 May 2002. After bouncing five times he freed himself from the cord and parachuted to the ground.

HABITATION: 6,600 M

In April 1961, a three-room dwelling believed to date from the late pre-Columbian period c. 1480 was discovered at 6,600 m (21,650 ft) on Cerro Llullaillaco (6,723 m; 22,057 ft) on the Argentine–Chilean border.

DEEPEST CONCERT: 303 M

The deepest concert was performed by Katie Melua (UK) and her band at 303 m (994 ft) below sea level, in the leg of Statoil's Troll A gas rig, off the coast of Bergen, Norway, on 1 October 2006. Ms Melua performed two, 30-minute concerts to an audience of 20 rig staff.

LIVE INTERNET BROADCAST: 2,800 M

On 24 July 2001, live footage of the HMS *Hood* was broadcast over the internet from a depth of 2,800 m (9,200 ft) at the bottom of the Denmark Strait, where she sank in 1941. The broadcast, from an ROV (remotely-operated vehicle), followed the discovery of the wreck by David Mearns (UK) of Blue Water Recoveries Ltd (UK).

SALVAGE: 5,258 M

The remains of a helicopter that had crashed into the Pacific Ocean in August 1991 with the loss of four lives was salvaged from a depth of 5,258 m (17,251 ft) by the crew of the USS *Salvor* and personnel from Eastport International (USA) on 27 February 1992. This is the greatest depth at which a salvage operation of any kind has been undertaken and successfully carried out.

MANNED DESCENT: 10,911 M

Dr Jacques Piccard (Switzerland) and Lt Donald Walsh (USA) piloted the Swiss-built US Navy bathyscaphe *Trieste* to a depth of 10,911 m (35,797 ft) in the Challenger Deep section of the Mariana Trench on 23 January 1960. The Challenger Deep is thought to be the **deepest point on Earth** and is situated 400 km (250 miles) south-west of Guam in the Pacific Ocean.

DEEPEST SCUBA DIVE BY A DOG: 4 M

Dwane Folsom (USA) regularly takes his dog, Shadow, scuba diving off the coast of Grand Cayman Island. The deepest the pair usually go is approximately 4 m (13 ft). When diving, Shadow wears a specially adapted diving suit made up of a helmet, weighted dog jacket and breathing tube connected to his owner's air tank. Mr Folsom rescued Shadow, a black mongrel – half retriever, half labrador – as a puppy from a dog pound in Boynton Beach, Florida.

LIVE TV BROADCAST: 2,400 M

Abyss Live (BBC, UK) was broadcast live from an underwater depth of 2.4 km (1.5 miles) on 29 September 2002. The programme, presented by Alastair Fothergill (UK), was broadcast from inside a MIR submersible along the Mid-Atlantic Ridge off the east coast of the USA. The main attraction of the event was live views of hydrothermal vents, fissures in the ocean floor from which mineral-rich water heated by moten rocks flows up in great dark coulds.

DEEPEST SALVAGE (COMMERCIAL): 4,500 M

On 20 July 1999, the US spacecraft *Liberty Bell 7* was commericaly salvaged from the bottom of the Atlantic Ocean, where it had sat since its splashdown on 21 July 1961. The spacecraft rested at a depth of 4,500 m (15,000 ft) before being raised by the ship *Ocean Project*. The salvage was financed by the Discovery Channel.

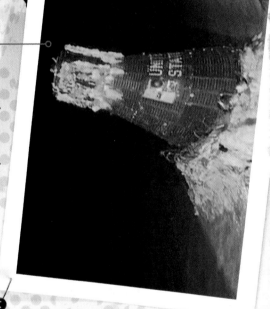

DEEPEST...

CYCLE RIDE: 66.5 M

Vittorio Innocente (Italy) cycled at a depth of 66.5 m (214 ft 10 in) in Santa Margherita Ligure, Liguria, Italy, on 21 July 2008.

SCUBA DIVE (FEMALE): 221 M

Verna van Schaik (South Africa) dived to 221 m (725 ft) in the Boesmansgat cave in South Africa's Northern Cape province on 25 October 2004. The dive lasted 5 hr 34 min, of which only 12 minutes were spent descending.

SCUBA DIVE (MALE): 318.25

Nuno Gomes (South Africa) dived to a depth of 318.25 m (1,044 ft) in the Red Sea off Dahab, Egypt, on 10 June 2005. Nuno also achieved the **deepest scuba dive in a fresh-water cave** with a depth of 282.6 m (927 ft 2 in) at Boesmansgat cave, South Africa, on 23 August 1996.

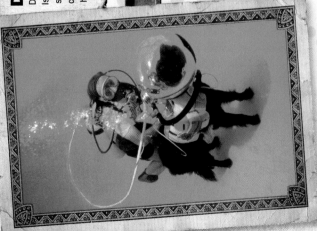

DEEPEST WATCH DIVING LIMIT: 6,000 M

The 20,000 feet model from CX Swiss Military Watch is a mechanical divers wristwatch made by Montres Charmex SA (Switzerland) that can function, as its name suggests, at depths of 6,000 m (20,000 ft). The watch was tested for water resistence at the Oceanographic Institute of the University of Southampton, UK, on 5 January 2009 and passed with flying colours.

Apr 15: A team of 12 players at the Castle Mona Pub, Newcastle, UK, knocked down 116,047 table skittles to gain the **highest table skittle score in 24 hours** on this day in 1990.

Apr 16: On 16 April 1976, the unmanned spacecraft *Helios 2* came within 43.5 million km (27 million miles) of the Sun – the **closest approach to the Sun by any spacecraft.**

Apr 17: The **highest speed attained on a ski-bob** is 201.79 km/h (125.38 mph) by Romuald Bonvin (Switzerland) at Les Arcs, Rhone-Alpes, France, on this day in 2003.

RULING THE WAVES

FASTEST TRANSATLANTIC SAILING

In July 2007, Franck Cammas (France) skippered the trimaran *Groupama 3* across the Atlantic, setting off west to east from Ambrose in New York, USA, to Lizard Point, Land's End, UK, in 4 days 3 hr 57 min 54 sec, at an average speed of 29.26 knots (54.1 km/h; 33.6 mph). The crew also broke the record for the **greatest distance sailed in 24 hours:** 794 nautical miles (1,470 km; 913.7 miles).

YOUNGEST PERSON TO SAIL THE ATLANTIC (SOLO)

Michael Perham (UK, b. 16 March 1992) left Gibraltar in his boat *Cheeky Monkey* on 18 November 2006, aged 14 years 247 days, and sailed west across the Atlantic Ocean, arriving in Nelson's Dockyard, Antigua, on 3 January 2007.

★ FASTEST TIME TO SAIL THE INDIAN OCEAN

Cheyenne, skippered by Steve Fossett (USA), sailed across the Indian Ocean at its widest point in a time of 9 days 20 hr 29 min from 25 February to 6 March 2004. At 38 m (125 ft) long and with a beam of 18 m (60 ft), *Cheyenne* is the **largest racing catamaran**.

★ FASTEST TIME TO SAIL THE PACIFIC OCEAN

Olivier de Kersauson (France) sailed from Los Angeles, California, USA, to Honolulu, Hawaii, USA – a total distance of 2,925 nautical miles (5,417.1 km; 3,366 miles) – in 4 days 19 hr 31 min 37 sec in November 2005. His *Geronimo* trimaran achieved an average speed of 19.17 knots (35.5 km/h; 22 mph).

★ FASTEST HONG KONG TO LONDON SAILING

In September 2008, Lionel Lemonchois (France) and his nine-man crew sailed *Gitana 13* from Hong Kong, China, to London, UK, in 41 days 21 hr 26 min 34 sec. The distance covered was 12,948 nautical miles (23,979.6 km; 14,900.2 miles), giving an average speed of 12.88 knots (23.8 km/h; 14.8 mph).

FASTEST TIME TO ROW THE ATLANTIC OCEAN

The fastest row across the Atlantic in any direction, land to land, is 33 days 7 hr 30 min and was achieved by the 14-man crew of *La Mondiale*, led by Leven Brown (UK). The British/Irish team left Puerto Mogan in Gran Canaria, Spain, on 15 December 2007 and arrived at Port St Charles, Barbados, on 17 January 2008.

YOUNGEST OCEAN ROWER

As part of the four-woman crew of *Silver Cloud*, Rachel Flanders (UK, b. 3 September 1990) became the youngest person to row across an ocean. On 2 December 2007, she left La Gomera, Canary Islands, aged 17 years 91 days, and rowed across the Atlantic, reaching Antigua on 14 February 2008.

FASTEST CROSSING OF THE ENGLISH CHANNEL BY AMPHIBIOUS VEHICLE

Professor Hans Georg Näder (Germany) and Captain Henry Hawkins (UK) made a successful crossing of the English Channel between Dover, UK, and Calais, France, in an amphibious vehicle named *Tonic* on 1 July 2008. The record-breaking feat was achieved in a time of 1 hr 14 min 20 sec and broke the previous record of 1 hr 40 min 6 sec set by Sir Richard Branson (UK) in June 2004.

Apr 18: The **oldest mother to have quadruplets** is Merryl Thelma Fudel (Australia), who gave birth to three girls and one boy on 18 April 1998, at the age of 55 years 286 days.

★ GREATEST DISTANCE SAILED SINGLEHANDED IN 24 HOURS

Thomas Colville (France) sailed an unprecedented 628.5 nautical miles (1,163.9 km; 723.2 miles) in his 32-m (105-ft) trimaran *Sodebo* on 7 December 2008. In doing so, Colville broke his own record, which had been set the year before, of 619 nautical miles (1,146 km; 712 miles).

★ NEW RECORD
UPDATED RECORD

YOUNGEST OCEAN ROWER (SOLO & UNSUPPORTED)

The youngest person to row the Atlantic solo and unsupported is Oliver Hicks (UK, b. 3 December 1981), who crossed west to east between 27 May and 28 September 2005 on board *Miss Olive, Virgin Atlantic* at the age of 23 years 175 days (at the start). He rowed from Atlantic Highlands, New Jersey, USA, to St Mary's, Isles of Scilly, UK, in 123 days 22 hr 8 min, to become the **first person to row from mainland USA to mainland UK solo and unsupported** and the **youngest person to row any ocean solo and unsupported**.

TOP 100 Records of the Decade

X-REF

If all this talk of water has whetted your appetite for more aquatic achievements, why not dive headfirst into Water Sports on p.258?

FASTEST SPEED UNDER SAIL

The fastest speed sailing over 500 m (1,640 ft) is 49.84 knots (92.3 km/h; 57 mph) and was achieved by Robert Douglas (USA) at Lüderitz, Namibia, on a kite surfer on 19 September 2008 – the first time that a kite surfer has set an outright speed sailing record.

★ FASTEST SPEED BY A KITE SAIL (FEMALE)

Sjoukje Bredenkamp (South Africa) reached a top kite-sail speed of 45.20 knots (83.7 km/h; 52 mph) during the 2009 Lüderitz Speed Challenge event in Lüderitz, Namibia, in October 2008. This is the third time in succession that Bredenkamp has set the female kite-sailing world record, having first claimed the title in 2006.

LONGEST JOURNEY BY AQUABIKE (JETSKI)

Adriaan Marais and Marinus du Plessis (both South Africa) followed the west coast of North America south to the Panama Canal on aquabikes (Yamaha FX Cruisers), starting out from Homer, Alaska, USA, and arriving in Panama City, Panama, after 95 days of navigation. Averaging 10 hours a day, they covered a total of 9,323 nautical miles (17,266 km; 10,729 miles) between 16 June and 19 September 2006.

GREATEST DISTANCE SAILED IN A MONOHULL YACHT IN 24 HOURS

Torben Grael (Brazil) skippered the monohull yacht *Ericsson 4* for 589 nautical miles (1,090 km; 677 miles) in 24 hours during the first leg (Alicante to Cape Town) of the Volvo Ocean Race in the Southern Atlantic Ocean, on 29 October 2008. This beat the previous record, which had been set during the 2006–07 race, by around 34 nautical miles (63 km; 39 miles).

SCALING THE HEIGHTS

★ FASTEST ICE CLIMBER

Pavel Gulyaev (Russia, below) climbed a 15-m-high (49-ft) vertical ice wall in a record time of 8.748 seconds at the Ice Climbing World Cup held in Bustemi, Romania, on 8 February 2009. Competitors at the Ice Climbing World Cup are each given six attempts to reach a top speed.

OLDEST PERSON TO CLIMB MOUNT EVEREST

According to Nepal's Senior Citizen Mt Everest Expedition (SECEE), Min Bahadur Sherchan (Nepal, b. 20 June 1931) reached the highest point on Earth on 25 May 2008 at the age of 76 years 340 days.

MOST CONQUESTS OF MOUNT EVEREST

Apa Sherpa (Nepal) reached the summit of Mount Everest for the 18th time in 2008, the most times anyone has ever successfully climbed the world's highest mountain.

FASTEST TIME TO CLIMB MOUNT EVEREST AND K2

In 2004, Karl Unterkircher (Italy) became the **first mountaineer to summit Everest and K2** – the world's two highest mountains – **in the same season without bottled oxygen**. He repeated this feat between 24 May and 26 July 2006 in a record time of 63 days.

FASTEST TIME TO CLIMB THE SEVEN SUMMITS – CARSTENSZ LIST (MALE)

Henrik Kristiansen (Denmark) climbed the highest peak on each continent (according to the

MOST 8,000-M PEAKS CLIMBED (FEMALE)

Three female climbers share the record for conquering the greatest number of 8,000ers, with 11 each. They are Nives Meroi (Italy, pictured), Gerlinde Kaltenbrunner (Austria) and Edurne Pasaban (Spain).

The term "8,000er" refers to any peak more than 8,000 m (26,246 ft) high.

Carstensz list) in 136 days between 21 January 2008 (when he ascended Vinson Massif in Antarctica) and 5 June 2008 (when he conquered Mount McKinley in Alaska, USA, the highest peak in North America).

DRIVING TO THE HIGHEST ALTITUDE (MOTORCYCLE)

Roland Hess (Chile/Switzerland), German Hess (Chile/Switzerland), Johann Janko (Chile/Austria) and Giovanni Sanguedolce (Argentina/Italy) rode to an altitude of 6,220 m (20,406 ft 9 in) on the slopes of Ojos del Salado, Atacama, Chile, using Honda 4RT 2007 motorcycles, on 19 March 2008.

Apr 21: Happy birthday to the **longest-reigning living queen**. Her Majesty Queen Elizabeth II (UK, b. 21 April 1926) succeeded to the throne on 6 February 1952 on the death of her father, King George VI.

TOP 100 Records of the Decade

7–8,000 m (23–26,000 ft): known as the **Dead Zone**, at or beyond which no human being can acclimatize – at such altitudes, the body uses up oxygen faster than it can be replenished naturally.

★ FASTEST TIME TO CLIMB EL CAPITAN

Hans Florine (USA, pictured right) and Yuji Hirayama (Japan, left) climbed the "Nose" of the 1,095-m-tall (3,593-ft) El Capitan in Yosemite National Park, California, USA, in 2 hr 48 min 50 sec in September 2002. On 30 July 2005, Florine climbed the entire vertical face of El Cap on his own in 11 hr 41 min, the ★**fastest solo ascent**.

FASTEST TIME TO CLIMB THE SEVEN SUMMITS (BOTH LISTS) BY A MARRIED COUPLE

Rob and Joanne Gambi (UK) achieved the fastest (and **first**) seven-summits ascent by a married couple, climbing the highest peak on each continent in 404 days for the Kosciuszko list (which assumes Mt Kosciuszko as the highest point in Australasia). The couple later climbed the Carstensz Pyramid (aka Puncak Jaya, the continent's highest point if Indonesia is included) in 799 days. Joanne is also the **fastest woman to climb the seven summits**.

FIRST PERSON TO CLIMB ALL PEAKS OVER 8,000 M

Reinhold Messner (Italy) became the first person to climb the 14 peaks over 8,000 m (26,246 ft) when he summitted Lhotse (8,501 m; 27,890 ft) on the Nepal/Tibet border on 16 October 1986. His quest started in June 1970.

FASTEST ASCENT OF ALL PEAKS OVER 8,000 M

Jerzy "Jurek" Kukuczka (Poland) climbed the 14 peaks higher than 8,000 m (26,246 ft) in 7 years 11 months 16 days between 4 October 1979, when he reached the summit of Lhotse (8,501 m; 27,890 ft) on the Nepal/Tibet border, and 18 September 1987, when he successfully completed an ascent of Shisha Pangma (8,012 m; 26,286 ft) in Tibet.

★ MOST DEATHS ON K2 IN ONE DAY

ExplorersWeb identifies 1 August 2008 as the deadliest day on K2, with 11 fatalities on the southeast face from an avalanche. A *serac* – a large block or column of ice, often the size of a house – crumbled and fell from an ice field near the summit, killing at least one climber and cutting the lines of a group of climbers descending the dangerous peak, the second highest in the world. Further ice falls claimed more lives during the night, while others died trying to recover the dead. The 11 dead hailed from Serbia, Pakistan, Norway, South Korea, Nepal, Ireland and France.

★ FIRST PERSON TO COMPLETE THE THREE POLES CHALLENGE

The first person to reach the North Pole, the South Pole and the peak of Mount Everest – known as the Three Poles Challenge – was Erling Kagge (Norway), who completed the trio on 8 May 1994. The **first** – and only – **person to complete the three poles challenge without the use of oxygen** on Everest was Antoine De Choudens (France, 1969–2003) between 25 April 1996 and 10 January 1999.

★ NEW RECORD
UPDATED RECORD

★ DEADLIEST MOUNTAIN TO CLIMB

Annapurna I, in the 55-km-long (34-mile) Annapurna Massif, has been climbed by 130 people, 53 of whom died along the way, giving the peak a 41% mortality rate – making it statistically the world's most dangerous mountain. The latest fatality came in 2008 when Iñaki Ochoa de Olza (Spain) had a seizure and pulmonary oedema near the summit.

On 28 October 2007, Tomaž Humar (Slovenia, inset below) became the ★**first person to "solo" Annapurna I**. Humar chose to climb a new route along the right side of the south face in a pure "alpine" style (meaning that he carried all of his food and equipment with him, as opposed to "expedition" style, in which the climber benefits from porters and fixed lines).

DEADLY PURSUITS

Annapurna I may be the deadliest climb, but, in absolute terms, more deaths occur on Mont Blanc (4,810 m; 15,781 ft) in the Alps than any other mountain. Six people died in the first month of 2009; 58 died (with 10 still missing, presumed dead) in 2008; and 30 died in the summer of 2007.

TOP **100** Records of the Decade

Apr 22: Released on this day in 1993, NCSA Mosaic became the world's **first Internet browser**.

Apr 23: The **farthest human-powered flight** was by Kanellos Kanellopoulos (Greece), who pedalled his *Daedalus 88* aircraft 115.11 km (71.52 miles) from Heraklion, Crete, to Santorini, Greece, on this day in 1988.

CIRCUMNAVIGATING THE GLOBE

FIRST SOLO CIRCUMNAVIGATION BY AIRCRAFT

Wiley Post (USA) made the first solo flight around the world from 15 to 22 July 1933 in a Lockheed Vega aircraft called *Winnie Mae*. He covered 25,089 km (15,596 miles), starting and ending in Brooklyn, New York City, New York, USA. Post is pictured wearing his experimental pressure suit – the *Winnie Mae* could not be pressurized, so Post adapted a diver's helmet and three-layered suit that would allow him to travel at ever greater altitudes.

CIRCUMNAVIGATION BY AMPHIBIOUS CAR

Ben Carlin (Australia) made the first, and so far only, circumnavigation of the globe in an amphibious vehicle, driving a modified Ford GPA jeep called *Half-Safe*. He completed the last leg of the Atlantic crossing (the English Channel) on 24 August 1951. He arrived back in Montreal, Canada, on 8 May 1958, having completed a circumnavigation of 62,765 km (39,000 miles) over land and 15,450 km (9,600 miles) by sea and river. He was accompanied on the trans-Atlantic stage by his ex-wife Elinore (USA) and on the long trans-Pacific stage (Tokyo, Japan to Anchorage, Alaska, USA) by Boye Lafayette De Mente (USA).

CIRCUMNAVIGATION ON FOOT

Proving circumnavigations on foot is notoriously difficult. George Matthew Schilling (USA) is reputed to have walked round the world between 1897 and 1904. However, the first verified circumnavigation on foot was by David Kunst (USA), who walked 23,250 km (14,450 miles) through four continents from 20 June 1970 to 5 October 1974.

★ LARGEST PASSENGER SHIP TO SAIL AROUND THE WORLD

Queen Mary II, at 148,528 tonnes (163,724 tons), is the largest passenger ship to circumnavigate the globe. The last great ocean liner (as opposed to passenger cruiser), towering as high as a 23-storey building and covering an area almost as large as four football fields, set off on her first world cruise on 10 January 2007 from Fort Lauderdale, Florida, USA, and completed the trip in 81 days.

LAST PERSON TO SAIL AROUND THE WORLD NON-STOP WESTBOUND, SOLO

In April 2008, Tomasz Lewandowski (Poland) became only the sixth sailor ever to successfully circumnavigate the globe single-handedly, sailing east to west, against the prevailing wind.

Lewandowski set out in his Mikado 56, *Luka*, from Ensenada, Baja California, Mexico, on 6 March 2007 and returned on 1 April 2008. His only company for the 28,710-nautical-mile (53,170-km; 33,038-mile) trip was his Jack Russell terrier, Wacek.

FIRST...

CIRCUMNAVIGATION BY AIRCRAFT WITHOUT REFUELLING

Richard G "Dick" Rutan and Jeana Yeager (both USA) circumnavigated the world in a westward direction from Edwards Air Force Base, California, USA, in nine days from 14 to 23 December 1986 without refuelling. The key to their success was their specially constructed aircraft *Voyager*, which was designed and constructed by Dick's brother Burt Rutan, owner of the company Scaled Composites, which achieved the **first private space flight** during 2004.

SOLO CIRCUMNAVIGATION BY BALLOON

Steve Fossett (USA) circumnavigated the globe in *Bud Light Spirit of Freedom*, a 42.6-m-tall (140-ft) mixed-gas balloon, from 19 June to 2 July 2002, becoming the first person ever to do so alone. He took off from Northam, Western Australia, and landed at Eromanga, Queensland, Australia, after covering 33,195 km (20,627 miles).

TOP 100 Records of the Decade

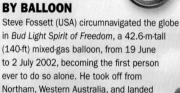

Queen Mary 2
CUNARD

Apr 24: Chad Fell (USA) blew the **largest ever bubblegum bubble**, boasting a diameter of 50.8 cm (20 in) at the Double Springs High School, Winston County, Alabama, USA, on 24 April 2004.

GUINNESS WORLD RECORDS

★ NEW RECORD
☆ UPDATED RECORD

★ FIRST FEMALE TO SAIL NON-STOP AROUND THE WORLD IN BOTH DIRECTIONS

On 16 February 2009, former PE teacher Dee Caffari (UK) made history when she finished the Vendée Globe round-the-world yacht race in 6th place. This achievement means that Dee is the first woman – and only the 4th person ever – to sail both ways around the world, alone and unaided. The first part of her double world first was achieved between November 2005 and May 2006, when she became the **first solo woman to circumnavigate westwards non-stop.**

☆ SOLO ROUND-THE-WORLD MONOHULL SAIL (MALE)

The fastest circumnavigation sailing solo in a monohull is 84 days 3 hr 9 min and was achieved by Michel Desjoyeaux (France) for winning the 2008/2009 Vendée Globe single-handed yacht race, starting and finishing at Les Sables d'Olonne, France, from 9 November 2008 to 1 February 2009. This is the second time Desjoyeaux has won this race (becoming the first person to win it twice) and he broke the record in both wins.

CIRCUMNAVIGATION BY BICYCLE

The fastest circumnavigation by bicycle is 194 days 17 hours, and was achieved by Mark Beaumont (UK), who cycled a distance of 29,445.81 km (18,296.74 miles) and travelled over 40,100 km (24,916 miles) in total (including transfers). The journey started and finished in Paris, France, from 5 August 2007 to 15 February 2008 and covered Europe, Pakistan, Malaysia, Australia, New Zealand and the USA.

★ YOUNGEST PERSON TO FLY SOLO AROUND THE WORLD

Barrington Irving (Jamaica/USA), an aerospace student at Florida Memorial University, USA, circumnavigated the globe in *Inspiration*, an aeroplane manufactured and assembled by the Columbia Aircraft Manufacturing Company, between 23 March and 27 June 2007. He completed the feat aged 23 years 227 days. His landmark 97-day flight was also the first solo circumnavigation flight by a black pilot.

FASTEST...

SOLO CIRCUMNAVIGATION BY HELICOPTER (FEMALE)

Jennifer Murray (UK) piloted her Robinson R44 helicopter around the world solo in 99 days from 31 May to 6 September 2000. The journey started and finished at Brooklands airfield in Surrey, UK, and crossed 30 countries. Murray, along with Colin Bodill (UK), also holds the record for the **first** and **fastest circumnavigation via both poles by helicopter**, which was completed in 170 days 22 hr 47 min on 23 May 2007.

CIRCUMNAVIGATION BY CAR

The record for the first and fastest man and woman to have circumnavigated the Earth by car, covering six continents under the rules applicable in 1989 and 1991 and embracing more than an equator's length of driving (24,901 road miles; 40,075 km), is held by Saloo Choudhury and his wife Neena Choudhury (both India). The journey took 69 days 19 hr 5 min from 9 September to 17 November 1989. The couple drove a 1989 Hindustan "Contessa Classic", starting and finishing in Delhi, India.

CUNARD

Queen Mary 2

SPLASHING OUT

Almost 500 passengers signed up for the entire round-the-world trip on the *Queen Mary II*, some paying in excess of $100,000. On a typical trip, the ship starts out with 6,000 bottles of Champagne; the library is the largest afloat, with 8,000 volumes, as is the dance floor.

WWW.GUINNESSWORLDRECORDS.COM

Apr 25: The record for the **most heads shaved in an hour** is 44, achieved by Anne Armstrong (UK) in Maginns of Castlewellan in County Down, UK, on 25 April 2008.

Apr 26: The **largest waltz** consisted of 242 pairs who danced at Austria Center Vienna, Vienna, Austria, on 26 April 2008.

★ LONGEST JOURNEY BY MOUTH-CONTROLLED MOTORIZED WHEELCHAIR

Chang-Hyun Choi (South Korea) covered 28,000 km (17,398 miles) in a mouth-controlled motorized wheelchair between 10 May 2006 and 6 December 2007. Chang Hyun Choi, who is affected by cerebral palsy and is paralysed from the neck down, travelled at a maximum speed of 13 km/h (8 mph) across 35 countries in Europe and the Middle East.

LONGEST SNOWMOBILE JOURNEY

Robert G Davis (USA) covered 19,574 km (12,163 miles) on his Yamaha RS Venture snowmobile during a 60-day period between 11 January 2008 and 11 March 2008.

★ GREATEST DISTANCE TRAVELLED BY TRAIN (24 HOURS)

Corey Pedersen and Michael Kim (both USA) travelled between Kanazawa and Sendai, Japan, covering 2,901.4 km (1,802.84 miles) without duplicating any part of the journey from 6 to 7 October 2008.

★ FASTEST SOLO, UNSUPPORTED AND UNASSISTED JOURNEY TO THE SOUTH POLE

Todd Carmichael (USA) completed a solo trek to the South Pole in a record time of 39 days 7 hr 49 min, arriving on 21 December 2008. In doing so, Carmichael also became the first American to reach the Pole solo and unaided.

QUAD BIKES...

The highest speed on a quad bike (ATV) is 249.51 km/h (155.04 mph), achieved by Terry Wilmeth (USA) on the AlbaAction/Fullbore/Powroll Rocket Raptor version 5.0 at Madras Airport, Madras, Oregon, USA, on 16 June 2007.

★ MOST COUNTRIES VISITED IN A CONTINUOUS JOURNEY BY CAR

Jim Rogers and Paige Parker (both USA) visited 111 countries and three territories (Western Sahara, French Polynesia and Gibraltar) by car between 1 January 1999 and 5 January 2002. They covered more than 245,000 km (152,000 miles) across six continents in their custom-built Mercedes off-road vehicle and trailer.

LONGEST LAWNMOWER RIDE

Over 260 consecutive days, Gary Hatter (USA) travelled 23,487.5 km (14,594.5 miles) on his lawnmower. Hatter started his drive in Portland, Maine, USA, on 31 May 2000 and passed through all 48 contiguous US states, as well as Canada and Mexico, before arriving in Daytona Beach, Florida, on 14 February 2001.

★ FASTEST UNSUPPORTED AND UNASSISTED JOURNEY TO THE SOUTH POLE

Ray Zahab (pictured), Kevin Vallely and Richard Weber (all Canada) reached the South Pole from the Hercules Inlet on 7 January 2009 after just 33 days 23 hr 30 min.

★ FIRST WINTER EXPEDITION TO THE NORTH POLE

Matvey Shparo and Boris Smolin (both Russia) began the earliest winter expedition to the North Pole on 22 December 2007, the day of winter solstice, from the Arktichesky Cape on the northern point of the Severnaya Zemlya Archipelago. They reached the North Pole on 14 March 2008, eight days before the vernal equinox, the official beginning of the polar day. Travelling in complete darkness, the only light source was the light on their headlamps.

★ LONGEST JOURNEY ON A QUADBIKE (ATV)

Josh and Anna Hogan (USA) covered 27,141 km (16,865 miles) on two Top 1 450 Quads (ATVs) from 24 August 2007 to 27 March 2008, starting in Mombassa, Kenya, and finishing in Elche, Spain, passing through 17 countries along the way.

Apr 27: The **fastest time to run a mile while balancing an egg on a spoon** is 7 min 8 sec by Ashrita Furman (USA) in Jamaica, New York, USA, on 27 April 2007.

Apr 28: The **most participants in a relay race** was 7,841 at the 35th Batavierenrace from Nijmegen to Enschede in the Netherlands on this day in 2007.

LONGEST LIFEBOAT JOURNEY

After his ship, the *Endurance*, became trapped in Antarctic sea ice, Sir Ernest Shackleton (UK) escaped with his crew of 28. In three lifeboats, they set course for Elephant Island, around 160 km (100 miles) away. Once there, Shackleton selected five of his best men to take the largest lifeboat towards a whaling station in South Georgia, 1,300 km (800 miles) away. In a journey that is still regarded as one of the greatest in history, Sir Ernest and his men reached the island after 17 days, on 19 May 1916.

LONGEST JOURNEY SWIMMING

Between 10 June and 30 July 2004, Martin Strel (Slovenia) swam the entire length of the Yangtze River, China, covering a record 4,003 km (2,487 miles).

X-REF
You can discover more record-breaking swimming achievements on pp.258–259.

FIRST PERSON TO REACH THE NORTH POLE (SOLO)

Dr Jean-Louis Etienne (France) was the first person to reach the North Pole solo and without dogs on 11 May 1986 after 63 days. He had the benefit of being resupplied several times during the journey.

★ MOST JOURNEYS FROM JOHN O'GROATS TO LAND'S END

The UK's most famous journey is from Land's End to John O'Groats (or vice versa), a 1,407 km (874 miles) trip by road (or 1,900 km; 1,200 miles off-road) that has been completed a record 19 times by John Taylor (Australia) on foot, by cycling or by car from 14 January 1980 to 29 November 2007.

★ OLDEST MARRIED COUPLE TO VISIT THE NORTH POLE

Heinz G Fischer (USA, b. 10 March 1929) and his wife Linda G Burdet (USA, b. 29 November 1931) skied to the North Pole together, aged 79 and 76 respectively, on 12 April 2008. The couple were dropped by helicopter at ice camp Barneo (1 degree south of the pole) and skied 6.39 km (4 miles) to the Pole.

★ FASTEST TIME TO VISIT EVERY SOVEREIGN COUNTRY

Dubai-based businessman Kashi Samaddar (India) visited all 194 United Nations member countries in 12 years 8 months 13 days, between 15 September 1995 and 27 May 2008. The globetrotting Mr Samaddar – who has actually visited 205 different countries – travelled with an Indian passport, which resulted in extensive delays because of visa issues. He hopes to have visited a total of 250 countries by 2010.

FIRST MOTHER AND SON TEAM TO REACH A POLE

At 9:15 p.m. local time (GMT 5 a.m.) on 2 May 2007, Daniel Byles and his mother Jan Meek (both UK) reached the magnetic North Pole (N 78° 35.724', W 104° 11.940') following a 24-day trek on foot and skis from Resolute Bay in Canada – a journey of around 560 km (350 miles).

LONGEST JOURNEY ON INLINE SKATES

Khoo Swee Chiow (Singapore) covered 6,088 km (3,782.9 miles) on inline skates, departing from Hanoi, Vietnam, on 20 October 2007 and arriving in Singapore on 21 January 2008.

OLDEST PERSON TO SKI TO BOTH POLES

The oldest person to ski to both Poles is Norbert H Kern (Germany, b. 26 July 1940), who skied to the South Pole on 18 January 2007 and to the North Pole on 27 April 2007, completing the task at the age of 66 years 275 days.

★ **NEW RECORD**
UPDATED RECORD

WWW.GUINNESSWORLDRECORDS.COM

Apr 29: The **oldest male tennis player to be ranked number one** by the **Association of Tennis Professionals** is Andre Agassi (USA), born on this day in 1970. He became the highest seeded men's player on 11 May 2003, aged 33 years 13 days.

TOP 100 Records of the Decade

★ FIRST AFRICAN-AMERICAN PRESIDENT OF THE USA

Barack Hussein Obama II (USA) was inaugurated as the 44th President of the USA on 20 January 2009, following a record-breaking campaign. In the September before election, Obama raised a monthly record of $150 million (£82.5 million), taking his fundraising total to over $605 million (£332.9 million) – also a record. Much of this went on advertising – an unprecedented $250 million (£137.5 million) was spent on TV ads in just five months. Over 136 million voters turned out on election day – the most since 1960 – and more than two million descended on the Capitol in Washington, DC for his inauguration (inset).

$5.3 billion: money raised and spent on the 2008 race to the White House – the **costliest election in history**

CONTENTS

USA

AT A GLANCE

- **AREA:** 9,826,630 km² (3,794,083 miles²)
- **POPULATION:** 303.8 million
- **HOUSEHOLDS:** 113.9 million
- **KEY FACTS:** The average calorie intake in the USA is 3,774.1 per day, the **highest daily consumption of calories**. The country also holds the record for the **highest percentage of gun ownership (country)** – a 1999 survey found that approximately 40% of households contain a gun.

★ MOST CHRISTMAS TREES CHOPPED IN TWO MINUTES

Erin Lavoie (USA) used an axe to cut down 27 Christmas trees in two minutes on the set of *Guinness World Records: Die Größten Weltrekorde* in Germany, on 19 December 2008.

LARGEST PUB CRAWL

More than 4,000 participants took part in the SaintPattys.com 11th Annual "Luck of the Irish" St Patrick's Pub Crawl on 14 March 2009, in Manhattan, New York City, USA. However, only 3,163 of the drinkers followed the official guidelines, which required attendees to have a card stamped at each of the 86 pubs visited along the east side of Manhattan. The route covered more than 8 km (5 miles), and everyone taking part wore green clothing in honour of St Patrick, the patron saint of Ireland. As per the guidelines, non-alcoholic drinks were allowed.

★ FASTEST LAWNMOWER

The fastest speed on an unaltered lawnmower is 98 km/h (61 mph) by Tommy Passemante (USA) at Miller Motorsports Park in Tooele, Utah, USA, on 18 November 2008. The record attempt was filmed for the MTV show *Nitro Circus*.

★ GREATEST PURCHASE OF PROPERTY

On 22 November 2006, US private equity firm Blackstone paid $20 billion (£10.5 billion) for 580 office buildings across the USA belonging to Equity Office Property Trust – itself part of the largest leveraged buyout in history with a total of $36 billion (£17 billion).

★ TALLEST MARIGOLD

The tallest marigold measured 3.07 m (10 ft 1 in) in December 2007 and was grown by Rebecca Shanks (USA), who lives in Berlin Heights, Ohio, USA.

FIRST ALL-TALKING CARTOON

Paul Terry's (USA) *Dinner Time* (USA, 1928) was premiered at the Mark Strand Theater, New York, USA, on 1 September 1928. The film preceded Disney's *Steamboat Willie* (USA, 1928) by a month.

FIRST CARTOON STRIP

The first cartoon strip ever printed is "The Yellow Kid", which first appeared in the *New York Journal* on 18 October 1896.

LARGEST ECONOMY

In terms of Gross Domestic Product (GDP), the USA has the biggest economy with a figure of $13.8 trillion for 2007, according to the International Monetary Fund.

★ FASTEST TIME TO SAIL FROM NEW YORK TO SAN FRANCISCO

Gitana 13, crewed by a team of nine and skippered by Lionel Lemonchois (France), sailed the Route de l'or, taking it from New York to San Francisco via Cape Horn in 43 days 3 min 18 sec between 16 January and 28 February 2008.

FIRST PRIVATELY-FUNDED MANNED SPACEFLIGHT

On 21 June 2004, *SpaceShipOne*, piloted by Mike Melvill (South Africa) and built by Scaled Composites (US), took off from Mojave Airport, California, USA, and reached an altitude of 100,124 m (328,492 ft), above the 100,000 m threshold set out by the Fédération Aéronautique Internationale (FAI) as the point where space begins. On 4 October 2004, *SpaceShipOne* went on to claim the $10 million (£5.5 million) Ansari X-Prize for non-government funded manned spaceflight.

TOP 100 Records of the Decade

★ FIRST DARK SKY PARK

In April 2007, the International Dark Sky Association named Utah's Natural Bridges National Monument, USA, as the first Dark Sky Park – that is, an area in which the night sky can be viewed clearly, without any "light pollution".

Apr 30: The **largest bonfire** had an overall volume of 1,715.7 m³ (60,589 ft³). It was built by ŠKD mladi Boštanj and lit on 30 April 2007 in Boštanj, Slovenia, to celebrate Labour Day.

May 1: The **tallest maypole** was erected by the town of Eicherloh, Germany, and stood 50.35 m (165 ft) high on this day in 2005.

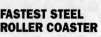

79.28 million: passengers carried within the USA in 2004 by Delta, the world's **busiest airline for domestic passengers**.

FASTEST STEEL ROLLER COASTER

Kingda Ka at Six Flags Great Adventure near Jackson, New Jersey, USA, has a design speed of 206 km/h (128 mph) and opened in the Spring of 2005. It is also the **tallest steel roller coaster**, with riders reaching 139 m (456 ft) above ground level.

TOP 100 Records of the Decade

★ HIGHEST DEFENCE BUDGET

The USA has the highest government budget for defence with $622 billion (£311.6 billion) approved for the 2007 financial year.

LARGEST HAMBURGER EVER

Loran Green and Friends of Hi Line Promotions (all USA) made a 2.74-tonne (3-ton) burger at the Sleeping Buffalo Resort at Saco, Montana, on 5 September 1999. The burger was a promotional item and not sold commercially.

TALLEST LIVING HORSE

Born in Iowa, USA, in 1998, the tallest living horse is Radar, a Belgian draft horse who was measured at 19 hands 3.5 in (202 cm; 79.5 in) without shoes on 27 July 2004 at the North American Belgian Championship in London, Ontario, Canada. Radar is owned by Priefert Manufacturing, Inc., in Mount Pleasant, Texas.

FASTEST TIME TO RUN THE NEW YORK MARATHON (MALE)

The fastest time to complete the New York Marathon by a male athlete is 2 hr 07 min 43 sec by Tesfaye Jifar (Ethiopia) on 5 November 2001. The **fastest time to run the New York marathon by a woman** is 2 hr 22 min 31 sec by Margaret Okayo (Kenya) on 2 November 2003.

★ HIGHEST-GROSSING YEAR FOR BROADWAY THEATRES

According to the League of American Theatres and Producers, the highest-grossing year for theatres on Broadway, New York City, was 2006, with $910 million (then £470 million) in ticket sales. Attendance figures matched those of 2005, with over 12 million people going to watch Broadway's musicals and plays.

★ MOST PERFORMANCES BY AN ACTOR IN THE SAME ROLE

Theatre actor Catherine Russell (USA) appeared as Magaret Thorne Brent in 8,820 performances of the play *Perfect Crime* in a number of New York City theatres between 18 April 1987 and 1 December 2008.

FIRST BUILDING TO HAVE A SAFETY ELEVATOR (LIFT)

On 23 March 1857, the world's first modern "safety elevator" went into service at a department store in New York City, USA. It was installed by Elisha Otis, who is widely credited with having advanced the development of the modern skyscraper by allowing buildings above five storeys to become practical living places for their occupants.

MOST STARS ON THE HOLLYWOOD WALK OF FAME

Actor, composer and songwriter Gene Autry (USA, 1907–98) has five stars on the Hollywood Walk of Fame strip – 6,384, 6,520, 6,644, 6,667 and 7,000 Hollywood Boulevard – for Recording, Motion Pictures, Television, Radio and Theatre.

★ NEW RECORD
UPDATED RECORD

★ LONGEST TAIL ON A HORSE

The longest tail on a horse is 381 cm (12 ft 6 in) and was measured on the mare JJS Summer Breeze on 23 August 2007. She is owned by Crystal and Casey Socha (both USA) of Augusta, Kansas, USA.

TALL TALES

The tallest horse ever was Sampson, bred by Thomas Cleaver of Toddington Mills, Bedfordshire, UK. This horse, foaled 1846, measured 21.2½ hands (219 cm; 86.5 in) in 1850 and is said to have weighed 1,524 kg (3,359 lb).

May 2: The **largest picnic** was set by 8,000 people, who sat down to eat prepared meals brought from home at the Plaza de España, Santa Cruz, Tenerife, Spain, on this day in 1999.

MEXICO

AT A GLANCE

- **AREA:** 1,972,545 km² (761,603 miles²)
- **POPULATION:** 108.3 million
- **HOUSEHOLDS:** 25.1 million
- Mexico is home to the **largest taco**, weighing 750 kg (1,654 lb), and Sistema Sac Actun, the **largest explored underwater cave system** at 153 km (95 miles) long.

HAIRIEST FAMILY

Victor "Larry" and Gabriel "Danny" Ramos Gomez (both Mexico) are two of a family of 19 that span five generations all suffering from the rare condition called Congenital Generalized Hypertrichosis, characterized by excessive body hair, particularly on the face and torso. The women are covered with a light to medium coat of hair, while the men of the family have thick hair on approximately 98% of their body apart from their hands and feet.

TALLEST UNDERWATER STALACTITE

Known locally as Tunich Ha, the world's largest underwater stalactite measures 12.8 m (42 ft) and is found in a cave formation called Sistema Chac Mol in Mexico. Salt water from the Caribbean penetrates the limestone in the region, creating astonishing visual effects as it meets fresh water seeping into the cave.

LARGEST ATTENDANCE AT A BOXING MATCH

The greatest paid attendance at any boxing match is 132,274 for four world title fights at the Aztec Stadium, Mexico City, Mexico, on 20 February 1993, headed by the successful WBC super lightweight defence by Julio César Chávez (Mexico) over Greg Haugen (USA).

★ LARGEST BALL COURT

The largest ball court in ancient Mesoamerica is the Great Ball Court in Chich'en Itza, Mexico. It was used to play the Mesoamerican ballgame, a sport with ritual associations played for over 3,000 years by the pre-Columbian peoples (a modern version of the game, known as Ulama, is still played today). The court measures 166 x 68 m (545 x 232 ft). The imposing walls are 12 m (39 ft) high, and in the centre, high up on each of the long walls, are rings carved with intertwining serpents.

★ NEW RECORD
★ UPDATED RECORD

★ LARGEST FOOTBALL TOURNAMENT (PLAYERS)

The Copa Telmex was held between February and November 2008 in Mexico and contested by 10,457 teams totalling 172,692 players.

★ LARGEST DISPLAY OF PIÑATAS

A display of 504 piñatas was organized by Union de Locatarios del Mercado Municipal, in Hermosillo, Sonora, Mexico, on 27 April 2008.

★ LARGEST DRAWING

"Artistic Electrocardiogram 411" has an overall surface area of 205.5 m² (221.97 ft²) and was completed by Filemon Trevino Berlanga of Monterrey, Mexico, on 13 March 2008.

MOST GAMES OF CHESS PLAYED SIMULTANEOUSLY

The most simultaneous games of chess ever played in one location is 13,446 on 21 October 2006 during the Third Mexico City Chess Festival in Mexico.

HIGHEST BOX OFFICE FILM GROSS FOR A MEXICAN FILM

Directed by Guillermo del Toro (Mexico), *El Laberinto del Fauno* (*Pan's Labyrinth*, Mexico/Spain/USA, 2006) made $42.6 million (£21.7 million) worldwide following its release in 2006.

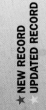

May 3: The world's **first spam email** was sent on this day in 1978 by Gary Thuerk (USA). It was sent to 397 email accounts on the ARPAnet of the US Defence Department.

May 4: The **most expensive sculpture sold at auction** is Constantin Brancusi's (Romania) *Bird in Space* (1923), which sold at Christie's, New York City, USA, for $27,456,000 (£14,431,204) in 2005.

CENTRAL AMERICA & CARIBBEAN

AT A GLANCE

- **AREA: Central America:** 523,780 km² (202,232 miles²); **Caribbean:** 127,753 km² (49,325 miles²)
- **POPULATION: C. America:** 44,934,014; **Caribbean:** 22,636,621 (2007 est.)
- **COUNTRIES: C. America:** Belize, Costa Rica, El Salvador, Guatemala, Honduras, Nicaragua, Panama; **Caribbean:** Anguila, Antigua and Barbuda, Aruba, The Bahamas, Barbados, British Virgin Is., Cayman Is., Cuba, Dominica, Dominican Republic, Grenada, Guadeloupe, Haiti, Jamaica, Martinique, Montserrat, Netherlands Antilles, Puerto Rico, St Barthélemy, St Kitts & Nevis, St Lucia, St Martin, St Vincent & The Grenadines, Trinidad & Tobago, Turks & Caicos, US Virgin Isles.

DEEPEST DIVE BY A MAMMAL

The deepest authenticated dive by a mammal was made by a bull sperm whale (*Physeter macrocephalus*) off the coast of Dominica, in the Caribbean, in 1991. Scientists from the Woods Hole Oceanographic Institute recorded the dive to be 2,000 m (6,500 ft) deep, lasting a total of 1 hour 13 minutes.

OLDEST AND YOUNGEST PRESIDENTS

Joaquin Balaguer (1906–2002, above left) was president of the Dominican Republic 1960–62, 1966–78 and 1986–96. When he finally left office at the age of 89, Balaguer was the world's **oldest president** and had held the presidency for more than 23 years in total.

Jean-Claude Duvalier (b. 3 July 1951, above right), became president of Haiti on 22 April 1971, becoming the world's **youngest president**, aged just 19 years 293 days. He served until 1986.

MOST PEOPLE BRUSHING THEIR TEETH IN A SINGLE VENUE

On 5 November 2005, 13,380 people brushed their teeth simultaneously at the Cuscatlán Stadium, City of San Salvador, El Salvador, at an event arranged by Colgate Palmolive (Central America) Inc.

LOWEST SUICIDE RATE

According to the World Health Organization's latest figures for May 2003, Antigua and Barbuda (1995), the Dominican Rebublic (1994), St Kitts and Nevis (1995) and St Vincent and The Grenadines (1986) all recorded the lowest suicide rates with no cases reported in the years shown.

WORST CYCLONE DISASTER – HOMELESS TOLL

Hurricane Mitch, which struck Central America (Honduras and Nicaragua) between 26 October and 4 November 1998, left approximately 2.5 million people dependent on international aid efforts when it destroyed 93,690 dwellings.

WORST OIL TANKER SPILL

The collision of the *Atlantic Empress* with the *Aegean Captain* off the coast of Tobago in the Caribbean Sea on 19 July 1979 resulted in the loss of 42.7 million US gallons of oil (287,000 tonnes).

★ LARGEST ANCIENT STONE BALLS

Known locally as *Las Bolas Grandes* ("the giant balls"), there are more than 1,000 perfectly spherical granitic globes scattered over the Diquis Delta in Costa Rica. Carved by an unidentified race of pre-Columbian people, the largest of the balls measures 2.5 m (8 ft 2 in) in diameter and weighs over 16 tonnes (17.6 tons).

OLDEST PLAYER IN MAJOR LEAGUE BASEBALL (MLB) TO HIT A HOME RUN

At 48 years 254 days, Julio Franco (Dominican Republic, b. 23 August 1958) became the oldest player in major league history to hit a home run when he connected off Randy Johnson (USA) for a two-run home run to help lead the New York Mets (USA) to a 5–3 win over the Arizona Diamondbacks (USA) at Chase Field in Phoenix, Arizona, USA, on 4 May 2007.

WHALE TALES...

The largest jaw ever recorded on a mammal belongs to a sperm whale. Measuring 5 m (16 ft 5 in) long, the massive lower jaw belonged to a male whale nearly 25.6 m (84 ft) in length. Sperm whales are also the largest-toothed whales.

May 5: The **most valuable painting sold at auction** is Pablo Picasso's *Garçon á la Pipe* (1905), which was sold to an anonymous buyer for $104 million (£58 million) on this day in 2004 at Sotheby's, New York City, USA.

SOUTH AMERICA

ACTUAL SIZE

AT A GLANCE

- **AREA:** 17,840,000 km² (6,888,062 miles²)
- **POPULATION:** 371 million
- **DENSITY:** 20.8 people/km² (53.8 people/mile²)
- **KEY FACTS:** the South American continent (which does not include Central America) covers 3.5% of the Earth's surface.
- **COUNTRIES:** Argentina (**fastest turn-around of presidents**: five in two weeks in December 2001), Bolivia (**highest train station**, Cóndor station, at 4,786 m; 15,702 ft), Brazil, Chile (**driest place** on Earth is Quillagua, with just 5 mm of rainfall in 1964–2001), Colombia, Ecuador, French Guiana, Guyana, Paraguay, Peru, Suriname, Uruguay and Venezuela.

LARGEST TRUMPET ENSEMBLE

On 19 February 2006, at a concert organized by Napoleón Gómez Silva in Oruro, Bolivia, an unprecedented 1,166 participants formed a trumpet ensemble.

★ MOST BALLOONS DEFLATED IN ONE MINUTE

To celebrate International Women's Day, yoghurt manufacturer Activia Argentina assembled a group of women numbering in their thousands to deflate as many balloons as they could in a minute at Parque Tres de Febrero in Buenos Aires, Argentina, on 8 March 2009. After a 60-second flurry of activity, the band of women managed to deflate a grand total of 9,768 balloons, setting a new world record in the process.

★ LARGEST CHARANGO

The largest charango (South American guitar) ever made measures 6.13 m (20 ft 1 in) long and 1.13 m (3 ft 8 in) across. It was commissioned by the Town Hall of Belisario Boeto, Villa Serrano, Chuquisaca, Bolivia, and presented on 15 January 2004.

LARGEST HORSE PARADE

On 29 July 2006, at an event organized by Fair of Flowers Cavalgade (Colombia), 8,233 horses and their riders took part in a parade at Medellín, Antioquia, Colombia.

LONGEST BEETLE

The longest beetle in terms of body size alone is the titan beetle *Titanus giganteus* of South America, with a body length of 15 cm (6 in). In terms of total length, the record holder is the hercules beetle *Dynastes hercules* (above, also of South America), which is 17.7 cm (7 in) long, owing to its pair of horns – one extending from the head, the other from the thorax.

HIGHEST TOLL PAID FOR PASSING THROUGH THE PANAMA CANAL

The highest toll ever paid for passing through the Panama Canal (the man-made waterway that joins the Atlantic and Pacific Oceans, and which opened in 1914) is $226,194.25 (£136,259.42), by the cruise ship *Coral Princess* on 25 September 2003. *Coral Princess* is 294 m (965 ft) long and can accommodate a total of 1,974 passengers.

May 6: The **youngest person to appear in football's World Cup** is Souleymane Mamam, who played for Togo against Zambia, aged 13 years 310 days, in a preliminary qualifying game on 6 May 2001.

May 7: The **fastest guitar player** is Tiago Alberto de Quadros (Brazil), aka Tiago Della Vega, who played "Flight of the Bumblebee" without error at 320 BPM at EM&T, Sao Paulo, Brazil, on this day in 2008.

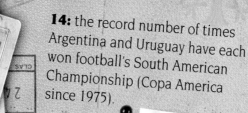

★ LARGEST GUINEA PIG FESTIVAL

At the annual Festival of the Cuy (guinea pig) in Huacho, Peru, guinea pig is pitted against guinea pig in a series of contests to find the fattest, fastest and even best dressed. The stakes are high: only the winners are spared entry to the final contest, the *tastiest* guinea pig of the day, in which they are stuffed, roasted, smoked and grilled. Guinea pig is a traditional (and almost inexhaustible) source of low-fat protein in the Andes.

LARGEST SWIMMING POOL

The world's largest swimming pool, in terms of area, is the San Alfonso del Mar seawater pool in Algarrobo, Chile. It is 1,013 m (3,324 ft) long and has an overall area of 8 ha (19.77 acres) – larger than 15 American football pitches. The prodigious pool was completed in December 2006.

★ HEAVIEST POTATO PIE

The heaviest potato pie weighed 5.37 tonnes (11,838 lb) and was created by the District Municipality of Carmen de la Legua Reynoso and displayed in the main square of Miguel Grau Seminario, Carmen de la Legua Reynoso, Callao, Peru, on 16 July 2004.

MOST DANGEROUS ROAD

The road considered by many to be the most lethal in the world is the North Yungas Road, which runs for 69 km (43 miles) from La Paz to Coroico in Bolivia and is held to be responsible for up to 300 deaths annually – or 4.3 per km (6.9 per mile)! For the majority of the stretch, the single-lane mud road (which caters for two-way traffic) is accompanied by an unbarricaded vertical drop, measuring 4,700 m (15,420 ft) at its highest, which becomes even more deadly during the rainy season.

HIGHEST CONCERT ON LAND

The highest concert ever staged on land took place at an altitude of 6,069 m (19,911 ft) and was performed by Musikkapelle Roggenzell – 10 musicians from Germany and Bolivia – on Mount Acotango, Bolivia, on 6 August 2007.

FASTEST TIME TO CYCLE THE LENGTH OF SOUTH AMERICA

Giampietro Marion (Italy) cycled the South American portion of the Pan-American Highway – starting in Chigorodo, Colombia, and finishing in Ushuaia, Argentina – in a time of 59 days between 17 September and 15 November 2000. Chigorodo is the closest town (and road) geographically to the border with Panama, and is therefore a logical starting point for an attempt on the South American portion of the Pan-American highway.

★ LARGEST COLLECTION OF CACHAÇA BOTTLES

José Moisés de Moura from Pernambuco, Brazil, has collected a total of 6,850 different cachaça bottles since 1986. Cachaça, the most traditional and most consumed spirit in Brazil, is made from sugar cane and is similar to white rum.

LARGEST CEVICHE

A ceviche (a dish of raw seafood marinated in citrus juices) weighing 6,791.3 kg (14,972 lb) was served up at the Coliseo Cerrado Miguel Grau del Callao in Callao, Peru, on 7 December 2008. The recipe required 5 tonnes (5.5 tons) of raw fish (perico or dorado), 500 kg (1,102 lb) of lemons, 400 kg (881 lb) of onions, 100 kg (220 lb) of peppers and 100 kg (220 lb) of salt.

HIGHEST LIVING WILD CAMELID

The term "camelid" refers to any member of the family Camelidae, including camels, llamas and dromedaries. The vicuña (*Vicugna vicugna*) is the highest-living wild camelid, found at altitudes of up to 4,800 m (15,750 ft) in the Andes of South America, along with the alpaca, a domestic camelid.

May 8: Reinhold Messner (Italy) and Peter Habeler (Austria) made **the first successful ascent of Mount Everest without supplemental oxygen** on 8 May 1978.

CANADA

10

AT A GLANCE
- **AREA:**
9,984,670 km² (3,855,102 miles²)
- **POPULATION:**
33,212,696
- **HOUSEHOLDS:**
12.3 million
- **KEY FACTS:** Canada and the USA share the **longest boundary**, which (including the Great Lakes boundaries) extends for 6,416 km (3,986 miles). Canada also has the **longest coastline**, with 243,798 km (151,489 miles), including islands.

★ **NEW RECORD**
UPDATED RECORD

LONGEST STREET

The longest designated street in the world is Yonge Street, running north and west from Toronto, Canada. The first stretch, completed on 16 February 1796, ran 55 km (34 miles). Its official length, now extended to Rainy River on the Ontario–Minnesota border, is 1,896.3 km (1,178.3 miles).

★ FIRST UFO LANDING PAD

The world's first official UFO landing pad was built in the small Canadian prairie town of St Paul in Alberta, and was formally opened on 3 June 1967. A sign next to the pad includes the following words: "… future travel in space will be safe for all intergalactic beings; all visitors from earth or otherwise are welcome to this territory and to the Town of St Paul."

OLDEST NUN

Sister Anne Samson (Canada, b. 27 February 1891) became the oldest nun on 5 May 2003 when, at the age of 112 years 67 days, she beat the record set by Sister Julia (France, b. Augustine Teissier, 1869–1981). Sister Anne died on 29 November 2004, aged 113 years 276 days, at Maison Provinciale Des Filles De Jésus, Moncton, New Brunswick, Canada.

BUSIEST ROUTE FOR INTERNATIONAL TELEPHONE CALLS

According to TeleGeography, the busiest international telephone route is between the USA and Canada. In 2002, there were some 10.9 billion minutes of two-way traffic between the two countries.

CRAWLING – FASTEST MILE

The fastest time to crawl 1 mile (1.6 km) is 23 min 45 sec, set by Suresh Arulanantham Joachim (Canada) in Toronto, Ontario, Canada, on 23 January 2007.

DEEPEST LIVE RADIO BROADCAST

On 24 May 2005, Dan Lessard (Canada) of CBC Radio Points North hosted a two-hour show consisting of recorded material, live music and interviews from a refuge station located 2,340 m (7,680 ft) beneath Creighton Mine, Sudbury, Ontario, Canada.

LONGEST SURVIVING KIDNEY-TRANSPLANT PATIENT

Johanna Leanora Rempel (Canada, b. 24 March 1948) was given a kidney from her identical twin sister Lana Blatz on 28 December 1960 in an operation performed at the Peter Bent Brigham Hospital, Boston, Massachusetts, USA. Both Johanna and her sister have continued to enjoy excellent health and both have had healthy children.

HIGHEST BLOOD-SUGAR LEVEL

Travis Maynard (Canada, b. 13 May 1960) survived a blood-sugar level of 141 millimoles/litre (mmol/L), or 2,538 milligrams/deciliter (mg/dl), when admitted to the Chalmers Regional Hospital, Fredericton, Canada, in a hyperosmolar non-ketotic coma on 6 February 2003. The normal blood-sugar range is between 4.4 and 6.6 mmol/L (80–120 mg/dl).

LARGEST HOCKEY STICK

The largest hockey stick is 62.48 m (205 ft) long, weighs 28.12 tonnes (30.9 tons) and was commissioned by Canada's Federal Government for the Canadian Pavilion at the Expo 1986 in Vancouver, Canada. Since 21 May 1988, the hockey stick has been displayed alongside the Cowichan Community Centre in Duncan, Vancouver Island, Canada.

May 9: The Chicago White Sox and the Milwaukee Brewers (both USA) played the **longest baseball match** on this day in 1984. It lasted 8 hr 6 min and the Chicago White Sox eventually won 7–6.

May 10: The record for the **most people to parachute from a balloon simultaneously** is held by 20 members of the Paraclub Flevo (Netherlands), who jumped from 2,000 m (6,560 ft) on 10 May 2003.

1,025: the most push-ups (one arm, using back of hand) in one hour, set by Doug Pruden (Canada) on 8 November 2008.

MOST EXPENSIVE POP MEMORABILIA

John Lennon's (UK) 1965 Phantom V Rolls Royce was bought for $2,229,000 (£1,702,733) by Jim Pattison (Canada, above), Chairman of the Expo 86 World Fair in Vancouver, Canada, at Sotheby's, New York City, USA, on 29 June 1985.

FASTEST REVERSE DRIVE OVER 500 MILES

Rob Gibney (Canada) covered 807.39 km (501.69 miles) at an average speed of 66.67 km/h (41.42 mph) in a Ford Crown Victoria in Calgary, Canada, on 22 August 2004.

FASTEST TALKER

Sean Shannon (Canada) recited Hamlet's soliloquy "To be or not to be" (260 words) in a time of 23.8 seconds (655 words per minute) in Edinburgh, Scotland, UK, on 30 August 1995.

FARTHEST DISTANCE ON A SNOWMOBILE ON WATER

Riding a snowmobile, Kyle Nelson (Canada) covered 69.28 km (43.04 miles) on Cowan Lake, Saskatchewan, on 3 September 2005.

LARGEST JAZZ FESTIVAL

The Festival International de Jazz de Montreal in Quebec, Canada, attracted 1,913,868 people for its 25th anniversary year in July 2004.

HIGHEST TIDE EVER

A tidal range of 16.6 m (54 ft 6 in) was recorded at springs in Leaf Basin, Ungava Bay, Quebec, Canada, in 1953.

FASTEST RUN ACROSS CANADA (FEMALE)

Ann Keane (Canada) ran across the country from St John's, Newfoundland, to Tofino, British Columbia, in 143 days between 17 April and 8 September 2002. She covered a total of 7,831 km (4,866 miles) and ran for all but three of the days.

LONGEST MARATHON PLAYING STREET HOCKEY

The longest street-hockey marathon lasted 105 hr 17 min and was achieved in the fundraiser "Hockey for Life" in Lethbridge, Alberta, from 20 to 24 August 2008.

MOST BRIDESMAIDS TO ONE BRIDE

Accompanied by 79 bridesmaids, aged one to 79, bride Christa Rasanayagam married Arulanantham Suresh Joachim (both Canada) at Christ the King Catholic Church, Mississauga, Ontario, Canada, on 6 September 2003.

MOST LETTERS TO SANTA COLLECTED IN A CHRISTMAS SEASON

During the Christmas season in 2006, Santa received 1.06 million letters and 44,166 emails. More than 11,000 Canada Post volunteers helped respond to these letters in 11 languages, including Braille.

SHORTEST TV COMMERCIAL

The world's shortest TV commercial is just half a frame (one field) and lasts for 1/60 of a second. Twelve different versions of the commercial were produced, all advertising MuchMusic – a Canadian music and video TV channel – and the first was aired on 2 January 2002.

LONGEST CANTILEVER BRIDGE

The Quebec Bridge (Pont de Quebec) over the Saint Lawrence River in Canada has the longest cantilever truss span of in the world at 549 m (1,800 ft) between the piers and 987 m (3,239 ft) overall. It carries a railway track and two carriageways.

May 11: Marek Turowski (UK) achieved the record for the **fastest furniture** with a speed of 148 km/h (92 mph), driving a motorized sofa in Leicestershire, UK, on 11 May 2007.

AT A GLANCE
- **AREA:** UK 244,820 km² (94,526 miles²) **Ireland** 70,280 km² (27,135 miles²)
- **POPULATION:** 60,943,912
- **HOUSEHOLDS:** 27.6 million
- The UK's flag is the Union Jack, or Union Flag. It combines the Scottish Saltire (possibly dating as far back as 1385), the Irish Saltire (St Patrick's cross) and the St George cross. Interestingly, the flag has been adopted as the UK's national symbol but it is not recognized by any UK law.

LARGEST GATHERING OF ROBIN HOODS

Despite high winds and low temperatures, 1,119 people dressed in full Robin Hood costumes gathered at Castle Green, Nottingham, UK, on 8 March 2008. The attempt was to celebrate the link that the city has with the legend of Robin Hood – an English folkloric hero whose band of "merry men" famously "stole from the rich to give to the poor".

LARGEST MAYPOLE DANCE

Maypole dancing, common in England and parts of western Europe, involves dancing around a pole festooned with ribbons and flowers, and is thought to be part of a fertility rite. Each dancer holds a ribbon attached to the top of the pole and plaits the pole as they dance around it. The largest maypole dance involved 146 participants at an event organized by Congleton Town Council in Congleton, Cheshire, UK, on 21 May 2008.

MOST STYLES DANCED SIMULTANEOUSLY TO ONE MUSIC TRACK

The most styles danced simultaneously to one music track is 48 in an event organized by One Leicester and Leicester City Council at Humberstone Gate in Leicester, UK, on 5 October 2008.

★ LONGEST-WORKING PACEMAKER (PRESENT DAY)

The longest-working pacemaker still in use (as of July 2008) was fitted into Lesley Iles (UK) on 15 January 1982. The superfit mother remains active and has even run the London Marathon.

★ FIRST UFO SIGHTING BY A PILOT

On 31 January 1916, a British pilot near Rochford, Essex, reported seeing a row of lights, resembling the lighted windows on a train carriage, rising up into the sky and disappearing. Such "UFO" sightings are common, but those witnessed by pilots are given more credence as they are trained to identify objects in the night sky.

FIRST BUS SERVICE

The first municipal motor omnibus service in the world was inaugurated on 12 April 1903 and ran between Eastbourne railway station and Meads in East Sussex, UK.

BEST-SELLING ALBUM IN THE UK

Greatest Hits (released 2 November 1981) by UK rock band Queen is the top-selling album of all time in the UK, with sales of 5.75 million copies.

FACT
The popular image of Robin Hood – the original "man in tights" with the feathered cap and green tunic – was defined by the 1930's movie star Errol Flynn (Australia).

MOST TRACTORS PLOUGHING SIMULTANEOUSLY

On 5 August 2007, an incredible 4,572 veteran tractors (i.e. older than 30 years) ploughed the same field simultaneously at Cooley, County Louth, Ireland. Tractors turned up from more than 30 countries – including South Africa and Australia – and ranged from a 1903 Ivel to dozens of 1977 Massey Fergusons.

YOUNGEST GAMEKEEPER

The youngest gamekeeper is Robert Mandry (UK, b. 1 January 1994), who, at the age of 11 years 312 days, led his first professional shoot on his family's estate, Holdshott Farm, Hampshire, UK, on 9 November 2005. Robert led three further shoots during that season (October 2005–February 2006), all following the retirement of his predecessor, Colin Parsons (UK).

★ NEW RECORD ★ UPDATED RECORD

May 12: The **most expensive house sale** was set by Eric Hotung at 6-10 Black's Link, Hong Kong, China. It sold for HK$778.88 million (£62,767,500; $101,909,312) on 12 May 1997.

May 13: The **smallest rowboat to cross an ocean** is *Puffin*, measuring 4.65 m (15 ft 6 in) long, which was rowed by Graham Walters (UK) across the Atlantic, east to west, between 3 February and 13 May 2007.

14 min 34.69 sec: the fastest three-legged climb up the Canary Wharf Tower – the UK's tallest building – by Heather Derbyshire and Karen Fingerhut (both UK) on 6 April 2008.

LARGEST PHOTO MOSAIC

The largest photo mosaic measures 860.83 m² (9,265 ft²) and contains 112,896 individual photographs donated by the public. It was created by The Big Picture project and was unveiled in the Thinktank at the Millennium Point in Birmingham, UK, on 23 August 2008.

★ FIRST HABITABLE SAND HOTEL

In summer 2008, holidaymakers on Weymouth beach in Dorset, UK, could spend the night in a hotel made entirely of sand. A total of 600 hours were needed to build the open-air 15-m² (50-ft²) hotel. A family room with a double and single bed and a sea view (but no toilet!) cost £10 ($21) a night. The hotel was the brainchild of sculptor Mark Anderson (UK), who was commissioned by the website LateRooms.com.

LONGEST PLAY

We were saddened to hear of the death in August 2008 of British writer/performer Ken Campbell (UK), who was known for, among other things, directing the longest recorded theatrical production: The Warp. This ten-part play cycle, written by Neil Oram, was performed for 18 hr 5 min at London's Institue of Contemporary Art on 18–20 January 1979.

FASTEST-SELLING BOOKER PRIZE-WINNING BOOK

Roddy Doyle's (Ireland) 1993 Booker-winning novel Paddy Clarke Ha Ha Ha sold 27,000 copies in hardback within 30 minutes of bookshops opening on the day after the prize was awarded.

★ LARGEST FISHING VESSEL

The 145.6-m (477-ft), 14,055 gross-registered-tonnage Irish trawler Atlantic Dawn is the world's largest fishing vessel. Built at a cost of $72 million (£50 million) in Norway, she was launched in 2001. She has a crew of 60, is capable of processing 300 tonnes (661,386 lb) of fish per day and can carry 7,000 tonnes (7,716 tons) of frozen catch.

FASTEST ACCORDION PLAYER

Liam O'Connor (Ireland) played "Tico Tico" at a speed of 11.67 notes per second on the Rick O'Shea show on 2FM radio in Dublin, Ireland, on 8 November 2006.

★ LARGEST HOT CROSS BUN

Hot cross buns – spiced fruit buns marked with a cross (thought to represent a crucifix) – are traditionally eaten at Easter. The largest hot cross bun weighed 81.62 kg (179 lb 14 oz) and was made by Allied Bakeries Ireland at their factory in Belfast, UK, on 16 March 2005. Staff at the bakery used 37.5 kg (82 lb 10 oz) of flour, 16.8 kg (37 lb) of water, 7 kg (15 lb 7 oz) of currants and 6.3 kg (13 lb 14 oz) of sultanas to make the bun.

★ MOST SIBLINGS TO COMPLETE A MARATHON

The 15 siblings of the O'Donoghue family – Willie, Kieran, Teresa, Joseph, Pat, Robert, Mary, Margaret, Noel, Adelaide, James (Jim-bob), Brenda, Kevin, Louise and Cronan (all Ireland) – completed the Dublin City Marathon, Dublin, Ireland, on 29 October 2007.

UK & IRELAND

The UK comprises Great Britain (England, Wales and Scotland) and Northern Ireland (which occupies one-sixth of the island of Ireland). The country Ireland (or Eire) occupies the remaining five-sixths of the island.

★ LONGEST CAMOGIE MARATHON

A game of camogie – the women's varient of the Celtic game hurling – played by Croydon Camogie Club (UK) at Emerald GAA Grounds in Ruislip, UK, on 23–24 August 2008 lasted 24 hr 7 min.

May 14: The longest steak was produced by Jean-Yves Renard (France) and a group of butchers from Evron, France. It measured 27.68 m (90 ft 9 in) long on 14 May 2002.

GUINNESS WORLD RECORDS

FRANCE

AT A GLANCE

- **AREA:** 543,965 km² (210,026 miles²)
- **POPULATION:** 60.7 million
- **HOUSEHOLDS:** 25.5 million
- **KEY FACTS:** According to 2006 figures, France is the **most popular country for tourism**, with 79.1 million out of a total of 842 million international arrivals. Paris is also the **most popular city for tourism**, with 31 out of every 150 foreign tourists to the country arriving in the French capital.

LARGEST ATTENDANCE FOR A SPORTING EVENT

The largest attendance for a sporting event is an estimated crowd of 10 million over a period of three weeks for the annual Tour de France cycling race.

★ MOST KISSES GIVEN IN A MINUTE

Valentin Pasquier (France) kissed 94 people in one minute in Nantes, France, on 12 November 2008. The record for the **most kisses received in one minute** is 108, set by Solene Oudet (France) in Nantes, France, also on 12 November 2008.

★ MOST EXPENSIVE WALLPAPER

The most expensive wallpaper is entitled "Les Guerres D'Independence" (The Wars of Independence) and in January 2006 was priced at £24,896.50 ($44,091; €36,350) for a complete set of 32 panels, each measuring 3.8 m (12 ft 5 in) high and 0.47 m (18.5 in) wide. If the panels could be sold separately, the price per 1 m² (3 ft²) would be £432.83 ($766.53; €631.95). The military scene is created from 19th-century woodblock prints and takes over one year to finish. The wallpaper is made by Zuber in Rixheim, France, and exports mainly to the USA.

★ HIGHEST TRIPLE BACK SOMERSAULT

Jerry and Jary Souza (France) achieved a triple back somersault at a height of 10.5 m (34 ft 4 in) at the studios of *L'Émission des Records* in Paris, France, on 30 November 2001.

TALLEST BRIDGE

The 2,460-m-long (8,070-ft) Millau Viaduct across the Tarn Valley, France, is supported by seven concrete piers, the tallest of which measures 333.88 m (1,095 ft 4.8 in). The bridge, which was designed by Foster and Partners (UK) and opened in December 2004, has a maximum height of 343 m (1,125 ft) from its highest point to the deepest part of the valley below.

TOP 100 Records of the Decade

LARGEST FASHION SHOW AUDIENCE

The Victoria's Secret Fashion Show held in Cannes, France, on 18 May 2000, was watched by more than two million people around the world, who logged on to VictoriasSecret.com. Featuring models Tyra Banks (above), Karen Mulder and Stephanie Seymour, it raised over $2 million (£1.25 million) for charity.

LARGEST FESTIVAL OF FILMS

The largest film festival is the Festival international du film de Cannes held in the south of France every May. The event attracts between 40,000 and 50,000 movie industry workers each year.

LARGEST COLLECTION OF JET-FIGHTERS

Michel Pont (France) currently owns 110 jet-fighters. His hobby started in 1985 and includes Russian MiGs, British Jaguars, and French Mirages. He buys them from foreign governments but is not allowed to fly them in French airspace.

May 15: The **largest orchestra** consisted of 6,452 musicians and music students from throughout British Columbia, who gathered in Vancouver, Canada, on 15 May 2000.

ITALY
VISAS

AT A GLANCE
- **AREA:** 301,245 km² (116,311 miles²)
- **POPULATION:** 58.1 million
- **HOUSEHOLDS:** 22.6 million
- **KEY FACTS:** Italy played host to the **largest zoetrope**, a device 9.9 m (393 ft 6 in) in diameter built to create the illusion of moving images, on 4 December 2008. The capital Rome is home to the **largest masonry dome** – the Pantheon measures 43 m (142 ft) across and has the greatest span of any dome built only of masonry.

★ LARGEST COOKED HAM
The largest cooked ham weighed 25.82 kg (56 lb) and was made by Magrí SRL in Ancona, Italy, on 23 April 2008.

★ LARGEST PINZINO
A pinzino is a bread made of wheat, flour, water and lard, fried on both sides. The largest weighs 18 kg (39.6 lb) and was made by the residents of Vigarano Pieve, Italy, on 22 June 2002.

★ LONGEST COOKED SALAMI
A cooked salami measuring 11.55 m (37 ft 10 in) was made by the Pro Loco Association of Viguzzolo, Italy, on 22 February 2009.

YOUNGEST OPERA SINGER
Ginetta Gloria La Bianca (USA, b. 12 May 1934) sang the part of Gilda in *Rigoletto* at Velletri, Italy, on 24 March 1950, aged 15 years 316 days. She also appeared as Rosina in *The Barber of Seville* at the Teatro dell'Opera, Rome, Italy, on 8 May 1950, 45 days later.

LARGEST ACCORDION
The largest playable accordion is 2.53 m (8 ft 3.5 in) tall, 1.9 m (6 ft 2.75 in) wide, 85 cm (2 ft 9.5 in) deep and weighs approximately 200 kg (440 lb). Built by Giancarlo Francenella (Italy), the instrument bears the name "Castelfidardo", after the town of Ancona in which it was constructed.

FASTEST CANONISATION
St. Peter of Verona, Italy, died on 6 April 1252 and was canonised on 9 March 1253, just 337 days after his death. In modern times, Mother Teresa of Calcutta is the record holder, with her beatification being within two years of her death on 5 September 1997.

MOST POINTS BY A CONSTRUCTOR IN A FORMULA ONE SEASON
In the 2004 Formula One season, the Ferrari team (Italy) amassed 262 World Championship points. The team's drivers that year were Michael Schumacher (Germany, 148 points) and Rubens Barrichello (Brazil, 114 points). The team won 15 races out of a possible 18, Schumacher with 13 victories and Barrichello chipping in with two.

LONGEST PORCHETTA
Nicola Genobile (Italy) and her team made a porchetta measuring 31.08 m (102 ft) and weighing 1,214 kg (2,926 lb). It was presented to the public in the Auchan shopping centre in Pescara, Italy, on 17 January 2009.

LARGEST CHOCOLATE SCULPTURE
Mirco Della Vecchia (Italy) built a chocolate sculpture in the shape of the Dolomite mountains in Limana, Italy, on 15 March 2009. His creation weighed 3.55 tonnes (3.91 tons) and measured 2.4 m (8 ft 2 in) tall, 6.39 m (9 ft 10 in) wide and 1 m (3 ft 3 in) deep.

May 16: The **first Academy Awards** were held at the Hollywood Roosevelt, California, USA, on 16 May 1929 for films made in 1927–28.

May 17: The **most expensive diamond** is a "D" colour Internally Flawless pear-shaped gem weighing 100.10 carats. It was sold at auction for $16,561,171 (£10,548,444) on this day in 1995.

SPAIN

AT A GLANCE

- **AREA:** 504,782 km² (194,897 miles²)
- **POPULATION:** 40.4 million
- **HOUSEHOLDS:** 15.3 million
- **KEY FACTS:** On the last Wednesday in August, the town of Buñol, near Valencia, holds its annual tomato festival, the Tomatina – the **largest annual food fight**. In 2004, around 38,000 people spent one hour throwing about 124.96 tonnes (137.75 tons) of tomatoes at each other.

MOST PROLIFIC PAINTER

Pablo Diego José Francisco de Paula Juan Nepomuceno de los Remedios Crispín Cipriano de la Santísima Trinidad Ruíz y Picasso (Spain, 1881–1973) was the most prolific of all professional painters, boasting a career that lasted 75 years. Picasso produced an estimated 13,500 paintings and designs, 100,000 prints and engravings, 34,000 book illustrations and 300 sculptures and ceramics – an output valued at $788 million (£500 million).

MOST FLAMENCO TAPS IN ONE MINUTE (FEMALE)

Flamenco dancer Rosario Varela (Spain) rapped out 1,274 taps in one minute on the set of the *Guinness World Records* TV show in Madrid, Spain, on 23 January 2009.

LARGEST NIGHTCLUB

Privilege nightclub in San Rafael, Ibiza, Spain, can hold up to 10,000 people and covers an area of 6,500 m² (69,940 ft²). The club has been the island's main attraction since 1994.

★ FASTEST TIME TO SOLVE FIVE RUBIK'S CUBES ONE-HANDED

Using just one hand, David Calvo (Spain) solved five Rubik's Cubes in 2 min 27.78 sec on the set of *Guinness World Records* in Madrid, Spain, on 16 January 2009. Calvo is able to solve one cube with one hand in just 28 seconds!

★ LARGEST SEVILLANAS DANCE

A Sevillanas dance is performed to a type of folk music originating from Seville in the south of the country. The largest dance was performed by 492 people for an event organized by Embrujo Andaluz (Spain) at Luis Mariano Square, Irun, Spain, on 11 May 2008.

★ FASTEST TIME TO BREAK FIVE BOTTLES WITH THE PALM

Alberto Delgado (Spain) broke five glass bottles using the palm of one hand in 40.46 seconds on the set of *Lo Show Dei Record* in Madrid, Spain, on 23 February 2008.

HEAVIEST MAYOR

José Manuel Barros González, Mayor of Porriño, Spain, weighed in at 179.330 kg (395 lb 4 oz; 28 stone) in July 1999.

OLDEST RESTAURANT

Restaurante Botín in Calle de Cuchilleros, Madrid, was opened in 1725 by Jean Botín (France) and his Asturian wife. The restaurant is now run by the third generation of the Gonzalez family, and the original 18th-century interiors and firewood oven remain intact.

MOST WINS OF THE FOOTBALL (SOCCER) EUROPEAN CUP

Real Madrid (Spain) has won the European Champions Cup nine times: 1955–56, 1956–57, 1957–58, 1958–59, 1959–60, 1965–66, 1997–98, 1999–2000 and 2002. It is also the world's ★ **richest soccer club**, with an income of $577.9 million according to Deloitte's annual Football Money League.

LARGEST CHAIR

The world's largest chair measures 26 m (85 ft 4 in) tall with a seat 10 m (32 ft 10 in) wide. The outsize chair was created by the company Grupo Hermanos Huertas to advertise their furniture factory and was completed in April 2005. It was constructed in, and sits outside, the company's factory in Lucena, Spain.

May 18: The volcanic explosion of Mount St Helens in Washington State, USA, on 18 May 1980 triggered the **fastest recorded avalanche**, with a velocity of 402.3 km/h (250 mph).

May 19: The **largest magazine** measures 90.5 x 102.1 cm (35.63 x 40.20 in). Created by publisher Bayard Revistas S.A., it was unveiled in the Palacio de Congresos in Madrid, Spain, on this day in 2007.

PORTUGAL

GUINNESS WORLD RECORDS

AT A GLANCE
- **AREA:** 92,391 km² (35,672 miles²)
- **POPULATION:** 10.6 million
- **HOUSEHOLDS:** 3.9 million
- **KEY FACTS:** The **longest reign of any European monarch** was that of Afonso I Henriques of Portugal, who ascended the Portuguese throne on 30 April 1112 and died on 6 December 1185 after a reign of 73 years 220 days, first as Count and then (after 25 July 1139) as King.

★ **NEW RECORD**
★ **UPDATED RECORD**

COUNTRY FILE: PORTUGAL
During the 15th and 16th centuries, Portugal was an international power to rival Spain, England and France. However, the Napoleonic Wars, the devastation of its capital Lisbon in an earthquake and the loss of its colony, Brazil, in 1822 greatly weakened the country. In 1910, a revolution ended the reigning monarchy; its place was taken by a succession of hardline governments over the following 60 years. A more democratic form of government was established by a left-wing military takeover in 1974. Portugal became a member of the European Community (now the European Union) in 1986.

★ LARGEST SADDLE
Carlos Almeida and Manuel Nogueira (both Portugal) manufactured a saddle 2.92 m (9 ft 6 in) long, 1.20 m (3 ft 11 in) high at the front and 1.55 m (5 ft 1 in) high at the back. It was presented and measured in Torre de Dona Chama, Portugal, on 3 February 2008.

LARGEST HUMAN LOGO
On 24 July 1999, 34,309 people organized by Realizar Eventos Especias gathered at the National Stadium of Jamor, Lisbon, Portugal, to create the Portuguese logo for Euro 2004, as part of Portugal's bid to UEFA to hold the European football championships in 2004.

★ LARGEST EASTER EGG
A giant Easter egg was built and decorated by Freeport in Alcochete, Portugal, in March 2008. The enormous egg was 14.79 m (48 ft 6 in) long and 8.40 m (27 ft 6 in) in diameter when measured by Guinness World Records.

★ LONGEST REEF-KNOT CHAIN
On 14 April 2007, 224 participants tied 8,841 reef knots in five minutes, which resulted in a chain measuring a record 7,848 m (25,748 ft) long. The event was organized by Agrupamento 626 – Corpo Nacional de Escutas (Portugal) at the National Stadium in Linda-a-Velha, Portugal.

MOST WATCHES IN A CHAIN
A chain of 1,382 Swatch watches buckled together was displayed in Oeiras Parque, Lisbon, Portugal, on 2 December 2003.

HIGHEST UNDERWATER MOUNTAIN FACE
Monte Pico in the Azores, Portugal, has an altitude of 2,351 m (7,711 ft) above sea level and extends a record 6,098 m (20,000 ft) from the surface to the sea floor, making it the highest underwater mountain face.

LONGEST PAINTING
A 4,001.8-m-long (13,129-ft 2-in) painting was created by the Círculo Artístico e Cultural Artur Bual and the City of Amadora in Amadora, Portugal, on 15 September 2007.

LONGEST LOAF
The lengthiest loaf ever baked measured 1,211.6 m (3,975 ft) and was created by Município de Vagos, Ferneto, Máquinas e Artigos Para a Indústria Alimentar, Lda. and Comissião de Festas de Vagos in Vagos (Portugal) during the Bread and Bakers' Party on 10 July 2005. Over 100 bakers, mainly from Vagos' municipality, worked for over 60 hours to produce dough for the loaf.

LARGEST POCKET KNIFE
The world's largest pocket knife measures 3.9 m (12 ft 8 in) when open and weighs 122 kg (268 lb 14 oz). The handle is made of wood, weighs 97 kg (213 lb 12 oz) and measures 1.95 m (6 ft 4 in); the steel blade also measures 1.95 m (6 ft 4 in), but weighs 25 kg (55 lb). It was designed by Telmo Cadavez of Bragança, Portugal, and handmade by Virgílio, Raúl and Manuel Pires (all Portugal) on 9 January 2003.

May 20: The **most premature baby** was James Elgin Gill (Canada), born to Brenda and James Gill on 20 May 1987 in Ottawa, Ontario, Canada; 128 days premature, he weighed 624 g (1 lb 6 oz).

NORDIC COUNTRIES

AT A GLANCE

SWEDEN
- **AREA:** 449,964 km² (173,732 miles²)
- **POPULATION:** 9.2 million
- **HOUSEHOLDS:** 4.2 million

FINLAND
- **AREA:** 338,145 km² (130,558 miles²)
- **POPULATION:** 5.3 million
- **HOUSEHOLDS:** 2.4 million

NORWAY
- **AREA:** 323,802 km² (125,020 miles²)
- **POPULATION:** 4.7 million
- **HOUSEHOLDS:** 2.0 million

ICELAND
- **AREA:** 103,000 km² (39,768 miles²)
- **POPULATION:** 319,355
- **HOUSEHOLDS:** 116,000

DENMARK
- **AREA:** 43,094 km² (16,638 miles²)
- **POPULATION:** 5.5 million
- **HOUSEHOLDS:** 2.5 million

GREENLAND
(part of the Kingdom of Denmark)
- **AREA:** 2,166,086 km² (836,330 miles²)
- **POPULATION:** 57,600
- **HOUSEHOLDS:** 21,302

★ **NEW RECORD**
UPDATED RECORD

★ FASTEST GLIDER ASSEMBLY

Kouvola's Glider Association (Finland) assembled a glider and launched it to an altitude of 400 m (1,310 ft) in 1 min 40 sec at Selänpää Airport, Valkeala, Finland, on 10 July 2001.

★ MOST NORTHERLY FAST-FOOD RESTAURANT

The most northerly fast-food restaurant is The Red Polar Bear, a kebab shop owned by Kazem Ariaiwad (Iran). It is located on the island of Spitsbergen, far within the Arctic Circle, in the Svalbard archipelago 482 km (300 miles) off the northern tip of Norway.

OLDEST LIVING TREE

A 4-m-tall (13-ft) Norway Spruce discovered in the Dalarna province of Sweden in 2004 has been growing for 9,550 years.

★ MOST PEACEFUL COUNTRY

According to the 2008 Global Peace Index – which measures internal and external turmoil such as organized conflict and violent crime in an attempt to quantify peace – Iceland ranks as the most peaceful country. Denmark was in second place, with Iraq ranked last.

HIGHEST SCORE ON THE HUMAN DEVELOPMENT INDEX

The United Nations' Human Development Index takes into account income levels, adult literacy rates, number of years schooling and life expectancy to provide an indicator of quality of life. The more recent study, in 2008, places Iceland and Norway at joint first place, with an index of 0.968 (out of 1). At the foot of the list is Sierra Leone, with just 0.329.

LONGEST SKIS

The world's longest pair of skis measured an incredible 534 m (1,751 ft 11 in) – roughly 300 times longer than a regular pair – and were worn by 1,043 skiers simultaneously in an event organized by Danske Bank on Drottninggatan in Örebro, Sweden, on 13 September 2008. Owing to the warm weather conditions, the participants needed artificial snow in order to ski.

MOST PRODUCTIVE ICE FLOE

Disko Bay in northern Greenland, 300 km (185 miles) north of the Arctic Circle, produces an average of 18.14 million tonnes (20 million tons) of ice and icebergs a day. The glacier that produces the ice advances at around 2,530 m (8,300 ft) per day and produces icebergs from a front 10 km (6 miles) long.

May 21: The **largest walk** was The New Paper Big Walk 2000, which had 77,500 participants and started from the National Stadium, Singapore, on this day in 2000.

May 22: The **youngest successful climber of Mt Everest** is Ming Kipa Sherpa (Nepal), who reached the summit on 22 May 2003 at the age of 15.

GUINNESS WORLD RECORDS 2010

11

$0: amount spent by Iceland on defence in 2009, the **lowest military spending by capita** of any country in the world.

FASTEST UNSUPPORTED NORTH POLE TREK BY A FEMALE

The fastest unsupported trek to the North Pole by a female is 48 days 22 hr by Cecilie Skog, who left Ward-Hunt Island in the Arctic Ocean with teammates Rolf Bae and Per Henry Borch (all Norway) on 6 March 2006 and reached the North Pole on 24 April 2006.

HIGHEST-TAXED COUNTRY

In Denmark, the highest rate of personal income tax is, as of 2009, 52%. Overall tax revenue as a percentage of the country's Gross Domestic Product (GDP) is 50.0%.

LONGEST SPAN OF ELECTRICAL OVERHEAD POWERLINE

The Ameralik Span is the longest electrical overhead powerline in the world. It is situated near Nuuk on Greenland and crosses Ameralik fjord, which is 5.37 km (3.34 miles) wide.

DEEPEST CONCERT UNDER GROUND

On 4 August 2007, Agonizer (Finland) performed a concert staged 1,271 m (4,169 ft 11 in) below sea level at Pyhäsalmi Mine Oy in Pyhäjärvi, Finland.

NORDIC WALKING...

... is a fitness technique that involves walking with special poles that help work the upper body. The **most people Nordic walking simultaneously was 1,026 at the Lidingöloppet course in Sweden on 22 September 2006. Participants were required to walk a minimum of 3 km (1.8 miles).**

OLDEST NATIONAL FLAG IN CONTINUOUS USE

The oldest continuously used national flag is that of Denmark. The current design of a white Scandinavian cross on a red background was adopted in 1625 and its square shape in 1748. In Denmark, it is known as the "Dannebrog" or "Danish cloth".

★ LARGEST CAT WING-SPAN

So-called "winged cats" are domestic cats suffering from a rare genetic skin disorder called feline cutaneous asthenia (FCA). With this condition, the skin is exceptionally extensible, so that when the cat grooms itself or rubs itself against an object, the skin stretches into long, furry wing-like extensions. Sometimes, these "wings" can contain muscle tissue and can be raised up and down by the cat.

The largest confirmed wing-span was recorded in northern Sweden in June 1949. Examined by the State Museum of Natural History, the cat's wings were 58 cm (23 in) across. Pictured is a more recent case (2008) of FCA from Sichuan in southern China.

LEAST CORRUPT COUNTRY

As of 2008, the world's least corrupt countries were Denmark, New Zealand and Sweden, all of which achieved a score of 9.3 on Transparency International's Corruption Perceptions Index. This index compares the misuse of public office for private gain in more than 180 countries, as perceived by business and country analysts. Finland was fifth with a score of 9.0, and Somalia last with 1.0.

★ MOST NOBEL PRIZE LAUREATES PER CAPITA

According to the Nobel Foundation, Iceland has 3.36 Nobel Laureates for every 1 million head of population. Sweden runs a close second with 3.33 Laureates per million. The Foundation, established in 1900, is based on the last will of Alfred Nobel (Sweden, 1833–96), the inventor of dynamite, and recognizes achievements in physics, chemistry, physiology or medicine, literature and for peace.

May 23: The **most amount of money paid for a mobile phone number** is 10 million QAR ($2.75 million; £1.46 million), by an anonymous bidder for the number 666-6666 during a charity auction in Qatar on 23 May 2006.

GERMANY

AT A GLANCE
- **AREA:** 357,021 km² (137,846 miles²)
- **POPULATION:** 82.3 million
- **HOUSEHOLDS:** 39.4 million
- **KEY FACTS:** Munich's Oktoberfest 99 attracted 7 million visitors – the **largest beer festival**. Germany is a formidable sporting nation, winning the **most medals at a winter Olympic Games** – 35 at the XIX Winter Games, Salt Lake City, Utah, USA, in 2002.

★ LARGEST PET STORE
The Zoo Zajac, owned and managed by Norbert Zajac (Germany) and situated in Duisburg, Germany, covered an area of 8,070.26 m² (86,867.56 ft²) as of September 2005.

FURTHEST LEANING TOWER
The bell tower of the Protestant church in Suurhusen leaned at an angle of inclination of 5.1939 degrees when measured on 17 January 2007.

★ FASTEST VIOLINIST
The fastest recorded violin player is David Garrett (Germany), who played "Flight of the Bumblebee" in 1 min 5.26 sec on the set of *Guinness World Records: Die Größten Weltrekorde* in Germany on 20 December 2008.

LARGEST RAT KING
A rat king occurs when young rats living close to each other get their tails entangled and encrusted with dirt. The knot tightens when the rats pull and, being trapped, they cannot feed themselves and they die. The rat king with the greatest number of rats was found in a miller's chimney at Buchheim, Germany, in May 1828. It contained 32 individual rats.

★ LARGEST EASTER EGG TREE
The record for the largest Easter egg tree was set by Zoo Rostock, Rostock, Germany, who decorated a tree with 76,596 painted hen's eggs on 8 April 2007.

LARGEST INDOOR WATER PARK
The Tropical Islands Resort near Berlin, Germany is situated in a giant former airship hangar and is 360 m (1,181 ft) long, 210 m (689 ft) wide and covers 66,000 m² (710,400 ft²). The facility features a large body of water called the South Sea as well as a smaller lagoon, a rain forest area and a number of large beaches.

LARGEST PRETZEL
A prodigious pretzel weighing 382 kg (842 lb), measuring 8.20 m (26 ft 10 in) long and 3.10 m (10 ft 2 in) wide was made by Olaf Kluy and Manfred Keilwerth of Müller-Brot GmbH (both Germany) in Neufahrn, Germany, on 21 September 2008.

★ MOST JUICE EXTRACTED FROM GRAPES IN ONE MINUTE
The greatest amount of juice successfully extracted by treading grapes for one minute is 5.4 litres (1.19 gal). This pressing task was achieved by Martina Servaty (Germany) in Mesenich on 9 November 2008 in celebration of Guinness World Records Day.

LONGEST TIME TO HOLD ONE'S BREATH
Tom Sietas (Germany) held his breath under water for 17 min 33 sec on the set of *Guinness World Records* in Madrid, Spain, on 30 December 2008. The feat saw Sietas reclaiming the record from the illusionist David Blaine (USA), who held his breath for 17 min 4.4 sec on the set of The Oprah Winfrey Show in Chicago, Illinois, USA on 30 April 2008.

★ MOST MILK EXTRACTED FROM A COW IN TWO MINUTES
Gunther Wahl (Germany) squeezed 2 litres (0.4 gal) of milk from a cow on the set of *Guinness World Records: Die Größten Weltrekorde* in Germany on 19 December 2008.

May 24: Kåre Walkert (Sweden), who suffers from apnea – a breathing disorder – recorded the **loudest snore** at 93 dBA, while sleeping at the Örebro Regional Hospital, Sweden, on 24 May 1993.

May 25: The **fastest time to score a goal in a Champions League final** is 52 seconds, by Paolo Maldini (Italy) playing for AC Milan against Liverpool on 25 May 2005.

NETHERLANDS

AT A GLANCE
- **AREA:** 41,526 km² (16,033 miles²)
- **POPULATION:** 16.6 million
- **HOUSEHOLDS:** 7.2 million
- **KEY FACTS:** The **largest painting** (a seascape) measured 8,586 m² (92,419 ft²) and was completed by ID Culture at The Arena, Amsterdam, on 14 August 1996. The **largest solar energy roof** covered the exposition hall of the Floriade 2002, Haarlemmermeer. It was 26,110 m² (281,045 ft²) in size and had a generating capacity of 2.3 MW.

★ **NEW RECORD**
UPDATED RECORD

MOST DOMINOES TOPPLED BY A GROUP

A total of 4,345,027 dominoes were toppled on the set of Domino Day 2008 in Leeuwarden on 14 November 2008. At the same event, the **largest domino mosaic** was created, comprising 1,011,732 dominoes and measuring 500 m² (5,382 ft²).

LARGEST CLOG DANCE
Introdans Education and Dance and Child International organized a clog dance involving 475 participants at the Spuiplein in the Hague, the Netherlands, on 8 July 2006.

FIRST EVIDENCE OF *HOMO ERECTUS*
Homo erectus (upright man), the direct ancestor of *Homo sapiens*, was discovered by Eugéne Dubois (Netherlands) at Trinil, Java, in 1891. The Javan *H. erectus* remains were dated to 1.8 million years in 1994.

FACT
The greatest distance covered on a land rowing machine is 5,278.5 km (3,280 miles), by Rob Bryant of Fort Worth, Texas, USA, who rowed across the USA in 1990.

★ TALLEST POPULATION
The Dutch are the world's tallest citizens, with the average male measuring 184 cm (6 ft) tall. Studies show that by 2012, Dutch men will average 186 cm (6 ft 1 in) and Dutch women 172 cm (5 ft 7 in). In early 2000, activists persuaded the Dutch government to raise the ceiling levels stipulated in the nation's building codes by 20 cm (7.8 in).

MOST PEOPLE ON ROWING MACHINES
The largest rowing class consisted of 165 people rowing simultaneously in an event organized by Boekel De Neree Advocaten and civil law notaries at Gustav Mahlerplein in Amsterdam, the Netherlands, on 14 August 2008.

★ LONGEST PERGOLA
A pergola measuring 40.42 m (132 ft 7 in) long and covered by leaves and grapes was created by Lidy and Niek Reijnen (both Netherlands). It was measured in Noord Beveland, the Netherlands, on 22 August 2005.

TALLEST WORKING WINDMILL
De Noord Molen at Schiedam, the Netherlands, is a windmill that stands 33.33 m (109 ft 4 in) tall. However, there are other – disused – Dutch windmills that are taller.

GREATEST ART ROBBERY
On 14 April 1991, 20 paintings, together estimated to be worth $500 million (£281.6 million), were stolen from the Van Gogh Museum in Amsterdam, the Netherlands.

FASTEST KNITTER
Miriam Tegels (Netherlands) hand-knitted 118 stitches in one minute at the Swalmen Townhall, the Netherlands, on 26 August 2006.

DID YOU KNOW?
Scientists think the reason that Dutch people are so tall is the amount of milk and cheese in their diet. These foods are rich in the nutrients needed for growth.

May 26: On this day in 1969, the crew of the *Apollo 10* command module reached a speed of 39,897 km/h (24,790.8 mph) – the **fastest speed at which humans have ever travelled.**

EASTERN & CENTRAL EUROPE

AT A GLANCE
- **AREA:** 3,554,034 km² (1,372,220 miles²)
- **POPULATION:** 216.8 million
- **COUNTRIES:**

Central Europe: Austria, Czech Republic, Hungary, Liechtenstein, Poland, Slovakia, Slovenia and Switzerland.

Eastern Europe: Belarus, Estonia, Latvia, Lithuania, Moldova, Romania and Ukraine.

South-eastern Europe: Albania, Bulgaria, Bosnia and Herzegovina, Croatia, Greece, Kosovo, Macedonia, Montenegro, Serbia and part of Turkey.

★ LARGEST ENAMEL IMAGE
Susanne Zemrosser (Austria) created an enamel mural measuring 50.63 m (166 ft 1 in) long and 2.61 m (8 ft 6 in) high. It was installed at the Praterstern subway station in Vienna, Austria, on 10 May 2008.

★ FARTHEST FLIGHT BY A PARAGLIDER (FEMALE)
Petra Krausova (Czech Republic) flew a distance of 302.9 km (188.2 miles) by paraglider from Quixada, Brazil, on 18 November 2005.

★ LARGEST COFFEE POT
The food and coffee-processing company Vispak d.d. completed a coffee pot measuring 1.24 m (4 ft 1 in) tall with a base diameter of 95 cm (37.4 in) in Visoko, Bosnia and Herzegovina, in June 2004.

★ MOST ENDURING OLYMPIC TORCH BEARER
Pandelis Konstantinidis (Greece) took part in the 2008 Olympic torch relay procession, 72 years after taking part in the 1936 torch relay.

★ LARGEST CHOCOLATE FIREWORK
The food company Nestlé made a chocolate firework measuring 3 m (9 ft 9 in) high and 1.5 m (4 ft 10 in) in diameter, designed to fire 60 kg (132 lb) of Swiss Cailler chocolates into the air. The firework was released on 31 December 2002 and showered its chocolatey payload over Hechtplatz in Zürich, Switzerland.

FACT
After the event, the beach towel was cut into small pieces and given away to all involved as a memento of the occasion.

LARGEST BEACH TOWEL
To celebrate the start of the summer tourist season in Cyprus, Bookcyprus.com and Aeolos Travel organized the manufacture of a massive beach towel measuring 64.2 m (210 ft 8 in) long by 31 m (101 ft 9 in) wide. Fittingly, the towel was laid on the beach at Fig Tree Bay in Protaras, Cyprus, for a party held on 1 June 2008.

★ LARGEST CORK MOSAIC
Saimir Strati (Albania) built a cork mosaic on the theme "Mediterranea" measuring 12.94 m (42 ft 6 in) wide by 7.1 m (23 ft 4 in) tall at the Sheraton Tirana Hotel in Tirana, Albania, between 8 August and 4 September 2008. The mosaic, which has an area of 91.8 m² (988 ft²), required 229,675 bottle corks.

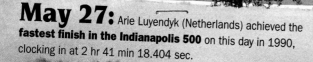

May 27: Arie Luyendyk (Netherlands) achieved the **fastest finish in the Indianapolis 500** on this day in 1990, clocking in at 2 hr 41 min 18.404 sec.

May 28: On this day in 2000, the **longest parade of Rolls-Royce cars** took place when 420 vehicles formed a 3.2-km (2-mile) procession on the A55 near Chester, UK.

15.52 m (50 ft 11 in): the longest **piece of chalk**, made by Vladimír Micenke and staff at his firm, Amice Košice, in Košice, Slovakia, in May 2000.

MOST MENTOS AND SODA FOUNTAINS

Students of the School of Business Administration Turiba in Riga, Latvia, celebrated their school's 15th anniversary by breaking a world record. On 19 June 2008, the students managed to make a total of 1,911 Mentos and soda fountains at the same time.

★ LARGEST RUBBER STAMP

A rubber stamp seal measuring 1.3 m (4 ft 3 in) tall and 1 m (3 ft 3 in) in diameter was unveiled at the Brand of the Year Awards in Kiev, Ukraine, on 6 June 2002. The stamp, which weighs 102.6 kg (226 lb), was made from rubber and walnut and cherry wood.

LONGEST STRAW CHAIN

Petru Pognaru, Marcu Cristi and 27 students (all Romania) made a straw chain measuring 11.29 km (7 miles) using 58,469 drinking straws. The chain was made at Dacia Square, Buzau, Romania, on 10 July 2008 and covered most of the surface of the public space.

LARGEST PARADE OF FIRE TRUCKS

Vogt Ltd Fire Service Accessories and Vehicles held a parade of 159 fire trucks in Oberdiessbach, Switzerland, on 28 April 2006.

HIGHEST RATE OF UNEMPLOYMENT (COUNTRY)

According to the International Labour Organization definition of unemployment, the country with the highest rate of unemployment is Macedonia, where 36% of the labour force is without a job, despite being available for work.

★ FASTEST SPEED WITH AN ICE STOCK

Ice stock is a winter sport similar to curling that uses gliding stones with long poles protruding from their middle. Bernhard Patschg (Austria) managed to accelerate his ice stock to an amazing speed of 67.16 km/h (41.73 mph) at Lake Stubenberg, Austria, on 30 January 2005.

★ LARGEST LEGAL DOCUMENT

The largest legal document is an insurance policy measuring 9 m (29 ft 4 in) tall by 6 m (19 ft 8 in) wide, issued by ING Asigurari de Viata of Romania. It was signed in Varna, Bulgaria, on 15 March 2008.

★ **NEW RECORD**
UPDATED RECORD

★ LARGEST DANCE (COUPLES)

A total of 1,635 couples danced the "cha-cha-cha" for five minutes in the market square in Kraków Old Town, Kraków, Poland, for the TV programme *You Can Dance* on 31 August 2008.

May 29: At 11:30 a.m. on 29 May 1953, Edmund Percival Hillary (New Zealand) and Sherpa Tenzing Norgay (Nepal) became the **first people to reach the summit of Mount Everest.**

RUSSIA

AT A GLANCE
- **AREA:** 17,075,200 km² (6,592,771 miles²)
- **POPULATION:** 140.7 m
- **HOUSEHOLDS:** 53.0 m
- **KEY FACTS:** Russia is facing a population crisis, with a growth rate in 2008 of -0.08%. Not only are there more abortions than births, the death rate is considerably higher than in mainland Europe (the average life expectancy for males in Russia is 61.5 years, which is 10 years below the European average).

BUSIEST METRO NETWORK
The Greater Moscow Metro carries up to 9 million passengers a day (compared with 4.5 million in the New York Subway and 3 million in the UK Tube) between its 177 stations. In all, 9,915 trains run over 12 lines totalling 292.2 km (81 miles) of track.

LARGEST COUNTRY
Russia is the largest country in the world. It has an area of 17,075,200 km² (6,592,771 miles²), or 11.5% of the world's total land area. It is 70 times larger than the UK, and had a population of 140,702,096 in July 2008.

HIGHEST PERSONAL MAJORITY
The highest ever personal majority for any politician has been 4,726,112 in the case of Boris Nikolayevich Yeltsin (b. 1 February 1931), the people's deputy candidate for Moscow, in the parliamentary elections held in the Soviet Union on 26 March 1989. Yeltsin received 5,118,745 votes out of the 5,722,937 that were cast in the Moscow constituency; his closest rival obtained 392,633 votes.

★ LARGEST AERIAL FIREFIGHTING FORCE
The Avialesookhrana of Russia, established in 1931, is the world's largest aerial firefighting force and was the first of its kind in the world. There are currently 4,000 "smokejumpers" in the force, who cover a forested area of 2 billion acres (809 million ha).

LONGEST JOURNEY BY TRACTOR
Vasilii Hazkevich (Russia) covered 21,199 km (13,172 miles) on an unmodified tractor from 25 April to 6 August 2005, starting and finishing in Vladimir, Russia.

MOST TANKS IN ONE ARMY
In 2006, the Russian Federation was credited with at least 22,831 Main Battle Tanks (MBT), making it the army with the most tanks in the world. China has about 7,580 MBTs, while the USA possesses approximately 7,620.

LARGEST BOARD GAME TOURNAMENT
A record 1,214 people played chess in the Central Park of Krasnoyarsk in Siberia, Russia, on 2 June 2007. A shot was fired to start the first round of games, and the 32 semi-finalists played a knock-out lightning tournament. The event was organized with the help of the city's Education Department.

HIGHEST CLOCK
Positioned 229 m (751 ft 3 in) above street level on top of the Federation Tower "West" in Moscow, Russia, the world's highest clock was activated on 24 April 2008.

GREATEST TEMPERATURE RANGE ON EARTH
The greatest recorded temperature ranges in the world are around the Siberian "cold pole" in the east of Russia. Temperatures in Verkhoyansk (67°33'N, 133°23'E) have ranged 105°C (188°F), from a coldest point of -68°C (-90°F) to a warmest of 37°C (98°F).

★ NEW RECORD   UPDATED RECORD

May 30: Ray Harroun (USA), driving the Marmon Wasp, was the **first ever winner of the Indianapolis 500** race (then known as the "International Sweepstakes") on this day in 1911.

May 31: The **oldest recorded bride** is Minnie Munro (Australia), who married 83-year-old Dudley Reid at Point Clare, New South Wales, Australia, on this day in 1991, aged 102 years!

ISRAEL

AT A GLANCE

- **AREA:** 20,770 km² (8,019 miles²)
- **POPULATION:** 6.8 m
- **HOUSEHOLDS:** 2.1 m
- **KEY FACTS:** Per capita, Israel has the ★ **greatest weapon holdings** of any country, with 2,546,600 weapons per 1 million people. According to the Center for International Policy, Israel is also the ★ **recipient of the most US military exports**, with the equivalent of $259.83 (£182.75) spent for every 1,000 people.

★ LARGEST *PAPIER MÂCHÉ* SCULPTURE

The largest *papier mâché* sculpture has a height of 2.10 m (6 ft 10 in) and a circumference of 6.60 m (21 ft 7 in). The model of the globe was presented at Ma'a lot Meshulam School in Rehovot, Israel, on 5 May 2008.

LONGEST-SERVING PRISONER IN SOLITARY CONFINEMENT

Mordecai Vanunu (Israel) spent nearly 12 years in a total isolation jail cell – the longest known term of solitary confinement in modern times. Born in 1954, Vanunu was convicted of treason for giving information about Israel's nuclear programme to *The Sunday Times* (UK) newspaper. He was sentenced to a total of 18 years, and spent from 1986 until March 1998 in total isolation. He remained incarcerated until he was released on 21 April 2004, although he has been arrested several times since then for violating the conditions of his release.

★ LARGEST TABBOULEH

A bowl of tabbouleh weighing 2,170 kg (4,784 lb) was made by the citizens of Majdal Shams, Israel, on 21 March 2008.

★ HIGHEST MALE YOUTH LITERACY RATE

In the 15–24 age group, male literacy rates are at a record high of 100% in Israel. According to the World Development Indicators database 2006, literacy is the ability of a person to "read and write a short, simple statement on their everyday life". Israeli women of the same age score 99.6% (at No.1 is Cuba, with a score of 100%).

★ MOST INJURIES FROM TERRORIST ATTACKS

In recent years (1968–2006), more Israelis have suffered injuries in terrorist attacks than any other people, with 1,165.73 injuries per 1 million of population, according to the Memorial Institute for the Prevention of Terrorism (MIPT) Terrorism Knowledge Base. Iraq is in second place with 706.49 injuries per million and the West Bank third with 653.39.

HEAVIEST LEMON

The world's heaviest lemon weighed 5.265 kg (11 lb 9.7 oz) on 8 January 2003 and was grown by Aharon Shemoel (Israel) on his farm in Kefar Zeitim, Israel. The lemon's circumference was 74 cm (29 in) and it was 35 cm (13.7 in) high. The record-breaking citrus fruit grew with another large lemon.

HIGHEST CONSUMPTION OF PROTEIN (COUNTRY)

Israel consumes more protein than any other country, according to the United Nations, with every Israeli eating 128.6 g (4.53 oz) every day. The world average is 75.3 g (2.65 oz).

Jun 1: Herbert Fisher and Zelmyra Fisher (both USA) achieved the **longest marriage of a living couple** on this day in 2008 at the grand old age of 84 years 50 days!

THE MIDDLE EAST

AT A GLANCE

- **AREA:** 7,158,624 km² (2,763,954 miles²)
- **POPULATION:** 340.7 m
- **COUNTRIES:** Bahrain, Egypt, Iran, Iraq, Jordan, Kuwait, Lebanon, Oman, Qatar, Saudi Arabia, Syria, Turkey, United Arab Emirates (UAE) and Yemen.

(As the Middle East is not a strictly definable region, we have opted to include the Gulf states and Egypt here. For information on Israel, see p.125.)

OFF ROAD

Hesham Nessim's journey began at 6:45 a.m. on 5 March 2009 when he set off from the north of El Gilf Plateau at the south of the Great Sand Sea. He covered a distance of 650 km (403 miles) in 5 hr 33 min when he reached the finish line in Siwa at 12:18 p.m. GWR judges were informed with location updates each hour via GPS.

OLDEST PAINTING ON A CONSTRUCTED WALL

On 2 October 2006, the French archaeological mission (leader Eric Coqueugniot, pictured right) at Dja'de al-Mughara – a Neolithic settlement on the Euphrates River near Aleppo, Syria – found walls of a house that bore a series of polychrome geometric paintings. Measuring 2 m x 2 m (6 ft 6.7 in x 6 ft 6.7 in), the wall is believed to date from c. 9000 BC.

LEAST TAXED COUNTRY

The sovereign countries with the least personal income tax are Bahrain and Qatar, where the rate, regardless of income, is nil.

LOWEST RATE OF DEATH

The United Arab Emirates has the fewest deaths per 1,000 population, with a projection of 1.4 per 1,000 for the period 2005–10.

HIGHEST RATE OF DIABETES

The United Arab Emirates (UAE) has the highest percentage of type-II diabetes in the population (20% between 20 and 79 years of age). Two other Gulf states feature in the top 10 list of diabetics: Kuwait (12.8%) and Oman (11.4%). At joint second place are Cuba and Puerto Rico, with 13.2%.

★ MOST CROWDED NETWORK OF ROADS

Qatar has 283.6 registered motor vehicles per kilometre (0.62 miles) of road, in theory making its roads the most crowded in the world, according to figures available in 2007.

★ LARGEST STEEL PLATE

A steel serving plate measuring 10.06 m x 2.03 m (33 ft x 6 ft 7 in) was crafted in Liwa, UAE, on 31 July 2008 for the 4th Liwa Festival. The dish was filled with 2 tonnes (2.2 tons) of dates.

★ LARGEST ACRYLIC PANEL

The largest single acrylic panel is an aquarium window at The Dubai Mall, Dubai, United Arab Emirates, that measures 32.88 m x 8.3 m (107 ft 10 in x 27 ft 2 in). It was completed on 25 July 2008.

FACT

The oldest painted wall features a geometric pattern of red (from burnt hematite rock), white (crushed limestone) and black (charcoal), not unlike the Persian art seen in carpets and rugs.

LARGEST SINGLE HUMANITARIAN OPERATION

The world's largest and most expensive humanitarian operation was undertaken by the United Nations World Food Programme (WFP), feeding the 27.1 million people in Iraq displaced by war. The food-aid operation began on 1 April 2003 and finished in late October 2003 with 2.2 million tonnes (2.4 million tons) of food commodities being delivered under a budget of $1.5 billion (£927 million; €1.3 billion).

★ FASTEST VEHICLE CROSSING THE GREAT SAND SEA

The record for the fastest crossing of the Great Sand Sea – the Sahara Desert – by a vehicle is 5 hr 33 min, achieved by Hesham Nessim (Egypt) between the Gilf Kebir Plateau and the Siwa Oasis in Egypt on 5 March 2009.

Jun 2: The **first radio patent** was granted on this day in 1896 to the Italian-Irish Marchese Guglielmo Marconi GCVO (1874–1937).

2,600,000 km² (1 million miles²): the area of the Arabian Desert, the world's **sandiest desert**, one third of which is completely covered in sand.

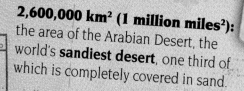

GUINNESS WORLD RECORDS

★ LARGEST MORTARBOARD

A giant mortarboard – a square academic headdress, so named because it resembles a bricklayer's cement palate – was made by HQ Link and the Bahrain Convention & Exhibition Bureau. The cap, which measured 6 m x 6 m (19 ft 8 in x 19 ft 8 in), was displayed at the Career, Education and Training Middle East 2006 exhibition in Manama, Bahrain, on 18 April 2006.

LARGEST ITEM ON A MENU

The largest item on any menu in the world is roasted camel, prepared very occasionally for Bedouin wedding feasts. The elaborate dish includes cooked eggs that are stuffed into fish; the fish are then stuffed into cooked chickens, and the chickens stuffed into a roasted sheep's carcass. Lastly, the sheep is stuffed into the whole camel.

LARGEST PERCENTAGE OF POPULATION TO ATTEND A FUNERAL

Official estimates gave the size of the crowds lining the 32-km (20-mile) route to Tehran's Behesht-e Zahra cemetery on 11 June 1989 for the funeral of Ayatollah Ruhollah Khomeini as 10,200,000 people. This figure represented one-sixth of Iran's population at that time.

THICKEST WALLS

Ur-nammu's city walls at Ur (now Muqayyar, Iraq), destroyed in 2006 BC, were 27 m (88 ft) thick and made of mud brick.

LONGEST PITA BREAD

Pita bread – or Arabic bread, as it's known in the Middle East – is widely used in many Middle Eastern and Mediterranean cuisines. The longest ever made measured 128.5 m (421 ft 6 in) – over two and a half times longer than an Olympic swimming pool – and was produced by a team from Jana Bakers LLC of Doha, Qatar, on 4 December 2008.

★ OLDEST SURVIVING PERSONAL NAME

The earliest surviving personal name is that of a predynastic king of Upper Egypt *ante* 3050 BC, who is indicated by the hieroglyphic sign for a scorpion. It has been suggested that the name should be read as Sekhen.

COSTLIEST CAVIAR

The most expensive of all caviar, and indeed the world's most expensive food, is "Almas", from the Iranian beluga fish. A single kilogram (2 lb 3 oz) of this "black gold" is regularly sold for £20,000 ($34,500). Almas is produced from the eggs of a rare albino sturgeon between 60 and 100 years old.

HIGHEST ALTITUDE MOSQUE

The King Abdullah Mosque on the 77th floor of the Kingdom Centre building in Riyadh, Saudi Arabia, is 183 m (600 ft) above ground level and was completed on 5 July 2004.

TOP 100 Records of the Decade

OLDEST CULTIVATED PLANT FOR DRINK

Among the oldest cultivated plants that are used primarily for drink are grapes (*Vitis vinifera*). The earliest evidence proving that grapes were cultivated to make wine dates to 6000 BC in Mesopotamia (modern-day Iraq). The earliest physical proof of wine being stored and drunk comes from pottery excavations made in 1968 in Iran and dating to c. 5000 BC. But it was the ancient Egyptians, in 3000 BC, who first recorded the process of winemaking, known as viticulture.

★ LARGEST BOOK

The world's largest book measures 3.85 m x 2.77 m (12 ft 7 in x 9 ft 1 in), weighs 1,060 kg (2,336 lb 9 oz) and consists of 304 pages. It is a recreation of a bestselling photography book, *Beirut's Memory*, which depicts the changing face of the Lebanese capital between 1991 and 2002. It was made by photographer Ayman Trawi (Lebanon) – the Lebanese Prime Minister Rafic Hariri's personal photographer – and displayed in Beirut on 27 February 2009.

★ **NEW RECORD**
★ **UPDATED RECORD**

HEAVIEST MEDALLION

A medallion with a 1 m (39.37 in) diameter and a thickness of 2.3 cm (0.9 in) weighed in at 185.88 kg (409 lb 12 oz) on 15 December 2008. It was made by Damas jewellery (UAE), one of the Middle East's leading jewellery retailers, to mark the 10th anniversary of the Sheikh Hamdan Al Maktoum Medical Science award. The medallion has a value of 1 million UAE dirhams or AED ($272,257; £186,006) and was made of solid fine silver plated with 22 carat gold. It took 85 jewellers a total of 30 days to craft this unique piece.

HH Sheikh Hamdan Bin Rashid Al Maktoum

(127)

WWW.GUINNESSWORLDRECORDS.COM

Jun 3: On this day in 2005, Fu Haifeng (China) hit a shuttlecock at a measured speed of 332 km/h (206 mph), the **fastest recorded speed of a shuttlecock**.

Jun 4: The **largest rideable bicycle**, as measured by the wheel diameter, is "Frankencycle", ridden by Steve Gordon (USA) on 4 June 1989. The wheel diameter is 3.05 m (10 ft) and the bike is 3.4 m (11 ft 1 in) high.

AFRICA

AT A GLANCE

- **AREA:** 31,107,983 km² (12,010,859 miles²)
- **COUNTRIES:** Algeria, Angola, Benin, Botswana, Burkina Faso, Burundi, Cameroon, Cape Verde, Central African Republic, Chad, Comoros, Côte d'Ivoire, D. R. Congo, Djibouti, Equatorial Guinea, Eritrea, Ethiopia, Gabon, Gambia, Ghana, Guinea, Guinea-Bissau, Kenya, Lesotho, Liberia, Libya, Madagascar, Malawi, Mali, Mauritania, Mauritius, Morocco, Mozambique, Namibia, Niger, Nigeria, Republic of the Congo, Réunion, Rwanda, Saint Helena, São Tomé and Príncipe, Senegal, Seychelles, Sierra Leone, Somalia, South Africa, Sudan, Swaziland, Tanzania, Togo, Tunisia, Uganda, Zambia, Zimbabwe.

★ OLDEST HUMAN ANCESTOR INFANT

"Selam" was a three-year-old female of the species *Australopithecus afarensis*, ancestors of human beings that lived 3.3 million years ago. Her remains were discovered on 10 December 2000 by a team led by Zeresenay Alemseged (Ethiopia) in Dikika, Ethiopia. The fossilized remains include a skull, a complete torso, fingers and a foot.

★ HIGHEST ECONOMIC GROWTH (COUNTRY)

In the period 1996–2006, Equatorial Guinea in Central Africa saw the highest annual percentage increase in real Gross Domestic Product (GDP), with a rise of 33.7%. GDP is the most commonly used indicator of an economy's health and is the combined sum of money made by the wealth-generating sectors of the economy, such as manufacturing, retailing and service industries.

★ LOWEST RATE OF CAR OWNERSHIP

Of the seven countries with the lowest rate of car ownership in the world, five are African: Burundi, Central African Republic, Ethiopia, Rwanda and Tanzania all have a rate of one car per 1,000 population, according to current figures. By contrast, the wealthy European state Luxembourg has 647 cars per 1,000, or one for every 1.5 people.

★ HIGHEST RATIO OF PATIENTS TO DOCTOR (COUNTRY)

Doctors in Malawi have more patients – 49,624 each, according to *The Economist* – than doctors in any other country.

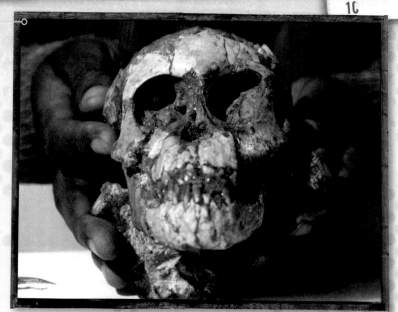

★ HIGHEST RATE OF DEATH

Swaziland has a projected death rate of 22.1 deaths per 1,000 population, for the period 2005–10. The landlocked kingdom in southern Africa also has the **lowest life expectancy in the world** – with the average male living to just 39.6 years – and the **highest rate of death from AIDS**, with 1,455 deaths per 100,000 population.

★ HIGHEST BIRTH RATE

Based on figures for 2007, the Democratic Republic of the Congo and Guinea-Bissau share the record crude birth rate of 50 births per 1,000 population. By contrast, Germany and Macau have eight births per 1,000 people.

LARGEST GAME OF PICK-UP STICKS

Sticks measuring 9.10 m (29 ft 10.3 in) long and 14.5 cm (5.7 in) in diameter were used in a giant game of pick-up sticks by pupils of St John's Preparatory School in Harare, Zimbabwe, on 21 July 2007.

LARGEST SCENTED GARDEN

The Kirstenbosch National Botanical Gardens on the slopes of Table Mountain, Cape Town, South Africa, covers 36 hectares (88.9 acres). The Fragrance Garden includes a braille trail and many aromatic plants, offering the opportunity for blind and visually impaired visitors to enjoy the experience.

FIRST FEMALE TO BE FIRST LADY OF MORE THAN ONE COUNTRY

Graca Machel was married to Samora Machel (1933–86), President of Mozambique, from 1975 to 1986. President Machel was killed in a plane crash on 19 October 1986. On 18 July 1998, Graca married Nelson Mandela (seated), President of South Africa, making her the first woman to be "First Lady" of two different countries.

Jun 5: On 5 June 1966, N. William Kennedy (Canada) slashed free the mooring lines of the 10,639-dwt SS Orient Trader, which then became the **largest object stolen by an individual**.

Jun 6: Minoru Saito (Japan) was 71 when he completed a non-stop solo circumnavigation in his 15-m (50-ft) yacht *Shuten-doji II* in 2005, becoming the **oldest person to sail around the world**.

160,000: the age, in years, of the **oldest remains of modern humans**. They were found in Ethiopia by a team of scientists led by Tim White (USA).

HIGHEST EDUCATION BUDGET

Lesotho, the landlocked country that is entirely surrounded by the Republic of South Africa, put 13% of its GDP into education, according to the latest annual figures available for 2003–07, which is more than any other nation.

The ★ **lowest budget for education** is Equatorial Guinea with 0.6%, according to the latest available figures.

LONGEST COMMERCIALLY OPERATED SINGLE-DROP ABSEIL

A single-drop abseil of 204 m (670 ft) can be experienced down the Maletsunyane waterfall at the Semonkong Lodge in Semonkong, Lesotho. The abseil is commercially operated on a daily basis but, because of the training required, only four people generally make the drop every day.

★ HIGHEST FERTILITY RATE (COUNTRY)

Fertility rates are determined by the ratio of children to each adult female. The country with the highest rate is Niger with 6.88 children per female, based on projected averages for 2010–15. Niger has one of the world's fastest growing populations, with a predicted increase of 41 million from 12 million (2004) to 53 million (2050).

SOUTH AFRICA

★ LONGEST KEBAB

A kebab measuring 2.047 km (1.271 miles) was prepared by the ArcelorMittal Newcastle Works on the occasion of the company's annual Community Day in Newcastle, South Africa, on 11 October 2008.

LARGEST WINE CELLAR

The wine cellars at Paarl of the Koöperatiewe Wijnbouwers Vereniging in Cape Province, in the centre of the wine-growing district of South Africa, cover an area of 22 ha (54 acres) – the equivalent of over 40 football fields – and have a capacity of 121 million litres (26.6 million gal) – enough to fill approximately 1.5 million bathtubs with wine!

★ LARGEST CARDBOARD BOX PYRAMID

The largest cardboard box pyramid consisted of 21,345 Air Wick Freshmatic boxes that were stacked into 20 layers, measuring 4.3 m (14 ft 1 in) tall. It was built by two teams of 10 in an event organized by Air Wick at the East Rand Mall in Bocksburg, South Africa, on 18 September 2008.

★ MOST SEAFOOD PREPARED

A record preparation of 1,739.56 kg (3,835 lb 1 oz) of large seafish, sardines, prawns, mussels and calamari was cooked by South Coast Tourism and Wozani Africa Events (both South Africa) at Silver Beach in Port Edward, South Africa, on 19 July 2008. The event drew a crowd of 7,200 people.

★ YOUNGEST POPULATION

In Uganda, the median age – that is, the age at which there are an equal number of people above and below – is just 14.8 years old. African countries dominate the list of nations with the lowest median ages, according to *The Economist*. Uganda is followed by Niger, with a median age of 15.5 years and Mali with 15.8 years.

★ NEW RECORD
UPDATED RECORD

Jun 7: The **highest score in a game of** *Space Invaders* is 55,160 points (also the highest possible score on that game), set by Donald Hayes (USA) on this day in 2003.

AT A GLANCE

- **AREA:** 3,600,292 km² (1,390,080 miles²)
- **POPULATION:** 1.619 billion*
- **COUNTRIES:** Afghanistan, Bangladesh, Bhutan, British Indian Ocean Territories, India, Kazakhstan, Kyrgyzstan, Maldives, Nepal, Pakistan, Sri Lanka, Tajikistan, Turkmenistan and Uzbekistan.

Population figures are estimated for July 2008; statistics for Iran are included as part of the Middle East – see p.126–127.

★ MOST FOUNTAIN POOLS

The city with the greatest number of fountain pools in a public place is the Turkmenistan capital city of Ashgabat, where a major intersection near the entrance to the airport contains 27 synchronized, illuminated and fully programmable fountains covering an area of 14.82 ha (36.62 acres).

★ LARGEST FLAMING IMAGE USING CANDLES

A total of 30,500 lit candles were arranged into the shape of a cross at an event organized by the Mar Sleeva Association for Rural Guidance in Irinjalakuda, Kerala, India, on 8 September 2008.

LARGEST OPIUM CROP

United Nations officials in Afghanistan are hoping that 2008 was a turnaround year for opium production in the country, as output fell by 6% to 7,700 tonnes (8,487 tons). While still the largest opium crop in the world – worth $3.4 billion (£2.3 billion) in illegal heroin trade – it is a sign that government and military pressure (as well as market forces and the weather) is reducing the number of people involved in the growing and selling of poppies (the source of the opium). An estimated 1 million fewer farmers cultivated poppies in 2008, opting instead for the more lucrative wheat and maize, which has risen in price.

LONGEST HAND-DRUMMING MARATHON

Kuzhalmannam Ramakrishnan (India) played a mridangam (a double-sided drum played with the hands and fingers) for a total of 301 hours at the Nada Layaa auditorium in Nehru College of Aeronautics and Applied Sciences, Coimbatore, Tamil Nadu, India, from 1 to 13 August 2008.

★ LARGEST BLOOD DONATION

A blood-donation drive organized by Dera Sacha Sauda (India) was held at Bapu Ji village in Srigarganagar, India, on 10 October 2004 and attracted 17,921 donors.

★ LONGEST DOSA

A dosa is a rice-flour pancake, and the largest on record was 9.14 m (30 ft), prepared by chefs at the Sankalp Restaurant in Andheri, Mumbai, India, on 12 February 2006.

★ LARGEST TEA PARTY

The largest tea party involved 32,681 participants and was achieved by Dainik Bhaskar (India) for the City of Indore at Nehru Stadium, Indore, India, on 24 February 2008.

FACT

First set in Switzerland in 2002, the flaming candle image world record has subsequently been held in Pakistan, Singapore, Japan, India and Belgium.

LARGEST YOGA CLASS

A record 29,973 students from 362 schools performed a sequence of yogic *kriyas* called Suryanamaskar ("Salute to the Sun") simultaneously for 18 minutes, led by Vivekanand Kendra (India) in Gwalior, India, on 19 November 2005.

MOST REFUGEES RECEIVED (COUNTRY)

The country that hosts more refugees than any other is Pakistan. According to the United Nations High Commission for Refugees (UNHCR), Pakistan received 1,044,500 refugees in 2006.

FLATTEST COUNTRY

The country with the lowest point of elevation is the Maldives at just 2.4 m (8 ft).

Jun 8: The **largest pizza delivery** was made by Papa John's pizza company on this day in 2006, when 13,500 pizzas were delivered to the NASSCO Shipyard in San Diego, California, USA.

Jun 9: The **fastest time to type the alphabet** is 7 seconds exactly and was achieved by Nick Watson (UK) at the Guinness World Records headquarters in London, UK, on 9 June 2006.

161.3 km/h (100.2 mph): the fastest delivery of a cricket ball, by Shoaib Akhtar (Pakistan) against England on 22 February 2003.

LARGEST CANOE CREW

It may not be the **longest canoe** – that record is held by the 45.44-m-long (149-ft 1-in) boat built by students of Nokomis Regional High School in Newport, Maine, USA, in 2006 – but the 43.7-m-long (143-ft 4-in) "Snake Boat" *Aries Punnamada Urukku Chundan* from Alleppey in Kerala, India, had a record crew of 143, which included 118 rowers, two rhythm men, five helmsmen and 18 singers. It was rowed in Kerala, India, on 1 May 2008.

LARGEST QUIZ

The largest quiz held at one location was attended by 1,566 participants during a stage of the "TIME Aqua Regia – The Science Quiz" event organized by TIME (Triumphant Institute of Management Education Pvt. Ltd) at Hari Hara Kala Bhavan, Hyderabad, India, on 3 December 2007.

LARGEST RANGOLI IMAGE

Nilesh Rajaram Naik (India) made a rangoli painting – a decorative artform using coloured powders or sands – measuring 70 x 70 m (229 x 229 ft) at Murda Ground in Tiswadi, Goa, India, on 22 May 2008. The portrait depicted Shivaji (1627–80), founder of the Maratha Empire.

HIGHEST INHABITED BUILDING

The highest inhabited buildings in the world are those in the border fort of Basisi by the Mana Pass (Lat. 31°04'N, Long. 79°24'E) at *c.* 6,000 m (19,700 ft), which is manned by the Indo-Tibetan Border Police (India). Because of lower air pressures at high altitudes and the corresponding decrease in the amount of oxygen in each breath taken, many people begin to feel the effects of altitude sickness at heights above 2,500 m (8,200 ft). It takes several days to acclimatize to the altitude at Basisi and most people become ill if airlifted directly to that height.

★ LARGEST TUNIC

Ariel Pakistan (Pakistan) made a kurta – a traditional shirt worn by both men and women in Afghanistan, Bangladesh, India and Pakistan – measuring 30.78 m (101 ft) long and 18 m (59 ft 3 in) wide in Karachi, Pakistan. It was put on display on 3 January 2008.

★ LONGEST HORN ON A SHEEP

The longest horn found on a species of sheep measured 191 cm (75 in) and belonged to a Marco Polo sheep (*Ovis ammon polii*), a species indigenous to the Pamir Mountains bordering Tajikistan, Afghanistan, Pakistan and China.

FASTEST GLACIER SURGE

In 1953, the Kutiah Glacier in Pakistan advanced more than 12 km (7.4 miles) in three months, averaging 112 m (367 ft) per day – the fastest glacial surge ever recorded.

LARGEST LANDLOCKED COUNTRY

The largest country with no border access to the open ocean is Kazakhstan, which has an area of 2,724,900 km² (1,052,089 miles²) and is bordered by Russia, China, Kyrgyzstan, Uzbekistan, Turkmenistan and the landlocked Caspian Sea.

★ LARGEST EASEL

In April 2008, Rajasekharan Parameswaran (India) of Meenachal, Tamilnady, India, unveiled an easel 17.22 m (56 ft 6 in) tall and 9.45 m (31 ft) wide.

LARGEST VOLUNTEER AMBULANCE ORGANIZATION

Abdul Sattar Edhi (Pakistan) began his ambulance service in 1948, ferrying injured people to the hospital. Today, his radio linked ambulance fleet is 500 vehicles strong and operates all over Pakistan.

MOST CINEMA ADMISSIONS

India – which produces **more feature-length films than any other country**, with 1,164 films released in 2007 – had a total of 3.29 billion cinema admissions in 2007, more than double the US figure and 20 times that of the UK. Pictured is Bollywood star Shilpa Shetty (India).

★ **NEW RECORD**
UPDATED RECORD

Jun 10: On this day in 1989, Alain Ferté (France) set the **fastest lap in the Le Mans 24-hour race**: 3 min 21.27 sec (at an average speed of 242.093 km/h, or 150.429 mph) in a Jaguar XJR-9LM.

SOUTH-EAST ASIA

AT A GLANCE

- **AREA:** 3,600,292 km² (1,390,080 miles²)
- **POPULATION:** 585 million
- **COUNTRIES:** Brunei, Burma (home of the mingun bell, the **heaviest bell in use** at 92 tonnes), Cambodia, East Timor, Indonesia (site of the **largest Buddhist temple** at 60,000 m³; 2,118,880 ft³), Laos, Malaysia (where the world's **heaviest mango**, weighing an impressive 3.1 kg; 6 lb 13 oz, was grown), the Philippines, Singapore, Thailand and Vietnam.

MOST PEOPLE IN A MINI

A classic challenge, the most people crammed into a Mini Cooper is 21 and was achieved by students of INTI College Subang Jaya at their campus in Selangor, Malaysia, on 17 June 2006. The rules for this record state that at the end of the attempt all participants must be within the car and all doors and windows must be fully closed.

LARGEST MONKEY BUFFET

The Kala Temple (also known as Monkey Temple) in Lopburi provence, north of Bangkok, Thailand, provides an annual spread of tropical fruit and vegetables, weighing 3,000 kg (6,613.86 lb) for the local population of monkeys, which numbers over 2,000.

★ MOST COUNTRIES IN A MILITARY TATTOO

Armed forces from 13 different counties participated in the Brunei Darussalam International Tattoo 2006, which was organized by the Ministry of Defence and the Royal Brunei Armed Forces at the Hassanal Bolkiah National Stadium in Brunei Darussalam from 29 July–1 August 2006.

★ HIGHEST DEFENCE BUDGET (PERCENTAGE GDP)

In 2006, Burma's military government allocated 18.7% of its GDP to defence spending.

LARGEST LEGAL BANKNOTE

On 22 May 1998, the Central Bank of Manila, the Philippines, issued a special 100,000-peso legal tender banknote measuring 22 x 33 cm (8½ x 13 in). Only 1,000 notes, which commemorated the centenary of the first declaration of Philippine independence, were issued.

★ HEAVIEST JICAMA

The Jicama, or yam bean, is an edible root vegetable popular in south-east Asian food. The heaviest Jicama weighed 21 kg (46 lb 4.8 oz). It was grown by Leo Sutisna (Indonesia) in Bandung, West Java, Indonesia, and was weighed on 25 January 2008.

RICHEST MONARCH

According to Forbes.com, the richest monarch in the world as of August 2007 was Sultan Haji Hassanal Bolkiah of Brunei, with an estimated wealth of $22 billion (£11 billion). In addition to being ruler of the oil-rich state, the 29th Sultan of Brunei inherited much of his wealth.

June 11: The **largest manufactured pure gold bar** weighs 250 kg (551 lb 2 oz) and was made by the Mitsubishi Materials Corporation on this day in 2005.

121,352,608: the population of Java, Indonesia, the world's **most populous island** as of the 2000 census.

LARGEST STICKER

On 5 September 2008, Focal Point Advertising and Golden Touch Imaging displayed a sticker made to advertise Levi Strauss jeans on the ESL Tower Building in Makati City, the Philippines. The sticker measured 61 x 71.26 m (200 ft x 235 ft) and had a total area of 4,366.46 m^2 (47,000 ft^2).

★ LONGEST BARBECUE

The longest barbecue measured 3,803.96 m (12,480 ft 2 in) and was created by Municipality of Santo Tomas (Philippines) in Santo Tomas, Pangasinan, the Philippines, on 11 February 2008. The massive meal took more than 3,500 cooks to prepare.

★ LARGEST EXPORTER OF RICE

According to information from the Food and Agriculture Organization of the United Nations, Thailand exported 8,094,000 tonnes (19,629,959,825 lb) of rice in 2007, giving it a 27% share of the global rice market.

LARGEST OBSERVATION WHEEL

Located in Marina bay, Singapore, the Singapore Flyer observation wheel comprises a 150-m (492-ft) diameter wheel, built over a three-story terminal building. The wheel has a total height of 165 m (541 ft).

★ **NEW RECORD UPDATED RECORD**

★ LARGEST DONATION CAN

A 6-m-high (19-ft) and 4-m-wide (13-ft) donation can was displayed by the Nanyang Technological University Student's Union and y.e.s. 93.3 fm at the Civic Plaza, Ngee Ann City, Singapore, on 10 July 1998. It was on show for three days to help raise money for a variety of local charities.

★ FASTEST TEXT MESSAGE

Jeremy Sng Gim (Singapore) typed a prescribed 160-character text on his mobile phone in 41.40 sec during the SingTel SMS Shootout 2008, held at Clarke Quay, Singapore, on 24 February 2008.

★ MOST DIABETES READINGS

The record for the most diabetes readings taken in 24 hours is 503, a feat that was achieved by Grace Galindez-Gupana, President of HalleluYAH Prophetic Global Foundation Philippines, with the sponsorship of ABS Gen Herbs International Corporation at the HalleluYAH Prayer Mountain for All Nations, in San Mateo, Rizal, the Philippines, on 15 March 2008.

DID YOU KNOW? Makati City, above, is the major financial, commercial and economic hub of the Philippines.

★ HIGHEST OWNER OCCUPANCY (COUNTRY)

According to the data available to the United Nations Human Settlement Programme, UN-Habitat, as of 1998, Cambodia had an amazing 95.3% of its population living in homes that they owned.

LARGEST EARWIG SANCTUARY

The largest, and only, earwig sanctuary is inside the Great Cave at Niah in Sarawak, northern Borneo. The species protected is the hairy earwig (*Arixenia esau*); the insects live in a single block of timber, which was fenced off in the early 1960s, thus creating the sanctuary.

★ FASTEST GAME OF HOPSCOTCH

Multiple record holder Ashrita Furman (USA) completed the fastest single game of hopscotch in just one min 23 sec at the fitness centre of the Awana Kijal Resort and Spa in Kijal, Malaysia, on 19 January 2006.

★ FASTEST GROWING CITY

Naypyitaw, the new capital of Burma, was built in the scrublands of central Burma 460 km (300 miles) north of the old capital, Rangoon. Most of the construction workers involved in building it have to travel great distances to reach the city. Naypyitaw is projected to have grown an amazing 57.8% in the period 2005–10, making it the fastest growing of all conurbations in the world with a population exceeding 750,000.

June 12: The **longest rabbit jump** is 3 m (9 ft 9.6 in) and was achieved by a rabbit called Yabo in Horsens, Denmark, on this day in 1999. Yabo was handled by Maria Brunn Jensen (Denmark).

June 13: The **most children born at a single birth** to be medically recorded is nine, born to Geraldine Brodrick (Australia) at the Royal Hospital for Women, Sydney, Australia, on this day in 1971.

NORTH-EAST ASIA

AT A GLANCE
- **AREA:** 11,795,031 km² (4,554,087 miles²)
- **POPULATION:** 1.63 billion*
- **COUNTRIES:** China (the **most populous country** with 1.3 billion inhabitants), which includes two Special Administrative Regions (SARs): Macau (home of Venetian Macau, the **largest casino**, with a 51,100-m²; 550,000-ft² gambling area) and Hong Kong (the **busiest container port**, handling 22 million containers in 2004), Japan, Mongolia, North Korea, South Korea and Taiwan (which saw the **largest parade of bicycles**, consisting of 2,284 bikes, on 21 February 2009).

*only includes figures for China, Hong Kong, Japan, South Korea and Taiwan.

★ **NEW RECORD**
UPDATED RECORD

★ YOUNGEST PROFESSIONAL GUITARIST

As of 4 August 2008, Yuto Miyazawa (Japan) was aged 8 years 165 days and had played numerous paid engagements on national television throughout the world. Yuto started playing guitar when he was three and has played with many musicians, including the American jazz guitar legend Les Paul.

HEAVIEST VEHICLE PULLED USING EARRINGS

Gao Lin (China) attached a Volkswagen car weighing 1,562 kg (3,443 lb) to his earrings by means of a rope and pulled it for 10 m (33 ft). This lobe-stretching feat of strength was achieved on the set of *Zheng Da Zong Yi – Guinness World Records Special* in Beijing, China, on 19 December 2006.

★ LARGEST TAMBOURINE ENSEMBLE

The largest gathering of people playing the tambourine involved 9,902 participants in an event organized by Taipei County Government in Taipei, Taiwan, on 1 January 2008.

LARGEST AIRPORT CARGO TERMINAL

With a total floor area of 280,500 m² (3,019,277 ft²), Hong Kong Air Cargo Terminals Limited (HACTL) SuperTerminal 1 is the world's largest cargo terminal under one roof. The terminal has a design capacity of 2.6 million tonnes (2.8 million tons) per year. Hong Kong also boasts the **largest airport passenger terminal building** in the form of the Hong Kong International Airport passenger terminal building, a massive 1.3-km-long (0.8-mile) structure, covering 550,000 m² (5,920,150 ft²).

X-REF
You've seen the youngest, but what about the oldest? Read all about some fascinating life stories on pp.70–71...

★ MOST MAGAZINE COVERS DESIGNED

Keizo Tsukamoto (Japan) has illustrated the cover of *Shukan Manga Times* for 38 years and 5 months as of July 2008 without missing a single issue. During that time, Tsukamoto produced a grand total of 1,937 magazine covers.

Jun 14: The **first non-stop flight across the Atlantic**, in a Vickers Vimy biplane, took 16 hr 12 min on this day in 1919 by John William Alcock and Arthur Whitten Brown (both UK).

3,063: hot springs visited by Takashi Kasori (Japan) between 1 November 2006 and 31 October 2007, the **most hot springs visited in one year**.

LONGEST MODELLING CONTRACT

The actress and model Shima Iwashita (b. 3 January 1941) of Japan has been a house model for the Japanese cosmetic company Menard since 1972. She first signed with them on 1 April 1972 and her contract has continued to be renewed every year since.

GUINNESS WORLD RECORDS

CERTIFICATE

The fastest time to run 100 m on all fours was set by Kenichi Ito (Japan) at Setagaya Kuritsu Sogo Undojyo, Tokyo, Japan, on 13 November 2008.

GUINNESS WORLD RECORDS LTD

★ FASTEST 100 M ON ALL FOURS

The fastest time to run 100 m on all fours is 18.58 seconds and was set by Kenichi Ito (Japan) at Setagaya Kuritsu Sogo Undojyo, Tokyo, Japan, on 13 November 2008. Ito came up with the idea of sprinting on all fours when he saw monkeys running very quickly in a zoo and trained every day for five years in preparation for the challenge.

★ FIRST CONFIRMED SURVIVOR OF TWO NUCLEAR ATTACKS

Tsutomu Yamaguchi (Japan) was in Hiroshima on a business trip on 6 August 1945, when a US B-29 aeroplane dropped the 12–15-kiloton "Little Boy" atomic bomb on the city, killing 140,000 people. Suffering burns to his upper body, Tsutomu managed to return to his hometown of Nagasaki on 8 August. The next day the US Army dropped "Fat Boy", a 20–22-kiloton bomb on the city, the ★ **first use of a plutonium weapon**. Around 73,000 people died in the attack, but Tsutomu again managed to survive with minor injuries. In both cities he was within 3 km (1.8 miles) of ground zero.

MOST BOUTS WON IN A YEAR BY A SUMO WRESTLER

In 2005, Yokozuna Asashoryu Akinori (Mongolia, birth name: Dolgorsuren Dagvadorj) won 84 of the 90 regulation bouts that top sumo wrestlers, or *rikishi*, fight annually.

★ MOST COUPLES HUGGING

A total of 1,451 couples hugged simultaneously at a World Children's Day charity event organized by McDonald's Restaurants, Taiwan, at Taipei Arena, Taipei, Taiwan, on 18 November 2007.

★ MOST BOOKS WRITTEN BY AN INDIVIDUAL IN A YEAR

The most books written in one year by an individual is six by Shinichi Kobayashi (Japan), who wrote and published the novels between 1 October 2007 and 15 September 2008.

★ LARGEST PRODUCER OF ENERGY (COUNTRY)

China is the largest producer of energy with 1,641.0 Mtoe (million tonnes of oil equivalent) as of 2005.

★ LARGEST MAHJONG TOURNAMENT

The largest Mahjong tournament is the First Super Cup Mahjong Tournament held by Gi Tiene International Co. Ltd (Taiwan) between 8 December 2007 and 3 February 2008. The competition featured 14,886 individual players from all over Taiwan.

LONGEST FIREWORK WATERFALL

The world's longest firework waterfall was the "Niagara Falls", which measured 3,517.23 m (11,539 ft 5 in) when ignited on 23 August 2008 at the Ariake Seas Fireworks Festival, Fukuoka, Japan.

★ LARGEST SHIPBUILDER

The world's largest shipbuilder is the Hyundai Heavy Industries Co. Ltd of Ulsan, South Korea, which in 1999 accounted for 13% of world ship production. In 2000, it produced 59 vessels with a gross deadweight of 4.2 million tonnes (4.6 million tons) and a total value of $3.8 billion (£2.5 billion). Hyundai's shipyard has nine dry docks, the largest of which is 640 m (2,100 ft) long and can hold several huge ships at once.

OLDEST POPULATION

According to the latest population figures available, in Japan, the median age – that is, the age at which there are an equal number of people above and below – was at the record high of 42.9 in 2007. In terms of Asian countries, Japan is exceptional in its high median age and is the only non-European country in the top ten. Italy has the second highest at 42.3 years.

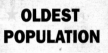

Jun 15: The **largest violin ensemble**, consisting of 4,000 child violinists playing "Recollections of England – Selection", performed at Crystal Palace, London, UK, on this day in 1925.

Jun 16: The **first woman in space** was Valentina Tereshkova (USSR) on this day in 1963. Born 6 March 1937, she was 26 years 102 days old at the time, also making her the **youngest woman in space**.

AUSTRALIA

AT A GLANCE
- **AREA:** 7,686,850 km² (2,967,909 miles²)
- **POPULATION:** 21 million
- **HOUSEHOLDS:** 7.7 million
- **KEY FACTS:** Australia is the world's **largest producer of raw wool**, with an output of 327,000 tonnes (360,455.8 tons) in 2006. China is the second largest producer of raw wool and New Zealand is third, with 168,000 tonnes (185,188 tons).

LARGEST HUMAN WHEELBARROW RACE

With 1,044 participants splitting up into 522 pairs, the largest human wheelbarrow race took place at the sports campus of Carey Baptist Grammar School, in Melbourne, Victoria, Australia, on 9 September 2008.

★ LARGEST SHEEP STATUE

A giant statue of a merino ram measuring 15 m tall, 18 m long and 4 m wide (49 x 59 x 13 ft) towers above the freeway in Goulburn, New South Wales, Australia. Named "Big Merino" but better known as "Rambo", the 97-tonne (106-ton) beast is constructed from steel and reinforced concrete and houses a gift shop and a wool exhibition. It opened to the public on 20 September 1985.

FASTEST TIME TO CLIMB THE EQUIVALENT HEIGHT OF EVEREST ON A MACHINE (MALE)
Richard Pemberton (Australia) climbed the equivalent of the height of Mount Everest (8,848 m; 29,028 ft) on a "Versaclimber" machine in 2 hr 53 min 47 sec at Executive Fitness Managment Gym, Adelaide, Australia, on 25 November 2006.

★ FASTEST TIME TO SHEAR ONE MERINO LAMB
Dwayne Black (Australia) successfully sheared a single merino lamb in 53.88 seconds on the set of *Zheng Da Zong Yi – Guinness World Records Special* in Beijing, China, on 20 September 2007.

LONGEST ROAD TRAIN
On 18 February 2006, a road train with a total length of 1,474.3 m (4,836 ft 11 in) was put together for an event sponsored by Hogs Breath Café in Clifton, Queensland, Australia. A single Mack Titan prime mover (road tractor), driven by 70-year-old veteran trucker John Atkinson (Australia), towed the 113 trailers weighing 1,299,986 kg (2,865,980 lb) for a distance of approximately 150 m (490 ft).

★ MOST EXPENSIVE CRICKET BAT
A cricket bat used by Sir Donald Bradman (Australia) in his debut test match was sold for A$145,000 (£66,000) at Leski Auctions, Melbourne, Australia, on 24 September 2008. Arguably the world's greatest cricketer, Bradman made his debut in the 1928/29 Ashes series. He scored just 18 runs in the first innings and 1 run in the second innings.

★ FASTEST CIRCUMNAVIGATION OF AUSTRALIA BY AQUABIKE
Paul Fua, Randall Jones and Lynden Parmenter (all Australia) circumnavigated Australia on an aquabike (jetski) in 106 days. They set out from Sydney Harbour on 20 August 2000 and covered around 16,500 km (10,250 miles) in a clockwise direction before arriving back in Sydney on 3 December 2000.

★ MOST WHISTLE BLOWERS
On 5 September 2008, a total of 37,552 people blew whistles simultaneously at an event organized by the Asthma Foundation of Queensland at Suncorp Stadium in Brisbane.

FASTEST 100 M WHEELBARROW RACE
Otis Gowa (Australia) pushed Stacey Maisel, who weighed 50 kg (110 lb), in a wheelbarrow over 100 m (328 ft) in a record time of 14 seconds. The wheelbarrow race was filmed on location for *Guinness World Records* at Davis Park, Mareeba, Queensland, on 15 May 2005.

June 17: The **first successful human kidney transplant** was performed by RH Lawler (USA) at Little Company of Mary Hospital, Chicago, Illinois, USA, on 17 June 1950.

NEW ZEALAND

AT A GLANCE
- **AREA:** 268,680 km² (103,737 miles²)
- **POPULATION:** 4.1 million
- **HOUSEHOLDS:** 1.5 million
- **KEY FACTS:** According to the latest available figures, which were released in 2006, New Zealand has **more CD players per member of the population** than any other country, with 88.5 per 100 people. The United Kingdom is only just behind New Zealand Kiwis with 88.4 per 100.

★ COIN FLICKING – FARTHEST DISTANCE

New Zealand's serial record breaker Alastair Galpin flicked a NZ$0.10 coin a distance of 10.64 m (34 ft 10 in) at the Old Homestead Community House, Auckland, New Zealand, on 2 November 2008.

★ TAP DANCING – MOST TAPS IN A MINUTE

Tony Adams (New Zealand) achieved 602 taps in one minute (averaging a fraction over 10 taps per second), live on Television New Zealand's *Good Morning Show* at Studio 11 in Wellington, New Zealand, on 4 August 2008.

X-REF
Can't get enough rugby records? Why not tackle the Rugby spread on pp.254–255?

FASTEST COAL SHOVELLING BY A TEAM OF TWO

The record for filling a 508-kg (0.5-ton) hopper with coal using a banjo shovel by a team of two is 14.8 seconds, by Brian Coghlan and Piet Groot (both New Zealand) at the opening of the Brunner Bridge, South Island, New Zealand, on 27 March 2004.

★ HIGHEST BUNGEE JUMP FROM A BUILDING

AJ Hackett (New Zealand) leaped 199 m (652 ft 10 in) off a platform situated at 233 m (764 ft 5 in) on the Macau Tower, Macau, China, on 17 December 2006.

LARGEST DEMOLITION DERBY

A demolition derby with 123 participants took place at Todd & Pollock Speedway, Mount Maunganui, New Zealand, on 16 March 2002. It took 47 minutes of mass automotive mayhem before the winner – the last car still moving – emerged.

FASTEST TEXT MESSAGE BLINDFOLDED

Elliot Nicholls (New Zealand) completed a 160-character text message, without error, while blindfolded in 45.09 seconds. The record was achieved at the Telecom shop on Filluel Street, in Dunedin, New Zealand, on 17 November 2007.

HEAVIEST COLOSSAL SQUID

TOP 100 Records of the Decade

On 22 February 2007, it was announced that fishermen in the Ross Sea of Antarctica had caught an adult male colossal squid (*Mesonychoteuthis hamiltoni*) weighing approximately 450 kg (990 lb) and measuring 10 m (33 ft). The squid was taken to New Zealand to be studied. Rarely-caught aquatic beasts, colossal squid are usually shorter than giant squid, but are much heavier.

★ FREEDIVING – CONSTANT WEIGHT NO FINS (MEN)

New Zealander William Trubridge dived to a depth of 86 m (282 ft 1 in) in the constant weight no fins category at the Vertical Blue 2008 Invitational Freediving competition, held at Dean's Blue Hole, Long Island, The Bahamas, on 10 April 2008. Constant weight no fins involves a totally unassisted descent and ascent (Inset).

MOST TRI NATIONS WINS

The Tri Nations, the annual rugby union tournament contested between Australia, New Zealand and South Africa, has been won a record nine times by New Zealand, who were victorious in 1996–97, 1999, 2002–03 and each year from 2005 to 2008.

★ NEW RECORD ★ UPDATED RECORD

June 18: On this day in 2005, Phil Naylor (UK) played the first hole of the Devlin course at St Andrews Bay Golf Resort and Spa, St Andrews, UK, in 1 min 52 sec, the **fastest single hole of golf**.

June 19: The **youngest scorer in a FIFA World Cup finals tournament** is Pelé, who was aged 17 years 239 days when he scored for Brazil against Wales at Gothenburg, Sweden, on 19 June 1958.

MODERN WORLD

CONTENTS

★ LARGEST COLLECTION OF *POOH & FRIENDS* MEMORABILIA

When Deb Hoffmann's (USA) collection of *Pooh & Friends* memorabilia was counted on 23 February 2009, it was found to contain 4,405 different items. Deb began her collection in 1967.

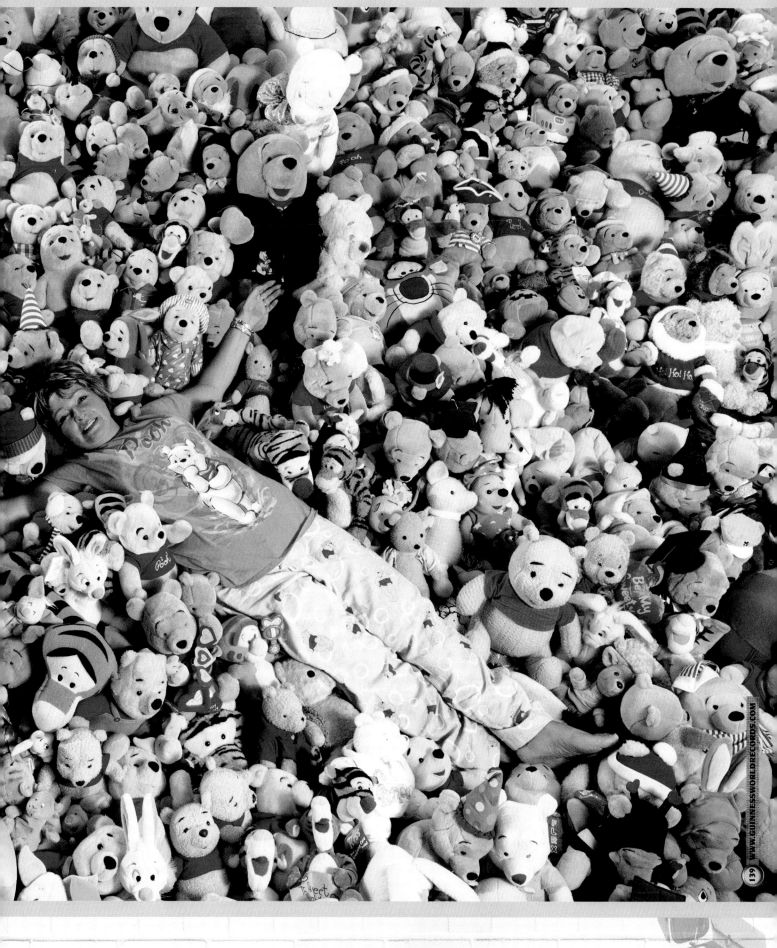

MAN'S BEST FRIEND

TOP DOG ONCE AGAIN

On 21 January 2009, the American Kennel Club (AKC) announced that, for the 18th consecutive year, the Labrador Retriever was the **most popular purebred dog**, with more than twice as many "Labs" registered in the country than any other breed. The Labrador is also the top dog in Canada and the UK.

LONGEST EARS ON A DOG

Tigger, a bloodhound who is owned by Bryan and Christina Flessner of St Joseph, Illinois, USA, has the longest ears of any dog. When measured on 29 September 2004, Tigger's right ear was found to be 34.9 cm (13.75 in) in length, while his left ear was slightly shorter at 34.2 cm (13.5 in).

★ MOST DOGS SKIPPING ON THE SAME ROPE

On 23 May 2007, Uchida Geinousha's "Super Wan Wan Circus" achieved the incredible canine feat of getting 12 dogs to skip together on the same rope at an event held for Sanyo Bussan Co. Ltd, Tokyo, Japan.

MOST SKIPS BY A DOG

IN ONE MINUTE

Sweet Pea, an Australian Shepherd/Border Collie cross, performed 75 rope skips in one minute on the set of *Live with Regis and Kelly* in New York City, USA, on 8 August 2007. Sweet Pea's owner Alex Rothaker (USA) helped out by swinging the rope.

★ FASTEST TIME TO POP 100 BALLOONS BY A DOG

Anastasia, a Jack Russell terrier owned by Doree Sitterly (USA), popped 100 balloons in 44.49 seconds on the set of *Live with Regis and Kelly* in Los Angeles, USA, on 24 February 2008. The balloons that Anastasia popped were standard party balloons inflated to a diameter of at least 20 cm (8 in).

WELL BALANCED

Sweet Pea (below) also holds the record for the **most steps climbed by a dog balancing a glass of water on the snout**. She successfully walked up 17 steps on the set of *Live with Regis and Kelly*, in New York City, USA, on 8 August 2007.

★ LARGEST DOG WALK

A leash-straining 10,272 dogs took part in the Butchers Great North Dog Walk, organized by Anthony Carlisle (UK). The walk was held in South Shields, UK, on 17 June 2007.

★ LARGEST DOG WEDDING CEREMONY

A "wedding" ceremony featuring 178 dog pairs took place at the "Bow Wow Vows" event organized by the Aspen Grove Lifestyle Center in Littleton, Colorado, USA, on 19 May 2007. The poochy partners sealed their marriage with a bark to the notes of the wedding march.

Jun 20: Bertha Wood (UK) became the **oldest person to have a debut book published** when *Fresh Air and Fun: The Story of a Blackpool Holiday Camp* came out on her 100th birthday on 20 June 2005.

Jun 21: The **highest recorded altitude in a helicopter** is 12,442 m (40,820 ft) by Jean Bouletan (France) flying an Aérospatiale SA315B "Lama" over Istres, France, on 21 June 1972.

HEAVIEST BREEDS OF DOG

The heaviest breeds of domestic dog *Canis familiaris* are the mastiff (pictured right) and the St Bernard, with males of both species regularly weighing 75–90 kg (165–200 lb). In its breed guidelines, the Kennel Club (UK) states that the ideal mastiff should have "a large, powerful, well knit frame", displaying "a combination of grandeur and courage".

⭐ OLDEST DOG (LIVING)

A dachshund called Chanel, who is owned by Karl and Denise Shaughnessy (both USA) of Port Jefferson Station, New York, USA, has a confirmed age of 20 years as of 6 May 2008.

OLDEST DOG (EVER)

The greatest reliable age recorded for a dog is 29 years 5 months for an Australian cattle-dog named Bluey, owned by Les Hall of Rochester, Victoria, Australia. Bluey was obtained as a puppy in 1910 and worked among cattle and sheep for nearly 20 years before being put to sleep on 14 November 1939.

TALLEST DOG LIVING

Gibson, a harlequin great Dane, measured 107 cm (42.2 in) tall on 31 August 2004. He was born on 26 April 2002, is owned by Sandy Hall of Grass Valley, California, USA, and works as a therapy dog, providing affection to people with special needs.

⭐ FASTEST POLE WEAVING

Alma, owned by Emilio Pedrazuela Cólliga (Spain), weaved through 24 poles in 5.88 seconds on the set of *Guinness World Records*, recorded in Madrid, Spain, on 16 January 2009. Alma was attempting the record as part of a three-dog challenge, with each dog having two attempts. Her first attempt was 6.10 seconds. The best attempts by the other two dogs, Yuna and King, were 6.79 seconds and 6.66 seconds respectively.

FACT
Pictured above are mastiffs Simba and Jorden, who appeared on a German Guinness World Records TV show in 2008 representing the world's heaviest dog breed.

LARGEST LITTER OF PUPPIES

Tia, a Neopolitan mastiff owned by Damian Ward (UK) and Anne Kellegher (Ireland) of Manea, Cambridgeshire, UK, gave birth to 24 puppies on 29 November 2004.

THE WET NOSE OF THE LAW

The ⭐**first sniffer dog trained to identify illegal mobile phones** was Murphy, a springer spaniel who was trained by the Eastern Area Drug Dog team, UK, to identify a certain scent emitted by mobile phones. Murphy began work with his handler, Mel Barker (UK), in autumn 2006 in an initiative to detect such contraband items among prisoners at Norwich Prison (HMP Norwich), Norfolk, UK. Murphy can even differentiate between prison officers' and prisoners' mobile phones, as well as locate phones that have been hidden in wall cavities or wrapped in plastic bags.

⭐ **NEW RECORD**
UPDATED RECORD

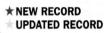

BIG FOOD

★ LARGEST SCONE

A scone weighing 49.89 kg (110 lb) and measuring 1 m (3 ft 2 in) in diameter was made by Mary, Nick and Amy Lovering of Sandford's Bakery in Torrington, Devon, UK, on 21 January 2009. The ingredients included 26.3 kg (58 lb) of flour, 15.87 kg (35 lb) of clotted cream and 5.44 kg (12 lb) of strawberry jam.

★ **NEW RECORD**
★ **UPDATED RECORD**

LARGEST...

LARGEST SCOTCH EGG

"Scotch egg" is the name given to a hard-boiled egg that is encased in spicy sausage meat, covered in breadcrumbs, then deep fried. The largest on record weighed 6.2 kg (13 lb 10 oz) and was made by Clarence Court (UK) and Lee Streeton (UK, pictured with his creation) at Rocco Forte Brown's Hotel in London, UK, on 30 July 2008. The entire cooking process took more than eight hours, with 90 minutes alone spent boiling an ostrich egg. The scotch egg is not a Scottish invention – it was conceived at the London, UK, food store Fortnum & Mason in 1738.

★ BIRYANI
A spicy biryani dish weighing 14.060 tonnes (15.498 tons) was prepared by Kohinoor Foods Ltd (India) in Delhi, India, on 1 March 2008.

★ BOUGATSA BREAD
Bougatsa is a pastry stuffed with custard, cheese or minced meat. The largest ever made weighed 182.2 kg (401 lb 11 oz) and was served in Serres, Greece, on 1 June 2008.

★ GAZPACHO
The Municipality of Campohermoso in Almeria, Spain, made a 4,520-litre (994-gal) gazpacho – a chilled tomato soup – on 2 August 2008.

★ JAMBALAYA
The Jambalaya Festival Association (USA) prepared a 1,379.3-kg (3,041-lb) jambalaya (a rice dish with meat and vegetables) in Gonzales, Louisiana, USA, on 24 May 2008.

MEATBALL
A 32.93-kg (72-lb 9-oz) mass of meat was prepared and cooked at Meatball Mike's in Cranston, Rhode Island, USA, on 6 June 2008.

★ PIZZA
The world's largest *commercially available* pizza has an area of 1.3 m² (14 ft²) and has been on sale at Mama Lena's Pizza House in McKees Rocks, Pennsylvania, USA, since 20 March 2006.

The **largest pizza ever cooked** weighed 12.19 tonnes (13.44 tons) and was prepared in Norwood, South Africa, in 1990.

TALLEST...

★ STACK OF POPPADOMS
Nahim Aslam and Fayaz Aslam (UK) stacked poppadoms to a height of 1.48 m (4 ft 10 in) at the Indian Ocean restaurant, Ashton-Under-Lyne, Lancashire, UK, on 9 October 2007.

★ COOKIE TOWER
The Mt Wilson Vista Council Girl Scouts erected a 1.62-m (5-ft 4-in) cookie tower at Paseo Colorado, Pasadena, California, USA, on 29 February 2008.

LARGEST RESTAURANT

The Bawabet Dimashq (Damascus Gate) restaurant in Damascus, Syria, has 6,014 seats and employs up to 1,800 staff during peak seasons. "In this part of the world, all people care about is their stomachs," says general manager Muhannad Samman, "so the food has to be the best."

STACK OF PANCAKES
Krunoslav Budiselic (Croatia) created a free-standing stack of 627 pancakes – each 23–25 cm wide (9–10 in) – at the Grand Hotel Toplice in Terme Catez, Slovenia, on 26 August 2008. The stack took 22 hours to complete and reached a total height of 74 cm (2 ft 5 in).

CHAMPAGNE-GLASS PYRAMID
Luuk Broos (Netherlands) and his team created a champagne fountain comprising 43,680 glasses, layered in an incredible 63 storeys, at the Wijnegem Shopping Center in Belgium on 25 January 2008.

CHOCOLATE SCULPTURE
A chocolate Christmas tree measuring 6.5 m (21 ft 4 in) tall was created by pastry chef Justo Almendrote (Spain) and unveiled in Madrid, Spain, on 10 December 2008. Approximately 300 kg (661 lb) of white chocolate was used!

INGREDIENTS...
- 1.7 kg (3 lb 11 oz) ostrich egg
- 4 kg (8 lb 13 oz) sausage meat
- 940 g (2 lb 1 oz) haggis
- 800 g (1 lb 12 oz) breadcrumbs

Jun 23: The **first brain cell transplant** was performed by a team of doctors from the University of Pittsburgh Medical Center, Pennsylvania, USA, on this day in 1998.

11,340 litres (3,602 gal): volume of the largest soda float, made at the Coca-Cola Museum in Atlanta, Georgia, USA, in May 2007... enough to fill 75 bath tubs!

LARGEST BOTTLE OF WINE

The world's largest bottle of wine measures 2.40 m (7 ft 10 in) tall and contains 480 litres (105.59 gal) of wine. The production of the wine bottle was organized by Emil Eberle (Switzerland) and Weinlaubenhof Kracher (Austria). The bottle, which has a diameter of 68 cm (2 ft 2 in) and weighs 630 kg (1,388 lb), was filled with 2005 Grand Cuvée TBA NV no.7 wine in Rehetobel, Switzerland, on 9 October 2007.

★ STRING OF LIQUORICE

The Junee Licorice and Chocolate Factory (Australia) made a liquorice string measuring 244 m (800 ft 6 in) in Junee, New South Wales, Australia, on 8 March 2008.

★ LINE OF PIZZAS

Chicago Town Pizzas (UK) produced a line of pizzas measuring 353.9 m (1,161 ft) in Preston, UK, on 10 December 2008.

LARGEST CHEESECAKE

A cheesecake weighing 2,133.5 kg (4,703 lb) was made by Philadelphia Kraft Foods Mexico at the Universidad del Claustro de Sor Juana in Mexico DF, Mexico, on 25 January 2009. The cheesecake had a diameter of 2.5 m (8 ft 2 in), a height of 56 cm (22 in), and included 800 kg (1,763 lb 11 oz) of cheese, 100 kg (220 lb 7 lb) of strawberries and 800 kg (1,763 lb) of yogurt!

LONGEST...

★ HOT DOG

A hot dog measuring 114.32 m (375 ft) was made by Empacadora Ponderosa (Mexico) in Monterrey, Mexico, on 27 September 2008.

★ LINE OF SANDWICHES

A line of sandwiches measuring 1,545.3 m (5,609 ft 11 in) was made by the Serravalle Scrivia shopping centre on 8 March 2009 in Alessandria, Italy.

HEAVIEST...

TOP 100 Records of the Decade

PUMPKIN

Joseph Jutras (USA) presented a pumpkin weighing 766.12 kg (1,689 lb) at the Topsfield Fair in Topsfield, Massachusetts, USA, on 29 September 2007.

★ LARGEST BURGER COMMERCIALLY AVAILABLE

A burger weighing a jaw-dropping 74.75 kg (164.8 lb) is available for $399 (£271.55) on the menu at Mallie's Sports Grill & Bar in Southgate, Michigan, USA, as of 29 August 2008. If you're feeling hungry, please notify the restaurant 24 hours in advance!

Jun 24: Wazir Muhammand s/o Abbass Ali Jagirani (Pakistan) had the world's **heaviest kidney stone** at 620 g (21.87 oz). It was removed from his right kidney in Sindh, Pakistan, on this day in 2008.

Jun 25: The **highest Scrabble score** recorded is 1,049, accomplished by Phil Appleby (UK). The winning match was played on 25 June 1989 at Wormley, Hertfordshire, UK.

FOOD FEATS

★ HIGHEST-POPPING TOASTER

Freddie Yauner (UK) designed and built a toaster that can toast a slice of bread and eject it to a height of 2.60 m (8 ft 6 in), as verified at the Guinness World Records offices in London, UK, on 13 June 2008. Just the thing for a high-class breakfast!

★ LONGEST CURRY DELIVERY

Newspaper journalists Jon Wise and James Crisp (both UK, above left and right, respectively) ordered a vegetable biryani and pilau rice from The Raj Mahal Restaurant in Christchurch, New Zealand, to the *Daily Sport* offices in Manchester, UK, where the pair work. Measuring the distance between the two points in a straight line, the curry travelled more than 18,830 km (11,701 miles) by the time it arrived at its destination on 29 February 2008.

LARGEST FEASTS

★ **Cooked meat**: A giant banquet of chicken, lamb, pork and beef weighing 26,145 kg (57,639 lb) was prepared by La Pastoral Social y Amigos for a charity event at La Asociacion Rural de Paraguay in Mariano Roque Alonso, Paraguay, on 26 October 2008.

★ **Ceviche**: See pp.108–109

★ **Cooked fish**: The Polish Union of America and visitors to the Polish Heritage Festival (both USA) ate 2,552 fish dishes, all provided by Krolick's Bar-B-Q, at Hamburg, New York City, USA, on 30 May 2008.

★ **Mixed seafood**: South Coast Tourism and Wozani Africa Events (both South Africa) prepared 1,739 kg (3,834 lb) of large sea fish, sardines,

prawns, mussels and calamari and served it to 7,200 visitors at an outdoor event held at Silver Beach, Port Edward, South Africa, on 19 July 2008.

★ FARTHEST CURLY WURLY STRETCH

Helen Weddle (UK) stretched a Curly Wurly – a chocolate-covered caramel lattice – a distance of 156.8 cm (5 ft 1 in) at Magna Science Centre, Rotherham, UK, on 26 July 2007. The Cadbury's candy usually measures 19–20 cm (7.4–7.8 in) long, despite its advertising slogan of "miles of chewy toffee..."!

★ MOST COCKTAILS MADE IN AN HOUR

Christopher Raph (USA) made 662 cocktails in one hour in Minneapolis, Minnesota, USA, on 16 April 2009. All the drinks were different and included at least three ingredients.

★ MOST NOODLE PORTIONS PREPARED (3 MINUTES)

Noodle chef Fei Wang (China) of Inn Noodle (London) prepared eight noodle portions in three minutes at Borough Market, London, UK, on 10 October 2008. The record was attempted as part of the *Gordon Ramsay's Cookalong Live* TV show.

During the same series of shows – in which chef Ramsay attempted (and failed) various head-to-head culinary challenges – Paul Kelly (UK) of Kelly Turkey Farms set the record for the ★ **fastest time to pluck three turkeys**, doing so in 11 min 30.16 sec at Little Claydon Farm, Essex, UK, on 13 November 2008.

Salmon monger Darren Matson (UK) of H Forman & Son appeared on the show and established the ★ **fastest time to bone and slice a salmon** (1 min 24.18 sec), also at Borough Market on 10 October 2008.

★ FASTEST TIME TO FILLET A 40-LB FISH

It took fishmonger Duncan Lucas (UK) just 4 min 25.31 sec to fillet and portion a 40-lb (18-kg) fish – at M & J Seafood, London, UK, on 1 October 2008.

★ LARGEST FRUIT MOSAIC

The People's Government of Pingyuan County and the local Committee of the Communist Party of China created a mosaic consisting of 372,525 fruits in Pingyuan County, Guangdong Province, China, on 1 December 2008. The mosaic was created for the county's Fourth Navel Orange Tourism Festival, had an area of 2,220 m² (23,895 ft²) and showed the county's flower and pictograms commemorating the achievement of its fruit growers.

4m
3m
2m
1m

Jun 26: Jennifer Capriati (USA, b. 29 March 1976) was just 14 years 89 days when she competed in her first match on 26 June 1990 and became the **youngest person to win a match at Wimbledon**.

MOST BIG MACS CONSUMED

Donald Gorske (USA) consumed his 23,000th McDonald's Big Mac on 17 August 2008. He is now in his 37th consecutive year of eating Big Macs on a daily basis.

MOST EGGS CRUSHED WITH THE HEAD IN ONE MINUTE

Serial record breaker Ashrita Furman (USA) crushed 80 eggs with his head in one minute at the Panorama Café, Jamaica, New York City, USA, on 10 December 2008. But this achievement is no flash in the frying pan – Furman also has the distinction of holding the **most Guinness World Records**, with a grand total of 164 records set, broken or re-established.

TALLEST CAKE

Students and staff at the Hakasima-Nilasari Culinary School baked a 33-m-tall (108-ft 3-in) cake to celebrate the Amazing Christmas event in Senayan City, Jakarta, Indonesia, from 28 November to 8 December 2008. The cake weighed 18.14 tonnes (19.99 tons) and included:
- 1,620 kg (3,571 lb) sugar
- 1,620 kg (3,571 lb) margarine
- 162 kg (357 lb) milk powder
- 243 kg (535 lb) chocolate powder
- 3,240 kg (7,143 lb) eggs
- 100 litres (211 pints) liquid sugar.

FASTEST EATERS

★ **Chocolate orange**: A chocolate orange is a ball of chocolate mixed with orange oil that is divided into 20 segments. Robert Jones (UK) unwrapped and ate an entire chocolate orange in 4 min 34.25 sec at the Balham Bowls Club in London, UK, on 29 November 2008.

Lemon (1): Ashrita Furman (USA) peeled and ate a lemon in 10.97 seconds at the Panorama Café in Jamaica, New York City, USA, on 24 August 2007.

Lemon (3): Gekidan Hitori (Japan) peeled and ate three lemons in 1 min 33 sec on the set of *Waratte Iitomo! Zokango* at Studio Alta, Tokyo, Japan, on 28 April 2008.

★ **Pickled eggs (3)**: Jonathan Armstrong (UK) ate three medium-sized pickled hen's eggs in 2 min 27.02 sec on 19 August 2008 at the Jeremy Bentham public house in London, UK.

★ **Hamburgers (3 min)**: The most hamburgers eaten in three minutes is five, by Sean Durnal (USA) in Fort Scott, Kansas, USA, on 11 July 2008.

Cream crackers: This food challenge is a classic Guinness World Records achievement that for years stood at about the 3-minute mark. Ambrose Mendy (UK), however, smashed this time by eating three crackers in 34.78 seconds at the studios of LBC radio, London, UK, on 9 May 2005.

LONGEST LINE OF SATAY

Staff of the Kopitiam Group (Singapore) put together a chicken satay measuring 140.02 m (459 ft 4 in) at Lau Pa Sat, Singapore, on 21 July 2007. Over 150 kg (330 lb) of chicken and 700 bamboo sticks were used to make the satay.

★ LONGEST CHOCOLATE BAR

Bakers Pasticceria Beddini created a ludicrously lengthy chocolate bar measuring 6.98 m (22 ft 10 in) long and 1.01 m (3 ft 4 in) wide for the Piazza Umbra shopping centre in Trevi, Italy, on 5 April 2009.

★ TALLEST SUGAR SCULPTURE

The tallest sugar sculpture ever (created in 11 hours) measures 4.97 m (16 ft 4.3 in) and was made by Regis Courivaud (France) in Minneapolis, Minnesota, USA, on 21 April 2006 during the filming of Guinness World Records Week for the Food Network channel.

TOP 100 Records of the Decade

★ MOST PARMESAN WHEELS CRACKED

When it comes to cracking the cheese, none can beat Whole Foods Market (USA). Staff at 176 Whole Foods Market stores cracked open 176 parmigiano reggiano wheels simultaneously at shops across North America and the UK on 12 April 2008.

MOST PEOPLE TOSSING PANCAKES

A record 405 people took part in a pancake toss hosted by Bram Zwiers on the television show *Mooi! Weer de Leeuw* in Almere, the Netherlands, on 24 October 2008.

Jun 27: The world's **first electronic cash dispenser** was installed at a branch of Barclays Bank, Enfield, Middlesex, UK, on this day in 1967.

Jun 28: The **largest band** ever assembled was formed of 20,100 members at the Ullevaal Stadium, Oslo, Norway, from Norges Musikkorps Forbund bands on this day in 1964.

MOST EXPENSIVE...

BICYCLE

A 24-carat gold-plated bicycle decorated with Swarovski crystals and featuring a hand-sewn leather saddle is sold by design firm Aurumania (Denmark) for €80,000 ($103,803; £74,468), making it the most expensive bicycle commercially available. A limited edition of 10 bikes will be made.

★ DUMMY/ PACIFIER

A $17,000 (£12,207) solid white gold dummy, studded with 278 diamonds, is available for sale from American company www. personalizedpacifiers.com. Although not recommended for actual use, the dummy does feature a silicone nipple and moving handle.

★ COMPUTER

The Japanese-owned Earth Simulator, which was completed in May 2002, cost an incredible $400,000,000 (£206,600,000). Although no longer the most powerful computer in the world, at the time of its construction, the *New York Times* reported it to be "so powerful that it matches the raw processing power of the 20 fastest American computers combined" – the Earth Simulator is available to international projects that need to simulate atmospheric, climate or oceanographic conditions.

MOST EXPENSIVE VETERAN CAR SOLD AT AUCTION

A UK collector paid £3,521,500 ($7,242,916) for the world's oldest surviving Rolls-Royce at Bonhams auctioneers, London, UK, on 3 December 2007. The two-seater, 10-hp car, was manufactured in Manchester, UK, in 1904, which puts it in the veteran (pre-1905) category.

★ NEW RECORD
UPDATED RECORD

INTERNET ADDRESS DOMAIN NAME

The internet domain name sex.com was sold by Gary Kremen (USA) for a reported $12 million (£6.7 million) in 2005, according to Forbes. The rights to this lucrative URL were fought over in court for many years.

★ LUNCH DATE SOLD AT AUCTION

A Hong Kong-based investor paid $2.1 million (£1.3 million) on 28 June 2008 for a lunch date with billionaire investor Warren Buffett. Zhao Danyang (Hong Kong) enjoyed a meal for himself and seven friends accompanied by Mr Buffett at Smith & Wollensky's steakhouse in New York City, USA.

FACT
A cheaper version without the crystals, and with the rims, handlebar, wheels and chain made of hand-polished aluminium, is available for €20,000 ($25,930; £18,626).

POP STAR'S COSTUME SOLD AT AUCTION

Elvis Presley's (USA) white peacock jumpsuit was bought for $300,000 (£214,711) in a sale by online auctioneer GottaHaveIt.com on 7 August 2008. The costume, which he wore on stage extensively during a five-month tour in 1974, was one of Elvis' favourites.

Jun 29: The **jigsaw puzzle with the most pieces** featured 212,323 pieces and had an overall measurement of 10.8 x 11.68 m (35 ft 5 in x 38 ft 4 in) when assembled in Singapore on 29 June 2002.

Jun 30: Jean François Gravelet, aka Charles Blondin (France), made the first crossing of the Niagara Falls on a 76-mm (3-in) rope 335 m (1,100 ft) long and 47.75 m (160 ft) above the falls on 30 June 1859.

£15,000 ($22,507): the price for 340 g (12 oz) of Puerth Hong Yin Yuan tea. It sells at $127 (£85) per cup – the world's **most expensive cup of tea** – at Harrods, London, UK.

★ BOTTLE OF WATER SOLD AT AUCTION

A 1 litre (0.21 gal) bottle of Evian natural mineral water sold for $23,000 (£15,401) to Shazzie Hoss (UAE) at an auction held in Dubai, UAE, on 12 November 2008. The handcrafted bottle, produced by French designer Christian Lacroix, was sold to raise funds for the Dubai Autism Center.

★ TURNTABLE

The price of the Continuum Caliburn turntable, manufactured by Continuum Audio Laboratories (Australia), reaches $112,000 (£57,800), depending on the finish. The tone arm alone costs an additional $12,000 (£6,200). The magnesium platter is magnetically levitated and suspended in a vacuum to ensure that the playing disc is unaffected by external vibrations.

WINE

The most expensive wine commercially available is the Chateau d'Yquem Sauternes (1787), a sweet, golden yellow dessert wine from Bordeaux, France, priced at an average of $60,000 (£31,402), depending on the retailer.

BATMAN MEMORABILIA SOLD AT AUCTION

A Batmobile used in *Batman Forever* (USA, 1995) sold at the Kruse International collector car auction in Las Vegas, USA, in September 2006 for $335,000 (£171,000) to John O'Quinn (USA). O'Quinn spent $690,000 (£351,870) on a 1975 Ford Escort GL once owned by Pope John Paul II at the 1995 Kruse auction.

★ BOOK

A book titled *Michelangelo: La Dotta Mano* costs €100,000 ($155,000; £78,500) per single edition. Each handmade copy takes six months to create and weighs 28.1 kg (62 lb), as the front cover is made from white marble.

INSECT

A giant 80-mm (3-in) stag beetle (*Dorcus hopei*) was reported to have been sold for ¥10,035,000 ($90,000; £57,000) at a store in Tokyo, Japan, on 19 August 1999.

★ VACUUM CLEANER

Vacuum cleaner manufacturer Electrolux celebrated its award-winning ErgoRapido model by teaming up with Gronowalski Crystal Fashion and designer Lukasz Jemioł (Poland) to make a unique Swarovski crystal encrusted cleaner. The bejewelled ErgoRapido comes with 3,730 Swarovski sparklers mounted on its body and is valued at €15,000 ($19,340, £13,825).

★ COMPUTER MOUSE

Swiss manufacturer Pat Says Now produces the world's most expensive computer mouse. Cast from 18-carat white gold and set with 59 individual diamonds, the mouse retails for $24,180 (£12,494).

★ COMPUTER KEYBOARD

The Happy Hacking Keyboard Professional HP Japan, produced by an affiliate of Fujitsu, retails at $4,240 (£2,190). Its extreme price is due in part to the fact that its keys are hand-coated in Urushi lacquer and then dusted with gold.

PIZZA

A pizza topped with onion puree, white truffle paste, fontina cheese, baby mozzarella, pancetta, cep mushrooms and wild mizuna lettuce, and garnished with fresh shavings of a rare Italian white truffle, is regularly sold for £100 ($178) in Gordon Ramsay's Maze restaurant, London, UK.

PAINTING BY A LIVING ARTIST SOLD AT AUCTION

Lucian Freud's (UK, b. 1922) painting *Benefits Supervisor Sleeping*, painted in 1995, sold for $33.64 million (£17.27 million) at an auction held at Christie's in Manhattan, USA, on 13 May 2008, making it the most expensive painting sold attributed to a living artist. The buyer was Russian billionaire Roman Abramovich.

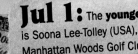

Jul 1: The **youngest female golfer to score a hole-in-one** is Soona Lee-Tolley (USA), aged 5 years 103 days at the par 3 7th at Manhattan Woods Golf Club, West Nyack, New York, USA, on 1 July 2007.

PLANET IN DANGER

★ COUNTRY WITH THE MOST
THREATENED MAMMALS

Indonesia has an estimated 667 mammal species – more than any other country – of which 146 are considered by the United Nations to be "threatened". The International Union for Conservation of Nature and Natural Resources lists 1,104 mammal species that face "a higher risk of global extinction"; Indonesia's threatened mammals, therefore, represent about 13% of the world total.

★ COUNTRY WITH THE LOWEST WATER POVERTY INDEX (WPI)

The Water Poverty Index (WPI) measures the impact of water scarcity and water provision on human populations. The WPI is a number between 0 and 100, where a low score indicates water poverty and a high score indicates good water provision. Niger is recognized by the Food and Agriculture Organization of the United Nations as having the lowest Water Poverty Index, with a mark of 35.2, and is followed closely by Ethiopia with 35.4. WPI is based on five factors: resources, access, capacity, use and environment. Finland has the highest Water Poverty Index with 78.0, while Canada sits in second place with a WPI of 77.7.

★ LARGEST CONSUMER OF ELECTRICITY

It is estimated that the United States consumed 3,892 billion kw/hr in 2007, which amounts to nearly a quarter of the whole world's consumption of electricity in that year, which came to 17,480 billion kw/hr. China was the second largest consumer, with a rate of 3,271 billion kw/hr.

★ LARGEST PRODUCER OF CARBON DIOXIDE PER CAPITA

Citizens of Qatar were responsible for the emission of 51.17 tonnes (56.40 tons) of carbon dioxide per person in 2004. Overall, in the same year, the USA produced more CO_2 than any other country, with emissions reaching 5.88 billion tonnes (6.48 billion tons). CO_2 is a potent greenhouse gas, produced during the combustion of solid, liquid and gaseous fuels.

★ HIGHEST LEVELS OF CARBON DIOXIDE

According to the World Meteorological Organization, the atmospheric abundance of carbon dioxide, a powerful greenhouse gas, was 383.1 ppm (parts per million) in 2007. This is the highest in recorded history and represents a 37% increase since the mid-18th century.

★ LARGEST PRODUCER OF SULPHUR DIOXIDE

China is responsible for the greatest production of sulphur dioxide – the primary contributor to acid rain – pumping out over 34.2 million tonnes (37.6 million tons) yearly.

Sulphur dioxide forms when fuel containing sulphur, such as coal and oil, is burned, when gasoline is extracted from oil or when metals are extracted from ore.

★ COUNTRY WITH THE LARGEST AREA OF PROTECTED LAND

According to the United Nations Environment Programme World Conservation Monitoring Centre (UNEP-WCMC), a total of 34.2% of land in Venezuela is protected. A protected area is defined as "an area of land and/or sea especially dedicated to the protection and maintenance of biological diversity, and of natural and associated cultural resources, and managed through legal or other effective means".

LAST CHANCE TO SEE...

Among the species under threat in Indonesia are the binturong (*Arctictis binturong*, top), also known as the Asian bearcat; the Bornean orangutan (*Pongo pygmaeus*, middle); and the Javan rhino (*Rhinoceros sondaicus*, bottom), with fewer than 60 in existence.

Jul 2: On this day in 2002, Steve Fossett (USA) completed the **fastest solo circumnavigation of the globe in a balloon**, taking *Bud Light Spirit of Freedom* around the world in 13 days 8 hr 33 min.

Jul 3: The **first transmission of colour television** occurred on this day in 1928 when John Logie Baird (UK) completed a demonstration at his studios in Long Acre, London, UK.

★ **NEW RECORD**
★ **UPDATED RECORD**

TOP 100 Records of the Decade

MOST UBIQUITOUS CONSUMER ITEM

Estimates for the global manufacture of plastic bags number in the trillions, making them the most abundant consumer product in the world. In the USA alone, consumers throw away 100 billion plastic bags every year; as plastic bags are manufactured from petroleum, this is equivalent to dumping nearly 12 million barrels of oil annually.

★ LARGEST BOTTLE ISLAND

The world's largest island made entirely from plastic bottles has been created just off Mexico by British expatriate Richard Sowa. The island is composed of over 100,000 empty, discarded plastic bottles held together in fishing nets and currently measures 14.6 x 12.8 m (47 ft 10 in x 41 ft 11 in). The sea-borne construction is growing ever larger in spiralling loops each day as Sowa canoes back and forth between his artificial island and the Mexican mainland, bringing more bottles to add to it. It even possesses a sand beach, a cabana and a compost toilet.

★ HIGHEST RATE OF GLASS RECYCLING

In 2007, the people of Switzerland recycled 320,000 tonnes (352,000 tons) of glass, which is 95% of the 336,000 tonnes (370,000 tons) of glass products they consumed – the highest rate of glass recycling in the world. By comparison, Germany recycled 87% of its glass and the UK managed 57%.

LARGEST REFORESTATION

The Chinese State Forestry Administration announced the beginning of a 10-year reforestation project to plant up an area the size of Sweden in May 2002. The replanted area, representing 5% of China's land mass, will measure about 440,000 km² (169,884 miles²) and should offset some of the environmental problems caused by logging in China.

TOP 100 Records of the Decade

★ GREATEST OCEAN POLLUTANT

According to the UN Environment Programme, plastic bags account for over 50% of all marine litter, with 46,000 pieces of plastic for every 2.5 km² (1 mile²) of ocean. The Blue Ocean Society for Marine Conservation estimates that more than 1 million birds and 100,000 marine mammals die each year because of this plastic.

WARMEST YEAR

A NASA report from January 2008 reveals that 2005 was the planet's warmest year on record. The report also revealed that Earth's 14 warmest years have all occurred since 1990.

TOP 100 Records of the Decade

FASTEST GROWING COMPONENT OF MUNICIPAL WASTE

According to the World Resources Institute, electronic waste is the fastest growing component of municipal waste worldwide with 20–50 million tonnes (22–55 million tons) generated annually. In the US alone, 14–20 million PCs are thrown out each year.

Jul 4: The **fastest time to boardsail across the English Channel** is 1 hr 4 min 33 sec, set by Baron Arnaud de Rosnay (France) on this day in 1982.

TOP **100** Records of the Decade

RICH LIST

On 5 March 2008, Warren Buffett (USA, pictured) ousted Microsoft's Bill Gates (USA) from the top of the Forbes rich list for the first time in 13 years. Buffett's wealth was estimated at $62 billion (£31 billion) while Gates' was a mere $58 billion (£29 billion). But the global credit crunch hit Buffett's fortune hard, reducing his wealth to $37 billion (£25.3 billion), while Gates fared slightly better and by April 2009 was once again **the world's richest man** with a $40-billion fortune (£27.3-billion).

FTSE 100

The Financial Times Stock Exchange (FTSE) 100 Index is a share index of the UK's 100 most valuable companies listed on the London Stock Exchange and is the most commonly used indicator of the health of the UK market.

• The **biggest rise of the FTSE 100** was posted on 24 November 2008, when it rose 372.00 to 4,152.96, a rise of 9.84%. It came on the back of news that the US Treasury had pumped over $13 billion (£8.98 billion) into the troubled banking giant Citigroup.

⭐ LARGEST POINTS FALL ON THE DOW JONES INDUSTRIAL AVERAGE (DJIA)

On 29 September 2008 – "Dark Monday" – the DJIA suffered a loss of 777.68 points, the largest one-day drop in its 114-year history. A dive of over 700 points was recorded shortly before 2:00 p.m. when the US Congress began to vote on the federal government's $700-billion (£482-billion) "bail-out bill" designed to protect the financial markets and the tax payers.

• The FTSE 100 closed at the end of 2008 at a level of 4,423.34, down from its opening level of 6,456.90 – the **greatest annual percentage fall of the FTSE 100**. This is a fall of more than 30%, making it the **index's worst year** in its 24-year history. This is the UK's second largest slide of all time, overshadowed only by the 55.3% fall of the FTSE All-Share Index in 1974.

• The **largest daily points loss on the FTSE 100** occurred on 11 September 2001, following the terrorist attacks in the USA, when the Index dropped 287.70 points.

DOW JONES INDUSTRIAL AVERAGE

The Dow Jones Industrial Average (DJIA) is an index compiled to monitor the health of the US stock market; it is based on the stock prices of 30 of the country's biggest companies.

• On 10 October 2008, the DJIA swung during the day from a low of 7,882.51 to a high of 8,901.28, the **largest swing ever recorded on the DJIA**. The day closed at 8,451.19, down 128.00. The top 10 largest swings ever on the DJIA occurred during the financial crises of 2008.

• The Dow closed on 13 October 2008 at 9,387.61, following a gain of 936.42 – the **largest daily points gain on the DJIA**.

LARGEST NATIONAL DEBT

The USA's national debt surpassed the $10-trillion mark for the first time on 30 September 2008 – rendering the famous Durst National Debt Clock in Times Square, New York City, USA, redundant. The sign, which clocks up the debt with every passing second, ran out of digits and required a hasty makeover.

TOP **100** Records of the Decade

CASH CAREFUL...

Warren Buffett is an investor and CEO of the conglomerate Berkshire Hathaway. Despite his great wealth, Buffett is notoriously frugal. He still lives in the same modest house in Omaha, Nebraska, USA, that he bought in 1958, and when he married his second wife, Astrid, in 2006, he purchased the wedding ring from a discount jewellery store.

OUR NATIONAL DEBT:
$10,149,940,844,092.
YOUR *Family share* **$86,019.**
THE NATIONAL DEBT CLOCK

Jul 5: On this day in 2001, six diners at Petrus, London, UK, spent £44,007 ($61,941) on one meal, making it the **most expensive meal per head**. The majority of the bill went on five bottles of wine.

$787 billion (£553 billion): the **largest single spending measure**, designed to stimulate the ailing US economy, approved by US Congress in February 2009.

★ HIGHEST COMPARATIVE PRICE LEVELS

By converting to a common currency and equalizing the purchasing power of different currencies, it is possible to calculate the comparative cost of goods around the world. The Comparative Price Index published by the OECD lists Switzerland as having the highest costs of any country (and a score of 135, where 100 = average price) – that is, a basket of shopping with a total average price internationally of $100 (£68.93) would cost you $135 (£93.07) in Switzerland.

● On 9 October 2007, the Dow closed at a record high of 14,164.53 – the ★ **highest closing of the DJIA** on record. Two days later, it peaked intraday at 14,198,10 but had fallen below the 9 October figure by the close of play.

★ COUNTRY WITH THE MOST BILLIONAIRES

According to Forbes, 42% of the world's billionaires live in the USA. Of the 1,125 world billionaires identified, 469 are from the USA.

★ GREATEST BUDGET DEFICIT

According to a White House estimate released in July 2008, the federal budget deficit will reach $482 billion (£319 billion) by the end of 2009. A deficit occurs when a country spends more money than it makes. Between 1998 and 2001, the USA was in surplus – the opposite, making more than it spent – but the sagging economy has sent debts through the roof.

★ POOREST CITIZENS

According to the World Resources Institute's Earthtrends report for the period 1989–2004, a total of 70.8% of the people of Nigeria existed on less than $1 a day (the equivalent today of $1.55, or £1.08), making it the nation with the poorest citizens.

The poorest nation, when based on the per person share of all monies made by a country's economic activity – that is, the ★ **country with the lowest Gross Domestic Product (GDP) per head of population** – is Burundi in Africa, with a figure of just $120 per head (as of 2006). By contrast, Luxembourg has the ★ **highest GDP per citizen**, with a figure of $87,490 per head.

★ LOWEST PRICE FOR FUEL

Given the large oil reserves in Venezuela, motorists in that country pay £0.025 ($0.037) per litre of fuel. In the UK, drivers were paying £1.15 ($1.68) per litre in February 2009.

RUNNERS-UP

The other top 10 countries listed by the OECD are:

2.	Japan	127
3.	Norway	123
4.	Denmark	117
5.	Iceland	112
6.	Sweden	110
7.	USA	109
8.	UK	107
9.	Ireland	105
10.	Finland	101

★ NEW RECORD
★ UPDATED RECORD

★ COUNTRY WITH THE GREATEST ECONOMIC FREEDOM

According to the 2009 Economic Freedom Index, the citizens of Hong Kong, China, enjoy the most economic freedom. This is defined by the Index as "the fundamental right of every human to control his or her own labour and property... to work, produce, consume and invest in any way they please, with that freedom both protected and unconstrained by the state". Hong Kong has held its position at the top of the chart for 15 consecutive years.

MOST ZEROS ON A BANKNOTE

The highest denomination banknote is a $100-billion-dollar note that features 11 zeros. It was issued in Zimbabwe on 22 July 2008, and because of inflation at that time it was enough to buy three eggs.

SPECIAL AGRO-CHEQUE

Pay the bearer on demand

ONE HUNDRED BILLION DOLLARS on or before 31st December 2008 for the Reserve Bank of Zimbabwe

Issue date: 1st July 2008

Dr. G Gono Governor

RESERVE BANK OF ZIMBABWE

100 000 000 000

100 BILLION

100000000000

AA0256829

02022900

Jul 6: The **oldest main draw Wimbledon tennis champion** is Martina Navratilova (USA), who was 46 years 261 days when she won the mixed doubles with Leander Paes (India) on this day in 2003.

Jul 7: Col. Ernest Loftus (Zimbabwe) had the **longest kept daily diary**. He began on 4 May 1896 at the age of 12 and continued it until his death 91 years later, on this day in 1987, aged 103 years 178 days.

CRIME

★ HIGHEST INCIDENCE OF PIRACY (YEAR)

According to the International Maritime Bureau, piracy and armed robbery attacks against ships increased significantly in 2008 with a total of 293 incidents – an increase of 11.4% on the previous year and an all-time high for modern piracy.

★ LARGEST SHIP HIJACKED

On 15 November 2008, pirates captured one of the world's largest oil tankers, the MV *Sirius Star* (UAE), off the coast of Somalia, East Africa. The 330-m-long (1,100-ft) VLCC (very large crude carrier) – which has a gross tonnage of 162,252 tons (147,192 tonnes) – was bound for the USA with a crew of 25 and a load of crude oil valued at $110 million (£74.2 million). The ship was taken to the Somali port of Haradheere and a ransom was demanded from the owners. The ship was eventually released on 9 January 2009 after an undisclosed sum was paid.

★ LARGEST PONZI FRAUD

A "Ponzi" scheme is a form of fraudulent investment in which returns are paid for by subsequent investors and not by the profit on real investments. They are named after Charles Ponzi (Italy/USA, 1882–1949, above right) who, in 1920, became notorious for establishing such a scheme.

The ★ **largest Ponzi fraud** to date was perpetrated by Bernard Lawrence Madoff (USA, above left), a former chairman of the NASDAQ stock market and hedge fund manager. According to a complaint filed in December 2008 by the US Attorney's Office and the FBI, Madoff told at least three employees that he had operated a giant "Ponzi" scheme that had lost $50 billion (£35 billion).

★ FIRST USE OF NINTENDO FOR CRIMINAL INVESTIGATION

Japanese police have used the Nintendo Wii Channel to generate a "wanted" poster of a hit-and-run suspect. Usually, police authorities use artists or photofit software for such purposes. However, by selecting a range of face shapes, hairstyles, ears and other features using the Nintendo "Mii" customizable avatar facility, police were able to create the mugshot of the male suspect. The wanted poster was displayed at the scene of the car accident next to a photograph of the type of car involved.

★ FIRST LEGAL SUMMONS SERVED ONLINE

In December 2008, Australian lawyers Mark MacCormack and Jason Oliver created internet and legal history when they used the Facebook social networking site to serve legal documents on a couple who had defaulted on their mortgage. A Supreme Court Judge in the Australia Capital Territory ruled that court notices served on the site were binding. Having tracked down one of the missing people by putting their email address into Facebook, the lawyers found information that was identical to that on the mortgage application, and also details of the second defendant.

HIGHEST HIJACK RANSOM

The MV *Faina* (pictured left), a Ukrainian vessel loaded with Russian tanks, was hijacked off the coast of Somalia by Somali pirates on 25 September 2008. The ship was eventually released after a ransom of $3.2 million (£2.2 million) was paid on 5 February 2009.

EXECUTIONS 2008

	COUNTRY	NUMBER	METHOD
1	China	1,718*	Lethal injection, shooting
2	Iran	346*	Hanging
3	Saudi Arabia	102*	Beheading
4	USA	37	Injection, electrocution
5	Pakistan	36*	Hanging
6	Iraq	34*	Hanging
7	Vietnam	19*	Shooting
8	Afghanistan	17	Shooting
9	North Korea	15*	Shooting
9=	Japan	15	Hanging

*Confirmed figure, actual figure may be higher
Source: Amnesty International
In total, 2,390 people were executed in 2008 and at least 8,864 people were sentenced to death

Jul 8: Svetlana Pankratova (Russia) has the world's **longest legs**, which were verified as measuring 132 cm (51.9 in) long in Torremolinos, Spain, on 8 July 2003.

841: the **most bicycles postcoded in a day**, during a crime prevention initiative held by Lancashire Constabulary at Beaumont College, Lancaster, UK, on 16 April 1994.

★ FIRST INTERNATIONAL CRIMINAL COURT

The International Criminal Court (ICC) came into being on 1 July 2002 and is the world's only permanent international criminal court. The ICC deals with the most serious crimes of international concern such as genocide and war crimes. The official seat of the court is in The Hague, the Netherlands (far left).

The ★ **first trial at the ICC** began on 26 January 2009, when Congolese warlord Thomas Lubanga (left) appeared on war crimes charges for his role in the civil war in the Democratic Republic of Congo.

DID YOU KNOW?
Although the official seat of the ICC is in the Hague, International Criminal Court proceedings may take place anywhere.

★ COUNTRY WITH THE MOST MURDERS

According to the Tenth United Nations Survey of Crime Trends and Operations of Criminal Justice Systems Report, the country with the highest number of intentional homicides in 2006, the latest year for which information is available, is India with 32,481. The USA was in second place with 17,034. Not all nations respond to the survey.

★ RICHEST DRUG DEALER

Joaquin Guzman Loera (Mexico), head of the Sinaloa Cartel and Mexico's most wanted man, has amassed a fortune of $1 billion (£680.2 million) from drug trafficking. The US government is offering a $5 million (£3.4 million) reward for the capture of Loera, who escaped from a Mexican prison in 2001 in a laundry van. He is the second alleged drug dealer to make *Forbes'* annual billionaire list – Colombia's Pablo Escobar was the world's seventh richest man in 1989.

★ LARGEST HASHISH HAUL

On 9 June 2008, 237 tonnes (261 tons) of hashish were seized in Khandahar, Afghanistan, by the UK's Special Boat Service and local commandos. Weighing the equivalent of 30 double-decker buses, the haul had a street value of $338 million (£171.6 million).

★ LARGEST ECSTASY HAUL

The largest ecstasy haul consisted of 15 million pills imported into Australia as 3,000 tins of tomatoes. Announced on 8 August 2008, the 4.4-tonne (4.8-ton) shipment was believed to have come from Italy and had an estimated street value of $400.3 million (£205.5 million).

★ MOST ADVANCED BIOMETRIC SECURITY METHOD

A new biometric system from the Hitachi Company (Japan), which is able to identify people from the unique pattern of veins inside their fingers, has been introduced into security systems in Europe and Japan. It is the fastest, and most secure, biometric method of identifying people.

★ LARGEST REWARD FOR COUNTER-TERRORISM

Osama bin Laden (Saudi Arabia), the terrorist leader of Al-Qaeda, has been on the FBI top ten wanted list since 1999, with a price of $25 million (£17.5 million) on his head. In July 2008, with fears growing that the threat from Al-Qaeda was stronger than at the time of the 9/11 terror attacks, the US Senate voted to double the reward for the death or capture of bin Laden to $50 million (£35 million).

★ GREATEST BANK ROBBERY

A gang of 6–10 robbers, previously "operating" as a landscape company in a nearby building, dug a tunnel measuring 78 m (256 ft) long at 4 m (13 ft) below street level, which ended directly below the Banco Central in Fortaleza, Brazil. On the weekend of 6–7 August 2005, the robbers broke through 1.1 m (3 ft 7 in) of steel-reinforced concrete to enter the bank vault and steal an estimated 164,755,150 Brazilian reais ($71.3 million; £40 million).

★ FIRST ARREST FOR MURDER OF A VIRTUAL VICTIM

In October 2008, a 43-year-old piano teacher was arrested in Miyazaki, Japan, after killing her online husband. The woman had been unexpectedly "divorced" in the context of the role-playing game *Maple Story*, in which avatars (such as the one pictured above) can marry. She was jailed on suspicion of illegally accessing a computer and manipulating data using her gaming partner's ID and password to log on to the game and "murder" her partner. If convicted, she could be jailed or fined up to $5,000 (£3,400).

★ NEW RECORD
★ UPDATED RECORD

★ BIGGEST MILITARY COMPUTER HACK

In 2002, Gary McKinnon (UK) was accused of hacking into 97 US military computers, as well as rendering 300 computers at a US Navy weapons station unusable after the 9/11 terrorist attacks in New York. In 2005, the US began extradition proceedings, alleging that McKinnon caused damage in the order of $800,000 (£550,000). McKinnon has admitted that his hacking constituted an offence in the UK and, as of March 2009, is contesting the extradition request in the UK courts.

Jul 9: The **largest limbo dance** involved 1,150 participants at the Music Under the Stars World Festival 2006 at the Chamizal National Memorial in El Paso, Texas, USA, on 9 July 2006.

Jul 10: When Willie Jones (USA) was admitted to hospital in Atlanta, Georgia, USA, on this day in 1980, his temperature was found to be 46.5°C (115.7°F), the **highest body temperature ever recorded.**

TERRORISM & WARFARE

MOST WANTED TERRORIST

Osama bin Laden (Saudi Arabia), figurehead of the terrorist organization Al-Qaeda, is sought by many nations for terrorist activities. He is also alleged to have been an inspiration for those responsible for the terrorist attacks on the USA on 11 September 2001.

According to the official count from the authorities, 2,749 people died as a result of the attacks, the **most individuals killed in a terrorist act**. A total of 157 people died aboard the two aircraft that crashed into the twin towers and a further 233 died in two other aircraft hijacked the same day.

★ OLDEST RESISTANCE HEROINE

On 3 February 2009, Andrée Peel (France) celebrated her 104th birthday, making her the oldest known surviving female member of the French Resistance. Known as Agent Rose, she helped to save 102 Allied pilots in a three-year period working for the Resistance during World War II.

★ FIRST EUROPEAN UNION TASK FORCE MISSION

In response to the growing problem of piracy off the coast of Somalia, the European Union, the political super bloc of Europe consisting of 27 member states, took the decision to deploy a naval force to the area from 15 December 2008 to take over from the NATO mission there. It is the first naval task force in the bloc's history and it will assist in the delivery of food aid to Somalia, as well as increasing maritime security in the hazardous Somali waters.

★ FIRST FEMALE COMBAT PILOT

Sabiha Gökçen (Turkey, b. 21 March 1913) enrolled in the Military Aviation Academy in Eskisehir, Turkey, in 1936 and undertook training at the First Aircraft Regiment there. She went on to fly fighter and bomber planes to become the first Turkish female aviator and the world's first female combat pilot.

★ LARGEST CONTRIBUTOR TO UN FORCES

In 2008, Pakistan was the largest contributor of police, military observers and troops to UN peacekeeping missions, with a total of 11,135 personnel. It was followed by Bangladesh with 9,567 and India with 8,693.

HIGHEST DEFENCE BUDGET

The USA has the world's largest defence budget, reported as $622 billion (£311.6 billion) by the International Institute for Strategic Studies in 2007. The budget request for 2009 will see it maintain that position, as the White House is seeking a record $711 billion (£483.7 billion).

The US accounts for 48% of the world's military spending – its defence budget is greater than the next 44 highest-spending countries combined.

FACT

Agent Rose was awarded France's highest award for bravery, the Legion d'Honneur, in 2004. She has also been awarded the War Cross with palm, the War Cross with purple star and the Medal of the Resistance.

★ MOST UN MISSIONS (CONTINENT)

Africa is currently home to seven authorized United Nations peacekeeping operations: Central African Republic and Chad; Darfur; Sudan; Côte d'Ivoire; Liberia; DR Congo; and Western Sahara. In Europe and the Middle East there are three each, while there are two in Asia and the Pacific and one in the Americas. Pictured are Nigerian peacekeepers with the UN on a mission to Darfur.

TOP 100 Records of the Decade

Jul 11: The **most hamburgers eaten in three minutes** is five and was achieved by Sean Durnal (USA) in Fort Scott, Kansas, USA, on 11 July 2008.

500,000: hours of flying time clocked up by the *Predator* unmanned aerial vehicle (UAV) as of 18 February 2009 – making it the world's **most deployed military UAV**.

★ FIRST FEMALE FOUR-STAR GENERAL

On Friday 14 November 2008, after 33 years in the US Army and at the age of 55, Ann E Dunwoody (USA) was promoted to full general rank – four-star general – the first in the history of the US armed forces.

★ LARGEST EU MISSION

On 9 December 2008, the European Union (EU) commenced its largest-ever mission, EULEX, when it deployed the first of nearly 1,900 officials to take over police, customs and justice responsibilities from the United Nations staff in Kosovo. The EU officials will be supported by 1,100 local staff, and the aim is not to govern but to oversee the running of the courts, police and customs services as well as helping the authorities to combat organized crime.

★ WORST EFFECT OF WEATHER IN WAR

The worst weather, in military terms, was the extremely bad winter of 1941–42 during World War II, when Germany invaded Russia. The troops were badly equipped for the cold, with temperatures dropping to at least -40°C (-40°F) – bad by even Russian standards. Casualty figures for the German campaign and the Siege of Stalingrad vary, but for both sides by the beginning of 1943 the total casualty figure was probably over 250,000, with troops dying from the effects of cold weather, disease, starvation, exhaustion and battle.

★ LARGEST NAVAL RAID

On 28 March 1942, during World War II, the British Royal Navy initiated *Operation Chariot* to destroy the Normandie dock in St Nazaire, France, the largest dry dock in the world at that time. HMS *Campbeltown*, an obsolete 1,090-ton (1,107-tonne) destroyer, was stripped out to reduce her draught for transit through the shallow waters to the dock, and the bows were packed with 4.5 tonnes (4.9 tons) of high explosive attached to delayed fuses. At 1:34 am, the ship rammed the dock gates, and in the hours that followed, the ship was examined by German soldiers; at 11:35 am, the explosives blew up, killing the soldiers, destroying the dock and putting it out of action until 1948.

★ MOST ADVANCED LONG-RANGE AIRBORNE SURVEILLANCE SYSTEM

With the introduction of the fifth and final new Sentinel R1 (spy jet) into Royal Air Force service on 10 February 2009, the UK armed forces have gained a long-range battlefield intelligence, target imaging and surveillance capability that is the most advanced of its kind in the world. Located at RAF Waddington, Lincolnshire, UK, No.5 (Army Co-operation) Squadron now has five modified Bombardier Global Express aircraft equipped with the Raytheon Airborne Stand-off Radar (ASTOR). This will provide high-quality radar images of a surveyed area, while the Moving Target Indicator (MTI) will detect moving vehicles operating in the area.

★ MOST FEMALE SUICIDE BOMBERS RECRUITED

On 21 January 2009 in Baghdad, Iraq, Samira Ahmed Jassim (Iraq) was arrested on suspicion of recruiting more than 80 women to become suicide bombers. In a taped confession, Jassim – nicknamed "Mother of the Believers" – confirmed that at least 28 of the recruits had carried out attacks.

★ MOST PROLIFIC EXECUTIONER

Personally selected in 1926 by Stalin, leader of the former USSR, Vasili M Blokhin (USSR) acted as chief executioner to the NKVD (People's Commissariat of Internal Affairs), where he led a company of executioners. Under him, they carried out most of the executions ordered by Stalin. Not only is he recorded as having executed all significant prisoners of the regime, as well as many others by his own hand, he also personally executed 7,000 Polish officers at the Ostachkov prison camp in 1940 over precisely 28 nights – 250 executions a night – thereby ranking him as the world's most prolific official executioner. He died in 1955.

★ NEW RECORD
★ UPDATED RECORD

★ WORST YEAR OF AFGHAN INSURGENCY

With a total of 294 coalition military deaths, 2008 was the worst year of the Afghan insurgency since NATO operations started there. Civilian deaths are more difficult to ascertain; it has nonetheless been estimated that, based on media reports, the number of civilian deaths ranges from 4,800 to 7,000 since October 2001.

AFGHANISTAN

Afghanistan produced around 87% of the world's opium crop in 2005, and more than 90% of the heroin in the UK alone comes from this one country.

Jul 12: The **highest speed to crash a motorcycle and survive** is an estimated 322 km/h (200 mph) by Ron Cook (USA) at El Mirage Dry Lake, California, USA, on 12 July 1998.

Jul 13: The **longest walk by a funambulist** (tightrope walker) is 3,465 m (11,368 ft) by Henri Rochetain (France). The wire was placed across a gorge at Clermont Ferrand, France, on 13 July 1969.

★ MOST EXPENSIVE TRAINERS

Ken Courtney (USA), founder of fashion label Ju$t Another Rich Kid, created these high-top Nike Dunks dipped in 18-carat gold as part of a fashion show in New York in 2007. Five pairs were made, costing $4,053 (£2,702) each.

MOST EXPENSIVE COIN SOLD AT AUCTION

The most expensive coin in the world is the 1933 Double Eagle, a $20 gold coin that was auctioned at Sotheby's, New York City, USA, on 30 July 2002 and which fetched substantially more than $20 – $7,590,020 (£4,856,370), in fact, including buyer's premium.

★ NEW RECORD
UPDATED RECORD

MOST DUCTILE ELEMENT

Gold is not only a precious metal, it's also exceptionally malleable and can even be spun into a thread suitable for embroidery. One gram of gold can be drawn to 2.4 km (1.4 miles), or 1 oz to 69.2 km (43 miles).

LARGEST GOLD NUGGET

The Holtermann Nugget, which weighed 235.14 kg (7,257 oz, or 7,560 troy oz), was found on 19 October 1872 in the Beyers Holtermann Star of Hope mine in New South Wales, Australia. It contained some 82.11 kg (2,534 oz; 2,640 troy oz) of gold.

LARGEST BAR OF GOLD

The largest manufactured pure gold bar weighs 250 kg (551 lb 2 oz) and was created by the Mitsubishi Materials Corporation on 11 June 2005 at the Naoshima Smelter & Refinery in Kagawa Prefecture, Japan.

DEEPEST MINE

With a depth of 3,777 m (12,391 ft) as of 2005, the Savuka Mine in South Africa is the largest and deepest gold mine. Miners extract rock that contains about 20 cm (1.2 in) of gold in each cubic metre.

請勿觸摸

★ LARGEST PRODUCER OF GOLD

China mined 276 metric tons (9.7 million oz) of gold in 2007, representing one-tenth of world supply. This was the first time since 1905 that South Africa was not responsible for the greatest output.
The **largest gold production company** is Barrick (Canada), with 27 mines in five continents and over 20,000 personnel. It also has the **largest gold reserves for a company**, with 124.6 million oz.

LARGEST GOLD RESERVES

The United States Treasury currently holds 8,133.5 tonnes of gold, worth $241 billion at July 2008 prices – the largest reserve of any single country.

MOST EXPENSIVE BATHROOM

In October 2008, we heard the sad news of the death of self-made jewellery tycoon Lam Sai-wing at the age of just 53. Lam was famous for spending HK$27 million (£2.4 million; $3.5 million) on a lavish loo in his Hong Kong shop. The toilet bowls, wash basins, mirror frames, wall tiles, floors and doors are all made out of solid 24-carat gold. Not everyone can "spend a penny" in Lam's loo, however – only customers spending over a certain amount in his store!

Jul 14: Richard Presley (USA) spent 69 days 19 min in a module under water – the **longest time spent living under water** – at a lagoon in Key Largo, Florida, USA, from 6 May to 14 July 1992.

Jul 15: The **largest firework** was the Universe I Part II, exploded in Hokkaido, Japan, on 15 July 1988. The 700-kg (1,543-lb) shell was 139 cm (54.75 in) in diameter.

> **145,000 tonnes:** the weight of all the gold ever mined as of 2001. This would form a solid gold cube with a length of 20 m (66 ft) and, at October 2008 prices, be worth $3.39 trillion!

LARGEST COIN

You'd need a pretty big pocket for the world's largest coin. It weighs 100 kg (220 lb 7 oz), measures 50 cm (19.6 in) in diameter and 3 cm (1.1 in) in thickness, and is made from bullion with a purity of 99.999%. The legal-tender coin was introduced on 3 May 2007 by the Royal Canadian Mint and has a face value of CAN$1 million ($900,375; £451,585).

MOST VALUABLE RELGIOUS ARTEFACT

The 15th-century gold Buddha in Wat Trimitr Temple in Bangkok, Thailand, measures 3 m (10 ft) tall and weighs an estimated 5.5 tonnes (12,125 lb). At the December 2008 price of $821.48 (£567) per fine ounce, its intrinsic worth was over $159 million (£109 million). The gold was only discovered under a layer of plaster in 1954.

★ MOST EXPENSIVE MUG

A 23-carat gold mug made by Yoo Long Kim Kee Gold Store (Thailand) was bought for 1,000,023 Thai Baht ($33,842; £17,293) by Nestlé Thai Ltd on 9 January 2008.

MOST LEAD TURNED INTO GOLD

In 1980, the renowned scientist Glenn Seaborg (USA) transmuted several thousand atoms of lead into gold at the Lawrence Berkeley Laboratory in California, USA. His experimental technique, which uses nuclear physics to remove protons and neutrons from the lead atoms, is far too expensive to enable routine manufacturing of gold from lead. Even so, Seaborg's work is the closest thing yet to the Philosopher's Stone – a mythical object that would reputedly turn base metal into gold.

LARGEST GOLD RING

The Najmat Taiba (which means "Star of Taiba") was created by Taiba (United Arab Emirates) for the Gold and Jewellery Co. Ltd of Saudi Arabia. No ordinary piece of finger jewellery, this ring is 70 cm (27.5 in) wide – the same diameter as a hula hoop! – and weighs 63.8 kg (140 lb 12 oz), about the same as a fully grown man! It consists of 5.17 kg (11.39 lb) of precious jewels set on a 58.68-kg (129-lb 5-oz), 21-carat gold ring. It took 55 workers 45 days to construct.

★ FIRST GOLD-PLATED PORSCHE

In 2005, German company Visualis commissioned an artist to gild a Porsche Boxster in 22-carat beaten gold. There are now plans to release a limited-edition model and plate nine further Porsches, though a price for this ultimate symbol of wealth and luxury has not yet been fixed.

★ LARGEST KNOWN GOLD REPOSITORY

The Federal Reserve Bank of New York, at 33 Liberty Street, Manhattan, holds an estimated 5,000 tonnes of gold bullion, worth $160 billion (£80.2 million) as of March 2008. The vault – which lies 26 m (86 ft) below sea level – is only the largest *known* repository; Swiss banks famous for not revealing details of their gold stocks may hold more.

LARGEST TRANSACTION FOR A NUMISMATIC ITEM

The largest known transaction for a single numismatic item (i.e. one relating to coins, currency or medals) took place on 7 November 2001, when a 30-kg (80-lb) pioneer gold bar retrieved from the SS *Central America*, wrecked in 1857, was bought anonymously for $8 million (£5.5 million).

DEEPEST SALVAGE WITH DIVERS

HM cruiser *Edinburgh* sank on 2 May 1942 off northern Norway in 245 m (803 ft) of water. For a period of 31 days (from 7 September to 7 October 1981), 12 divers worked on the wreck in pairs, recovering 460 gold ingots in all.

DID YOU KNOW?

The largest coin may have a face value of CAN$1 million but at December 2008 gold prices, it would cost CAN$3.60 million ($2.89 million; £1.93 million) to buy! With gold, it is the mass and purity that matters, not the face value of coins.

HEAVIEST GOLD HOARD

On 25 January 1917, the White Star Liner HMS *Laurentic* sank after striking a mine in 40 m (132 ft) of water off Malin Head, Donegal, Ireland. A hoard of gold ingots weighing 43 tonnes (96,320 lb) (worth £5 million ($23.8 million) in 1917) has been recovered from the wreck over the years.

MOST VALUABLE SHIPWRECK

Mel Fisher (USA), one of the most famous treasure hunters of the 20th century, found the *Nuestra Señora de Atocha* off Florida, USA, on 20 July 1985. When it sank in a hurricane in 1622, it had been carrying a cargo worth hundreds of millions of dollars, among it 44 tonnes (40 tons) of gold and silver, some 31.75 kg (70 lb) of emeralds, 20 bronze cannon, 525 bales of tobacco and countless items left unregistered to avoid taxation. So vast was the cargo that it had taken two months to load; no surprise, then, that it all sank in a matter of minutes.

Jul 16: The **greatest recorded crowd at any football match** was 199,854 for the Brazil v. Uruguay World Cup match in Rio de Janeiro, Brazil, on 16 July 1950.

Jul 17: Professional stuntman Ted A. Batchelor (USA) endured the **longest full-body burn (without oxygen)** for 2 min 38 sec on an island at Ledges Quarry Park, Nelson, Ohio, USA, on 17 July 2004.

TOYS & GAMES

★ LARGEST DISPLAY OF LEGO *STAR WARS* CLONE TROOPERS

The world's largest construction and display of Lego *Star Wars* Clone Troopers was composed of 35,210 individual models and was built by Lego in Slough, UK, on 27 June 2008.

MOST HOOPS HULA-HOOPING

Jin Linlin (China) successfully hula-hooped 105 hoops on the set of *Zheng Da Zong Yi – Guinness World Records Special* in Beijing, China, on 28 October 2007. The guidelines require three full revolutions of standard-size hula hoops between the shoulders and hips.

★ LARGEST MARBLE TOURNAMENT

The largest marble tournament was set by 677 participants playing the game Ringer in an event organized by the Toy & Miniature Museum of Kansas City in Missouri, USA, on 23 August 2008.

★ LARGEST TEDDY BEAR MOSAIC

A teddy bear mosaic measuring 57.04 m² (614 ft²) was made by the Chelsea Teddy Bear Company in Chelsea, Michigan, USA, on 26 July 2008. Members of the public contributed bears to help create a large peace symbol mosaic in the company car park.

★ MOST TRAVELLED TOY MASCOT

A bear called Rex Lancaster, owned by Rex Travel Organization Inc. (USA), travelled 453,056 km (281,516 miles) from 9 November 2005 to 5 May 2006, passing through seven continents and 30 countries on his journey.

★ FASTEST SLOT CAR

A Scalextric Honda F1 replica reached a speed of 1,583.4 scale km/h (983.88 scale mph) when it was controlled by Dallas Campbell (UK) of *The Gadget Show* at the Chatsworth Rally Show, Chatsworth, UK, on 6 June 2008.

★ MOST EXPENSIVE TOY CAR

A red-and-green model delivery van with the name W E Boyce on the side sold for a record £19,975 ($39,852) in March 2008. First sold in the 1930s for about £0.10 (then $0.30), the van was sold by Vectis Auctions of Teeside, UK.

LARGEST IMAGE BUILT WITH LEGO

A picture made from 1.2 million Lego bricks was found to have an area of 80.84 m² (870.15 ft²) when measured on 24 October 2007. Completed by The Toy Museum during August 2007 in Bellaire, Ohio, USA, the picture was 13.61 x 5.95 m (44 ft 8 in x 19 ft 6 in) in size and took over 2,000 hours to complete. The image was essentially that of a truck with different designs created in the "cargo" being carried by the vehicle.

★ LARGEST GATHERING OF SOFT TOYS

The Girl Scouts of Southeast Florida, USA, organized a record-breaking gathering of 5,884 soft toys at Roger Dean Stadium in Jupiter, Florida, USA, on 6 September 2008.

HAND-IN-PAW

The longest human/soft-toy chain included 2,623 people, each with a soft toy, and was achieved in an event organized by the JJ van der Merwe Primary School in Ermelo, South Africa, on 29 August 2008.

21,600: the number of pieces in the world's **largest jigsaw puzzle**, which was 5,428 m² (58,435 ft²) when measured in Hong Kong, China, on 3 November 2002.

LARGEST PLAYABLE TWISTER BOARD

A playable Twister board measuring 39 m (128 ft) long and 36.2 m (119 ft) wide was put together at the University of Tulsa in Oklahoma, USA, on 23 October 2008. In total, 600 standard Twister boards were used, covering an area of 1,415.1 m² (15,232 ft²).

★ **NEW RECORD**
★ **UPDATED RECORD**

FASTEST TIME TO SOLVE A RUBIK'S CUBE BY A ROBOT

Invented by Peter Redmond (Ireland), "Rubot2" solved a Rubik's cube in 1 min 4 sec at the BT Young Scientist & Technology Exhibition, Dublin, Ireland on 8 January 2009.

FACT
The fastest time to solve the Cube by a human is 9.55 sec by Ron van Bruchem (Netherlands) on 24 November 2007.

★ **MOST EXPENSIVE TOY SOLDIER SOLD AT AUCTION**
The most valuable toy soldier in the world is the first handcrafted 1963 GI Joe prototype, which was sold on 7 August 2003 by its creator Don Levine to businessman Stephen A Geppi (USA) for $200,000 (£124,300) during an auction conducted by Heritage Comics Auctions of Dallas, Texas, USA.

★ **LARGEST TEDDY BEAR (STITCHED)**
Dana Warren (USA) constructed a stitched teddy bear measuring a record 16.86 m (55 ft 4 in) in length. The bear was completed on 6 June 2008 and displayed at the Exploration Place, Wichita, Kansas, USA.

★ **LONGEST TOY TRAIN TRACK**
A wooden toy train track measuring 1,650.14 m (5,413 ft 10 in) – that's 1.65 km (1.02 miles) long – was built by Friends of Thomas "Team Japan" in collaboration with Fuji Television Network Inc., Fuji Television Kids Entertainment Inc. and Sony Creative Products Inc. at Mediage/Aqua City Odaiba, Japan, on 23 August 2006.

★ **SCRABBLE, MOST SIMULTANEOUS OPPONENTS**
On 7 November 2007, Ganesh Asirvatham (Malaysia) played Scrabble against 25 opponents simultaneously, winning 21 of the 25 games. The attempt took place in Mumbai, India, and was organized by Mattel Toys (India) Pvt. Ltd.

EARLIEST CARTOON MERCHANDISE
Pat Sullivan's (USA) Felix the Cat, who appeared in 1919 as the animal that "kept on walking", was not only the first cartoon character to attain the celebrity of a human star but also the first to be used as an image on packaging, in 1924. Felix was also merchandized as a hugely successful cuddly toy two years later.

TALLEST LEGO STRUCTURE

The tallest structure built from Lego was 29.48 m (96 ft 8 in) high and was constructed by Per K. Knudsen, Finn Flou Laursen and Karsten Niebuhr (all Denmark) from Lego CE in collaboration with Die Kinderfreunde at the Rathausplatz in Vienna, Austria, 2 to 5 October 2008. The tower used more than 450,000 stones (bricks), almost all of them having eight studs. The bricks were put together in blocks by Viennese children, and the architects added the blocks in the tower.

Jul 18: Michael O'Shaughnessy (USA) accomplished the **fastest crossing of the English Channel by paddleboard** in a time of 5 hr 9 min on this day in 2006.

Jul 19: The **largest rocking horse** measured 4.8 m x 4.8 m x 2.7 m (15 ft 7 in x 15 ft 7 in x 8 ft 9 in). The horse was made by citizens of Hanno, Saitama, Japan, and completed on 19 July 2004.

CLOTHES

★ MOST PANTS WORN AT THE SAME TIME

Carl Saville (UK, far left) wore 137 pairs of underpants at the same time on the set of *Guinness World Records – Smashed*, in London, UK, on 3 October 2008.

Jef Van Dijck (Belgium, left) holds the record for the **most T-shirts worn at the same time** – a total of 227 – at an attempt organized by Unizo in Brecht, Belgium, on 24 April 2008.

BRA

In September 1990, Triumph International Japan Ltd developed a brassiere with an underbust measurement of 24 m (78 ft 8 in) and a bust measurement of 28 m (91 ft 10 in).

★ UNDERPANTS

Giant underpants measuring 17.75 m (58 ft 3 in) across the waist and 11.82 m (38 ft 9 in) from waistband to crotch were manufactured by Angajala Venkata Giri (India). They were presented and measured in Jeypore, India, on 15 December 2007.

T-SHIRT

A T-shirt measuring 57.19 m (187 ft 7 in) long and 40.88 m (134 ft 1 in) wide was made by OMO Safe Detergent in Ho Chi Minh City, Vietnam, and displayed on 9 March 2006.

★ RETAILERS OF MEN'S SUITS

Aoyama Trading Company (Japan) are the largest menswear retailers of suits in the world. From January to December 2007, the company sold 2,725,359 men's suits.

LARGEST...

HAWAIIAN SHIRT

In March 1999, Hilo Hattie (USA), a retailer of Hawaiian fashions in Hawaii, USA, created an aloha shirt with a chest measurement of 4.26 m (14 ft), a waist of 3.5 m (11 ft 5 in) and a neck of 1.53 m (5 ft).

TROUSERS

Trousers measuring 10.83 m (35 ft 6 in) long with a 6.4-m (20-ft 10-in) waist were made by Value Planning Co., Ltd, on 27 December 2006.

★ **NEW RECORD**
UPDATED RECORD

★ APRON

A kitchen apron measuring 17.6 m (57 ft 8 in) long and 15.4 m (50 ft 6 in) wide – and weighing 50 kg (110 lb) – was manufactured by Ignacio Rodriguez (Spain) in San Sebastian, Spain, on 15 January 2007.

PAIR OF SOCKS

A pair of long nylon socks, measuring 114 cm (45 in) from top to toe and 25 cm (10 in) wide, were made by Michael Roy Layne (USA) in October 1986 and displayed outside City Hall in Boston, USA, to celebrate the Red Sox baseball team entering the World Series.

★ LARGEST HIKING BOOT

A hiking boot measuring 7.1 m (23 ft 5 in) long, 2.5 m (8 ft 2 in) wide and 4.2 m (13 ft 9 in) tall was made by Schuh Marke (Germany) and presented in Hauenstein, Germany, on 30 September 2006. The boot weighs 1,500 kg (3,306 lb), the leather used weighs 300 kg (661 lb) and the shoelace is 35 m (114 ft 9 in) in length. Pictured measuring the boot are Guinness World Records adjudicators Kristian (top) and Andrea.

BEST FOOT FORWARD

The ★ **largest cowboy boot** measures 2.50 m (8 ft 2 in) in height and 2.38 m (7 ft 9 in) in length and was made by Belachew Tola Buta (Ethiopia). The boot was measured in Addis Ababa, Ethiopia, on 24 January 2008.

Jul 20: The **largest mirrored disco ball** measures 7.35 m (24 ft 1.3 in) in diameter and was made by Raf Frateur of Frateur Events. It was displayed at "Studio 54" in Antwerp, Belgium, on this day in 2007.

Jul 21: A temperature of -89.2°C (-128.6°F) was registered at Vostok, Antarctica, on 21 July 1983, the **lowest recorded temperature on Earth**.

20: the number of underpants Joel Nathan (Australia) put on in one minute in Perth, Australia, on 27 July 2007 – a record shared with Alastair Galpin (NZ).

LARGEST MEN'S SUIT

Between 14 February and 7 March 2001, tailors from Raymond Ltd constructed the world's largest men's suit at their factory in Mumbai, India. From shoulder to trouser hem, the suit measured 19.5 m (64 ft) long.

SOCKS WORN ON ONE FOOT

Alastair Galpin (New Zealand) managed to fit 74 socks on one foot for Guinness World Records Day in Auckland, New Zealand, on 7 November 2006.

LARGEST PAIR OF JEANS

Workers from textile company Corporacion Wama Pieers (Peru) created a pair of jeans measuring 40 m (131 ft) long, 30 m (98 ft) wide and weighing more than 2 tonnes (2.2 tons). The jeans, which were cut from 3,000 m (9,842 ft) of cloth, were unveiled in Lima, Peru, on 30 October 2008.

FACT
The most expensive pair of jeans (commercially available) are Escada's Couture Swarovski Crystal Jeans, which could be bought from Neiman Marcus Stores in 2006 for a mere $10,000 (£5,800)!

EXPENSIVE JEANS

An original pair of 115-year-old Levi Strauss & Co. (USA) 501 jeans were sold by Randy Knight (USA) to an anonymous collector from Japan for $60,000 (£33,230) through internet auction site eBay on 15 June 2005.

★ SOCKS SORTED IN ONE MINUTE

Kristina Ilieva (Bulgaria) sorted socks into 16 correct pairs at the Guinness World Records Pavilion in Global Village, Dubai, United Arab Emirates, on 24 November 2008.

★ GLOVES WORN ON ONE HAND

Multiple record-holder Alastair Galpin (New Zealand) was able to get 24 gloves on to one hand at the Old Homestead Community House in Auckland, New Zealand, on 2 November 2008.

EXPENSIVE DRESS SOLD AT AUCTION

The flesh-coloured beaded Jean Louis (France) gown worn by actress Marilyn Monroe (USA) when she sang "Happy Birthday" to President John F. Kennedy on 19 May 1962 was sold at auction on 27 October 1999 for $1,267,000 (£767,042) at Christie's, New York, USA. It was sold to New York dealers Robert Schagrin and Peter Siegel of Gotta Have It! Collectibles. The sale, of more than 100 of Monroe's belongings, raised $13,405,785 (£8,115,862).

EXPENSIVE SHOES FROM A FILM SOLD AT AUCTION

The ruby slippers worn by Judy Garland (USA) in the film *The Wizard of Oz* (USA, 1939) sold at Christie's, New York, USA, on 24 May 2000 for $666,000 (£450,948). Made by Innes Shoe Co., Los Angeles, the shoes are constructed from red silk faille overlaid with hand-sequined georgette and lined with white kid leather.

★ MOST GARTERS REMOVED WITH THE TEETH

Ivo Grosche (Germany) removed 26 garter belts from the legs of willing volunteers using just his teeth in a period of two minutes on the set of *Guinness World Records: Die Größten Weltrekörde* in Germany, on 18 December 2008.

MOST...

★ EXPENSIVE COSTUME FROM A FILM

A black cocktail dress designed by Hubert de Givenchy (France) and worn by Audrey Hepburn (Belgium) in the iconic film *Breakfast at Tiffany's* (USA, 1961) was sold to an anonymous bidder by the author Dominique Lapierre (France) at Christie's, London, UK, for £467,200 ($924,401) on 5 December 2006.

EXPENSIVE JACKET SOLD AT AUCTION

The most valuable jacket sold at auction belonged to rock legend Jimi Hendrix (USA) and was sold to the Hard Rock Cafe chain on 19 September 2000 for £35,000 ($49,185). The sale was organized by Sotheby's at the London, UK, branch of the Hard Rock Cafe.

Jul 22: The **oldest panda ever** in captivity was Dudu, who was born in 1962 and lived for most of her life in Wuhan Zoo, Chengdu, China, until her death on 22 July 1999, aged 37 years.

MODERN WORLD
COLLECTIONS

★ CAN YOU BEAT THIS?

Is *your* collection a world beater? Contact us if:
1. You've amassed the items personally over time (not just inherited or bought the lot).
2. Every object is different.
3. You have a log book in which the items are numbered and described.

Find out more about how to be a record breaker on p.14 or visit www.guinnessworldrecords.com

★ POKÉMON

As of 1 April 2008, Belle Starenchak (USA) of Dunnellon, Florida, USA, had amassed 5,456 different items of Pokémon memorabilia over 10 years of collecting. Starenchak's favourite Pokémon is Pikachu and her collection boasts one of the official Volkswagen beetle Pikachu Cars, which she named "PikaBug".

BADGES

As of 19 June 2008, Seppo Mäkinen (Finland) had collected 30,105 different badges from over 50 countries.

★ DONALD DUCK MEMORABILIA

The largest collection of Donald Duck memorabilia belongs to Mary Brooks (USA), with 1,285 different items as of 28 May 2008. Her collection is over 30 years old.

★ DEMITASSE CUPS

Paul Pisasale (Australia) had a collection of 650 different demitasse cups, as of 11 March 2008. Pisasale has been collecting the cups, which are used to serve espresso, since 1993.

★ ELEPHANTS

Janet Mallernee-Briley (USA) – aka The Elephant Lady – has a collection of elephant-related items that numbered 5,779 as of 8 April 2008. The previous holder – Sandy Rosen-Hazen (USA) – died in May 2007, leaving behind a collection of 4,233 objects, but not before the two women could meet in an online elephant-collecting community.

★ MINIATURE CHAIRS

Barbara Hartsfield (USA) has collected miniature chairs for over 10 years and owned 3,000 examples as of 13 March 2008.

★ MOBILE PHONES

Carsten Tews (Germany) had 1,260 different mobile phones, as of 12 April 2008, collected over the last decade. The oldest item in his collection is a TeKaDe BSA 31 car phone.

★ MOUSE MATS

As of 19 April 2008, Daniel Evans (UK) had 3,673 different mouse mats, amassed since 2001. His first mat was a gift from his mother, who had won it in a competition.

PENGUINS

Birgit Berends (Germany) had a 5,098-strong penguin collection, as of 12 March 2008. Birgit started her collection in 1990 because of the animated series *Pingu*. Her favourite penguin is a real living specimen named Alfred, whom she has adopted in the Cuxhaven Kurpark in Germany.

"DO NOT DISTURB" SIGNS

Jean-François Vernetti (Switzerland) has collected 8,888 different "Do Not Disturb" signs from hotels in 189 countries across the world since 1985. Jean-François began his collection after spotting a spelling error on a "Do Not Disturb" sign he was using at a hotel in Sheffield, UK.

Jul 23: The **heaviest combined weight balanced on the head in one hour** is 5,180.09 kg (11,420 lb 2 oz) by John Evans (UK) in Lowestoft, Suffolk, UK, on 23 July 2000.

Jul 24: The **longest inverted flight** lasted 4 hr 38 min 10 sec, and was performed by Joann Osterud (Canada) flying from Vancouver to Vanderhoof, Canada, on 24 July 1991.

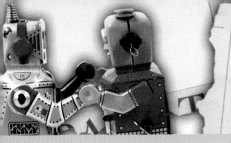

20,202: the number of unique items in Mark Hendrickx's (Netherlands) **largest collection of beer bottles**. It includes bottles from 2,302 breweries across 120 countries.

★ DALMATIANS

Kazzy Ferrier (UK) has been collecting dotty dalmatian-related objects since 1992, when Ditto, a real dalmation puppy, entered her life. She currently owns over 5,000 items, including teapots, snow globes, curtains, keyrings, toilet paper and 1,117 different ornaments. She even drives a spotty Smart car!

★ PANDA ITEMS

Janice Kennedy (New Zealand) has been collecting panda items since 1960 and had a total of 252 as of 7 August 2008.

★ SILVER COINS

The largest collection of silver coins consists of 1,600 non-duplicate coins from around the world. The collection – which was assessed in person by a Guinness World Records adjudicator on 1 July 2008 – belongs to a Mexican man who does not want his name published for fear of being kidnapped or having his collection stolen.

SNOW GLOBES

Wendy Suen's (China) love of snow globes – and in particular mini globes no larger than a golf ball – has resulted in a unique collection that numbered 1,888 as of 7 April 2008.

★ STAMPS FEATURING EYEGLASSES

Jane Lippert Hushea (USA) of Pompano Beach, Florida, USA, has a total of 1,476 stamps featuring people wearing eyeglasses, an unusual collection that she started in 1952.

SICKBAGS

Niek Vermeulen's (Netherlands) collection of airline sickness bags has now grown to an incredible 5,468. He has accumulated the sick sacks since the 1970s from 1,065 different airlines – as well as from the Space Shuttle and *Air Force One.*

★ THIMBLES

Donna Decator (USA) has been collecting thimbles since 1986 and owned a grand total of 4,930 unique items as of 15 October 2008.

★ TOOTHBRUSHES

Grigori Fleicher (Russia) owns 1,320 different toothbrushes; he has also amassed over 3,000 other dental healthcare products.

★ NEW RECORD
UPDATED RECORD

CLOCKS

One man with time on his hands – or at least walls – is Jack Schoff (USA), owner of a record 1,094 working time pieces of varying types as of 17 June 2008. "Collecting clocks keeps me sane," says Jack.

TROLLS

Sophie Marie Cross's (UK) army of 490 different trolls is the largest in the world. She started collecting the cute little critters in 2003. A troll can be identified by its colourful, long, wild hair, its squashed nose and its forward-pointing ears.

163

Jul 25: Louise Brown (UK), the **first test-tube baby**, was delivered by Caesarean section from Lesley Brown (UK) in Oldham General Hospital, Lancashire, UK, on this day in 1978.

1,000 m (3,281 ft): proposed height of the Nakheel Tower, currently under construction in Dubai, UAE.

ENGINEERING & TECHNOLOGY

TOP **100** Records of the Decade

★ TALLEST STRUCTURE

On 17 January 2009, the Burj Dubai ("Dubai Tower"; architects: Skidmore, Owings & Merrill LLP) in Dubai, United Arab Emirates, topped out at a record-breaking 818 m (2,684 ft), making it the ★ **tallest man-made structure** on Earth, surpassing the 628.8-m-tall (1,815-ft 5-in) KVLY-TV mast in North Dakota, USA. It is also the ★ **tallest man-made structure ever** (surpassing the 646.38-m-tall; 2,120-ft 8-in Warszawa radio mast in Poland, which fell down during renovation in 1991) and the ★ **tallest free-standing structure** (beating the 553.34-m-tall; 1,815-ft 5-in CN Tower in Canada).

The construction also established a new record for the ★ **highest vertical concrete pumping** (601 m; 1,972 ft), beating the 532 m (1,745 ft) height achieved during the building of the Riva del Garda hydroelectric plant in Italy.

At the time of going to press (May 2009), the Burj Dubai had yet to be named as the world's **tallest building**, as it had not been officially opened – a key criteria for the Guinness World Record, as agreed with the Council on Tall Buildings and Urban Habitat. At the time of press, Taipei 101 in Taiwan remains the record holder at 508 m; 1,666 ft.

CONTENTS

ECO TRANSPORT

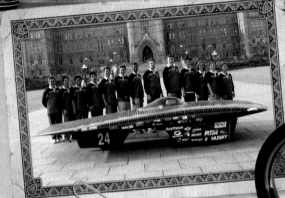

LONGEST JOURNEY BY SOLAR ELECTRIC VEHICLE

The *Midnight Sun* solar car team from the University of Waterloo in Ontario, Canada, travelled 15,070 km (9,364 miles) through Canada and the USA, departing from Waterloo on 7 August and finishing back in Ottawa on 15 September 2004.

★ LOWEST FUEL CONSUMPTION ACROSS 48 US STATES

Between 3 and 25 September 2008, Helen and John Taylor (both Australia) achieved an average fuel consumption of 3.99 litres/100 km (70.64 miles/UK gallon) while driving a 2009 VW Jetta TDI powered with Shell diesel over 15,158 km (9,419 miles) through all 48 contiguous US states.

The Taylors also set the record for the ★ **lowest fuel consumption driving around Australia** when they covered a distance of 14,580 km (9,059 miles) on just 453.94 litres (99.85 UK gallons; 119.91 US gallons) of Shell diesel, in a Peugeot 308 HDi, between 3 and 26 February 2008 – a fuel consumption of 3.13 litres/100 km (90.75 miles/gallon).

LARGEST PEDAL-POWERED VEHICLE

The largest pedal-powered vehicle is capable of carrying 104 riders and was built by Alloy Fabweld in conjunction with the Great Dunmow Round Table at Duxford Airfield, Cambridgeshire, UK, on 22 September 2007.

★ LONGEST JOURNEY ON AN ELECTRIC MOBILITY VEHICLE (SCOOTER)

John Duckworth (UK) travelled 2,662.8 km (1,654.6 miles) around mainland UK on a Horizon Mayan electric mobility scooter between 20 June and 27 July 2004, finishing in Hincaster, Cumbria, UK.

★ FASTEST ELECTRIC MOTORCYCLE

The *KillaCycle* electric motorcycle can accelerate from 0 to 60 mph in less than a second and is powered by a lithium ion phosphate battery pack. It has a top speed of 270 km/h (168 mph) and covers a quarter of a mile in 7.95 seconds (500 m in 9.85 seconds).

BEST-SELLING HYBRID CAR

Global sales of the Toyota Prius exceeded the 1 million mark in 2008, with a total of 1,028,000 sold by the end of April. As of February 2009, US sales alone reached 1 million. "Hybrid" vehicles use two or more power sources, typically an internal combustion engine and electric motor(s).

MOST FUEL-EFFICIENT CAR

The PAC-Car II from the Swiss Federal Institute of Technology Zurich used 0.01857 litres (0.00408 gallons) of petrol for 100 km (62 miles, equivalent to 24,481 km/g 15,212 mpg) on 26 June 2005.

Jul 26: The **largest permanent Monopoly board** measures 9.44 x 9.44 m (31 x 31 ft). Located in San Jose, California, USA, it was officially opened to the public on this day in 2002.

395.821 km/h (245.523 mph): the **highest speed achieved by an electric vehicle**, set by Patrick Rummerfield (USA) on 22 October 1999.

★ MOST FUEL-EFFICIENT 40-TON TRUCK

The Mercedes Benz Actros used 19.44 litres per 100 km (6.88 gallons per 100 miles) under test drive conditions at the high speed track of Nardò in Brindisi, Italy, in May 2008. This average was established by driving the truck for one week – 24 hours a day – over 12,728 km (7,908 miles) of track.

★ FIRST HYDROGEN FUEL CELL CAR

The FCX Clarity was developed by Honda and introduced in 2008. Its hydrogen fuel cell (the red unit pictured right) produces no carbon monoxide (CO), carbon dioxide (CO_2), hydrocarbons (HC) or oxides of nitrogen (NOx) – its only emissions are heat and water vapour (H_2O). The company plan to lease 200 of the cars between 2008 and 2010.

★ FIRST FLIGHT BY A COMMERCIAL AIRLINER USING NATURAL GAS FUEL

On 1 February 2008, an Airbus A-380 MSN004 – the world's **largest passenger airliner** – successfully completed the first ever flight by a commercial aircraft using a liquid fuel processed from gas (a GTL, or "gas to liquid" fuel). The flight from Filton in Bristol, UK, to Toulouse, France, took three hours. The aircraft uses Rolls-Royce Trent 900 engines, and Shell International Petroleum provided the GTL jet fuel. During the flight, one engine was fed with a blend of GTL and jet fuel while the remaining three were fed with standard jet fuel.

The flight marks the start of a programme to evaluate sustainable alternative fuels for the future. Airbus predicts that about 25% of fuel used in aviation will come from alternative sources by 2025.

★ FIRST JET AIRCRAFT POWERED BY BIODIESEL

On 2 October 2007, the first flight of a jet-fighter powered only with 100% biodiesel fuel took place at Reno, Nevada, USA. The aircraft was an unmodified Czech Delfín L-29 (Albatross). It reached an altitude of 5,181 m (17,000 ft) without any significant loss of performance compared with a flight using conventional fuel.

A series of tests had been undertaken with a blend of jet fuel and biodiesel; the amount of biodiesel was gradually increased until test data with 100% biodiesel – made from vegetable oil used to fry chips – was found to be acceptable.

★ FASTEST BIODIESEL-FUELLED BOAT

Running entirely on biodiesel and incorporating hemp for the first time in any boat construction, *Earthrace* is one of the most environmentally friendly vessels in the world. Skippered by Pete Bethune (New Zealand), the wave-piercing trimaran completed a round-the-world trip on 27 June 2008 after just 60 days 23 hr 49 min, shaving 13 days off the record for powerboats.

Jul 27: The world's **largest lollipop** weighed 2.1 tonnes (2.3 tons) and was made by Franssons (Sweden) for a festival in Gränna, Sweden, on 27 July 2003.

Jul 28: The **largest button mosaic** measured 66.89 m² (720 ft²), contained 296,981 buttons and was made at Maritime Square, Tsing Yi District, Hong Kong, between 23 and 28 July 2006.

CARS & BIKES

FASTEST POLICE CAR IN SERVICE

With a top speed of 370 km/h (230 mph) and a power output of 372 kW (500 bhp), the fastest police car is the Lamborghini Gallardo LP560-4, which is in service with the Italian State Police. A pool of just 30 policemen and women are permitted to drive the car after taking special training.

★ FARTHEST REVERSE RAMP JUMP BY CAR

A stuntman reversed an Austin Allegro car up a ramp, clearing a distance of 18.62 m (61 ft 2 in) over a "cushion" of cars in Woodbridge, Suffolk, UK, on 27 May 2008. The Allegro that was used in the stunt, which was filmed for the motor vehicle-based television programme *Top Gear* (BBC, UK), was only modified with a roll-cage and cleared 10 cars before smashing into the 11th. The anonymous stuntman was unhurt.

LONGEST CAR

Jay Ohrberg of Burbank, California, USA, designed a 26-wheel limousine measuring 30.5 m (100 ft) long. A truly luxurious vehicle, the car includes a swimming pool with diving board and a king-sized water bed.

CHEAPEST PRODUCTION CAR

The cheapest production car is the Tata Nano, a four-door, five-seater family car with a 33 bhp, 623 cc rear-engine (with a maximum speed of 70 km/h, or 43 mph), which went on sale on 23 March 2009 for 100,000 rupees ($1,979; £1,366). Tata Motors (India) launched the car at the 9th Auto Expo in New Delhi, India, on 10 January 2008, with the aim of providing car ownership to millions of people across the developing world.

LONGEST MOTORCYCLE

Colin Furze (UK) built a motorcycle that was found to be 14.03 m (46 ft 3 in) long when it was measured at Saltby Aerodrome, Leicestershire, UK, on 14 October 2008. Furze's bike, made from two 50 cc Honda Sky mopeds and an aluminium trellis, was long in the making – he found he was constantly walking from one end of his creation to the other to find his tools!

★ FASTEST SPEED ON A TOP-FUEL DRAGBIKE

Top Fuel Dragbiker Larry "Spiderman" McBride (USA, pictured) achieved a speed of 394.87 km/h (245.36 mph) over a quarter of a mile, a record for Top Fuel Dragbike racing, on 6 March 2006 at South Georgia Motorsports Park, Valdosta, Georgia, USA.

★ LARGEST AUTOMATED TRUCK

Engineers from Caterpillar Inc. (USA) and computer scientists from Carnegie Mellon University (USA) are working together to automate 635-tonne (700-ton) Caterpillar trucks designed to haul loads up to 217.7 tonnes (240 tons) as part of the US Defence Advanced Research Projects Agency (DARPA) Urban Challenge. The goal is to use automation technology including Global Positioning Satellite (GPS) receivers to improve efficiency and reduce the risk of injury to people in the hazardous environments in which high-capacity trucks operate.

LARGEST MONSTER TRUCK

Bigfoot 5 is 4.7 m (15 ft 6 in) tall with 3-m-high (10-ft) tyres and weighs 17,236 kg (38,000 lb). Built in the summer of 1986, the monster truck is one of a fleet of 17 Bigfoot vehicles created by Bob Chandler of St Louis, Missouri, USA.

SMALLEST PRODUCTION CAR

Smaller than an average fairground "dodgem" car, the Peel P50 is 134 cm (53 in) long, 99 cm (39 in) wide and 134 cm (53 in) high. The vehicle, which weighs a mere 59 kg (130 lb) and has a top speed of 61 km/h (38 mph), was constructed by Peel Engineering Co. at Peel, Isle of Man, between 1962 and 1965.

Jul 29: Born on this day in 1977, Balamurali Ambati (USA) became the world's **youngest doctor** on 19 May 1995 at the age of 17 years 294 days when he graduated from medical school.

4.749 tonnes (5.234 tons): the weight of the **heaviest motorcycle**, the *Harzer Bike Schmiede*, built by Tilo and Wilfried Niebel of Zilly, Germany.

★ FIRST "ROADABLE" AIRCRAFT

The *Terrafugia Transition*, an aeroplane described by its manufacturers, Terrafugia (USA), as "roadable" because it can become a car, successfully completed its first flight at Plattsburgh International Airport in Plattsburgh, New York, USA, on 5 March 2009. The two-seater aircraft has a range of 724 km (450 miles) and can reach speeds of 185 km/h (115 mph). The plane converts into a car in just 15 seconds, with the wings folding automatically at the touch of a button.

FASTEST PRODUCTION CAR

An Ultimate Aero TT Super Car, manufactured by Shelby Supercars (USA), achieved two-way timed speeds in excess of 412 km/h (256.14 mph) on Highway 221, Washington, USA, on 13 September 2007.

TOP 100 Records of the Decade

FASTEST LAND SPEED

On 15 October 1997, Andy Green (UK) achieved a speed of 1,227.985 km/h (763.035 mph) over a distance of one mile in his car *Thrust SSC* in the Black Rock Desert, Nevada, USA.

FASTEST STEAM CAR

On 19 August 1985, Robert E Barber (USA) broke the 79-year-old record for a steam car when *Steamin' Demon*, built by Barber-Nichols Engineering Co., reached a speed of 234.33 km/h (145.58 mph) at Bonneville Salt Flats, Utah, USA.

LARGEST CAR PARADES

★ **Ferrari:** Cornes & Company Ltd assembled 490 Ferrari cars at the Fuji Speedway Circuit, Shizuoka, Japan, on 11 May 2008.

★ **Mitsubishi:** Mitsubishi Lancer Register (UK) arranged 273 Mitsubishi cars in Chippenham, Wiltshire, UK, on 12 July 2008.

★ **Mustang:** Michel Bourassa (Canada) organized 620 Mustangs to be driven between St-Eulalie and Victoriaville, Quebec, Canada, on 7 June 2008.

★ **Mini:** The Dutch Mini People gathered 884 Mini cars of varying types in Lelystad, the Netherlands, on 11 May 2008.

★ SMALLEST ALL-TERRAIN ARMOURED VEHICLE

Built by Howe and Howe Technologies and measuring less than 1 m (3 ft 3 in) wide, the *PAV1 Badger* is the world's smallest all-terrain armoured vehicle. Powerful enough to break down doors but small enough to fit in a lift, the vehicle was designed to increase officer safety in SWAT team duties and was commissioned by Civil Protection Services (CPS) of California, USA.

★ **NEW RECORD**
UPDATED RECORD

Jul 30: Between 10 June and 30 July 2004, Martin Strel (Slovenia) swam the entire length of the Yangtze River, China, covering 4,003 km (2,487 miles) – **the longest journey ever swum.**

Jul 31: The **highest recorded jump by an insect**, set on this day in 2003, is 70 cm (28 in) by the froghopper (*Philaenus spumarius*). When jumping, it accelerates at 4,000 m (13,000 ft) per second.

★ FASTEST PRODUCTION DIESEL BOAT

The fastest diesel boat currently in production is the XSR48, a 14.63-m (48-ft) stiff Kevlar/carbon-fibre monocoque-hull, luxury superboat, which can achieve speeds in excess of 161 km/h (100 mph) with its 1,900 hp race-tuned engine option. Developed by XSMG World Ltd (UK) and launched in Lymington, UK, in December 2006, production will be limited to 100 models and prices start around £1 million ($1.5 million).

★ FIRST CATAMARAN MADE FROM PLASTIC

In spring 2009, David de Rothschild (UK), founder of Adventure Ecology, will set sail in an 18-m (60-ft) catamaran made entirely from plastic bottles, self-reinforcing plastic (polyethylene terephthalate) and recycled waste products. His 19,446-km (12,083-mile; 10,500-nautical mile) voyage across the Pacific from San Francisco, USA, to Sydney, Australia, takes him through an area popularly termed the "great Pacific garbage patch", a mass of floating debris five times the size of the UK that sits just below the surface between California and Hawaii. The aim of the voyage is to highlight the threat of pollution.

★ LARGEST CHARTERED YACHT

The largest private yacht that is available for charter is the 124-m (407-ft) *Savarona*, built for Mrs Emily Roebling Cadwallader (USA) in 1931. It was sold to the Turkish government in 1938, but privatized in 1992. It features a swimming pool, jacuzzis, two separate saunas and steam rooms and a Turkish bath built from 260 tonnes (286 tons) of carved marble.

★ LARGEST MARINE ENGINE

The Wärtsilä RT-flex96C is a turbocharged, two-stroke reciprocating diesel engine designed to power large container ships. Built in the Aioi Works of Japan's Diesel United Ltd, it has a length of 27 m (88 ft 7 in), is 13.5 m (44 ft 4 in) high and weighs over 2,300 tonnes (2,535 tons). In 2008, the power output of the 14-cylinder version of this engine attained 84.42 megawatts (114,800 bhp).

LARGEST CONTAINER SHIP

At 397 m (1,300 ft) long and with a beam of 56 m (184 ft), the MV *Emma Maersk* is the largest container vessel in the world. The 20-storey ship has a top speed in excess of 25 knots (46.2 km/h; 28.7 mph).

FACT

The *Visby* class is designed principally for anti-submarine operations and has a top speed of 35 knots (64 km/h; 40 mph). The vessel costs £100 million ($150 million).

★ LARGEST CARBON FIBRE SHIP

The first of the five new Swedish *Visby* class corvettes came into service in January 2009, having completed sea trials in 2008. The vessel is the largest ship to be made of carbon fibre – an extremely hard, lightweight material that enables it to be faster and lighter than a conventional ship, making it one of the stealthiest afloat. The *Visby* is 73 m (239 ft 6 in) long, weighs 600 tonnes (661 tons) – about half the weight of a conventional corvette – and has a crew of 43.

LARGEST SHIP

The world's largest ship of any kind is the oil tanker *Jahre Viking* at 564,763 tonnes (622,544 tons) deadweight and 260,815 grt. The tanker is 458.45 m (1,504 ft) long, has a beam of 68.8 m (226 ft) and a draught of 24.61 m (80 ft 9 in).

The ship went out of service in 2004, and is currently a permanently moored storage tanker. It also has a new name: the *Knock Nevis*.

★ FIRST LITTORAL COMBAT SHIP

In order to operate more effectively in coastal (littoral, or near-shore) waters, the US Navy has created a new class of littoral combat ship. The first test version, known as *Sea Fighter*, is a high-speed aluminium catamaran that will test a variety of technologies designed for greater operational effectiveness in littoral waters. It weighs 950 tonnes (1,047 tons), is 79.9 m (262 ft) long with a beam of 22 m (72 ft) and has a top speed of around 50 knots (92.5 km/h; 57.5 mph). It has been in service since May 2005.

Aug 1: The **first men to row the Atlantic** were George Harbo and Frank Samuelson (both Norway), who departed on 6 June 1896 and arrived on this day after rowing 5,262 km (3,270 miles).

Aug 2: Excluding singalongs by stadium crowds, the **greatest choir** is one of 60,000, which sang at a choral contest in Breslau, Germany (now Wrocław, Poland), on 2 August 1937.

275.97 knots (511.09 km/h; 317.58 mph): the official **world water speed record** set by Ken Warby (Australia) on 8 October 1978.

★ **NEW RECORD**
☆ **UPDATED RECORD**

TOP 100 Records of the Decade

LARGEST
PASSENGER LINER

Weighing 160,000 gross tons (162,567 tonnes) and measuring 338.9 m (1,112 ft) in length and 72 m (237 ft) in height, the 15-deck MS *Independence of the Seas* is the world's largest passenger liner. The boat, registered in Nassau, The Bahamas, can carry 5,700 passengers and crew, and its amenities include a theatre, water park, wave simulator, rock-climbing wall, an ice-skating rink and a boxing ring.

The MS *Oasis of the Seas*, due to take its maiden voyage on 1 December 2009, will be even bigger. It resembles a floating city, complete with tropical gardens, a 100-m-long (328-ft) landscaped park and seven "neighbourhoods" that can support over 6,500 people. Some of the facilities can be seen in the artist's impression, right.

Oasis of the Seas

ZIPLINE (not on artwork)
Thrill-seekers can try out the 25-m-long (82-ft) zipline suspended nine decks above the boardwalk.

2,700 STATE ROOMS
The ship can accommodate 5,400 passengers in its state rooms.

CLIMBING WALL
Oasis of the Seas has two rock-climbing walls; they flank each side of the AquaTheater, facing aft toward the wake.

SHOPS & RESTAURANTS
Cafes, restaurants, a jazz bar, snack bar, wine bar, steakhouse and a three-deck cocktail bar.

DIVING PLATFORMS
Two 10-m-high (33-ft) platforms connected by a bridge that also supports a trapeze for evening circus acts.

AQUATHEATER POOL
By day: Largest and deepest freshwater pool at sea – 6.6 x 15.7 m (21 x 51 ft) with a depth of 5.4 m (17 ft).

WATER & LIGHT SHOW
By night: Programmable nozzles provide a colourful, synchronized water show with 20-m-high (65-ft) fountains.

AMPHITHEATRE
The size of a football field, the outdoor amphitheatre has its own micro-climate.

GIANT LED SCREENS
Two giant Barco LED screens flank the AquaTheater pool, displaying images filmed by cameras located under the water.

Aug 3: The **oldest cat ever** is Creme Puff, who was born on 3 August 1967 and lived until 6 August 2005 – 38 years 3 days in total. Creme Puff lived with her owner, Jake Perry, in Austin, Texas, USA.

★ MOST EXPENSIVE AIRCRAFT LOSS

On 23 February 2008, a USAF B-2 Spirit bomber crashed due to moisture in three of its 24 air-pressure sensors giving false readings to its flight computer. The incident marked the first crash of a B-2 bomber. Introduced into service in 1997 at a unit cost of around $737 million (£456 million), the aircraft were so expensive that only 21 were made. According to experts, the cost to replace the B-2 would be around $1.4 billion (£2 billion).

★ FIRST SUPERSONIC FLIGHT WITH SYNTHETIC FUEL BLEND

On 19 March 2008, a Boeing B-1B Lancer from 9th Bomb Squadron at Dyess Air Force Base in Texas, USA, became the first aircraft to fly at supersonic speed using synthetic fuel. The fuel is a 50/50 blend of synthetic gas derived from natural gases and standard petroleum gas. It is being tested as part of a United States Air Force programme to help the environment and reduce reliance on imported fuels. The flight was made in the airspace over the White Sands Missile Range in Texas and New Mexico, USA.

★ HIGHEST ALTITUDE BY AN AUTOGYRO

Andrew Keech (USA) flew a Little Wing LW-5 autogyro to a height of 8,049 m (26,407 ft) in Frederick, Maryland, USA, on 20 April 2004. Invented by Juan de la Cierva, autogyros are aircraft that achieve lift using rotating wings.

★ LONGEST PRODUCTION RUN FOR A MILITARY AIRCRAFT

The Lockheed C-130 first flew on 23 August 1954 and was introduced into service with the USAF in December 1956. It has been in continuous production ever since, with more than 40 different models produced, serving the air forces of over 50 nations.

★ NEW RECORD
UPDATED RECORD

★ MOST EXPENSIVE PRIVATE JET

The Airbus A380 purchased by HRH Prince Waleed Bin Talal of Saudi Arabia in November 2007 for his personal use (the first private sale of an A380) had a list price of $319 million (£152 million). The world's **largest private jet**, it has a wing-span of 79.8 m (261 ft 8 in) and a maximum take-off weight of 560 tonnes (617 tons). Rumour has it that the Prince has asked for the double-decker plane to be fitted with a marble dining area, a sauna and a gym – as well as having the exterior covered in gold leaf.

TOP 100 Records of the Decade

★ LARGEST AIRLIFT OF PENGUINS

On the weekend of 1–2 July 2000, between 15,000 and 20,000 penguins were airlifted by helicopter after an oil spill off the coast of western South Africa. The operation to save the birds, part of the largest colony of African penguins, was mobilized by the International Fund for Animal Welfare (IFAW).

GLOBEMASTER III

A total of 20 C-17 Globemaster IIIs from Charleston Air Force Base, South Carolina, USA, took part in the ★ **largest formation of cargo aircraft from a single base** on 21 December 2006 to demonstrate the US Air Force's strategic airdrop capability.

★ FIRST FLIGHT FROM HAWAII TO NORTH AMERICA

On 11 January 1935, Amelia Earhart (USA) flew a Lockheed Vega 5b solo from Wheeler Field, Honolulu, Hawaii, to Oakland Airport in Oakland, California, USA. The flight lasted 18 hours, covered a distance of 3,862 km (2,400 miles) and netted the pilot a $10,000 (£2,040) prize for her achievement. Earhart disappeared two years later, on 2 July 1937, somewhere in the South Pacific while attempting to fly around the world.

Aug 4: The **longest standing jump on a motorcycle** is 4.2 m (13 ft 9 in), a mark held jointly by Jeroni Fajardo and Toni Bou (both Spain) who both achieved the record on this day in 2004.

853: maximum seating capacity on a double-decker Airbus 380 – the world's **largest passenger plane by weight and by capacity**.

★ MOST SUCCESSFUL AIRCRAFT DITCHING

The "success" of an aircraft ditching into water can be judged on the number of passengers who survive. The most successful ditch, therefore, was US Airways Airbus A320 flight 1549, flown by Captain Chesley B "Sully" Sullenberger (inset), which landed in the Hudson River, New York, USA, on 15 January 2009. All of the 155 passengers and crew survived the incident, caused by birds flying into the aircraft's engines.

LARGEST AIRLINE

As of June 2007, the airline with the largest fleet of active aircraft is American Airlines, with 978 planes, including 47 Boeing 777s. Orders have also been placed for 42 Boeing 787-9 Dreamliners for delivery in 2012.

FACT

Sullenberger, an ex-US Air Force fighter pilot and keen glider pilot, received the key to New York City in recognition of his fantastic flying.

★ LARGEST MODEL AIRCRAFT BY LENGTH

Dyna Might is a 1:4.9 scale model of the B-29 Superfortress, built by Vercruyesse Bart, Honore Ignace and Lamaire Pieter (all Belgium). The plane – which has a wing-span of 8.8 m (28 ft 10 in), is 6.05 m (19 ft 10 in) long and weighs 200 kg (441 lb) – made its maiden flight on 22 May 1998.

★ SMALLEST COAXIAL HELICOPTER

The GEN H-4 made by Gen Corporation (Japan) has a rotor length of only 4 m (13 ft). The aircraft weighs just 70 kg (154 lb 5 oz) and consists of a single seat, a basic landing gear and a single power unit. Unlike more traditional helicopters, it has two coaxial (mounted on a common axis) contra-rotating rotors, which eliminate the need for a tail rotor for balancing.

★ FIRST JET WING FLIGHT ACROSS THE ENGLISH CHANNEL

On 26 September 2008, Yves "Jet Man" Rossy, a Swiss pilot and inventor, took just 9 min 7 sec to cross the English Channel wearing a jet wing. Rossy attained a speed of 299 km/h (186 mph) during the flight.

★ LONGEST FLIGHT BY AN UNMANNED AERIAL VEHICLE (UAV)

On 21 March 2001, a Northrop Grumman Ryan Aeronautical RQ-4A Global Hawk flew for a total of 30 hr 24 min 1 sec at Edwards Air Force Base, California, USA. It was 13.5 m (44 ft 3 in) long, had a wing-span of 35 m (114 ft 9 in) and a gross take-off weight of 10,704 kg (23,600 lb). The Global Hawk later became the **first UAV to fly across the Pacific Ocean**.

★ FIRST MANNED HYDROGEN-POWERED AIRCRAFT

A two-seat Dimona motor glider, powered by a modified exchange membrane fuel cell/lithium battery hybrid system designed by Boeing Research and Technology Europe Proton, flew in tests from an airfield at Ocana, Spain, during February and March 2008.

★ MOST ADVANCED MILITARY AIRLIFTER

The C-17 Globemaster III is the most advanced military airlifter in service today, with a strategic, unrefuelled range of 2,400 nautical miles (4,445 km; 2,762 miles) carrying a payload of 78,657 kg (169,000 lb), and a speed of 450 knots (Mach 0.76; 833 km/h; 518 mph). It can airdrop 102 paratroops with their equipment and operate on airfields with runways as short as 1,066 m (3,500 ft). There are currently around 190 C-17s, which are 53 m long (174 ft) and have a wing-span of 51.75 m (169 ft 9 in), operational worldwide.

Aug 5: The **most participants in a didgeridoo ensemble** was 238 musicians, all participating at Didge Fest UK held in Escot Park, Devon, UK, on this day in 2006.

Aug 6: The **first website** was launched on this day in 1991. The site – http://nxoc01.cern.ch/hypertext/WWW/TheProject.html – was created by Tim Berners-Lee (UK) to explain the World Wide Web.

★FASTEST MAXIMUM OPERATING SPEED FOR A TRAIN

On the 114-km-long (70.84-mile) Beijing–Tianjin Intercity Rail line in China, trains run at a maximum operating speed of 350 km/h (217.48 mph). Tests have shown an unmodified capability of 394 km/h (244.82 mph) but the speed has been limited for safety reasons.

★TUNNEL BORING

During August 2008 construction of a 6.9-km (4.2-mile) underground route between Atocha and Chamartin stations in Madrid, Spain, a tunnelling speed record of 92.8 m (304 ft 5 in) per day was reached using a double-shield tunnel-boring machine.

MAGLEV TRAIN

The MLX01, a manned superconducting, magnetically levitated (maglev) train, operated by the Central Japan Railway Company and Railway Technical Research Institute, reached a record high speed of 581 km/h (361 mph) on the Yamanashi Maglev Test Line, Yamanashi Prefecture, Japan, on 2 December 2003.

TRAIN IN REGULAR PUBLIC SERVICE

The maglev train linking China's Shanghai International Airport and the city's financial district reaches a top speed of 431 km/h (267.8 mph) on each 30-km (18-mile) run. The train, built by Germany's Transrapid International, had its official maiden run on 31 December 2002.

LONGEST...

EXHIBITION TRAIN

The Opel *Millennium Express* is the world's longest exhibition train and measures 284 m (931 ft) in length. It was "rolled out" at the Opel plant at Russelsheim, Germany, on 28 July 1999. The *Millennium Express,* which is made up of 14 wagons, was created to celebrate the 100th anniversary of Opel car production.

FASTEST...

★SCHEDULED SPEED BETWEEN TWO RAIL STOPS

Between the French rail stops of Lorraine and Champagne-Ardennes, trains reach an average speed of 279.4 km/h (173 mph), covering the 167.6-km (104-mile) route in 36 minutes, according to the last official *Railway Gazette International* World Speed Survey study in 2005. While this figure is almost half the speed of the **fastest train speed ever** – 574.8 km/h (357.2 mph) achieved by a French SNCF modified version of the TGV called V150 (with larger wheels than usual and two engines driving three double-decker cars) on 3 April 2007 – it represents a realistic, affordable, environmentally sound and safe top speed.

★ NEW RECORD
UPDATED RECORD

★MOST EXPENSIVE HIGH-SPEED RAIL LINK

The 108-km-long (67-mile) Channel Tunnel Rail Link connecting the British end of the Channel Tunnel to London cost £5.8 billion ($11.6 billion) and is the world's most expensive high-speed rail link. The finding came after construction costs were investigated for Britain's Commission for Integrated Transport.

ON TRACK...

The Fortescue Metals Group track, which carries the world's heaviest haul, is 1,435-mm standard gauge line made from 38,000 tonnes of continuously welded 68-kg/m rail. The entire line was built from scratch in just 18 months.

★HEAVIEST HAUL RAILWAY

On 14 May 2008, the Fortescue Metals Group (Australia) completed 230 km (142 miles) of single-track railway line from their Cloudbreak iron ore mine in Pilbara to Port Hedland. The track is capable of running trains of up to 2.5 km (1.55 miles) long, hauling a gross load of up to 38,400 tonnes (42,328 tons) of ore. The fleet of 15 locomotives and 976 ore cars make up four trains, with each of the ore cars designed to operate at a nominal 40-tonne (44-ton) axle load.

Aug 7: The **longest sandwich** measured 634.50 m (2,081 ft) and was created by Pietro Catucci and Antonio Latte of EuroSpin in Mottola, Taranto, Italy, on 7 August 2004.

Aug 8: The **longest skateboard ramp jump** was performed by Danny Way (USA) with a 24-m (79-ft) 360 air on his Mega Ramp at X Games X in Los Angeles, California, USA, on 8 August 2004.

FREIGHT TRAIN

A freight train measuring 7.35 km (4.5 miles) long and consisting of 682 ore cars pushed by eight powerful diesel-electric locomotives was assembled by BHP Iron Ore. The train travelled 275 km (171 miles) from the company's Newman and Yandi mines to Port Hedland, Western Australia, on 21 June 2001.

HOSPITAL TRAIN JOURNEY

The Indian Army, as a part of their contribution to the Golden Jubilee Celebrations of India's Independence, organized a hospital train that provided specialized medical treatment to retired personnel of the Indian Army Forces in 11 Indian states. The train departed from New Delhi on 15 August 1997 and returned five months later on 13 January 1998.

SUSPENDED MONORAIL

The Chiba Urban Monorail near Tokyo, Japan, is the longest suspended monorail train system in the world, at 15.2 km (9.45 miles). The first 3.2-km (1.99-mile) stretch opened on 20 March 1979, and the line has been expanded three times since.

PASSENGER TRAIN

A passenger train created by the National Belgian Railway Company measured 1,732.9 m (5,685 ft) and consisted of 70 coaches pulled by one electric locomotive. It travelled 62.5 km (38.9 miles) from Ghent to Ostend, Belgium, on 27 April 1991.

NON-STOP INTERNATIONAL TRAIN JOURNEY

Leaving London, UK, at 9:40 a.m. on 16 May 2006, a Eurostar train travelled the 1,421 km (883 miles) to Cannes, France, in 7 hr 25 min without stopping. The journey was part of an event promoting *The Da Vinci Code* (USA, 2006) movie, and the film's stars Tom Hanks and Audrey Tatou were on board.

FACT

The Siemens-built locomotive (above) needed just 30 km (18.6 miles) of free track to first set the record at 344 km/h (213.7 mph) and then raise it to 357 km/h (221.8 mph).

DISTANCE COVERED BY A RUNAWAY TRAIN

A record run of 161 km (100 miles) was made on the Chicago, Burlington & Quincy Railroad east of Denver, Colorado, USA, on 26 March 1884 when a wind of great force set eight coal cars on the move at Akron, Colorado. The cars ran on to the main line, where the wind drove them along at around 64 km/h (40 mph). A freight engine eventually brought the cars under control in just under three hours.

★ FASTEST ELECTRIC LOCOMOTIVE

The multi-system electric 1216 050 (type ES 64 U4), built by Siemens and owned by Austrian Federal Railways (ÖBB) is the fastest electric locomotive on record.

On 2 September 2006, the locomotive reached a speed of 357.0 km/h (221.8 mph) while being driven by Alex Dworaczek of Munich, Germany, on the high speed line between Ingolstadt and Nuremberg, Germany.

SUPER POWER

Each train on the Fortescue Metals Group's (FMG) Pilbara to Port Hedland line will be hauled by two GE Dash 9-4400CW engines, with two banker locomotives assisting through the Chichester range, a distance of 57 km (34 miles). From the 200-km (120-miles) mark, the trains are moved to the port with two locomotives at the head end of the train. This configuration makes them the **longest and heaviest head-end-powered trains** in operation worldwide.

Aug 9: The **longest-running advertising campaign** features Smokey Bear, a mascot of the United States Forest Service, who was first portrayed on a fire-prevention poster displayed on 9 August 1944.

175

WWW.GUINNESSWORLDRECORDS.COM

WEAPONS

WINDOWS
The car's tinted windows are tough enough to withstand armour-piercing bullets. The passenger windows are sealed to protect against the risk of chemical or biological attack.

DOOR
Each door is thought to have 20-cm-thick (8-in) armour plating, and a 12.7-cm-thick (5-in) steel alloy plate under the car provides bomb protection.

BODYWORK
The mixed metal and ceramic bodywork is designed to break up projectiles.

★ FIRST WEARABLE SNIPER DETECTOR

The EARS sniper detection system is a device designed for soldiers fighting in urban war zones or other places where enemy snipers are likely to be present. Weighing under 170 g (6 oz), the device is based on a single miniature integrated acoustic sensor and uses just 1 watt of power to give the soldier audio-visual alerts to identify the direction and distance of small-arms fire from a variety of weapons.

★ FIRST DEPLOYED BATTLEFIELD RAY GUN

The Zeus ray gun, named after the Greek god of the sky and thunder, is used to neutralize explosives such as roadside bombs and unexploded ordnance at a safe distance (300 m; 984 ft). The weapon, which was field-tested in Afghanistan in 2003, has since been sent to Iraq, and approximately 12 more are likely to be deployed by the end of 2009.

★ OLDEST SAMPLE OF WEAPONS-GRADE PLUTONIUM

The oldest known sample of weapons-grade plutonium was produced in 1944 at the Hanford nuclear site in Washington DC, USA, from the spent nuclear fuel that came from the prototype X-10 reactor at Oak Ridge in Tennessee, USA. The sample – a jar of white liquid slurry that had been locked in a safe and deposited in a trench at the Hanford nuclear site – was rediscovered in 2004 by workers attempting to clean up the contaminated facility where the first nuclear weapons were built.

★ MOST ADVANCED NIGHT VISION SYSTEM

The BugEye developed by BAE Systems for missile tracking applications is based on the eyes of the male wasp parasite *Xenos peckii*. The parasite's visual system – not found in any other living creature – uses 50 lenses to provide a 120° field of vision. The BugEye is not quite so advanced yet, using nine lenses to create 60° of peripheral vision, but is still far more than the 20° field of vision currently available on most standard lighter cameras for missile-tracking systems.

★ MOST ADVANCED SNIPER RIFLE

First operationally deployed by the British Army's 16 Air Assault Brigade in Afghanistan in May 2008, the L115A3 sniper rifle made by Accuracy International weighs just 6.8 kg (15 lb). It fires large 8.59-mm calibre rounds that are less likely to be deflected over extremely long ranges. Under optimal conditions, it can achieve a first-round hit at 600 m (1,968 ft) and harassing fire at a range of more than 1,100 m (3,608 ft).

★ SAFEST PRESIDENTIAL LIMOUSINE

Nicknamed "Cadillac One" or "the Beast", the presidential limousine built for Barack Obama (USA) is an extended Cadillac DTS built by General Motors. The exact technical specifications are confidential for security reasons, but defence technology includes: Kevlar reinforced run-flat tyres that are shred- and puncture-proof; 20-cm-thick (8-in) armour-plated doors with bulletproof windows; and a 12.7-cm-thick (5-in) bomb-proof reinforced steel plate chassis. The cabin area is believed to be sealed against chemical attacks and contains a coded communications suite. The mobile fortress is unlikely to manage more than 12.8 km (8 miles) to the gallon.

★ MOST ROBUST WAR ROBOT

The Dragon Runner is a robot that can be thrown into caves and buildings to perform mine clearance, explosives disposal and reconnaissance tasks. Weighing just 9 kg (19.8 lb), it has all its electronics encased in a tough plastic shell and can operate either side up. It can also be further equipped with a manipulator arm with rotating shoulder, wrist and grippers, night vision cameras, motion detectors, a microphone and caterpillar tracks.

Aug 10: The **longest surfboard rideable by one person** is 9.2 m (30 ft 2 in) long and was displayed by Murasaki Sports at Hama Atsuma, Tomakomai, Japan, on this day in 2008.

63 tonnes (69.4 tons): the weight of the M1A2 Abrams tank, the **heaviest tank** currently in service.

★ FIRST TRUE AUTOMATIC WEAPON

In 1883, Hiram Maxim (later Sir Hiram Maxim) built and developed the first self-powered, single-barreled machine gun. It used the recoil force of the fired round to extract the fired case and place another in the chamber, cocking the action in the process. By holding the trigger down, the gun fired continuously.

★ FIRST MACHINE GUN

In 1862, Richard Gatling (USA) produced the first workable, hand-cranked, multiple-barrel machine gun. First used during the American Civil War of 1861–65, loose cartridges were gravity fed into the open breach from a top-mounted funnel device. It was this feature rather than the multi-rotating barrels that permitted unskilled operators to achieve high rates of fire.

★ **NEW RECORD**
★ **UPDATED RECORD**

★ MOST EXPENSIVE TANK

The K2 Black Panther Main Battle Tank, developed and produced in South Korea, costs around 8,300,000,000 South Korean Won ($8.5 million; £5.96 million) per unit. The tank, which requires a three-man crew, has a 1,500 hp engine and can travel at 70 km/h (43.5 mph) on paved roads and 50 km/h (31 mph) off-road. The Republic of Korea Army currently has 390 of the tanks on order.

users to input various factors, such as weather conditions and distance, while the accelerometer measures angles to the target, providing detailed data on how to set up the ideal shot at distances of up to 2,000 m (6,561 ft). The programme also has built-in profiles for three major sniper rifles, including the M110 semi-automatic, and allows the user to add further profiles to suit their needs.

★ MOST LETHAL IPOD APPLICATION

On 22 December 2008, Runaway Technology Inc. released BulletFlight, an application for the iPhone and iPod Touch that helps marksmen make more accurate shots. The application turns the iPod into a ballistics computer and allows

★ MOST UAVS SHOT DOWN BY A LASER WEAPON SYSTEM

In December 2008, a Humvee mounted laser weapon system, dubbed the Laser Avenger by its manufacturer, Boeing Combat Systems, shot down three small Unmanned Aerial Vehicles (UAVs) at the White Sands Missile Range, New Mexico, USA.

Aug 11: The **lowest resting heart beat** on record is 27 bpm by Martin Brady (UK), recorded on this day in 2005.

Aug 12: The **youngest chess player to qualify as an International Grand Master** is Sergey Karjakin (Ukraine, b. 12 January 1990), aged 12 years 212 days on this day in 2002.

SUPERSTRUCTURES

LOFTY AMBITIONS

The history of the world's **tallest structures** tells the story of man's towering ambitions. The earliest superstructures were grandiose final resting places for Ancient Egyptian pharaohs. As Christianity flowered across Europe in the Middle Ages, gargantuan churches and cathedrals rose up as epic paeans to God. The skyscrapers of the modern era are a tribute both to leaps in technology and to good old-fashioned human ingenuity. So, if you've got a head for heights, sit back and let us take you on a tour of history's larger-than-life structures. *Note: dates in parenthesis indicate the building's period as tallest in the world.*

COLOGNE CATHEDRAL (1880–84)

Although construction of Cologne Cathedral began in 1248, this striking example of Gothic architecture was not completed until 1880. From that year until 1884, the cathedral was the world's tallest building, until it was superseded by the Washington Monument. Only Ulm Cathedral has taller spires than those of Cologne, which top out at 157 m (515 ft) – more than 10 times the height of a London double-decker bus. It has now been designated a World Heritage Site.

RED PYRAMID OF SNEFERU (c. 2600–2560 BCE)

So called because of the pinkish limestone from which it is constructed, this 104-m (341-ft) pyramid is one of three at the Dahshur Necropolis in Egypt. Built by the fourth-dynasty pharaoh Sneferu, who ruled c. 2613–2589 BCE, it remained the world's tallest man-made structure until overtaken by the Great Pyramid of Giza.

ST MARY'S CHURCH (1625–47)

Located in Stralsund, Germany, and another famous example of Gothic architecture, St Mary's Church stretched to a height of 151 m (495 ft). This pre-1400 construction finally lost its title as the world's tallest building when its tower (which had already been rebuilt after a storm toppled it) was destroyed by a lightning strike in 1647. (The baton then passed to Strasbourg Cathedral.) It currently rises to a relatively modest 104 m (341 ft).

OSTANKINO TOWER (1967–75)

Still the tallest man-made structure in Europe – and the first structure to exceed 500 m (1,640 ft) – this free-standing TV and radio tower in Moscow, Russia, is 540 m (1,772 ft) tall. Construction began in 1963 and lasted four years. It finally lost its title as the tallest structure on land to Toronto's CN Tower.

ST NIKOLAI (1874–76)

Located in Hamburg, Germany, this gargantuan Gothic Revival building was the world's tallest for just two years before it was overtaken by Rouen Cathedral. Several buildings dedicated to St Nikolai, the earliest dating back to the 11th century, had been erected on the spot, but this church – whose spire topped out at 147.3 m (483 ft 3 in) – was built between 1846 and 1874.

EIFFEL TOWER (1889–1930)

This much-loved Parisian landmark – named after its designer, Gustave Eiffel (France) – was originally intended to serve as a grand gateway to the city's Universal Exhibition and was planned to stand for just 20 years. (It took two years to erect, finally opening in 1889.) Despite provoking a storm of outrage, the tower – which at 324 m (1,063 ft) is three times the height of London's St Paul's Cathedral – swiftly became a tourist favourite. The Chrysler Building took its crown in 1930.

LINCOLN CATHEDRAL (1311–1549)

Built between 1185 and 1311, and with a 160-m-tall (525-ft) central spire, Lincoln Cathedral is commonly regarded as having been the world's tallest structure until 1549. In that year, the spire burned down and its record was assumed by St Olaf's Church in Tallinn, Estonia.

EMPIRE STATE BUILDING (1931–67)

This iconic New York landmark was the first building to exceed 100 storeys and is today officially one of the Seven Wonders of the Modern World, as put forward by the American Society of Civil Engineers in 1994. Completed in 1931 and topping out at 381 m (1,250 ft), it was succeeded as the world's tallest structure by the Ostankino Tower in 1967.

PYRAMID OF DJOSER (c. 2700–c. 2600 BCE)

Located in Egypt's Saqqara Necropolis and built for the eponymous pharaoh in the 27th century BCE, this pyramid reached 62 m (203 ft) in height – or about the same as that of the sculpted heads of the four US presidents immortalized on Mount Rushmore. In around 2600 BCE, it was superseded by the Red Pyramid of Sneferu.

Aug 13: On this day in 2003, Scott Hammell (Canada) executed the **highest suspension straitjacket escape** dangling from a hot-air balloon 2,194.5 m (7,200 ft) over Knoxville, Tennessee, USA.

320.94 m (1,053 ft): the height of the **tallest hotel**, the sail-shaped, 202-suite Burj Al Arab ("The Arabian Tower"), located in Dubai, UAE.

BURJ DUBAI (2009–)

The world's **tallest structure** is currently the Burj Dubai in Dubai, United Arab Emirates, which reached a vertiginous 688 m (2,257 ft) on 1 September 2008. That's more than twice the height of the Eiffel Tower! It is due to reach its maximum height of 818 m (2,684 ft) upon completion in September 2009.

★ **NEW RECORD**
UPDATED RECORD

CN TOWER (1975–2009)

At a dizzying 553.33 m (1,815 ft 5 in), Toronto's CN Tower overtook Moscow's Ostankino Tower as the tallest structure in 1975, during its construction. It was completed the following year and held its title for an impressive 32 years until the Burj Dubai took its place. Like the Empire State Building, the CN Tower has been voted one of the Seven Wonders of the Modern World.

ST OLAF'S CHURCH (1549–1625)

Dating from the 12th century and located in Tallinn, Estonia, St Olaf's Church was the tallest building in the world from 1549 to 1625, when St Mary's Church in Stralsund claimed its throne. It was originally 159 m (522 ft) tall; after repeated lightning strikes and reconstructions, today it reaches only 123 m (404 ft).

STRASBOURG CATHEDRAL (1647–1874)

At 142 m (465 ft) tall, the spire of Strasbourg Cathedral is 3 m (9 ft 10 in) taller than the Sydney Harbour Bridge. The building was the tallest structure in the world from 1647 (when Stralsund's St Mary's Church lost its spire) to 1874 (when it was overtaken by St Nikolai's Church in Hamburg). This much-revered Gothic cathedral was begun in 1015 and completed in 1439.

ROUEN CATHEDRAL (1876–80)

Officially the Cathédrale Notre-Dame de Rouen, this splendid Gothic cathedral was built between 1202 and 1880 and was the tallest building in the world for the last four years of this period, after which it was overtaken by Cologne Cathedral. Its spire topped out at 151 m (495 ft).

WASHINGTON MONUMENT (1884–89)

Opened in 1888, but officially the world's tallest structure for four years previously, this striking obelisk rises to 169.29 m (555 ft 5.1 in). In 1889, the Eiffel Tower took its record. (For more about this famous monument, see below.)

CHRYSLER BUILDING (1930–31)

An Art Deco masterpiece, this famous Manhattan skyscraper was erected between 1928 and 1930 and reached 318.9 m (1,046 ft) in height – over three times the height of the Red Pyramid of Sneferu. It was the world's tallest building for less than a year, before losing its title to another New York icon – the Empire State Building.

GREAT PYRAMID OF GIZA (c. 2560 BCE–1311)

Egypt's largest pyramid once rose to 146 m (479 ft), though erosion has now reduced its height. Also known as the Pyramid of Cheops (or Khufu), it is one of three pyramids at the Giza Necropolis near Cairo, Egypt. Completed c. 2560 BCE, it was the world's tallest structure for more than 3,800 years, until the erection of Lincoln Cathedral.

CITY LIMITS

The Washington Monument is the tallest building in Washington, DC, USA – and will remain so. How can we be so sure? It's the law. The 1910 Heights of Buildings Act restricted the height of any new building in the city to the width of the adjacent street, plus an additional 6.1 m (20 ft).

179

Aug 14: Svetlana Masterkova (Russia) ran the **fastest mile by a woman** – in a time of 4 min 12.56 sec – in Zurich, Switzerland, on 14 August 1996.

Aug 15: Opened on 15 August 1956, the Algiers Drive-in of Detroit, Michigan, USA, had a screen measuring 65.8 m (216 ft) wide and covering 445.9 m² (4,800 ft²) – the **largest drive-in movie screen**.

ATOM SMASHERS

★ LARGEST MACHINE EVER BUILT

The Large Hadron Collider (LHC) is not just the world's **largest particle accelerator** – it's the largest and most complex machine ever built (and the **largest fridge**!). Located on the Franco-Swiss border near Geneva, Switzerland, it consists of a 27-km-long (16.7-mile) circular tunnel under the ground.

The LHC was built with the aim of smashing together two opposing beams of protons at extremely high energies in order to witness the results of their collisions. The most famous goal of this experiment is to find the theorized Higgs boson – the so-called "God particle" – which so far has eluded discovery. The first beam of protons was steered around the LHC on 10 September 2008 but operations were halted on 19 September when a fault was discovered.

On this page are a selection of the world records established by this extraordinary science project.

French Alps

LARGE HADRON COLLIDER
The LHC and its four detectors are located between 50 and 150 m (164 and 490 ft) underground

Geneva
SWITZERLAND
Lac Leman
FRANCE

4 LHCb
Large Hadron Collider beauty – to study the b-quark ("beauty quark")

3 CMS
Compact Muon Solenoid – a general particle detector with a solenoid magnet

Super Proton Synchrotron
7-km-long (4.3-mile) particle pre-injector

1 ATLAS
A Toroidal LHC Apparatus – a general particle detector with a giant, doughnut-shaped magnet

2 ALICE
A Large Ion Collider Experiment – to recreate conditions just after the Big Bang

Accelerator
Protons race around a 27-km (16.7-mile) track 11,245 times every second

★ HEAVIEST PARTICLE DETECTOR

The Compact Muon Solenoid (CMS) **3** is one of the general-purpose detectors in the LHC. Built around a huge solenoid magnet, the whole detector is 21 m long, 15 m wide and 15 m high (68 ft 10 in x 49 ft 2 in x 49 ft 2 in), and weighs 12,500 tonnes (13,778 tons). Its job is to observe aspects of high-energy physics including the possibility of extra dimensions.

★ NEW RECORD
UPDATED RECORD

★ HIGHEST-ENERGY PARTICLES IN A PARTICLE ACCELERATOR

The proton beams in the LHC can be accelerated by magnets up to within around one-millionth of a per cent of the speed of light (299,792,458 m/s; 983,571,056 ft/s), circumnavigating the accelerator 11,245 times per second. This means each proton will have around 7 TeV of energy (7 tera electron volts), equivalent to the energy used by seven flying mosquitoes. Combined, all the protons in the active beams have the energy equivalent to 900 cars travelling at 100 km/h (62 mph).

★ LARGEST SILICON DETECTOR

The Compact Muon Solenoid 2 (CMS2) Silicon Stop Tracking Detector is designed to track the three-dimensional positions of particles produced in collisions inside the LHC's Compact Muon Solenoid experiment **3**. This array has a total surface area of 205 m² (2,206 ft²) – roughly the area of a tennis court.

★ LARGEST COMPUTING GRID

In order to tackle the vast amounts of data from the LHC, scientists around the world have collaborated to create the Worldwide LHC Computing Grid. It consists of 100,000 computers across 140 computer centres in 33 countries and was unveiled in October 2008. The LHC detectors are expected to generate 300 gigabytes of data (equivalent to 35 full-length DVDs) per second.

★ LARGEST SUPERCONDUCTING MAGNET

The Barrel Toroid consists of eight magnet coils in an array 25 m long and 5 m wide (82 x 16 ft). It weighs 100 tonnes (110 tons). Part of the Atlas Detector **1**, it was first tested in 2006 at an operating temperature of -269°C (-452.2°F) and is designed to use a 4-Tesla magnetic field to bend the paths of particles produced in the collisions in the LHC.

★ LARGEST REFRIGERATOR

The 9,300 magnets inside the Large Hadron Collider are designed to be refrigerated for operational use. Around 10,080 tonnes (11,111 tons) of liquid nitrogen are needed to cool them down to just -193.2°C (-315.76°F) before they are filled with nearly 60 tonnes (66 tons) of liquid helium, which cools them further to just -271.3°C (-456.34°F).

★ LONGEST VACUUM SYSTEM

The beams of particles that travel around the accelerator ring at the Large Hadron Collider must operate in a vacuum in order to avoid

Aug 16: Usain Bolt (Jamaica) ran the **fastest ever men's 100 m** in 9.69 seconds in The Bird's Nest, Beijing, China, during the Olympic Games on this day in 2008.

MOST SENSITIVE GAMMA RAY DETECTOR

Gammasphere at the Argonne National Laboratory, Illinois, USA, is the most sensitive gamma ray "microscope" in the world. It is a cylinder measuring 3 m (10 ft) high-pierced with 110 gamma ray detectors. These focus on a central target area that is blasted with ions. Gammasphere is so sensitive that it can detect gamma rays produced in these collisions that are 300,000 times weaker than the strongest produced in the collisions.

★ LARGEST CYCLOTRON

Cyclotrons are a type of particle accelerator in which charged particles, such as protons, are accelerated using a high-frequency alternating voltage. The particles move in a spiral so that they meet the same accelerating voltage numerous times. The largest is the 18-m (59-ft) diameter machine at TRIUMF, the Canadian lab for particle and nuclear physics. The protons inside this cyclotron travel 45 km (27.9 miles) as they spiral outwards, gradually reaching their maximum energy of 520 mega electron volts. The TRIUMF cyclotron has been in operation since 1974.

collisions with gas molecules. In total, the LHC contains a vacuum some 54 km (33.5 miles) long and is rated as a UHV, or Ultra High Vacuum – which means that it has 10 times *less* gas pressure than the almost-vacuum conditions experienced at the surface of the Moon.

★ HIGHEST-ENERGY OPERATIONAL ACCELERATOR

The LHC is due to become operational once more in September 2009, so as of June 2009 – the time of going to press – the Tevatron at the Fermi National Accelerator Laboratory in Batavia, Illinois, USA, remains the world's most powerful particle accelerator. The Tevatron is a "synchrotron", the most powerful type of accelerator using synchronized magnetic and electric fields that can accelerate protons and antiprotons in a ring 6.3 km (3.9 miles) long up to energies of 1 tera electron volt.

LONGEST LINEAR ACCELERATOR

The Stanford Linear Accelerator Center (SLAC) in California, USA, is a particle accelerator some 3.2 km (2 miles) long. Since beginning operations in 1966, its key achievements include the discovery of the charm quark and tau lepton subatomic particles. The accelerator is located underground and is among the world's longest and straightest objects.

★ LAST MAJOR UNDISCOVERED PARTICLE

The current theory of particles, such as the proton, neutron and electron, and how they interact, is known as the Standard Model. All major high-energy physics experiments since the mid-20th century have yielded discoveries or results that agree with this theory. It is, however, incomplete. One phenomenon which remains unexplained is exactly why these particles have mass. The Higgs boson is a theoretical particle which, if it exists, would explain why matter in the Universe has mass at all. Its existence is predicted by the Standard Model, and it remains the last such predicted particle to be undiscovered by science. One of the major goals of the Large Hadron Collider project is to discover the Higgs boson.

★ MOST COMMON PARTICLE ACCELERATOR

The television set in its earliest form is based on a cathode ray tube, in which electrons are emitted from a hot metal cathode, accelerated by electric fields and directed by magnets on to the inside of the screen, making the individual pixels glow to form a moving image. Estimates of the number of these "domestic particle accelerators" range from 1 to 2 billion globally.

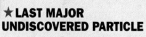

Aug 17: The **largest mosaic of wrapped bubblegums** measured 19.4 m² (209 ft²) and was created in Johannesburg, South Africa, on this day in 2004.

Aug 18: The **largest ukulele ensemble** involved 401 participants at "Ukulele 07" on Långholmen Island in Stockholm, Sweden, on 18 August 2007.

THINK BIG!

LARGEST BALL OF CLINGFILM

At the beginning of 2006, Jake Lonsway's (USA) clingfilm ball was the size of a softball; as of 14 June 2007, it had grown to 3.51 m (11 ft 6 in) wide and weighed 127.7 kg (281 lb 8 oz) – five times heavier than Jake!

★ BEACH BALL

An inflatable beach ball measuring 10.99 m wide (36 ft) – about three storeys – was made by Carnival Cruise Lines (USA) and bounced through the streets of Dallas, Texas, USA, on 26 October 2008.

LARGEST RUBBER-BAND BALL

An estimated 700,000 rubber bands have gone into Joel Waul's (USA) giant band ball. "Megaton", as Joel calls it, was measured in Lauderhill, Florida, USA, on 13 November 2008 and found to weigh 4,097 kg (9,032 lb) – about the same as a young bull elephant! It is 2 m (6 ft 7 in) high and 7.72 m (25 ft 4 in) in diameter.

LARGEST...

TOILET ROLL

Kimberly-Clark Perú unveiled a roll of toilet paper with a diameter of 1.7 m (5 ft 6 in) in Lima, Peru, on 7 June 2008. With a surface area of 56,000 m² (602,000 ft²), it has enough paper to last the average human 100 years.

BED

A bed measuring 23.47 m (77 ft) long and 14.17 m (46 ft 6 in) wide was created by Mark Gerrick (USA) and Royal Sleep Products in Fort Worth, Texas, USA, on 11 September 2008.

PILLOW

Every big bed needs a big pillow... The largest ever measured 225 m² (2,422 ft²) and was created by AAROVA vzw (Belgium) in Oudenaarde, Belgium, on 3 October 2008.

CUP OF COFFEE

On 11 October 2007, Mauricio Cadavid (Colombia) created a 4,143-litre (911.5-gal) cup of coffee – enough to fill over 50 bath tubs or 17,511 cups! It contained an estimated 1.5 million mg of caffeine.

EYELASHES
Made from 16 skis

EYES
Made from giant Christmas wreaths

NOSE
2.5 m (8 ft) long

MOUTH
Made from five car tyres painted red

SCARF
30 m (100 ft) long

ARMS
Made from two 9-m-tall (30-ft) spruce trees

BODY
5,890 tonnes (6,500 tons) of snow packed into concentric rings; cranes used to shift snow to a height of 35 m (113 ft 7 in) – just 9 m (30 ft) shorter than the Statue of Liberty!

★ LARGEST WHOOPEE CUSHION

In order to demonstrate the scientific principles behind wind instruments, Steve Mesure (UK) crafted a giant whoopee cushion measuring 3.05 m (10 ft) in diameter. It was made on behalf of the Street Vibe Festival of Sound held at The Scoop near Tower Bridge in London, UK, on 14 June 2008.

TALLEST SNOWMAN

Olympia – a snowman, or more accurately a snow-woman, built by residents of Bethel in Maine, USA, and its surrounding towns – measures 37.21 m (122 ft) tall. She was built over a period of one month, and completed on 26 February 2008.

Aug 19: The **oldest functioning car** is La Marquise, a steam-powered vehicle manufactured in France in 1884. It was sold for $3,520,000 (£1,767,000) on this day back in 2007.

Aug 20: The **largest cup of soft drink** contained 3,791.4 litres (834 gal) of lemonade and was created by Arthur Greeno and Chick-fil-A (both USA) on this day in 2008.

GUINNESS WORLD RECORDS

BIG GUS

LARGEST CHAINSAW

A working chainsaw measuring 6.98 m (22 ft 11 in) long, 1.83 m (6 ft) high and powered by a V-8 engine was made by Moran Iron Works, Inc., of Onaway, Michigan, USA, in 1996. Named "Big Gus", it was put on display by James A DeCaine (USA) at Da Yoopers Tourist Trap at Ishpeming, Michigan, USA. DeCaine calls items such as this – and his **largest rifle** (see right) – as "Yoopervations": novelty items built not out of necessity but "out of whimsy".

★ KNITTING NEEDLES

Knitting needles measuring 3.5 m (11 ft 5.8 in) long, with a diameter of 8 cm (3.15 in), were used by Ingrid Wagner (UK) to knit a tension square of ten stitches by ten rows at the Metro Radio Arena, Newcastle upon Tyne, UK, on 10 March 2008.

CANNED FOOD STRUCTURE

On 4 July 2008, students from the School of Architecture at Montana State University – in partnership with non-profit organization Conscious Alliance (both USA) – used 45,725 cans of food to build a structure in the shape of a human hand. The sculpture measured 9.75 m (32 ft) long, 4.88 m (16 ft) wide and 3.05 m (10 ft) tall.

★ FLUTE OF SPARKLING WINE

The world's largest wine flute was filled with 16.5 litres (3.63 gal) of sparkling wine by Fede & Tinto at the Vini nel Mondo 2008 wine-lovers event in Spoleto, Umbria, Italy, on 30 May 2008.

PAIR OF SCISSORS

A pair of scissors measuring 1.78 m (5 ft 10 in) from tip to handle were manufactured by Michael Fish (Canada) and his team from Keir Surgical Ltd. The scissors were displayed at the Operating Room Nurses Association of Canada's (ORNAC) 20th National Conference in Victoria, Canada, on 24 April 2007.

★ GLASS OF BEER

A glass of beer containing 384.21 litres (84.5 gal) – that's about 676 pints – of Budweiser was produced by Harry Caray's Restaurant Group and WLS AM 890 (both USA) in Chicago, Illinois, USA, on 21 February 2008.

★ LANTERN

A stone lantern built for the Nenbutsushu Sanpouzan Muryojuji Temple in Kato City, Hyogo, Japan, measured 12 m (39 ft 4 in) tall and 7.4 m (24 ft 3 in) wide on 10 March 2008.

★ LARGEST WORKING RIFLE

On display at Da Yoopers Tourist Trap at Ishpeming, Michigan, USA, is a working rifle 10.18 m (33 ft 4 in) long belonging to James A DeCaine (USA). It can shoot projectiles by using propane and oxygen and is capable of firing a rock wrapped in duct tape a distance of 4 km (2.5 miles).

LARGEST SKATEBOARD

A skateboard measuring 9.4 m (31 ft 0.5 in) long, 2.4 m (8 ft) wide and 1.19 m (47 in) high was designed and produced by a team of students attending Jerry Havill's Team Problem Solving course at Bay de Noc Community College in Escanaba, Michigan, USA, on 17 August 2007.

★ **NEW RECORD**
★ **UPDATED RECORD**

View this clip

Aug 21: The **oldest athlete to win an Olympic gold** was Patrick Joseph "Babe" McDonald (USA), who was 42 years 26 days when he won the 25.4-kg-weight (56-lb) throw at Antwerp, Belgium, today in 1920.

ALTERNATIVE ENERGIES

A WHAT? NO, A WATT

A watt is a unit of measurement used to describe the rate at which electrical power flows – a 100-watt lightbulb, for example, uses up 100 joules of energy every second. A 100 megawatt (mega = 1,000,000) power station therefore produces 100,000,000 joules of energy per second – a lot of lightbulbs! Here is a rough guide to the outputs of various forms of technology:

- Wind turbines: 1–5 MW
- Geothermal: 1–100 MW
- Solar: 10–500 MW
- Hydro: 1–18,000 MW

★ MOST POWERFUL PUMPED STORAGE STATION

The Bath County Pumped Storage Station in Virginia, USA, consists of a pumping station and two reservoirs, separated in height by 380 m (1,247 ft). When demand on the electricity grid is low, excess power pumps water from the lower into the higher reservoir. When demand is high, water is released back into the lower, via turbines, which can generate 2,100 megawatts of power at maximum flow, at a rate of 915 m³ (32,242 ft³) per second.

SOLAR POWER

★ NEW RECORD
UPDATED RECORD

★ LARGEST INVESTMENT IN RENEWABLE ENERGIES

Germany's investment in renewable energies increased to over $14 million (£7 million) in 2007, mostly for solar photovoltaics and wind power.

★ FASTEST-GROWING ENERGY TECHNOLOGY

Grid-connected solar photovoltaic technology – the harnessing of solar power – has seen a 50% annual increase in installed capacity in 2006–07, reaching an estimated 7.8 gigawatts (GW). Hydro power remains the ★ largest contributor to renewable energy, reaching a capacity of 770 GW in 2007.

★ HIGHEST POWER OUTPUT FROM A TIDAL STREAM TURBINE

In December 2008, Marine Current Turbines (UK) announced the successful operation of their SeaGen turbine. Operating like an underwater wind farm, its two huge turbines are driven by the tidal flow in Strangford Lough, UK. SeaGen can generate up to 1.2 megawatts of power.

★ MOST WIDELY DEPLOYED SOLAR TECHNOLOGY

At the beginning of 2007, the installed capacity for solar water heating was approximately 154 GW. Israel has the **highest per capita use of solar-power heaters**, with one heater for every 10 people.

LARGEST SOLAR POWER FACILITY

In terms of capacity, the Harper Lake Site (LSP 8 & 9) in the Mojave Desert, California, USA, which is operated by UC Operating Services, is the largest solar electric power facility in the world. Its two solar electric-generating stations have a nominal capacity of 160 megawatts (80 megawatts each). The station site covers 1,280 acres (5.2 km²; 2 miles²) and houses 400,000 solar collectors (mirrors that concentrate solar energy) over an area equal to 750 football fields.

★ HIGHEST SOLAR EFFICIENCY

In July 2007, a team led by the University of Delaware, USA, announced the creation of a photovoltaic cell system with an energy efficiency of 42.8%. Currently, mass-produced cells have an efficiency of 15–20%, while high-end cells operate at roughly 25%.

The US Defense Advanced Research Projects Agency (DARPA) considers the potential of solar cells so great – primarily for lightening the load of soldiers on the battlefield – that they initiated the Very High Efficiency Solar Cell (VHESC) programme to develop cells that are at least 50% efficient. The market value of cells is around $100 million (£68 million).

LARGEST SOLAR-SLATE ROOF

A former barn in Berne, Switzerland, is fitted with a roof measuring 2,050 m² (22,066 ft²) and containing 16,650 photovoltaic-cell-embedded slates known as "sunslates". The project was engineered by Atlantis Energy Ltd and is expected to generate 167,000 kWh (kilowatt-hours) of electrical energy.

MOST POWERFUL SOLAR CHIMNEY

Enviromission's (Australia) solar-chimney power station in Manzanares, Spain, produced 50 kilowatts between 1982 and 1989. It consisted of a large area of greenhouses in which air, heated by the Sun, expanded upwards through a central tower, powering turbines as it escaped into the atmosphere.

Aug 22: At 92 years 156 days, Smoky Dawson (Australia, b. 19 March 1913) is the **oldest person to release a new album of original material** when *Homestead Of My Dreams* came out on this day in 2005.

Aug 23: The **largest Mexican wave** involved a total of 157,574 participants and was achieved by the TUMS wave at Bristol Motor Speedway in Bristol, Tennessee, USA, on 23 August 2008.

4,244,020: the record number of free energy-saving light bulbs distributed by Scottish and Southern Energy, *The Sun* newspaper and Cool nrg across the UK on 19 January 2008.

GUINNESS WORLD RECORDS

★ HIGHEST-CAPACITY CHICKEN-MANURE POWER STATION

In September 2008, a biomass power plant in Moerdijk, the Netherlands, was opened that converts chicken manure into electricity. With a generating capacity of 36.5 megawatts, the plant is carbon neutral, as the burning of the manure releases less greenhouse gases than if it were spread on fields. The plant consumes around 440,000 tonnes (440,925 tons) of chicken manure each year – around a third of the annual production in the Netherlands.

★ HIGHEST-CAPACITY WIND FARM

The Horse Hollow Wind Energy Centre consists of 421 wind turbines spread over nearly 190 km² (73 miles²) of Texas, USA. At its peak, it can produce 735.5 megawatts of electricity. The wind farm is owned by Florida Power & Light (FPL) Energy, which owns 47 such sites providing power for nearly 1 million US homes.

★ MOST POWERFUL SOLAR POWER TOWER

The PS10 power plant near Seville, Spain, uses a total of 624 moveable mirrors (heliostats), each with an area of 120 m² (1,292 ft²) to focus the Sun's light on to the top of a 115-m-high (377-ft) tower, where the combined heat drives a turbine to produce electricity. With a maximum generating capacity of 11 megawatts, the PS10 – which became operational in March 2007 – has the potential capacity to power up to 60,000 homes.

GEO, HYDRO, TIDAL & WIND

GREATEST GEOTHERMAL GENERATING CAPACITY

The USA has the world's largest geothermal generating capacity, able to produce 2,700 megawatts of electricity directly from the Earth. ("Geothermal" comes from the Greek for "earth-heat".)

The Geysers Power Plant in California, USA, is the world's **largest complex of geothermal plants**. The 22 power plants on site draw on the power from 350 steam wells and are capable of generating 1,700 megawatts of electricity.

MOST POWERFUL HYDROELECTRIC STATION

The Itaipu hydroelectric power station, on the border between Paraguay and Brazil, can generate 12,600 megawatts of electricity – or enough to power the state of California, USA.

FACT
The Moerdijk plant will produce enough renewable energy for 90,000 homes. Each year, the Netherlands produces around 1.2 million tonnes (1.3 million tons) of chicken manure.

MOST POWERFUL TIDAL POWER STATION

The La Rance tidal barrage, which is situated in the mouth of the La Rance river estuary in Bretagne, France, has been operating since 1966. It generates 240 megawatts of electricity from its 24 turbines, which are driven by the rising and falling tides. The electricity generated would meet the power needs of a city of 300,000 people.

LARGEST WIND GENERATOR

With a hub height of 135 m (443 ft) and a rotor diameter of 127 m (416 ft), the Enercon E-126 is the world's largest wind turbine. Its capacity is rated at 6 megawatts (or 20 million kilowatt-hours each year) — enough to fuel 5,000 European households of four! The wind generator was manufactured by Enercon GmbH (Germany) and installed on the Rysumer Nacken in Emden, Germany. It began operation in November 2007.

★ LARGEST WIND FARM

In terms of absolute numbers, Altamont Pass in California, USA, has the largest concentration of wind turbines in the world. With around 7,300 turbines spread over an area of 140 km² (54 miles², or twice the size of Manhattan in New York, USA), it has a maximum generating capacity of 576 megawatts – that is, an annual generation of about 1.1 terawatt-hours (TWh) of electricity. Construction of the first turbines began in 1981 as a reaction to the 1970s energy crisis, making them among the oldest in the USA.

CUTTING EDGE SCIENCE

★ SMALLEST NANOCAR

In 2005, scientists at Rice University in Texas, USA, led by James Tour, revealed a "car" made from a single molecule of mostly carbon atoms. It contains a chassis, axles and four wheels made from "buckyballs" (a sphere of 60 carbon atoms). The entire assemblage – which "rolls on four wheels in a direction perpendicular to its axles," according to Tour – measures just 3–4 nanometres across, slightly wider than a strand of DNA. The car is moved using a scanning tunnel microscopy (STM) probe.

★ HIGHEST ACHIEVED RPM (REVOLUTIONS PER MINUTE)

Researchers from the Department of Power Electronics at the Swiss Federal Institute of Technology, Zürich, announced in November 2008 that they had created a drive system which can spin at a rate of one million revolutions per minute. The drive system – which has applications in drill and compressor technology – has a titanium shell that prevents it from flying apart.

BEND OVER BACKWARDS

The M-2000iA has six axes of motion – equivalent, say Fanuc, to a human waist, shoulder, elbow, wrist and fingers; it is even more flexible than a human shoulder, being able to contort into any position.

STRONGEST ROBOTIC ARM

The M-2000iA/1,200 – an industrial robot created by Fanuc Robotics (USA) and unveiled in October 2008 – can lift a payload of 1,199 kg (2,645 lb). "Armed" with artificial intelligence sensors and video cameras, the M-2000iA can lift a tonne of metal 6 m (20 ft) into the air.

★ FASTEST TRANSISTOR

In 2007, US security company Northrop Grumman announced that they had created a transistor with an operating frequency of over 1,000 gigahertz. Transistors are the basic elements of electronic components, amplifying, detecting or switching electrical signals. "These advancements will enable a new generation of military and commercial applications that operate at higher frequencies with improved performance," said Dwight Streit, vice president, at the company's Space Technology sector.

Aug 25: The **youngest sports commentator** is Zach Spedden (USA, b. 8 July 1992), who called an entire nine-inning baseball game aged 10 years 48 days on this day in 2002.

★ MOST ACCURATE GRAVITY MAPPING SATELLITE

The European Space Agency's Gravity field and steady-state Ocean Circulation Explorer (GOCE, artist's impression above) satellite was launched on 17 March 2009. Its mission is to orbit the Earth while performing very high resolution measurements of Earth's gravity field. GOCE will, over 24 months in orbit, provide a map of Earth's "geoid" (that is, its idealized shape – smooth but irregular – based on the varying strength of gravity across the globe) with an accuracy of just 1–2 cm (0.5 in) in altitude and 100 km (62 miles) across. The GOCE map will provide an advanced baseline from which sea-level changes and ice-sheet evolution can be monitored with very high accuracy.

★ HIGHEST INTENSITY POSITRON BEAM

Positrons are the antimatter equivalent of electrons, and the two annihilate each other upon collision. The PULSTAR nuclear reactor, operated by North Carolina University, USA, uses the intense radiation in the vicinity of its reactor core to produce a low-energy beam of positrons with an intensity of 600 million positrons per second. Positrons are used to detect damage in nuclear reactors, as well as probe the scale of nanotechnological materials.

NANOTECHNOLOGY

★ SMALLEST ELECTRIC MOTOR

In 2005, US researchers at the Lawrence Berkeley National Laboratory and University of California at Berkeley, USA, unveiled a motor which operates by moving atoms between two molten droplets of metal. Completely contained within a carbon nanotube, the motor measures less than 200 nanometres across – hundreds of times smaller than the width of a human hair.

ACTUAL SIZE

★ HEAVIEST MAN-MADE WATER STRIDER

In 2008, a team led by Wei Pan at Tsinghua University in Beijing, China, announced the development of a technique for coating the wire legs of an artificial water strider with extremely water repellent polymer nanofibres. This makes the strider's legs so hydrophobic that they do not break the surface tension of water even when holding a weight of 1 gram – around 100 times heavier than a real water strider.

★ SMALLEST NANO CALLIGRAPHY

In 1991, scientists at the Hitachi Central Research Laboratory (Japan) reproduced the message "Peace 91 HCRL" on the surface of a molybdenum disulphide crystal using a scanning tunnelling microscope to blast out atoms of sulphur from the crystal one at a time. The letters are less than 1.5 nanometres in height.

★ STRONGEST CARBON NANOTUBE

In 2008, a team led by Alan Windle (UK) at the University of Cambridge announced they had developed a method of making carbon nanotubes around 1 cm (0.4 in) long with a tensile strength of 9 gigapascals. This corresponds to around four times stronger than Kevlar, the strong synthetic fibre used in body armour. Further refinements of this material could theoretically make it the best candidate for the construction of a space elevator for reaching space without the use of rockets.

★ LARGEST GRAPHENE SHEET

Scientists at UCLA in California, USA, reported the successful fabrication of sheets of graphene with surface areas up to 800 microns (0.0000012 in²). The sheets are just one atom of carbon in thickness and, at the atomic scale, resemble a chain-link fence.

Graphene, a nanofabric, is the **thinnest man-made material**, with a thickness of just one single atom of carbon. Graphene is similar to carbon nanotubes and buckyball carbon-60 molecules, but can exist as a single sheet of theoretically an infinite size.

★ NEW RECORD   UPDATED RECORD

★ MOST COMPLEX LASER SYSTEM

The goal of the National Ignition Facility (NIF) at the Lawrence Livermore National Laboratory in California, USA, is "creating a miniature star on Earth". To do this, 192 laser beams housed in a 10-storey chamber will focus 2 million joules of energy on to a tiny target (inset) containing hydrogen fuel. This will fuse (ignite) the atoms' nuclei and recreate the conditions that exist in the cores of stars. The practical aim of the project is self-sustaining nuclear fusion in the laboratory.

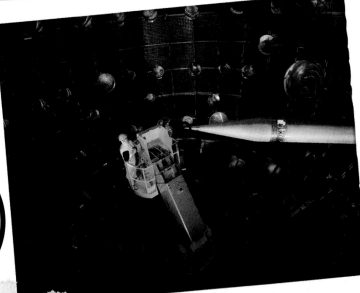

Aug 26: The **youngest club DJ** is Jack Hill (UK, b. 20 May 2000), who played at CK's Bar and Club in Weston-Super-Mare, UK, on 26 August 2007 aged 7 years and 98 days.

Aug 27: The **loudest noise ever recorded** was produced when the island-volcano Krakatoa exploded in an eruption on this day in 1883. The sound was heard 5,000 km (3,100 miles) away.

INTERNET

LARGEST FINE FOR SPAMMING

Three US companies were together ordered to pay $1.08 billion (then £619.8 million) to Robert Kramer (USA) for spamming the customers of his Iowa-based Internet Service Provider with junk email between August and December 2003, breaking local anti-spam law. Since the federal CAN-SPAM Act became US law in January 2004, the largest damages for spamming is $873 million (£603 million), which was awarded to Facebook against Adam Guerbuez (Canada) in 2008.

LONGEST BROADBAND

WI-FI CONNECTION

In April 2007, Ermanno Pietrosemoli (Venezuela) shot an 802.11 wireless signal 382 km (237 miles) between two mountains in the Venezuelan Andes. Pietrosemoli – president of the Latin American networking association Escuela Latino-america de Redes – sent a signal with a data throughput of 3 Mb/s.

★ LARGEST SOCIAL NETWORK

In April 2008, social networking websites Facebook and MySpace both had 115 million unique viewers using their services. By May 2009, Facebook surged ahead of its rival to claim over 200 million users, with 100 million logging on once a day.

LARGEST VIDEO-SHARING SERVICE

Founded in February 2005 and bought by Google in November 2006 for $1.65 billion (£863 million), YouTube allows Internet users to upload and watch video clips. As of 2009, around 13 hours of video are uploaded every minute. In July 2008, US users watched more than 558 million hours of video on the site.

★ MOST CYBER-DISSIDENTS IMPRISONED (COUNTRY)

According to Reporters Without Borders, the country that has incarcerated the most people for violating its web-surfing laws is China, with 69 people in prison as of 13 March 2009.

★ MOST INTERNET "FRIENDS"

Tom Anderson (USA), president and co-founder of MySpace, is automatically added as your first "friend" when you open a MySpace account. Because of this, Anderson had a total of 262,838,285 "friends" on his contacts list as of 31 May 2009.

★ MOST VISITED PERSONAL BLOG IN 24 HOURS

Japanese TV presenter Yusuke Kamiji's personal weblog attracted 230,755 unique visitors on 12 April 2008.

★ HIGHEST-ALTITUDE COMPUTER VIRUS

In August 2008, NASA revealed that laptops orbiting the Earth at an altitude of around 350 km (217 miles) on board the International Space Station had been infected with a virus. The laptops were for email and minor experiments only and were not integral to the space station. According to SpaceRef.com, the virus was the W32.Gammima.AG worm, which installs malware that steals online game data.

HIGHEST BROADBAND COVERAGE PER CAPITA

According to figures published by the Organization for Economic Co-operation and Development (OECD) in July 2007, Denmark has the highest broadband coverage per capita, with 34.3 per 100 people having internet connections with download speeds equal to or faster than 256 kbit/s.

ONE IS AMUSED!

Pictured is Queen Elizabeth II (UK) during a visit to the London headquarters of Google in October 2008. She was shown a YouTube clip of the "Laughing Baby" video – in which a child is made to laugh by someone saying "boo". "Lovely little thing, isn't it?" remarked the Queen.

YOUTUBE

Her Majesty Queen Elizabeth II launched a YouTube channel for the British monarchy in December 2007, 50 years after her first televised Christmas message in 1957. The channel is regularly updated with footage from various royal events.

Aug 28: The **oldest person to visit the North Pole** is Dorothy Davenhill Hirsch (USA, b. 11 May 1915), who visited the Pole on the Russian nuclear icebreaker *Yamal* on this day in 2004.

97: the percentage of all emails considered to be spam by Microsoft UK. The "vast majority" of these emails are stopped at source, said a Microsoft spokesperson.

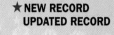

★ LONGEST-RUNNING HACKER CONVENTION

Originally started in 1993 as a party for members of "Platinum Net", a now-defunct Canada-based hacking network, DEFCON is the oldest continuously running hacker convention. Held at the Riviera Hotel & Casino in Las Vegas, Nevada, USA, the event regularly attracts crowds of 5,000–7,000. Tickets cost $120 and can only be purchased only on the door in cash to avoid attempts by police to track attendees through their credit card details.

★ FIRST US PRESIDENT WITH REGULAR EMAIL ACCESS

Among the first few announcements made when Barack Obama took office in January 2009 was the news that the President, an avid emailer, would use email to stay in touch with senior staff and personal friends during his term of office. However, the title for the ★ **first US President to use email in office** goes to Bill Clinton (USA), who sent one e-mail as a test and another, with the help of his staff, to astronaut John Glenn while he was in orbit on the Space Shuttle.

MOST SEARCHED-FOR NEWS ITEM

Alaskan governor Sarah Palin (USA, below) was named as the most searched-for person on the internet in 2008, according to the Google Zeitgeist list, which identifies the fastest-growing global search terms. Palin, the Republican Party's Vice-President nominee in the 2009 presidential elections, may have lost at the polls but she beat even President Barack Obama (USA) to the top of the list – as well as ousting last year's No.1, Britney Spears (USA), from the top spot!

TOP 100 Records of the Decade

YOUNGEST BILLIONAIRE

Facebook CEO Mark Zuckerberg (USA, b. 14 May 1984) had an estimated net worth of $1.5 billion (£756 million) when listed on Forbes.com on 5 March 2008, aged just 23 years 296 days.

★ LARGEST ONLINE AND INTERACTIVE MAP

Launched under its current title in 2005, Google Earth is an internet-linked application that produces a virtual 3D globe depicting the entire Earth from satellite data. Since 2005, Google Earth has been expanded to include areas under the sea and in space. It has also added new applications to its suite of map services, including Google Street View, which provides 360° horizontal and 290° vertical panoramic photographic views of streets of the major cities in Australia, France, Italy, Japan, Netherlands, New Zealand, Spain, the UK and USA.

FACT

DEFCON usually features talks, events and a Wi-Fi network where attendees can show off their hacking skills to their peers.

★ MOST SOFTWARE DOWNLOADS IN 24 HOURS

Mozilla's Firefox 3.0 is a free web browser that is developed by a team of volunteer programmers. It was downloaded 8,002,530 times on June 17–18, 2008, the launch day of the new Firefox web browser.

★ LARGEST "RICKROLL"

"Rickrolling" is an internet phenomenon where links purporting to lead somewhere else instead lead to a music video of 80s' pop star Rick Astley (UK) singing "Never Gonna Give You Up". The ★ **biggest online "Rickroll"** occurred on 1 April 2008, when all the featured links on YouTube's front page linked to the music video. The same month, Survey USA estimated that at least 18 million Americans had been "Rickrolled".

Aug 29: Sir Ranulph Fiennes and Charles Burton (both UK) completed the **first surface circumnavigation via both the geographical poles** on this day in 1982.

Aug 30: Carl F Haupt (USA, b. 21 April 1926) became the **oldest climber to summit Mount Kilimanjaro** in Tanzania, on 30 August 2004, aged 78 years 131 days.

GADGETS

★ MOST SECURE SMART-PHONE

The Sectera Edge is the first and only smartphone/PDA to be certified by the US National Security Agency as able to connect to classified US Government networks. With a touch of one button, users can switch between unclassified and classified (top secret) phone calls using the NSA Type 1 encryption algorithms. It was developed and built by General Dynamics (USA) to meets US military standards for ruggedness, including water, shock and temperature resistance.

★ QUADRUPED ROBOT DISTANCE RECORD

BigDog, developed by Boston Dynamics (USA) in 2005, is a four-legged robot designed to be a "pack mule" for soldiers travelling on rough terrain. It measures 1 x 0.7 m (3.2 x 2.2 ft) tall and weighs 75 kg (165 lb). In February 2009, the developers announced that it had walked 20.5 km (12.8 miles) autonomously, using GPS tracking.

★ FIRST USB PROSTHETIC

In May 2008, Finnish computer programmer Jerry Jalava lost part of a finger in a motorcycle accident. To "replace" the lost digit, Jalava made a prosthetic finger, inside which he installed a 2-GB USB memory stick, allowing him to carry his data around with him constantly. The idea came to him when doctors, having learned of his profession, joked that he should make a "finger drive" for his hand.

★ SMALLEST COLOUR SCANNER

Planon System Solutions (Canada) have produced a pen-sized (226-mm-long x 12-mm-thick; 8.9 in x 0.5 in) colour scanner that can digitize a sheet of paper in four seconds. The DocuPen RC800 has 8 MB of flash memory supplemented by a 1 GB micro CD card.

★ FIRST GPS PROJECTILE TRACKING DEVICE

StarChase is a tracking system developed by the US company of the same name. It is a small cannon that fires a golf ball-sized sticky projectile at a vehicle being pursued by law-enforcement personnel. The projectile contains a small GPS tracker, receiver and power supply and allows the police to track fugitives without having to enter into a car chase.

★ FASTEST COMPUTER

Built by IBM (US) for the US National Nuclear Security Administration, the Roadrunner computer, unveiled on 10 June 2008, is capable of operating at one petaflop (1,000 trillion floating point operations per second).

TOP 100 Records of the Decade

★ THINNEST BLU-RAY PLAYER

In January 2009 at the Consumer Electronics Show in Las Vegas, Nevada, USA, Samsung (South Korea) revealed its wall-mountable, Wi-Fi-enabled BDP 4600 Blu-ray player, which has a thickness of just 39 mm (1.5 in).

★ NEW RECORD
★ UPDATED RECORD

★ LONGEST RANGE BLUESNARF

Bluesnarfing is the act of stealing data such as telephone numbers and addresses from insecure Bluetooth devices. In 2004, mobile security expert John Hering (USA) used an antenna attached to a gun-like stock to bluesnarf a mobile phone from a distance of 1.7 km (1.1 miles). As part of the experiment, he used "exploits" (mobile-phone hacks) to attack the phone, steal its contact list and send sms messages from it. The attack was performed on one of the phones owned by the wireless research and development company that Hering worked for, in order to demonstrate vulnerabilities in Bluetooth devices at the time.

Aug 31: The **longest distance swum without flippers in open sea** is 225 km (139.8 miles) by Veljko Rogosic (Croatia) in the Adriatic Sea from Grado to Riccinoe (both Italy) from 29 to 31 August 2006.

1 billion: the number of iPod/iTouch software downloads from Apple's App Store, as of April 2009 – just nine months after opening. It would reportedly cost you $71,442 (£49,386) to buy all 25,000 Apps.

ACTUAL SIZE

SMALLEST CAMERA PLANE

In July 2008, researchers at the University of Delft, the Netherlands, unveiled the DelFly Micro. The dragonfly-shaped prototype aerial drone weighs just 3 g (0.1 oz) and has a wing-span of 10 cm (4 in). It carries a camera that transmits live video to a controller on the ground. The camera and transmitter weigh 0.4 g (0.015 oz) and the onboard lithium ion battery can keep the plane flying for up to three minutes.

SMALLEST FUEL CELL

In January 2009, chemical engineers at the University of Illinois, USA, revealed a prototype fuel cell measuring just 3 x 3 x 1 mm. The metal hydride fuel cell contains just four components: a metal hydride chamber, a water reservoir, a thin membrane separating them and an electrode assembly. It can generate 0.7 volts and 0.2 milliamps for 30 hours before needing refuelling.

★ MOST EXPENSIVE ICE-CREAM MAKER

The G Series ice-cream makers, made by NitroCream LLC (USA), are customized and signed by artists. Prices start at $75,000 (£51,484) for these machines, which are designed for restaurants or home kitchens. They use liquid nitrogen to create ice cream almost instantly, by mixing the nitrogen, which turns into gas at -196°C (-321°F), directly with the ice cream mixture. The G Series was launched in March 2009 but for those with a smaller wallet, a cheaper version, the N2-G4, costs just $34,900 (£23,952).

★ LARGEST BLUETOOTH DEVICE

In February 2007, London's Tower Bridge was modified to be a giant Bluetooth-enabled device. Bluetooth detectors on the bridge scanned people crossing below 15 times per second and displayed the location of people with Bluetooth devices as brightly coloured pixels on a lighting array on the bridge's upper walkway, allowing spectators to watch the movement of people along the bridge.

★ HAPTIC JACKET WITH THE MOST ACTUATORS

Philips Electronics (Netherlands) have produced a "haptic" feedback system fitted to a wearable jacket. The jacket is lined with 64 actuators – vibration motors – that provide the wearer with the sensation of being touched, adding heightened interaction with movies or video games. Two AA batteries are sufficient to replicate the feel of a punch, a shiver running up the spine or the beating of a heart.

BEST-SELLING SMARTPHONE

According to analyst firm iSuppli, Apple's iPhone outsold all other models of smartphone in the USA in July 2007, its first full month on sale. In the last four months of 2007, Apple sold 2,315,000 units, helping to push their net quarterly profits to $1.58 billion (£805,326,016) and making the iPhone the fastest-selling smartphone ever. As of March 2009, global sales have reached 17 million units.

TOP 100 Records of the Decade

★ FIRST VIDEO WATCH PHONE

With a thickness of 1.39 cm (0.55 in) and a 3.6-cm (1.43-in) colour screen, the LG GD910 Watch Phone is the first model in the world that allows video calls. First announced at the Consumer Electronics Show in Las Vegas, Nevada, USA, the phone includes features such as a touchscreen, voice recognition and Bluetooth. It is due to be available to the public sometime in 2009.

FARTHEST DISTANCE FLOWN WITH ROCKET BELT

On 24 November 2008, Eric Scott (USA) flew 457 m (1,500 ft) across a 320-m-deep (1,053-ft) part of the Royal Gorge, Colorado, USA, using a rocket belt. He completed the flight, without parachute, in 21 seconds, leaving just 12 seconds of reserve fuel.

193

Sept 1: The Burj Dubai tower in Dubai, United Arab Emirates, reached a height of 688 m (2,257 ft) on this day in 2008, making it the **world's tallest building**.

Sept 2: The **longest carrot** measured 5.841 m (19 ft 1.96 in) and was grown by Joe Atherton (UK). The carrot was measured in Somerset, UK, on 2 September 2007.

ART & MEDIA

CONTENTS

8,361.31 m² (90,000 ft²): the area of the **largest chalk pavement art**, created by 5,678 schoolchildren in Alameda, California, USA, in June 2008.

★LARGEST ANAMORPHIC PAVEMENT ART

Covering an area of over 270 m² (2,906 ft²), *Waterfall* is the largest piece of 3D pavement art ever created. Artist Edgar Mueller (Germany) turned River Street in Moose Jaw, Saskatchewan, Canada, into a virtual raging torrent of a river during the city's Prairie Arts Festival in Summer 2008. Mueller's work celebrates the phenomenon and technique of "perspectival anamorphosis"; this involves creating a distorted image that can only be seen properly from one view point.

ART & SCULPTURE

★ LARGEST PAPIER-MÂCHÉ PANDA DISPLAY

The World Wildlife Fund (WWF) set up a display of 1,600 papier-mâché pandas in Paris on 18 October 2008 to draw attention to the continuing plight of giant pandas, the emblem of the organization, and to encourage the protection of their environment. The number of papier-mâché pandas represented the number of the animals remaining in the wild.

★ MOST EXPENSIVE ILLUSTRATION SOLD AT AUCTION

An anonymous British collector bought a Beatrix Potter (UK) watercolour titled "The Rabbits' Christmas Party" for £289,250 ($575,400) at Sotheby's in London, UK, in July 2008. The illustration, created in the 1890s, had been part of the collection of the artist's brother, Bertram Potter.

LARGEST ORIGAMI MOSAIC

More than 2,000 children trained by 150 origami experts assembled a mosaic measuring 320.87 m² (3,453 ft²) at an event to celebrate the Beijing Olympics organized by the Hong Kong Youth Visual Art Association, Chinese Arts Festival, Lo Fung Art Gallery Ltd and the Union of Visual Artists Limited, at Hiu Kwong Street Sports Centre, in Kwun Tong, Hong Kong, China, on 26 July 2008.

MOSAICS...

STONE
On 29 July 2001, a team of 2,001 students, teachers and parents completed a stone mosaic depicting three figures hand-in-hand (parent, student, teacher) dancing on six beans representing the cultivation of youth. The mosaic, which was organized by HK Talent Foundation Ltd and HK United Youth Association Ltd, has a surface area of 4,720 m² (50,805.65 ft²) and is located in the Luozuling Park, Shiyan Town, Shenzhen, China.

CANDY
Around 5,000 schoolchildren and customers created a mosaic of the Haribo logo measuring 15 m (49 ft) in length and 3 m (10 ft) in height using 350,000 Haribo sweets for the Centro Commerciale Curno shopping centre and Aldino srl (both Italy) in Curno, Bergamo, Italy, on 2 November 2008.

★ CAR
Rally organizer Tequenitune (Japan) arranged a car mosaic of the Subaru company logo covering an area of 3,795 m² (40,849 ft²) and made from 339 Subaru cars at Ryugasaki Airfield, Ibaraki, Japan, on 7 March 2009.

★ COOKIE
Visual artist Laurent Gagnon (Canada) designed a cookie mosaic measuring 16.53 m² (177.9 ft²) to celebrate the 400th anniversary of the founding of Québec City, using biscuits provided by the Canadian baking company Leclerc in St-Augustin-de-Desmaures, Québec, Canada, on 26 June 2008.

★ CONFETTI
Nikki Douthwaite (UK) created a 2.4 x 1.5-m (8 x 5-ft) portrait of Formula 1 driver Lewis Hamilton (UK) from 250,000 discarded hole-punched dots in October 2008.

LARGEST...

★ HANDPRINT PAINTING
Erdem Örnek and students of Tevfik Kusoglu Primary Education School (all Turkey) in Kayseri, Turkey, created a handprint painting measuring 2,944.62 m² (31,695.5 ft²) on 20 June 2008.

MURAL BY ONE ARTIST
Pontus Andersson (Sweden) created a mural measuring 696.3 m² (7,494.9 ft²) depicting the north and south waterfronts of Gothenburg in Gothenburg, Sweden, on 4 September 2007.

★ PAINTING BY NUMBERS
A group of 2,409 volunteers created a paint-by-numbers picture measuring 1,328.52 m² (14,300 ft²) during the "Lilly Global Day of Service" on 15 May 2008 in Indianapolis, Indiana, USA.

★ PERMANENT COIN MURAL
Jin Jeonggun (South Korea) created a permanent coin mural depicting the South Korean flag consisting of 110,000 10-won coins measuring 24 m² (258.33 ft²) in Seoul, South Korea, on 16 April 2008.

★ ART COMPETITION
The Federal Ministry of Transport, Building and Urban Affairs of Germany organized an art competition to promote traffic safety among young children that attracted a total of 122,942 entries from children from all over Germany. The pictures were eventually displayed at the Olympiastadion in Berlin, Germany, on 3 June 2008, in an event organized by 2sense event GmbH and Zeitgeist Media (both Germany).

★ CARDBOARD BOX SCULPTURE
Volunteers from Cheney and surrounding areas and Allpak Containers, Inc., in Cheney, Washington, USA, built a replica of a medieval castle measuring 34.06 x 2.03 x 22.04 m (111 ft 9 in x 6 ft 8 in x 72 ft 4 in) out of cardboard boxes on 18 August 2007. A total of 147 boxes were used in the sculpture.

Sept 3: On this day in 1906, Joe Gans (USA) beat Oscar Nelson (Denmark) after an epic 2-hr 6-min, 42-round boxing match, the **longest world boxing title fight**, in Goldfield, Nevada, USA.

Sept 4: The **most consecutive boomerang catches** from juggling two boomerangs, keeping at least one aloft at all times, is 555, by Yannick Charles (France) at Strasbourg, France, on this day in 1995.

3,398 m³ (120,000 ft³): the volume of the **largest snow sculpture**, built by a team of 600 sculptors in Heilongjiang Province, China, in December 2007.

★ LARGEST
COFFEE CUP MOSAIC

In September 2008, German documentary film makers assembled a mosaic depicting a huge cup of coffee from 77,244 coffee cups outside the Brandenburg Gate in Berlin to illustrate the amount of coffee consumed by an average German in a lifetime.

PICTURE MADE OF LITE-BRITE

Representatives from advertising agency Vitrorobertson LLC and ASICS America Corporation (both USA) created a Lite-Brite picture of an ASICS Gel-Lyte III trainer using 347,004 lite-brite pegs in New York City, USA, on 7 October 2008.

WOODEN SCULPTURE

Michel Schmid (Switzerland) built a 22.92-m (75-ft 2-in) wooden Sioux Indian head in Porrentruy, Switzerland, on 19 August 2008.

TALLEST...

CHOCOLATE SCULPTURE

Pastry chef Justo Almendrote (Spain) created a chocolate sculpture measuring 6.5 m (21 ft 4 in) in the shape of a Christmas tree. It was unveiled to the public in Madrid, Spain, on 10 December 2008.

LARGEST
CHALK PAVEMENT ART

The largest chalk pavement art measured 8,361.31 m² (90,000 ft²) and was created by 5,678 children from schools in Alameda, California, USA, for the Kids' Chalk Art Project between 27 May and 7 June 2008.

STAINED-GLASS WINDOW

The tallest stained-glass window in the world is the 41.14-m-high (135-ft), 9-m-wide (29-ft 6-in) back-lit glass mural installed in 1979 in the atrium of the Ramada Hotel, Dubai, United Arab Emirates.

LONGEST...

GRAFFITI SCROLL

The longest graffiti scroll measured 700.92 m (2,299 ft 7 in) and was crafted by children's charity "To hamogelo tou pediou" in an event organized by Anemos Events in Kerkyra, Greece, on 15 December 2008.

PAINTING BY AN INDIVIDUAL

The longest painting by an individual measured 2,008 m (6,587 ft 10 in) and was created by Tommes Nentwig (Germany) in Vechta, Germany, on 10 July 2008.

GUM WRAPPER CHAIN

Since 11 March 1965, Gary Duschl of Virginia, USA, has been making a gum wrapper chain which currently measures 13,526 m (44,378 ft). The chain is made up of 2,071,148 links from 1,036,574 wrappers.

TOP 100 Records of the Decade

CARTOON STRIP

Pupils of De Eindhovense School in Eindhoven, the Netherlands, created a cartoon strip measuring 309.90 m (1,016 ft 8 in) long and 70 cm (2 ft 3 in) high entitled "Look at us – De Eindhovense School" on 25 January 2008.

★ MOST MONEY MADE AT AUCTION BY A SINGLE ARTIST

Damien Hirst (UK) made £111 million ($200.8 million) during a two-day auction of his works on 15–16 September 2008. Only three of the 167 items on sale at Sotheby's in London, UK, went unsold at the end of the auction.

★ NEW RECORD
UPDATED RECORD

TOP 100 Records of the Decade

LARGEST
ICE HOTEL

The Ice Hotel in Jukkasjärvi, Sweden, has a total floor area of between 4,000 m² and 6,000 m² (43,000–64,000 ft²), and in the winter of 2008–09 featured 80 rooms, many decorated with ice sculptures, as well as an ice bar and an ice church. Lying 200 km (120 miles) north of the Arctic circle, the hotel has been re-created (and enlarged) for the winter season every December since 1990.

Sept 5: Employees of Pidy, a company based in Ypres, Belgium, completed a cream-puff pastry, or mille-feuille, 1,037.25 m (3,403 ft) in length on this day in 1992, the **longest mille-feuille**.

PHOTOGRAPHY

OLDEST SURVIVING PHOTOGRAPH

The grainy image on the left shows the view from the window of the home of inventor Joseph Niépce (France, 1765–1833). To look at, it is far from special until you realize that it was taken in 1827 using a *camera obscura* and is in fact the oldest known surviving photograph. (Beneath it is the pewter plate on to which the image was originally exposed.) Rediscovered by the historian Helmut Gernsheim in 1952, it is now in the Gernsheim Collection at the University of Texas, Austin, USA.

CAMERA OBSCURA

View from the Window at Le Gras (top) took eight hours to expose using a precursor of the camera called a *camera obscura* ("veiled chamber"). A simple box with a pinhole lens, light enters and exposes a plate coated with light-sensitive bitumen.

★ LARGEST DAGUERREOTYPE

David Burder (UK) built *Big Bertha*, a 2-m² (6.5-ft²) camera capable of taking daguerreotype images measuring up to 0.6 x 2.12 m (4 x 2 ft). Daguerreotype – named after its inventor, Louis Jacques Mandé Daguerre (France, 1789–1851) – was the first truly successful form of photography, with the subjects captured on light-sensitive, silver-coated copper plates.

☀ LARGEST PANORAMIC DIGITAL PHOTOGRAPH

Michael Høeltermand of SUN-ADvertising (Denmark) snapped a panoramic digital photograph of 15.33 gigapixels – that is, containing 15.33 billion "picture elements". The image, which covers an area of 3,958.5 m² (42,608 ft²) – half the size of a regular football pitch – was created for "Event 2006" on 20 May 2006, which was held at the Messecenter Herning, Denmark.

LARGEST COLLECTION OF CAMERAS (STILLS PHOTOGRAPHY)

Dilish Parekh of Mumbai, India, has a collection of 4,425 antique cameras that he has amassed since 1977. Parekh, who works as a photojournalist, has within his collection cameras made by Rolliflex, Canon, Nikon and a Royal Mail Postage stamp camera that dates back to 1907.

FIRST JPEGS

The well-known digital image format JPEG – which stands for Joint Photographic Experts Group – was developed in order to standardize the techniques for digital image compression and is used on the internet and by digital cameras. The first images that use the JPEG compression method are a set of four test images used by the JPEG group called "Boats", "Barbara", "Toys" and "Zelda", created on 18 June 1987 in Copenhagen, Denmark.

LARGEST PHOTOGRAPHIC EXHIBITION

A photographic exhibition entitled "The Running Line" featured a record 138,355 photographs, all taken by the people of Tyneside, UK, during the 2006 Great North Run half marathon. The images were mounted side by side on a roll and draped around Saltwell Park in Gateshead, UK, on 19 October 2007.

Sept 6: The worldwide TV audience for the funeral of Diana, Princess of Wales (UK, 1961–97) on this day in 1997 was estimated at 2.5 billion – the **largest TV audience for a live broadcast**.

Sept 7: The **highest speed reached on a conventional motorcycle** is 406.62 km/h (252.662 mph), by John Noonan (USA) at Bonneville Salt Flats, Utah, USA, on this day in 2005.

11,811: the **largest collection of sporting photographs**, owned by Alex McFadyen (Canada) and collected since October 1977.

LENS

The lens was salvaged from a used-parts bin on the Kodak Super-8 movie-camera production line. The camera's resolution of just .01 megapixels – which is 10,000 pixels of image data – resulted in a 100-line black and white image.

DIGITAL TAPE

A "portable digital instrumentation recorder" – i.e. a regular cassette tape – was used to store images. It took 23 seconds to record an image to tape and another 23 seconds to read the tape and display the image on a television screen.

CCD CHIPS

Charge-coupled devices (CCD) – electronic sensors used to gather the optical information – had just been introduced in 1973 and were the inspiration behind the digital camera.

CIRCUITRY

Steve Sasson, the camera's inventor, amassed "several dozen digital and analogue circuits all wired together on approximately half a dozen circuit boards".

LARGEST NUDE PHOTO SHOOT

A total of 18,000 people volunteered to collectively pose naked in Zocalo Square, Mexico City, Mexico, for photographer Spencer Tunick (USA) on 6 May 2007.

★ NEW RECORD
UPDATED RECORD

★ MOST EXPENSIVE CELEBRITY PHOTOS

People magazine and *Hello!* magazine each paid $6.08 million (£3.5 million) – $12.16 million (£7 million) in total – to Brad Pitt and Angelina Jolie (both USA) for images of their twins Vivienne and Knox Jolie-Pitt when they were three weeks old in July 2008. It is thought the money was donated to a foundation created by Pitt and Jolie that helps children in need around the world.

A/D CONVERTER

An analogue-to-digital converter was cannibalized from a Motorola digital voltmeter.

★ FIRST DIGITAL CAMERA

Steve Sasson (USA) of Kodak built the first digital camera prototype in 1975. It weighed 3.6 kg (8 lb) and was the size of a toaster. The camera took black and white images with a resolution of 0.01 megapixels and its on-board storage medium was magnetic tape. Images were viewed by removing the tape and placing it in a cassette-reader playback device, which then displayed images on a TV monitor.

★ LARGEST PINHOLE CAMERA

A pinhole camera created from a 13.71 x 48.76 x 24.38 m (45 x 160 x 80 ft) aircraft hangar in El Toro, California, USA, produced a photograph on canvas measuring 9.62 x 33.83 m (31 ft 7 in x 111 ft) in June 2006. A pinhole camera works on the same principle as a *camera obscura* (see opposite page).

★ LONGEST PHOTOGRAPHIC CAREER

GHF Atkins (UK) had his first photograph published in 1927 and had photos published in every subsequent decade until he retired in 2004. He specialized in photographs of buses.

★ LARGEST PHOTO ALBUM

A photo album measuring 4 m x 5 m (13 ft 1 in x 16 ft 4 in) was created by Johnson's Baby China and unveiled in Beijing, China, on 10 June 2008.

★ MOST EXPENSIVE PHOTOGRAPH SOLD AT AUCTION

German photographer Andreas Gursky's image *99 Cent II, Diptych* (2001) is a chromogenic colour print of the interior of a discount store, showing racks of packaged food. One of six copies of the photograph, which measures 206 x 341 cm (81.1 x 134.2 in), was sold at auction by Sothebys, London, UK, on 7 February 2007 for £1,700,000 ($3,351,720) including premium.

MOST SUCCESSFUL INSTANT CAMERA

In 1947, Edwin Land (USA), created the Polaroid instant camera, which used the principle of diffusion transfer to reproduce the image recorded by the camera lens directly on to a photosensitive surface; this was then dispensed from the camera "instantly" as a photograph. In 1998, the Polaroid Corporation generated revenue of $1.86 billion (£1.12 billion), with sales peaking at $3 billion (£2.04 billion) in 1991. The company stopped making the film used in their cameras in 2008, after digital photography took over the market and made the Polaroid concept largely redundant.

MOST EXPENSIVE BOOK BY A SINGLE PHOTOGRAPHER

Helmut Newton's Sumo, a retrospective of German-born Australian photographer Helmut Newton's work, retails at $8,563 (£6,000) on the website of the book's publisher Taschen.

★ MOST EXPENSIVE CAMERA SOLD AT AUCTION

An 1839 daguerreotype camera, made by Susse Freres, was sold at auction in Vienna, Austria, on 26 May 2007 for €588,613 ($792,000; £399,385).

The wooden box structure, which was in its original state, had been lying forgotten in a loft in Munich, Germany, since 1940 until the owner of the premises accidentally came across it.

Sept 8: The **fastest harmonica player** is Nicky Shane (USA) who played "Oh When the Saints Go Marching In" at a speed of 285 bpm in SRS Studios, Santa Barbara, California, USA, on this day 2005.

WHAT'S ON TV

★ MOST WINS OF THE ESPN ULTIMATE COUCH POTATO

The aim of the ESPN Ultimate Couch Potato award is to watch a continuous sports TV broadcast from a recliner for as long as possible without falling asleep. Three Americans have each won twice: Jason Pisarik (lasting 32 hr and 39 hr 55 min), Jeff Miller (40 hr 30 min and 39 hr 2 min) and Stan Friedman (pictured, 29 hr and 19 hr 48 min).

★ MOST WATCHED NATIONAL NETWORK TV BROADCAST

China Central Television's New Year's Eve Gala (aka *Spring Festival*) regularly attracts viewing figures of over 300 million. The 2009 broadcast of song, dance and news review was seen by 95.6% of all families watching television in China.

Internationally broadcast events (such as Live Aid) or global sporting events (such as the Olympics and the World Cup) attract higher viewing figures.

HIGHEST TV ADVERTISING RATE (SINGLE DAY)

On 1 February 2008, NBC Sports (USA) secured a record $206 million (£141 million) in TV advertising from its slots during the Super Bowl XLIII game between the Pittsburgh Steelers and Arizona Cardinals (both USA). Many of the 69 available 30-second time slots sold for $2–3 million (£1.3–2.06 million). All 69 slots were sold to 32 advertisers; this, plus pre- and post-match advertising resulted in a record day's ad sale of $261 million (£179 million).

HIGHEST-PAID TV STARS

Two and a Half Men (CBS, USA, 2003–present) star Charlie Sheen (USA) is currently the highest-paid actor on TV, earning $20 million (£13.6 million) for his role as eternal bachelor Charlie Harper in the hit comedy show.

The highest-paid actress on TV for this period was Katherine Heigl (USA), aka Dr Izzie Stevens from *Grey's Anatomy* (ABC, USA, 2005–present). According to Forbes, she earned $13 million (£8.8 million) in 2007–08.

★ GREATEST PRODUCT PLACEMENT (TV SERIES)

Product placement involves promoting a branded product or service subtly (or sometimes not so subtly) within the context of a TV show. There were a record 6,248 incidences of product placement throughout 2008 on the TV series *Biggest Loser* (NBC, USA, 2004–present), according to a study by Nielsen. In this game show, obese contestants compete for cash prizes by losing as much weight as possible.

MOST WATCHED TV EVENT OF THE YEAR (2008)

The Nielsen Company estimated that – worldwide – up to 4.7 billion viewers tuned into the Beijing Olympics at some point. This equates to approximately 70% of the global population.

• The **most watched TV show of the year in the UK** was *Wallace and Gromit: A Matter of Loaf and Death* (BBC), which aired on Christmas Day and attracted an audience of 16.15 million.

• The **most watched TV show of the year in the USA** Was Super Bowl XLII (Fox), in which the New York Giants achieved a thrilling win over the New England Patriots. This was the **largest TV audience for a Super Bowl** ever; the huge average viewing figures of 97.5 million places this Super Bowl second only to the *M*A*S*H* series finale in the list of all-time viewing figures (see TV comedies & soaps on pp.200–01).

★ HIGHEST-RATED TV SCI-FI

The re-imagined sci-fi series *Battlestar Galactica* (2004–present) is currently the highest-rated science-fiction and fantasy show on TV, according to an aggregation of reviewers' ratings. The last three series (out of four) appear in the Metacritic.com sci-fi top 10, with Season 3 peaking in ratings with a score of 9.4/10.

Sept 9: The record for the **longest distance walking over hot plates** is 19.10 m (62 ft 7 in) and was achieved by Rolf Iven (Germany) in Cologne, Germany, on this day in 2006.

635: the **most seizures caused by a TV show**; strobing effects in an episode of *Pokémon* shown in Japan in December 1997 left dozens hospitalized.

★ LONGEST TV ADVERT

To celebrate the launch of their new route from Dubai, UAE, to São Paulo, Brazil, the Emirates airline created a TV commercial lasting 14 hr 40 min – the same length of time as the journey itself. It features Fernando Ferreira (Brazil, aka Non-Stop Fernando), who talks (without cuts) for the entire time about the delights of his home country and the benefits of flying Emirates.

★ MOST SUCCESSFUL FEATURE-FILM SPIN-OFF

The most successful feature-film spin-off from a TV show is *Transformers* (USA, 2007), based on the syndicated 1984–87 TV series of the same name. The movie grossed over $700 million (£488 million) worldwide and was a live-action version of the 1980s' cartoon series, which itself was based on the Hasbro toy line.

• The ★ **most successful feature-film spin-off from a live-action TV show** is *Mission Impossible II* (USA, 2000), based on the *Mission Impossible* series (USA, CBS 1966–73; ABC 1988–90). The second and most lucrative instalment in the feature-film franchise grossed over $545 million (£365 million) worldwide.

A potential candidate for breaking this record is JJ Abrams' (USA) "reboot" of *Star Trek* (USA, 2009), which has been heavily marketed since January 2008.

LONGEST RUNNING SCI-FI TV SERIES

Doctor Who (BBC, UK) has chalked up 753 episodes to date (April 2009), encompassing 204 storylines, numerous specials, five spin-off series and 10 official Doctors. The relaunched show is set to return for a fifth season in 2010 with 26-year-old Matt Smith (pictured) as the eleventh – and youngest – Doctor.

★ MOST PORTRAYED SUPERHERO ON TV

The character of Superman has featured in four live-action TV series and been played by five different US actors: George Reeves (*The Adventures of Superman*, syndicated 1951–57, pictured above left); John Haymes Newton and Gerard Christopher (*Superboy*, syndicated 1988–91); Dean Cain (*Lois & Clark: The New Adventures of Superman*, ABC 1993–97); and Tom Welling (*Smallville*, Warner Bros., later CW, 2001–present, pictured above right). A sixth actor, Johnny Rockwell (USA), played the character in *The Adventures of Superboy* (1961), an untransmitted pilot for an unrealized series.

The characters of Superman and Batman have also appeared in numerous cinema serials and animated TV series over the years.

★ LARGEST DVD BOX SET

The 2007 DVD release of *Prisoner – Cell Block H: The Complete Collection* (Australia, 1979–1986) comprises 179 discs containing 692 episodes. The gritty women's-prison drama series has an overall running time of 22 days 14 hr 4 min.

HIGHEST-RATED TV SERIES

The fourth season of the Baltimore-set crime drama *The Wire* (HBO, USA, 2002–09) achieved a record high rating of 98/100 on the aggregator website Metacritic.com, making it the highest-rated series on TV. Season five also appears in the top 10 list of highest-rated shows. Created by David Simon (USA), the multi-award-winning series explores the nature of street and drug crime from various points of view, and was heralded as a unique – and most successful – take the "cop show" genre.

Sept 10: The **longest measured home run in a major league game** is 193 m (634 ft) by Mickey Mantle (USA) for the New York Yankees at Briggs Stadium, Detroit, Michigan, USA, on this day in 1960.

Sept 11: The **youngest astronaut** is Major (later Lt-Gen.) Gherman Stepanovich Titov (Russia, born on this day in 1935), who was aged 25 years 329 days when launched in *Vostok 2* on 6 August 1961.

TV COMEDIES & SOAPS

★ LONGEST UNINTERRUPTED TRANSMISSION OF A TV SERIES

From 7 to 11 June 2008, the German pay TV channel Sat.1 Comedy broadcast – without any interruptions – all 236 episodes of the US TV series *Friends*. The comedy marathon was broadcast primarily to give viewers the chance to watch something other than Euro 2008, the UEFA European Football Championship, in which Germany finished runners-up.

★ MOST POPULAR COMEDY OF THE DECADE

According to TV.com, *Scrubs* (NBC/ABC, USA, 2001–present) was the most popular comedy on TV in the 2000s. Its average visitor review score of 9.2 out of 10 was also the highest for this period, a record shared with *Friends* (NBC).

In terms of reviewer ratings collated on Metacritic.com, the ★ **highest–rated comedy of the decade** was season five of *Curb Your Enthusiasm* (HBO, USA, 2000–present) starring *Seinfeld* co-creator Larry David (USA) as a fictional version of himself.

★ MOST EMMY AWARDS FOR BEST COMEDY SERIES

Frasier (NBC, USA, 1993–2004) won a record 37 Emmys during its run, including five consecutive wins for Best Comedy Series. Its star, Kelsey Grammer (USA), appeared in three different shows as Dr Frasier Crane, and for each series received Emmy acknowledgement: twice for *Cheers* (NBC, USA), once for his guest appearance on *Wings* (NBC, USA), and nine times (winning four) for *Frasier* – the **most TV shows to receive Emmy nominations for the same character**.

LARGEST TV AUDIENCE FOR A COMEDY SHOW

The 2.5-hour-long finale of *M*A*S*H* (CBS, USA) – *Goodbye, Farewell and Amen* – had an estimated audience of 125 million (from 50.15 million households) on 28 February 1983. The black comedy/medical drama recounted the experiences of field doctors in the Korean War, and the final episode was seen by 77% of the viewing public – or 60.2% of all US households.

★ BIGGEST-SELLING TV SHOW ON DVD (2008)

The hour-long season six premiere special *Family Guy: Blue Harvest* (FOX, USA) achieved DVD sales of 1,141,575 – of which a record 442,000 were Blu-ray – in 2008. The DVD of the show's seventh series occupied the number 2 spot, making *Family Guy* the TV comedy show of the year in terms of home entertainment sales. "Blue Harvest" was the fake working title used to maintain the secrecy of the making of *Star Wars VI: Return of the Jedi* (USA, 1983).

COMEDIES

★ FIRST TV SITCOM

The first television sitcom was *Pinwright's Progress* (BBC, UK, 1946–47) starring character actor James Hayter (UK) as J Pinwright, owner of the smallest multiple store in the world. The show ran for 10 half-hour episodes, which were broadcast fortnightly, live from studios at Alexandra Palace, London, UK.

★ LONGEST-RUNNING SITCOM (LONGEVITY)

The longest-running sitcom is *Last of the Summer Wine* (BBC, UK), which debuted in 1973 and is still on air. Having completed its 30th season, it boasts 292 episodes, all written by the show's creator, Roy Clarke.

★ LONGEST-RUNNING SITCOM (MOST EPISODES)

During its 20th season (2008–09), *The Simpsons* (USA) became the longest-running TV sitcom by number of episodes broadcast. The classic cartoon sitcom, which first broadcast on Fox (USA) on 17 December 1989, has now seen 443 episodes (and counting) aired, overtaking the 435 episodes of former record holder *The Adventures of Ozzie and Harriet* (ABC, USA), which ran from 1952 to 1966.

★ NEW RECORD
  UPDATED RECORD

TOP 100 Records of the Decade

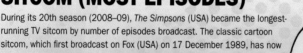

Sept 12: The **longest contract in National Hockey League history** is the 15-year deal given to goaltender Rick DiPietro (USA) by the New York Islanders (USA) on this day in 2006.

Sept 13: The **fastest production car** is an Ultimate Aero TT Super Car that achieved a speed of 412 km/h (256.14 mph) on Highway 221, Washington, USA, on 13 September 2007.

19: the number of Primetime Emmys won by *The Simpsons'* writer and producer James L Brookes – the **most Emmys won by an individual**.

★ MOST SUCCESSFUL TELENOVELA

In terms of its global reach, the most successful telenovela is *Yo Soy Betty, La Fea* ("I am Ugly Betty"), created by Fernando Gaitán (Colombia), which aired on Colombia's RCN Television network from 1999 to 2001. It has gone on to be the first truly global telenovela, being shown in its original form throughout Latin America and Spain, and dubbed for at least 15 other countries. Adaptations or remakes have also been produced in 19 other languages, with the US remake alone showing on at least 50 TV networks around the world.

SOAP OPERAS

★ FIRST SOAP OPERA

Soap operas began life on US radio in the 1930s; the name refers to the soap manufacturers that often sponsored these continuing dramas. The mother of the soap opera was Irna Phillips (USA, 1901–73), who created the first radio soap, *Painted Dreams*, which debuted on 20 October 1930. Phillips would later go on to create three giants in the field: *The Guiding Light* (USA, NBC Radio, 1937–1956; CBS TV, 1952–present), *As the World Turns* (USA, CBS TV, 1956–present) and *Another World* (USA, NBC TV, 1964–present).

★ FIRST TV SOAP OPERA

In 1944, Lever Brothers sponsored TV versions of two radio soaps – *Big Sister* and *Aunt Jenny's Real Life Stories* – on Dumont's

New York station. Two years later, *Faraway Hill* (2 October to 18 December 1946) became the first networked soap opera.

★ LONGEST-RUNNING SOAP OPERA

The Guiding Light (later just *Guiding Light*) began on NBC radio on 25 January 1937 and first aired on television on 30 June 1952. The classic soap, which is based around the central themes of family, love, romance, community and the trials and tribulations of human life, continues to run today on US TV (CBS).

The longest-running soap on UK television is *Coronation Street* (ITV), which debuted on 9 December 1960 and is still on air today.

LONGEST-SERVING SOAP STAR

Helen Wagner (USA) has played Nancy McClosky in *As the World Turns* (USA, CBS) since it premiered on 2 April 1956. Britain's longest-serving soap star is William Roache

(UK), who has played Ken Barlow in *Coronation Street* (ITV) since its first episode on 9 December 1960.

★ MOST PROLIFIC SOAP OPERA PRODUCER

Telenovelas (the Latin American version of soap opera) are the most widely watched shows in Latin American and are exported in huge numbers to many different territories. It's estimated that telenovelas from Mexico and Brazil are more globally popular than US, British and Australian soap operas combined. The market leader in this field is Mexico's Televisa, closely followed by Brazil's Globo.

★ MOST POPULAR SOAP

The Young and the Restless (CBS, USA, 1973–present) rated as the most watched soap of the 2007–08 TV season in the USA – and the **most watched soap of the decade** (and the 1990s). The daytime drama – shown in 22 countries – has rated no.1 every week for over 1,000 consecutive weeks US daytime ratings.

MOST BAFTA NOMINATIONS

The British Academy of Film and Television Arts (BAFTA) TV awards are the UK equivalent of the Emmys, and the most frequent nominee is comedienne Victoria Wood (UK), whose record 12th nomination came in 2007 for her role in *Housewife, 49* (ITV, UK).

MOST SUCCESSFUL TV SOAP

Dallas (CBS, USA) began in 1978 as a mini-series and went on to become the most successful soap opera of all time. By 1980, it was watched by an estimated 83 million people in the USA – giving it a record 76% share of the TV audience – and had been seen in more than 90 countries. The final episode was broadcast in the USA on 3 May 1991.

CERTIFICATE

The most successful TV soap was Dallas (USA), which ran from 1978 until 1991 and was broadcast in 90 countries around the globe.

GUINNESS WORLD RECORDS LTD

Sept 14: Edward Charon (USA) holds the record for the **most telephone directories torn in three minutes (male)**. He ripped 56 directories, each with 1,006 pages, in just three minutes in Branson, Missouri, USA, on 14 September 2006.

GAME SHOWS & REALITY TV

★ MOST SYNDICATED GAME SHOW

Who Wants to be a Millionaire?, created by Celador (UK) and first broadcast in the UK in 1998, can now be seen in over 100 countries around the world. Pictured is US host Regis Philbin (USA), who won the 2001 Daytime Emmy Award for Outstanding Game Show Host. Most recently, the Indian version of the show featured in the Oscar-winning hit movie *Slumdog Millionaire* (UK, 2008).

★ NEW RECORD
UPDATED RECORD

★ FIRST GAME SHOW

Canada-based journalist and former teacher Roy Ward Dickson (UK, 1910–78) effectively invented the game-show format when he adapted quizzes he had set for his pupils to the radio. *Professor Dick and His Question Box* aired on CKCL Radio on 15 May 1935, and Dickson went on to produce many pioneering game-show formats, including the first panel game, *Claim to Fame*.

★ FIRST TV GAME SHOW

Spelling Bee was first transmitted on BBC television at 10:00 p.m. on 31 May 1938. Beamed live from Alexandra Palace, London, UK, the 15-minute show involved host Freddie Grisewood (UK) asking adult contestants to spell various words and was based on a successful radio format adapted by the BBC from the US schools' Spelling Bee competitions. The show ran monthly for just five episodes.

★ LARGEST FINE IMPOSED ON A BROADCASTER

In May 2008, ITV plc (UK) were fined a record £5,675,000 ($11,218,000) for irregularities and misconduct over its premium phone line services by Ofcom, the independent regulator for the communication industries in the UK. "Serious editorial issues" were raised over *Ant & Dec's Saturday Night Takeaway* (pictured), *Gameshow Marathon* and *Soapstar Superstar*. Uncounted votes to the value of £7.8 million ($15.4 million) were logged.

★ MOST SUCCESSFUL REALITY TV FORMAT

The UK's *Strictly Come Dancing*, which pairs celebrities with professional dancers and asks the public to vote on which of the couples is the best dancing duo, has spawned more international spin-offs than any other programme.

The BBC format has been sold to 38 countries as *Dancing With the Stars*, including the USA where the eighth season's premiere had 22.8 million viewers on 9 March 2009, which was a record for the show.

★ FIRST GAME-SHOW CONTESTANT TO WIN $100,000

US television networks were required to cap game-show winnings after a series of scandals in the 1950s, but NBC limited their contestants' earnings by capping the number of games that could be played by a champion. On the 1980s version of NBC's *Sale of the Century* (USA), contestant Barbara Phillips (USA) retired with winnings of over $150,000 (£100,000).

The **largest cash prize won on a TV game show** is $2,520,700 (£1,331,309) by Ken Jennings of Salt Lake City, Utah, USA, on CBS show *Jeopardy!*, winning 74 games between 2 June and 30 November 2004.

★ MOST PROLIFIC TV GAME-SHOW HOST (USA)

Bill Cullen (USA, 1920–90) hosted 23 different game shows during a television career that spanned five decades. Cullen's shows included *Winner Take All* (his first, in 1952), *The Price is Right*, *Blockbusters* and *The Joker's Wild*. The Bill Cullen Career Achievement Award is now awarded by The Game Show Congress, a non-profit organization that promotes the game-show industry.

Sept 15: 171 members of the Chilli Club International (Australia) performed at the opening of the Sydney Olympics, Australia, on 15 September 2000 – the **most people simultaneously fire-eating**.

83 4 56

($19,300; £10,887) led to 30,000 people vying to be at the front of a queue leading into the Ultra Stadium in Manila, the Philippines. When the gates finally gave way, hundreds were crushed by the desperate mob.

★ FIRST FLY-ON-THE-WALL REALITY TV SERIES

The 12-part *An American Family* (PBS, filmed 1971; aired 1973) is considered to be the first TV show to feature a prolonged fly-on-the-wall look at real people. Over 10 million viewers would tune in each week to watch as the "stars" – the Louds, a typical nuclear family from Santa Barbara, California, USA – went about their everyday lives. Viewing figures peaked when mother Ann asked father Bill for a divorce.

PICK IT UP and Smile...
YOU MAY BE ON CANDID CAMERA
PHILADELPHIA DEPT. OF STREETS — SANITATION

FIRST REALITY TV SHOW

The first TV show to regularly feature members of the public as its stars was the USA's *Candid Camera*, which premiered (as *Candid Microphone*) in 1948. The premise was to perform practical jokes on members of the public and film their reactions.

★ MOST SYSTEMATIC GAME-SHOW STUDY

Economists keen to understand decision-making processes have analyzed clips from the game show *Deal or No Deal* (Endemol, 2002). The resulting paper, *Deal or No Deal? Decision Making under Risk in a Large-Payoff Game Show* (Post, Van den Assem, Baltussen and Thaler; March 2008), explores the choices made by 151 contestants on the show. The conclusion? Players who suffer setbacks early in the game take more risks later on, rather than taking decisions based on guaranteed returns – an established economic concept known as "prospect theory".

★ MOST PROLIFIC PRODUCERS

Together, Mark Goodson and Bill Todman (both USA) created more than 25 game-show formats, producing over 21,830 hours of TV. Goodson alone produced over 39,000 shows.

★ COSTLIEST GAME-SHOW PRODUCTION ERROR

The Plinko minigame on the *Price is Right* requires the contestant to drop a token down a board studded with pegs; as the chip falls, it is deflected by the pegs and ends up in one of a number of slots worth various amounts of prize money. During the filming of an episode on 22 July 2008, the producers forgot that the Plinko board had been rigged to always result in a $10,000 (£5,011) win and the contestant managed three wins before the fault was detected. The contestant was allowed to keep the $30,000 (£15,033).

HIGHEST DEATH TOLL FROM A GAME SHOW

On 4 February 2006, at least 74 people died during a stampede for tickets for the Filipino game show *Wowowee* (ABS-CBN). The chance to win 1 million pesos

★ LARGEST GAME-SHOW SET

Hosted by Richard O'Brien (UK, left), UK game-show *The Crystal Maze* (Chatsworth Television/Channel 4, 1990–95) boasted the world's largest game-show set, which was, at the time, the largest TV set in Europe. Technically not a maze but a set of four interconnected "time zones", the Crystal Maze was the size of two football pitches and cost about £250,000 ($480,000) to build.

★ FASTEST-SELLING DOWNLOAD SINGLE (UK)

UK reality TV talent show *The X Factor* has been producing record breakers ever since it first hit the small screen in 2004. Series winners Shayne Ward, Leona Lewis and Alexandra Burke (all UK) have each held the record for **fastest-selling download single in the UK**, with Burke's (pictured) track "Hallelujah" being the current holder with 289,621 downloads sold in the week ending 27 December 2008.

203

Sept 16: The **largest school reunion** involved 3,299 former pupils of Stadium High School, Tacoma, Washington, USA, attending the centennial event on this day in 2006.

Sept 17: The **shortest radio show** is *The Maurie Show*, presented by Maurie Sherman (Canada), which lasts one minute and was first broadcast on Virgin Radio Toronto, Canada, on 17 September 2008.

HOLLYWOOD HEROES

HIT MAN

Following his role in *The Dark Knight* (USA, 2008), his death at just 28 and his posthumous Oscar award, Heath Ledger (Australia) topped the list of ★ **"fastest rising"** male searched for on Google in 2008.

DANIEL RADCLIFFE

Daniel Radcliffe's (UK) starring roles in the five *Harry Potter* movies – plus parts in *The Tailor of Panama* (USA/Ireland, 2001) and *December Boys* (Australia, 2007) – means that he remains unbeaten as the **highest-average-grossing box-office star in a leading role**, raking in an average of $558 million (£383 million) per film. He is also, therefore, the ★ **highest-grossing actor of the decade**.

TOM CRUISE

With 20 movies in his filmography classed as "blockbusters", Tom Cruise has appeared in the ★ **most $100-million grossing movies**. His first blockbuster was *Top Gun* (USA, 1986), which earned $345 million (£235 million); his most recent – *Valkyrie* (USA/Germany, 2008), a real-life story about the attempted assassination of Adolf Hitler – grossed just over $165 million (£117 million). Despite this, Cruise was named as the ★ **most overpaid actor** of the year (see below).

★ MOST OVERPAID ACTOR

Forbes magazine has named Tom Cruise (USA) as the world's most overpaid actor, based on the relationship between the profitability of his movies and the size of his fees. Cruise – named as the most powerful actor in Hollywood in 2008 – had a recent run of movies that under-performed at the box office, including *Lions for Lambs* (USA, 2007), which earned just $1.88 (£0.94) for every $1 (£0.50) he was paid. For his last three movies (plus their first three months of DVD sales), Cruise grossed an average of $4 (£2) for every $1 he was paid. See *Screen Goddesses* on p.207 for a full explanation of the formula *Forbes* used to come to this ruling.

HIGHEST PAID ACTOR

Keanu Reeves (USA) received a salary of $15 million (then £9.17 million) for each of the two *Matrix* sequels, *Reloaded* and *Revolutions* (both USA/Australia, 2003), plus 15% of the box-office gross. *The Matrix* (USA/Australia, 1999) earned the actor $10 million (£6.18 million) plus 10% of the gross, putting his earnings for the trilogy at an estimated $260 million (£159 million) – an average of $87 million (£53 million) per movie.

JAMES DEAN & HEATH LEDGER

In 2009, Heath Ledger (Australia, 1979–2008, below left) became only the second person ever to win an acting Oscar after his death (for the role of The Joker in the 2008 blockbuster *The Dark Knight*, USA). The **first actor to win an acting Oscar posthumously** was Peter Finch (UK) for his role as Howard Beale in *Network* (USA, 1975). The ★ **most posthumous Oscar nominations for an actor** is two, by James Dean (USA, 1931–55, below) as Cal Trask in *East of Eden* (USA, 1955) and as Jett Rink in *Giant* (USA, 1956).

MAGIC TOUCH...

According to the UK *Daily Mail* newspaper, Daniel Radcliffe will earn $50 million (£35 million) for reprising his role as Harry Potter in the last two movies in the series – not bad, considering that his first Potter pay cheque was for just $362,000 (£250,000)!

Sept 18: In 2006, Anousheh Ansari (Iran) spent $20 million (£10.5 million) to become the **first female space tourist**, blasting off on this day for an eight-day stay on the *International Space Station*.

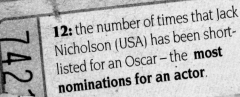

12: the number of times that Jack Nicholson (USA) has been short-listed for an Oscar – the **most nominations for an actor**.

BEST ACTOR: MOST OSCAR NOMINATIONS FOR A CHARACTER

One character has inspired more Best Actor Oscar nominations than any other: Henry VIII of England (1491–1547). Pictured right to left are Charles Laughton (UK) in *The Private Life of Henry VIII* (UK, 1933), for which he won the Oscar; Robert Shaw in *A Man for All Seasons* (UK, 1966); and Richard Burton (UK) in *Anne of the Thousand Days* (UK, 1969).

MOST ACADEMY AWARDS (OSCARS) FOR BEST ACTOR

With his win for portraying gay activist Harvey Milk in *Milk* (USA, 2008), Sean Penn (USA) became the ninth actor to share the accolade of winning two Oscar trophies for Best Actor. His other was for *Mystic River* (USA, 2003). Marlon Brando (USA), Gary Cooper (USA), Daniel Day-Lewis (UK), Tom Hanks (USA), Dustin Hoffman (USA), Fredric March (USA), Jack Nicholson (USA) and Spencer Tracy (USA) round off the list.

★ SHORTEST SCREEN TIME FOR A BEST ACTOR OSCAR WIN

Anthony Hopkins (UK) won a Best Actor Oscar for his performance in *The Silence of the Lambs* (USA, 1991), despite appearing on screen for little more than 16 minutes.

★ MOST RAZZIE NOMINATIONS

Sylvester Stallone (USA) has the dubious honour of being nominated in the annual Golden Raspberry "Worst in Film" Awards a record 30 times (winning 10); nine of the nominations (1984–92) were consecutive, also a record. The Razzies were first awarded in 1981 by US copywriter John Wilson as a light-hearted complement to the American Academy Awards (Oscars).

★ MOST RAZZIE NOMINATIONS IN A SINGLE YEAR

In 2004, Ben Stiller (USA) received a record five Golden Raspberry Worst Actor nominations in one year, for *Along Came Polly*, *Anchorman*, *Dodgeball*, *Envy* and *Starsky & Hutch* (all USA).

In 2007, Eddie Murphy (USA) won five Razzie nominations for just one film: *Norbert* (USA). He played three characters, all of whom won a Worst Actor trophy; two of the characters were nominated for Worst Couple and Murphy was nominated for Worst Screenplay.

★ HIGHEST-GROSSING ACTOR

Over the past year, the movies of Samuel L Jackson (USA) have grossed a further $150.3 million (£105.8 million) at the box office, taking his total career box-office gross to $7.57 billion (£5.35 billion).

TOP 100 Records of the Decade

MARLON BRANDO

The ★ **first actor to break the $1 million threshold** was Marlon Brando (USA), who was paid $1.25 million (£400,500) – equivalent today to $8.8 million; £6.1 million – for his starring role as Fletcher Christian in *Mutiny on the Bounty* (USA, 1962).

With his small part as Jor–El in *Superman* (1978), he also broke the $3 million mark; he also negotiated a share of the profits, thereby earning $14 million ($46 million or £32 million today) for just 10 minutes of screen time.

JOHNNY DEPP

Pirates star Johnny Depp (USA) this year regains his position as the ★ **most powerful actor** in Hollywood. Candidates for this role are assessed on their salary, web hits, news agency and magazine coverage, Celebdaq rating, IMDB star rating, and so on, for a 12-month period.

Sept 19: The **pumpkin-chuckin' world record** was set on this day in 1998 when an Aludium Q-36 Pumpkin Modulator was used to fire a pumpkin 1,368 m (4,491 ft) at Morton, Illinois, USA.

Sept 20: The **first world circumnavigation** was completed on this day in 1522 – not by Ferdinand Magellan, as often thought (he was killed in the Philippines), but by his navigator, Juan Sebastián Elcano (Spain).

SCREEN GODDESSES

CAMERON DIAZ

The **highest annual earnings for an actress** in 2007–08 was $50 million (£26.9 million) by Cameron Diaz (USA, below – she's the one on the right, obviously, next to Princess Fiona from *Shrek*). Since her debut in *The Mask* (USA, 1994), Diaz has appeared in a string of hit movies, including *My Best Friend's Wedding* (USA, 1997), *Charlie's Angels* (USA, 2000) and its sequel, and most recently *What Happens in Vegas* (USA, 2008, inset), as well as providing the voice of Fiona in the *Shrek* movies. (See opposite for a list of the 10 richest actresses in Hollywood.)

A DECADE OF SUCCESS

As of June 2008, Emma Watson (UK, right) had starred in six movies and grossed an average $753,700,000 (£554,880,000) per movie – the ★ **highest average box-office gross for an actress**. The reason for Watson's massive success? The five phenomenally successful *Harry Potter* movies that she has starred in since 2001.

Keira Knightley (UK, far right) has starred in 15 movies since 2000, including the three films in the massive hit series *Pirates of the Caribbean*. According to the Internet Movie Database, the total box-office gross for Knightley's movies in the last decade is $3.42 billion (£2.52 billion), which is the ★ **highest box-office gross for an actress in multiple roles** (three or more).

★ MOST POWERFUL ACTRESS

Angelina Jolie (USA) has retained her position as the top actress in Hollywood's power league thanks to her Oscar-nominated performance in *Changeling* (USA, 2008) and the public's seemingly endless appetite for stories about her relationship with Brad Pitt (USA) and their ever-expanding family – including the couple's most recent additions, twins Knox Léon and Vivienne Marcheline.

MOST CONSECUTIVE $100 MILLION-GROSS MOVIES

Jada Pinkett (USA) has appeared in seven movies with a domestic gross of over $100 million, four of which were consecutive, a record for an actress: *The Matrix Reloaded* (USA, 2003), *The Matrix Revolutions* (USA, 2003), *Collateral* (USA, 2004) and *Madagascar* (USA, 2005). Her other +$100 million movies were *Scream 2* (USA, 1997), *The Nutty Professor* (USA, 1996) and *Madagascar: Escape 2 Africa* (USA, 2008).

HIGHEST SALARY PER FILM

In February 2006, it was revealed that Reese Witherspoon (USA) had struck a pay deal worth $29 million (£17 million) to star in and produce horror movie *Our Family Trouble* (USA, 2009). The deal is based on her wage as an actress, plus a percentage of box-office takings. This beats the $25 million (£15.1 million) earned by Julia Roberts (USA) for *Mona Lisa Smile* (USA, 2003).

★ MOST SCREEN CREDITS FOR A LIVING ACTRESS

Marianne Stone (UK) has been credited for appearances in a record-breaking 159 movies from 1943 to 1985. Usually appearing in supporting roles or as a bit-part actress, she is best known for her regular appearances in the *Carry On...* movies.

OSCARS

★ SHORTEST ROLE TO WIN AN ACTING OSCAR

Beatrice Straight (USA, 1914–2001) won the Best Actress in a Supporting Role award at the 1977 American Academy Awards for her portrayal of Louise Schumacher in *Network* (USA, 1976) – despite appearing on screen for a mere 5 min 40 sec!

Sept 21: The **fastest time to play a concert in each of the 50 states of the USA** is 50 days by Adam Brodsky (USA) between 3 August and 21 September 2003.

Sept 22: The **most people to perform a synchronized swimming routine** was 105 at the Big Sync in London, UK, on this day in 2007.

1965: year in which *The Avengers'* Diana Rigg (UK) became the ★**first western actress to perform kung fu on TV**.

MILEY CYRUS

The **highest-earning child actor** is currently Miley Cyrus (USA, b. 23 November 1992), who earned an estimated $25 million (£12.5 million) in 2008 according to Forbes. Born Destiny Hope Cyrus (her father is the US country singer Billy Ray Cyrus), the singer-songwriter shot to fame in 2006 as the star of the Disney Channel's *Hannah Montana* series. She subsequently released two solo studio LPs – *Meet Miley Cyrus* (2007) and *Breakout* (2008) – both of which entered the *Billboard* 200 at No.1. In 2008, *Time* magazine declared her to be one of the 100 Most Influential People in the World.

★MOST OSCAR NOMINATIONS FOR THE SAME CHARACTER IN ONE FILM

Only two movie characters have ever had two Oscar nominations in the same film: Rose DeWitt Bukater in *Titanic* (USA, 1997) led to nominations for both Kate Winslet (UK) and Gloria Stuart (USA); and Iris Murdoch, played by nominees Dame Judi Dench (UK) and Winslet again, in *Iris* (UK/USA, 2001).

MOST NOMINATIONS

Meryl Streep (USA, b. 22 June 1949) was nominated for a total of 15 Oscars from 1979 to 2008. She has been nominated 12 times for Best Actress, winning in 1983 for *Sophie's Choice* (USA, 1982), and three for Best Actress in a Supporting Role, winning in 1980 for *Kramer vs. Kramer* (USA, 1979). Her 15th nomination followed her starring role in *Doubt* (USA, 2008).

MOST BEST ACTRESS WINS

Katharine Hepburn (USA, 1907–2003) won four Best Actress Oscars, for *Morning Glory* (USA, 1933) in 1934, *Guess Who's Coming to Dinner* (USA, 1967) in 1968, *The Lion in Winter* (UK, 1968) in 1969 and *On Golden Pond* (USA, 1981) in 1982.

OLDEST BEST ACTRESS

Jessica Tandy (UK, 1909–94) won the Best Actress Oscar for *Driving Miss Daisy* (USA, 1989) on 29 March 1990 at the age of 80 years 295 days. The **youngest winner of a Best Actress Academy Award** was Marlee Matlin (USA, b. 24 August 1965), who won on 30 March 1987 for her role as Sarah Norman in *Children of a Lesser God* (USA, 1986), aged 21 years 218 days.

NICOLE KIDMAN

According to data supplied by Forbes, the ★**most overpaid actress** is Nicole Kidman (Australia), with a box-office gross of $1 for every $1 paid in salary. To calculate this "payback", the following formula is applied to the star's last three movies to gross over $5 million:

$$\frac{\left(\dfrac{\text{worldwide box-office}}{2}\right)^* + \text{first 3 months of DVD sales} - \text{budget}}{\text{salary}} = \text{payback}$$

The box-office figure is halved to approximate the studios' return on each ticket sold

With *The Golden Compass* (USA, 2007), *Invasion* (USA, 2007) and *Bewitched* (USA, 2005) all under-performing, Kidman appears to have had a run of bad luck!

BRIGITTE NIELSEN

When it comes to actresses, almost everyone looks up to Brigitte Nielsen (Denmark, b. 15 July 1963) – literally. Along with Sigourney Weaver (USA, b. 8 October 1949), Margaux Hemingway (USA, 1955–96) and Geena Davis (USA, b. 21 January 1957), the statuesque blonde tops out at 1.82 m (6 ft). All four share the record for **tallest actress in a leading role**.

WEALTHIEST ACTRESSES (2007–08)

1. Cameron Diaz (USA) $50 m (£26.9 m)
2. Keira Knightley (UK) $32 m (£21.5 m)
3. Jennifer Aniston (USA) $27 m (£18.1 m)
4= Reese Witherspoon Gwyneth Paltrow (both USA) $25 m (£16.8 m)
6. Jodie Foster (USA) $23 m (£15.4 m)
7. Sarah Jessica Parker (USA) $18 m (£12.1 m)
8. Meryl Streep (USA) $16 m (£10.7 m)
9. Amy Adams (USA) $14.5 m (£9.7 m)
10. Angelina Jolie (USA) $14 m (£9.4 m)

Source: *Forbes*

Sept 23: The **youngest winner of golf's Open championship** is Tom Morris Jr (UK, b. 20 April 1851). He was 17 years 156 days old when he won the Open at Prestwick Golf Club, Prestwick, UK, on this date in 1868.

AT THE MOVIES

★ FIRST FULLY DIGITAL FEATURE FILM

The Rescuers Down Under (USA, 1990), the first ever animated sequel made by Disney (USA), was also the first movie to be made using the Computer Animation Production System (CAPS) – Disney's digital ink-and–paint system developed with Pixar (USA). CAPS allowed for, among other things, the digital colourization of scanned elements, multi-plane backgrounds and complex camera movements never before available to animators.

★ **NEW RECORD**
★ **UPDATED RECORD**

★ MOST OSCARS WON BY A FILM

Three films have won 11 Oscars. The first to achieve the record was *Ben-Hur* (USA, 1959), which won from 12 nominations on 4 April 1960, *Titanic* (USA, 1997) from 14 nominations on 23 March 1998 and *The Lord of the Rings: The Return of the King* (NZ/USA, 2003), which completed a clean sweep to win all 11 of its nominations on 29 February 2004.

★ HIGHEST-GROSSING MOVIE BY A FEMALE DIRECTOR

With a global box-office gross of over $351 million (£244 million), *Twilight* (USA, 2008), directed by Catherine Hardwicke (USA), is the highest-grossing movie directed by a woman. Based on the best-selling novel by Stephenie Meyer, *Twilight* explores the relationship between a teenage schoolgirl and her vampire boyfriend. A sequel, *The Twilight Saga: New Moon* (2009), is currently in production.

TOP 100 Records of the Decade

★ FIRST FULL-LENGTH FEATURE FILMED IN DIGITAL HIGH RES

The French movie *Vidocq* (2001) – about the life of Eugène François Vidocq, founder of the *Sûreté Nationale*, France's National Police – was the first theatrical release of a movie shot on digital 1080p24 cameras. This revolutionary movie was released a whole year before *Star Wars II – Attack of the Clones* (USA, 2002) made it to the screen.

HIGHEST-GROSSING STUDIO

In 2008, over 248 million tickets were sold for the 31 movies released by Warner Bros., earning it a gross of $1.78 billion (£1.22 billion) and a record 18.13% market share.

Sept 24: The **fastest tennis serve by a man** is 249.4 km/h (155 mph) by Andy Roddick (USA) during a Davis Cup semi-final match against Russia on 24 September 2006.

Sept 25: The **most valuable chocolate bar** – a piece from Robert Scott's (UK) 1901–04 *Discovery* expedition to the Antarctic – sold at auction in London, UK, on this day in 2001 for £470 ($687).

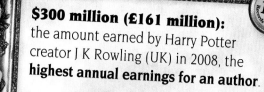

$300 million (£161 million): the amount earned by Harry Potter creator J K Rowling (UK) in 2008, the **highest annual earnings for an author**.

★ BEST SELLING DOWNLOAD ALBUM IN THE

Viva La Vida Or Death And All His Friends by Coldplay (UK) is the top with sales of 115,000 to the end of 2008. The album sold 30,378 on sale (week ending 21 June 2008).

★ FASTEST-SELLING UK TOUR

All 600,000 tickets for British band Take That's 2009 UK tour sold out within five hours when they went on sale on 31 October 2008. Originally a five-piece, including Robbie Williams (UK), the current incarnation (pictured below, left to right) comprises Howard Donald, Mark Owen, Gary Barlow and Jason Orange (all UK).

★ BEST-SE SINGLES W

For the first tim sold (actually 4 week ending 2 highest total si The figure (of w included a reco album downloa

In the same 115.1 million s making 2008 f **sales year in** previous record Downloads acc of the 2008 to

★ MOST POPULAR FILM GENRE

Comedies accounted for 30.26% of the movies released in 2008, the highest market share of any genre. Analysing the box-office results from this year's releases, it is possible to formulate the elements for the ideal Hollywood movie: a contemporary, live-action, adult (but PG-13-rated) comedy based on an original screenplay.

★ FIRST ANIMATION NOMINATED FOR BEST FOREIGN FILM

Vals Im Bashir (*Waltz with Bashir*, Israel/Germany/France/USA; 2008) was the first animation to be Oscar-nominated for Best Foreign Language Film. The movie, directed by Ari Folman (Israel), tells the story of an ex-soldier piecing together his shattered memories of an Israeli Army mission in the First Lebanon War (1982).

★ HIGHEST EARNINGS FOR A FILM PRODUCER

TV and movie producer Jerry Bruckheimer (USA) – the man responsible for bringing *Pirates of the Caribbean: At World's End* (USA, 2008) and *National Treasure: Book of Secrets* (USA, 2008) to the big screen, as well as *CSI*, *Cold Case* and *Without a Trace* to the small screen – has overtaken Stephen Spielberg as Hollywood's highest earning mogul. The Forbes Celebrity 100 estimated his earnings for 2007–08 at a cool $145 million (£101 million).

Spielberg, however, remains the **most powerful person in motion pictures** according to Forbes, having recently produced *Transformers* (USA, 2007) and directed *Indiana Jones and the Kingdom of the Crystal Skull* (USA, 2008).

★ MOST DOWNLOADED MOVIE TRAILER (24 HOURS)

The trailer for JJ Abram's (USA) reboot of the *Star Trek* (USA, 2009) franchise was downloaded from apple.com a record 1.8 million times in 24 hours, starting on 6 March 2009. It became the site's most popular high-definition (HD) download ever, with more than five million downloads in its first five days. The movie, which opened on 8 May 2009, returns to the roots of the TV series and follows the characters as they first meet.

★ MOST GOLDEN RASPBERRIES WON BY A MOVIE

Three cinematic clangers share the record for winning nine trophies at the Golden Raspberry Awards, which celebrate the worst in Hollywood movie making. The most recent was *I Know Who Killed Me* (USA, 2007), starring Lindsay Lohan (USA), who earned two Razzies for both the roles she played; the other two were John Travolta's (USA) *Battlefield Earth* (USA, 2000) and *Showgirls* (USA, 1995).

HIGHEST BOX-OFFICE GROSS (OPENING DAY)

With a worldwide box-office gross of $997 million (£693 million), *Batman: The Dark Knight* (USA, 2008) is the second most successful movie of all time, behind *Titanic* (USA, 1997). *The Dark Knight* opened on 18 July 2008 and raked in $66.4 million (£33.2 million), setting new box-office records for **opening-** and **single-day takings**. See table below for more Dark Knight achievements.

THE DARK KNIGHT RECORDS

Highest-grossing opening day	$66.4 million
Highest-grossing single day	$66.4 million
Highest-grossing weekend	$158 million
Highest gross from a midnight screening	$18.5 million
Highest-grossing PG-13	$997 million
Widest film release in a single country	4,366 screens (USA)
Highest-grossing first release on IMAX	$55 million
Fastest time to gross $100 million	2 days
Fastest time to gross $200 million	5 days
Fastest time to gross $500 million	45 days

Oct 8: The **level-flight duration record fo** **launched paper aircraft** is 27.6 seconds by Ken B at the Georgia Dome, Atlanta, Georgia, USA, on 8 Oc

Sept 26: The **longest speech made in the United Nations** lasted 4 hr 29 min. It was made on this day in 1960 by President Fidel Castro Ruz (Cuba).

BIGGEST-S[ELLING]
DIGITAL DOW[NLOAD]
SINGLE IN TH[E ...]

"Sex On Fire" by Kings of [...]
sold 560,000 digital cop[ies ...]
as of March 2009. Their [...]
Only By The Night is the [...]
selling digital album [...]
download sales in exce[ss ...]

BEST-SELLING UK ALBUM SERIES BY VARIOUS ARTISTS

Sales of the *Now!* series
of albums passed the
85-million mark in August
2008. Up until then,
70 albums had been
released in the series, which
began in October 1983. *Now!*
70 sold a record 383,002
copies in its first week of
release. The artist with the
most tracks featured in the
series is Robbie
Williams (UK), with 28.

★ BEST-SELLING ACT W[ITH]
NO CONCERT APPEAR[ANCE]
Irish singer/songwriter Enya, who [...]
70 million albums since 1988, h[as ...]
end of 2008) never performed a[...]

★ HIGHEST CLIMB TO [...]
ON THE BILLBOARD HO[T ...]
Kelly Clarkson's (USA) single "M[y Life Would]
Suck Without You" rose from No[...]
after it sold 280,000 downloads [...]
week of release on 7 February 2[009 ...]

★ MOST NEW ENTRIE[S ...]
ON THE BILLBOARD
HOT DIGITAL SONGS C[...]
David Cook (USA) registered 14 [...]
on the Hot Digital Songs chart [...]
including the No.1 "The Time Of [...]
sold 260,000 downloads.

MOST OFFICIAL REAL-LIFE STAND-INS IN A VIDEO GAME

The most real-life stand-ins are found
in the *Tomb Raider* series. Lara Croft
has been officially portrayed by
10 different models since 1996,
including actress Rhona Mitra and
TV presenter Nell McAndrew (both
UK). The current real-life Lara
is UK gymnast/model Allison Carroll
(pictured left).

★ BEST-SELLING VIDEO GAME SERIES (STEALTH)
The best-selling stealth video game
franchise is the *Metal Gear* series,
which sold over 22 million units in
the 20 years between its launch in
1987 and March 2009.

★ LARGEST IN-GAME SOUNDTRACK

Grand Theft Auto IV boasts 214 licensed tracks
played over 18 in-game radio stations. This
beats the previous record of 156 licensed
songs featured in *GTA: San Andreas*.
   The release of *GTA IV*, on 29 April 2008, is
also the **most successful entertainment
product launch**, generating $310 million
(£159 million) in first-day sales worldwide.

★ BEST-SELLING ADVENTURE GAME SERIES ON NINTENDO DS
The best-selling point-and-click adventure game
series for Nintendo DS is the *Ace Attorney*
series, based on the role of a defence attorney
in a fictional courtroom setting, which has sold
over 2.8 million copies as of May 2008.

★ LARGEST COLLECTION OF PLAYABLE GAMING SYSTEMS
Richard Lecce (USA) owns 483 unique video
gaming systems, including a variety of home
consoles, portable games and LCD mini-
systems, as of August 2008.

★ HIGHEST SCORE FOR AN ORIGINAL *DONKEY KONG* ARCADE GAME
The highest-ever recorded score is 1,050,200
points, set by Billy Mitchell (USA) on 16 July
2007, in a game lasting 2 hr 39 min. He beat
previous record holder Steve Wiebe (USA) by
just 1,100 points, but, unlike Wiebe, did not
play the game through to completion.
   The titanic struggle between these gaming
giants served as the basis for the film *The King
of Kong* (USA, 2007), the **★ highest grossing
video game documentary**. Mitchell offered
$10,000 to anyone who could beat his score
at the 2007 Classic Gaming Expo.

★ MOST POPULAR MMORPG GAME

In terms of numbers of online subscribers,
World of Warcraft is the most popular Massively
Multiplayer Online Role-Playing Game (MMORPG),
with 11.6 million subscribers as of January
2009. According to developers Blizzard
Entertainment, *WoW* hosts over 2 million
subscribers in Europe, more than 2.5 million
in the USA and around 5.5 million in Asia.

★ FASTEST COMPLETION OF *H2OVERDRIVE*
(FROZEN TUNDRA COURSE)
The fastest completion of the Frozen Tundra
course on *H2overdrive* (Arcade, 2009) is 1 min
34.35 sec, achieved by Kevin Williams (UK) at
the Arcades Trade Exhibition International (ATEI),
Earl's Court, London, UK, on 27 January 2009.

Oct 6: The **longest bridal wedding veil** was w[orn by ...]
Schlott at her wedding to Michael Stöpke (both German[y ...]
2007 in Loxstedt-Dedesdorf, Germany. It was 3,168 m ([...]

Oct 9: The **largest free-floating soap bubble**, made using a
wand, had a volume of 2.98 m³ (105.4 ft³). It was produced by XTREME
Bubbles LLC in Farmington, Minnesota, USA, on this day in 2005.

Oct 10: On this day in 1993, a total of 44,158 people
descended on Warwick Farm Racecourse, Sydney, Australia, for a
huge barbecue, the **largest attendance for a one-day barbecue**.

42,611,601: the number of downloads of *America's Army*, the **most downloaded war video game**.

★ BEST-SELLING VIDEO GAME

Wii Sports, which came bundled with the Wii console, has achieved worldwide sales of over 43 million copies since its launch in 2006. This eclipses the previous record held for over 20 years by another Nintendo favourite, *Super Mario Bros*, with 40 million copies sold worldwide.

★ LONGEST WINNING STREAK ON *STREET FIGHTER IV*

Zack Bennett (UK) remained unbeaten in 108 matches of *Street Fighter IV* at HMV in Oxford Street, London, UK, on 20 February 2009.

★ FIRST PROTEIN NAMED AFTER A VIDEO GAME CHARACTER

In July 2008, biologists from the Osaka Bioscience Institute in Suita, Osaka Prefecture, Japan, identified a protein that is necessary to efficiently transmit visual information to the brain. Having determined that the protein is used in kinetic vision (being able to detect fast-moving objects), they named it pikachurin after Pikachu, the Pokémon creature who is also known for high speed.

★ HIGHEST SCORE FOR A SINGLE TRACK ON *GUITAR HERO III* (XBOX 360)

Former *Guitar Hero III* record holder Danny Johnson (USA) reclaimed his title in style on 4 February 2009, scoring 965,364 points playing *Through the Fire and the Flames*, the game's hardest track, on the set of

Pix 11 Morning News, in New York City, USA.

Johnson then went on to break his own record, scoring 973,954 points at the Best Buy electronics store, also in New York City, later the same day.

★ MOST EXPENSIVE HOME FLIGHT SIMULATOR COCKPIT

Matthew Sheil (Australia) has spent eight years constructing a flight simulator cockpit based round the 747-400. The project has cost $300,000 (£132,000) and features 12 computers controlling motion, audio and the flight simulator game itself. Motion is provided by a hydraulic system fitted to the cockpit.

★ FASTEST COMPLETION OF *SONIC THE HEDGEHOG 3*

James Richards (UK) of Maidstone, Kent, UK, completed *Sonic the Hedgehog 3* in 49 min 1 sec on the Sega Genesis/Mega Drive using Sonic as his character on 9 August 2008.

★ FASTEST COMPLETION OF *RESIDENT EVIL 4*

Derek Taylor (UK) completed *Resident Evil 4* (Wii) in 2 hr 12 sec at the Nottingham GameCity event in Nottingham, UK, on 31 October 2008.

★ NEW RECORD
UPDATED RECORD

YOUNGEST PRO GAMER

The youngest professional video gamer is Lil Poison. Born on 6 May 1998, Victor De Leon III – aka Lil Poison – started gaming at the age of two and took part in his first competition at the age of four. Major league gaming recruiters signed him as a Pro Gamer when he was just six, making him the world's youngest signed professional gamer.

GUINNESS WORLD RECORDS: THE VIDEOGAME

(Wii leaderboards as of 9 March 2009)

CHALLENGE	ACHIEVEMENT	HOLDER	COUNTRY	DATE
One minute melon smash	198 melons smashed	Romaap	Netherlands	13/12/2008
Plane eating	19.10 seconds	DBER87	USA	27/02/2009
Plunger throwing	157 plungers	CACA	UK	03/02/2009
Phone book tear	29.44 seconds	rsimpson	UK	14/01/2009
Longest fingernails	28 m 37 cm	siddie	UK	01/01/2009
Human cannonball	790.02 m	TITOU	France	30/12/2008
Plane pulling	11.62 m	Wiinner	UK	23/11/2008
Turkey plucking	11.05 seconds	CASE123	UK	03/01/2009
Cockroach eating	14.71 seconds	MELLORS	UK	02/01/2009
Most tattooed person	5,001 cm²	SANDRE	France	29/11/2008

Oct 11: The **fastest time to make an omelette** is 49 seconds. It was achieved by Howard Helmer (USA) on the set of *This Morning* (ITV) at the London Studios, London, UK, on this day in 2006.

GUINNESS WORLD RECORDS

219

WWW.GUINNESSWORLDRECORDS.COM

SPORTS

CONTENTS

GUINNESS WORLD RECORDS

TOP **100** Records of the Decade

⭐ LIGHTNING BOLT

Having set a world record time of 9.72 seconds for the 100 m in May 2008, Jamaican sprinter Usain Bolt went to the Beijing Olympic Games in August of that year as huge favourite to take the gold medal in the blue riband track event. "Lightning" Bolt didn't disappoint: in the Olympic 100 m final on 16 August, he lowered his record to 9.69 seconds, even though he eased up before the finish line (pictured). But Bolt's record breaking had only just begun – on 20 August, the world's **fastest man** won the 200 m gold with a record time of 19.30 seconds, and two days later he was part of the Jamaica 4 x 100 m relay team (Bolt, Asafa Powell, Michael Frater, Nesta Carter) that won gold in a new world record time of 37.10 seconds.

ACTION SPORTS

★ LONGEST SOMERSAULT ON SPRING-LOADED STILTS

John Simkins (UK) of Team 101 bounced to a height of 4.57 m (14 ft 11 in) on the set of *Guinness World Records* in Madrid, Spain, on 23 December 2008, using spring-loaded stilts.

Spring-loaded stilts consist of a footplate with ski-type bindings, a rubber foot pad and a fibreglass leaf spring to produce lift. They date back as far as 1957, when acrobats Bill Gafney and Tom Weaver demonstrated a type of pogo stick/stilt in the pages of *Time* magazine. Today, the sport is known as "powerbocking", after Alexander Böck (Germany), who originally obtained the patent.

★ OLDEST BUNGEE JUMPER

The oldest person to bungee jump is Helmut Wirz (Germany, b. 2 December 1924), who was 83 years 8 months and 7 days on the date of his latest jump in Duisburg, Germany, on 9 August 2008. He took up the extreme sport when he retired from work and could no longer afford his hobby of flying a Cesna light aircraft.

★ FASTEST 20-CONE SLALOM ON INLINE SKATES

Guo Fang (China) negotiated a 20-cone slalom course on inline skates in 5.04 seconds on the set of *Zheng Da Zong Yi – Guinness World Records Special* in Beijing, China, on 14 November 2008.

★ LONGEST JOURNEY KITE-SURFING (MALE)

The longest continuous kite-surfing journey by a male was 149.05 nautical miles (276.04 km; 171.52 statute miles) by Philipp Knecht (Switzerland), who travelled from Cumbuco through Jericoacoara to Camocim (Brazil) in 12 hr 9 min on 6 November 2006.

★ MOST CONTINUOUS LOOPS WITH A PARAGLIDER

Multiple paragliding world champion Raul Rodriguez (Spain) achieved a record 108 continuous loops with a paraglider in Passy Plaine Joux, France, on 15 June 2006.

★ LOWEST INDOOR PARACHUTE JUMP

The lowest-ever indoor parachute jump was performed by Andy Smith and Paul Smith (both USA) from a height of just 58.5 m (192 ft) in the Houston Astrodome, Texas, USA, on 17 January 1982.

★ LONGEST RAIL GRIND ON A SNOWBOARD

Luis Chamarro "Toto" (Spain) ground his snowboard for 59.10 m (193 ft 11 in) at Madrid SnowZone in Madrid, Spain, on 27 September 2008.

★ GREATEST DISTANCE IN 24 HOURS ON A SNOWMOBILE (WOMAN)

Roxann Weidner (USA) covered 1,640.11 km (1,019.12 miles) on a snowmobile in 24 hours on a circular course at Tug Hill, New York, USA, from 24 to 25 January 2001. She made 118 laps of the course, which was just short of 14 km (9 miles) long, at an average speed of 68 km/h (42.25 mph).

★ FASTEST SPEED ON A SNOWMOBILE

Chris Hanson (USA) reached 277.13 km/h (172.2 mph) on Lake Nipissing in North Bay, Ontario, Canada, on 13 March 2004.

FASTEST SPEED BY A MALE PARAGLIDER (25-KM COURSE)

The highest speed achieved over a 25-km (15.53-mile) triangular course for an official Fédération Aéronautique Internationale (FAI) world record is 41.15 km/h (25.56 mph) by Charles Cazaux (France) at Aiguebelette, France, on 23 July 2006.

BACK FLIPS...

Aaron Fotheringham is 16 years old and suffers from spina bifida. He has been in a wheelchair since he was 13, and began practising stunts and tricks soon after. His unofficial record is six consecutive back flips.

★ FIRST WHEELCHAIR BACK FLIP

Aaron Fotheringham (USA) successfully landed the first wheelchair back flip at the Doc Romeo skate park in Las Vegas, Nevada, USA, on 25 October 2008.

Oct 12: The **greatest number of theatrical performances** is 47,250 for *The Golden Horseshoe Revue* staged at Anaheim, California, USA, from 16 July 1955 to 12 October 1986.

GUINNESS WORLD RECORDS

RULES OF ENGAGEMENT

The UK's Royal Air Force state that "canopy formation is a visually impressive discipline involving intentional controlled collisions, or docking, of canopies. Once under canopy, the skydivers fly into each other and form an array of stacks and formations."

HIGHEST JUMP ON A POGO STICK

David Barabé (Canada) – a mechanical engineering student – achieved 243.84 cm (8 ft) on a customized pogo stick at the Université de Sherbrooke in Québec, Canada, on 24 April 2008. The pogo stick used for the attempt was a Vurtego modified with an air-injection system.

FASTEST SPEED BY A FEMALE PARAGLIDER (25-KM COURSE)

The highest average speed achieved over a 25-km (15.53-mile) triangular course for an official FAI world record by a woman is 24.5 km/h (15.2 mph) by Fiona Macaskill (UK) at Plaine Joux, France, on 17 April 2007.

TOP 100 Records of the Decade

HIGHEST ALTITUDE BALLOON SKYWALK

Mike Howard (UK) walked on a beam between two balloons at an altitude of 6,522 m (21,397 ft) near Yeovil, Somerset, UK, on 1 September 2004 as part of a recording for the *Guinness World Records: 50 Years, 50 Records* television show.

★ FASTEST SPEED FOR A TOWED SKATEBOARD

Professional skateboarder Danny Way (USA) – the first person to jump the Great Wall of China on a skateboard – was towed to a speed of 119 km/h (74 mph) in California City, California, USA, on 4 November 2008.

FASTEST SPEED ON A GRAVITY-POWERED STREET LUGE

Tom Mason (USA) reached a speed of 130.8 km/h (81.28 mph) on a street luge at Mount Whitney, California, USA, on 29 May 1998.

★ FASTEST 50-CONE SLALOM ON A SKATEBOARD

The fastest time to slalom 50 cones with a skateboard is 12.83 seconds, achieved by Martin Drayton (Trinidad and Tobago) in Hyde Park, London, UK, on 2 October 2007.

★ SMALLEST PARACHUTE

The smallest parachute canopy used for a jump is the JVX-37 measuring 3.43 m² (37 ft²), which was landed by Luigi Cani (Brazil) on 1 February 2008 in Perris Valley, California, USA.

LARGEST CANOPY FORMATION

The largest canopy formation consisted of 100 parachutes and was formed by an international team over Lake Wales, Florida, USA, on 21 November 2007. The formation was in the shape of a diamond, with each parachutist in contact with the canopy of the person below them.

WWW.GUINNESSWORLDRECORDS.COM

Oct 13: The record for the **most simultaneous conkers matches** played is 197 (394 players), achieved at Redland High School for Girls in Bristol, UK, on 13 October 2006.

Oct 14: The **first ever supersonic flight** was achieved on this day in 1947 by Captain Charles "Chuck" Elwood Yeager (USA), with a speed of Mach 1.015 (1,078 km/h; 670 mph).

AMERICAN FOOTBALL

LONGEST NFL INTERCEPTION RETURN

The longest interception return for a touchdown was one of 107 yards by Ed Reed (USA, far right), playing for the Baltimore Ravens against the Philadelphia Eagles (both USA) on 23 November 2008. Reed broke his own record of 106 yards set against the Cleveland Browns (USA) on 7 November 2004.

★ LONGEST TOUCHDOWN IN A SUPER BOWL

The longest touchdown in Super Bowl history is 100 yards, scored by James Harrison (USA) of the Pittsburgh Steelers in Super Bowl XLIII at the Raymond James Stadium, Tampa, United States, on 1 February 2009. The linebacker intercepted a throw from Kurt Warner (USA) and ran the full length of the field to score at the end of the first half. Pittsburgh went on to win the game 27–23.

MOST CONSECUTIVE NFL GAMES PLAYED

Punter Jeff Feagles (USA) has played 336 NFL games, for the New England Patriots (1988–89), Philadelphia Eagles (1990–93), Arizona Cardinals (1994–97), Seattle Seahawks (1998–2002) and New York Giants (2002–07) (all USA). Feagles is also the **oldest player in Super Bowl history** – he was 41 years 333 days old when he appeared for the New York Giants in Super Bowl XLII on 3 February 2008.

★ NEW RECORD
UPDATED RECORD

★ MOST CONSECUTIVE NFL GAMES RECORDING A SACK

Two players have gained the distinction of sacking the quarterback in 10 consecutive games. DeMarcus Ware (USA, pictured right) of the Dallas Cowboys (USA) got his 10 from 16 December 2007 to 19 October 2008; Simon Fletcher (USA) of the Denver Broncos (USA) took down his quarterbacks between 15 November 1992 and 20 September 1993.

★ FASTEST TIME TO REACH 2,000 RUSHING YARDS IN AN NFL CAREER

Adrian Peterson (USA) of the Minnesota Vikings (USA) topped 2,000 career rushing yards during the 2008 season. Peterson reached the milestone in 21 games, becoming the fastest player in NFL history to reach 2,000 career rushing yards.

Peterson also holds the record for the **most yards gained rushing in an NFL game**: he rushed 296 yards against the San Diego Chargers (USA) at the Metrodome in Minneapolis, Minnesota, USA, on 4 November 2007.

FIRST UNDEFEATED SEASON BY AN NFL TEAM

The New England Patriots scored a 16-0 record in 2007, the first team to go undefeated in a regular season since the league went to a 16-game schedule in 1978.

YOUNGEST NFL COACH

The youngest coach ever hired in the NFL's modern era is Lane Kiffin (USA, b. 9 May 1975), who was 31 years 259 days old when he signed on to coach the Oakland Raiders (USA) on 23 January 2007. He was controversially dismissed in September 2008, having lost 15 out of 20 regular season games.

★ MOST CONSECUTIVE PLAY-OFFS BY A HEAD COACH

Superstar coach Tony Dungy (USA) has led his teams, Tampa Bay Buccaneers (1999–2001) and Indianapolis Colts (2002–08), into the play-offs for 10 consecutive seasons.

★ MOST CONSECUTIVE NFL PLAY-OFF GAMES THROWING A TOUCHDOWN PASS

Brett Favre (USA) threw at least one touchdown pass in 18 postseason games while playing for the Green Bay Packers (USA) from 1992 to 2007.

TOP 100 Records of the Decade

Oct 15: The official **land-speed record** (measured over one mile) is 1,227.985 km/h (763.035 mph), set by Andy Green (UK) on 15 October 1997 in the Black Rock Desert, Nevada, USA.

Oct 16: The **tallest free-standing house of cards** measured 7.86 m (25 ft 9 in) and was built by Bryan Berg (USA) on this day in 2007 in Dallas, Texas, USA.

TOP 100 Records of the Decade

9,280: the **most pass attempts in an NFL career**, set by Brett Favre (USA) between 1992 and retirement in 2008.

★ MOST RECEPTIONS, NFL POSTSEASON

The most receptions in one postseason is 30 by Larry Fitzgerald (USA) playing for the Arizona Cardinals during the 2008 postseason (four games).

★ MOST WATCHED NFL CHAMPIONSHIP GAME

The New York Giants' 17–14 upset of the New England Patriots in Super Bowl XLII on 3 February 2008 was the most watched NFL championship game ever. It was seen by an average of 97.5 million viewers, according to Nielsen Media Research. The game eclipsed the previous Super Bowl record of 94.08 million, set when the Dallas Cowboys defeated the Pittsburgh Steelers in 1996.

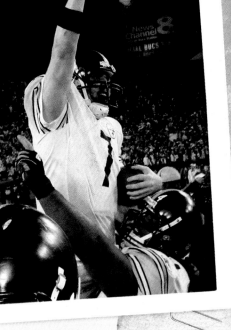

★ MOST TOUCHDOWN CATCHES IN AN NFL POSTSEASON

Playing for the Arizona Cardinals, wide receiver Larry Fitzgerald (USA) scored seven touchdown catches during the four games of the 2008 postseason.

★ MOST SEASONS PASSING 4,000 YARDS IN AN NFL CAREER

Peyton Manning (USA) of the Indianapolis Colts (USA) reached 4,000 passing yards in a season for the ninth time in his career. During the 2008 season, Manning also extended his record streak of consecutive seasons with at least 25 touchdown passes to 11 years.

MOST WINS IN AN NFL CAREER AS A STARTING QUARTERBACK

Brett Favre (USA) has had 169 victories as a starting quarterback between 1992 and 2008.

★ FEWEST TURNOVERS IN AN NFL SEASON (TEAM)

The fewest turnovers in a 16-game season by a team is 13 by the New York Giants (USA) and Miami Dolphins (USA) in 2008.

★ OLDEST PLAYER

Paul L Morton (USA, b. 12 January 1941) was 67 years old when he played a regular season for the semi-professional Stateline Miners (USA) in 2008.

★ MOST TOUCHDOWNS BY A TIGHT END IN AN NFL CAREER

Tight end Tony Gonzalez (USA, right) of the Kansas City Chiefs (USA) has scored 76 touchdowns in his career through to the end of the 2008 season. He also holds career records for the **most catches** (916) and **most receiving yards by a tight end** (10,940).

MOST SUPER BOWL WINS

The Pittsburgh Steelers (USA) have recorded more Super Bowl victories than any other team, with a total of six titles, winning in the 1974, 1975, 1978, 1979, 2005 and 2008 seasons.

At 36 years 323 days, the Steelers' Mike Tomlin (USA, b. 15 March 1972) is the **youngest head coach to lead his team to a Super Bowl win**, when the Steelers defeated the Arizona Cardinals (USA) 27–23 in Tampa, Florida, USA, on 1 February 2009.

LIONS LOSS

The **most losses in an NFL season** is 16 by the Detroit Lions – they ended the 2008 season with an unprecedented 0–16 record.

Oct 17: A total of 43,716,440 participants – in 6,540 global events – took part in the **largest stand up in 24 hours**, as part of the UN's "Stand Up Against Poverty 2007": the largest record ever staged.

TOP 100 Records of the Decade

ATHLETICS

MOST TEAM WINS OF THE EUROPEAN CUP

Three teams have won the European Cup a record six times: East Germany in 1970 and 1975–83 (when it was held biennially); Germany in 1994–96, 1999 and 2004–05; and Great Britain in 1989, 1997–98, 2000, 2002 and 2008 (pictured).

Russia holds the record for the **most European Cup wins by a women's team** with 14 victories, in 1993, 1995, 1997–2008. From 2009, the Cup will be replaced by the European Team Championships.

For a comprehensive list of all IAAF athletics world records, please turn to the Sports Reference section on pp.266–275.

★ MOST 20 KM WORLD RACE WALKING CUP WINS (FEMALE)

The 20 km event at the women's World Race Walking Cup has been contested five times and been won by a different athlete on each occasion: Liu Hongyu (China) in 1999, Erica Alfridi (Italy) in 2002, Yelena Nikolayeva (Russia) in 2004, Ryta Turava (Belarus) in 2006 and Olga Kaniskina (Russia) in 2008.

★ MOST MEDALS WON AT A SINGLE WORLD RACE WALKING CUP (COUNTRY)

At the 2008 World Race Walking Cup held in the streets of Cheboksary in Chuvashia, Russia, the home nation collected a record 15 out of a possible 20 medals: six individual golds, three silvers and a bronze, plus five team golds.

★ MOST TEAM GOLDS WON AT THE WORLD CHAMPIONSHIPS

The athletics World Championships were inaugurated in 1983, when they were held in Helsinki, Finland. The championships were originally held every four years, but this changed in 1991 when the event became biennial. To date, the most golds won by a team is 114 by the USA, between 1983 and 2007. Far behind in second place is Russia with 33 golds.

The USA also boasts the ★ **most medals won at the world championships** with 234 (compare this with Russia's 121).

★ MOST ATHLETES TO COMPETE IN THE WORLD CHAMPIONSHIPS

A record 1,978 athletes took part in the Athletics World Championships held in Osaka, Japan, from 24 August to 2 September 2007 – the 11th staging of the competition.

MOST ATHLETICS WORLD RECORDS SET ON ONE DAY

Jesse Owens (USA, 1913–80) set five world records in 45 minutes at Ann Arbor, Michigan, USA, on 25 May 1935. At 3:15 pm, he equalled the world record for the 100 yard dash with a 9.4-second sprint; he achieved an 8.13-m (26-ft 8.25-in) long jump at 3:25 pm; a 20.3-second 220 yards (and 200 m, although this is considered a separate race) at 3:45 pm, and a 22.6-second 220 yard low hurdles (and 200 m) at 4:00 pm.

FASTEST 50 KM RACE WALK (MALE)

Denis Nizhegorodov (Russia, above) completed the 50 km race walk at the World Cup in Cheboksary, Russia, in a new record time of 3 hr 34 min 14 sec, on 11 May 2008. Italy's Alex Schwazer finished the World Cup race in second place, trailing by 2 min 50 sec, but went on to win the gold medal in the event at the Beijing Olympic Games.

FASTEST 110 M HURDLES (MALE)

On 12 June 2008, Dayron Robles (Cuba) shaved 0.01 seconds off the world best for the 110 m hurdles in Ostrava, Czech Republic, setting a new record time of 12.87 seconds. Later that year, Robles added the Olympic title to his world record, winning the final of the event at the 29th Olympic Games held at the National Stadium, Beijing, China, in 12.93 seconds on 21 August 2008.

GUINNESS WORLD RECORDS 2010

Oct 18: The **largest cobweb** was discovered by Ken Thompson (UK) on 18 October 1998. It covered the entire 4.54-hectare (11.23-acre) playing field at Kineton High School, Kineton, Warwick, UK.

Oct 19: On 19 October 2002 the **world's longest line of firecrackers** was detonated in Sueca, Valencia, Spain, measuring 11 km (6.83 miles) long.

30.86 seconds: the time that 100-year-old Philip Rabinowitz (South Africa) took to run the 100 m in July 2004.

MOST PEOPLE RUNNING 100 M IN A 24-HOUR RELAY

A record 3,807 participants took part in a 24-hour 100-m relay for Latvia's 90th Anniversary Celebrations at the Daugava Stadium in Riga, Latvia, on 19 October 2008. The youngest participant on the day was a one-year-old toddler!

FASTEST 100 MILES ON A TREADMILL (TEAM)

On 13 November 2008, a team of 12 set a record in Bickershaw, Wigan, UK, when they ran 100 miles (160 km) on a treadmill in 9 hr 5 min 17 sec. The team consisted of Adam Balmer, Anthony Battersby, Adam Bibby, Michael Dawes, Joseph Donald, Lee Double, Mark Foster, Ray Hill, Simon Holland, Farrell Kilbane, Mark Livingston and Steven Turnbull (all UK).

FASTEST 5,000 M (FEMALE)

On 6 June 2008 at the Exxon Mobil Bislett Games in Oslo, Norway, Tirunesh Dibaba (Ethiopia) smashed the world record for the 5,000 m when she recorded a time of 14 min 11.15 sec. Dibaba's time beat the previous best time, set by Meseret Defar (Ethiopia), by more than 5 seconds.

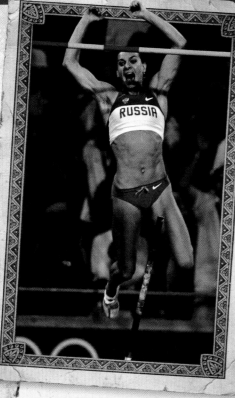

GREATEST DISTANCE RUN IN 48 HOURS ON A TREADMILL

Ultra runner Tony Mangan (Ireland) covered 405.22 km (251.79 miles) on a treadmill at St Mel's College in Longford, Ireland, from 22 to 24 August 2008.

FASTEST 1,000 X 400 M

The fastest time for 1,000 runners to run 400 m in a relay is 21 hr 57 min 46 sec and was achieved by Turn und Sportgemeinde (Germany) in Lollar, Germany, on 14–15 July 2008.

★LONGEST HAMMER THROW (HIGHLAND GAMES)

The longest throw of the light hammer (16 lb; 7.25 kg) is 47.76 m (156 ft 8.5 in) by Bruce Aitken (UK) at the Aboyne Games, Aberdeenshire, UK, in August 2000. Other challenges at the Highland Games include caber tossing (throwing a large wooden pole), stone putting (similar to the shot put but using actual stones), tug o' war and bagpiping.

HIGHEST POLE VAULT (FEMALE)

Having set new world records of 5.03 m (16 ft 6.0 in) in Rome, Italy, on 11 July 2008 and 5.04 m (16 ft 6.4 in) Monaco on 29 July 2008, Yelena Isinbayeva (Russia) capped an amazing couple of months of pole-vaulting excellence by securing the gold medal at the Beijing Olympics with another world best of 5.05 m (16 ft 6.8 ft) at the National Stadium, Beijing, China, on 18 August 2008.

COMBINED EVENTS

The World Combined Events Challenge is an annual worldwide competition series for Decathlon (Men) and Heptathlon (Women). The three best scores of the year are accumulated to find out who has the highest points total.

● The ★**most points scored in the World Combined Events Challenge by a male** is 26,476, by Tomáš Dvorák (Czech Republic) in 1999.

● The ★**most points scored by a female** is 20,541, by Carolina Kluft (Sweden) in 2004.

● The ★**most wins by a female** is four by Carolina Kluft (Sweden), who claimed the title each year from 2003 to 2006.

● The ★**most wins by a male** is four, by Roman Šebrle (Czech Republic) in 2002, 2004–05 and 2007.

★ **NEW RECORD**
UPDATED RECORD

FASTEST 3,000 M STEEPLECHASE (FEMALE)

In an event that was new to the Olympic Games, Russia's Gulnara Galkina (née Samitova) won the 3,000 m steeplechase final in a record time of 8 min 58.81 sec at the National Stadium, Beijing, China, on 17 August 2008.

Oct 20: The **lowest note by a human voice** was achieved on this day in 2000 by Tim Storms (USA), who produced a recognizable B-2 note that was measured electronically at 8 Hz.

227

MARATHONS

FASTEST MARATHON (MALE)

On 28 September 2008, at the age of 35, Haile Gebrselassie won the Berlin Marathon, Berlin, Germany, with a world record time of 2 hr 03 min 59 sec, breaking his own world best time by 27 seconds. It was the first occasion that anyone had run under 2 hr 4 min for the race over 26 miles 385 yards (42.195 km).

FASTEST MARATHON (FEMALE)

Paula Radcliffe (UK) ran the fastest marathon ever recorded by a woman when she completed the 2003 London Marathon in 2 hr 15 min 25 sec in London, UK, on 13 April 2003.

FASTEST AGGREGATE TIME TO COMPLETE A MARATHON ON EACH CONTINENT (MALE)

The fastest aggregate time to complete a marathon on each of the seven continents is 23 hr 43 min 55 sec, which was achieved by David Smith (UK), who ran marathons around the world between 12 November 1995 and 5 March 2008. With a fastest time of 2 hr 52 min 43 sec and a slowest of 3 hr 45 min 19 sec Smith averaged just over 3 hr 23 min for each race.

★ **NEW RECORD**
UPDATED RECORD

YOUNGEST PERSON TO COMPLETE A MARATHON ON ALL SEVEN CONTINENTS (MALE)

Timothy Harris (UK, b. 26 February 1983) was 23 years 339 days old when he completed the Marrakech Marathon, Marrakech, Morocco, on 28 January 2007 in a time of 3 hr 34 min. It was the final race in a sequence of seven marathons that Harris ran on each of the seven continents, which had begun at the K42 Patagonia Mountain Marathon, Neuquen, Argentina, on 29 October 2006 (a race that Harris completed in 4 hr 45 min).

★ MOST MARATHONS RUN ON CONSECUTIVE DAYS (FEMALE)

Michelle Atkins (UK) ran 10 marathons on consecutive days in Brathay, UK, from 9 to 18 May 2008.

★ MOST MARATHONS RUN ON CONSECUTIVE DAYS (MALE)

Enzo Caporaso (Italy) ran 51 marathons on consecutive days in Turin, Italy, from 23 February to 13 April 2008.

★ FASTEST MARATHON BACKWARDS ON INLINE SKATES

Werner Fischer (Germany) completed a marathon travelling backwards on inline skates in 1 hr 45 min 56 sec at the 2006 Berlin Marathon, Berlin, Germany, on 23 September 2006.

★ MOST POINTS SCORED TO WIN THE WORLD MARATHON MAJORS

Inaugurated in 2006, the World Marathon Majors championship encompasses the five annual marathon races in Boston (USA), London (UK), Berlin (Germany), Chicago and New York City (both USA), with athletes scoring points for top five finishes over two calendar years. The World Championship and Olympic marathons are also included in the years they are run. Gete Wami (Ethiopia) won the 2006–07 women's competition with 80 points. Robert Cheruiyot (Kenya, above) won the men's competition in 2006–07, also scoring 80 points.

FASTEST HALF MARATHON PUSHING A PRAM (FEMALE)

Nancy Schubring (USA) ran a half marathon in 1 hr 30 min 51 sec while pushing a pram at the Mike May Races Half Marathon, Vassar, Michigan, USA, on 15 September 2001. For comparison, Lornah Kiplagat (Netherlands) ran the **fastest half marathon (female)** in 1 hr 6 min 25 sec in Udine, Italy, on 14 October 2007.

FASTEST TIMES FOR THE FIVE MAJOR MARATHONS

M: Male
F: Female

MARATHON	ATHLETE	TIME	DATE
Berlin (Germany)	M: Haile Gebrselassie (Ethiopia)	2:03:59	28 Sep 2008
	F: Mizuki Noguchi (Japan)	2:19:12	25 Sep 2005
Boston (USA)	M: Robert Cheruiyot (Kenya)	2:07:14	17 Apr 2006
	F: Margaret Okayo (Kenya)	2:20:43	15 Apr 2002
Chicago (USA)	M: Khalid Khannouchi (Morocco)	2:05:42	24 Oct 1999
	F: Paula Radcliffe (UK)	2:17:18	13 Oct 2002
London (UK)	M: Martin Lel (Kenya)	2:05:15	13 Apr 2008
	F: Paula Radcliffe (UK)	2:15:25	13 Apr 2003
New York City (USA)	M: Tesfaye Jifar (Ethiopia)	2:07:43	4 Nov 2001
	F: Margaret Okayo (Kenya)	2:22:31	2 Nov 2003

Oct 21: The **world's largest shoe** measured 5.29 m long, 2.37 m wide and 2.03 m high (17 ft 4 in x 7 ft 8 in x 6 ft 7 in) and was unveiled in Marikina City, Philippines, on this day in 2002.

3 hr 50 min 31 sec: the ★fastest marathon in military desert uniform by Jennifer Jenks (UK) at the Flora London Marathon 2009.

MOST PEOPLE LINKED TOGETHER

Neal Gardner (UK) and 29 of his friends set the record for the **most people linked together to run a marathon**. The 30 runners set a time of 6 hr 18 min 41 sec.

FLORA
LONDON MARATHON
2009

The 2009 Flora London Marathon took place on 27 April on the streets of London, UK. On a day of stifling heat there were more Guinness World Records attempts than ever in the marathon's history; over 60 runners took part in 29 official record attempts, and 11 new Guinness World Records were achieved. All of the new record holders feature on this page – well done to them and everyone who took part.

SANTA CLAUS & CARTOON CHARACTER

Paul Simons (UK, left) recorded the ★ **fastest marathon dressed as Santa Claus** in 2 hr 55 min 50 sec. Meanwhile "Bananaman" Darren Stone (UK, above left) ran the ★**fastest marathon dressed as a cartoon character** with a time of 3 hr 36 min 7 sec.

FULL SUIT & FILM CHARACTER

Thomas Day (UK, right) completed the race in 4 hr 19 min 37 sec – the ★**fastest marathon dressed in a full suit**. Ian Benskin (UK, below right) dressed as a Thunderbird to run the ★**fastest marathon in a film character costume (male)** in 3 hr 11 min 50 sec.

FRUIT

Sally Orange (UK), wearing an orange costume, ran the ★**fastest marathon dressed as a fruit** in 4 hr 32 min 28 sec.

LEPRECHAUN

Jack Lyons (UK) ran the ★**fastest marathon dressed as a leprechaun** in 4 hr 22 min 08 sec.

VEGETABLE

Robert Prothero (UK) wore a carrot costume to run the ★**fastest marathon dressed as a vegetable** in 3 hr 34 min 55 sec.

ANIMAL COSTUME

Alastair Martin (UK) ran the ★**fastest marathon in an animal costume (male)**, in 3 hr 42 min 27 sec while dressed as an ostrich.

BACKPACK

Gordon Chaplin (UK) achieved the ★**fastest marathon carrying a 40-lb pack** when he recorded a time of 5 hr 35 min 19 sec.

Oct 22: The **fastest speed at which a car has been driven in reverse** is 165.08 km/h (102.58 mph) by Darren Manning (UK) in a Caterham 7 Fireblade in Gloucester, UK, on this day in 2001.

Oct 23: The **world's largest doner kebab** weighed 413 kg (910 lb 7 oz) and was made by the Maroosh Lebanese Café at the Applause Festival, Albury, New South Wales, Australia, on this day in 2004.

AUTOSPORTS

FORMULA ONE

• The record for the **most wins in a Formula One season by a rookie** is four, set by Jacques Villeneuve (Canada) in 1996 and equalled by Lewis Hamilton (UK) in 2007.

• Italian constructor Ferrari has amassed a total of 209 Grands Prix, the ★ **most Grand Prix wins by a manufacturer**, between 1961 and 2008.

• A Formula One legend, Michael Schumacher (Germany) recorded 148 points in the 2004 season, the **most points by a driver in a single season**. Schumacher dominated Formula One in the 1990s and 2000s and also holds the records for the **most Grands Prix wins by a driver**, with 84 chequered flags between 1991 and 2005, and the **most points scored in a Formula One career**, with an intimidating total of 1,248 points scored between 1991 and 2005.

• The **oldest Formula One World Champion** was Juan Manuel Fangio (Argentina, b. 24 June 1911), who won his last World Championship on 4 August 1957, aged 46 years 41 days.

• Rubens Barrichello (Brazil) holds the record for ★ **most Formula One Grand Prix starts** with 257 starts from 1993 to 2008. Barrichello has raced for Jordan (1993–96), Stewart Grand Prix (1997–99), Ferrari (2000–05) and Honda (2006–08). He has amassed 519 career points including nine wins and 61 podium finishes. The driver is said to have grown up idolizing the multiple Formula One World Champion and fellow Brazilian Ayrton Senna (1960–1994).

★ FIRST FEMALE INDYCAR WINNER

When Danica Patrick (USA) won the Indy Japan 300 in Motegi, Japan, on 20 April 2008, she became the first woman to take the chequered flag in the history of IndyCar racing.

Patrick was also the **first woman to lead the Indianapolis 500** race when she headed the field for 19 laps in the May 2005 event.

NASCAR TRUCK SERIES

• Ted Musgrave (USA) won his first NASCAR title in 2005, taking that year's NASCAR Craftsman Truck Series championship. It was the ★ **first vehicle carrying the number "1" to win a NASCAR championship** in any of NASCAR's three national touring series.

• Jack Sprague (USA) earned $7,276,475 (£4,952,165) in the 2008 season, giving him the distinction of the ★ **highest earnings in a NASCAR career**. Sprague also claimed the ★ **greatest prize money from one series race**, taking home a purse of $93,375 (£47,639) at Daytona on 16 February 2007.

• Mike Skinner (USA) recorded 47 poles in the 2008 season, an achievement that gave him the **most career poles won in the NASCAR Truck series**. A trucking king, Skinner currently drives the #5 Exide Toyota Tundra for Randy Moss Motorsports in the NASCAR Camping World Truck Series.

GLOSSARY

FIA: Fédération Internationale de l'Automobile
NASCAR: National Association for Stock Car Auto Racing
NHRA: National Hot Rod Association
TT: Touring Trophy

MOST CONSECUTIVE WORLD RALLY CHAMPIONSHIP TITLES

The most consecutive FIA World Rally Championship titles won is five, by Sébastien Loeb (France) between 2004 and 2008. Loeb won all of his titles driving for the Citroën team.

TT RACES

• Joey Dunlop (Ireland, 1952–2000) accumulated the **most Isle of Man TT race wins in a career**, with 26 victories between 1977 and 2000.

• Maria Costello (UK) lapped the 60.75-km (37.75-mile) Isle of Man TT course in a time of 19 min 43.8 sec, at an average speed of 184.64 km/h (114.73 mph), on 8 June 2004, the ★ **fastest lap time for a female driver**.

★ FIRST NASCAR WIN FOR A JAPANESE AUTOMAKER

Kyle Busch (USA) gave Toyota its first NASCAR Sprint Cup victory, winning the Kobalt Tools 500 at Atlanta Motor Speedway on 9 March 2008. The win came in Toyota's 40th race and is the first NASCAR victory by a foreign manufacturer since Al Keller (USA) drove a Jaguar (UK) to a road-course win in 1954.

Oct 24: The **youngest player in a baseball World Series** was Fred Lindstrom, who was 18 years 339 days old when he played for the New York Giants (NL) on this day in 1924.

MOST CONSECUTIVE NASCAR TITLES

Jimmy Johnson (left) and Cale Yarborough (both USA) are the only drivers to win three consecutive NASCAR Cup championships. Jimmy took his third straight title in 2008; Cale accomplished the feat in 1978.

• Mike Ashley (USA) hit a terminal velocity of 573.02 km/h (356.06 mph) from a standing start over 440 yd (402 m) in a Dodge Charger in Las Vegas, Nevada, USA, on 13 April 2007, the **fastest speed in an NHRA Funny Car drag race**.

• The **highest lap speed for the Isle of Man TT races** is 208.33 km/h (129.45 mph) by John McGuinness (UK, riding for England). McGuinness achieved this feat on a Honda CBR1000 Fireblade on 9 June 2006.

• Melanie Troxel (USA) reached a terminal velocity of 531.58 km/h (330.31 mph) after a 440-yd (402-m) run at the Texas Motorplex in Dallas, USA, in October 2005 – the ★**fastest speed in Top Fuel NHRA drag racing (female)**.

NHRA DRAG RACING

• John Force (USA) is the first drag racer to win 1,000 career rounds, the ★**most Funny Car rounds won in a career**. Force attained this landmark achievement at the Gateway International Raceway in Madison, Illinois, USA, on 4 May 2008. Force also holds the records for the ★**most career finals for a drag racer**, with 202 appearances, and the ★**most career wins for a drag racer**, with 126 race victories.

YOUNGEST F1 WORLD CHAMPION

Lewis Hamilton (UK, b. 7 January 1985) won his first F1 World Championship on 2 November 2008 at Interlagos, Brazil, aged 23 years and 298 days. Hamilton, driving for McLaren Mercedes, won the title by just one point from Brazilian Felipe Massa.

Oct 25: Verna van Schaik (South Africa) dived to a depth of 221 m (725 ft) in a cave in South Africa's Northern Cape province on 25 October 2004 – the **deepest scuba dive by a woman**.

Oct 26: The **fastest ascent of Mount Kilimanjaro** is by Gerard Bavato (France), who ran the 34 km (21.1 miles) from the base to the summit in a time of 5 hr 26 min 40 sec on 26 October 2007.

BALL SPORTS

★ MOST EUROPEAN KORFBALL CHAMPIONSHIPS (TEAM)

Korfball is played in over 50 countries worldwide. It is similar to mixed netball and takes place on a rectangular court, either indoors or outdoors. ("Korf" refers to the basket into which teams attempt to shoot a ball.) The Netherlands have won the European Korfball Championships a record three times, in 1998, 2002 and 2006.

● The ★ oldest AFL coach was Allan Jeans (Australia), who coached Hawthorn in a 1989 match, aged 56 years 9 days.

● Fred Fanning (Australia) holds the record for the ★ most goals kicked in a match, scoring 18 goals for Melbourne against St Kilda in a single AFL match in 1947.

BEACH VOLLEYBALL

● The most tournament titles won by a woman was 105, by Misty May-Treanor (USA) between 2000 and 2008.

● The beach volleyball World Championships were first staged for both men and women in 1997 and are held biennially. The ★ most wins by a women's team is four, by the USA in 2003, 2005 and 2007–08.

● The most men's beach volleyball World Tour titles won by the same pair is five, consecutively, by Emanuel Rego and Ricardo Santos (both Brazil) in 2003–07.

● Beach volleyball has been part of the Olympic Games since 1996, and the most Olympic wins by a men's team is three, by the USA: Karch Kiraly and Kent Steffes in Atlanta 1996; by Dain Balanton and Eric Fonoimoana in Sydney 2000; and by Phil Dalhausser and Todd Rogers in 2008.

BEACH HANDBALL

The men's World Championships has been staged three times, and the most wins is just one, by three countries: Egypt (2004), Brazil (2006) and Croatia (2008).

★ MOST WINS OF THE ANZ CHAMPIONSHIPS

The ANZ Championship is the newly created elite netball competition in Australia and New Zealand, replacing Australia's Commonwealth Bank Cup and New Zealand's National Bank Trophy. It was contested for the first time in 2008 between 10 teams from each country. In the inaugural event, the New South Wales Swifts (Australia, playing in red) beat the Waikato-Bay of Plenty Magic (New Zealand, in black) 65–56.

AUSTRALIAN FOOTBALL LEAGUE

● The ★ most AFL games coached is 713, by Jock McHale (Australia) for Collingwood between 1912 and 1949.

● Charlie Ricketts (Australia) was 24 years 91 days old when he coached South Melbourne in 1909, making him the AFL's ★ youngest coach.

CANADIAN FOOTBALL LEAGUE

● The ★ most kicks blocked in a CFL career is 12, by Gerald Vaughn (Canada) playing for the Calgary Stampeders, Winnipeg Blue Bombers and Hamilton Tiger-Cats, between 1993 and 2004.

● The Grey Cup is the name of the trophy given to the CFL champions and also the name of the championship itself. The player to win the ★ most consecutive Grey Cup Final Most Valuable Players awards is two, by Doug Flutie (USA) playing for the Toronto Argonauts in 1996–97.

● The ★ most career fumbles returned for touchdowns is five, by Michael Allen (USA) for the Winnipeg Blue Bombers in 1988–93.

HANDBALL

● The highest score in an international handball match occurred when the USSR beat Afghanistan 86–2 in the "Friendly Army Tournament" at Miskolc, Hungary, in August 1981.

● The most wins of the women's European Championships is four, by Norway – in 1998, 2004, 2006 and 2008.

HOCKEY (FIELD)

● The Champions Trophy was first held in 1978, and since 1980 it has been contested annually by the top six men's hockey teams in the world. The most wins of the men's hockey Champions Trophy is nine and was achieved by Australia in 1983–85, 1989–90, 1993, 1999, 2005 and 2008. Germany also has a tally of nine victories, but some of these occurred before reunification: 1986–88 (as West Germany) and 1991–92, 1995, 1997, 2001 and 2007 (as Germany).

Oct 27: An audience at the BBC's Big Bash event held between 24 and 27 October 1997 at the NEC, Birmingham, UK, clapped with a reading of 100 dB – the **loudest applause ever measured**.

1,109: the **most goals scored by at korfball World Championship (team)** was by the Netherlands between 1978 and 2007.

★ NEW RECORD ★ UPDATED RECORD

★ MOST PASSING YARDS IN GREY CUP FINALS

Canadian Football quarterback Anthony Calvillo (USA) – the League's Most Outstanding Player of 2008 – achieved a record 1,458 passing yards in Grey Cup finals games between 2000 and 2006.

NETBALL

- The ★ **most international appearances** is 164, recorded by Irene van Dyk (New Zealand) playing for South Africa and New Zealand between 1994 and 2008.

VOLLEYBALL

- The ★ **most wins of the volleyball Grand Prix** – a women-only tournament played annually since 1993 – is seven by Brazil in 1994, 1996, 1998, 2004–06 and 2008.
- The ★ **most wins of the men's Olympic Volleyball title** is three, by the USSR in 1964, 1968 and 1980, and the USA in 1984, 1988 and 2008.
- The ★ **most medals won in the volleyball World League** is 13, by Italy and Brazil. Italy have the **most gold medals in the World League**, with eight.

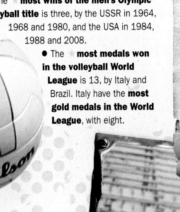

MOST ALL-IRELAND HURLING FINALS

The greatest number of All-Ireland hurling Championships won by a team is 31, by Kilkenny between 1904 and 2008.

X-REF
Fanatical football fans will relish our four pages of outstanding soccer records. Ready? Then turn now and shoot straight for p.246!

KORFBALL
The ★ **most team wins in the korfball World Championships** (instituted 1978) is seven, by the Netherlands, in 1978, 1984, 1987, 1995, 1999, 2003 and 2007.

- The Asia Cup was introduced by the Asia Hockey Foundation (ASHF) in 1982 (with the first women's tournament following in 1985). The ★ **most Asia Cup wins by a men's team** is three, by Pakistan in 1982, 1985 and 1989. The ★ **most wins by a women's team** is also three, by South Korea in 1985, 1993 and 1999.
- Anne Graves (UK, b. 5 March 1935) is the ★ **oldest regular hockey player**. She has played the majority of the 2008/09 season for the Stevenage Ladies 5s in the Five Counties Division 7 Hockey League in Stevenage, UK, aged 74.

HIGHEST CAREER EARNINGS FROM THE BEACH VOLLEYBALL AVP TOUR (WOMEN)

Misty May-Treanor (USA) has won a record $1,824,158 (£1,236,527) in official Association of Volleyball Professionals (AVP) Tour earnings through to the end of the 2008 season.

MOST BEACH HANDBALL CHAMPIONSHIPS (FEMALE)

The women's beach handball World Championships has been staged on three occasions. Three countries share the record for the most wins, with one each: Russia in 2004; Brazil in 2006 (pictured); and Croatia in 2008.

Oct 28: The record for **hula-hooping the most hoops at once** is 105 and was set by Jin Linlin (China) on the set of *Zheng Da Zong Yi – Guinness World Records Special* in Beijing, China, on this day in 2007.

Oct 29: On this day in 2007, Beverley Lateo (Italy) paid £8,000 ($16,420) for the **most expensive haircut** on the rate card at the Stuart Phillips Salon in Covent Garden, London, UK.

BASEBALL

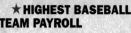

★ HIGHEST BASEBALL TEAM PAYROLL

The New York Yankees (USA) had a payroll of $218.3 million (£109.35 million) for the 2007 season, a Major League Baseball (MLB) record for a single season. The Yankees have had the highest payroll for nine straight years. The team's total rose from $207.5 million (£106.1 million) in 2006.

★ MOST GAMES PLAYED AT SHORTSTOP – CAREER

Omar Vizquel (Venezuela) played in 2,654 games with the Seattle Mariners, Cleveland Indians and San Francisco Giants (all USA) from 1989 to 2008.

★ MOST CONSECUTIVE GAMES WITHOUT AN ERROR – FIRST BASE

Kevin Youkilis (USA) played 238 consecutive games as a first baseman for the Boston Red Sox (USA) in 2007 and 2008. Youkilis also handled a record 2,002 consecutive catches at first base without an error.

★ MOST DURABLE BAT BOY

Stan Bronson Jr (USA) began his service for the Memphis Tigers (USA) baseball team on 15 February 1958 at the age of 29 years 211 days and continues to do so.

★ MOST SAVES IN A MAJOR LEAGUE BASEBALL SEASON

The Major League Baseball (MLB) record for most saves in a season is 62, by Francisco Rodriguez (Venezuela) playing for the Los Angeles Angels (USA) in 2008.

★ NEW RECORD
★ UPDATED RECORD

★ MOST CONSECUTIVE SCORELESS INNINGS BY A RELIEF PITCHER

Brad Ziegler (USA) had 39 scoreless innings playing for the Oakland Athletics (USA) in 2008. Ziegler also broke the mark for the **longest shutout streak for any pitcher at the start of his career**.

★ MOST CAREER POSTSEASON RUNS BATTED IN

Bernie Williams (Puerto Rico) had 80 career postseason runs batted in while playing for the New York Yankees (USA) from 1991 to 2006.

MOST SAVES IN AN MLB CAREER

Trevor Hoffman (USA) recorded 554 career saves playing for the Florida Marlins and San Diego Padres (both USA) from 1993 to 2008.

★ MOST CONSECUTIVE SEASONS HITTING 35 HOME RUNS

Alex Rodriguez (USA) has played 11 consecutive seasons where he has scored at least 35 home runs while batting for the Seattle Mariners, Texas Rangers and New York Yankees (all USA) from 1998 to 2008.

FACT
Fenway Park in Boston, USA, has been the Red Sox's home since 1912. It has a capacity of 37,400 (night) and 36,984 (day) as of 2008.

★ MOST CONSECUTIVE BASEBALL CROWD SELL-OUTS

The Boston Red Sox (USA) had 468 consecutive sell-outs, playing every home game at Fenway Park since 15 May 2003. The Cleveland Indians (USA) held the previous record – 455 consecutive sellouts – at Jacobs Field from 12 June 1995 to 4 April 2001.

MOST STRIKEOUTS IN AN MLB CAREER BY A LEFT-HANDED PITCHER

Randy Johnson (USA) recorded 4,789 strikeouts playing for the Montreal Expos (Canada), Seattle Mariners, Houston Astros, Arizona Diamondbacks and New York Yankees (all USA) from 1988 to 2008.

★ MOST DOUBLE PLAYS IN AN MLB CAREER BY A PITCHER

Greg Maddux (USA) participated in 98 double-plays in his career with the Chicago Cubs, Atlanta Braves, Los Angeles Dodgers and San Diego Padres (all USA) from 1986 to 2008.

★ MOST DOUBLE PLAYS IN AN MLB CAREER BY A SHORTSTOP

Omar Vizquel (Venezuela) participated in 1,698 double-plays in his career with the Seattle Mariners, Cleveland Indians and San Francisco Giants (all USA) from 1989 to 2008.

Oct 30: Matthew "Matt the Knife" Cassiere (USA) achieved the **fastest handcuff escape** with a time of five seconds at Rhode Island, New England, USA, on this day in 2004.

Oct 31: The **largest Jack o'lantern** was carved by Scott Cully (USA) from the world's **largest pumpkin**, weighing 666.32 kg (1,469 lb), on 31 October 2005 in Northern Cambria, Pennsylvania, USA.

1,406: bases stolen by Rickey Henderson (USA), playing for various teams between 1979 and 2003.

MOST STRIKEOUTS IN A GAME BY A BATTER

Many players have equalled the record of five strikeouts in a game, but the most recent is Craig Monroe (USA) of the Detroit Tigers (USA). Craig is pictured looking at the home-plate umpire after a called second strike in the ninth innings of a 6–5 loss to the Milwaukee Brewers (USA) in an interleague baseball game on 14 June 2007.

★ FASTEST BASEBALL PITCH (FEMALE)

The fastest pitch by a woman is 104.6 km/h (65 mph), achieved by Lauren Boden (USA) at Lakeside High School, Atlanta, USA, on 19 April 2008.

MOST EJECTIONS IN AN MLB CAREER

Bobby Cox (USA), manager of the Toronto Blue Jays (Canada) and Atlanta Braves (USA) from 1978 to 2008, has been ejected from 143 games.

MOST RUNS SCORED IN AN MLB SEASON BY A SWITCH-HITTER

Switch-hitter Mark Teixeira (USA) scored 144 runs for the Texas Rangers (USA) in 2005.

★ MOST HOME RUNS LEADING OFF A GAME

Rickey Henderson (USA) achieved a record-breaking 81 home runs leading off a game while playing for the Oakland Athletics, New York Yankees, San Diego Padres, Anaheim Angels, New York Mets, Seattle Mariners, Boston Red Sox, Los Angeles Dodgers (all USA) and the Toronto Blue Jays (Canada) from 1979 to 2003.

★ MOST HOME RUNS SCORED ALL FOR ONE MANAGER IN AN MLB CAREER

Chipper Jones (USA) recorded all 408 of his career home runs playing for manager Bobby Cox (USA) of the Atlanta Braves (USA) from 1993 to 2008. Jones' 408 home runs are the most ever hit by a National League switch-hitter.

★ MOST HOME RUNS HIT IN ONE POSTSEASON

Carlos Beltran (Puerto Rico) hit eight home runs in one postseason playing for the Houston Astros (USA) in the 2004 postseason. This record is shared with Barry Bonds (USA), who played for the San Francisco Giants (USA) in the 2002 postseason.

MOST CONSECUTIVE SEASONS WITH 200 OR MORE HITS

Ichiro Suzuki (Japan) had at least 200 hits in eight consecutive seasons playing for the Seattle Mariners (USA) from 2001 to 2008, equalling Wee Willie Keeler's (USA) record in 1894–1901.

MOST STRIKEOUTS IN AN MLB SEASON BY A BATTER

Mark Reynolds (USA) achieved 204 strikeouts playing for the Arizona Diamondbacks (USA) in the 2008 season.

★ MOST HOME RUNS IN AN MLB CAREER BY A DESIGNATED HITTER

Frank Thomas (USA) scored 269 home runs in his career as a designated hitter playing for the Chicago White Sox, Oakland Athletics (both USA) and the Toronto Blue Jays (Canada) from 1990 to 2008.

★ MOST WILD PITCHES THROWN IN AN INNINGS

This record is held by various pitchers with a score of four, most recently by R A Dickey (USA) playing for the Seattle Mariners (USA) on 17 August 2008.

MOST HOME RUNS HIT IN A POSTSEASON BASEBALL CAREER

The record for the most career home runs hit in the postseason is 25 by Manny Ramirez (Dominican Republic) playing for the Cleveland Indians, Boston Red Sox and Los Angeles Dodgers (all USA) since 1995.

MOST TIMES HIT BY A PITCH IN A BASEBALL MATCH

Several players have been hit three times by a pitch. The most recent were Nomar Garciaparra (USA), playing for the Los Angeles Dodgers (USA) on 3 July 2006, Reed Johnson (USA), playing for the Toronto Blue Jays (Canada) on 29 April 2006, Manny Ramirez (Dominican Republic), playing for the Boston Red Sox (USA) on 5 July 2008, and Chase Utley (USA), playing for the Philadelphia Phillies (USA) on 8 April 2008.

EYE ON THE BALL...

Greg Maddux (USA, b. 14 April 1966) was the first pitcher in major league history to win the Cy Young Award for four consecutive years (1992–1995).

MOST GOLD GLOVE AWARDS IN AN MLB CAREER

The Rawlings Gold Glove Award (usually known as the Gold Glove) is given annually to the MLB player judged to have the most "superior individual fielding performance". Greg Maddux (USA) has been awarded 18 while playing for the Chicago Cubs, Atlanta Braves, Los Angeles Dodgers and San Diego Padres (all USA) from 1986 to 2008.

Nov 1: Eugene Andreev (USSR) experienced the **longest free-fall parachute jump**, falling 24,500 m (80,380 ft) after jumping from a balloon at 25,458 m (83,523 ft) near Saratov, Russia, in 1962.

BASKETBALL

★ FIRST TWINS SELECTED IN FIRST ROUND OF THE SAME NBA DRAFT

Twins Brook (right) and Robin Lopez (left) from North Hollywood, California, USA, are the first twins selected in the opening round of the same NBA draft. Brook was the 10th overall selection by the New Jersey Nets and Robin was the 15th overall pick by the Phoenix Suns (both USA).

NBA

★ BEST SINGLE-SEASON IMPROVEMENT (TEAM)

The biggest single-season turnaround is 42 wins by the Boston Celtics (USA) during the 2007–08 season. The Celtics won 24 games in 2006–07 but improved to 66 wins in 2007–08.

★ BEST 30-GAME START (TEAM)

The Boston Celtics also achieved to a 27–3 record with their 97–93 win over the Houston Rockets (USA) on 2 January 2008, which ties them with five other teams for the best start in NBA history after 30 games. The 1966–67 Philadelphia 76ers, 1969–70 New York Knicks, 1971–72 Los Angeles Lakers, 1990–91 Portland Trail Blazers and 1995–96 Chicago Bulls (all USA) each began the season 27–3.

★ MOST THREE-POINT FIELD GOALS IN AN NBA GAME (TEAM)

The Orlando Magic scored 23 three-point shots in an NBA match against the Sacramento Kings (both USA) on 13 January 2009.

★ NEW RECORD
UPDATED RECORD

HIGHEST PERCENTAGE OF THREE-POINT FIELD GOALS

Since 2003, Jason Kapono (USA) has shot a 45.6 percentage of field goals for the Cleveland Cavaliers, Charlotte Hornets, Miami Heat (all USA) and Toronto Raptors (Canada).

★ FEWEST FIELD GOALS SCORED IN A GAME (TEAM)

The Miami Heat (USA) scored 17 goals in an 88–62 loss against the Boston Celtics on 30 March 2008.

★ MOST PLAYOFF GAMES WON BY A COACH

Phil Jackson (USA) recorded 193 playoff game wins while coaching the Chicago Bulls (1989–97) and the Los Angeles Lakers (1999–2008).

FEWEST POINTS SCORED IN A HALF (TEAM)

The New Orleans Hornets scored 16 points in the second half of their 89–67 loss to the Los Angeles Clippers (both USA) on 1 March 2006.

★ MOST PLAYOFF GAME APPEARANCES (INDIVIDUAL)

Robert Horry (USA) has made 244 appearances playing for the Houston Rockets, Los Angeles Lakers and San Antonio Spurs (all USA) from 1992 to 2008.

★ MOST STEALS IN A FINAL

The Boston Celtics achieved 18 steals in Game 7 of the NBA Finals against the Los Angeles Lakers on 17 June 2008.

MOST THREE-POINT FIELD GOALS IN AN NBA CAREER

Reggie Miller (USA) scored 2,560 three-point field goals for the Indiana Pacers (USA) between 1987 and 2005, a career record for an NBA player.

★ YOUNGEST PLAYER TO APPEAR IN 1,000 GAMES (NBA CAREER)

At the age of 32 years 165 days, Kevin Garnett (USA, b. 19 May 1976) became the youngest individual to appear in 1,000 NBA career games. He achieved this landmark while playing for the Boston Celtics in a 96–80 victory over the Chicago Bulls (all USA) on 31 October 2008, breaking Shawn Kemp's (USA) record of 33 years 24 days set in December 2002.

MOST BLOCKS IN A WNBA CAREER

Margo Dydek (Poland, wearing white) achieved 877 blocks in 323 games playing for the Utah Starzz (1998–2002), San Antonio Silver Stars (2003–04), Connecticut Sun (2005–07) and Los Angeles Sparks (2008). She also holds the record for the **most blocks per game**, with a 2.72 average.

Nov 2: The world's **largest truffle** was a white truffle weighing 1.31 kg (2 lb 8 oz), found by Giancarlo Zigante (Croatia) on 2 November 1999. It was estimated to be worth £3,175 (then $5,080).

34: the **most points scored in a WNBA debut game** – by Candace Parker (USA), playing for the Los Angeles Sparks (USA) on 18 May 2008.

★ YOUNGEST INDIVIDUAL TO SCORE 12,000 POINTS

At 24 years 35 days, Lebron James (USA, b. 30 December 1984) is the youngest player in NBA history to score 12,000 career points. James reached the mark while playing for the Cleveland Cavaliers (USA) on 3 February 2009.

WNBA

★ MOST GAMES PLAYED

Vickie Johnson (USA) has played in 378 games during her Women's National Basketball Association (WNBA) career with the New York Liberty (USA) between 1997 and 2005, and the San Antonio Silver Stars (USA) between 2006 and 2008. Johnson also holds the record for the ★ **most minutes played in a WNBA career** with a total of 11,698 minutes played over the same period.

★ HIGHEST POINT-SCORING AVERAGE

Named Rookie of the Year in her 2006 debut season, Seimone Augustus (USA) has scored 2,104 points in 99 games for the Minnesota Lynx (USA) since starting her professional career, giving her a record point-scoring average of 21.3.

★ MOST ASSISTS

Ticha Penicheiro (Portugal) provided 2,023 assists in 339 games playing for the Sacramento Monarchs (USA) between 1998 and 2008.

★ LONGEST-TENURED NBA COACH

Jerry Sloan (USA) has spent 22 seasons coaching the Utah Jazz (USA), a post he took up in 1988. Jerry also holds the record for the **most technical fouls in an NBA career**. As of 15 March 2007, he was whistled for 413 fouls in his career as a player – with the Baltimore Bullets and Chicago Bulls – and as a coach – with the Bulls and Utah Jazz (all USA).

★ MOST POINTS SCORED

Lisa Leslie (USA) scored a record-breaking 5,909 points playing for the Los Angeles Sparks (USA) from 1997 to 2008. A four-time women's basketball Olympic gold medalist, Leslie also holds three other records: the ★ **most field goals**, with 2,188; the ★ **most free throws made**, with 1,412; and the ★ **most rebounds**, with 3,156 – all achieved over the course of her career with the Los Angeles Sparks.

★ MOST MINUTES PLAYED PER GAME IN AN WNBA CAREER

Veteran WNBA player Katie Smith (USA) averaged 34.8 minutes per game over the course of her career for the Minnesota Lynx (USA) from 1995 to 2005 and the Detroit Shock (USA) from 2005 to 2008. She also racked up the ★ **most three-point field goals in an WNBA career**, with 674 three-pointers over the same period.

RECORD-BREAKING LEBRON

Lebron James (above in yellow) currently holds six Guinness World Records, including the **youngest individual to win a Most Valuable Player award in an All-Star game** (he was 21 years 51 days when he won on 19 February 2006) and the **youngest player to score 50 points in an NBA match** – he was 20 years 80 days when he set this record on 20 March 2005.

★ MOST POINTS SCORED IN ONE QUARTER BY AN INDIVIDUAL, NBA

Carmelo Anthony (USA) scored 33 points in the third quarter playing for the Denver Nuggets against the Minnesota Timberwolves (both USA) on 10 December 2008. Anthony tied the mark set by George Gervin (USA) playing for the San Antonio Spurs against the New Orleans Jazz (both USA) on 9 April 1978.

Nov 3: The **first known attack using an unmanned aerial vehicle** occurred in Yemen on 3 November 2002, when a CIA-operated AGM-114 Hellfire missile was fired at six alleged Al-Qaeda operatives.

Nov 4: The record for the **most yo-yos spun simultaneously** was set by Eric Lindeen (Sweden), who managed to spin nine yo-yos up on hooks in Stockholm, Sweden, on 4 November 2006.

NBA ALL-STAR JAM SESSION

NBA All-Star Jam Session presented by Adidas gives fans the once in a lifetime experience of participating in NBA All-Star excitement, where the chance to meet and collect free autographs from NBA Players and Legends is just the beginning. With over 46,451 m² (500,000 ft²) of NBA All-Star action, Jam Session is non-stop basketball nirvana! Fans of all ages can shoot, slam and dribble all day on several different courts, compete against their friends in skills challenges, watch mascots, dance teams, and celebrities compete in basketball competitions or get basketball tips from NBA players and legends.

★ FASTEST
BASELINE TO BASELINE DRIBBLE

Basketball pro Devin Harris (USA) of the New Jersey Nets (USA) showed the crowd his athletic abilities by dribbling the length of the court, baseline to baseline, in just 3.93 seconds during NBA All-Star Jam Session on 16 February 2009.

MOST...

★ BLINDFOLDED FREE THROWS IN TWO MINUTES

Australian basketball legend Ed Palubinskas is so well known for shooting, he even set up the Palubinskas Basketball Academy to teach players to improve their shooting skills. At NBA All-Star Jam Session in Phoenix, Arizona, USA, on 16 February 2009, he really put himself to the test, netting a record eight free throws in two minutes – not all that impressive until you realize that he was blindfolded at the time!

LONGEST TIME...

★ SPINNING A BASKETBALL ON THE HEAD

Harlem Globetrotter Scooter Christensen (USA) spun a basketball on his head for 6.07 seconds at NBA All-Star Jam Session in Phoenix, Arizona, USA, on 12 February 2009. Christensen also broke the record for the **longest time spinning a basketball on the nose**, with a time of 5 seconds.

SPINNING A BASKETBALL ON ONE FINGER

Joseph Odhiambo (USA) span a basketball on one finger, using one hand and giving the ball just one spin, for 1 min 54.88 sec on 14 February 2009 at NBA All-Star Jam Session in Phoenix, Arizona, USA, breaking his previous record of 37.46 seconds, set at the 2008 event.

A renowned basketball freestyler, Odhiambo has a number of world records to his name, including the **longest time to spin a basketball on one finger, maintaining spin** – an impressive 4 hr 15 min on 19 February 2006 in Houston, Texas, USA during NBA All-Star Jam Session.

★ HIGHEST SLAM DUNK
WITH A BACK FLIP

Jerry Burrell (USA), a member of the acrobatic basketball skills group Team Acrodunk, thrilled the crowds at NBA All-Star Jam Session when he sunk a slam dunk while back flipping from a platform 4.67 m (15 ft 4 in) high in Phoenix, Arizona, USA, on 16 February 2009.

TWO BALLS A-SPINNING

Basketball skills specialist Tommy Baker (UK) spun out the record for the ★ **longest duration spinning two basketballs on one hand** to 32.88 seconds at NBA All-Star Jam Session in Phoenix, Arizona, USA, on 14 February 2009.

BALL ACROBATICS

Athletic basketball performers Team Acrodunk (USA) set two records at NBA All-Star Jam Session 2009. The ★ **most backboard passes to a dunk in 30 seconds using a trampoline (team)** saw four of the group complete 35 passes on the trampoline before finishing off with a slam dunk. The ★ **farthest six-person tandem using a trampoline** saw the team passing the ball on a trampoline 6 m (20 ft) from the basket before shooting a slam dunk.

Nov 5: On 5 November 2001, Tesfaye Jifar (Ethiopia) achieved the **fastest time to finish the New York Marathon by a male athlete**, completing the course in just 2 hr 7 min 43 sec.

38: the **most free throws in a minute (female)**, set by Becky Hammon (USA) of the San Antonio Silver Stars at NBA All-Star Jam Session in 2008.

★ MOST CONSECUTIVE THREE-POINTERS ON NBA 2K9

The 2K Sports Gaming Area was a popular venue with video game fans throughout NBA All-Star Jam Session. It was here, on 14 February 2009, that Marcus Platt (USA, above left) established a new world record by scoring a total of eight three-pointers on the run in the video game NBA 2K9.

★ BASKETBALL HEADERS WHILE SPINNING TWO BASKETBALLS

Ball skills entertainer Tommy Baker (UK, pictured far left) managed 40 basketball headers while spinning another basketball on each of his hands at NBA All-Star Jam Session in Phoenix, Arizona, USA, on 16 February 2009.

Baker also set the record for the ★ **most consecutive chest and head rolls using three basketballs** at the same event, keeping three basketballs rolling in a circular motion – around his arms, up his shoulders and over his head – a total of 10 times.

★ BASKETBALL NECK CATCHES IN ONE MINUTE

Luis "Trikz" Da Silva Jr (USA) really got it in the neck at NBA All-Star Jam Session – he caught an impressive total of 24 basketballs with his neck in one minute on 14 February 2009.

CONSECUTIVE FREE THROWS FROM A WHEELCHAIR

National Wheelchair Basketball Association (NWBA) player Jeff Griffin (USA) scored three consecutive free throws from a wheelchair at NBA All-Star Jam Session in Phoenix, Arizona, USA, on 12 February 2009.

★ THREE-POINTERS SCORED IN ONE MINUTE ON NBA 2K9

Video gamer Chad Heathcote (USA) scored 26 three-point shots in one minute on NBA 2K9 at NBA All-Star Jam Session in Phoenix, Arizona, USA, on 12 February 2009. Heathcote used the player Steve Nash to beat off strong competition and triumph in the record-breaking video game challenge.

★ CONSECUTIVE FREE THROWS ON NBA 2K9

Blaine Griffin (USA) showed off his video-gaming skills by racking up 15 consecutive free throws on NBA 2K9 at NBA All-Star Jam Session in Phoenix, Arizona, USA, on 15 February 2009.

★ FREE THROWS SCORED IN ONE MINUTE ON NBA 2K9

Just a minute was all it took for Phil Ramirez (USA) to score 13 free throws on NBA 2K9 at NBA All-Star Jam Session on 13 February 2009.

MOST BLINDFOLDED FREE THROWS IN ONE MINUTE

Chauncey Billups (USA) equalled Jack Ryan's (USA) record of five free throws scored blindfolded in one minute at NBA All-Star Jam Session in Phoenix, Arizona, USA, on 14 February 2009.

★ NEW RECORD   UPDATED RECORD

Nov 6: The world's **largest Hindu temple** – the BAPS Swaminarayan Akshardham in New Delhi, India – has a total area of 8,021.43 m² (86,342 ft²) and was inaugurated on this day in 2005.

Nov 7: The **most expensive dessert** is the Frrrozen Haute Chocolate ice cream sundae, added to the menu at Serendipity 3 in New York City, USA, on 7 November 2007 – at a cost of $25,000 (£12,000)!

233

COMBAT SPORTS

MOST GOLD MEDALS WON AT THE OLYMPICS FOR WRESTLING (MALE)

Five men have each won three Olympic wrestling titles: Carl Westergren (Sweden) in 1920, 1924 and 1932; Ivar Johansson (Sweden) in 1932 (twice) and 1936; Aleksandr Vasilyevich Medved (USSR) in 1964, 1968 and 1972; Aleksandr Karelin (Russia) in 1988, 1992 and 1996; and Buvaysa Saytiev (Russia) in 1996, 2004 and 2008.

FASTEST 100-MAN KUMITE-KARATE

The 100-Man Kumite is the ultimate test in full-contact karate. It involves fighting 100 opponents in full-contact knockdown fighting with each bout lasting two minutes. On 9 June 2002, Paddy Doyle (UK) took just 3 hr 6 min to defeat his 100 opponents. He won 59 fights by Ippon (full points) and 29 by decision, drew 12 and did not lose a single fight.

FACT

Pictured is Russia's Buvaysa Saytiev (blue) fighting Uzbekistan's Soslan Tigiev (red) during the 2008 Beijing Olympic Games.

★ MOST WORLD CHAMPIONSHIP MEDALS WON (FEMALE)

For an individual female judoka, the record for the most Judo World Championships medals won is 11, by Ingrid Berghmans (Belgium), with six gold, four silver and one bronze between 1980 and 1989.

Ryoko Tani (Japan) has won the **most World Championship titles (female)**, with seven wins in the - 48 kg category between 1993 and 2007.

KARATE

LONGEST BOXING MATCH

Andy Bowen boxed Jack Burke (both USA) in New Orleans, Louisiana, USA, on 6–7 April 1893. The match lasted 110 rounds – or 7 hr 19 min – before being declared a no contest.

MOST TEAM KATA WORLD CHAMPIONSHIPS (FEMALE)

Kata is the detailed choreographed patterns of karate moves, practised either solo or in pairs. In competitive kata, Japan has won the Karate Kata World Championships on eight occasions between 1988 and 2008.

★ MOST CONSECUTIVE KATA WORLD CHAMPIONSHIPS (FEMALE)

Atsuko Wakai (Japan) has won four consecutive World Karate Federation (WKF) World Championships, in 1998, 2000, 2002 and 2004.

JUDO

★ MOST WORLD CHAMPIONSHIP MEDALS WON (MALE)

Judo, which means "gentle way", uses only throws in combat, with no punching, kicking or striking. The most medals won by an individual male at a world championships is seven, by two judoka: Naoya Ogawa (Japan), with four gold and three bronze between 1987 and 1995; and Robert Van de Walle (Belgium) with two silver and five bronze between 1979 and 1989.

TAEKWONDO

★ MOST WORLD CUP HEAVYWEIGHT WINS (MALE)

Taekwondo is the national sport of Korea and one of the most widely practised martial arts in the world. The most Taekwondo World Cup Heavyweight class wins by a man is three, by Pascal Gentil (France) from 2000 to 2002.

★ MOST WORLD CUP HEAVYWEIGHT WINS (FEMALE)

Myoung Sook Jung (Korea) recorded three World Cup Heavyweight class wins, in 1997, 2000 and 2001.

MOST CONSECUTIVE WORLD SUPER-MIDDLEWEIGHT TITLE DEFENCES

Joe Calzaghe (UK, right) successfully defended his super-middleweight world title on 21 occasions. He completed his 21st defence by beating Mikkel Kessler (Denmark, left) on points in Cardiff, UK, on 3 November 2007.

Nov 8: The **smallest newspaper**, measuring 32 x 22 mm (1.25 x 0.86 in), was an edition of the children's newspaper First News (UK) published on 8 November 2007.

Nov 9: The **fastest office** is a roadworthy desk travelling at a top speed of 140 km/h (87 mph). It was created and driven by Edd China (UK) in London, UK, on this day in 2006.

30,648: participants in the **largest martial arts display**, held in China on 10 April 2004.

★ **NEW RECORD**
UPDATED RECORD

★ MOST WORLD JUDO CHAMPIONSHIP TEAM COMPETITION WINS (FEMALE)

The Japan women's team has won the World Judo Championships on two occasions, in 2002 and 2008 (pictured).

★ MOST WORLD CUP LIGHTWEIGHT WINS (MALE)

Hadi Saeibonehkohal (Iran) has more World Cup lightweight class wins than any other competitor, triumphing on four occasions, first in 1998 and then from 2000 to 2002.

★ MOST WORLD CUP LIGHTWEIGHT WINS (FEMALE)

Eun Kyung Jun (South Korea) has won the World Cup lightweight class on two occasions, in 2002 and 2006.

★ MOST COUNTRIES COMPETING AT A TAEKWONDO WORLD CHAMPIONSHIPS

The 18th (11th Women's) World Taekwondo Championships held between 18 and 22 May 2007 in Beijing, China, welcomed a record 116 participating nations.

UFC

★ MOST HEAVYWEIGHT CHAMPIONSHIPS

Ultimate Fighting Championship (UFC) is a US-based mixed martial arts competition. Randy Couture (USA) won seven UFC heavyweight championship bouts between 1997 and 2008.

★ HEAVIEST FIGHTER

Teila Tuli (USA) weighed 188 kg (414 lb) for his one and only UFC carrer fight. He lost to Gerard Gordeau (Netherlands) at UFC 1 on 12 November 1993, despite far outweighing his opponent.

★ LIGHTEST FIGHTER

Thiago Alves (Brazil), Jeff Curran, Jens Pulver and Leonard Garcia (all USA) each weigh in at 63.5 kg (140 lb), making them the lightest UFC fighters.

★ MOST UFC MIDDLEWEIGHT CHAMPIONSHIPS

Anderson Silva (Brazil) has won five UFC middleweight championship bouts, which is the most by an individual fighter. Silva set the record between 2006 and 2008. The middleweight championship was reinstituted in 2001 when the old middleweight championship became the light heavyweight championship.

★ LARGEST AUDIENCE FOR A UFC TELEVISION SHOW

UFC 66, held at the MGM Arena in Las Vegas, USA, on 30 December 2006, attracted a pay-per-view television audience of 1 million viewers. The event was headlined by a bout between Chuck Liddell and Tito Ortiz (both USA), in which Liddell defeated Ortiz to retain the UFC light heavyweight championship.

★ MOST WINS OF THE WKF WORLD KARATE CHAMPIONSHIPS KATA CLASS (MALE)

The most titles won by a man is three, a record shared by Tsuguo Sakumoto (Japan) in 1984, 1986 and 1988; Michael Milan (France) in 1994, 1996 and 2000; and Luca Valdesi (Italy, above) in 2004, 2006 and 2008.

MOST WINS OF THE WORLD WRESTLING ENTERTAINMENT CHAMPIONSHIP (MALE)

One male wrestler has won the World Wrestling Entertainment (WWE) Championship on eight occasions: Triple H (USA, b. Paul Levesque, pictured right) took the title between 1999 and 2008.

Nov 10: The record for the **largest salad** is 10,260 kg (22,619 lb 6 oz) and was achieved by the Sde Warburg Agricultural Association in Sde Warburg, Israel, on 10 November 2007.

CRICKET

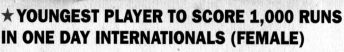

★ YOUNGEST PLAYER TO SCORE 1,000 RUNS IN ONE DAY INTERNATIONALS (FEMALE)

When Sarah Taylor (UK, b. 20 May 1989) scored her 1,000th run in women's One-day International cricket at the age of 19 years 104 days, she became the youngest woman to reach that milestone in the one-day form of the game. Taylor achieved the feat playing for England against India at the County Ground, Taunton, Somerset, UK, on 1 September 2008.

TWENTY20 MATCHES

★ HIGHEST INDIVIDUAL SCORE IN AN INNINGS

Brendon McCullum (New Zealand) scored 158 not out (from 73 deliveries) for the Kolkata Knight Riders against Bangalore Royal Challengers in a Twenty20 match in Bangalore, India, on 18 April 2008.

★ HIGHEST INDIVIDUAL SCORE IN AN INTERNATIONAL INNINGS

Chris Gayle (Jamaica) scored 117 (from 57 deliveries) for the West Indies against South Africa in a Twenty20 match in Johannesburg, South Africa, on 11 September 2007. Gayle hit 10 sixes in his innings – the ★ **most sixes in an international Twenty20 innings**.

**★ NEW RECORD
★ UPDATED RECORD**

MOST CATCHES BY A FIELDER IN AN INTERNATIONAL CAREER

Ross Taylor (New Zealand) has taken 13 catches for New Zealand in Twenty20 internationals spanning 17 matches between 2006 and 2008.

★ MOST SIXES IN AN INNINGS

Graham Napier (UK) hit 16 sixes in his innings of 152 not out (from 58 deliveries) for the Essex Eagles in a Twenty20 match against Sussex Sharks in Chelmsford, UK, on 24 June 2008.

MOST WICKETS IN A TWENTY20 INTERNATIONAL CAREER

Daniel Vettori (New Zealand, pictured left) has taken 21 wickets in Twenty20 internationals, playing for New Zealand between 2007 and 2009.

★ MOST WICKETS IN A TWENTY20 CAREER

Tyron Henderson (South Africa) has taken 74 wickets in Twenty20 spanning 62 matches between 13 April 2004 and 30 October 2008.

ONE DAY INTERNATIONAL (ODI) MATCHES

HIGHEST MARGIN OF VICTORY (RUNS)

New Zealand scored 402–3 to beat Ireland (112 all out) by 290 runs in an ODI match at Aberdeen, UK, on 1 July 2008.

MOST CATCHES BY A FIELDER IN AN ODI CAREER

Mahela Jayawardene (Sri Lanka) held 159 catches in 299 ODI matches between 1998 and 2009, an average of 0.535 catches per match.

★ MOST ODI MATCHES PLAYED

Sanath Jayasuriya (Sri Lanka) played a record 432 ODI matches for his country between 1989 and 2009.

MOST WICKET-KEEPING DISMISSALS IN AN ODI CAREER

Wicket-keeper Adam Gilchrist (Australia) secured a total of 472 dismissals (417 catches, 55 stumpings) in 287 ODI matches from 1996 to 2008.

Gilchrist also holds the record for the **most wicket-keeping dismissals in a cricket World Cup career** with 52 in 31 matches in World Cup tournaments from 1992 to 2007.

MOST WICKETS TAKEN IN A ONE-DAY INTERNATIONAL CAREER

Muttiah "Murali" Muralitharan (Sri Lanka) has taken 505 wickets (at an average of 22.74 per wicket) in 329 ODI matches for Sri Lanka, Asia and the ICC World XI. His tally was amassed in matches between 12 August 1993 and 8 February 2009.

MOST WICKET-KEEPING CATCHES IN A TEST CAREER

Wicket-keeper Mark Boucher (South Africa) took 453 catches in 126 matches playing Test cricket for South Africa between October 1997 and March 2009.

Add 22 stumpings to that figure and you get a career total of 475 Test dismissals, the **most wicket-keeping dismissals in a Test cricket career**.

Nov 11: The **largest animal sculpture** (a cow), measuring 14.18 m (46 ft 6 in) tall, 11.77 m (38 ft 7 in) wide and 21.24 m (69 ft 8 in) long, was created by Milka (Germany) in Berlin, Germany, on this day in 2007.

52: the number of stumpings claimed by William Oldfield (Australia) in a career of 54 tests, 1920–1937.

★ MOST FOURS IN A TWENTY20 INTERNATIONAL INNINGS

Herschelle Gibbs (South Africa) hit 14 fours in his innings of 90 (from 55 deliveries) for South Africa against the West Indies in Johannesburg, South Africa, on 11 September 2007. No other player has scored more fours in an international Twenty20 innings.

★ MOST TRIPLE CENTURIES IN A TEST CAREER

Only three batsmen in the history of Test match cricket have scored two innings of more than 300 runs: Sir Don Bradman (Australia) hit 334 against England in 1930 and 304 against England in 1934, both scores coming at Leeds, UK; Brian Lara (Trinidad and Tobago), playing for the West Indies, hit 375 against England at St Johns, Antigua, in 1994, and 400 against England at the same ground in 2004; and Virender Sehwag (India) scored 309 against Pakistan in Multan, Pakistan, in 2004, and 319 against South Africa in Chennai, India, in 2009.

★ MOST MAN OF THE MATCH AWARDS

Jaques Kallis (South Africa) has won 20 Test match Man of the Match awards between 1985 and 2009.

TEST NATIONS

There are currently 10 Test cricket playing nations: Australia, Bangladesh, England, India, New Zealand, Pakistan, Sri Lanka, South Africa, West Indies and Zimbabwe (Zimbabwe has not played a Test match since 2005).

MOST CENTURIES IN A CAREER

In a One-day International (ODI) career that has encompassed 425 matches between December 1989 and March 2009, modern-day cricket marvel Sachin Tendulkar (India) has scored 43 centuries, the **most centuries scored in an individual ODI career**.

Tendulkar, known as "Little Master" by his fans, also holds the record for the **most centuries scored by an individual batsman in Test matches** – 42 in 159 Tests between November 1989 and April 2009.

TEST MATCHES

★ MOST DOUBLE CENTURIES IN A TEST SERIES

Sir Donald Bradman (Australia) scored three double centuries in the 1930 Ashes series against England – the most by an individual batsman in a Test match series.

★ MOST APPEARANCES AS A TEST MATCH REFEREE

Ranjan Madugalle (Sri Lanka) has officiated at a total of 110 Test matches between 1993 and 2009.

★ MOST TIMES TO SCORE IN THE 90S

The most Test match scores in the 90s by an individual batsman is 10, by "Iceman" Steve Waugh (Australia) between 1985 and 2004, and Rahul Dravid (India) between 1996 and 2009. A score in the 90s is unenviable as it means getting out before reaching the milestone of a century.

★ MOST WICKETS TAKEN

Muttiah Muralitharan (Sri Lanka) is the leading Test match wicket-taker, with 770 wickets (at an average of 22.18 runs per wicket) in 127 matches from 28 August 1992 to 5 March 2009.

FACT

Gibbs (above) hit six sixes in an over against the Netherlands in the 2007 World Cup in St Kitts – the first person to achieve the feat in an international match.

★ MOST CENTURIES IN A TEST SERIES

Clyde Walcott (Barbados) hit five centuries for the West Indies in the 1955 series against Australia from 26 March to 17 June 1955.

★ MOST CONSECUTIVE INNINGS BEFORE SCORING FIRST DUCK

AB de Villiers (South Africa) batted for 78 innings before scoring his first duck (zero runs) between 17 December 2004 and 27 November 2008.

RUN MACHINE...

In his incredible career, Sachin Tendulkar has scored the **most runs** in One Day Internationals, with 16,684, the **most runs in Test cricket**, with 12,773, and the **most runs in the Cricket World Cup**, with 1,796 in World Cup tournaments from 1992 to 2007.

Nov 12: Paul McCartney (UK) became the **first singer to broadcast live to space** when he sent a "wake up call" to the International Space Station during a concert on this day in 2005.

Nov 13: The **largest teepee** stands 15.61 m (51 ft 2 in) high and is 16.34 m (53 ft 7 in) in diameter. It was constructed by the fire fighters of Horgenberg, Switzerland, on this day in 2004.

CYCLING

★ GREATEST DISTANCE CYCLED (24 HR)

Extreme cyclist Marko Baloh (Slovenia) cycled a total of 890.2 km (553.14 miles), solo and unpaced, over 24 hours in Lenart, Slovenia, over 6–7 September 2008.

MOST UCI BMX WORLD TITLES (MALE)

Kyle Bennett (USA, above) racked up a record three Union Cycliste Internationale (UCI) BMX World Championship titles, in 2002–03 and 2007. Bennett also jointly holds the record for the **most consecutive BMX World Championship titles** with Gary Ellis (USA), who won the title in both 1987 and 1988. The **most UCI BMX World Championships (female)** is three, held by Gabriela Diaz (Argentina), who won in 2001, 2002 and 2004.

★ NEW RECORD
★ UPDATED RECORD

OLYMPIC CYCLING

● The **most Olympic cycling medals won (male)** is five, shared by Daniel Morelon (France) and Chris Hoy (UK). Hoy also set the ★**fastest Olympic 1-km standing start race win** with a time of 1 min 0.711 sec.

● Leontien Zijlaard-Van Moorsel (Netherlands) has won four individual gold medals at two Olympic Games – the **most Olympic cycling gold medals (female)**. She struck gold in the road race, time trial and pursuit categories at the 2000 Sydney Olympics and in the time trial at the 2004 Athens Olympics. Her tally of six medals also gives her the record for the **most Olympic cycling medals** overall.

MOUNTAIN-BIKING

● Nicolas Vouilloz (France) achieved the **most downhill World Championship wins (male)** with a total of 10 titles — three in the junior championships (1992–94) and seven in the senior class (1995–99 and 2001–02). Vouilloz also holds the **most downhill World Cup titles (male)** with five, winning in 1995–96 and 1998–2000.

● The **most mountain-biking cross-country World Championships (female)** is four, achieved by Gunn-Rita Dahle Flesjå (Norway) in 2002 and 2004–06. A truly extraordinary record-breaking cyclist, she's also won the **most mountain-biking cross-country World Cups (female)**, with four consecutive victories from 2003 to 2006.

Dahle Flesjå's near total dominance of women's cross-country mountain-biking is only challenged by Pia Sundstedt (Finland), who gained the **most wins of the UCI Mountain Bike Marathon World Cup (female)** with a grand total of three victories between 2006 and 2008.

● In the men's marathon categories, Thomas Frischknecht (Switzerland) scored victories in 2003 and 2005 to claim the **most wins of the UCI Mountain Bike Marathon World Championship (male)**. Meanwhile, Leonardo Paez (Colombia) has the distinction of the **most wins of the UCI Mountain Bike Marathon World Cup (male)**, with titles in 2006 and 2008.

● In the field of women's four-cross mountain-biking, Jill Kintner (USA) and Anneke Beerten (Netherlands) rule the roost, each winning two World Cups; Kintner in 2005–06 and Beerten in 2007–08. This distinction makes them joint holders of the record for the ★ **most four-cross mountain-biking World Cup titles (female)**.

MOST FOUR-CROSS MOUNTAIN-BIKING WORLD CUPS (MALE)

Four-cross mountain-bike racing features four riders racing simultaneously down a prepared track, with the first rider down winning the race. Brian Lopes (USA) won three four-cross world cups, in 2002, 2005 and 2007, and holds the record for the **most four-cross mountain-biking World Championship titles by a man**, with three wins also in 2002, 2005 and 2007.

Nov 14: Frank Brown, Marcelo Prieto and Rafael Monteiro Saladini (all Brazil) paraglided 461.6 km (286.8 miles), the **farthest flight in a paraglider**, on this day in 2007.

★ FIRST CYCLIST TO BE KNIGHTED

Chris Hoy (UK) became the first sports cyclist to be knighted, when honoured by Her Majesty Queen Elizabeth II in the 2009 New Year Honours List. Hoy's knighthood came shortly after he won three golds at the 2008 Olympic Games and was in recognition of his services to sport.

ROAD CYCLING

FACT
Years before finding Olympic success, Chris Hoy raced BMX bikes, becoming the Scottish champion in his early teens.

• Rubén Plaza Molina (Spain), riding for team Comunidad Valenciana–Puerta Castalla, averaged a record 56.218 km/h (34.932 mph) over the 38.9-km (24.1-miles) time trial from Guadalajara to Alcalá de Henares in the 2005 Vuelta a España (Tour of Spain), the **fastest time trial of a major Tour**.

• The **most stage wins of the Tour of Spain** is 39, by Delio Rodriguez (Spain), between 1941 and 1947. The **most wins of the Tour of Spain** is three, with honour for this achievement shared between Tony Rominger (Switzerland), who won in 1992–94, and Roberto Heras Hernandez (Spain), who won in 2000 and 2003–04. Heras Hernandez also won the race in 2005, but he tested positive for a banned substance and his victory was handed to Denis Menchov (Russia).

• Mathias Clemens (Luxembourg) won five Tours of Luxembourg (1935–37, 1939 and 1947) – the ★**most wins of the Tour of Luxembourg**.

• Lance Armstrong (USA) has the **most wins in the Tour de France**, with seven titles between 1999 and 2005.

• Three cyclists can claim the record for the **most wins of the Tour of Italy**, with five titles apiece for: Alfredo Binda (Italy, 1925, 1927–29, 1933); Fausto Coppi (Italy, 1940, 1947, 1949, 1952–53); and Eddy Merckx (Belgium, 1968, 1970, 1972–74). In the points competition, it is a different story, with two riders having scored a record four points wins. Francesco Moser (Italy) in 1976–78 and 1982 and Giuseppe Saronni (Italy) in 1979–81 and 1983 are both able to claim the ★**most Tour of Italy points competition victories**.

TOP 100 Records of the Decade

CYCLO-CROSS

• Hanka Kupfernagel (Germany) has won the **most cyclo-cross World Championships (female)**, with four title victories in 2000–01, 2005 and 2008.

• In the men's event, Eric De Vlaeminck (Belgium) still holds the record for the **most cyclo-cross World Championships (male)**, with seven wins, in 1966 and 1968–73.

TRIALS

• Karin Moor (Switzerland) has won seven cycling World Championships trials titles, with seven consecutive wins from 2001 to 2007, earning her the record for **most trials cycling World Championship titles (female)**.

• The rider with the **most wins of the trials cycling World Championships (male, elite)** is Benito Ros Charral (Spain), who racked up five titles in 2003–05 and 2007–08.

★ MOST MOUNTAIN BIKE MARATHON WORLD CHAMPIONSHIPS (FEMALE)

Norwegian cyclist Gunn-Rita Dahle Flesjå has achieved four wins of the Union Cycliste Internationale Mountain Bike Marathon World Championship. Flesjå took the top title in 2004–06 and, after illness impeded her performance in 2007, came back fighting to claim victory in 2008.

FASTEST 4-KM TEAM PURSUIT

The GB team of Ed Clancy, Bradley Wiggins, Paul Manning and Geraint Thomas scored a world record, and Olympic gold, with a time of 3 min 53.31 sec in Beijing, China, on 18 August 2008.

Nov 15: On this day in 2005, A US collector paid $690,000 (£393,300) for an original poster for the film *Metropolis* (Germany, 1927), the **most money paid for a poster**.

Nov 16: The **greatest recorded meteor shower** occurred on this night in November 1966, when the Leonid meteors were visible between western North America and eastern Russia (then USSR).

FOOTBALL

★ NEW RECORD
UPDATED RECORD

CLUB FOOTBALL

MOST UEFA CHAMPIONS LEAGUE GOALS

Raúl González Blanco (Spain) scored 64 goals in UEFA Champions League matches playing for Real Madrid (Spain) between 1995 and 2009.

Raúl also holds the record for the **most UEFA Champions League appearances**, having played in 125 matches since his debut on 13 September 1995.

★ MOST GOALS SCORED IN AN MLS CAREER

Jamie Moreno (Bolivia) scored 112 goals in 295 Major League Soccer (MLS) games playing for D C United and MetroStars (both USA) between 1996 and 2007.

MOST UEFA CHAMPIONS LEAGUE WON BY AN INDIVIDUAL PLAYER

Clarence Seedorf (Suriname) claimed his fourth UEFA Champions League winning title as a player when his team, AC Milan (Italy), beat Liverpool in Athens, Greece, on 23 May 2007. Seedorf also won with AC Milan in 2003 and triumphed with two other clubs: Ajax (Netherlands) in 1995 and Real Madrid (Spain) in 1998.

★ YOUNGEST PLAYER IN THE CHAMPIONS LEAGUE

Celestine Babayaro (Nigeria) was 16 years 87 days old when he played for Anderlecht (Belgium) against Steaua Bucharest (Romania) in a UEFA Champions League match on 23 November 1994. The **oldest player in the UEFA Champions League** is Marco Ballota (Italy), who was 43 years 252 days old when he played for Lazio (Italy) against Real Madrid (Spain) on 11 December 2007.

★ MOST APPEARANCES IN THE UEFA EUROPEAN CHAMPIONSHIPS

Both defender Lilian Thuram (France) and goalkeeper Edwin van der Sar (Netherlands, pictured above) have played in 16 UEFA European Championship matches. Both players' international careers spanned the tournaments played from 1996 to 2008.

HIGHEST TRANSFER FEE

Zinedine Zidane (France) moved from Juventus (Italy) to Real Madrid (Spain) for a reported 13,033,000,000 Spanish pesetas (£47 million; $66.36 million) on 9 July 2001.

TOP 100 Records of the Decade

★ MOST WINS OF THE TOP DIVISION IN ENGLISH FOOTBALL BY A FEMALE TEAM

The FA Women's Premier League is the top division of league football competition in England for women and has been won a record 11 times by Arsenal Ladies between 1993 and 2009.

★ MOST UEFA EUROPEAN CHAMPIONSHIP MATCHES PLAYED

The most matches played by a team in all UEFA European Football Championships is 38 by Germany (West Germany 1960–88) between 1960 and 2008.

The German national side has also won the ★ **most matches by a team in all UEFA European Football Championships** with a total of 19 victories, which have included titles, in 1972, 1980 and 1996.

MOST CONSECUTIVE ENGLISH PREMIER LEAGUE APPEARANCES

US goalkeeping veteran Brad Friedel (USA, pictured left) has recorded 188 consecutive appearances in the English Premier League, playing for Blackburn Rovers and Aston Villa, between 14 August 2004 and 31 January 2009.

Nov 17: The **fastest time to pluck a turkey** is 1 min 30 sec by Vincent Pilkington of Cootehill, Co. Cavan, Ireland, who achieved the feat on RTE television in Dublin, Ireland, on this day in 1980.

31-0: the highest score in an international match, by Australia against American Samoa at Coffs Harbour, NSW, Australia on 11 April 2001.

★ YOUNGEST PLAYER IN ENGLISH LEAGUE FOOTBALL

Reuben Noble-Lazarus (UK, b. 16 August 1993, pictured right wearing black) came on as a substitute for Barnsley, aged 15 years 45 days, at Portman Road, Ipswich, UK, on 30 September 2008, making him the youngest player to appear in an English league match.

YOUNGEST PERSON TO PLAY IN THE TOP DIVISION OF ENGLISH FOOTBALL

The youngest player to appear in the English Premier League, which is the top division of English professional football, is Matthew Briggs (UK, b. 9 March 1991), who came on as a substitute playing for Fulham in their 3–1 defeat against Middlesborough on 13 May 2007, aged 16 years 65 days.

★ MOST ENGLISH FOOTBALL PREMIER LEAGUE RED CARDS

The most red cards received by an individual player in the English Premier League is eight, by three players: Richard Dunne (Ireland) playing for Everton and Manchester City

between 1996 and 2008; Duncan Ferguson (UK) playing for Everton and Newcastle between 1994 and 2006; and Patrick Vieira (France), who played for Arsenal between 1996 and 2005

INTERNATIONALS

★ MOST GOALS SCORED IN A SINGLE FIFA CONFEDERATIONS CUP TOURNAMENT

The most goals scored by an individual player in a single Confederations Cup tournament is seven by Romario (Brazil) in 1997.

★ MOST UEFA EUROPEAN CHAMPIONSHIP GOALS SCORED BY AN INDIVIDUAL

Michel Platini (France) has scored a record nine goals in UEFA European Championship finals tournaments. Platini scored all nine goals playing in midfield for France in the 1984 European Championships, which were held in his home country from 12–27 June 1984.

LONGEST-RUNNING FOOTBALL COMPETITION FOR NATIONAL TEAMS

The oldest surviving international football competition in which national teams compete is the South American Championship (known as the Copa America since 1975), organized by the South American Football Confederation, Conmebol. The competition was first held in Argentina in 1916, with Venezuela hosting Copa America 2007, its 42nd tournament. Argentina and Uruguay have each won the tournament on 14 occasions.

★ OLDEST INTERNATIONAL FOOTBALL GROUND

The Racecourse Ground, Wrexham, Wales, UK, is the oldest international football ground that is still in use. The first international match was played at the Racecourse on 5 March 1877, when Scotland beat Wales 2–0.

Wales are the third oldest international football team after England and Scotland.

MOST GOALS SCORED IN EUROPEAN CLUB COMPETITIONS

Between 1995 and 19 February 2009, Filippo Inzaghi (Italy) scored a record 66 goals playing in European club competitions for Parma, Juventus and AC Milan (all Italy).

MOST INTERNATIONAL CAPS WON (FEMALE)

Kristine Lilly (USA, b. 22 July 1971) has played in 342 international matches for the US women's soccer team, a record for any international footballer, male or female. Lilly's debut for her national team took place on 3 August 1987, just 12 days after her 16th birthday, in a match against China.

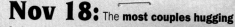

Nov 18: The **most couples hugging simultaneously** is 1,451 at a World Children's Day charity event held at Taipei Arena, Taipei, Taiwan, on this day in 2007.

Nov 19: A total of 1.6 million tickets, valued at £80 million ($142,825,258.47), were sold on 19 November 2005 for Robbie Williams' 2006 World Tour – **the most tour tickets sold in a day**.

FOOTBALL: WORLD CUP

MOST WINS OF THE FIFA WORLD CUP

The Fédération Internationale de Football Association (FIFA) instituted the first World Cup on 13 July 1930 in Montevideo, Uruguay. Brazil have won the tournament, which is held every four years, on five occasions: in 1958, 1962, 1970, 1994 and 2002. After winning their third title, Brazil were awarded the original World Cup trophy, the Jules Rimet Trophy (far left), to keep. In 1974, a new trophy, the FIFA World Cup Trophy (left), was introduced.

★ **NEW RECORD**   **UPDATED RECORD**

MOST CONSECUTIVE WINS IN WORLD CUP FINALS (TEAM)

Between 2002 and 2006, Brazil won a record 11 World Cup finals matches in a row. The sequence began on 3 June 2002 with a 2–1 victory over Turkey in Ulsan, South Korea, and ended on 27 June 2006 when the Brazilian team beat Ghana 3–0 in Dortmund, Germany. The winning streak included the 2002 World Cup Final in Tokyo, Japan, on 30 June 2002, in which Brazil defeated Germany 2–0 to secure their fifth World Cup (pictured).

★ FIRST HAT-TRICK SCORED IN THE FIFA WORLD CUP

Bert Patenaude (USA) was the first player to score a hat-trick (three goals) in a World Cup finals match, playing for the USA against Paraguay in Montevideo, Uruguay, on 17 July 1930. Until 2006, Argentinian Guillermo Stabile was credited with the record, having scored three times in his country's 6–3 victory over Mexico on 19 July 1930. But research by FIFA indicated that a goal that was initially credited to the USA's Tom Florie in the match against Paraguay should instead be attributed to Patenaude, thus confirming his hat-trick.

MOST FIFA WORLD CUP CLEAN SHEETS

Two goalkeepers have each achieved 10 clean sheets (a match in which they have conceded no goals) in their World Cup finals career. Peter Shilton (UK) achieved the feat playing for England from 1982 to 1990 and Fabien Barthez (France) equalled the record playing for France in finals from 1998 to 2006.

★ HIGHEST GOAL AVERAGE IN A FIFA WORLD CUP FINALS

At the 1954 World Cup finals in Switzerland, 16 teams contested a total of 26 matches, during which an incredible 140 goals were scored at an average of 5.38 goals per match. Hungary alone scored 25 goals in four matches to progress to the Final, where they lost 3–2 to West Germany. The ★ **lowest goal average** was 2.21 per game at the 1990 finals in Italy. The overall average for the 18 World Cup finals is 2.91 goals per match.

Nov 20: The **largest serving of currywurst** weighed 150.07 kg (330 lb 13 oz) and was made in an event organized by Volkswagen AG (Germany) in Wolfsburg, Germany, on 20 November 2008.

Nov 21: The **oldest known divorcee** was 101-year-old Harry Bidwell of East Sussex, UK. He divorced his 65-year-old wife on this day in 1980.

11: the number of seconds it took Hakan Suker of Turkey to score against South Korea during the 2002 World Cup finals – the **fastest World Cup goal.**

GUINNESS WORLD RECORDS

★ FIRST FIFA WORLD CUP GOAL

Lucien Laurent (France, circled left), scored the first ever World Cup goal playing for France against Mexico in Montevideo, Uruguay, on 13 July 1930. The goal, a 19th-minute volley, was the opener in France's 4–1 victory over the Mexico team. France lost their two remaining group games and were eliminated from the tournament after the opening stages.

★ OLDEST REFEREE AT THE FIFA WORLD CUP FINALS

George Reader (UK) was 53 years 236 days old when he officiated at the final match of the 1950 World Cup finals at the Maracana stadium, Rio de Janeiro, Brazil, on 16 July 1950. The match was won by Uruguay, who beat the hosts Brazil 2–1.

★ MOST FIFA WORLD CUP FINALS MATCHES REFEREED

Joel Quiniou (France) refereed eight World Cup finals matches in a career that spanned the 1986, 1990 and 1994 tournaments.

Quiniou took charge of his first match on 13 June 1986, when Uruguay drew 0–0 with Scotland, and sent off Uruguay's Jose Batista after just one minute, which was the **fastest expulsion in a FIFA World Cup finals** match.

FIRST PERSON TO WIN THE FIFA WORLD CUP AS BOTH CAPTAIN AND COACH

Franz Beckenbauer (Germany) captained West Germany to a 2–1 victory in the FIFA World Cup Final match against the Netherlands in Munich, Germany, on 7 July 1974. On 8 July 1990, Beckenbauer coached the German team to a 1–0 win in the FIFA World Cup Final match against Argentina in Rome, Italy.

★ LARGEST ATTENDANCE AT A FIFA WORLD CUP FINALS

The 52 matches played at the 1994 World Cup finals tournament in the USA, held from 17 June to 17 July 1994, attracted a total of 3,587,538 spectators at a record high average of 68,991 spectators per game.

The 1994 World Cup finals also had the **★ largest television audience of any World Cup finals tournament**, when a record 32,115,652 viewers in 188 broadcast countries watched a total of 16,392 hours 37 minutes of transmission.

MOST CARDS ISSUED
IN A FIFA WORLD CUP FINALS MATCH

An incredible 20 cards (16 yellow and four red) were issued during the Portugal v Netherlands match played in Nuremburg, Germany on 25 June 2006, during the 2006 FIFA World Cup finals. The four red cards issued were the **most expulsions in a single World Cup finals tournament match**, with each team having two players sent off.

MOST MINUTES PLAYED IN WORLD CUP FINALS

Italian defender Paolo Maldini has featured on the pitch for a total of 2,217 minutes in World Cup finals, playing for Italy in the 1990, 1994, 1998 and 2002 tournaments.

Nov 22: The **highest average speed achieved in a glider by a woman** is 227.8 km/h (141.54 mph) by Ghislaine Facon (France) at Chos Malal, Argentina, on this day in 2005.

249

WWW.GUINNESSWORLDRECORDS.COM

GOLF

★ MOST PGA CHAMPIONS TOUR MAJOR TOURNAMENT VICTORIES

Jack Nicklaus (USA) secured an unprecedented eight victories in PGA Champions Tour major tournaments between the years 1990 and 1996.

★ HIGHEST CAREER EARNINGS ON THE EUROPEAN SENIOR TOUR

The European Senior Tour career earnings record stands at €1,799,375 (£1,712,274; $2,336,395) and was achieved by Carl Mason (UK) between 2003 and 2008.

★ MOST PGA CHAMPIONS TOUR WINS

Between 1995 and 2008, Hale Irwin (USA) secured 45 victories in Professional Golfers' Association (PGA) Champions Tour events. The Champions Tour is held in the UK and US and is open to golfers aged 50 and upwards.

Irwin is also the ★ oldest US Open golf champion. He was aged 45 years 15 days when he won the tournament at Medinah Country Club, Illinois, USA, in 1990.

★ HIGHEST SEASON'S EARNINGS FOR THE US LPGA

The season's record for earnings on the US Ladies Professional Golf Association (LPGA) Tour is $4,364,994 (£3,198,973) by Lorena Ochoa (Mexico) in 2007.

★ GREATEST PRIZE MONEY FOR A GOLF TOURNAMENT

The PGA Tour Players Championship, contested between 8 and 11 May 2008 at Sawgrass, Florida, USA, had a total prize pool of $9,500,000 (£6,614,445), with $1,710,000 (£1,190,814) going to the winner.

THE OPEN/US OPEN

★ MOST APPEARANCES AT THE OPEN CHAMPIONSHIP

The greatest number of appearances at the annual Open Championship (known as the Open, or – outside the UK – as the British Open), is 46 by Gary Player (South Africa), between 1956 and 2001. The Open is the sole major golf tournament to be staged outside the USA.

★ MOST TIMES TO HOST THE OPEN CHAMPIONSHIP BY A COURSE

The Royal and Ancient Golf Club of St Andrews (UK) has hosted the Open Championship on 27 occasions between 1873 and 2005.

★ OLDEST CHAMPION

The oldest winner of the Open is Tom Morris Sr (UK, b. 16 June 1821), who was aged 46 years 99 days when he won the 1867 Championship at Prestwick Golf Club, Prestwick, UK, on 26 September 1867.

FASTEST GOLF ROUND (TEAM)

The fastest round of golf took 7 min 56 sec and was achieved by the News/Talk 760 WJR team of golfers (USA) at the Monument Course, Boyne Mountain, Michigan, USA, on 20 July 2008. In total, 22 players and 19 volunteers took part in the event.

★ YOUNGEST CHAMPION

The youngest Open Championship winner is Tom Morris Jr (UK, b. 20 April 1851), who was 17 years 156 days old when he won the 1868 Open Championship at Prestwick, UK, on 23 September 1868. Tom also holds the record for the ★ most consecutive wins of the Open Championship, with four from 1868 to 1872 (there was no Open Championship in 1871).

★ OLDEST COMPETITOR

The oldest competitor at the Open Championship was Gene Sarazen (USA, b. 27 February 1902). He entered the 1976 Championship, aged 74 years 132 days, at Royal Birkdale golf course, Southport, UK, on 10 July 1976.

★ NEW RECORD
UPDATED RECORD

GREAT LENGTHS

The par-77 International GC in Bolton, Massachusetts, USA, is the world's longest golf course at 7,612 m/ 8,325 yd (24,973 ft) – that's over 7.6 km or 4.7 miles long! The course was remodelled in 1969 by prolific golf course architect Robert Trent Jones (USA).

HIGHEST EUROPEAN TOUR CAREER EARNINGS (MALE)

The European tour career earnings record stands at €23,595,864 (£22,453,678; $30,638,010) and is held by Colin Montgomerie (UK) for the years 1986–2009.

PUTT IT THERE

The longest putt holed in a major tournament is 33.5 m (110 ft) by Jack Nicklaus (USA) in the 1964 Tournament of Champions and Nick Price (Zimbabwe) in the 1992 US PGA. Bob Cook (USA) sank a 42.74-m (140-ft 2¾-in) putt in the International Fourball Pro-Am Tournament in 1976.

Nov 23: The **greatest number of plates spun simultaneously** is 108, achieved by Dave Spathaky (UK) for the *Tarm Pai Du* television programme in Thailand on 23 November 1992.

Nov 24: The **fastest time to solve a Rubik's Cube** is 9.55 seconds by Ron van Bruchem (Netherlands) in the Dutch Championship 2007 Rubik's Cube competition held on this day in 2007.

4 years 195 days: the age of Christian Carpenter (USA, b. 6 June 1995) when he became the **youngest golfer to record a hole-in-one**.

★ MOST CURTIS CUP WINS (TEAM)

The ladies' Curtis Cup competition, held between the USA and a combined team of Great Britain and Ireland, was first staged in 1932 and won by the USA. The USA has subsequently won the tournament on 27 occasions, up to 2008.

★ MOST WINS OF THE SENIOR BRITISH OPEN

Two golfers share this record. Gary Player (South Africa) won the Senior British Open three times, in 1988, 1990 and 1997. Tom Watson (USA) achieved the same feat in 2003, 2005 and 2007.

★ MOST CONSECUTIVE MATCH WINS (INDIVIDUAL)

Two players share the record for the longest unbeaten streak in the Ryder Cup, each going undefeated for 12 matches. Lee Westwood (UK) was unbeaten from 2002 to 2008 and Arnold Palmer (USA) from 1965 to 1971.

★ MOST MATCHES HALVED BY AN INDIVIDUAL

Two golfers have halved eight matches in their Ryder Cup careers: Tony Jacklin (UK) from 1967 to 1979, and Gene Littler (USA) from 1961 to 1975. A match is halved when all competitors record the same score and thus share the match points.

★ YOUNGEST CAPTAIN

Arnold Palmer (USA) captained the United States team at the age of 34 years 1 month 1 day at East Lake Country Club, Atlanta, Georgia, USA, in the 1963 competition.

MOST US OPEN TITLES

Four US players have won the US Open four times: Willie Anderson (1901, 1903–05), Bobby Jones Jr (1923, 1926, 1929, 1930), Ben Hogan (1948, 1950, 1951, 1953) and Jack Nicklaus (1962, 1967, 1972, 1980).

Two women jointly share the record for the **most US Women's Open titles** with four victories: Betsy Earle-Rawls (USA) in 1951, 1953, 1957 and 1960, and Mickey Wright (USA) in 1958, 1959, 1961 and 1964.

With four wins (1958, 1960–61, 1963), Wright also holds the record for the **most LPGA Championships won (individual)**.

RYDER CUP

MOST MATCH WINS (TEAM)

Instituted in 1927, the Ryder Cup is staged every two years between the USA and Europe (British Isles or Great Britain prior to 1979). The USA has won 25 to 10 (with two draws) up to 2008.

★ MOST CONSECUTIVE CUP WINS (TEAM)

The USA has won the Ryder Cup seven times consecutively on two separate occasions, first from 1935 to 1955, and most recently from 1971 to 1983.

★ MOST MATCH WINS (INDIVIDUAL)

The most Ryder Cup match wins by an individual is 23 (out of 46) by Nick Faldo (UK). The Brit also holds the world record for the **most Ryder Cup tournaments played**, with 11 (the US record is eight, shared by Billy Casper, Ray Floyd and Lanny Wadkins).

★ HIGHEST CAREER EARNINGS ON THE US PGA TOUR

The all-time career earnings record on the US PGA circuit is held by Tiger Woods (USA) with $82,354,376 (£60,355,051) between 1996 and 2009.

Among other records, Woods also achieved the **★ lowest score under par after four rounds at the Open Championship:** a score of -19 (19 under par) at St Andrews, UK, on 23 July 2000.

HIGHEST US LPGA TOUR CAREER EARNINGS

Annika Sorenstam (Sweden) won a record $22,573,192 (£17,292,700) on the US LPGA Tour in a career stretching from 1993 to 2009.

TOP 100 Records of the Decade

Nov 25: Joakim Lundblad (Sweden) took the record for the **most sushi made in two minutes** when he made 12 norimaki sushi in two minutes in Stockholm, Sweden, on 25 November 2001.

ICE HOCKEY

LONGEST ICE HOCKEY MARATHON

Brent Saik (Canada) and friends at Saiker's Acres, Strathcona, Alberta, Canada, played ice hockey for 241 hr 21 min from 8 to 18 February 2008.

HIGHEST SCORE IN AN ICE HOCKEY MATCH

The highest score in an international ice hockey match occurred when Slovakia beat Bulgaria 82–0 in a pre-Olympic women's qualification game that took place in Liepaja, Latvia, on 6 September 2008.

★ YOUNGEST PLAYER TO APPEAR IN 200 NHL GAMES

At 20 years 111 days, Jordan Staal (Canada, b. 10 September 1988) became the youngest player to appear in 200 National Hockey League (NHL) games while playing for the Pittsburgh Penguins (USA) since the 2006–07 season. Staal also holds the rookie record for most shorthanded goals scored in a season, with seven in 2006–07.

LARGEST ICE HOCKEY TOURNAMENT – PLAYERS

The Hockey Calgary 37th Annual Minor Hockey Week Tournament was contested by 664 teams (10,922 players) in Calgary, Alberta, Canada, from 5 January to 13 January 2007.

MOST...

★ STANLEY CUP PLAYOFF GAMES PLAYED

Chris Chelios (USA) has played 248 games in Stanley Cup playoffs, for the Montreal Canadiens (Canada), Chicago Blackhawks and Detroit Red Wings (both USA) in the National Hockey League since 1984. Chelios also holds the record for the **most seasons playing in the postseason**, with 23.

Chelios's amazing career longevity has seen him rack up 1,629 games in the NHL up to 8 February 2009, the **most NHL games played by an American-born player**.

★ GOALS SCORED BY A PLAYER IN FIRST NHL GAME

Fabian Brunnstrom (Sweden) scored three goals in his first NHL game playing for the Dallas Stars against the Nashville Predators (both USA) on 15 October 2008. Only two other players have scored a hat-trick in their debut game: Alex Smart of the Montreal Canadiens (both Canada) on 14 January 1943; and Real Cloutier of the Quebec Nordiques (both Canada) on 10 October 1979.

MEN'S ICE HOCKEY WORLD CHAMPIONSHIPS

Canada has won 24 men's ice hockey world titles: 1920, 1924, 1928, 1930–32, 1934–35, 1937–39, 1948, 1950–52, 1955, 1958–59, 1961, 1994, 1997, 2003–04 and 2007.

DURABLE ICE HOCKEY PLAYER

John Burnosky (USA) played ice hockey on a regular basis for 76 years. He began playing at Kelvin Technical High School, Winnipeg, Manitoba, Canada, in 1929 and continued playing until 2005.

GOALS SCORED IN A SEASON

Alex Ovechkin (Russia) scored 65 goals playing in the NHL for the Washington Capitols (USA) during the 2007–08 season, the ★ **most goals scored by a left wing in a season**.

Brett Hull (Canada) scored 86 goals playing on the right wing for the St Louis Blues (USA) during the 1990–91 season, the ★ **most goals scored by a right wing in a season**.

Multiple world record holder Wayne Gretzky (Canada) – aka "The Great One" – scored 92 goals playing as centre for the Edmonton Oilers (Canada) during the 1981–82 season, the ★ **most goals scored by a centre in a season**.

★ MOST OVERTIME GOALS SCORED IN A SEASON

Daniel Sedin (Sweden, left), playing for the Vancouver Canucks (Canada) during the 2006–07 season, and Patrik Elias (Czech Republic), playing for the New Jersey Devils (USA) in the 2003–04 season, each scored a record four National Hockey League (NHL) goals in overtime.

Nov 26: The **largest serving of risotto** weighed 7.51 tonnes (8.27 tons) and was made by the Ricegrowers' Association of Australia and displayed on this day in 2004.

Nov 27: The **highest start to a marathon** is for the Everest Marathon, first run on 27 November 1987. It begins at Gorak Shep, at 5,212 m (17,100 ft) and ends at Namche Bazar, at 3,444 m (11,300 ft).

2.06 m (6 ft 9 in): the height of Zdeno Chara (Czech Republic) of the Boston Bruins (USA) – the **tallest NHL player ever**.

★ FASTEST SHOT IN NHL HISTORY

Zdeno Chara (Czech Republic) of the Boston Bruins (USA) hit a slap shot measured at 169.7 km/h (105.4 mph) during the SuperSkills competition at the NHL All-Star Weekend in Montreal, Canada, on 25 January 2009. Chara broke Al Iafrate's 16-year-old record of 169.3 km/h (105.2 mph).

★ OVERTIME GOALS SCORED IN A CAREER

The NHL record for the most overtime goals scored in a regular season career stands at 15 and is shared by three players: Patrik Elias (Czech Republic) playing for the New Jersey Devils (USA) since the 1997–98 season; Mats Sundin (Sweden) playing for the Quebec Nordiques and Toronto Maple Leafs (both Canada) since the 1990–91 season; and Jaromir Jagr (Czech Republic) playing for the Pittsburgh Penguins, Washington Capitals and New York Rangers (all USA) from the 1990–91 season to the 2007–08 season.

★ SAVES IN A SHUTOUT

Goaltender Craig Anderson (USA) made 53 saves while minding the net for the Florida Panthers (USA) in a 1–0 victory over the New York Islanders (USA) on 2 March 2008. Anderson also has the **most saves in consecutive shutouts**, 93, when he made another 40 saves in a 1–0 win over the Boston Bruins (USA) on 4 March 2008.

ART ROSS TROPHY WINS

The Art Ross Trophy is awarded each year to the player who has scored the most points in NHL regular season play. The most Art Ross Trophies won by an individual player is 10 by the legendary Wayne Gretzky (Canada) between 1981 and 1994.

★ BEST 30-GAME START BY A TEAM

The best start through 30 games in National Hockey League history is 52 points by the San Jose Sharks (USA) at the beginning of the 2008–09 season. The Sharks won 25 games to equal the record set by the Boston Bruins (USA) in 1929–30 for **most victories in the first 30 games of the season**.

★ SHOOTOUT VICTORIES IN A SEASON BY AN NHL TEAM

Edmonton Oilers (Canada) recorded 15 shootout victories playing in the NHL during the 2007–08 season.

★ TEAM SHUTOUTS IN A SEASON

The single-season record for being shut out is 16 by the Columbus Blue Jackets (USA) during the 2006–07 season.

GOALS SCORED BY A PLAYER IN AN INTERNATIONAL MATCH

Chris Bourque (USA) scored five goals to help the USA beat Norway 11–2 in the International Ice Hockey Federation World Junior Championship in Vancouver, Canada, on 26 December 2005. Bourque equalled the USA Hockey record first set by Wally Chapman (USA) in January 1984.

★ NEW RECORD
UPDATED RECORD

★ MOST CONSECUTIVE SEASONS WINNING 40 GAMES BY AN NHL GOALTENDER

Martin Brodeur (Canada), the goaltender of the New Jersey Devils (USA), had three consecutive seasons winning at least 40 games: in 2005–06, 2006–07 and 2007–08. Brodeur also has the **★ most 40-win seasons for a goaltender**, with seven: 1997–98, 1999–2000, 2000–01, 2002–03, 2005–06, 2006–07 and 2007–08.

Nov 28: On this day in 2000, Madonna (USA) performed a concert that was broadcast live on the internet by Microsoft Network and was watched by 11 million people online, making it the **largest internet pop concert**.

SPORTS
RUGBY

★ MOST SUPER LEAGUE TRIES

"Try Machine" Keith Senior (UK) scored 169 tries playing rugby league for Sheffield Eagles and Leeds Rhinos (both UK) in Europe's Super League from 1996 to 2009.

RUGBY UNION

★ FASTEST TRY IN THE ENGLISH PREMIERSHIP

Lee Blackett (UK) scored a try in 8.28 seconds playing for Leeds Carnegie against Newcastle Falcons at Headingley, Leeds, UK, on 21 March 2008. Leeds went on to win the game 16–15.

★ OLDEST RUGBY LEAGUE PLAYER

Dennis Gleeson (Australia, b. 17 August 1936) was 70 years 9 days old when he played for the State Rail Apprentice RLFC in the New South Wales Tertiary Student Rugby League Competition at the Peter Hislop Oval, Auburn, Australia, on 26 August 2006.

★ MOST PENALTIES IN AN INTERNATIONAL CAREER

The reliable boot of Welshman Neil Jenkins kicked 248 penalties in 91 matches for his country between 1991 and 2002.

MOST HONG KONG SEVENS WINS

First held in 1976, the Hong Kong Sevens seven-a-side tournament has been won 12 times by Fiji, in 1977–78, 1980, 1984, 1990–92, 1997–99, 2005 and 2009.

★ MOST CONVERSIONS IN ONE HOUR (TEAM)

Haddington Rugby Football Club Under 17s scored 374 conversions in one hour at Neilson Park, Haddington, Scotland, UK, on 15 November 2008. The club's achievement broke the previous record of 124 held by Bicester Rugby Union Club Under 12s.

★ MOST TRIES IN A BRITISH LIONS & IRISH LIONS CAREER

Tony O'Reilly (Ireland) scored six tries playing for the British & Irish Lions in Test matches in 1955 and 1959.

★ MOST TRIES IN AN IRB SEVENS CAREER

Santiago Gomez Cora (Argentina) scored 213 tries in International Rugby Board (IRB) Sevens competitions between 1999 and 2009. However, the record for the **most points in an IRB Sevens career** goes to Ben Gollings (UK), who scored 1,907 points while playing for England from 2001 to 2009.

★ HIGHEST ATTENDANCE FOR A GUINNESS PREMIERSHIP RUGBY UNION MATCH

The largest paying attendance for a single Guinness Premiership regular season match is 50,000 for a Harlequins match against Leicester (pictured) on 27 December 2008.

★ MOST TRIES
IN A TRI-NATIONS MATCH

Jongikhaya "Jongi" Nokwe of South Africa scored four tries against Australia at Ellis Park, Johannesburg, South Africa, on 30 August 2008. The Springboks romped home to an emphatic 53–8 victory against the Wallabies.

Nov 29: Rajat Kumar Mishra (India, b. 28 November 1992) played a tabla, a traditional indian hand drum, live on All India Radio at the age of seven, making him the **youngest tabla player**.

Nov 30: The **most concerts performed in 24 hours** was 50 by N Karthik (India) at venues in and around Bangalore, India, on 29–30 November 2005.

7,337: points scored by William Henry Dusty Hare (UK), the **most points scored in a Rugby Union career by an individual player**.

★ MOST POINTS IN AN ENGLISH PREMIERSHIP CAREER

Charlie Hodgson (UK) broke rival fly-half Jonny Wilkinson's record for the most points in an English Premiership rugby union career with a 65th-minute penalty scored for Sale Sharks against Newcastle Falcons (coincidentally, Wilkinson's team) at Edgeley Park, Newcastle, UK, on 8 March 2009. By the end of the match, Hodgson had amassed an impressive career total of 1,492 points, but, despite this feat, Sale still lost the game 32–25.

RUGBY LEAGUE

MOST CONSECUTIVE HAT-TRICKS

The most consecutive matches in which an individual player scored three tries is 12 by Richard Lopag of Deighton New Saracens, Huddersfield, West Yorkshire, UK, in the 2000/01 season.

★ MOST TRIES IN A NATIONAL RUGBY LEAGUE SEASON

Terry Lamb (Australia) scored 38 tries playing for Eastern Suburbs, Sydney, Australia, in the 1938 season.

★ MOST INTERNATIONAL APPEARANCES

New Zealander Ruben Wiki made 55 international appearances for his country between 1994 and 2006.

★ MOST APPEARANCES IN A NATIONAL RUGBY LEAGUE SEASON

Dave Brown (Australia) made 349 appearances for Western Suburbs and Canterbury-Bankstown between 1980 and 1996.

MOST STATE OF ORIGIN SERIES WINS

Australia's State of Origin series is an annual best-of-three series fought between Queensland and New South Wales. Queensland has had the most wins, with 17 between 1980 and 2008.

MOST POINTS IN A NATIONAL LEAGUE CAREER

Andrew Johns (Australia) scored 2,176 points in league matches between 1993 and 2007, playing for the Newcastle Knights, but the record for the **most points in a National League season** belongs to Hazem El Masri (Lebanon), who scored 342 points in the 2004 season playing for the Canterbury Bulldogs.

★ MOST TRIES IN AN INTERNATIONAL RUGBY UNION CAREER

Speedy winger Daisuke Ohata (Japan), who started his career playing Rugby Sevens, scored an amazing 65 tries for his country, Japan, in 68 internationals between 1996 and 2006, an average of more than one try per game. Since 2006, Ohata has been dogged by injuries, first to his left Achilles tendon and then to his right. The first of these cost him the chance to compete in the 2007 Rugby World Cup.

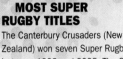

MOST SUPER RUGBY TITLES

The Canterbury Crusaders (New Zealand) won seven Super Rugby titles between 1998 and 2008. The Super Rugby competition is the largest club rugby competition in the southern hemisphere. It was renamed the Super 14 competition from the Super 12 for the 2006 season with the admission of two new teams.

★ MOST SIX NATIONS WINS

The top northern-hemisphere competition was renamed from the Five Nations to the Six Nations in 2000 when Italy were invited to join the series. England have won the championship 25 times over the event's history. The **most Grand Slams**, where one team wins against all the other teams, is 12, also held by England.

★ LARGEST ATTENDANCE AT A CLUB MATCH

A crowd of 81,600 watched the Guinness Premiership final between Leicester Tigers and London Wasps (both UK) at Twickenham Stadium, London, UK, on 31 May 2008. Wasps won 26–16.

★ MOST CONVERSIONS IN AN INTERNATIONAL CAREER

Andrew Mehrtens (New Zealand) kicked 169 conversions in 70 matches for the All Blacks in a career than ran between 1995 and 2004.

MOST HEINIKEN CUP TITLE WINS

Inaugurated in 1995, the Heineken Cup, or H-cup, is Rugby Union's premier European club competition. It has been won three times by Toulouse (France), in 1996, 2003 and 2005.

Dec 1: The **fastest piggyback race** over 1 mile (1.61 km) is 13 min 1 sec, set by Ashrita Furman (USA) carrying Bipin Larkin at the Egilshöll Sports Complex, Reykjavik, Iceland, on this day in 2006.

TENNIS & RACKET SPORTS

BADMINTON

MOST BADMINTON SINGLES WINS (MALE)

Two players have won the Badminton World Championships men's singles title twice: Yang Yang (China) in 1987 and 1989 and, more recently, Lin Dan (China, above) in 2006 and 2007.

TEAM LEADER

The **largest annual team competition in world sport** is the Davis Cup, organized by the International Tennis Federation (ITF), which is based in London, UK. A knockout competition, the 2007 event saw 137 countries enter, with Spain emerging victorious.

LONGEST MATCH

In the men's singles final at the World Championships in Glasgow, UK, on 1 June 1997, Peter Rasmussen (Denmark) beat Sun Jun (China) 16/17, 18/13, 15/10 in a match lasting 2 hr 4 min.

★ MOST NATIONS IN THE SUDIRMAN CUP

A total of 59 nations competed in the 1997 staging of the Sudirman Cup, named after the famous Indonesian player Dick Sudirman.

MOST WINS...

- **Overall championships**: five, by Park Joo-bong (South Korea): men's doubles (1985, 1991), mixed doubles (1985, 1989, 1991).
- **Badminton World Championships singles (female)**: two, by China's Li Lingwei (1983, 1989), Han Aiping (1985, 1987), Ye Zhaoying (1995, 1997) and Xie Xingfang (2005, 2006).
- **Sudirman Cup**, inst. 1989, held every two years (**World Mixed Team Badminton Championship**): six, by China, 1995–2001.

- **Uber Cup**, inst. 1956 (**World Team Badminton Championships – female**): 11, by China, between 1984 and 2008.

REAL TENNIS

MOST WORLD CHAMPIONSHIPS (MEN)

Jacques Edmond Barre (France) held the title for a record 33 years from 1829 to 1862; however, the **first recorded real tennis World Champion** was a Frenchman known only as Clerg c. 1740. Since 1996, the competition has been held biennially on even-numbered years. The record for the **most defences of the real tennis World Championships** belongs to Robert Fahey (Australia), who fought off strong opposition to retain the title on nine occasions between 1994 and 2008.

OLDEST TABLE TENNIS PLAYER

Dorothy de Low (Australia, b. 5 October 1910) was aged 97 years 232 days when she represented Australia at the XIV World Veterans Table Tennis Championships at Rio de Janeiro, Brazil, on 25 May 2008. She won the gold medal at the 1992 championship in Dublin, Ireland, in the Over-80s Women's Singles category.

★ MOST MONEY WON IN A TENNIS CAREER (FEMALE)

Lindsay Davenport (USA) has really cashed in on her tennis success, winning an impressive $22,144,735 (£16,229,211) in tournament play over the course of her professional tennis career between 1993 and 2008.

MOST WORLD CHAMPIONSHIPS (WOMEN)

Penny Lumley (UK, née Fellows) has won the Women's World Championships (inst. 1985) six times between 1989 and 2003.

TABLE TENNIS

OLYMPIC GAMES

The **most women's medals won** is four, by Deng Yaping (China) with four golds (1992–96), which is also the **most women's gold medals won**; and Yoo Nam-kyu (South Korea) with one gold and three bronze (1988–96).

The **most men's gold medals** is two by Liu Guoliang (China) for singles and doubles (1996); and Ma Lin (China) for singles and team (2008).

Dec 2: The **largest game of bingo** involved a total of 70,080 participants and took place at an event organized by Almacenes Exito S.A. in Bogotá, Colombia, on 2 December 2006.

Dec 3: The **largest group of carol singers** comprised 7,514 lusty-voiced warblers who performed at the Bob Jones University, South Carolina, USA, on 3 December 2004.

16 years 182 days: the age at which Martina Hingis (Switzerland) became the **youngest person to be ranked tennis number one**.

GUINNESS WORLD RECORDS

★ MOST CONSECUTIVE US OPEN SINGLES TITLES (FEMALE)

Three women have won four consecutive US Open singles titles each: Molla Mallory (Norway) in 1915–18, Helen Jacobs (USA) in 1932–35 and Chris Evert (USA) in 1975–78.

MOST WIMBLEDON SINGLES TITLES

Martina Navratilova (USA) won a record nine Wimbledon singles tennis titles, in 1978–79, 1982–87 and 1990.

Two players hold the record for the **most men's Wimbledon singles titles**, with a total of seven each: W C Renshaw (UK), with wins in 1881–86 and 1889, and more recently Pete Sampras (USA), with victories in 1993–95 and 1997–2000.

★ LONGEST FINAL (MALE SINGLES)

Rafael Nadal (Spain) beat Roger Federer (Switzerland) 6-4, 6-4, 6-7(5), 6-7(8), 9-7 in a match lasting 4 hr 48 min at the Wimbledon Championships in London, UK, on 6 July 2008.

WHEEL SKILLS

A record 60 wheelchair athletes took part in a tennis tournament organized by Business Clubs of America (USA) in San Diego, California, USA, on 20 June 2008 – the world's ★largest wheelchair tennis tournament.

● The record for the most International Tennis Federation Wheelchair Tennis World Championships won by a female player is nine by Esther Vergeer (Netherlands) in 2000–08.

LONGEST RALLY

Ettore Rossetti and Angelo Rossetti (both USA, seen here with GWR's Stuart Claxton) played a tennis rally of 25,944 strokes at North Haven Tennis & Racquet in North Haven, Connecticut, USA, on 9 August 2008.

The **most men's team gold medals won** is eight by China, from 1988 to 2008. The **most women's team gold medals won** is nine, also by the Chinese team and also from 1988 to 2008.

X-REF
Do sports statistics make you ecstatic? Then turn to p.266 for our **Sports Reference section** – a numerical nirvana of sporting facts and figures!

The ★**highest annual earnings for a female** is an estimated $26 million (£13.2 million) earned by Maria Sharapova (Russia) from June 2007 to June 2008.

★ MOST CONSECUTIVE US OPEN SINGLES TITLES (MALE)

Richard Dudley "Dick" Sears (USA) won seven consecutive US Open singles tennis titles from 1881 to 1887 while still a student. His 18-match unbeaten streak remained a record until 1921.

MOST FRENCH OPEN TITLES

Between 1962 and 1973, Margaret Court (Australia) won a record 13 French Open tennis titles: five singles titles, four doubles titles and four mixed doubles titles.

The **greatest number of French Open tennis titles won by a man** is nine, by Henri Cochet (France): four singles titles, three doubles titles and two mixed doubles titles, between 1926 and 1930.

WORLD TABLE TENNIS CHAMPIONSHIPS (TEAM)

In addition to their strong performances in the Olympics, China also dominates the World Table Tennis Championships. Between 1961 and 2008, China won the Swaythling Cup (inst. 1926) 17 times, the **most men's team titles**.

China also won the Corbillon Cup (inst. 1926) 18 times between 1965 and 2008, the **most women's team titles**.

TENNIS

★ HIGHEST ANNUAL EARNINGS (FROM ALL SOURCES)

Roger Federer (Switzerland) earned an estimated $35 million (£17.5 million) between June 2007 and June 2008.

He also holds the record for the **most money won in a tennis career (male)**: $44,644,857 (£32,718,876) between 1998 and 2008.

GREATEST EVER?

Roger Federer's record for the most consecutive finals victories (24 back-to-back wins between October 2003 and September 2005) is considered one of the greatest achievements of the Open era. It is also one of our Top 100 Records of the decade.

★ MOST CONSECUTIVE FRENCH OPEN SINGLES TITLES (MALE)

The French Open is the tennis world's premier clay court tournament. Two players have each won the French Open, four times consecutively: Björn Borg (Sweden) in 1978–81 and Rafael Nadal (Spain, left) in 2005–08. Nadal's record on clay is formidable – he has also scored the **most consecutive clay-court men's singles wins**, with 60 victories.

TOP 100 Records of the Decade

Dec 4: The **greatest distance covered by wheelchair in 24 hours** is 182.4 km (113.34 miles), by Mario Trindade (Portugal) at the Vila Real Stadium in Vila Real, Portugal, on 3–4 December 2007.

257

WWW.GUINNESSWORLDRECORDS.COM

WATERSPORTS

★ MOST GOLD MEDALS WON AT A SINGLE OLYMPIC GAMES (MALE)

The most gold medals won at a single Olympic Games is eight by Michael Phelps (USA), who won gold in the following swimming disciplines at the 2008 Beijing Olympics, between 9 and 17 August 2008: 400 m individual medley, 4 x 100 m freestyle relay, 200 m freestyle, 200 m butterfly, 4 x 200 m freestyle relay, 200 m individual medley, 100 m butterfly and the 4 x 100 m medley relay.

DIVING

MOST WORLD CHAMPIONSHIPS

Greg Louganis (USA) has won a record five world titles: highboard in 1978 and both highboard and springboard in 1982 and 1986. Louganis shares the record for the ★ most consecutive FINA championship titles with Philip Boggs (USA), who scored springboard wins in 1973, 1975 and 1978.

FACT
Phelps earns an estimated $5 million (£3.4 million) per year through endorsements, including a deal to be the face of Mazda in China.

HIGHEST DIVE FROM A DIVING BOARD (MALE)

The world record high dive from a diving board is 53.9 m (176 ft 10 in) by Olivier Favre (Switzerland) at Villers-le-Lac, France, on 30 August 1987. The record highest dive from a diving board (female) is 36.80 m (120 ft 9 in) by Lucy Wardle (USA) at Ocean Park, Hong Kong, China, on 6 April 1985.

MOST FINA GRAND PRIX MEN'S SPRINGBOARD TITLES

The most Fédération Internationale de Natation Diving Grand Prix Springboard titles won by an individual male diver is seven by Dmitri Sautin (Russia) in 1995–2001. Sautin also holds the record for the ★ most FINA grand prix men's platform titles, with four in 1995–96, 1998 and 2000.

MOST GOLDS WON (MALE)

The most Olympic gold medals won is 14, achieved by swimmer Michael Phelps (USA). He won six gold medals at the 2004 Olympics and eight gold medals at the 2008 Olympics.

★ MOST FINA GRAND PRIX WOMEN'S 10 M PLATFORM TITLES

Na Li (China) has won the Grand Prix 10 m Platform title three times (1999–2000, 2002).

MOST OLYMPIC DIVING MEDALS WON (MALE)

Dmitri Sautin (Russia) won a total of eight Olympic medals, two gold, two silver and four bronze, between 1992 and 2008. His most recent was a silver in the men's synchronized springboard event.

YOUNGEST GOLD MEDALLIST

The youngest individual Olympic winner was Marjorie Gestring (USA, b. 18 November 1922), who took the springboard diving title at the age of 13 years 268 days at the Olympic Games in Berlin, Germany, on 12 August 1936.

FASTEST SWIM, LONG COURSE, 800 M FREESTYLE (FEMALE)

Rebecca Adlington (UK) set a time of 8 min 14.10 sec to complete the 800 m on 16 August 2008 at the Beijing Olympics, China. She was a full 6 seconds ahead of the silver medallist and 2 seconds ahead of the former world record held by Janet Evans (USA) – a record set in 1989, the year Rebecca was born.

WATER POLO

★ MOST OLYMPIC WATER POLO TITLES WON (WOMEN)

Since women's water polo was introduced at the 2000 Olympic Games, the winners have been Australia in 2000, Italy in 2004 (Manuela Zanchi is pictured below right) and the Netherlands (Danielle de Bruijn is pictured below left) in 2008.

MOST OLYMPIC WINS

Hungary's men's team has won the Olympic tournament most often, with nine wins between 1932 and 2008. With an additional three silver medals and three bronze, the Hungarians also top the table for the most Olympic water polo medals, with 15.

Dec 5: A total of 23,930 people attended the premiere of *Brewster McCloud* (USA, 1970) at the Houston Astrodome, Texas, USA, on 5 December 1970, the **largest premiere for any movie**.

6: the **most synchronized swimming Olympic golds**, won by Russia between 1984 and 2008.

TOP 100 Records of the Decade

ROWING

FASTEST 2,000 M, ROWING EIGHT (FEMALE)

The women's record time for 2,000 m on non-tidal water is 5 min 55.50 sec by a USA eight at Eton, UK, on 27 August 2006.

MOST OLYMPIC GOLDS (FEMALE)

The most Olympic golds for rowing won by a woman is five, a record shared by Elisabeta Lipa (Romania), who won in 1984, 1992, 1996, 2000 and 2004, and Georgeta Damian (Romania) in 2000, 2004 and 2008.

WINDSURFING

★ MOST FORMULA WORLD CHAMPIONSHIPS (MALE)

Formula windsurfing is a class of race windsurfing that has developed over the last 15 years in order to surf in light and moderate winds. The most World Championships won by a man is two, by four sailors: Wojtek Brzozowski (Poland) in 2000 and 2008; Kevin Pritchard (USA) in 2001–02; Steve Allen (Australia) in 2003 and 2006; and Antoine Albeau (France) in 2005 and 2007.

The ★ **most Formula Windsurfing World Championships won by a woman** is four, by Dorota Staszewska (Poland) in 2000–02 and 2004.

A. VAN KOEVERDEN

CANADA

★ FASTEST CANOE/ KAYAK K1 500 M FLATWATER (MALE)

Adam van Koeverden (Canada) completed the men's kayak K1 500 m flatwater event in 1 min 35.55 sec in Beijing, China, on 19 August 2008.

FASTEST SWIM LONG COURSE RELAY 4 X 100 M FREESTYLE (FEMALE)

The Netherlands team (Inge Dekker, Ranomi Kromowidjojo, Femke Heemskerk and Marleen Veldhuis) completed the 4 x 100 m freestyle in a record-breaking time of 3 min 33.62 sec in Eindhoven, the Netherlands, on 18 March 2008.

Dec 6: The **most coconuts smashed in 1 minute with one hand** is 81, set by Muhamed Kahrimanovic (Germany) in Hamburg, Germany, on this day in 2007.

Dec 7: The band Grabowsky (Germany) were applauded for 1 hr 30 min after a performance at Altes-Brauhaus-Musicclub in Frankenthal, Germany, on 7 December 2002 – the **longest applause**.

WHEEL SKILLS

★ TIGHTEST PARALLEL PARKING IN REVERSE

Terry Grant (UK) parked a Renault Twingo GT in reverse in a space that was only 15 cm (5 in) longer than the car at ExCeL London, UK, on 3 February 2008.

★ FIRST SKATEBOARD TRICK

The ollie is a skateboarding trick in which the skateboarder pops the board into the air, making him appear to be jumping with the skateboard stuck to his feet. It was first performed by Alan "Ollie" Gelfand (USA) in 1976 and was originally known as a "no-hands aerial".

★ MOST OLLIES IN ONE MINUTE

Rob Dyrdek (USA) popped 42 skateboard ollies in a minute on MTV's *The Rob & Big Show* in Los Angeles, California, USA, on 17 September 2007. On the same show, on the same day, Rob managed the ★ **most consecutive ollies**, with 215 non-stop, the ★ **most frontside ollies in one minute** (32), and the ★ **most back-side, back-foot ollie-impossibles** – 15.

★ MOST CONSECUTIVE KICK FLIPS ON A SKATEBOARD

Zach Kral (USA) pulled off 1,546 consecutive kick flips at 4 Seasons Skate Park, Milwaukee, Wisconsin, USA, on 30 November 2008.

FASTEST SKATEBOARD SPEED (STANDING)

Douglas da Silva (Brazil) reached a speed of 113 km/h (70.21 mph) on a skateboard in a standing position at Teutonia, Rio Grande do Sul, Brazil, on 20 October 2007. The run was a qualifier for the International Downhill Malarrara Pro Teutonia and was measured using a radar speed gun.

★ LONGEST ONE-WHEEL MANUAL (WHEELIE)

Stefan Akesson (Sweden) skateboard wheelied for 68.54 m (224 ft 10 in) at Gallerian Shopping Centre, Stockholm, Sweden, on 2 November 2007.

★ LONGEST CONTINUOUS UNICYCLE RIDE

On 18 October 2004, Joze Voros (Slovenia) unicycled for 143.46 km (89.14 miles) without his feet touching the ground.

FASTEST 100 M ON A UNICYCLE

Peter Rosendahl (Sweden) set a sprint record for 100 m of 12.11 seconds (29.72 km/h; 18.47 mph) from a standing start at Las Vegas, Nevada, USA, on 25 March 1994.

★ **NEW RECORD**
★ **UPDATED RECORD**

★ FASTEST MOTORCYCLE HANDLEBAR WHEELIE

Enda Wright (Ireland) reached a speed of 173.81 km/h (108 mph) while performing a handlebar or "highchair" wheelie in Elvington, York, UK, on 11 July 2006. To perform a handlebar wheelie, the rider sits on the petrol tank with his legs hanging over the handlebars.

Dec 8: The **highest score in any NFL game** is 73 by the Chicago Bears against the Washington Redskins (0) in the NFL Championship game at Washington, USA, on 8 December 1940.

30.62 m (100 ft 5 in): the **longest skateboard slide**, set by Rob Dyrdek (USA) on 17 September 2007.

LONGEST RAMP-TO-RAMP JUMP ON A QUADBIKE

Jon Guetter (USA) jumped a distance of 53.92 m (176 ft 11 in) ramp to ramp on a quadbike at the Crusty Demons Night of World Records at Calder Park Raceway in Melbourne, Victoria, Australia, on 29 March 2008. Guetter smashed the previous record of 45.38 m (148 ft 11 in).

★FASTEST ATV SIDE-WHEELIE

Travis Pastrana (USA) proved that it was possible to perform a side-wheelie on an all-terrain vehicle (ATV) at a speed of 75.6 km/h (47 mph) at the Miller Motorsports Park in Tooele, Utah, USA, on 18 November 2008.

At the same event, Pastrana and Jolene Van Vugt (USA) performed the **★longest tandem ATV side-wheelie**, covering 5.29 km (3.29 miles).

★LONGEST UTV WHEELIE

Andy Bell (USA) performed a 1,544.97-m (960-ft) wheelie on a utility terrain vehicle (UTV) at the Miller Motorsports Park in Tooele, Utah, USA, on 18 November 2008.

ATVs AND UTVs

An all-terrain vehicle (ATV) is defined by the American National Standards Institute (ANSI) as a vehicle that travels on low-pressure tyres, with a seat that is straddled by the driver, along with handlebars for control. A utility terrain vehicle (UTV) is basically a pickup truck crossed with an ATV – they are used on farms, building sites or places where equipment needs transporting over rough terrain. They are also used to perform tricks.

LONGEST MOTORCYCLE RAMP JUMP

Robbie Maddison (Australia) achieved a 106.98-m (351-ft) ramp jump in Melbourne, Australia, on 29 March 2008.

★TIGHTEST GAP DRIVEN THROUGH ON TWO WHEELS

Filmed for *Zheng Da Zong Yi – Guinness World Records Special*, the Zhengzhi Driving School drove a car through a gap on two wheel 66 cm (2 ft 1 in) wide in Linyi City, Shandong Province, China, on 2 November 2008.

★LONGEST MINI-BIKE JUMP WITH BACK FLIP

Ben Fiez (Australia) jumped 20.21 m (66 ft 4 in) while performing a back flip on a Honda CRF at Calder Park Raceway in Melbourne, Australia, on 29 March 2008.

LONGEST BICYCLE WHEELIE JOURNEY

Kurt Osburn (USA) travelled 4,569 km (2,839.6 miles) from the Guinness World of Records Museum in Hollywood, California, USA, to the Guinness World of Records Museum in Orlando, Florida, USA, between 13 April and 25 June 1999. He wheelied all the way!

★LONGEST BICYCLE NO-FOOT WHEELIE (BACK WHEEL)

The longest no-foot wheelie on a mountain bike is 52.93 m (173 ft 8 in) by Jim DeChamp (USA) at Miller Motorsports Park in Tooele, Utah, USA, on 18 November 2008 for the MTV show *Nitro Circus*.

★MOST CONSECUTIVE BACK FLIPS ON INLINE SKATES (HALFPIPE)

Kevin Lopez (Belgium) achieved a record 31 consecutive back flips on inline skates on a halfpipe at ZDF Inliner Days 2007, Mainz, Germany, on 23 September 2007.

★LONGEST RAMP-TO-RAMP BACK FLIP ON A MOTORCYCLE

Cameron Sinclair (Australia) achieved a ramp-to-ramp motorcycle back flip of 39.49 m (129 ft 7 in) at the Crusty Demons Night of World Records at Calder Park Raceway in Melbourne, Victoria, Australia, on 29 March 2008.

Dec 9: The **largest Santa Claus gathering** was achieved by 13,000 participants in the Guildhall Square in Derry City, Northern Ireland, UK, on 9 December 2007.

Dec 10: The **oldest message in a bottle** spent 92 years 229 days at sea. It was released by the Marine Laboratory, Aberdeen, UK, on 25 April 1914 and recovered by Mark Anderson (UK) on this day in 2006.

261

WWW.GUINNESSWORLDRECORDS.COM

X GAMES

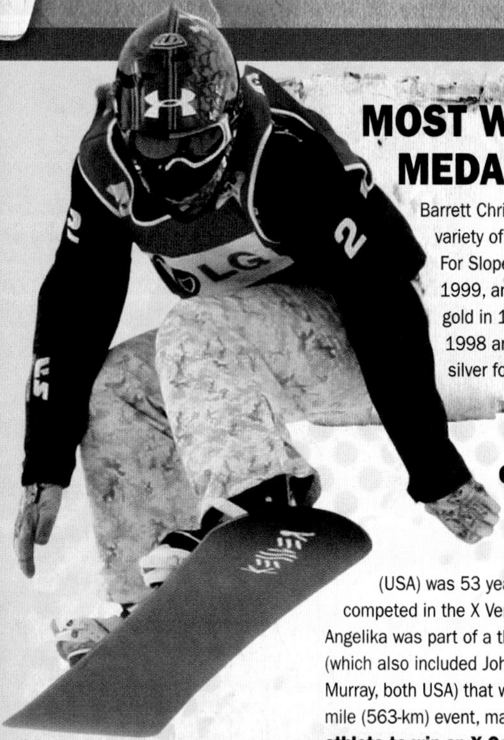

MOST WINTER X GAMES MEDALS WON (FEMALE)

Barrett Christy (USA) won 10 Winter X Games medals in a variety of snowboard disciplines between 1997 and 2001. For Slopestyle, she won gold in 1997, silver in 1998 and 1999, and bronze in 2000 and 2002; in Big Air, she won gold in 1997 and 1999, and silver in 1998 and 2001; finally, she earned a silver for SuperPipe in 2000.

OLDEST X GAMES ATHLETE

Angelika Casteneda (USA) was 53 years old when she competed in the X Venture Race in 1996. Angelika was part of a three-person team (which also included John Howard and Keith Murray, both USA) that won the six-day, 350-mile (563-km) event, making her the **oldest athlete to win an X Games gold medal**.

★ MOST KICK FLIPS IN 30 SECONDS

Zachary Kovacs (USA, left) and Michael Sohheh (USA, right) each completed 13 kick flips in 30 seconds at the X Games 14 Guinness World Records Break Fest in Los Angeles, California, USA, on 2 August 2008.

YOUNGEST X GAMES ATHLETE

Nyjah Huston (b. 30 November 1994, USA) was just 11 years 246 days old when he made his debut at X Games 12 in Los Angeles, California, USA, on 3–6 August 2006, when he competed in Men's Skateboard Street. In the finals, Huston placed eight out of the 19 skaters taking part in the event.

YOUNGEST X GAMES GOLD MEDALLIST

Ryan Sheckler (USA, b. 30 December 1989) was 13 years 230 days old when he won the Skateboard Park gold medal at ESPN X Games Nine in Los Angeles, California, USA, on 17 August 2003.

MOST WINTER X GAMES MEDALS WON (MALE)

Shaun White (USA) has won 14 Winter X Games medals in the snowboard disciplines between 2002 and 2009: for Slopestyle he won silver (2002), five golds (2003–2006 and 2009) and two more bronze (2007–2008), and for SuperPipe he won two silvers (2002, 2007) and four golds (2003, 2006 and 2008–2009).

Guinness World Records is proud to partner with the X Games – the world's **largest action sports event**. At X Games 14 in August 2008, for example, we sponsored the GWR Break Fast and challenged all-comers to break records for the **most ollies in 30 seconds** and the **most kick flips in 30 seconds**.

GAMES

GUINNESS WORLD RECORDS 2010

Dec 11: The **oldest permanent circus building** is Cirque d'Hiver (originally Cirque Napoléon), which opened in Paris, France, on this day in 1852.

Dec 12: The **greatest dressed weight for a turkey** is 39.09 kg (86 lb) for a stag reared by Philip Cook of Leacroft Turkeys Ltd, Peterborough, UK, which was weighed on 12 December 1989.

MOST WAKEBOARDING MEDALS WON

US wakeboarders Darin Shapiro (left), Dallas Friday and Tara Hamilton (right) have each earned six Summer X Games medals in the sport of wakeboarding, a water sport that employs a combination of water-skiing, snowboarding and surfing techniques.

★ NEW RECORD
UPDATED RECORD

MOST OLLIES IN 30 SECONDS

Willy Apodaca (USA) completed 33 ollies in 30 seconds at the X Games 14 Guinness World Records Break Fest in Los Angeles, California, USA, on 2 August 2008.

LONGEST BMX 360° RAMP JUMP

Mike Escamilla (USA, aka "Rooftop") completed a 15.39-m (50-ft 6-in) BMX 360-degree ramp jump on the Mega Ramp at X Games 11 in Los Angeles, California, USA, on 3 August 2005.

LONGEST HANDSTAND ON A SNOWSKATE BOARD

Trenton R Schindler (USA) performed a snowskate-board handstand lasting a record 4.38 seconds during the GWR Break Fest at Winter X Games 11 in Aspen, Colorado, USA, on 28 January 2007.

X-REF

Like incredible achievements with a watery theme? Why not turn to pp.258–259 and check out the exciting Water Sports records?

FIRST "900" ON A SKATEBOARD

Skateboard legend Tony Hawk (USA) became the first person to achieve a "900" (two and a half airborne rotations) in competition at the ESPN X Games Five in San Francisco, California, USA, on 27 June 1999. The so-called "900" is regarded as one of the most difficult tricks in vert skateboarding.

MOST X GAMES MEDALS (SKATEBOARD)

TOP 100
Records of the Decade

Skateboarders Andy Macdonald and Tony Hawk (both USA) have each won 16 X Games medals during their careers.

KING OF SNOWSKATE

On consecutive days in January 2007, snowskate boarder Phil Smage (USA) set three new ollie records during the GWR Break Fest at Winter X Games 11 in Aspen, Colorado, USA. On 25 January, Smage achieved the **most consecutive ollies on a snowskate board**, making 14 in a row. The next day, he achieved the **highest ollie on a snowskate board** with a height of 70.5 cm (27.75 in). On 27 January, Smage made the **longest ollie on a snowskate board** with an effort measured at 3.45 m (11 ft 4 in).

FIRST NON-US SNOWBOARDER TO EARN SUPERPIPE GOLD AT AN X GAMES

Antii Autti (Finland) became the first snowboarder from outside the USA to earn a gold medal in SuperPipe. He landed back-to-back 1080s (three full 360° rotations) in Aspen, Colorado, USA, in 2005, at Winter X Games Nine to take the top spot over Danny Kass and Shaun White (both USA).

MOTO X HIGHEST STEP UP JUMP

The greatest height achieved in the X Games Moto X Step Up event is 10.67 m (35 ft), by Tommy Clowers (USA) in August 2000. Essentially a "high jump" on a motorcycle, riders must try to clear a bar placed at the top of a steep take-off ramp. The height obtained is the equivalent of jumping on to the roof of a two-storey building.

LONGEST MOTO X DIRT-TO-DIRT BACK FLIP

Jeremy Stenberg and Nate Adams (both USA) did a dirt-to-dirt back flip measuring 30.48 m (100 ft) in the Moto X Freestyle finals at X Games 11 in Los Angeles, California, USA, on 6 August 2005.

LONGEST SKATEBOARD RAMP JUMP

The longest skateboard ramp jump was performed by professional skateboarder Danny Way (USA) with a 24-m (79-ft) 360° air on his Mega Ramp at X Games 10 in Los Angeles, California, USA, on 8 August 2004.

WWW.GUINNESSWORLDRECORDS.COM

Dec 13: The **oldest film director**, Manoel de Oliveira (Portugal), made his most recent film, *Cristóvão Colombo – O Enigma* (Portugal, released on 13 December 2007) at the age of 99 years 2 days.

BOGGED DOWN AND DIRTY

Bog snorkelling is a challenging event that requires participants to "swim" two lengths of a 60-yard (54-m; 180-ft) water-and mud-filled trench cut into a peat bog. Competitors must complete the course using just the power generated by the flippers on their feet and must not use traditional swimming strokes.

The World Bog Snorkelling Championships have been taking place annually at the Waen Rhydd Peat bog, Llanwrtyd Wells, Powys, UK, since 1985. In recent years, the Bog Snorkelling Triathlon has been added to the programme; it starts with a 12-km (7.5-mile) run, followed by two lengths of bog snorkelling and then a 30.5-km (19-mile) mountain cycle.

MOST PEOPLE RUNNING IN HIGH-HEELED SHOES

In an event organized by Gillette Venus Embrace and *Shop Til You Drop* magazine, 265 people took part in a 150-m (492-ft) race wearing high-heeled shoes in Sydney, Australia, on 2 September 2008. Heels had to be at least 7 cm (2.75 in) high and no more than 1.5 cm (0.6 in) wide at the tip.

FASTEST RACING SNAIL

The World Snail Racing Championship has been held every July since 1970 at Congham, Norfolk, UK, where races are conducted over a 33-cm (13-in) course located outside the local church. The all-time record holder is a snail named Archie, trained by Carl Bramham (UK), who sprinted to the winning post in 2 min 20 sec in 1995.

★ FASTEST TIME TO RUN 150 M IN HIGH-HEELED SHOES

Jill Stamison (USA) ran 150 m (492 ft) in high-heeled shoes in 21.95 seconds during the "High-Heel-a-Thon" on *Live with Regis and Kelly* on 9 July 2008 in New York City, USA.

FASTEST WIFE-CARRYING CHAMPIONSHIPS WIN

The World Wife-Carrying Championships is held annually in Sonkajärvi, Finland (first held 1992). The contest is a race in which each contestant carries his/her wife over a 253.5-m (831-ft 8-in) obstacle course as quickly as possible. The record time is 56.9 seconds by Margo Uusarj and Sandra Kullas (both Estonia) on 1 July 2006. This is the fastest time for the event since a minimum wife-weight of 49 kg (7 st 10 lb) was introduced in 2002.

LARGEST TOURNAMENT OF ROCK, PAPER, SCISSORS

A Rock, Paper, Scissors tournament with 793 participants was organized by Renee Tomas at Brigham Young University, Provo, Utah, USA, on 11 April 2008.

★ FASTEST COMPLETION OF THE WORLD BOG SNORKELLING TRIATHLON

The fastest female to complete the bog snorkelling triathlon course is Natalie Bent (UK, pictured), who got through the gruelling challenge in 3 hr 9 min 59 sec at the 2008 World Bog Snorkelling Triathlon, Llanwrtyd Wells, UK, on 6 July 2008. Natalie's brother Daniel Bent (UK) holds the male record for the event, having completed the triathlon in 2 hr 23 min 46 sec on the same day.

MOST WORMS CHARMED

At the first World Worm Charming Championship held at Cheshire, UK, on 5 July 1980, Tom Shufflebotham (UK) charmed 511 worms out of a 3-m² (32-ft²) plot in the allotted time of 30 minutes.

★ MOST WINS OF THE SAUNA WORLD CHAMPIONSHIPS

The World Sauna Championships, held in Heinola, Finland, challenges contestants to see who can stay in a sauna for the longest time. Two men have won this competition four times each: Leo Pusa (Finland, pictured) won in 2000–02 and 2004, and Timo Kaukonen (Finland) won in 2003 and 2005–07.

GUINNESS WORLD RECORDS 2010

Dec 14: The South Pole was first reached at 11:00 a.m. on this day in 1911 by a Norwegian party of five men led by Captain Roald Amundsen (Norway), after a 53-day march with dog sledges.

Dec 15: The **farthest accurate archery shot** was 200 m (656 ft) and was made on this day in 2005 by Peter Terry (Australia) at the Kalamunda Governor Stirling Archery Club, Perth, Australia.

5: the number of times Alan "Nasty" Nash (UK) has won the Toe Wrestling Championships.

MOST AIR-GUITAR WORLD CHAMPIONSHIP WINS

The Oulu Music Video Festival's Air Guitar World Championships has been held annually in Finland since 1996. Zac "The Magnet" Monro (UK), who rocked his way to the title in 2001 and 2002, is the only person to have won the event more than once since its inauguration.

LARGEST WELLINGTON BOOT RACE

A record 1,022 wellie-boot-wearing participants completed a 2-km (1.24-mile) course in Callendar Park, Falkirk, UK, for an event organized by Kidney Kids Scotland on 17 May 2007.

★ FARTHEST GRAPE SPIT

Anders Rasmussen (Norway) spat a grape a record distance of 8.72 m (28 ft 7.25 in) at Myra, Arendal, Norway, on 4 September 2004.

★ FARTHEST MATCH THROW

Michael Ottosson (Sweden) threw a matchstick measuring 4.7 cm (1.85 in) long and weighing 4.8 g (0.16 oz) a distance of 18.75 m (61 ft 6 in) at Smögens tennis hall in Stockholm, Sweden, on 31 January 2001.

FARTHEST COW-PAT THROW

Records in the sport of throwing dried cow pats or "chips" depend on whether or not the projectile may be "moulded into a spherical shape". The greatest distance achieved under the "non-sphericalization and 100 % organic" rule (established in 1970) is 81.1 m (266 ft) by Steve Urner (USA) at the Mountain Festival in Tehachapi, California, USA, on 14 August 1981.

MOST OYSTERS EATEN IN THREE MINUTES

Colin Shirlow (UK) ate 233 oysters in three minutes at the World Oyster Eating Championship held in Hillsborough, County Down, UK, on 3 September 2005.

FASTEST SPEED FOR A MORSE CODE TRANSMISSION

On 6 May 2003, Andrei Bindasov (Belarus) transmitted 216 Morse code marks of mixed text in one minute. The attempt was part of the International Amateur Radio Union's 5th World Championship in High Speed Telegraphy.

FARTHEST TOBACCO SPIT

David O'Dell (USA) spat a tobacco wad 16.23 m (53 ft 3 in) at the World Tobacco Spitting Championships held in California, USA, on 22 March 1997.

FIRST SHEEP COUNTING CHAMPIONSHIPS

The first National Sheep Counting Championships were held in New South Wales, Australia, on 14–15 September 2002. Sheep are herded past competitors, who try to guess the precise figure. Peter Desailly (Australia) took the inaugural title by correctly counting 277 sheep.

FASTEST TIME TO BOIL A BILLY CAN

Frank Ryder (Australia) boiled a billy can (a lightweight cooking pot used on a campfire) containing 2 litres (3.5 pints) of water in 7 min 29.3 sec in a competition held in Queensland, Australia, on 3 June 1989.

MOST ELEPHANT POLO WORLD CHAMPIONSHIPS

The Tiger Top Tuskers have won the World Elephant Polo Association Championships on eight occasions: 1983–85, 1987, 1992, 1998, 2000 and 2003. The invitational tournament is held every December in Megauly, on the edge of the Royal Chitwan National Park in Nepal.

★ NEW RECORD
UPDATED RECORD

★ OLDEST ROACH RACES

As the story goes, the Story Bridge Hotel Cockroach Races were started when two bar regulars argued over which suburb had the biggest and fastest roaches. Races have now been held at the Story Bridge Hotel, Brisbane, Australia, on 26 January (Australia Day) every year for 28 years. Races are held on a circular track and roaches are released in the middle... the first to the edge is the winner.

STEWARD

Dec 16: Many happy returns today to Dexter Dunworth (Australia), the **oldest licensed boxer** – he was 52 years 139 days old at the time of his most recent bout in May 2008.

ATHLETICS – OUTDOOR TRACK EVENTS

MEN	TIME/DISTANCE	NAME & NATIONALITY	LOCATION	DATE
100 m	9.69	Usain Bolt (Jamaica)	Beijing, China	16 Aug 2008
200 m	19.30	Usain Bolt (Jamaica)	Beijing, China	20 Aug 2008
400 m	43.18	Michael Johnson (USA)	Seville, Spain	26 Aug 1999
800 m	1:41.11	Wilson Kipketer (Denmark)	Cologne, Germany	24 Aug 1997
1,000 m	2:11.96	Noah Ngeny (Kenya)	Rieti, Italy	5 Sep 1999
1,500 m	3:26.00	Hicham El Guerrouj (Morocco)	Rome, Italy	14 Jul 1998
1 mile	3:43.13	Hicham El Guerrouj (Morocco)	Rome, Italy	7 Jul 1999
2,000 m	4:44.79	Hicham El Guerrouj (Morocco)	Berlin, Germany	7 Sep 1999
3,000 m	7:20.67	Daniel Komen (Kenya)	Rieti, Italy	1 Sep 1996
5,000 m	12:37.35	Kenenisa Bekele (Ethiopia)	Hengelo, the Netherlands	31 May 2004
10,000 m	26:17.53	Kenenisa Bekele (Ethiopia)	Brussels, Belgium	26 Aug 2005
20,000 m	56:26.00	Haile Gebrselassie (Ethiopia)	Ostrava, Czech Republic	26 Jun 2007
1 hour	21,285 m	Haile Gebrselassie (Ethiopia)	Ostrava, Czech Republic	27 Jun 2007
25,000 m	1:13:55.80	Toshihiko Seko (Japan)	Christchurch, New Zealand	22 Mar 1981
30,000 m	1:29:18.80	Toshihiko Seko (Japan)	Christchurch, New Zealand	22 Mar 1981
3,000 m steeplechase	7:53.63	Saif Saaeed Shaheen (Qatar)	Brussels, Belgium	3 Sep 2004
110 m hurdles	12.87	Dayron Robles (Cuba)	Ostrava, Czech Republic	12 Jun 2008
400 m hurdles	46.78	Kevin Young (USA)	Barcelona, Spain	6 Aug 1992
4 x 100 m relay	37.10	Jamaica (Asafa Powell, Nesta Carter, Michael Frater, Usain Bolt)	Beijing, China	22 Aug 2008
4 x 200 m relay	1:18.68	Santa Monica Track Club, USA (Michael Marsh, Leroy Burrell, Floyd Heard, Carl Lewis)	Walnut, USA	17 Apr 1994
4 x 400 m relay	2:54.29	USA (Andrew Valmon, Quincy Watts, Harry Reynolds, Michael Johnson)	Stuttgart, Germany	22 Aug 1993
4 x 800 m relay	7:02.43	Kenya (Joseph Mutua, William Yiampoy, Ismael Kombich, Wilfred Bungei)	Brussels, Belgium	25 Aug 2006
4 x 1,500 m relay	14:38.80	West Germany (Thomas Wessinghage, Harald Hudak, Michael Lederer, Karl Fleschen)	Cologne, Germany	17 Aug 1977

WOMEN	TIME/DISTANCE	NAME & NATIONALITY	LOCATION	DATE
100 m	10.49	Florence Griffith-Joyner (USA)	Indianapolis, USA	16 Jul 1988
200 m	21.34	Florence Griffith-Joyner (USA)	Seoul, South Korea	29 Sep 1988
400 m	47.60	Marita Koch (GDR)	Canberra, Australia	6 Oct 1985
800 m	1:53.28	Jarmila Kratochvílová (Czechoslovakia)	Munich, Germany	26 Jul 1983
1,000 m	2:28.98	Svetlana Masterkova (Russia)	Brussels, Belgium	23 Aug 1996
1,500 m	3:50.46	Qu Yunxia (China)	Beijing, China	11 Sep 1993
1 mile	4:12.56	Svetlana Masterkova (Russia)	Zürich, Switzerland	14 Aug 1996
2,000 m	5:25.36	Sonia O'Sullivan (Ireland)	Edinburgh, UK	8 Jul 1994
3,000 m	8:06.11	Wang Junxia (China)	Beijing, China	13 Sep 1993
5,000 m	14:11.15	Tirunesh Dibaba (Ethiopia)	Oslo, Norway	6 Jun 2008
10,000 m	29:31.78	Wang Junxia (China)	Beijing, China	8 Sep 1993
20,000 m	1:05:26.60	Tegla Loroupe (Kenya)	Borgholzhausen, Germany	3 Sep 2000
1 hour	18,517 m	Dire Tune (Ethiopia)	Ostrava, Czech Republic	12 Jun 2008
25,000 m	1:27:05.90	Tegla Loroupe (Kenya)	Mengerskirchen, Germany	21 Sep 2002
30,000 m	1:45:50.00	Tegla Loroupe (Kenya)	Warstein, Germany	6 Jun 2003
3,000 m steeplechase	8:58.81	Gulnara Samitova-Galkina (Russia)	Beijing, China	17 Aug 2008
100 m hurdles	12.21	Yordanka Donkova (Bulgaria)	Stara Zagora, Bulgaria	20 Aug 1988
400 m hurdles	52.34	Yuliya Pechonkina (Russia)	Tula, Russia	8 Aug 2003
4 x 100 m relay	41.37	GDR (Silke Gladisch, Sabine Rieger, Ingrid Auerswald, Marlies Göhr)	Canberra, Australia	6 Oct 1985
4 x 200 m relay	1:27.46	United States "Blue" (LaTasha Jenkins, LaTasha Colander-Richardson, Nanceen Perry, Marion Jones)	Philadelphia, USA	29 Apr 2000
4 x 400 m relay	3:15.17	USSR (Tatyana Ledovskaya, Olga Nazarova, Maria Pinigina, Olga Bryzgina)	Seoul, South Korea	1 Oct 1988
4 x 800 m relay	7:50.17	USSR (Nadezhda Olizarenko, Lyubov Gurina, Lyudmila Borisova, Irina Podyalovskaya)	Moscow, Russia	5 Aug 1984

MEN'S 4 X 100 M RELAY

Asafa Powell, Nesta Carter, Michael Frater and Usain Bolt (all Jamaica) celebrate after winning the gold medal in the 4 x 100 m relay final on 22 August 2008 at the Beijing Olympics.

WOMEN'S 1 HOUR

Dire Tune (Ethiopia) in the 1 hour event at the IAAF World Athletics Grand Prix meeting on 12 June 2008 in Ostrava, Czech Republic, where she ran 18,517 m.

Dec 17: The **first controlled and sustained power-driven flight** occurred at 10:35 a.m. on 17 December 1903, when Orville Wright flew the 9-kW (12-hp) *Flyer I* for a distance of 36.5 m (120 ft).

Dec 18: The **largest secret Santa game** involved 1,270 participants in an event organised by Boots UK Limited in Nottingham, UK, on 18 December 2008.

29: years that ultrarunner Jeff Norman (UK) has held the 50 km track world record of 2 hr 48 min 6 sec.

ATHLETICS – INDOOR TRACK EVENTS

MEN	TIME/DISTANCE	NAME & NATIONALITY	LOCATION	DATE
50 m	5.56	Donovan Bailey (Canada)	Reno, USA	9 Feb 1996
60 m	6.39	Maurice Green (USA)	Madrid, Spain	3 Feb 1998
	6.39	Maurice Green (USA)	Atlanta, USA	3 Mar 2001
200 m	19.92	Frankie Fredericks (Namibia)	Liévin, France	18 Feb 1996
400 m	44.57	Kerron Clement (USA)	Fayetteville, USA	12 Mar 2005
800 m	1:42.67	Wilson Kipketer (Denmark)	Paris, France	9 Mar 1997
1,000 m	2:14.96	Wilson Kipketer (Denmark)	Birmingham, UK	20 Feb 2000
1,500 m	3:31.18	Hicham El Guerrouj (Morocco)	Stuttgart, Germany	2 Feb 1997
1 mile	3:48.45	Hicham El Guerrouj (Morocco)	Ghent, Belgium	12 Feb 1997
3,000 m	7:24.90	Daniel Komen (Kenya)	Budapest, Hungary	6 Feb 1998
5,000 m	12:49.60	Kenenisa Bekele (Ethiopia)	Birmingham, UK	20 Feb 2004
50 m hurdles	6.25	Mark McKoy (Canada)	Kobe, Japan	5 Mar 1986
60 m hurdles	7.30	Colin Jackson (GB)	Sindelfingen, Germany	6 Feb 1994
4 x 200 m relay	1:22.11	Great Britain & N. Ireland (Linford Christie, Darren Braithwaite, Ade Mafe, John Regis)	Glasgow, UK	3 Mar 1991
4 x 400 m relay	3:02.83	USA (Andre Morris, Dameon Johnson, Deon Minor, Milton Campbell)	Maebashi, Japan	7 Mar 1999
4 x 800 m relay	7:13.94	Global Athletics & Marketing, USA (Joey Woody, Karl Paranya, Rich Kenah, David Krummenacker)	Boston, USA	6 Feb 2000
5,000 m walk	18:07.08	Mikhail Shchennikov (Russia)	Moscow, Russia	14 Feb 1995

WOMEN	TIME/DISTANCE	NAME & NATIONALITY	LOCATION	DATE
50 m	5.96	Irina Privalova (Russia)	Madrid, Spain	9 Feb 1995
60 m	6.92	Irina Privalova (Russia)	Madrid, Spain	11 Feb 1993
	6.92	Irina Privalova (Russia)	Madrid, Spain	9 Feb 1995
200 m	21.87	Merlene Ottey (Jamaica)	Liévin, France	13 Feb 1993
400 m	49.59	Jarmila Kratochvílová (Czechoslovakia)	Milan, Italy	7 Mar 1982
800 m	1:55.82	Jolanda Ceplak (Slovenia)	Vienna, Austria	3 Mar 2002
1,000 m	2:30.94	Maria de Lurdes Mutola (Mozambique)	Stockholm, Sweden	25 Feb 1999
1,500 m	3:58.28	Yelena Soboleva (Russia)	Moscow, Russia	18 Feb 2006
1 mile	4:17.14	Doina Melinte (Romania)	East Rutherford, USA	9 Feb 1990
3,000 m	8:23.72	Meseret Defar (Ethiopia)	Stuttgart, Germany	3 Feb 2007
5,000 m	14:24.37	Meseret Defar (Ethiopia)	Stockholm, Sweden	18 Feb 2009
50 m hurdles	6.58	Cornelia Oschkenat (GDR)	Berlin, Germany	20 Feb 1988
60 m hurdles	7.68	Susanna Kallur (Sweden)	Karlsruhe, Germany	10 Feb 2008
4 x 200 m relay	1:32.41	Russia (Yekaterina Kondratyeva, Irina Khabarova, Yuliya Pechonkina, Yulia Gushchina)	Glasgow, UK	29 Jan 2005
4 x 400 m relay	3:23.37	Russia (Yulia Gushchina, Olga Kotlyarova, Olga Zaytseva, Olesya Krasnomovets)	Glasgow, UK	28 Jan 2006
4 x 800 m relay	8:18.54	Moskovskaya Region (Anna Balakshina, Natalya Pantelyeva, Anna Emashova, Olesya Chumakova)	Volgograd, Russia	11 Feb 2007
3,000 m walk	11:40.33	Claudia Stef (Romania)	Bucharest, Romania	30 Jan 1999

ATHLETICS – ULTRA LONG DISTANCE (TRACK)

MEN	TIME/DISTANCE	NAME & NATIONALITY	LOCATION	DATE
50 km	2:48.06	Jeff Norman (GB)	Timperley, UK	7 Jun 1980
100 km	6:10:20	Donald Ritchie (GB)	London, UK	28 Oct 1978
100 miles	11:28:03	Oleg Kharitonov (Russia)	London, UK	20 Oct 2002
★ 1,000 km	5 days 16:17:00	Yiannis Kouros (Greece)	Colac, Australia	26 Nov–1 Dec 1984
1,000 miles	11 days 13:54:58	Peter Silkinas (Lithuania)	Nanango, Australia	11–23 Mar 1998
6 hours	97.2 km (60.4 miles)	Donald Ritchie (GB)	London, UK	28 Oct 1978
★ 12 hours	162.4 km (100.91 miles)	Yiannis Kouros (Greece)	Montauban, France	15–16 Mar 1985
★ 24 hours	303.506 km (188.59 miles)	Yiannis Kouros (Greece)	Adelaide, Australia	4–5 Oct 1997
★ 48 hours	473.495 km (294.21 miles)	Yiannis Kouros (Greece)	Surgères, France	3–5 May 1996
★ 6 days	1,038.851 km (645.51 miles)	Yiannis Kouros (Greece)	Colac, Australia	20–25 Nov 2005

WOMEN	TIME/DISTANCE	NAME & NATIONALITY	LOCATION	DATE
50 km	3:18:52	Carolyn Hunter-Rowe (GB)	Barry, South Wales, UK	3 Mar 1996
★ 100 km	7:00:27	Norimi Sakurai (Japan)	Winschoten, the Netherlands	8 Sep 2007
100 miles	14:25:45	Edit Berces (Hungary)	Verona, Italy	21–22 Sep 2002
★ 1,000 km	7 days 01:28:29	Eleanor Robinson (GB)	Nanango, Australia	11–18 Mar 1998
1,000 miles	13 days 1:54:02	Eleanor Robinson (GB)	Nanango, Australia	11–23 Mar 1998
6 hours	83.2 km (57.7 miles)	Norimi Sakurai (Japan)	Verona, Italy	27 Sep 2003
12 hours	147.6 km (91.71 miles)	Ann Trason (USA)	Hayward, USA	3–4 Aug 1991
24 hours	250.106 km (155.40 miles)	Edit Berces (Hungary)	Verona, Italy	21–22 Sep 2002
★ 48 hours	382.777 km (237.85 miles)	Inagaki Sumie (Japan)	Surgères, France	16–18 May 2008
6 days	883.631 km (549.06 miles)	Sandra Barwick (New Zealand)	Campbelltown, Australia	18–24 Nov 1990

OFFICIAL WEBSITES

Athletics:
www.iaaf.org

Ultrarunning:
www.iau.org.tw

★ NEW RECORD
UPDATED RECORD

Dec 19: The **greatest distance covered by an electric vehicle in 24 hours** is 2,142.317 km (1,330.828 miles) on 19–20 December 1999 by the Mitsubishi FTO-EV.

SPORTS REFERENCE

ATHLETICS – ROAD RACE

MEN	TIME	NAME & NATIONALITY	LOCATION	DATE
10 km	27:02	Haile Gebrselassie (Ethiopia)	Hoha, Qatar	11 Dec 2002
15 km	41:29	Felix Limo (Kenya)	Nijmegen, the Netherlands	11 Nov 2001
	•41:29	Deriba Merga (Ethiopia)	Ras Al Khaimah, UAE	20 Feb 2009
20 km	55.48	Haile Gebrselassie (Ethiopia)	Phoenix, USA	15 Jan 2006
Half marathon	58.33	Samuel Wanjiru (Kenya)	The Hague, the Netherlands	17 Mar 2007
25 km	1:12:45	Paul Malakwen Kosgei (Kenya)	Berlin, Germany	9 May 2004
30 km	1:28:00	Takayuki Matsumiya (Japan)	Kumamoto, Japan	27 Feb 2005
Marathon	2:03:59	Haile Gebrselassie (Ethiopia)	Berlin, Germany	28 Sep 2008
100 km	6:13:33	Takahiro Sunada (Japan)	Tokoro, Japan	21 Jun 1998
Road relay	1:57:06	Kenya (Josephat Ndambiri, Martin Mathathi, Daniel Mwangi, Mekubo Mogusu, Onesmus Nyerere, John Kariuki)	Chiba, Japan	23 Nov 2005

WOMEN	TIME	NAME & NATIONALITY	LOCATION	DATE
10 km	30:21	Paula Radcliffe (GB)	San Juan, Puerto Rico	23 Feb 2003
15 km	46:55	Kayoko Fukushi (Japan)	Marugame, Japan	5 Feb 2006
20 km	1:02:57	Lornah Kiplagat (Netherlands)	Udine, Italy	14 Oct 2007
Half marathon	1:06:25	Lornah Kiplagat (Netherlands)	Udine, Italy	14 Oct 2007
25 km	1:22:13	Mizuki Noguchi (Japan)	Berlin, Germany	25 Sep 2005
30 km	1:38:49	Mizuki Noguchi (Japan)	Berlin, Germany	25 Sep 2005
Marathon	2:15:25	Paula Radcliffe (GB)	London, UK	13 Apr 2003
100 km	6:33:11	Tomoe Abe (Japan)	Tokoro, Japan	25 Jun 2000
Road relay	2:11:41	China (Jiang Bo, Dong Yanmei, Zhao Fengdi, Ma Zaijie, Lan Lixin, Li Na)	Beijing, China	28 Feb 1998

• *Still awaiting ratification at the time of going to press*

15 KM ROAD RACE

Deriba Merga (Ethiopia) runs the marathon at the 2008 Olympic Games in Beijing, China. On 20 February 2009, Merga equalled Kenyan Felix Limo's 15 km road race record in a time of 41 min 29 sec in Ras Al Khaimah, UAE.

ATHLETICS – RACE WALKING

MEN	TIME	NAME & NATIONALITY	LOCATION	DATE
20,000 m	1:17:25.6	Bernardo Segura (Mexico)	Bergen, Norway	7 May 1994
20 km (road)	1:17:16	Vladimir Kanaykin (Russia)	Saransk, Russia	29 Sep 2007
30,000 m	2:01:44.1	Maurizio Damilano (Italy)	Cuneo, Italy	3 Oct 1992
50,000 m	3:40:57.9	Thierry Toutain (France)	Héricourt, France	29 Sep 1996
50 km (road)	3:34:14	Denis Nizhegorodov (Russia)	Cheboksary, Russia	11 May 2008

WOMEN	TIME	NAME & NATIONALITY	LOCATION	DATE
10,000 m	41.56.23	Nadezhda Ryashkina (USSR)	Seattle, USA	24 Jul 1990
20,000 m	1:26:52.3	Olimpiada Ivanova (Russia)	Brisbane, Australia	6 Sep 2001
20 km (road)	1:25:41	Olimpiada Ivanova (Russia)	Helsinki, Finland	7 Aug 2005

ATHLETICS – INDOOR FIELD EVENTS

MEN	RECORD	NAME & NATIONALITY	LOCATION	DATE
High jump	2.43 m (7 ft 11.66 in)	Javier Sotomayor (Cuba)	Budapest, Hungary	4 Mar 1989
Pole vault	6.15 m (20 ft 2.12 in)	Sergei Bubka (Ukraine)	Donetsk, Ukraine	21 Feb 1993
Long jump	8.79 m (28 ft 10.06 in)	Carl Lewis (USA)	New York City, USA	27 Jan 1984
Triple jump	17.83 m (58 ft 5.96 in)	Aliecer Urrutia (Cuba)	Sindelfingen, Germany	1 Mar 1997
	17.83 m (58 ft 5.96 in)	Christian Olsson (Sweden)	Budapest, Hungary	7 Mar 2004
Shot	22.66 m (74 ft 4.12 in)	Randy Barnes (USA)	Los Angeles, USA	20 Jan 1989
Heptathlon*	6,476 points	Dan O'Brien (USA)	Toronto, Canada	14 Mar 1993

WOMEN	RECORD	NAME & NATIONALITY	LOCATION	DATE
High jump	2.08 m (6 ft 9.8 in)	Kajsa Bergqvist (Sweden)	Arnstadt, Germany	4 Feb 2006
Pole vault	•5.00 m (16 ft 4 in)	Yelena Isinbayeva (Russia)	Donetsk, Ukraine	15 Feb 2009
Long jump	7.37 m (24 ft 2.15 in)	Heike Drechsler (GDR)	Vienna, Austria	13 Feb 1988
Triple jump	15.36 m (50 ft 4.72 in)	Tatyana Lebedeva (Russia)	Budapest, Hungary	6 Mar 2004
Shot	22.50 m (73 ft 9.82 in)	Helena Fibingerová (Czechoslovakia)	Jablonec, Czechoslovakia	19 Feb 1977
Pentathlon†	4,991 points	Irina Belova (Russia)	Berlin, Germany	15 Feb 1992

* 60 m 6.67 seconds; long jump 7.84 m; shot 16.02 m; high jump 2.13 m; 60 m hurdles 7.85 seconds; pole vault 5.20 m; 1,000 m 2 min 57.96 sec

† 60 m hurdles 8.22 seconds; high jump 1.93 m; shot 13.25 m; long jump 6.67 m; 800 m 2 min 10.26 sec

• *Still awaiting ratification at the time of going to press*

Dec 20: The world's **largest Christmas cracker** measured 63.1 m (207 ft) long and 4 m (13 ft) in diameter and was made at Ley Hill School, Chesham, Buckinghamshire, UK, on 20 December 2001.

Dec 21: The **first crossword clue** appeared in the US newspaper *New York World* on 21 December 1913. The clue was "What bargain hunters enjoy." The answer? "Sales."

26: Guinness World Records broken by Haile Gebrselassie (Ethiopia), making him one of the greatest distance runners in history.

ATHLETICS – OUTDOOR FIELD EVENTS

MEN	RECORD	NAME & NATIONALITY	LOCATION	DATE
High jump	2.45 m (8 ft 0.45 in)	Javier Sotomayor (Cuba)	Salamanca, Spain	27 Jul 1993
Pole vault	6.14 m (20 ft 1.73 in)	Sergei Bubka (Ukraine)	Sestriere, Italy	31 Jul 1994
Long jump	8.95 m (29 ft 4.36 in)	Mike Powell (USA)	Tokyo, Japan	30 Aug 1991
Triple jump	18.29 m (60 ft 0.78 in)	Jonathan Edwards (GB)	Gothenburg, Sweden	7 Aug 1995
Shot	23.12 m (75 ft 10.23 in)	Randy Barnes (USA)	Los Angeles, USA	20 May 1990
Discus	74.08 m (243 ft 0.53 in)	Jürgen Schult (USSR)	Neubrandenburg, Germany	6 Jun 1986
Hammer	86.74 m (284 ft 7 in)	Yuriy Sedykh (USSR)	Stuttgart, Germany	30 Aug 1986
Javelin	98.48 m (323 ft 1.16 in)	Jan Železný (Czech Republic)	Jena, Germany	25 May 1996
Decathlon*	9,026 points	Roman Šebrle (Czech Republic)	Götzis, Austria	27 May 2001

WOMEN	RECORD	NAME & NATIONALITY	LOCATION	DATE
High jump	2.09 m (6 ft 10.28 in)	Stefka Kostadinova (Bulgaria)	Rome, Italy	30 Aug 1987
Pole vault	5.05 m (16 ft 6 in)	Yelena Isinbayeva (Russia)	Beijing, China	18 Aug 2008
Long jump	7.52 m (24 ft 8.06 in)	Galina Chistyakova (USSR)	St. Petersburg, Russia	11 Jun 1988
Triple jump	15.50 m (50 ft 10.23 in)	Inessa Kravets (Ukraine)	Gothenburg, Sweden	10 Aug 1995
Shot	22.63 m (74 ft 2.94 in)	Natalya Lisovskaya (USSR)	Moscow, Russia	7 Jun 1987
Discus	76.80 m (252 ft)	Gabriele Reinsch (GDR)	Neubrandenburg, Germany	9 Jul 1988
Hammer	77.80 m (255 ft 3 in)	Tatyana Lysenko (Russia)	Tallinn, Estonia	15 Aug 2006
Javelin	72.28 m (253 ft 6 in)	Barbora Spotáková (Czech Republic)	Stuttgart, Germany	13 Sep 2008
Heptathlon†	7,291 points	Jacqueline Joyner-Kersee (USA)	Seoul, South Korea	24 Sep 1988
Decathlon**	8,358 points	Austra Skujyte (Lithuania)	Columbia, USA	15 Apr 2005

* *100 m 10.64 seconds; long jump 8.11 m; shot 15.33 m; high jump 2.12 m; 400 m 47.79 seconds; 110 m hurdles 13.92 seconds; discus 47.92 m; pole vault 4.80 m; javelin 70.16 m; 1,500 m 4 min 21.98 sec*

† *100 m hurdles 12.69 seconds; high jump 1.86 m; shot 15.80 m; 200 m 22.56 seconds; long jump 7.27 m; javelin 45.66 m; 800 m 2 min 8.51 sec*

** *100 m 12.49 seconds; long jump 6.12 m; shot 16.42 m; high jump 1.78 m; 400 m 57.19 seconds; 100 m hurdles 14.22 seconds; discus 46.19 m; pole vault 3.10 m; javelin 48.78 m; 1,500 m 5 min 15.86 sec*

CYCLING – ABSOLUTE TRACK

MEN	TIME/DISTANCE	NAME & NATIONALITY	LOCATION	DATE
200 m *(flying start)*	9.772	Theo Bos (Netherlands)	Moscow Russia	16 Dec 2006
500 m *(flying start)*	24.758	Chris Hoy (GB)	La Paz, Bolivia	13 May 2007
1 km *(standing start)*	58.875	Arnaud Tournant (France)	La Paz, Bolivia	10 Oct 2001
4 km *(standing start)*	4:11.114	Christopher Boardman (GB)	Manchester, UK	29 Aug 1996
Team 4 km *(standing start)*	3:53.314	Great Britain (Ed Clancy, Paul Manning, Geraint Thomas, Bradley Wiggins)	Beijing, China	18 Aug 2008
1 hour	*49.7 km	Ondrej Sosenka (Czech Republic)	Moscow, Russia	19 Jul 2005

WOMEN	TIME/DISTANCE	NAME & NATIONALITY	LOCATION	DATE
200 m *(flying start)*	10.831	Olga Slioussareva (Russia)	Moscow, Russia	25 Apr 1993
500 m *(flying start)*	29.655	Erika Salumäe (Estonia)	Moscow, Russia	6 Aug 1987
500 m *(standing start)*	33.588	Anna Meares (Australia)	Palma de Mallorca, Spain	31 Mar 2007
3 km *(standing start)*	3:24.537	Sarah Ulmer (New Zealand)	Athens, Greece	22 Aug 2004
1 hour	*46.065 km	Leontien Zijlaard-Van Moorsel (Netherlands)	Mexico City, Mexico	1 Oct 2003

Some athletes achieved better distances within an hour with bicycles that are no longer allowed by the Union Cycliste Internationale (UCI). The 1-hour records given here are in accordance with the new UCI rules

OFFICIAL WEBSITES

Athletics & Race Walking:
www.iaaf.org

Cycling:
www.uci.ch

★ **NEW RECORD**
UPDATED RECORD

4 KM TEAM CYCLING

Gold medallists Paul Manning, Ed Clancy, Geraint Thomas and Bradley Wiggins (all GB) celebrate after the men's team pursuit finals at the Laoshan Velodrome on Day 10 of the 2008 Olympic Games on 18 August 2008 in Beijing, China. They achieved a time of 3 min 53.314 sec.

Dec 22: The record for the **most lights lit simultaneously on a Christmas tree** is 150,000 by RTL Television GmbH, Germany, on 22 December 2006 at Cologne Cathedral, Cologne, Germany.

WWW.GUINNESSWORLDRECORDS.COM

SPORTS REFERENCE

FREEDIVING

MEN'S DEPTH DISCIPLINES	DEPTH/TIME	NAME & NATIONALITY	LOCATION	DATE
Constant weight with fins	120 m (393 ft 8 in)	Herbert Nitsch (Austria)	The Bahamas	11 Apr 2009
Constant weight without fins	88 m (288 ft 8 in)	William Trubridge (New Zealand)	The Bahamas	10 Apr 2009
Variable weight	140 m 259 ft 4 in)	Carlos Coste (Venezuela)	Sharm el Sheikh, Egypt	9 May 2006
No limit	214 m (702 ft)	Herbert Nitsch (Austria)	Spetses, Greece	14 Jun 2007
Free immersion	109 m 357 ft 7 in)	Herbert Nitsch (Austria)	The Bahamas	6 Apr 2009
MEN'S DYNAMIC APNEA				
With fins	250 m (800 ft 2 in)	Alexey Molchanov (Russia)	Lignano, Italy	5 Oct 2008
Without fins	213 m (698 ft 9 in)	Tom Sietas (Germany)	Hamburg, Germany	2 Jul 2008
	213 m (698 ft 9 in)	Dave Mullins (New Zealand)	Wellington, New Zealand	12 Aug 2008
MEN'S STATIC APNEA				
Duration	10 min 12 sec	Tom Sietas (Germany)	Athens, Greece	7 Jun 2008
WOMEN'S DEPTH DISCIPLINES				
Constant weight with fins	96 m (314 ft 11 in)	Sara Campbell (UK)	The Bahamas	2 Apr 2009
Constant weight without fins	60 m 196 ft 10 in)	Natalia Molchanova (Russia)	Dahab, Egypt	12 Jun 2008
Variable weight	122 m (400 ft 3 in)	Tanya Streeter (USA)	Turks and Caicos Islands	19 Jul 2003
No limit	160 m (524 ft 11 in)	Tanya Streeter (USA)	Turks and Caicos Islands	17 Aug 2002
Free immersion	85 m (278 ft 10 in)	Natalia Molchanova (Russia)	Crete, Greece	27 Jul 2008
WOMEN'S DYNAMIC APNEA				
With fins	214 m (702 ft 1 in)	Natalia Molchanova (Russia)	Lignano, Italy	5 Oct 2008
Without fins	151 m (495 ft 4 in)	Kathryn McPhee (New Zealand)	Wellington, New Zealand	9 Aug 2008
WOMEN'S STATIC APNEA				
Duration	8 min 0 sec	Natalia Molchanova (Russia)	Maribor, Slovenia	6 Jul 2007

MEN'S DEPTH

Herbert Nitsch (Austria) dives at Dean's Blue Hole, Bahamas. He holds the world record in three depth disciplines: constant weight with fins, constant weight without fins as well as free immersion.

ROWING

MEN	TIME	NAME & NATIONALITY	LOCATION	DATE
Single sculls	6:35.40	Mahe Drysdale (New Zealand)	Eton, UK	26 Aug 2006
Double sculls	6:03.25	Jean-Baptiste, Adrien Hardy (France)	Poznan, Poland	17 Jun 2006
Quadruple sculls	5:36.20	Christopher Morgan, James McRae, Brendan Long, Daniel Noonan (Australia)	Beijing, China	10 Aug 2008
Coxless pairs	6:14.27	Matthew Pinsent, James Cracknell (GB)	Seville, Spain	21 Sep 2002
Coxless fours	5:41.35	Sebastian Thormann, Paul Dienstbach, Philipp Stüer, Bernd Heidicker (Germany)	Seville, Spain	21 Sep 2002
Coxed pairs*	6:42.16	Igor Boraska, Tihomir Frankovic, Milan Razov (Croatia)	Indianapolis, USA	18 Sep 1994
Coxed fours*	5:58.96	Matthias Ungemach, Armin Eichholz, Armin Weyrauch, Bahne Rabe, Jörg Dederding (Germany)	Vienna, Austria	24 Aug 1991
Coxed eights	5:19.85	Deakin, Beery, Hoopman, Volpenhein, Cipollone, Read, Allen, Ahrens, Hansen (USA)	Athens, Greece	15 Aug 2004
LIGHTWEIGHT				
Single sculls*	6:47.82	Zac Purchase (GB)	Eton, UK	26 Aug 2006
Double sculls	6:10.02	Mads Rasmussen, Rasmus Quist (Denmark)	Amsterdam, the Netherlands	23 Jun 2007
Quadruple sculls*	5:45.18	Francesco Esposito, Massimo Lana, Michaelangelo Crispi, Massimo Guglielmi (Italy)	Montreal, Canada	Aug 1992
Coxless	6:26.61	Tony O'Connor, Neville Maxwell (Ireland)	Paris, France	1994
Coxless fours	5:45.60	Thomas Poulsen, Thomas Ebert, Eskild Ebbesen, Victo Feddersen (Denmark)	Lucerne, Switzerland	9 Jul 1999
Coxed eights*	5:30.24	Altena, Dahlke, Kobor, Stomporowski, Melges, März, Buchheit, Von Warburg, Kaska (Germany)	Montreal, Canada	Aug 1992
WOMEN				
Single sculls	7:07.71	Rumyana Neykova (Bulgaria)	Seville, Spain	21 Sep 2002
Double sculls	6:38.78	Georgina and Caroline Evers-Swindell (New Zealand)	Seville, Spain	21 Sep 2002
Quadruple sculls	6:10.80	Kathrin Boron, Katrin Rutschow-Stomporowski, Jana Sorgers, Kerstin Köppen (Germany)	Duisburg, Germany	19 May 1996
Coxless pairs	6:53.80	Georgeta Andrunache, Viorica Susanu (Romania)	Seville, Spain	21 Sep 2002
Coxless fours*	6:25.35	Robyn Selby Smith, Jo Lutz, Amber Bradley, Kate Hornsey (Australia)	Eton, UK	26 Aug 2006
Coxed eights	5:55.50	Mickelson, Whipple, Lind, Goodale, Sickler, Cooke, Shoop, Francia, Davies (USA)	Eton, UK	27 Aug 2006
LIGHTWEIGHT				
Single sculls*	7:28.15	Constanta Pipota (Romania)	Paris, France	19 Jun 1994
Double sculls	6:49.77	Dongxiang Xu, Shimin Yan (China)	Poznan, Poland	17 Jun 2006
Quadruple sculls*	6:23.95	Hua Yu, Haixia Chen, Xuefei Fan, Jing Liu (China)	Eton, UK	27 Aug 2006
Coxless pairs*	7:18.32	Eliza Blair, Justine Joyce (Australia)	Aiguebelette-le-Lac, France	7 Sep 1997

*Denotes non-Olympic boat classes

Dec 23: The **youngest band to have a recording banned** from radio play is Who's Ya Daddy? (Australia; average age 12 years 26 days). "I Like Fat Chicks" was banned from ZZZ FM on 23 December 2004.

Dec 24: The world's **first passenger-carrying car** was a steam-powered road vehicle carrying eight passengers, built by Richard Trevithick (GB). It first ran at Camborne, Cornwall, UK, on 24 December 1801.

8: minutes that Natalia Molchanova (Russia) can hold her breath without using supplemental oxygen.

SPEED SKATING – LONG TRACK

MEN	TIME/POINTS	NAME & NATIONALITY	LOCATION	DATE
500 m	34.03	Jeremy Wotherspoon (Canada)	Salt Lake City, USA	9 Nov 2007
2 x 500 m	68.31	Jeremy Wotherspoon (Canada)	Calgary, Canada	15 Mar 2008
1,000 m	1:06.42	Shani Davis (USA)	Salt Lake City, USA	7 Mar 2009
1,500 m	1:41.80	Shani Davis (USA)	Salt Lake City, USA	6 Mar 2009
3,000 m	3:37.28	Eskil Ervik (Norway)	Calgary, Canada	5 Nov 2005
5,000 m	6:03.32	Sven Kramer (Netherlands)	Calgary, Canada	17 Nov 2007
10,000 m	12:41.69	Sven Kramer (Netherlands)	Salt Lake City, USA	10 Mar 2007
500/1,000/500/1,000 m	137.230 points	Jeremy Wotherspoon (Canada)	Calgary, Canada	18–19 Jan 2003
500/3,000/1,500/5,000 m	146.365 points	Erben Wennemars (Netherlands)	Calgary, Canada	12–13 Aug 2005
500/5,000/1,500/10,000 m	145.742 points	Shani Davis (USA)	Calgary, Canada	18–19 Mar 2006
Team pursuit (8 laps)	3:37.80	Netherlands (Sven Kramer, Carl Verheijen, Erben Wennemars)	Salt Lake City, USA	11 Mar 2007

WOMEN	TIME/POINTS	NAME & NATIONALITY	LOCATION	DATE
500 m	37.02	Jenny Wolf (Germany)	Calgary, Canada	16 Nov 2007
2 x 500 m	74.42	Jenny Wolf (Germany)	Salt Lake City, USA	10 Mar 2007
1,000 m	1:13.11	Cindy Klassen (Canada)	Calgary, Canada	25 Mar 2006
1,500 m	1:51.79	Cindy Klassen (Canada)	Salt Lake City, USA	20 Nov 2005
3,000 m	3:53.34	Cindy Klassen (Canada)	Salt Lake City, USA	18 Mar 2006
5,000 m	6:45.61	Martina Sáblíková (Czech Republic)	Salt Lake City, USA	11 Mar 2007
500/1,000/500/1,000 m	149.305 points	Monique Garbrecht-Enfeldt (Germany)	Salt Lake City, USA	11–12 Jan 2003
	149.305 points	Cindy Klassen (Canada)	Calgary, Canada	24–25 Mar 2006
500/1,500/1,000/3,000 m	155.576 points	Cindy Klassen (Canada)	Calgary, Canada	15–17 Mar 2001
500/3,000/1,500/5,000 m	154.580 points	Cindy Klassen (Canada)	Calgary, Canada	18–19 Mar 2006
Team pursuit (8 laps)	2:56.04	Germany (Daniela Anschütz, Anni Friesinger, Claudia Pechstein)	Calgary, Canada	13 Nov 2005

SPEED SKATING – SHORT TRACK

MEN	TIME/POINTS	NAME & NATIONALITY	LOCATION	DATE
500 m	41.051	Sung Si-Bak (South Korea)	Salt Lake City, USA	10 Feb 2008
1,000 m	•1:23.454	Charles Hamelin (Canada)	Montreal, Canada	18 Jan 2009
1,500 m	2:10.639	Ahn Hyun-Soo (South Korea)	Marquette, USA	24 Oct 2003
3,000 m	4:32.646	Ahn Hyun-Soo (South Korea)	Beijing, China	7 Dec 2003
5,000 m relay	•6:38.486	South Korea (Kwak Yoon-Gy, Lee Ho-Suk, Lee Jung-Su, Sung Si-Bak)	Salt Lake City, USA	19 Oct 2008

WOMEN	TIME/POINTS	NAME & NATIONALITY	LOCATION	DATE
500 m	•42.609	Wang Meng (China)	Beijing, China	29 Nov 2008
1,000 m	1:29.495	Wang Meng (China)	Harbin, China	15 Mar 2008
1,500 m	2:16.729	Zhou Yang (China)	Salt Lake City, USA	9 Feb 2008
3,000 m	4:46.983	Jung Eun-Ju (South Korea)	Harbin, China	15 Mar 2008
3,000 m relay	•4:07.179	China (Liu Qiuhong, Wang Meng, Zhang Hui, Zhou Yang)	Salt Lake City, USA	18 Oct 2008

•*Still awaiting ratification at the time of going to press*

★ **NEW RECORD**
UPDATED RECORD

MEN'S 500 M SHORT TRACK

Sung Si-Bak (South Korea) competes at the Samsung ISU Short Track World Cup 2008/2009 in Nagano, Japan. On 10 February 2008, he achieved a time of 41.051 seconds in this event. He was also part of the team that holds the 5,000 m relay record.

OFFICIAL WEBSITES

Freediving:
www.aida-international.org

Rowing:
www.worldrowing.com

Speed skating:
www.isu.org

WOMEN'S 1,500 M SHORT TRACK

China's Zhou Yang leads, followed by Katherine Reutter (USA) and Jung Eun-Ju (South Korea) in the women's 1,500 m finals at the 2008 ISU Short Track World Cup on 9 February 2008. Zhou Yang won in a time of 2 min 16.729 sec.

Dec 25: From 1922 to 25 December 1973, Tommy Chambers (UK, 1903–84) rode a verified total of 1,286,517 km (799,405 miles), the **greatest distance cycled in a lifetime**.

SPORTS REFERENCE

SWIMMING – LONG COURSE (50 M POOL)

MEN	TIME	NAME & NATIONALITY	LOCATION	DATE
50 m freestyle	•20.94	Frederick Bousquet (France)	Montpellier, France	26 Apr 2009
100 m freestyle	•46.94	Alain Bernard (France)	Montpellier, France	23 Apr 2009
200 m freestyle	1:42.96	Michael Phelps (USA)	Beijing, China	12 Aug 2008
400 m freestyle	3:40.08	Ian Thorpe (Australia)	Manchester, UK	30 Jul 2002
800 m freestyle	7:38.65	Grant Hackett (Australia)	Montreal, Canada	27 Jul 2005
1,500 m freestyle	14:34.56	Grant Hackett (Australia)	Fukuoka, Japan	29 Jul 2001
4 x 100 m freestyle relay	3:08.24	USA (Michael Phelps, Garrett Weber-Gale, Cullen Jones, Jason Lezak)	Beijing, China	11 Aug 2008
4 x 200 m freestyle relay	6:58.56	USA (Michael Phelps, Ryan Lochte, Ricky Berens, Peter Vanderkaay)	Beijing, China	13 Aug 2008
50 m butterfly	•22.43	Rafael Munoz (Spain)	Malaga, Spain	5 Apr 2009
100 m butterfly	50.40	Ian Crocker (USA)	Montreal, Canada	30 Jul 2005
200 m butterfly	1:52.03	Michael Phelps (USA)	Beijing, China	13 Aug 2008
50 m backstroke	24.33	Randall Bal (USA)	Eindhoven, the Netherlands	5 Dec 2008
100 m backstroke	52.54	Aaron Peirsol (USA)	Beijing, China	12 Aug 2008
200 m backstroke	•1:52.86	Ryosuke Irie (Japan)	Canberra, Australia	10 May 2009
50 m breaststroke	•27.06	Cameron van der Burgh (South Africa)	Durban, South Africa	18 Apr 2009
100 m breaststroke	58.91	Kosuke Kitajima (Japan)	Beijing, China	11 Aug 2008
200 m breaststroke	2:07.51	Kosuke Kitajima (Japan)	Tokyo, Japan	8 Jun 2008
200 m medley	1:54.23	Michael Phelps (USA)	Beijing, China	15 Aug 2008
400 m medley	4:03.84	Michael Phelps (USA)	Beijing, China	10 Aug 2008
4 x 100 m medley relay	3:29.34	USA (Aaron Peirsol, Brendan Hansen, Michael Phelps, Jason Lezak)	Beijing, China	17 Aug 2008

WOMEN	TIME	NAME & NATIONALITY	LOCATION	DATE
50 m freestyle	•23.96	Marleen Veldhuis (Netherlands)	Amsterdam, the Netherlands	19 Apr 2009
100 m freestyle	52.88	Lisbeth Trickett (Australia)	Sydney, Australia	27 Mar 2008
200 m freestyle	•1:54.47	Federica Pellegrini (Italy)	Riccione, Italy	8 Mar 2009
400 m freestyle	•4:00.66	Joanne Jackson (UK)	Sheffield, UK	16 Mar 2009
800 m freestyle	8:14.10	Rebecca Adlington (UK)	Beijing, China	16 Aug 2008
1,500 m freestyle	15:42.54	Kate Ziegler (USA)	Mission Viejo, USA	17 Jun 2007
4 x 100 m freestyle relay	3:33.62	Netherlands (Inge Dekker, Ranomi Kromowidjojo, Femke Heemskerk, Marleen Veldhuis)	Eindhoven, the Netherlands	18 Mar 2008
4 x 200 m freestyle relay	7:44.31	Australia (Stephanie Rice, Bronte Barratt, Kylie Palmer, Linda Mackenzie)	Beijing, China	13 Aug 2008
50 m butterfly	•25.33	Marleen Veldhuis (Netherlands)	Amsterdam, Netherlands	19 Apr 2009
100 m butterfly	56.61	Inge de Bruijn (Netherlands)	Sydney, Australia	17 Sep 2000
200 m butterfly	2:04.18	Liu Zige (China)	Beijing, China	14 Aug 2008
50 m backstroke	27.67	Sophie Edington (Australia)	Sydney, Australia	23 Mar 2008
100 m backstroke	58.77	Kirsty Coventry (Zimbabwe)	Beijing, China	11 Aug 2008
200 m backstroke	2:05.24	Kirsty Coventry (Zimbabwe)	Beijing, China	16 Aug 2008
50 m breaststroke	30.31	Jade Edmistone (Australia)	Melbourne, Australia	30 Jan 2006
100 m breaststroke	1:05.09	Leisel Jones (Australia)	Melbourne, Australia	20 Mar 2006
200 m breaststroke	2:20.22	Rebecca Soni (USA)	Beijing, China	15 Aug 2008
200 m medley	2:08.45	Stephanie Rice (Australia)	Beijing, China	13 Aug 2008
400 m medley	4:29.45	Stephanie Rice (Australia)	Beijing, China	10 Aug 2008
4 x 100 m medley relay	3:52.69	Australia (Emily Seebohm, Leisel Jones, Jessicah Schipper, Lisbeth Trickett)	Beijing, China	17 Aug 2008

• *Still awaiting ratification at the time of going to press*

MEN'S 100 M FREESTYLE

French swimmer Alain Bernard (above) celebrates setting a new world record after winning the semi-final of the men's 100 m freestyle (long course) with a time of 46.94 seconds, during the French Swimming Championships on 23 April 2009 in Montpellier, France.

Three days later, at the same event, Frederick Bousquet (France) set a new world best for the 50 m freestyle with a time of 20.94 seconds.

WOMEN'S 200 M BUTTERFLY

Liu Zige (China) swims in the 200 m butterfly final on Day 6 of the 2008 Olympic Games on 14 August 2008 in Beijing, China. She won the race and set a new record of 2 min 4.18 sec.

Dec 26: On 26 December 2005, at the age of three years, Cranston Chipperfield (UK) became the **youngest person to take the stage as a circus ringmaster**, at the Circus Royale, Lanarkshire, UK.

Dec 27: Vesta Gueschkova (Bulgaria) was launched 22.9 m (75 ft) from a crossbow in Tampa, Florida, USA, on 27 December 1995 – the **longest distance a human has been fired as an arrow**.

SWIMMING – SHORT COURSE (25 M POOL)

MEN	TIME	NAME & NATIONALITY	LOCATION	DATE
50 m freestyle	20.48	Amaury Leveaux (France)	Rijeka, Croatia	11 Dec 2008
100 m freestyle	44.94	Amaury Leveaux (France)	Rijeka, Croatia	13 Dec 2008
200 m freestyle	1:40.83	Paul Biederman (Germany)	Berlin, Germany	16 Nov 2008
400 m freestyle	3:34.58	Grant Hackett (Australia)	Sydney, Australia	18 Jul 2002
800 m freestyle	7:23.42	Grant Hackett (Australia)	Melbourne, Australia	20 Jul 2008
1,500 m freestyle	14:10.10	Grant Hackett (Australia)	Perth, Australia	7 Aug 2001
4 x 100 m freestyle relay	3:04.98	France (Grégory Mallet, Fabien Gilot, William Meynard, Frédérick Bousquet)	Istres, France	20 Dec 2008
4 x 200 m freestyle relay	6:52.66	Australia (Kirk Palmer, Grant Hackett, Grant Brits, Kenrick Monk)	Melbourne, Australia	31 Jul 2007
50 m butterfly	22.18	Amaury Leveaux (France)	Rijeka, Croatia	14 Dec 2008
100 m butterfly	49.07	Ian Crocker (USA)	New York City, USA	26 Mar 2004
200 m butterfly	•1:50.53	Nikolay Skvortsov (Russia)	St Petersburg, Russia	11 Feb 2009
50 m backstroke	22.87	Randall Bal (USA)	Berlin, Germany	16 Nov 2008
100 m backstroke	•49.20	Aschwin Wildeboer (Spain)	Madrid, Spain	21 Dec 2008
200 m backstroke	1:47.84	Markus Rogan (Australia)	Manchester, UK	13 Apr 2008
50 m breaststroke	25.94	Cameron van der Burgh (South Africa)	Stockholm, Sweden	11 Nov 2008
100 m breaststroke	56.88	Cameron van der Burgh (South Africa)	Moscow, Russia	9 Nov 2008
200 m breaststroke	2:02.92	Ed Moses (USA)	Berlin, Germany	17 Jan 2004
100 m medley	51.15	Ryan Lochte (USA)	Manchester, UK	13 Apr 2008
200 m medley	1:51.56	Ryan Lochte (USA)	Manchester, UK	11 Apr 2008
400 m medley	3:59.33	Laszlo Cseh (Hungary)	Debrecen, Hungary	14 Dec 2007
4 x 100 m medley relay	3:24.29	Russia (Stanislav Donets, Sergey Geybel, Evgeny Korotyshkin, Alexander Sukhorukov)	Manchester, UK	13 Apr 2008

WOMEN	TIME	NAME & NATIONALITY	LOCATION	DATE
50 m freestyle	23.25	Marleen Veldhuis (Netherlands)	Manchester, UK	13 Apr 2008
100 m freestyle	51.70	Lisbeth Lenton (later Trickett, Australia)	Melbourne, Australia	9 Aug 2005
200 m freestyle	1:51.85	Federica Pellegrini (Italy)	Rijeka, Croatia	14 Dec 2008
400 m freestyle	3:56.09	Laure Manaudou (France)	Helsinki, Finland	9 Dec 2006
800 m freestyle	8:04.53	Alessia Filippi (Italy)	Rijeka, Croatia	12 Dec 2008
1,500 m freestyle	15:32.90	Kate Ziegler (USA)	Essen, Germany	19 Oct 2007
4 x 100 m freestyle relay	3:28.22	Netherlands (Hinkelien Schreuder, Inge Dekker, Ranomi Kromowidjojo, Marleen Veldhuis)	Amsterdam, the Netherlands	19 Dec 2008
4 x 200 m freestyle relay	7:38.90	Netherlands (Inge Dekker, Femke Heemskerk, Marleen Veldhuis, Ranomi Kromowidjojo)	Manchester, UK	9 Apr 2008
50 m butterfly	24.99	Marieke Guehrer (Australia)	Berlin, Germany	16 Nov 2008
100 m butterfly	55.74	Lisbeth Trickett (Australia)	Canberra, Australia	26 Apr 2008
200 m butterfly	2:03.12	Nakanishi Yuko (Japan)	Tokyo, Japan	23 Feb 2008
50 m backstroke	26.23	Sanja Jovanovic (Croatia)	Rijeka, Croatia	13 Dec 2008
100 m backstroke	56.15	Sakai Shiho (Japan)	Tokyo, Japan	22 Feb 2009
200 m backstroke	2:00.91	Kirsty Coventry (Zimbabwe)	Manchester, UK	11 Apr 2008
50 m breaststroke	29.58	Jessica Hardy (USA)	Manchester, UK	10 Apr 2008
100 m breaststroke	1:03.72	Leisel Jones (Australia)	Canberra, Australia	26 Apr 2008
200 m breaststroke	•2:17.50	Annamay Pierse (Canada)	Toronto, Canada	14 Mar 2009
100 m medley	58.80	Natalie Coughlin (USA)	New York City, USA	23 Nov 2002
200 m medley	2:06.13	Kirsty Coventry (Zimbabwe)	Manchester, UK	12 Apr 2008
400 m medley	4:25.06	Mireia Belmonte (Spain)	Rijeka, Croatia	14 Dec 2008
4 x 100 m medley relay	3:51.36	USA (Margaret Hoelzer, Jessica Hardy, Rachel Komisarz, Kara Denby)	Manchester, UK	11 Apr 2008

• Still awaiting ratification at the time of going to press

MEN'S 50 M & 100 M BREASTSTROKE

Cameron van der Burgh (South Africa) dives in for the 50 m breaststroke on 11 November 2008 at the Short Course World Cup held in Stockholm, Sweden. He swam the event in a record 25.94 seconds.

Two days earlier, on 9 November 2008, van der Burgh also broke the 100 m breaststroke (short course) record by swimming it in 56.88 seconds in Moscow, Russia.

★ NEW RECORD
UPDATED RECORD

OFFICIAL WEBSITE

Swimming:
www.fina.org

WOMEN'S 50 M BUTTERFLY

A jubilant Marieke Guehrer (Australia) after swimming the women's 50 m butterfly at the FINA Short Course Swimming World Cup on 16 November 2008 in Berlin, Germany, in a time of 24.99 seconds.

Dec 28: The **first operating cinema** was the Cinématographe Lumière at the Salon Indien in Paris, France, opened under the management of Clément Maurice (France) on 28 December 1895.

273 WWW.GUINNESSWORLDRECORDS.COM

SPORTS REFERENCE

WEIGHTLIFTING

MEN	CATEGORY	WEIGHT LIFTED	NAME & NATIONALITY	LOCATION	DATE
56 kg	Snatch	138 kg	Halil Mutlu (Turkey)	Antalya, Turkey	4 Nov 2001
	Clean & jerk	168 kg	Halil Mutlu (Turkey)	Trencín, Slovakia	24 Apr 2001
	Total	306 kg	Halil Mutlu (Turkey)	Sydney, Australia	16 Sep 2000
62 kg	Snatch	153 kg	Shi Zhiyong (China)	Izmir, Turkey	28 Jun 2002
	Clean & jerk	182 kg	Le Maosheng (China)	Busan, South Korea	2 Oct 2002
	★ Total	326 kg	Zhang Jie (China)	Kanazawa, Japan	28 Apr 2008
69 kg	Snatch	165 kg	Georgi Markov (Bulgaria)	Sydney, Australia	20 Sep 2000
	Clean & jerk	197 kg	Zhang Guozheng (China)	Qinhuangdao, China	11 Sep 2003
	Total	357 kg	Galabin Boevski (Bulgaria)	Athens, Greece	24 Nov 1999
77 kg	Snatch	173 kg	Sergey Filimonov (Kazakhstan)	Almaty, Kazakhstan	9 Apr 2004
	Clean & jerk	210 kg	Oleg Perepetchenov (Russia)	Trencín, Slovakia	27 Apr 2001
	Total	377 kg	Plamen Jelyazkov (Bulgaria)	Doha, Qatar	27 Mar 2002
85 kg	Snatch	187 kg	Andrei Rybakou (Belarus)	Chiang Mai, Thailand	22 Sep 2007
	Clean & jerk	218 kg	Zhang Yong (China)	Ramat Gan, Israel	25 Apr 1998
	★ Total	394 kg	Andrei Rybakou (Belarus)	Beijing, China	15 Aug 2008
94 kg	Snatch	188 kg	Akakios Kakhiasvilis (Greece)	Athens, Greece	27 Nov 1999
	Clean & jerk	232 kg	Szymon Kolecki (Poland)	Sofia, Bulgaria	29 Apr 2000
	★ Total	412 kg	Akakios Kakhiasvilis (Greece)	Athens, Greece	27 Nov 1999
105 kg	Snatch	200 kg	Andrei Aramnau (Belarus)	Beijing, China	18 Aug 2008
	Clean & jerk	237 kg	Alan Tsagaev (Bulgaria)	Kiev, Ukraine	25 Apr 2004
	★ Total	436 kg	Andrei Aramnau (Belarus)	Beijing, China	18 Aug 2008
105+ kg	Snatch	213 kg	Hossein Rezazadeh (Iran)	Qinhuangdao, China	14 Sep 2003
	Clean & jerk	263 kg	Hossein Rezazadeh (Iran)	Athens, Greece	25 Aug 2004
	Total	476 kg	Hossein Rezazadeh (Iran)	Sydney, Australia	26 Sep 2000
WOMEN	CATEGORY	WEIGHT LIFTED	NAME & NATIONALITY	LOCATION	DATE
48 kg	Snatch	98 kg	Yang Lian (China)	Santo Domingo, Dominican Republic	1 Oct 2006
	Clean & jerk	120 kg	Chen Xiexia (China)	Taian City, China	21 Apr 2007
	Total	217 kg	Yang Lian (China)	Santo Domingo, Dominican Republic	1 Oct 2006
53 kg	Snatch	102 kg	Ri Song-Hui (North Korea)	Busan, South Korea	1 Oct 2002
	Clean & jerk	129 kg	Li Ping (China)	Taian City, China	22 Apr 2007
	Total	226 kg	Qiu Hongxia (China)	Santo Domingo, Dominican Republic	2 Oct 2006
58 kg	Snatch	111 kg	Chen Yanqing (China)	Doha, Qatar	3 Dec 2006
	Clean & jerk	141 kg	Qiu Hongmei (China)	Taian City, China	23 Apr 2007
	Total	251 kg	Chen Yanqing (China)	Doha, Qatar	3 Dec 2006
63 kg	Snatch	116 kg	Pawina Thongsuk (Thailand)	Doha, Qatar	12 Nov 2005
	Clean & jerk	142 kg	Pawina Thongsuk (Thailand)	Doha, Qatar	4 Dec 2006
	Total	257 kg	Liu Haixia (China)	Chiang Mai, Thailand	23 Sep 2007
69 kg	★ Snatch	128 kg	Liu Chunhong (China)	Beijing, China	13 Aug 2008
	★ Clean & jerk	158 kg	Liu Chunhong (China)	Beijing, China	13 Aug 2008
	★ Total	286 kg	Liu Chunhong (China)	Beijing, China	13 Aug 2008
75 kg	Snatch	131 kg	Natalia Zabolotnaia (Russia)	Chiang Mai, Thailand	25 Sep 2007
	Clean & jerk	159 kg	Liu Chunhong (China)	Doha, Qatar	13 Nov 2005
	Total	286 kg	Svetlana Podobedova (Russia)	Hangzhou, China	2 Jun 2006
75+ kg	★ Snatch	140 kg	Jang Mi-Ran (South Korea)	Beijing, China	16 Aug 2008
	★ Clean & jerk	186 kg	Jang Mi-Ran (South Korea)	Beijing, China	16 Aug 2008
	★ Total	326 kg	Jang Mi-Ran (South Korea)	Beijing, China	16 Aug 2008

• *Still awaiting ratification at the time of going to press*

MEN'S 105 KG SNATCH

Andrei Aramnau (Belarus) competes in the men's 105 kg group at the 2008 Olympic Games in Beijing, China. He holds the Snatch record of 200 kg as well as the total of 436 kg, both achieved at the Beijing Olympics on 18 August 2008.

★ **NEW RECORD**
UPDATED RECORD

WOMEN'S 69 KG

Weightlifter Liu Chunhong (China) shows off the gold medal she was awarded for a lift of 128 kg during the women's 69 kg Snatch on Day 5 of the 2008 Olympic Games on 13 August 2008 in Beijing, China. She holds all the world records in this weight category: she also lifted 158 kg in the clean & jerk at the same event, and so achieved a Total of 286 kg.

OFFICIAL WEBSITES

Weightlifting:
www.iwf.net

Waterskiing:
www.iwsf.com

Dec 29: The **oldest mother** is Maria del Carmen Bousada Lara (Spain). She was 66 years 358 days old when she gave birth to twin boys, Christian and Pau, in Barcelona, Spain, on 29 December 2006.

Dec 30: In the week ending 30 December 2007, almost 43 million tracks were legally downloaded in the USA – a figure 42.5% higher than the record set in the same week the previous year.

WATERSKIING

MEN	RECORD	NAME & NATIONALITY	LOCATION	DATE
Slalom	1.5 buoy | 9.75-m line | 58 km/h	Chris Parrish (USA)	Trophy Lakes, USA	28 Aug 2005
Barefoot slalom	20.6 crossings of wake in 30 sec	Keith St Onge (USA)	Bronkhorstspruit, South Africa	6 Jan 2006
Tricks	12,400 points	Nicolas Le Forestier (France)	Lac de Joux, Switzerland	4 Sep 2005
Barefoot tricks	10,880 points	Keith St Onge (USA)	Adna, USA	17 Sep 2006
Jump	74.2 m (243 ft 5 in)	Freddy Krueger (USA)	Seffner, USA	5 Nov 2006
Barefoot jump	27.4 m (89 ft 11 in)	David Small (GB)	Mulwala, Australia	8 Feb 2004
Ski fly	91.1 m (298 ft 10 in)	Jaret Llewellyn (Canada)	Orlando, USA	14 May 2000
Overall	2,818.01 points*	Jaret Llewellyn (Canada)	Seffner, USA	29 Sep 2002

WOMEN	RECORD	NAME & NATIONALITY	LOCATION	DATE
Slalom	1 buoy | 10.25-m line | 55 km/h	Kristi Overton Johnson (USA)	West Palm Beach, USA	14 Sep 1996
		Karina Nowlan (Australia)	Sacramento, USA	22 Sep 2008
Barefoot slalom	17.0 crossings of wake in 30 sec	Nadine de Villiers (South Africa)	Witbank, South Africa	5 Jan 2001
Tricks	8,740 points	Mandy Nightingale (USA)	Santa Rosa, USA	10 Jun 2006
Barefoot tricks	4,400 points	Nadine de Villiers (South Africa)	Witbank, South Africa	5 Jan 2001
Jump	56.6 m (186 ft)	Elena Milakova (Russia)	Rio Linda, USA	21 Jul 2002
Barefoot jump	20.6 m (67 ft 7 in)	Nadine de Villiers (South Africa)	Pretoria, South Africa	4 Mar 2000
Ski fly	69.4 m (227 ft 8.2 in)	Elena Milakova (Russia)	Pine Mountain, USA	26 May 2002
Overall	2,850.11 points**	Clementine Lucine (France)	Lacanau, France	9 Jul 2006

*5@11.25 m, 10,730 tricks, 71.7 m jump   **4@11.25 m, 8,680 tricks, 52.1 m jump; calculated with the 2006 scoring method*

WOMEN'S SLALOM

Karina Nowlan (Australia) competes at the 2007 Waterskiing World Championships. She is joint world record holder in the women's slalom event after equalling Kristi Overton Johnson's (USA) feat on 22 September 2008 in Sacramento, USA.

LONGEST SPORTS MARATHONS

SPORT	TIME	NAME & NATIONALITY	LOCATION	DATE
Aerobics	24 hours	Duberney Trujillo (Colombia)	Dosquebradas, Colombia	26–27 Feb 2005
Archery	27 hours	Micheal Henri Dames (South Africa)	Grahamstown, South Africa	8–9 Aug 2005
Baseball	33 hr 15 min 45 sec	Boys of Slumber (USA)	Long Island, USA	24–26 May 2008
Basketball	81 hr 1 min	La Cuesta Youth Association LV Movement (Spain)	Tenerife, Spain	1–4 Jul 2008
Basketball (wheelchair)	26 hr 3 min	University of Omaha students and staff (USA)	Omaha, Nebraska, USA	24–25 Sep 2004
Bowling (tenpin)	120 hours	Andy Milne (Canada)	Mississauga, Ontario, Canada	24–29 Oct 2005
Bowls (indoor)	36 hours	Arnos Bowling Club (UK)	Southgate, UK	20–21 Apr 2002
Bowls (outdoor)	168 hours	Lloyd Hotel Bowling Club (UK)	Manchester, UK	25 Oct–1 Nov 2008
Cricket	66 hr 16 min	Raymond Terrace District Cricket Club (Australia)	Raymond Terrace, Australia	24–27 Jan 2009
Curling	40 hr 23 min	B Huston, C McCarthy, G Poole, K McCarthy, K Martin, M Witherspoon, R Martin, T Gouldie, T Teskey, W From (Canada)	Brandon, Manitoba, Canada	9–10 Mar 2007
Darts (doubles)	27 hr 22 min	Jeff Garland, Tony Gafa, Ian van Veen, John Goggin (Australia)	Wyee Point, Australia	30–31 Aug 2008
Darts (singles)	26 hr 42 min	Stephen Wilson and Robert Henderson (UK)	Palnackie, Scotland, UK	20–21 Jun 2008
Fistball (indoor)	24 hours	TG 1855 Neustadt bei Coburg e.V. (Germany)	Frankehalle, Neustadt, Germany	16–17 Apr 2005
Floorball	24 hr 15 min	TRM Floorball and Hornets Regio Moosseedorf Worblental (Switzerland)	Zollikofen, Switzerland	27–28 Apr 2007
Football	33 hr 36 min	Adesa & Stantec teams (Canada)	Edmonton, Alberta, Canada	9–10 Aug 2008
Football (five-a-side)	24 hr 30 min	Rossendale Mavericks and the Fearns Community Sports College (UK)	Waterfoot Rossendale, UK	23–24 Nov 2007
Handball	70 hours	HV Mighty/Stevo team (Netherlands)	Tubbergen, the Netherlands	30 Aug–2 Sep 2001
Hockey (ice)	241 hr 21 min	Brent Saik and friends (Canada)	Strathcona, Alberta, Canada	8–18 Feb 2008
Hockey (indoor)	50 hours	Bert & Macs and Mid-Town Certigard teams (Canada)	Lethbridge, Alberta, Canada	25–27 Mar 2008
Hockey (inline/roller)	24 hours	8K Roller Hockey League (USA)	Eastpointe, Michigan, USA	13–14 Sep 2002
Hockey (street)	105 hr 17 min	Molson Canadian and Canadian Tire teams (Canada)	Lethbridge, Alberta, Canada	20–24 Aug 2008
Korfball	30 hr 2 min	Kingfisher Korfball Club (UK)	Larkfield, Kent, UK	14–15 Jun 2008
Netball	58 hours	Sleaford Netball Club (UK)	Sleaford, Lincolnshire, UK	25–27 Jul 2008
Parasailing	24 hr 10 min	Berne Persson (Sweden)	Lake Graningesjön, Sweden	19–20 Jul 2002
Pétanque (boules)	40 hr 9 min	Bevenser Boule-Freunde (Germany)	Bad Bevensen, Germany	22–23 Jul 2006
Pool (singles)	53 hr 25 min	Brian Lilly and Daniel Maloney (USA)	Spring Lake, North Carolina, USA	10–12 Oct 2008
Skiing	202 hr 1 min	Nicky Willey (Australia)	Thredbo, NSW, Australia	2–10 Sep 2005
Snowboarding	180 hr 34 min	Bernhard Mair (Austria)	Bad Kleinkirchheim, Austria	9–16 Jan 2004
Spinning (static cycling)	185 hr 42 min	Tom Seabourne (USA)	Mt Pleasant, Texas, USA	5–12 Dec 2008
Table football	51 hr 52 min	Alexander Gruber, Roman Schelling, Enrico Lechtaler, Christian Nägele (Austria)	Bregenz, Austria	27–29 Jun 2008
Table tennis (doubles)	101 hr 1 min 11 sec	Lance, Phil and Mark Warren and Bill Weir (USA)	Sacramento, California, USA	9–13 Apr 1979
Table tennis (singles)	132 hr 31 min	Danny Price and Randy Nunes (USA)	Cherry Hill, New Jersey, USA	20–26 Aug 1978
Tai chi	25 hr 5 min	Ken Dickenson and Kevin Bartolo (Australia)	Sutherland, NSW, Australia	17–18 Mar 2006
Tennis (doubles)	50 hr 0 min 8 sec	Vince Johnson, Bill Geideman, Brad Ansley and Allen Finley (USA)	Hickory, North Carolina, USA	7–9 Nov 2008
Tennis (singles)	31 hr 35 min 30 sec	George L. Bolter and Athos Rostan III (USA)	Hickory, North Carolina, USA	8–9 Nov 2008
Volleyball (beach)	24 hr 10 min	K Garbulski, M Fuks, A Jankowski and T Konior (Poland)	Ustka, Poland	27–28 Jun 2008
Volleyball (indoor)	55 hr 3 min	SVU Volleybal (Netherlands)	Amsterdam, the Netherlands	20–22 Dec 2008
Wakeboarding	6 hr 17 min	Ian Taylor (UK)	Milton Keynes, UK	1 Sep 2004

PLEASE NOTE: *GWR sports marathon guidelines are constantly updated – please contact us for information before attempting a record.*

WWW.GUINNESSWORLDRECORDS.COM

Dec 31: The former Soviet Tupolev Tu-144 first flew on 31 December 1968, thereby becoming the **first supersonic airliner to fly**.

ACKNOWLEDGEMENTS/CREDITS

Guinness World Records would like to thank the following individuals, companies, groups, websites, societies, schools, collages and universities for their help in the creation of the 2010 edition: 3run, Brenden Adams & family, Willie Adams, Bender Helper Impact (Susan Bender, Adam Fenton, Mark Karges, Chrissy Kelleher, Brian Reinert, Shannon Swaggerty and Sally Triebel), Oliver Blagden, Blue Peter Production, BBC 1, Luke and Joseph Boatfield, Book Marketing Ltd (Steve Bohme and Rachel Levin), Alfie Boulton-Fay, Ceri, Katie and Georgie Boulton, Olivia Boulton, Box Office Mojo, Brand Museum, Notting Hill, CCTV (Guo Tong), Chulalongkorn Hospital, Bangkgok, Thailand, Clara and Camille Chambers, ChartTrack, Edd & Imogen China, Adam Cloke, Cobourg Fire Department, Ontario, Canada, Collaboration Inc (Miho Goto, Suzuki san), Mark Collins, Creo (Richard Saysell and Iain Johnstone), Kenneth & Tatiana Crutchlow (Ocean Rowing Society), Josh Cushins, Gordner Dan (X Games), Chi Danny (X Games), Davies Media (Ceri Davies and Charlotte O'Brien), Bryn Downing (INP Media), Malee Duangdee & family, Louis Epstein, Ermanno Pietrosemoli Escuela Latino-america de Redes, Europroducciones (Marco Fernandez de Araoz, Mar Izquierdo, Sheila Izquierdo, Maria Ligues, Stefano Torrisi, Gabriela Ventura, Amelia Ewen, Toby Ewen, explorersweb.com, Debbie Ezel, Rachel Falikoff, Imageworks, Molly and Isobel Fay, Flora London Marathon (Natasha Grainger and Nicola Okey), Kate Fisher (St Pancras Press Officer), Rob Fraser, Ansley Fuks, Thomasina Gibson, Dorotka Girton, Gladstone Skate Park, Michigan, USA, Ryan, Brandon and Jordan Greenwood, Victoria Grimsell, Greg Grusby (Industrial Light & Magic), Michael Hebranko, Stuart Hendry Hit Entertainment, Japan (Jun Otsuki and Frank Foley), Marsha

Hoover, Anne-Mareike Homfeld (European Space Agency), Hotel Arts, Barcelona, Bill Hughes (unofficial engineering consultant), Simon Hughes (unofficial car consultant), Caroline Iggulden (The Sun), imdb.com, Panoula Ioannidou (Manager, 40 Savile Row), ITV Productions (Laurence Blyth, Malcolm Donkin, Paul Ritz, Emma Wilkinson), Lodato Jason (NBA), Stokel John (Rob Dyrdek's Fantasy Factory), Richard Johnston, Simon Jones, Barberan Karen (NBA), Robshaw Kelly (X Games), Sultan Kosen & family, Lacey Leavitt, Don Levy (Sony Pictures, London Aquarium, All at Macmillan Distribution, Manda (Carey and Nick), Jim Manion (International Federation of Body Builders), Carla Maroussas (Ascent Media), metacritic.com, Morgan Middle School, Ellensburgh, WA, Motion Capture Society, Murphy Marc (X Games), Lori Mezhoff, Blackwell Michelle (NBA), Myrtle Beach Airport, South Carolina, USA, Nationmaster. com, Nitro Circus (Smoler Barry and Zablow Shanna), Norddeich TV (York Altendorf, Thomas Goseberg, Rainer Noseck, Ollie Wieberg), Olga TV (Jude, Bert and Paul O'Grady), Outline Productions (Rainer Chapman, Selina Ferguson, Ian Homans, Diana Hunter, Steve Kidgell, Laura Mansfield, Jamie Starr, Janine Terry, Helen Veale), Sullivan Patrick (NBA), Kate Perkins, Daniel Phillips, Julia Pistor, POD Worldwide (Yip Cheong, Christy Chin, Alex Liew), Sean Porter, The Queens Head & Artichoke Public House, London, Buchholz Rachel (NGK), R&G Productions (Stéphane Gateau, Patrice Parmentier, Jean-Francois Peralta, Jerome Revon), Martyn Richards Research (Martyn Richards), Michael Rummery, Anna Rutherford, Sassy (Nikki Gillespie and Steve Kemsley), Robyn Scott, Austin Scott, Thomas Sergeant, Sky1 (Helen Devonald, Kirsty Howell, Emma Read, Louise Snell, Ben Tattersal-Smith, James Townley, Sophie Turner-Laing, Nicky White), Marcela Soukupova, Wacharasindhu Suttipong (Chulalongkorn

Hospital, Thailand), Charlie Taylor, Holly Taylor, Television News Release (Amanda and Claire), Hand Theo (www. dannyway.com), Simon Thompson, TIHE (Peter Harper), Twin Galaxies, Jessica, Isabel and Samuel Way, Weezer, Kate White, Daniel Woods, Claire Woodward.

IN MEMORIA
Amy, the **longest rabbit**; Sandy Allen, **tallest living woman**; Maria de Jesus, **oldest woman**; Edna Parker, **oldest woman**.

PICTURE CREDITS
2 Rex Features; Rex Features/Maurice McDonald/PA **3** Getty Images; NASA/AP/PA **5** Paul Michael Hughes/GWR; Nick Garbutt/NHPA **6** Ranald Mackechnie/GWR; S Blair Hedges; Richard Bradbury/GWR; Rick & Nora Bowers/Alamy **7** Getty Images; Getty Images; Ranald Mackechnie/GWR; Getty Images; Drew Gardner/GWR

UK INTRO
8 Iain McLean; Andi Southam **9** Paul Michael Hughes/GWR; Richard Bradbury/GWR; Patrick Brown/GWR **10** Ken McKay/Rex Features; Jon Bond

USA INTRO
8 Nate Christenson; Rob Fraser/GWR; Paul Michael Hughes/GWR **9** Joe Murphy/Getty Images; Paul Michael Hughes/GWR **11** Adam Bouska

CANADA INTRO
8 Ranald Mackechnie/GWR **11** Ken Ardill; Richard Wahab

WORLD INTRO
8 Oleg Nikishin/Getty Images Paul Michael Hughes/GWR **10** Richard Bradbury/GWR; Richard Bradbury/GWR; Rob Fraser/GWR

12 Mary Evans Picture Library; Getty Images; Alamy; Charles Walker/Topfoto; J Wood/showhistory.com; Getty Images; Patrice Fury/Rex Features; Getty Images **13** Jeff Haynes/Getty Images; Getty Images; Getty Images; Getty Images; Getty Images **14** Paul Michael Hughes/GWR **15** Paul Michael Hughes/GWR **16** Griff Stefan

Gregorowius/RTL; Stefan Gregorowius/RTL; Andi Southam/Sky1; Paul Michael Hughes/GWR; Paul Michael Hughes/GWR **17** Yolanda de Santos; John Wright/GWR; Paul Michael Hughes/GWR **18** Paul Michael Hughes/GWR; Nick Hannes/Panos/GWR **19** Dave Nelson; PA **20** NASA **22** Astrium (P Dumas); NASA; Melinda Podor/Alamy **23** NASA; NASA; NASA; NASA **24** NASA **25** NASA; D Ducros/CNES; NASA **26** NASA; NASA; Ralph Morse/Getty Images **27** NASA; NASA; NASA **28** NASA; NASA; NASA; Getty Images **29** Detlev Van Ravensswaay/Science Photo Library; NASA; NASA; NASA **30** David Welling/Nature PL **32** Adam Woolfitt/Robert Harding; Science Photo Library; Alamy **33** Stephen Alvarez/National Geographic; Fabrizio Villa/Getty Images **34** Bill Frymire/Alamy; Paiwei Wei/Getty Images; W Robert Moore/Getty Images **35** Kevin Schafer/NHPA; Photolibrary; Dennis Flaherty/Getty Images **36** Galen Rowell/Alamy; Walter Bibikow/Reflex Stock; Rex Features **37** Yoshio Tomii/Photolibrary; Dr George Beccaloni/Science Photo Library; David Madison/Getty Images **38** NASA; Getty Images; Alamy; Getty Images **39** Philippe Bourseiller/Getty Images; David Tipling/Alamy; Alamy **40** Bruno Morandi/Photolibrary; John Pennock/Getty Images; Alamy; Alexander Walter/Getty Images **41** Pavel Filatov/Alamy; Jeff Foott/Getty Images **42** David B Fleetham/Photolibrary; Robin Smith/Photolibrary; Seapics **43** Getty Images; Geoscience Australia; Pete Atkinson/Getty Images **44** Science Photo Library; Fred Olivier/Nature PL **45** Denis Sarrazin/ArcticNet/Centre d'Etudes Nordiques; Gordon Wiltsie/National Geographic **46** Richard Du Toit/FLPA **48** Rob Lind; Natural History Museum/PA; Daniel Heuclin/NHPA; John S Ascher; Bruce Beehler/NHPA **49** Mark Webster/Photolibrary; Satoshi Kuribayashi/Photolibrary **50** David Bickford; Alamy; Lynda Richardson/Corbis **51** Mark Moffett/FLPA; Geoff Brightling/Getty Images;

Geoff Brightling/Getty Images **52** S Blair Hedges; Juan Carlos Ulate/Reuters Tony Crocetta/NHPA **53** David A Northcott/Corbis Nick Garbutt/NHPA; Gabriele Gentile **54** Johnny Jensen/Image Quest Marine; Burt Jones & Maurine Shimlock/NHPA; Jonathan Bird/SeaPics **55** R Nicholls; Peter Arnold/Alamy; William West/Getty Images **56** Lee Dalton/Photoshot; Ben Osborne/Getty Images; Joseph Van Os/Getty Images **57** Mike Briner/Alamy; Dave King/Getty Images; Peter Dazeley/Getty Images; Jeff Harris/Getty Images; Alex Cao/Getty Images; Catherine Ledner/Getty Images; Igor Shpilenok/Nature PL **58** Andrea Ferraril/NHPA; Yves Lefevre/Still Pictures; Reuters **59** Bela Szandelszky/Getty Images; Morales/Photolibrary; Rick & Nora Bowers/Alamy; Getty Images **60** Ranald Mackechnie/GWR **62** Chris Stowers/Panos **63** Paul Michael Hughes/GWR; Ranald Mackechnie/GWR; Richard Bradbury/GWR **64** Paul Michael Hughes/GWR; Richard Bradbury/GWR **65** George Legeros; John Wright/GWR **66** Survival International; Carol Becker/Angela Fisher/Getty Images **67** Getty Images; Getty Images; Gavin Hellier/Robert Harding; Tengku Bahar/Getty Images **68** Photolibrary; Rex Features; Splash News **69** ABC News; Jane Stockman/Getty Images **70** Polaris/Eyevine; Frazer Harrison/Getty Images; Barcroft Media **71** Adam Bouska; AP/PA Sanjit Das/Barcroft Media **72** Richard Bradbury/GWR; Patrick Brown/GWR **73** Nir Elias/Reuters; Rob Fraser/GWR **74** Ranald Mackechnie/GWR **76** John Wright/GWR; John Wright/GWR; Ranald Mackechnie/GWR **77** John Wright/GWR **78** John Wright/GWR; John Wright/GWR; John Wright/GWR **79** John Wright/GWR; Fahad Shadeed/Reuters; John Wright/GWR **80** Paul Michael Hughes/GWR; John Wright/GWR **83** Ian West/PA **85** Bjoern Sigurdsoen/Getty Images **87** Warren Lynam; Ken Platt Sr **88** Richard Bradbury/GWR **90** John Wright/GWR **92** Rex Features; Reuters; Ole Morte

Aanestad/Getty Images **93** Sebastian D'Souza/Getty Images; Gordon Sinclair/Rex Features; Getty Images **94** Marcel Mochet/Getty Images; Yvan Zedda / Gitana SA **95** odger Bosch/Getty Images; Guy Salter/Getty Images; Vivek Prakash/Reuters **96** Adrian Bitoiu **97** Michael Maloney/Corbis; Michael Maloney/Corbis; David Paterson/Alamy **98** Getty Images; AP/PA; Rex Features **99** Thierry Martinez/Getty Images; Joe Raedle/Getty Images **102** Chuck Kennedy/Getty Images; Robert Nickelsberg/Getty Images **104** John Wright/GWR; Nate Christenson; Wally Pacholka **105** Richard Bradbury/GWR **106** John Wright/GWR; Mireille Vautier/Alamy; Alamy; Holly Stein/Getty Images; Moviestore Collection **107** Roberto Schmidt/Getty Images; Corbis; Brad Mangin/Getty Images; Alamy; Yuri Cortez/Getty Images **108** Patrick Landmann/Science Photo Library; Eliseo Fernandez/Reuters **109** Mariana Bazo/Reuters; Pilar Olivares/Reuters; Paul Souders/Getty Images **110** Alamy; Mauro Azzura **111** Bill Zygmant/Rex Features; Andre Jenny/Alamy **112** WENN; Joe McGorty/GWR **113** Rex Features; Darren Staples/Reuters **114** Franck Fife/Getty Images; Frank Micelotta/Getty Images **115** Clive Rose/Getty Images **116** PA Jasper Juinen/Getty Images **118** Peter Adams/Getty Images **119** WENN; Nils-Johan Norenlind/Getty Images **120** John Wright/GWR; John Wright/GWR **121** Hoge Noorden/EPA; Alamy **124** Rex Features; Kazbek Basayev/Getty Images; Ziyah Gafic/Getty Images **125** Eliana Aponte/Reuters **126** Khaled al-Harir/Reuters **128** Euan Denholm/Reuters; Dave M. Benett/Getty Images; Robert Hollingworth/Alamy **129** David Preston/Alamy; David Sacks/Getty Images; Schalk van Zuydam/AP/PA **131** Ray Tang/Rex Features **132** Chris Jackson/Getty Images **133** Roslan Rahman/Getty Images; David Longstreath/AP/PA **134** Rex Features **135** Menard

3 million: the number of people who took part in the **largest anti-war rally** in Rome, Italy, on 15 February 2003, protesting against the US invasion of Iraq.

INDEX

This year's index is organized into two parts: by subject and by superlative. **Bold** entries in the subject index indicate a main entry on a topic, and entries in **BOLD CAPITALS** indicate an entire chapter. Neither index lists personal names.

32.2 cm (12.6 in): the width of the **thickest** book, *The Complete Miss Marple* by Agatha Christie, published by HarperCollins and unveiled on 20 May 2009.

STOP PRESS

LONGEST TIME CONTROLLING A FOOTBALL (MALE)

At an event organized by Sony PlayStation in Covent Garden, London, UK, on 30 April–1 May 2009, Dan Magness (UK) controlled a football, keeping it up in the air and in constant motion, for 24 hours. He completed an estimated 250,000 touches in total during his feat.

★ LARGEST SHAMPOO BOTTLE

A bottle of shampoo measuring 4.70 m by 1.54 m (15 ft 5 in by 5 ft 6 in) and weighing 1,045 kg (2,303 lb) was produced by Ismail Abu Dawood Trading Co. at Al-Andalus Hyper store of Panda, in Jeddah, Saudi Arabia, on 19 March 2009.

LARGEST BOWL OF PASTA

Wataniya restaurants-Sbarro (Qatar) made a bowl of pasta weighing 4,430 kg (9,760 lb) at the Doha golf club in Doha, Qatar, on 28 March 2009.

LARGEST COLLECTION OF NATIVITY SETS

The largest collection of nativity sets consisted of 1,802 different pieces, as of 14 March 2009. All are housed in the Museo dei Sogni e Della Memoria in Feltre, Italy.

★ LONGEST STAND-UP COMEDY SHOW BY AN INDIVIDUAL

Funnyman Tommy Tiernan (Ireland) performed stand-up at Nuns Island Theatre, Galway, Ireland, for 36 hours 15 minutes. The event started at 3:00 p.m. on Friday 10 April 2009, and finished at 3:15 a.m. on Sunday 12 April.

★ FASTEST 20 CONE BACKWARDS SLALOM ON INLINE SKATES

Paul Randles (UK) completed a 20 cone backwards slalom on inline skates in 5.62 sec on the set of *Guinness World Records* in Madrid, Spain, on 23 January 2009.

LARGEST BUFFET

The Kuşadası Professional Chefs Association displayed a buffet with 1,028 different dishes at the 5th Annual Kuşadası Food Festival, held at the Pine Bay Holiday Resort, Kuşadası, Turkey, on 18 April 2009.

DRIVING TO THE HIGHEST ALTITUDE BY MOTORCYCLE

The greatest altitude reached autonomously by a motorcycle is 6,245 m (20,488 ft 9 in), achieved by a team of six of the North Calcutta Disha Motorcycle Club (all India) with Hero Honda motorcycles on the Changchemno Range near Marsemikla, India, on 29 August 2008.

FACT

Fenerbahçe Sports Club isn't just home to a football team, it also has teams for athletics, men's and women's basketball, boxing, swimming and a variety of other sports too.

★ LARGEST FOOTBALL SHIRT

A Fenerbahçe football shirt measuring 71.35 m by 79.15 m (234 ft 1 in by 259 ft 8 in) was created by AVEA in an event organized by Efor Turizm Organizasyon VE TIC Ltd at the Sükrü Saracoglu Stadium, Istanbul, Turkey, on 5 April 2009.

FASTEST TIME TO PUT ON A DUVET COVER

In just 42.97 seconds, Alan Hughes (Ireland) set a new record for the fastest time to put on a duvet cover on the set of *Ireland AM*, TV3 in Dublin, Ireland, on 17 September 2008.

★ OLDEST BOXING WORLD CHAMPION (FEMALE)

Terri Moss (USA, b. 25 January 1966) was 41 years 105 days when she defeated Stephanie Dobbs (USA) to win the Women's International Boxing Federation (WIBF) minimumweight title in Tulsa, Oklahoma, USA, on 10 May 2007.

MOST PEOPLE KISSING SIMULTANEOUSLY

A total of 39,879 people kissed at the same time at an event organized by Gobierno del Distrito Federal in Mexico DF, Mexico, on 14 February 2009. The final figure is an odd number because kisses involving more than two people (such as two children kissing a parent) were allowed.

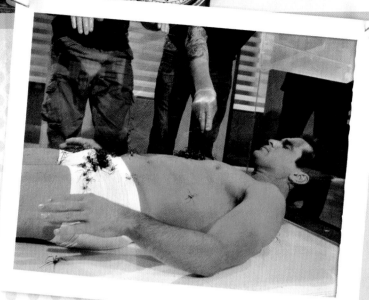

MOST SPIDERS ON A BODY FOR 30 SECONDS

Shane Crawford (Australia), an ex-professional sportsman and AFL champion, had 153 spiders placed on his body for 30 seconds on the set of *The Footy Show* in the Nine Network Studios in Melbourne, Victoria, Australia, on 23 April 2009.

MOST STEP UPS IN ONE HOUR WITH A 40-LB PACK

One for fitness fanatics, the most step ups completed in one hour with an 18-kg (40-lb) pack is 1,824 by Robin Simpson (UK) at the BT Heroes of Sport Exhibition at the GMEX Centre, Manchester, UK, on 25 October 2008.

This popular record has been broken three time this year alone. It was originally set by multiple record holder Paddy Doyle (UK) on 9 November 2006.

★ MOST POSITIONS HELD IN THE *NEW YORK TIMES* BESTSELLERS LIST

Thriller writer James Patterson (USA) has had 43 of his books listed in the *New York Times* bestsellers chart, with 31 of them making it to the No.1 position. Pictured is Patterson receiving his certificate from GWR's Sam Fay.

TOP **100** Records of the Decade

LARGEST SILVER-SERVICE DINNER PARTY

An epic silver-service dinner party took place on 17 July 2008, when 16,206 people were guests at the Alpha Kappa Alpha Sorority Inc., Centennial Celebration Dinner hosted by the Walter E Washington Convention Center (USA) in Washington DC, USA.

★ LONGEST CONCERT BY A SOLO ARTIST

Canadian pianist Jason Beck, aka Gonzales, performed in a solo concert for 27 hours 3 minutes 44 seconds at the Cine 13 in Paris, France, on 18 May 2009. Jason was keen to avoid repeating songs during his attempt and promised his audience "I will break the record without sounding like a broken record".

★ LARGEST CHOIR

On 12 May 2009, a confirmed choir of 100,000 people (plus an unconfirmed 60,000 additional singers) gathered in Hyderabad, Andhra Pradesh, India. The mass sing-along in Telugu, the language of the Andhra Pradesh state, broke the previous 72-year-old record held by a choir of 60,000 at a contest held in what is now Wroclaw, Poland.

★ LARGEST PHYSICS LESSON

A total of 5,401 students were taught by Steve Spangler Science (USA) during a presentation in Denver, Colorado, USA, on 7 May 2009.

★ FASTEST TIME TO SORT 500 g OF PEANUT M&MS

The fastest time to sort 500 g (17.64 oz) of Peanut M&Ms using one hand is 2 min 37 sec, achieved by Debbie Nugent (UK) at Pinewood Studios, UK, on 23 April 2009.

★ MOST SNAILS ON THE FACE

Mike Dilger (UK) managed to keep 37 snails on his face for the required 10 seconds while appearing on *The One Show* for BBC television in Covent Garden, London, UK, on 13 May 2009.

★ MOST EXPENSIVE MUSIC SINGLE SOLD AT AUCTION

A rare seven-inch copy of an unreleased 1965 single, "Do I Love You (Indeed I Do)" by Frank Wilson (USA), was sold at auction in April 2009 for £25,742 ($39,294) to a buyer who wished to remain anonymous.

★ NEW RECORD
★ UPDATED RECORD

★ LONGEST RABBIT

Alice, a Flemish giant rabbit owned by Annette Edwards (UK) and measuring 98 cm (3 ft 3 in), became the new longest rabbit after the sad news reached us of the death of Amy, the previous record holder, also owned by Annette. Alice was measured at Lowesmoor House Veterinary Centre, Worcester, UK, on 29 April 2009.

GUINNESS WORLD RECORDS

LAST...

★TITANIC SURVIVOR

Elizabeth Gladys "Millvina" Dean (UK, 2 February 1912–31 May 2009) was just 69 days old when she travelled third class on the cruise liner *Titanic* with her parents and 18-month-old brother, all hoping to start a new life in the USA. She, along with her mother and brother, survived to return to the UK when the "unsinkable" ship sank on 14 April 1912, but her father, Bert, was among the 1,517 passengers who perished in the tragedy.

★ PASSENGER PIGEON

Martha, the last living passenger pigeon (*Ectopistes migratorius*), died in Cincinnati Zoo, USA, on 1 September 1914. It was 29 years old and the very last of billions of these birds killed by mankind in less than a century.

The exact number of pink-breasted passenger pigeons that existed is impossible to determine, but an estimated 40% of the entire North American bird population was of this one species. The bird was largely shot for food, and a single shooter could easily kill 1,000 birds in one session. And incredible though it may seem today, despatching pigeons was even a sport at one time...

★ OLYMPIC PIGEON SHOOT

Live pigeon shooting was held for the first (and last) time in the extravagant 1900 Paris Olympics. Leon de Lunden (Belgium) snatched the gold, killing 21 birds in the process. France's Maurice Faure managed to down 20 birds, while Donald Mackintosh and Crittenden Robinson (both USA) tied for third place, with 18 pigeons each.

★ DEATH FROM SMALLPOX

The last case of smallpox that resulted in death occurred in August 1978, when a medical photographer at Birmingham University, UK, was infected with a sample kept for research purposes. There have been no cases of the disease since then.

★ FLIGHT OF CONCORDE

At 16.05 p.m. (BST) on 24 October 2003, Concorde made its last touchdown at the UK's Heathrow Airport. On its final transatlantic flight, it carried 100 celebrities from New York City, USA, to mark the end of its 27 years of service. Before the flight, Captain Mike Bannister said, "What we have tried to do is to make the retirement of Concorde a celebration."

★ WORLD WAR II VETERAN TO SURRENDER

Private Teruo Nakamura (Taiwan), who served during World War II in the Imperial Japanese Army, did not surrender until 1974. He was stationed on Morotai Island in Indonesia, which was captured by the Allies in September 1944. Private Nakamura remained there, in hiding, long after the Allies departed.

★ SOLDIER TO SEE ACTION IN BOTH WORLD WARS

Francesco Domenico Chiarello (Italy, 1898–2008) was called up in 1918 during World War I and served as an infantryman, seeing action in Trentino, Italy. In 1940, he was called up again at the age of 42 to fight in World War II at Reggio Calabria, Italy, but was discharged after a few months.

★ ORIGINAL OLYMPICS

In AD 393, the original Olympic Games – first held c. 776 BC – were staged for the final time. The Christian Emperor Theodosius I disapproved of the Games' Ancient Greek pagan origins and had them banned in AD 394 for being anti-Christian. Olympia, the original site of the Games on the Greek Peloponnese peninsula, is where the modern Olympic flame is kindled to light the torch for today's Games.

G-BOAF

1890: the year of the Battle of Wounded Knee between the US Cavalry and the tribal Sioux Indians, the **last battle on American soil**.

GUINNESS WORLD RECORDS

★ DODO

The last known specimen of Mauritian dodo (*Raphus cucullatus*, formerly *Didus ineptus*) died in 1681. The single remaining closest relative – a *Rodrigues solitaire* from the nearby Rodrigues Island – died in 1790. The dodo's downfall was brought about by its fearlessness and flightlessness, as it would inquisitively approach strangers (and predators). Unfortunately for the dodo, it was also rather tasty…

BRITISH PRIME MINISTER TO BE ASSASSINATED

The last (and, to date, only) British prime minister to be assassinated was the Honourable Spencer Perceval (UK, 1762–1812), who was shot in the lobby of the House of Commons, London, UK, by John Bellingham (UK) on 11 May 1812.

CASTRATO

The fashion for castrati – male opera singers whose testicles are removed before puberty, thus preserving their angelic boyhood voices – waned in the early 20th century. The last castrato was Alessandro Moreschi (Italy), who died in 1922. And on a similar note…

★ EUNUCH

The last court eunuch – a male castrated in order to look after a harem of women without succumbing to sexual temptation – was Sun Yaoting (China), who died in 1996.

★ NEW RECORD
☆ UPDATED RECORD

★ LONDON PEA SOUPER

When smoke from coal-burning fires mixes with fog, the result is a blinding, choking blanket of smog, known in London as a "pea souper". In December 1952, during the city's last pea souper, 3,500–4,000 people died from acute bronchitis. Visibility in the street was down to 30 cm (12 in) and cinemas closed because it was impossible to see the screens.

★ HIEROGLYPH

The last known and datable hieroglyphs – the "sacred carved letters" engraved on monuments by Ancient Egyptians to communicate their

X-REF
You've read about some amazing lasts, don't forget to check out some incredible firsts on pp.2–3.

religious beliefs – are those on Hadrian's Gate at the Temple of Philae on Philae Island on the Nile, Egypt. They date back to 24 August AD 394.

USE OF THE GUILLOTINE

The last use of the guillotine in France, before its abolition on 9 September 1981, was for the execution of Hamida Djandoubi, a torturer and murderer aged 28, at Baumettes Prison, Marseille, on 10 September 1977.

EXECUTION OF A WITCH

The last legal execution of a witch was that of Anna Göldi at Glarus, Switzerland, on 18 June 1782.

★ MAN ON THE MOON

On 14 December 1972, the USA's programme of manned lunar exploration came to an end when Gene Cernan, commander of the *Apollo XVII* mission, stepped off the Moon's surface and boarded the lunar excursion vehicle, *Challenger*. This was the last of six successful manned lunar landings; the Moon has not experienced human footfall from that day to this.

BRITISH AIRWAYS

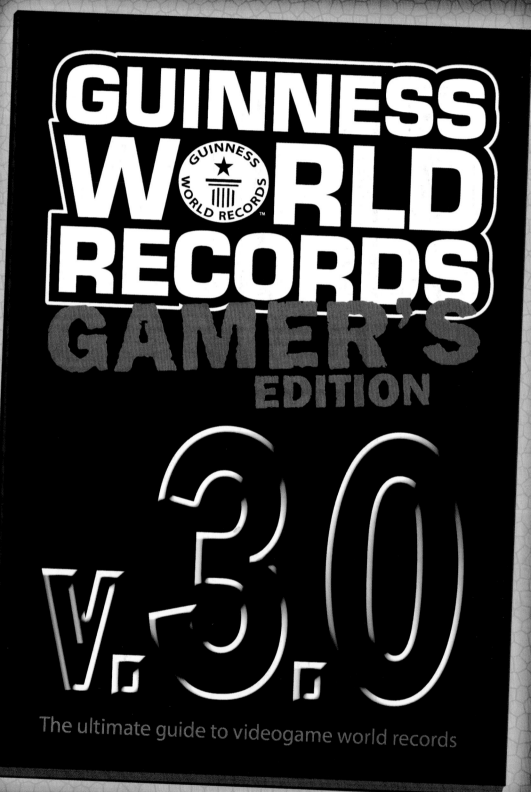